In the Shadow of the Prophet

ROY P. MOTTAHEDEH

In the Shadow of the Prophet

Essays in Islamic History

ONEWORLD ACADEMIC

Oneworld Academic

An imprint of Oneworld Publications

Published by Oneworld Academic in 2023

A CIP record for this title is available from the British Library

ISBN 978-0-86154-560-5
eISBN 978-0-86154-561-2

Typeset by Geethik Technologies
Printed and bound in Great Britain by Clays Ltd, Elcograf S.p.A.

Oneworld Publications
10 Bloomsbury Street
London WC1B 3SR
England

For my family, my wife Patricia,
my sons Rafi and Rostam,
and my granddaughter Deirdre Peri

Contents

About the Author

Roy Parviz Mottahedeh is the Gurney Professor of History, Emeritus, at Harvard University. He served as the Director of the Center for Middle Eastern Studies at Harvard from 1987 to 1990 and as Director of the Prince Alwaleed Bin Talal Islamic Studies Program at Harvard from 2006 to 2011. He founded the *Harvard Middle East and Islamic Review* as a medium for Harvard students and faculty to publish their work. He was elected a member of the Academy of Arts and Sciences and the Council on Foreign Relations and has served as a series editor for several academic publishers.

Roy Parviz Mottahedeh was born in New York City on July 3, 1940, the son of Rafi Y. and Mildred R. Mottahedeh. He received his primary and secondary education in Quaker schools in New York and Pennsylvania. In 1960 he received a *magna cum laude* B.A. in history from Harvard College and was awarded a Shaw Traveling Fellowship which he used to explore Europe, the Middle East, and Afghanistan. He then undertook a second B.A. in Persian and Arabic at the University of Cambridge in the U.K., where he received the E.G. Browne Prize. In 1962 he returned to Harvard to pursue a Ph.D. in history under Sir Hamilton Gibb and Richard Frye. He was elected a Junior Fellow in the Harvard Society of Fellows in 1967 and received his Ph.D. in 1970 for a dissertation on administration in the Buyid period of the tenth and eleventh centuries C.E.

He began his teaching career in the Department of Near Eastern Studies at Princeton University in 1970. The manuscript of his first book, *Loyalty and Leadership in an Early Islamic Society*, gained him tenure, and its publication in 1980 gained him a Guggenheim Fellowship. In 1981 he was appointed a MacArthur Prize Fellow in the first group awarded. The MacArthur Prize allowed him to write his second book, *The Mantle of the Prophet* (1985). This book, which was a study of contemporary Iran as understood through two millennia of history, has been widely translated and remains in print.

He returned to Harvard University in 1986 as Professor of Islamic History in the Department of History. In 1994 he was appointed Gurney Professor of History. With his colleague Angeliki Laiou he co-edited *The Crusades from the Perspective of Byzantium and the Muslim World* (2001). His interest in increasing understanding of Islamic law and jurisprudence in the West led to his translation of and introduction to *Lessons in Islamic Jurisprudence* (2003), which explains not only the terminology but also the philosophy and reasoning behind Islamic law. In 2006 he received an honorary degree in theology from the University of Lund in Sweden.

He is the author of numerous articles that demonstrate his wide range of interests from the Abbasid period in the eighth century C.E. to Islamic revival movements of the present day. His critique of Samuel Huntington's theory of the "clash of civilizations" (1995) has been translated into several languages and widely distributed. His work covers such diverse topics as the transmission of learning in the Muslim world, the social bonds that connected people in the early Islamic Middle East, the theme of "wonders" in *The Thousand and One Nights*, the concept of *Jihād* in the early Islamic period, echoes of the pre-Islamic past in the medieval Islamic world, perceptions of Persepolis among later Muslims, and the basis for an ethic of toleration in Islamic thought.

He lives in Watertown, Massachusetts, with his wife of forty years and is the father of two sons.

Preface

My publisher kindly asked me to collect my essays many years ago, but in my younger years it seemed that there was never time to do so. Now that I am eighty-one, I turned to this task because the pandemic forced me to stay at home. The task was difficult because I had failed to keep Word copies of my earlier published essays and had only PDFs of many of them. These PDFs had to be converted back to Word for the publisher. I could not have managed this task without the invaluable assistance of Johannes Makar, a Harvard Ph.D. student in the Department of Near Eastern Languages and Civilizations, who not only painstakingly converted the PDFs back into Word, correcting all the Arabic and Persian transliterations that were garbled in the conversion, but also provided useful editorial suggestions.

I wrote my dissertation and published my first article in the 1960s and only got my first computer in the late 1980s. Before this I had only carbon copies of my work prior to publication and offprints afterwards. In the age of early computers authors such as myself using Arabic and Persian transliterations had to submit both Word and PDF versions to publishers so that the two versions could be compared, and the correct transliteration inserted into the published book or article. Now transliterations of Arabic and Persian are standardized by unicode so that Word versions are not garbled when moving between computers and software programs.

This collection of essays is intended not only for those in Islamic studies but also for students of history and the general public who may not have a background in this field of study and may not know certain Arabic and Persian terms used in this volume. The Islamic world and Islamic history have become better understood in my lifetime but are still not well known or much understood in the Western world. I have organized these essays into sections and introduced the sections with the student or non-specialist reader in mind, in the hope that they might start reading the more general topics and then move on to the more specialized topics. At first, I sought to bring up to date the essays included here by adding postscripts about recent publications on the subject. Alas, that task demanded so much work that I regretfully gave it up. Nevertheless, I have included several postscripts to articles about recent history in the Middle East.

A number of the essays included here have been slightly modified; two of which were taken from larger works and needed modifications in order to stand alone. The other modified essays referred to current events at the time they were written and required changing the present tense to past tense and some updating of information. I have also removed small sections that were no longer relevant. These changes are noted in the "Author's notes" that precede the footnotes in each article. My writing betrays my partisanship for Islamic authors I favor, such as Jalāl al-Din Rumi, the 7th/13th-century Persian mystic and poet. At the end of this volume, I give a nearly complete bibliography of my work.

The vocabulary of my field of study, the medieval Islamic world, has changed somewhat during my lifetime. The ancient and medieval world that I studied in my youth was commonly called the Near East in contrast to the Far East. Now, however, the Near East is commonly used as a term only for the ancient, pre-Islamic period, while Middle East is commonly used for the Islamic period. Consequently, I have changed references in these articles from the Islamic Near East to the Islamic Middle East. Similarly, Orientalist was a favorable term in my youth when I was taught by H.A.R. Gibb who called himself an Orientalist. Early Western travelers to the Near or Middle East regarded themselves as explorers of the Orient, and nineteenth-century Orientalist painting is a well-known feature of art history. Now, however, the term Orientalist has by and large been abandoned within Middle Eastern studies due to Edward Said's 1978 book, *Orientalism*, which criticized Western scholars studying the "Orient" as being tainted by imperialism and colonialism. I have therefore removed the term in most places but still regard it as a benign, albeit old-fashioned term for a scholar of the Middle East. Another development in the vocabulary of my field has produced the two terms Islamist and Islamicist, which have been used interchangeably by some. However, here the term Islamist is used for those who believe that the primary ingredient of public life should be in accordance with Islam. In contrast, the term Islamicist is used here for those who study the culture of Muslims.

Many of the articles in this volume deal with Iran, the country of my father's birth, although the first of my articles to be published in Persian in Iran, my account of Iran under the Abbasids in the 2nd/8th through the 4th/10th centuries, appeared without my name. My first book, *Loyalty and Leadership in an Early Islamic Society* (1980), which was about the Buyid kingdom of Rayy, was belatedly translated into Persian twice (2009 and 2015). However, to my knowledge, my second book, *The Mantle of the Prophet* (1985), which has been translated into Arabic, Danish, German, and Turkish, and which focuses on the recent history of Iran within the background of two millennia of Iranian history, remains untranslated and unavailable in Iran.

Some of the articles here on relatively recent history in Iran stop well short of the present. I have not tried to bring them up to date, as I stopped reading the Iranian press more than a decade ago. These articles were focused on important events as they were unfolding at the time they were written, and they are now part of the recent history of the Middle East. I hope the information and perspectives in them are still useful. To everyone's great good fortune, many authors, including some of Iranian origin, write well about current events in Iran, including the much-admired Ervand Abrahamian.

Transliterations of Arabic and Persian can vary from one publication to another not only because each modern publication prefers a certain kind of transliteration but also because Arabic and Persian authors translated each other's work with the result that medieval texts survive in one or both languages. Proper names of people and places can therefore be transliterated differently. Moreover, Arabic and Persian versions of famous medieval Islamic names such as Ibn Sīnā for Avicenna, Ferdawsi for Firdausi, ʻUmar Khayyām for Omar Khayyam, and Shāhrzād for Scheherazade can confuse readers without a background in the language or history of the Middle East. For this reason, I have chosen to use the most common English form of these names. In order to make this volume a coherent whole, I have made a number of changes throughout the articles. I have tried to employ uniform transliterations and diacritical marks for names and terms in this volume. For the definite article (al-) in Arabic, I have chosen to write "al-" in all cases, even though it is pronounced differently when followed by words beginning with certain consonants. For example, some scholars choose to follow the pronunciation rather than the orthography and write ar-Rāghib rather than al-Rāghib, but I have not done this. I have also avoided using the *tā marbūṭa* in my Arabic transliterations except in instances in which there is liaison with the following word in the genitive—thus, Sūra by itself but Sūrat al-Baqara and madrasa by itself but Madrasat al-Mahdī. In most Persian loan words from Arabic the final *tā marbūṭa* (which in Arabic is both an "h" and a "t") becomes a "t" whether in liaison or not, as in *bid'at*. However, when the *tā marbuṭa* is silent in Persian loan words, as in *madrasah*, the final "h" is usually omitted in transliteration. Modern map names without diacritical marks have been used for certain places such as Kerbala for Karbalā, Khorasan for Khurāsān, Kufa for Kūfa, and Sistan for Sīstān. I have also treated terms in a uniform manner throughout this volume while choosing the most common form of the term in English. Thus, I have chosen to use Seljuk rather than Saljuq and Shi'ite rather than Shi'i, etc. I have also tried to explain words such as diwan/divan, which can have very different meanings, both in Arabic and in Persian, either office/ministry or a collection of poetic works.

Foreign words which are now in English-language dictionaries, such as ayatollah, mullah, ulema, imam, madrasa, jihad, and fatwa, are not italicized or given diacritical marks here, although Sūra and ḥadīth have been given diacritical marks out of respect for scripture. Medieval and pre-modern authors have been transliterated with diacritical marks, but Arabic and Persian authors and editors of the late nineteenth, twentieth and twenty-first centuries have been transliterated without diacritical marks except for *'ayn*s and internal *hamza*s. Persian place names such as Fin and Qazvin have been given without the long ī and w common in Arabic. Persian authors of medieval and pre-modern texts in Persian have usually been transliterated with the short vowels "o" and "e" common in that language and without the long "i" in Arabic, as, for example, Asadi Ṭusi rather than Asadī Ṭūsī and Ḥāfeẓ rather than Ḥāfiẓ. (Sometimes the choice is arbitrary.) For Persian authors writing in both Persian and Arabic, Arabic transliteration has usually been used, for example, Ghazālī. Titles in Arabic are given in Arabic even if the text that it accompanies is in Persian. The names of modern people such as the Ayatollahs Borujerdi, Khoei, and Khamenei have been given in the common form used in newspapers. In all of these tasks I have had the invaluable assistance of Johannes Makar.

Finally, I should mention the different calendars in use in this volume: the Gregorian (which replaced the Julian) calendar (C.E.) in use in the West, the lunar Hijri calendar (A.H.) in use in all Islamic countries, and the solar Hijri calendar (S.H.) also used in Iran and Afghanistan. Dates can differ widely; for example, 2000 C.E. equals 1420–21 A.H. but also 1378–79 S.H. Most often I have given dates in both A.H. and C.E. in the text, for example, 505/1111, or in equivalent centuries, for example, 6th/12th century. I have not tried to give Gregorian equivalents for modern publications that give only A.H. or S.H. solar dates because they usually cover parts of two years.

My immense debt to my teachers and colleagues is nowhere acknowledged in this book. I also owe a great debt to my many graduate students, who for half a century have sat through seminars and worried through Arabic and Persian texts with me. My greatest debt, however, is to my family and, in particular, to my wife Patricia, without whom this volume would not have been finished.

ROY P. MOTTAHEDEH
Watertown, Massachusetts
February 2022

Acknowledgments

1 "An Introduction to Islam," originally "Islam: A Primer," delivered at the Faith Angle Forum in Key West, January (2002) published online without the author's corrections as: *Center Conversations* 15 (Washington, D.C., Ethics and Public Policy Center: 2002), republished without the author's corrections in Michael Cromartie (ed.), *Religion, Culture, and International Conflict: A Conversation* (Lanham, MD, Rowman & Littlefield Publishers, Inc.: 2005) 53–59. © 2005 Rowman & Littlefield Publishers, Inc.

2 "The Foundations of State and Society," in Marjorie Kelly (ed.), *Islam: The Religious and Political Life of a World Community* (New York, Praeger Publishers: 1984) 55–72. ©1984 National Public Radio and the Foreign Policy Association. Reproduced by permission of ABC-CLIO, LLC.

3 "Does Pre-Modern Islamic Thought Allow for a Secular Realm?" in Bruce Fudge, Kambiz GhaneaBassiri, Christian Lange and Sarah Bowen Savant (eds.), *Non sola scriptura: Essays on the Qur'an and Islam in Honour of William A. Graham*, Routledge Studies in the Qur'an (London and New York, Routledge: 2022) 215–224. © 2022 Routledge. Reproduced by permission of Taylor & Francis Group.

4 "An Introduction to Islamic Law and Islamic Jurisprudence," originally "Introduction," in Muḥammad Bāqir aṣ-Ṣadr, *Lessons in Islamic Jurisprudence*, translated and with Introduction, Glossary and Summary by Roy Parviz Mottahedeh (Oxford, U.K., Oneworld Publications: 2003) 1–33. © 2003 Roy Mottahedeh.

5 "Consultation and the Political Process in the Islamic Middle East of the 9th, 10th, and 11th Centuries," in Moawiyah M. Ibrahim (ed.), *Arabian Studies in Honour of Mahmoud Ghul: Symposium at Yarmouk University, December 8–11, 1984*, Yarmouk University Publications, Institute of Archaeology and Anthropology Series 2 (Wiesbaden,

Otto Harrassowitz: 1989) 83–88. © Yarmouk University, Irbid, Jordan. Reproduced with permission.

6 "The Idea of the *Jihād* in Islam before the Crusades," with Ridwan al-Sayyid, in Angeliki E. Laiou and Roy Parviz Mottahedeh (eds.), *The Crusades from the Perspective of Byzantium and the Muslim World* (Washington, D.C., Dumbarton Oaks Research Library and Collection: 2001) 23–29. © 2001 Dumbarton Oaks Research Library and Collection, Trustees for Harvard University, Washington, D.C. Reproduced with permission.

7 "Friendship in Islamic Ethical Philosophy," in Alireza Korangy, Wheeler M. Thackston, Roy P. Mottahedeh and William Granara (eds.), *Essays in Islamic Philology, History, and Philosophy*, Studies in the History and Culture of the Middle East 31, A Festschrift in Celebration and Honor of Professor Ahmad Mahdavi Damghani's 90th Birthday (Berlin and Boston, De Gruyter: 2016) 229–239. © Walter de Gruyter GmbH, Berlin and Boston. Reproduced with permission of Walter de Gruyter and Company; permission conveyed through Copyright Clearance Center, Inc.

8 "Brother and Brotherhood," in Jane Dammen McAuliffe (gen. ed.), *Encyclopaedia of the Qur'ān*, 1 (Leiden, Brill: 2001) 259–263. © 2001 Koninklijke Brill nv, Leiden, The Netherlands. Reproduced with permission.

9 "The *Shu'ūbīyah* Controversy and the Social History of Early Islamic Iran," *International Journal of Middle East Studies* 7: 2 (1976) 161–182. © 1976 Cambridge University Press, Cambridge, U.K. Reproduced with permission.

10 "Bureaucracy and the Patrimonial State in Early Islamic Iran and Iraq," in Ihsan Abbas (ed.), *al-Abḥāth* 29 (1981) 25–36, Journal of the Center for Arab and Middle East Studies, Faculty of Arts and Sciences, American University of Beirut. © 1981 American University of Beirut. Reproduced with permission.

11 "Some Attitudes towards Monarchy and Absolutism in the Eastern Islamic World of the Eleventh and Twelfth Centuries A.D.," in Joel L. Kraemer, Ilai Alon (eds.), *Religion and Government in the World of Islam*, Proceedings of the Colloquium held at Tel-Aviv University 3–5 June 1979, *Israel Oriental Studies*, X (Tel-Aviv, Tel Aviv University: 1980) 86–91. © 1983 Faculty of the Humanities, Tel-Aviv University, Israel.

12 "Oaths and Public Vows in the Middle East of the Tenth and Eleventh Centuries," in Marie-France Auzépy and Guillaume Saint-Guillain (eds.), *Oralité et lien social au Moyen Âge (Occident, Byzance, Islam): parole donnée, foi jurée, serment,* College de France-CNRS, Centre de recherche d'histoire et civilisation de Byzance, Monographies 29 (Paris, ACHCByz: 2008) 117–122. © 2008 Association des amis de Centre d'histoire et civilisation de Byzance, Paris. Reproduced with permission.

13 "Qur'ānic Commentary on the Verse of *khums* (al-Anfāl VIII:41)," in Kazuo Morimoto (ed.), *Sayyids and Sharifs in Muslim Societies: The Living Links to the Prophet* (London and New York, Routledge: 2012) 37–48. © 2012 Morimoto Kazuo. Reproduced by permission of Taylor & Francis Group.

14 "The Transmission of Learning: The Role of the Islamic Northeast," in Nicole Grandin and Marc Gaborieau (eds.), *Madrasa: la transmission du savoir dans le monde musulman* (Paris, αρ éditions Arguments: 1997) 63–72. © 1997 αρ éditions Arguments.

15 "Traditional Shi'ite Education in Qom," in *Harvard Middle Eastern and Islamic Review,* 2:1 (1995) 89–98. © 1995 President and Fellows of Harvard College. Reproduced with permission.

16 "The Najaf Ḥawzah Curriculum," in the *Journal of the Royal Asiatic Society,* 3rd series, 26:1–2 (2016) 341–351. © 2016 The Royal Asiatic Society of Great Britain and Ireland. Reproduced with permission.

17 "A Note on the '*Ṭasbīb*,'" in Wadad al-Qadi (ed.), *Studia Arabica et Islamica: Festschrift for Iḥsān 'Abbās on his Sixtieth Birthday* (Beirut, American University of Beirut: 1981) 347–352. © 1981 American University of Beirut. Reproduced with permission.

18 "The Economic Thought of al-Rāghib al-Iṣfahānī," delivered in 2016 to planned but as yet unpublished Festshrift for Roger Owen.

19 "Administration in Buyid Qazwīn," in D.S. Richards (ed.), *Islamic Civilisation 950–1150* Papers in Islamic History, III (Oxford, U.K., Cassirer: 1973) 33–45. © 1973 Bruno Cassirer Ltd., Oxford.

20 "Medieval Kashan: Crossroads of Commerce and Culture," with Mehrdad Amanat, in David Durand-Guédy, Roy P. Mottahedeh and Jürgen Paul (eds.), *Cities of Medieval Iran, Eurasian Studies* 16 (Leiden, Brill: 2018) 395–429. © 2018 Koninklijke Brill nv, Leiden, The Netherlands. Reproduced with permission.

21 "Faith and Practice: Muslims in Historic Cairo," in Farhad Daftary, Elizabeth W. Fernea and Azim Nanji (eds.), *Living in Historic Cairo: Past and Present in an Islamic City* (Seattle, WA, Azimuth Editions, London, in association with the Institute of Ismaili Studies; University of Washington Press: 2010) 104–116. Reproduced with permission.

22 "Medieval Lexicography on Arabic and Persian Terms for City and Countryside," in David Durand-Guédy, Roy P. Mottahedeh and Jürgen Paul (eds.), *Cities of Medieval Iran, Eurasian Studies* 16 (Leiden, Brill: 2018) 465–478. © 2018 Koninklijke Brill nv, Leiden, The Netherlands. Reproduced with permission.

23 "Keeping the Shiʿites Straight," in Mark Silk (ed.), *Religion in the News* 6:2 (2003) 4–6, 27. © 2003 Center for the Study of Religion in Public Life, Trinity College, Hartford. Reproduced with permission.

24 "Shiʿite Political Thought and the Destiny of the Iranian Revolution," in Jamal S. al-Suwaidi (ed.), *Iran and the Gulf: A Search for Stability* (Abu Dhabi, The Emirates Center for Strategic Studies and Research: 1996) 70–80. © 1996 The Emirates Center for Strategic Studies and Research.

25 *The Quandaries of Emulation: The Theory and Politics of Shiʿi Manuals of Practice*, The Ninth Farhat J. Ziadeh Distinguished Lecture in Arab and Islamic Studies, May 2, 2011, The Department of Near Eastern Languages and Civilization, the University of Washington (Seattle, University of Washington: 2014). Reproduced with permission.

26 "Iran's Foreign Devils," in *Foreign Policy* 38 (Washington, D.C., Carnegie Endowment for International Peace: 1980) 19–34. © 1980 Carnegie Endowment for International Peace. Reproduced with permission.

27 "The Islamic Movement: The Case for Democratic Inclusion," in Nikki R. Keddie (ed.), *Contention: Debates in Society, Culture, and Science* 4:3 (1995) 107–127. © Indiana University Press, Vol. 4, No. 3 (Spring). Reproduced with permission.

28 "Toward an Islamic Theory of Toleration," in Tore Lindholm and Kari Vogt (eds.), *Islamic Law Reform and Human Rights: Challenges and Rejoinders* (Oslo, Nordic Human Rights Publications: 1993) 25–36. © 1993 Nordic Human Rights Publications and the individual authors. Reproduced with permission.

29 "Pluralism and Islamic Traditions of Sectarian Divisions," in *Svensk Teologisk Kvartalskrift* 82 (Lund, Wallin & Dalholm Boktryckeri AB: 2006) 155–161. Reproduced with permission.

30 "The Clash of Civilizations: An Islamicist's Critique," in *Harvard Middle Eastern and Islamic Review* 2:2 (1995) 1–26. © 1995 President and Fellows of Harvard College. Reproduced with permission.

31 "The Islamic Foundation for Citizenship and Pluralism," in *Kufa Review* 7 (2014) 9–15, International Academic Journal Sponsored by the University of Kufa, Iraq (Dar attanweer: 2014). Reproduced with permission.

32 "Some Islamic Views of the Pre-Islamic Past," in *Harvard Middle Eastern and Islamic Review* 1:1 (1994) 17–6. © 1994 President and Fellows of Harvard College. Reproduced with permission.

33 "The Eastern Travels of Solomon: Reimagining Persepolis and the Iranian Past," in Michael Cook, Najam Haider, Intisar Rabb, and Asma Sayeed (eds.), *Law and Tradition in Classical Islamic Thought: Studies in Honour of Professor Hossein Modarressi* (New York, Palgrave Macmillan: 2013) 247–267. Reproduced with permission of Palgrave Macmillan.

34 "The Idea of Iran in the Buyid Dominions," in Edmund Herzig and Sarah Steward 153–160. © 2012 London Middle East Institute. Reproduced by permission of Bloomsbury Publishing Plc.

35 "*'Ajā'ib* in *The Thousand and One Nights*," in Richard G. Hovannisian and Georges Sabagh (eds.), *The Thousand and One Nights in Arabic Literature and Society*. Giorgio Levi della Vida Series in Islamic Studies 12 (Cambridge, U.K., and New York, Cambridge University Press: 1997) 29–39. © 1997 Cambridge University Press. Reproduced by permission.

36 "Finding Iran in the Panegyrics of the Ghaznavid Court," in A.C.S. Peacock and D.G. Tor (eds.), *Medieval Central Asia and the Persianate World: Iranian Tradition and Islamic Civilisation* (London and New York, Cambridge University Press: 2015) 129–142. Reproduced by permission of Bloomsbury Publishing Plc.

Reflections on a Life in Middle Eastern History

My father emigrated from Iran in the 1920s, and his love of Iranian culture, especially its arts and crafts, is largely responsible for my early interest in the Middle East. We spoke English at home because my mother, who was born in New Jersey, never learned Persian. Although I lived in New York for only the first fourteen years of my life, I feel that I am essentially a New Yorker. I still speak American English with a few words of New York dialect, and Central Park is still the best place for a walk.

From kindergarten through high school, I studied at Quaker schools in New York and Pennsylvania. I acquired a deep respect for the Quaker approach to religion, which complemented my parents' religion as Baha'is. My interest in Iran (called Persia in my youth) was encouraged by my father's interest in Persian art, which formed the initial basis for his import business. We lived near the Metropolitan Museum, and I spent many weekends with my parents visiting the Met, especially its rooms for Near Eastern art.

As an undergraduate at Harvard, I was too much in a hurry. I graduated when I was nineteen, a terrible mistake. I was still uneducated and wish that I could have taken more courses. Harvard gave me a fellowship to travel for a year, and I spent three months in Persian-speaking Afghanistan (partly because I could not get a visa to go to Iran). Afghanistan was a little-known treasure and at that time seemed more an eighteenth- or nineteenth-century country than one of the contemporary period.

After my year of travel, I went to the University of Cambridge, England, in 1961–62 and took the final exam, the Tripos, in Persian and Arabic. For the book prize which I received, I chose the Persian mystical epic by Rumi. (I still hope to read it in its entirety before I die.) Shortly after my return to Harvard, my revered teacher, H.A.R. Gibb, with whom I had studied Middle Eastern history and literature, had a stroke and retired. Among my other teachers, was Robert Lee Wolf, with whom I studied Byzantine and Crusader history, and Richard Frye, with whom I studied Middle Iranian languages such as Soghdian, of which I remember nothing. I acquitted myself adequately in the four fields of history in my Ph.D. exams. One of my examiners in the field of medieval Islamic history of the Middle East, L. Carl Brown, later moved to Princeton and offered me an assistant professorship there when I completed my degree.

At Princeton I had a largely congenial set of colleagues in my Department of Near Eastern Studies although I missed being in a history department. As a good citizen of that Department, I taught both elementary and intermediate Arabic and Persian several times during my sixteen years at Princeton. However, it was the advanced language courses serving as history seminars that I most enjoyed. When I moved to Harvard I taught only history courses, basic and intermediate courses for undergraduates and advanced text-based seminars for graduate students. Many excellent scholars came as visiting professors from the Middle East, and I audited their classes with great benefit. Unlike most scholars I never lived in the Middle East except for several months in Cairo in 1988 with my young family. Nevertheless, I made brief visits fairly often. I enjoyed being a guest lecturer, occasionally for extended periods, in many Western countries, including Australia, Austria, Denmark, France, Germany, Great Britain, Italy, Japan, Norway and Sweden, as well as in the Middle East and Far East, in Egypt, Iran, Iraq, Israel, Jordan, Kuwait, Lebanon, Oman, Pakistan, Saudi Arabia, Turkey and the United Arab Emirates. My actual teaching abroad was limited to Koç University in Turkey where I was invited for several years to give a lecture in a world history class as well as in a faculty seminar.

For anyone like me of Iranian background, the problem of sectarianism and the occasional rejection of pluralism seems a central issue in the history of the Islamic Middle East. Consequently, in my research I was attracted to the history of the 4th/10th and 5th/11th centuries partly because it was a period of greater toleration in religious matters in the Middle East. I still dearly hope for growing acceptance in the Middle East of the variety of belief and advocacy that has been so important to the societies in which it exists.

My research on the Middle East began as an undergraduate at Harvard where I wrote my senior honors thesis on a 5th/11th-century Sufi named

Kāzeruni. My dissertation, which I never published, was written, with almost no input from my advisor, on administration and local history under the Buyids, the dynasty that ruled southern Iraq and western Iran from approximately 950 to 1050 C.E. As an Assistant Professor at Princeton, I decided I needed a more original topic for my first book in order to gain tenure. *Loyalty and Leadership in an Early Islamic Society*, published in 1980, was the result, and it did give me tenure. In this book I described the social structure of the societies ruled by the Buyids on the basis of language that showed commitment to the leaders who became rulers. The first part of the Buyid period has unusually rich sources that tell us how the Buyid kings interacted with their soldiers and society. These descriptions allowed me to discuss the manner in which commitments were made between the ruler, his army, his bureaucracy and his more powerful subjects.

While at Princeton I was influenced by the scholars at the Institute for Advanced Studies, in particular by Clifford Geertz, the eminent anthropologist, and Giles Constable, who had taught me medieval European history while at Harvard. Other scholars who greatly encouraged my career were Albert Hourani, Charles Issawi, Andras Hamori, and A.L. Udovitch.

Surprisingly, I won a MacArthur Prize Fellowship in 1981, which allowed me to write my second book, *The Mantle of the Prophet*, about the history of Iran over 2,000 years up to the Revolution of 1978–79. This book is both the biography of a mullah and a survey of critical moments in the history and culture of the past two millennia in Iran.

World events intrude upon any life and career spent in Middle Eastern Studies—the bombing of U.S. marines in Lebanon, the massacres at Sabra and Shatila, the Iranian Revolution, the hostage crisis, the Iran–Iraq war, the fatwa on Salman Rushdie, the Iraqi invasion of Kuwait, the U.S. coalition invasion of Iraq, the 9/11 attacks, the war in Afghanistan, and the Arab Spring—events which, unfortunately, divide scholars of the Middle East. I have tried to explain many aspects of Islamic culture to politicians, journalists, and the general public in the course of my career. For a few decades I was deeply absorbed in events in the Middle East and was invited to events in Washington, D.C., including seminars at the State Department. I wrote op-ed pieces about the massacres at Sabra and Shatila, the persecution of Baha'is, and American support for Arab education, the latter put into the Congressional Record. No matter how impartial one tries to be, it is impossible to avoid being attacked, sometimes viciously, especially if one's ancestry is partly Iranian and one teaches Islamic history. Now, over three decades later that have been full of revolution and war, the general public is, fortunately, much more knowledgeable about the Middle East and Islamic culture.

My third book, *Lessons is Islamic Jurisprudence*, which is a translation of and detailed explanation of Muhammad Baqir al-Sadr's book on Shi'ite jurisprudence as well as my own introduction to Islamic jurisprudence, was intended to offer both Muslims and non-Muslims a mutual ground for discussing the similarities and differences in Islamic and Western law.

My research interests have been wide and varied, which may explain why my book production has been limited. In literature I have focused on *The Thousand and One Nights*, the marvels of Qazvini and Ghaznavid poetry. In art I have focused on Islamic miniatures that illustrate history and the lusterware of Kashan. In history I have concentrated on the medieval period of the 4th/10th and 5th/11th centuries in Iraq, Iran, and Syria and on the modern period in Iran, my country of ancestry. Within history I have focused on aspects of pluralism, toleration, and emulation.

My favorite history book is *The Civilization of the Renaissance in Italy* by Jacob Burckhardt, and I was tempted to write such a book for the medieval Islamic period. Alas, I now see that the writing of such a book is beyond my reach.

I have been called an Orientalist and, more recently, an Islamicist. I regard myself as an historian. I have taught many undergraduate courses as well as numerous seminars for graduate students at Princeton and Harvard, and I have directed dissertations on a wide array of topics. From these students, now colleagues, I have learned much. They, among others, are continuing scholarship in the field of Middle Eastern studies. My students—and also students of my older students—are now spread across the country. Some even teach in Western Europe and the Middle East. I hope that they have benefited in some degree from my teaching and my writing.

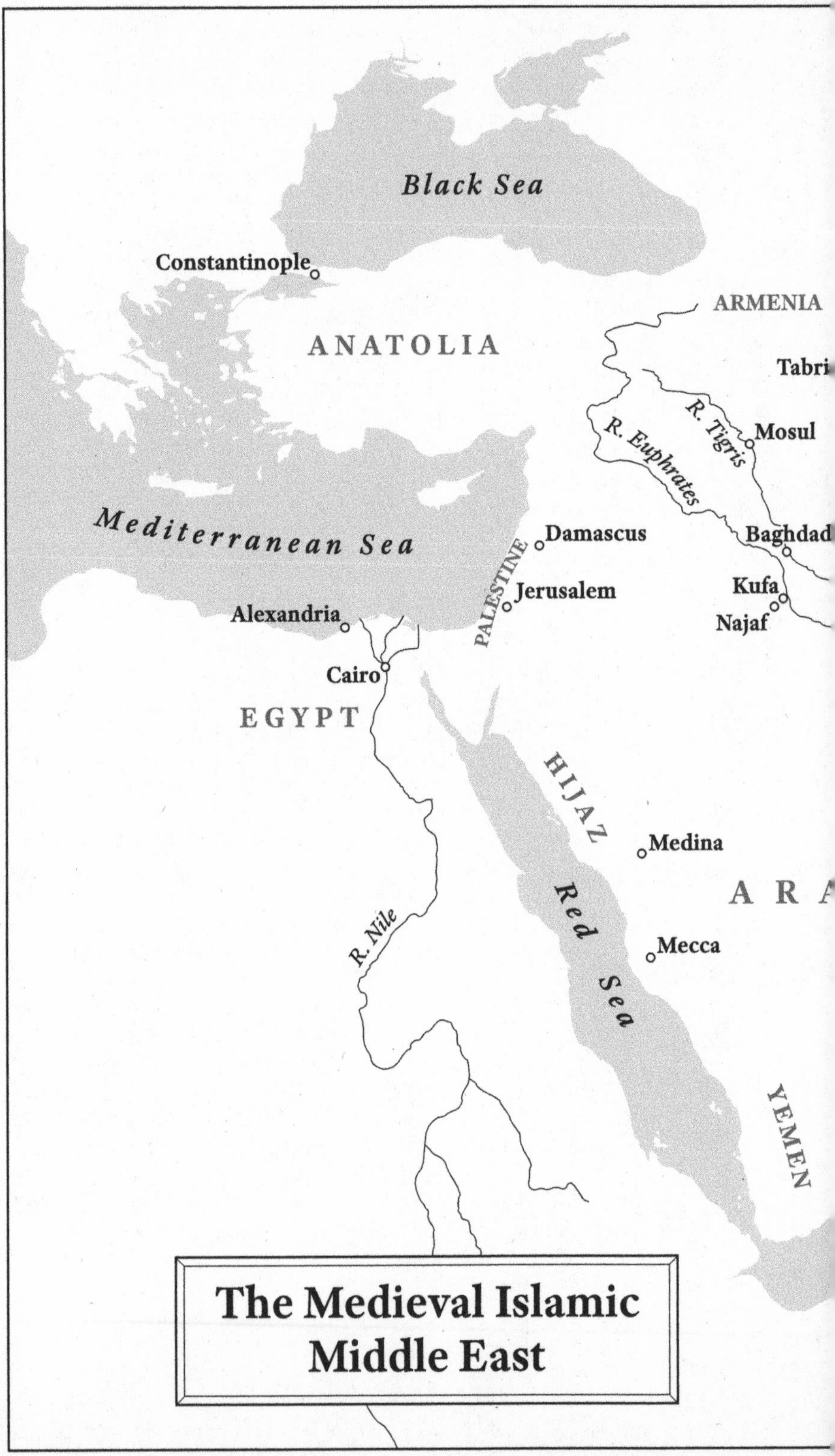
Black Sea
Constantinople
ANATOLIA
ARMENIA
Tabri
R. Tigris
Mosul
R. Euphrates
Mediterranean Sea
Damascus
Baghdad
PALESTINE
Jerusalem
Kufa
Najaf
Alexandria
Cairo
EGYPT
HIJAZ
Medina
ARA
Red Sea
R. Nile
Mecca
YEMEN
The Medieval Islamic Middle East

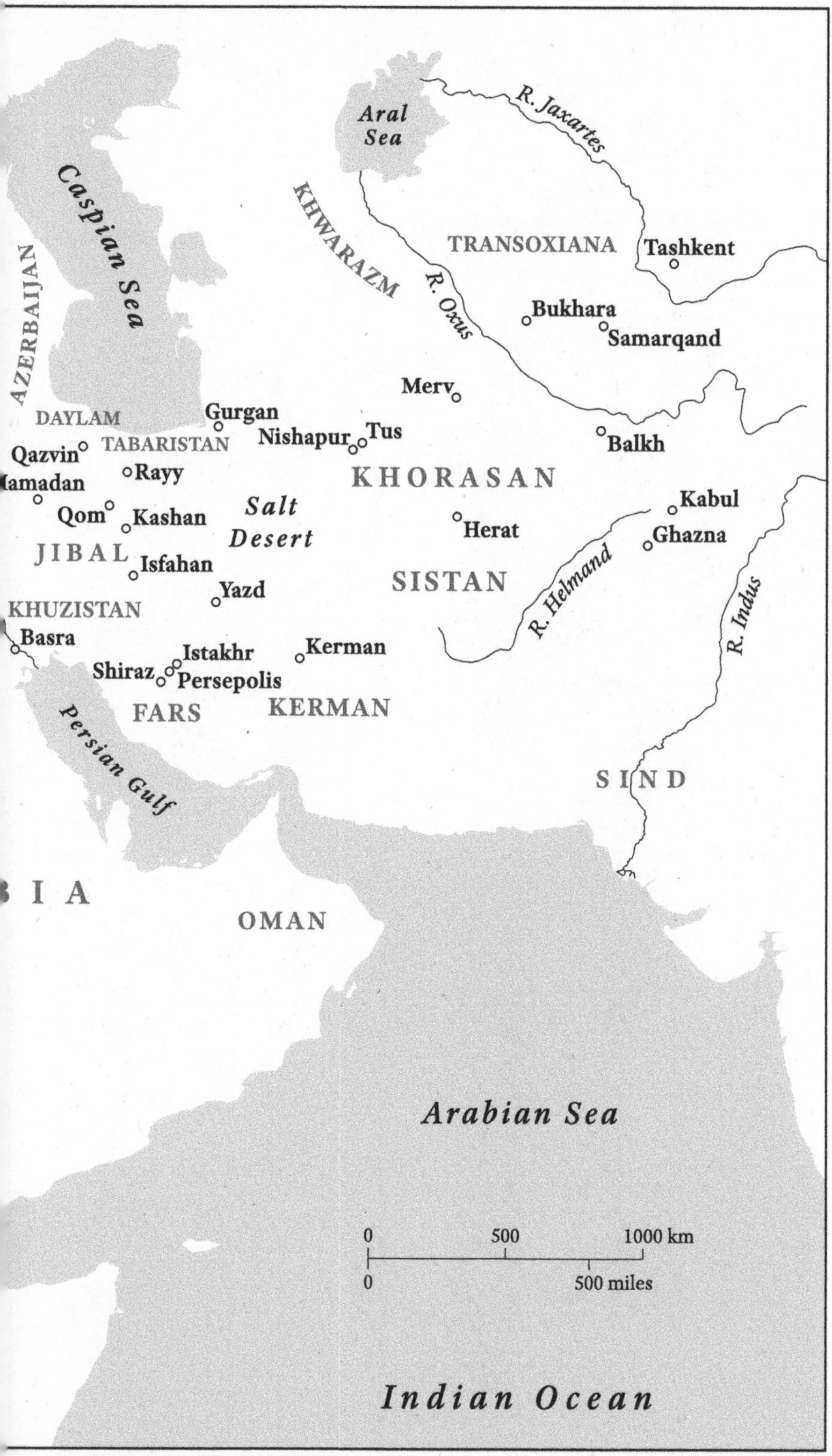

Aral Sea
R. Jaxartes
Caspian Sea
KHWARAZM
TRANSOXIANA
Tashkent
AZERBAIJAN
R. Oxus
Bukhara
Samarqand
Merv
DAYLAM
Gurgan
Tus
Balkh
Qazvin
TABARISTAN
Nishapur
Rayy
KHORASAN
amadan
Kabul
Salt Desert
Qom
Kashan
Herat
Ghazna
JIBAL
Isfahan
R. Helmand
SISTAN
Yazd
KHUZISTAN
R. Indus
Basra
Istakhr
Kerman
Shiraz
Persepolis
FARS
KERMAN
Persian Gulf
SIND
IA
OMAN
Arabian Sea
0
500
1000 km
0
500 miles
Indian Ocean

UNDERSTANDING ISLAM

Attempts to reduce the Islam practiced in the Middle East to simple formulas often fail. If I were thirty-one rather than eighty-one, I would write more about the harm of such reductionism. Of course, many analogues between human cultures exist; otherwise, we would not understand anything outside our own culture. Nor should we regard cultures as static. Very important scholars, such as the French Arabist Maurice Gaudefroy-Demombynes (d. 1957), have written helpful books on Muslim institutions, but the actual historically attested variety in most cases exceeds the space available in a book of ordinary size.

Almost all my work has been devoted to understanding the Islamic period in the Middle East. In its conventional meaning, the Middle East comprises the area from Egypt and Turkey to Afghanistan and the nearby area of Central Asia. There is no reason for omitting other areas of the Islamic experience except for my comparative ignorance about other Islamic areas, such as Morocco and South Asia, both of which interest me greatly but about which I do not feel competent to write.

Some authors correctly distinguish between Muslim as a religious designation and Islamic as a civilizational description for societies predominantly Muslim or dominated by Muslims. There is no question that Muslim belief plays a significant role in Islamic societies. Nevertheless, the historian must understand this role within specific historical contexts. Except for some Muslim practices, such as fasting during Ramadan, it is difficult to find historical universals for Islamic societies. However, even the beginning of the Ramadan fast is a subject of disagreement between Twelver Shiʿites and most Sunnis. It is surprising that democracy at this point exists far less in the Arab world than it does in the Muslim Far East such as Indonesia. Nevertheless, Muslims everywhere have a strong feeling of brother- and sisterhood and look to their mutual destinies with great interest. (This feeling is not dissimilar to that of Catholics and many other Christians.)

One universal on which Muslims agree is the starting date of their calendar. The "migration," or Hijra, of the Prophet Muḥammad from Mecca (where he was persecuted in the early years of his mission of spreading Islam, or "submission" to the message of the Qur'ān) to Medina (where many received him as head of state) took place on July 16, 622 C.E. (Julian calendar). This date was chosen as the beginning of the new Islamic calendar. The Muslim dates are marked A.H. (Anno Hegirae, "in the year of the Hijra"), referring to the Prophet's migration. Although there is agreement on the starting date of the calendar, some Muslims, while keeping the religious calendar in A.H., also use a solar calendar (S.H.) from the same starting date in 622 in order to keep track of the agricultural and astronomical year. The twelve months of the year in the lunar A.H. calendar are approximately eleven days shorter than the solar calendar. Thus, the new year in the A.H. calendar slowly rotates backwards and falls on earlier and earlier dates. Most Hijri dates in this volume are in the A.H. calendar.

The first article in this section, "An Introduction to Islam," began as a conversation in Key West in 2002 between journalists and scholars in The Faith Angle Forum, sponsored by the Ethics and Public Policy Center of Washington, D.C. It was first published online in 2002 as a Center Conversation and subsequently republished in 2005 in *Religion, Culture, and International Conflict: A Conversation*, edited by Michael Cromartie. This discussion was organized to inform some journalists who had no background in the history of Muslims and their religion. Because this article began as a conversation, it is intended for the intelligent lay reader with no background in Islam or Muslim societies. In this article, I, as an historian, have emphasized the history of Muslims from the Prophet Muḥammad in the seventh century C.E. to the present. The centrality of the Qur'ān, the transformation of Islamic society by the year 1000 C.E., and the development of Muslim societies from the seventeenth and eighteenth centuries to the present are also discussed. This brief introduction to Islam leaves out many very important things, but it may help readers understand the more technical articles that follow.

The second article in this section, "The Foundations of State and Society," was published in 1984 in a book intended for non-specialists entitled *Islam: The Religious and Political Life of a World Community*, edited by Marjorie Kelly. This article summarizes the main points of the introductory chapter in my book *Loyalty and Leadership* (1980). It attempts in a general way to present ideas of government common among Muslims from the beginning of Islam up to the present. Again, like the first article, it is intended for the intelligent lay reader. It discusses in some detail the difference between Sunni belief and Twelver Shiʿite belief and the evolution of political thought among Muslims. For many Muslims throughout their history their rulers were a lesser evil than anarchy, the most feared state of society. Many Muslims came to believe that their governments were not an important element in their salvation but a means of keeping order while they personally sought salvation through religious observance and behavior. The article also explains the continual hope of Muslims for an ideal of Islamic government, which motivated political change in some periods, although no such attempt at universal government was ever widely accepted.

The third article in this section, "Does Pre-Modern Islamic Thought Allow for a Secular Realm?", was delivered at a conference in 2018 honoring my close and admired friend and colleague William Graham on his retirement. It was published in 2022 in *Non sola scriptura: Essays on the Qur'an and Islam in Honour of William A. Graham*, edited by Bruce Fudge, Kambiz GhaneaBassiri, Christian Lange and Sarah Bowen Savant. The question of the possibility of a secular sphere in the history of Muslim societies has always interested me, and I have discussed the subject in my classes over the last forty years. In many systems of pre-modern Islamic thought the sacred and the forbidden share some characteristics. The emergence of a secular realm in Middle Eastern Islamic thought is indicated by titles that signal the ruler's command of both "the world" and "religion," occasionally among the Buyids and then regularly under the Seljuks. Islamic ethics came to emphasize individual moral development. Such ethics were concerned with the distinction between God's claims and human claims, thereby demonstrating a belief in the separation between the divine and the human spheres. Although Islamic distinctions between sacred and secular exist, they do not match the contemporary understanding of these terms in the West. I believe that describing the changing use of terms is one of the central tasks that historians of medieval Islam should undertake. Undoubtedly, the digitization of medieval texts will make such matters easier in the future, although there is no substitute for reading these texts through in their original language.

An Introduction to Islam

By and large, Muslims view Islam not as a human religion but as the most perfect revelation of God that has come to mankind. All human society needed revelation, and therefore the very first human being, Adam, had to be a prophet because he could not live without the guidance of revelation.

The word "Muslims" in the Qur'ān often means, simply, "believers." In some cases, "Muslims" includes other "People of the Book"—Christians and Jews—as well as followers of the Qur'ān, and sometimes it seems to mean simply "followers of the Qur'ān." Most Muslims do not believe in natural law (although the Shi'ites, who make up perhaps fifteen percent of the Muslim population, do). But Muslims do believe that human beings have an inner nature that is religious, and because of this, Muslims through the ages have believed that there *is* salvation outside of Islam (though some would say this is rare). They believe that human beings can discover some of the moral law by examining this inner nature.

Muslims see themselves as following the ultimate monotheism. Of course, both Islam and Christianity are, in a way, derivatives of Judaism, and both are ways of universalizing monotheism. But Muslims believe their monotheism is the perfect, the ultimate monotheism.

Now, the next thing to understand about Islam is that Muḥammad is not Christ. The self-revelation of God in Jesus is a concept that Muslims

---

Author's note: This article originated as a taped conversation between journalists and scholars that was transcribed and published online, without the author's corrections, as: *Center Conversations* 15 (Washington, D.C., Ethics and Public Policy Center: 2002). It was later republished, without the author's corrections, in Michael Cromartie (ed.), *Religion, Culture, and International Conflict: A Conversation* (Lanham, MD, Rowman & Littlefield Publishers, Inc.: 2005) 53–59. As a conversation it was an informal, spoken presentation without footnotes intended for the general public. For this introduction, the original conversation has been slightly modified due to the passage of time, small sections no longer relevant removed, the language made clearer and more formal, and the quotations footnoted.

do not accept. And the Qur'ān is not the Bible; maybe it corresponds to the Torah, but it is definitely not the Bible. Muslims believe that the entirety of the Qur'ān is a perfect, unerring revelation of God.[1] And just as the New Testament relates the things that Jesus said and did, there is a great deal in Islam about the sayings and doings of Muḥammad. These are the famous ḥadīth. It is a body of material—some tens of thousands of sayings are considered somewhat more authentic than five hundred thousand other sayings. It allows believers to construct several different varieties of Islam. And it is somewhat like the New Testament in that it shows the perfect exemplar, Muḥammad, of the religion.

Another basic fact is that there is no sacramental function by clergy in Islam. Ulema are the learned people, the religious authorities; they are not priests. Every Muslim can do everything necessary for personal salvation by himself or herself. This is important to understand because people keep saying, "Why don't the Muslim clergy speak out for this or that?" Well, they speak out for everything! One man's clergyman is simply another man's *ḥalāl* butcher. To understand Islam, one must set aside the perception of religion that is based on Christianity and look to a different model. Of course, there are some Muslim systems that are slightly more hierarchical than others. One is the system of the Twelver Shi'ites, the kind of clergy the Iranians have. But even they are absolutely incapable of keeping order among and within the clergy. There is great debate over who has the right to determine the meaning of scripture.

The Arabs make up only a minority of Muslims—two hundred or three hundred million out of more than a billion [421 million out of more than 1.9 billion in 2022]. And, of course, a significant number of Arabs are Christians [about 15 million in the Middle East in 2022]. But although Arabs constitute less than twenty percent of Muslims, people often claim to be talking about the Muslim world when what they are really describing is the Arab world. That error will hamper any ability to conceptualize what is happening among the Muslims.

Like Judaism and Christianity, Islam honors Abraham as a patriarch of the faith; he is considered an ancestor of the Prophet Muḥammad. There are some questions common to all the Abrahamic faiths. First, does anyone have more authority than anyone else to interpret salvation? Second, are

1 Perhaps Jesus Christ, as the Logos (the Word) and the perfect incarnation of God, is comparable.

God's commandments for the construction of the physical and moral world necessary? That is, was God in a sense constrained by logic? Or are these arrangements arbitrary? As logicians would say, is logic inherently logical, or is it in fact something that has been *constructed* to describe things? I think this is a fundamental difficulty of all human thought. And it turns out to be a central theological problem for Islam.

A third problem area is: How much, if at all, had God ceded to humans the responsibility to figure out his moral intentions for the world? Cardinal Ratzinger (before becoming Pope Benedict XVI) made this point when he wrote that it was within God's power to concede no control of the moral world to mankind; that it was within God's power to instruct mankind for every action, but that instead there is a sphere in which He has ceded to man the power to solve problems and puzzles by himself.[2] Judaism, Islam, and Christianity all wonder where that sphere is. A corollary is that both Judaism and Islam have a certain amount of law in their scripture—and there are certainly more commandments in the Old Testament and in the Qur'ān than in the New Testament—but this does not mean that Jews and Muslims believe all actions in this life are religiously determined. It is simply a matter of looking to scripture in the hope of finding guidance as to how to behave.

Christianity emphasizes the need for God's grace in order for human beings to be saved. A famous Islamic saying is, "Acts [are to be evaluated] according to their intentions [and not by outcomes]."[3] And there is great individual responsibility to God. At least three times the Qur'ān says, "Let no one bear the burden of another,"[4] meaning that one bears the

2 See Joseph Cardinal Ratzinger, *Gott und die Welt: Glauben und Leben in unserer Welt*, Ein Gesprach mit Peter Seewald (Stuttgart, Deutsche Verlags-Anstalt: 2000) and the English translation by Henry Taylor, *God and the World: Believing and Living in our Time, A Conversation with Peter Seewald* (San Francisco, Ignatius Press: 2002). Throughout this book Cardinal Ratzinger speaks of the freedom God has given to man: "God gives us a great deal of free play" (p. 105). He sometimes speaks of the "sphere of freedom" (pp. 188, 454). In the second part of an earlier book, *Salt of the Earth: The Church at the End of Millennium* (San Francisco, Ignatius Press: 1997), he discusses the relationship between Church and State. Cardinal Ratzinger clearly recognized the difference between God and the World. Interestingly, a similar recognition of "Religion" and the "World" can be seen in the Islamic "propaganda" of the Buyid rulers of the 4th/10th and 5th/11th centuries; see my articles "Does Pre-Modern Islamic Thought Allow for a Secular Realm" (Article 3 here) and "Finding Iran in the Panegyrics of the Ghaznavid Court" (Article 36 here).

3 A.J. Wensinck, "Niyya," in *The Encyclopaedia of Islam*, 2nd ed., VIII (Leiden, Brill: 1993) 66–67.

4 Qur'ān I:164, XII:15, XXXIX:7.

responsibility for his/her actions and for his/her salvation. There is an interesting word in Arabic that means to do good or to make something beautiful (*iḥsān*). A typical verse in the Qur'ān reads, "Vie with one another, hastening to the way which leads to forgiveness from your Lord, and to a garden whose breadth is the heavens and the earth, prepared for the pious, those who spend in charity in the times of both ease and adversity and who restrain their anger and pardon other human beings. God loves those who do what is beautiful (or, what is good)."[5]

Now, we come to my real discipline, which is not the theology of Islam but its history. By the year 1000 C.E.—an arbitrary but easily remembered date—a whole series of things had happened within the Islamic world, which I will discuss. Muḥammad died in 632. By 1000 it was clear that the experiment of a single Muslim ruler—the caliph—had failed. And a class of religious experts—the aforementioned ulema—had divided itself (though not to everybody's satisfaction) into certain discrete schools of law. In their development of a kind of scholastic learning, the ulema represent the unity of Islam. The high scholastic tradition that existed among the ulema in the Middle Ages was centripetal; people wrote referencing one another's works. A famous book by the celebrated theologian, Ghazālī (d. 505/1111), written to refute philosophy as it had developed in the area of Baghdad was called *The Incoherence of the Philosophers*. Then in the next century the Spanish Muslim philosopher Averroes, who was a great medieval thinker and influential on European scholasticism, wrote an attack on that book, calling his book *The Incoherence of the Incoherence*. It is a world in which at that high scholastic level there is continuous conversation.

In what way are Muslims a united community otherwise? Mainly in ritual observation. Now, there is some variation in that area as well. But the prayer is fairly uniform (though not entirely), as is the practice of the pilgrimage. However, as for the Qur'ān and what it means for life, there is some amount of disagreement. And therefore, in a sense, the Muslim world today is only one very specific instance of Qur'ānic observance. Now, I feel that Muslims throughout the ages have had a great deal of sympathy for one another and have been worried about the plight of fellow Muslims. They recognize the community of people who share the same ritual observation. But beyond that, I do not think the terms "Islamic

5 Qur'ān III:133–134.

world" and "Muslim world" are always useful units of reference. There are not enough commonalities for that.

In any case, by the year 1000 C.E. the ulema, although internally divided into schools of law, represent the unity of Islam. By the end of that century, around 1095, the theological schools called madrasas were established with large dormitories, enormous pious endowments, adequate stipends, abundant supplies of ink and paper, and the like. So, the scholastic system developed in most of the Muslim world through patronage for its particular kind of learning.

By the year 1000 C.E. it had also become clear that law was the queen of the sciences, the most important subject. That does not mean that students in the madrasas did not study algebra, astronomy, and other subjects; but always these subjects were given an Islamic wash. In studying Islamic thinkers, it is extremely difficult to distinguish a kind of Islamic patina from something that goes very deep and is really Islamic. The Qur'ān is the first lengthy piece of Arabic prose we have, and it really establishes Arabic. There was only poetry before. Aside from letters and little bits of translation of the Gospels, Arabic prose of any length did not exist before the Qur'ān. As a result, the language of the Qur'ān permeates Arabic in a way that I think the language of the King James Version of the Bible permeated English in the seventeenth and eighteenth centuries. But that is an imperfect parallel, and there is nothing recent in English that gives one any sense of the way a foundational document can permeate a language. Anyway, many things considered "Islamic" have no real connection with Islam. They appear to be Islamic because that is the baseline on which their language and thought exist.

Although law became the queen of the sciences, Islamic law is staggeringly unspecific about many aspects of the law of public governance. The lawbooks merely say that the community should have a totally just ruler. They say it in many different ways—the ruler should be kind, he should be merciful, he should be just, he should not be swayed by the people around him. However, by and large they leave aside the whole matter of public governance.

By the year 1000 C.E. the caliphate had disappeared, and there was great disagreement as to what Islamic government was. There are specific commands and prohibitions in the Qur'ān. But there are at most five hundred verses of law-making—much less than in, for example, Leviticus.

Also, by 1000 C.E., Sufism had developed. This is a kind of mystical Islam that emphasizes individual spiritual development. Rumi, the Persian poet and mystic of the 7th/13th century—the best-selling Muslim poet in the

United States—is an example of the Sufi tradition. Sufism is an extremely appealing interpretation of Islam, and it became an important way of spreading Islam throughout Central Asia, India, Indonesia, and elsewhere.

By the year 1000 C.E., people had come to realize that they were being ruled by governments that had come to power simply by deposing other regimes. The word "sultan" means "power," and by the year 1000 "Mr. Power" was beginning to be the title of the ruler. These rulers had imposed themselves on kingdoms. The ulema tended to say, "Okay, as long as the rulers prevent anarchy, they are acceptable." There's a famous line of Ibn Taymīya (d. 732/1332), the prominent Sunni rigorist: "It has been said that sixty years of an oppressive Imam is better than one night without a ruler, and experience confirms that."[6] So, a lot of the ulema were incredibly quietist. But they demanded certain things from the government—including patronage for themselves—which they got, and the defense of Islamic society against outside attacks.

In Egypt, the Mamluk dynasty ruled from 1250 to 1517 C.E. They were of slave origin; in fact, the whole dynasty was a group of slaves, succeeding one another as sultan. What did they do? Well, they kicked out the last Crusaders, and they defended the Muslims against the invading non-Muslim Mongols. They patronized learned Muslims; for example, they built madrasas. As long as they allowed Muslims to do what they needed to do for their own salvation, such as prayer and fasting, their regimes were considered more or less acceptable. There was a kind of understanding that the ulema would not endorse any specific regimes, but neither would they fight a regime as long as it allowed Muslims to do the things necessary for their own salvation.

Correspondingly, the Muslim learned tradition is concerned with orthopraxis—that is, behaving as a Muslim—as a standard for who is a Muslim. There is a verse in the Qur'ān that is translated, "Do not say to anyone who offers you peace, 'You are not a believer.'"[7] In general, Muslims do not call one another "unbelievers." Only in the direst circumstances would one charge a Muslim with failing to be a Muslim.

So, there was a de facto secular sphere. People think that in Islam, religion and government are one.[8] Yes, on a hypothetical level; people

---

6 Ibn Taymīya, *Majmū' al-Fatāwā*, 28:391. He is echoing the view of his predecessor, al-Ghazālī, the great Sufi thinker and theologian.

7 Qur'ān IV:94.

8 See my article "Does Pre-Modern Islamic Thought Allow for a Secular Realm?" (Article 3 here).

dreamed that it should be that way. But in reality it was not; it had ceased to be that way for a long time.

In the 3rd/9th century a law school was founded by Aḥmad ibn Ḥanbal (d. 241/855), whose followers are known as Ḥanbalīs. The founder was very much a literalist in his interpretations of scripture. He wanted to restore Islam to the purity of the faith as it was elucidated during the time of the Prophet and his Companions, those who were close to him during his lifetime. Ibn Ḥanbal's followers were much more ready than anybody else to call an opposing Muslim "unbeliever." The Ḥanbalīs and their school of law, which is still the smallest school of law in Islam, started to develop a kind of rigorist Islam that, in the hands of some of its interpreters, rejected even deductive logic.

The middle of the 7th/13th century brought the Mongol invasion, and the last caliph, who was only a shadowy figure, was killed. People speak about the Crusades as the great offensive campaign from the West, but the Mongols were much worse. They were pagans who conquered at least half of the Muslims around the world in their time. The Mongols had strange habits such as not washing because they believed that water was sacred and should not be put on the human body. This was deeply offensive to Muslims, for whom washing is ritually important. The Mongols were altogether terrifying, strange, non-Muslim people who suddenly ruled over half of the Muslims.

In the seventeenth century the Ottoman Empire was doing well. But in the eighteenth century it became glaringly obvious that European power and prosperity were far surpassing that of the Ottomans. Muslim states, though not yet subjected to direct colonialism, knew that they were lagging behind the European states. Two things happened: 1) Muslims developed a longing to discover the secret of European power, and 2) movements arose that were excessively concerned with purity.

In the mid-eighteenth century, Ibn 'Abd al-Wahhāb founded a rigorous, anti-Sufi system that came to be called Wahhabism. Ibn 'Abd al-Wahhāb was ready to apply the term "unbeliever" to anybody who was not a true monotheist according to his very narrow definition. Most later followers of Ibn 'Abd al-Wahhāb were not so ready to reject other Muslims. But from the rigorist thinkers of the eighteenth century, there was a succession of people leading up to Osama bin Laden in the twentieth century (not a mainstream Wahhābī), who expanded the idea that people could be called non-Muslim and said that entire existing governments in Islamic countries could be declared non-Muslim. Part of this trend was a reaction to the rise of an educated secular elite, who, while often intensely religious, did not believe that the ulema, the traditional scholastics, were the real interpreters of scripture.

The present-day Islamic militancy is a self-defeating movement. Its first aim had been to overthrow national governments. For instance, earlier pronouncements by Osama bin Laden were all about overthrowing the Saudi Arabian government, but later ones rambled all over the world and talked about Hiroshima and the situation of the Palestinians. In a national context the militants are almost always defeated; in fact, in certain countries, like Egypt, public sentiment turned against them. The massacre at the Tomb of Queen Hatshepsut near Luxor in 1997 was a kind of crest of the Islamic militant wave in Egypt. Fifty-eight foreign tourists and four Egyptians were brutally slain, and most Egyptians were horrified. The Islamic militant wave had crested in Egypt, and so these Muslim militants went off to the wildest, least controlled country in the world, Afghanistan.

Does the future belong to the moderates? They may not have their voice now, partly because many competing voices are stifled by autocratic governments. But among the educated the moderates seem to be in the majority. In the long term the moderates will, by and large, be followers of the reformist thinkers of Islam, of whom a significant number are in the Islamic diaspora. Remember how many Muslims are living in nations that are not majority Muslim, such as India.

What is the best way to counter the militants? Would a Fulbright plan to provide a better and more rounded education in these Islamic countries help? A lot of young Muslims go through engineering school but do not learn how one argues about history, about subjects that by their very nature are uncertain, like the social sciences. We should sponsor and help schools in the vernacular languages—Arabic, Pashtu, Urdu, whatever. This would not only create the human capital that is essential for the development of these countries but would also indigenize a certain way of conducting debate. It would give the students of these schools more understanding of their interlocutors in the West. Such a plan would also make the civil society—particularly the NGOs that exist in these countries—more powerful, in that the people who lead them would not be all Western-educated people.

The Foundations of State and Society

Islam at first allowed little room for the compartmentalization or separation of life into sacred and secular spheres, and hence little room for the dichotomy of church and state that has been such a familiar part of the Western Christian experience. Nevertheless, the practical historical experience of Muslims in trying to build an Islamic state did bring home to them that while there was a sphere of individual action for which one could be held accountable, there was also a sphere of collective action from which the individual might have to divorce himself or herself in part. This partial divorce arose because of disagreements about the nature and source of authority in the Islamic community after the death of the Prophet. Such a partial divorce of the individual Muslim from his government was always thought to be a temporary arrangement. But it proved to be a beneficial one, in that it has allowed Muslims to preserve a general sense of political community on an ideological level even though, on a practical level, the Muslim world has been divided among many governments for over a millennium.

Roughly two years before his death in 632 C.E., the Prophet Muḥammad made his last pilgrimage to Mecca. On this occasion he gave a moving (and often quoted) address to his followers, in the course of which he said, according to one source: "God has given two safeguards to the world: His Book [the Qur'ān] and the *sunna* [the example] of His Prophet [Muḥammad]." According to another source, Muḥammad said: "God has

Author's note: This article was first published as: "The Foundations of State and Society," in Marjorie Kelly (ed.), *Islam: The Religious and Political Life of a World Community* (New York, Praeger Publishers: 1984) 55–72. It had no footnotes, but I have added references to relevant articles in this volume. The article was adapted, with additions, from the introductory chapter in my *Loyalty and Leadership in an Early Islamic Society* (Princeton, Princeton University Press: 1980) 7–25. Reproduced by permission of ABC-CLIO, LLC.

given two safeguards to the world: His Book and the family of His Prophet." Taken together, these two statements contain all the basic ingredients of Muḥammad's legacy for the future political life of the community: the Qur'ān, the family of Muḥammad, and the example of Muḥammad. Yet the correct mix of these ingredients remained a subject of active (and sometimes bitter) disagreement.

Even before he led a political community, it had been clear to Muḥammad that the moral vision of Islam had political implications. Islam was a religion in which public life was very much a collective responsibility of the community, and the Qur'ān provided regulations according to which the community should discharge the responsibility. When, for the last twelve years of his life, Muḥammad was the actual leader of a political community, the political aspect of Islamic belief was confirmed and extensively elaborated.

When Muḥammad died, the Islamic community no longer had a divinely inspired leader, and quarrels over choosing a new leader immediately broke out. These quarrels have so preoccupied most historians, both Eastern and Western, that they have neglected the gradual emergence of a remarkable unanimity among Muslims on an issue even more fundamental than the choice of a successor to Muḥammad: the consensus of Muslims in the original centers of Islam in Arabia that the community should have a single leader. They agreed that the community of believers should neither be divided into separate Muslim political communities (like the separate Christian and Jewish political communities), nor accept some form of collective leadership, such as a governing council. In the decade after Muḥammad's death, the Muslims of the Ḥijaz (the province around Mecca and Medina) thoroughly defeated separatist movements in Arabia, after which the great majority of Muslims everywhere and for centuries accepted the idea that the Muslim community (*umma*) should be politically unified under a single leader.

This unity of the *umma* and of its leadership was in perfect agreement with the character of the Islamic revelation. In the view of Muslims, God had revealed in Islam a moral law intended for all mankind, and the vehicle of this revelation was a single man (Muḥammad) who lived a life of exemplary obedience to that law. Muḥammad, the single vehicle of revelation and perfect example, had maintained a unified community under his sole leadership. After his death, Muslims quite naturally felt that his example of single leadership should be followed.

QUR'ĀN AND SUNNA

The Muslim community also agreed on the status of the Qur'ān, the first "safeguard" that Muḥammad had left for his community. The Qur'ān is, in the belief of Muslims, the infallible word of God. The earlier revelations that are described in Jewish and Christian scripture have been distorted through time and were never intended to have the completeness of Islam. The Qur'ān is the undistorted revelation in which, as God tells the believers in the Qur'ān itself, "I have perfected your religion for you and completed My favor [or "benefit"] to you" (V:3). But the Qur'ān discusses leadership in general terms. It gives no direct indication as to how a new leader should be chosen, although later commentators constructed many and conflicting interpretations of the implications of Qur'ānic verses for this question.

If the agreement of the Islamic community on the status of the Qur'ān did not solve the constitutional problem of succession to leadership, it did guarantee the central importance of the Qur'ān for Islamic culture. The most complete revelation must have implicit in it something of relevance for every human situation, and most Muslim thinkers sought to make some connection between their ideas and the contents of the Qur'ān.

The second safeguard left for the Muslim community was the *sunna* of the Prophet. If there was widespread agreement as to the importance of the *sunna*, there was equally widespread disagreement as to its contents. The word *sunna* means customary practice; and in the context of Muḥammad's speech quoted above, it means the practice established by the example of Muḥammad (and, to a lesser extent, by his closest Companions, who were presumed to be most deeply influenced by him). The Qur'ān may have been comparable with the Christian Logos in its role and its preternatural perfection; but the Qur'ān did not directly legislate for all circumstances, and the Qur'ān was a book, not a person. Muḥammad was the perfect example of a Muslim; and his example, therefore, was a nearly indispensable guide to living the life of a Muslim and to making the implicit concepts of the Qur'ān explicit.

This example was known to later generations through ḥadīth. The word "ḥadīth" is often translated "tradition" and is explained as a report of a saying or action of Muḥammad. But ḥadīth is more than this; it is the body of accounts of what Muḥammad said and did, what was done in his presence and not forbidden by him, and even includes some of the sayings and doings of his close Companions. It is, in effect, all the historical material available to establish the *sunna*. To draw another analogy with Christianity, from the point of view of many Muslims, the Gospels are a form of Christian ḥadīth about Jesus.

The *sunna*, therefore, was very much a "safeguard" to the community. It gave the Islamic community a means for extending the teachings of Islam, and it assumed an underlying unity in these teachings. It assumed this unity not only because an extensive spiritual and ethical system needs some degree of harmony between its parts, but also because reverence for the *sunna* meant that such extensions would, if at all possible, be traced to a single historical source, the lives of the Prophet and his closest Companions. The study of the Qur'ān had primacy over the study of ḥadīth, but anyone who has looked at the earliest extant Qur'ānic commentaries knows that in the first two centuries of Islam, the greater part of such commentary consisted of ḥadīth. Together, the study of Qur'ān and ḥadīth gave a further unity of focus for future Islamic cultures, because Arabic philology developed in large part out of a desire to understand the sometimes difficult and often elliptical language of the Qur'ān and ḥadīth. As a result, wherever there were Muslim men of learning, they cultivated the "Arabic sciences" as an integral part of religious learning.

A body of material so important and so lacking in boundaries could not pass through history unmolested. Ḥadīth appeared that were generally thought to be forgeries; and the "science" or "knowledge" of ḥadīth, which studied the validity of ḥadīth, developed gradually but with ever growing elaboration over the first four centuries of the Islamic era. Ḥadīth was the central ingredient of religious "knowledge" (*'ilm*) and, consequently, "ulema" ("knowers" of religious knowledge) were above all knowers of Qur'ān and ḥadīth. The knowledge or science of ḥadīth involved a careful study of the chain (*isnād*) of transmitters through which a ḥadīth had been handed down from a Companion of Muḥammad to the generation of the scholar; and gatherings to transmit ḥadīth were probably the most common occasions on which ulema came together in formal meetings.[1]

Only in the 5th/11th century does the study of ḥadīth seem to have decreased in importance among the religious sciences. By this time, *isnād*s were becoming impossibly long, and there was increasing consensus as to

1 See my article "The Transmission of Learning: The Role of the Islamic Northeast" (Article 14 here).

which written ḥadīth collections were reliable. Moreover, other religious sciences had been more fully elaborated. For example, the implications, or pseudo implications, of ḥadīth for law had been distilled into law books; and however much early law and ḥadīth may have been intertwined, scholars—especially if they wanted a career involving law—could hardly study their subject without making the law books their principal concern.

THE FAMILY OF MUḤAMMAD AND SHIʿISM

The third "safeguard" was the family of Muḥammad. Neither of the other two safeguards was the cause of so much disagreement as was this one. Some believed that Muḥammad intended his family to succeed him in leadership of the community and saw in this safeguard the only correct understanding of Qur'ān and *sunna*; for how could there be agreement in interpreting the Qur'ān and the *sunna* without the (possibly infallible) leadership by a member of this family? Others saw in this legitimist attitude a denial of the whole rationale of the *sunna*. If the *sunna* was the example of Muḥammad as reported by his close Companions and confirmed by the subsequent actions of these Companions, how could anyone claim that the reports and actions of these Companions should be radically discounted unless confirmed by the interpretation and example of leaders from Muḥammad's family?

At the death of Muḥammad, the family-centered theory of leadership looked to ʿAlī, Muḥammad's cousin and son-in-law, as the obvious successor ("caliph") to the Prophet.[2] ʿAlī had been one of the very earliest (possibly the earliest male) to accept Muḥammad's message. He was, moreover, the adopted son of Muḥammad and, through his marriage to Fāṭima, he was the father of Muḥammad's only grandsons to reach maturity, Ḥasan and Ḥusayn. However, at the death of Muḥammad, the majority of Muslims did not accept the family-centered theory. The advocates of the family said that because the other Companions of Muḥammad wanted the leadership, they chose to disregard the obvious claims of ʿAlī and the expressed intention of Muḥammad that the descendants of ʿAlī should take over the leadership.[3]

---

2 See my discussion of the "Caliphate" in Bryan S. Turner *et al.* (eds.), *The Wiley Blackwell Encyclopedia of Social Theory* (Oxford, U.K., John Wiley & Sons Ltd.: 2017; also published online).

3 See my article "Keeping the Shiʿites Straight" (Article 23 here).

In contrast, the majority of Muslims did not believe that Muḥammad had clearly designated 'Alī as his successor, or that 'Alī was a choice clearly superior to other close Companions of Muḥammad. 'Alī did not press his claims, but after the third caliph was killed, many Muslims accepted him as the new caliph. The death of 'Alī's predecessor, however, had marked the beginning of the first civil war in Islam; and 'Alī was swept into this civil war without being able to bring it to an end. He was killed in 661 C.E., and the caliphate passed away from his branch of Muḥammad's family.

The descendants of 'Alī, the 'Alids, continued to play an important role in the Islamic world. Even those who rejected 'Alī's claim to be the appointed successor of Muḥammad revered the 'Alids for the family ties that had distinguished their ancestors. In fact, because most of the 'Alids were descended from Ḥasan and Ḥusayn, the sons of 'Alī and Fāṭima, they were, through their mother, lineal descendants of Muḥammad himself. Most Muslims considered it a religious duty to show the 'Alids signs of their great respect, signs that sometimes included gifts of money. Therefore, even 'Alids who did not claim any special right to the caliphate had a certain advantage in seeking political power; and there have been many 'Alid kings in Islamic history, including the present Kings of Morocco and Jordan.

There were always 'Alids, however, who regarded the honor of their ancestry not as a possible focus for the reverence of other Muslims, but as a positive claim for their political allegiance. The supporters of these 'Alid claimants were called *Shī'at 'Alī* (the party of 'Alī); hence they became known to Muslims as Shi'ites. Shi'ism was in the first instance based on a political claim; and for one branch of Shi'ites, the Zaydīs, the political claim continues to be the most important element of belief that distinguishes them from non-Shi'ites. The Zaydīs believe that any 'Alid who personally and militarily seeks the leadership of the Islamic community, and has the religious learning necessary for leadership, can be the caliph. The recent rulers of the northern Yemen, the Imams, are such leaders. The Zaydī theory recognizes that two or more 'Alids may make such a claim to leadership simultaneously. But the principle of unified rule is preserved in that, if the territories of two Zaydī leaders are close enough to be in effective contact, one of them must resign (or be forced to resign) leadership in favor of the other.

In the earliest Islamic period these political claims seem to have been the most important element in Shi'ism, but claims to spiritual leadership soon came to be of central importance to a large group of Shi'ites. As was discussed above, such claims allowed the Shiʿites to maintain a unified view of religious life by making a single ʿAlid leader the authoritative standard for the interpretation of legal, political, metaphysical, and all other matters. It was also natural that some branches of Shiʿism should emphasize the spiritual leadership of their leaders because, in most cases, real political leadership remained in the hands of non-Shiʿites. Many Shiʿites, therefore, came to distinguish between caliphate—actual political leadership—and "imamate," the theoretical right to leadership. Muslims in their collective daily prayer stand behind an imam who leads them and is the model for their movements; and where an imam is not officially appointed by the government, any group of Muslims is supposed to defer to the "best" among them as imam. The overall leader of authority and model for the Islamic community was, in the view of the Shiʿites, an ʿAlid, who was also called imam in this more particular sense. The Shiʿites held that the imam should also be caliph, though circumstances might prevent him from attaining this office. Even if he passed his life in unrelieved obscurity, the one God-given imam for any period was, in the view of his followers, the only real authority for the spiritual and political life of his age.

After a few generations, there were hundreds of descendants of ʿAlī. If only one of them could be the imam (and, it was hoped, the caliph), which one should it be? As we have seen, the Zaydī answer was both clear and confusing—the imam was any learned ʿAlid who was militarily successful in claiming leadership. But other Shiʿites laid much more emphasis than the Zaydīs on the imam's role as authoritative interpreter, and they therefore sought to explain the presence of this authority as the result of something more than individual initiative. Most Shiʿites other than Zaydīs felt that the ʿAlid imam could be identified because he had directly inherited his station and/or had been specifically designated by his predecessor.

Neither of these principles, however, could induce agreement among the non-Zaydī Shiʿites. Inheritance was essential to the overall claim of the ʿAlids, and the line of imams most widely recognized by present-day Shiʿites is a line in which the "imamate" usually passed to the eldest son. Yet the principle of primogeniture was never very strong in the Islamic Middle East; and even in this widely recognized line, the "imamate" passed from Ḥasan (ʿAlī's eldest son by Fāṭima, Muḥammad's daughter) to Ḥusayn (the second eldest son by this mother). Specific designation proved just as unreliable a means of guaranteeing an undisputed succession. Most non-Zaydī ʿAlid claimants to the "imamate" kept such claims secret or, at least, were wise enough not to discuss them publicly, for these claims implied a challenge to the existing non-Shiʿite leadership, especially to the non-ʿAlid caliphs. Therefore, specific designation was almost never performed publicly, and the claims of any supposed designee were hard to establish. Since most such designations seem to have been made orally by the dying imam in his last hours, their authenticity was almost inevitably suspect to some of the followers who had not been present.

It is not surprising, then, that Shiʿites often disagreed as to which ʿAlid was the imam. It is also not surprising that frequently, after the apparent death of an imam, some of his followers held either that he had not really died, or that his successor was living in such perfect secrecy that even those close to him did not know his station. ʿAlid pretenders had been repeatedly defeated, and God had allowed their opponents to continue in power. Therefore, some Shiʿites were not at all astonished to hear that their imam had not died, but disappeared, and would reappear in the fullness of time to become, with divine aid, the actual ruler of the Islamic community.

The most important instance of such an interruption to a line of visible imams took place in 873 C.E., when the Eleventh Imam in succession from ʿAlī through his son Ḥusayn died in Iraq. Some of his followers held that he was succeeded by his infant son, the Twelfth Imam, who had disappeared and would return as a messianic figure. The Shiʿites who awaited the return of this Twelfth Imam were called Twelvers: The Twelvers changed their allegiance from a visible to an unseen imam at a juncture in Islamic history when divisions had forever destroyed the political unity of the Islamic *umma*, and the caliphs who still ruled the core of the former empire, Iraq and surrounding territories, were being murdered periodically by their Turkish palace guard. It was a good moment for the Twelvers to put aside their aspirations for worldly power. Moreover, non-Shiʿite Muslims were willing to tolerate the Twelvers more than they did most other Shiʿite groups, especially if the Twelvers had no immediately present candidate for the caliphate. At present, the majority of the inhabitants of Iran and southern Iraq are Twelvers.

SUNNISM AND THE FIRST CALIPHS

While Shiʿites, deprived of power, were evolving a variety of political theories, historical events were hammering out the political theory of the non-Shiʿites. Later Muslims would look back and call these early non-Shiʿite Muslims Sunnis, as most non-Shiʿites came to be called in a later period.[4] In the early Muslim world, the Shiʿites had definite, strongly held positions on succession to the caliphate; but for most other Muslims, events moved faster than theory, and their theory was to a large extent an explanation of events and a reaction to the more exclusive political theories of the Shiʿites. Only later did this initially less well-defined theory become the basis of conscious sectarian self-definition.[5] Sunnism, the school of Islam espoused by the majority of present-day Muslims, was the historicist solution to the problems presented by Muḥammad's death. In light of the ḥadīth in which the Prophet had said his community would never "agree upon an error," the Sunnis could look back at the history of the Islamic community and, in retrospect, use the agreement of previous Muslims as a test for the validity of previous experiments by Muslims in creating a Muslim government. However, the formulation and the contents of this retrospective, historicist solution could (and did) emerge only after the Islamic community had lived through a fairly long historical experience.

On the day of Muḥammad's death, after heated discussion, a large meeting in Muḥammad's capital city of Medina chose Abū Bakr as his successor; and in token of their choice, each of them swore an oath of allegiance to him.[6] Abū Bakr had a measure of authority among Muslims because of his very long and close association with Muḥammad. He was, for example, Muḥammad's father-in-law, and had been appointed by the Prophet to be the prayer leader (*imām*) in his place during his final illness. Just as important was Abū Bakr's membership in the tribe of Quraysh, which ruled the nearby city of Mecca. The next day, when the Meccans heard that a fellow Meccan of Quraysh had been chosen caliph, they accepted the choice. These historical events were later to become fundamental points of reference for Sunni political theory.

In subsequent years in Medina, several further choices of caliph by discussion and/or acclamation followed; it was a procedure familiar from

4 See my article "Keeping the Shiʿites Straight" (Article 23 here) for the distinction between Shiʿites and Sunnis. See also my article "The Quandaries of Emulation: The Theory and Practice of Shiʿite Manuals of Practice" (Article 25 here) for some important modern differences between Shiʿites and Sunnis.

5 See my article "Pluralism and Islamic Traditions of Sectarian Division" (Article 29 here).

6 See my article "Consultation and the Political Process in the Middle East of the 9th, 10th and 11th Centuries" (Article 5 here).

the practice of Arab tribes before Islam and sanctioned by a verse in the Qur'ān that said, "[Better and more enduring is the reward of God] to those who obey their Lord, attend to their prayers, and conduct their affairs by consultation" (XL:38). No clear precedent for the method of consultation emerged in these early choices of caliph, and the Islamic world was soon plunged into a civil war that ended, after the murder of 'Alī, with the victory of the Umayyads, a clan of Muḥammad's tribe, the Quraysh. The Umayyads set up the first successful hereditary succession to the caliphate, though their right to this succession was not uncontested.

Finally, in 750 C.E., another family of the tribe of Quraysh, the descendants of Muḥammad's uncle 'Abbās, defeated the Umayyads and assumed the dignity of the caliphate. From their capital in Baghdad, they ruled virtually all of the Islamic world except Spain, which passed into the hands of a descendant of the Umayyads. The Abbasids tried to win the support of the ulema by their extensive patronage of religious learning. Even if they did not claim the infallibility that was attributed to various 'Alid leaders, the Abbasids hoped to be accepted as the spiritual guides of the Islamic community. Despite the caliphs' vacillating support of conflicting views of orthodoxy, however, the great majority of Muslims refused to concede to the Abbasid caliphs any special authority to regulate such matters. Yet their patronage of learning and their ostentatious use of religious symbols made the Abbasid caliphate itself a religious symbol. Therefore, Muslims who had lost any desire to obey the Abbasids nevertheless defended the principle that the Abbasid caliphs should, even if deprived of executive power, be maintained as a symbol of legitimate government and of unity among Muslims.

That the Abbasids should lose actual control of an empire stretching from the Atlantic to Central Asia was hardly surprising. What is surprising is the frequency with which both the Abbasids and their usurpers agreed to cover each loss with the fiction that the caliphs had kept full theoretical sovereignty over any province while granting actual control to the usurper. In token of this sovereignty, the actual ruler (often called an *amīr*, commander) had the name of the reigning Abbasid caliph mentioned in the Friday congregational prayer and on the coinage. By the 4th/10th century, these *amīr*s called themselves kings, a title that had rarely been used by rulers since the pre-Islamic period. Because of the pagan associations of kingship, the caliphs had always sought to disassociate themselves from this title, and kingship and caliphate continued to have separate existences.[7] In exchange for the recognition offered by an *amīr*, the Abbasid caliph often (but not invariably) sent a diploma investing the *amīr* with the right to rule his territories. Among the many advantages offered by this exchange of formalities was that it recognized the continuing agreement of most Muslims to the principles that had prevailed after the selection of the first caliph, Abū Bakr—an agreement that there was not, nor could there be, a plurality of Islamic communities. There was one Islamic community, by definition a unity of all Muslims; and the symbol of its unity was the single leader: the caliph, the "successor" of the Prophet.

CONSENSUS

If the ruler was the personal symbol of the unity of the Islamic community, the principle that symbolized the will to unity was *ijmāʿ* (consensus or agreement). Both Shiʿites and those groups who later came to be called Sunnis accepted the validity of the famous ḥadīth that "my community (*umma*) will never agree upon an error." The theory of most Shiʿite groups in some sense anticipated the basic political needs of the Islamic community and provided a precise means for their complete fulfillment: the community needed an ʿAlid leader chosen according to a definite principle and considered this leader to be the most authoritative interpreter of Islam for his age. Most non-Shiʿites believed that God had intended that the leader of the Islamic community be chosen by some sort of consultative process. Beyond that, they did not agree on the procedure to be used in this consultative process, or the scope of the authority of a leader so chosen. They believed in the historical mission of the community, which in the long term would not "agree upon an error."

The amazingly rapid territorial expansion of the Islamic state in the generation after the Prophet's death made it clear that from the start the community would perform this historical mission, not only in the confines of the Arabian Peninsula but also on the stage of world history. It seems likely that the earliest caliphs, Abū Bakr and ʿUmar, did not intend wars of conquest. But when their expeditions to subdue pro-Byzantine and

7 See my article "Some Attitudes towards Monarchy and Absolutism in the Eastern Islamic World of the 11th and 12th Centuries" (Article **11** here).

pro-Persian Arabs revealed the weakness of the Byzantine and Persian empires, they showed great genius at organizing and controlling subsequent conquests, which within a few decades put the caliph in Medina in control of Iran, Iraq, Syria, Egypt, and areas beyond. What might have been an uncoordinated migration of militarily aggressive Bedouin was, in fact, an orderly change of regimes in which much of the lower-level civil administration of the conquered areas was kept intact. In accord with the practice of Muḥammad and the precept of the Qur'ān, Jews and Christians, as "People of the Book"—that is, communities possessing revelations recognized by the Qur'ān—were allowed not only to continue to practice their religion but also to retain some authority to run their own communities; and non-Muslims continued to constitute the majority of the inhabitants of the new Muslim state for well over two centuries.

While the rapidity of the conquests encouraged the tolerance of Christians and Jews, it also encouraged some discrimination on the part of the early Muslims. The first generation of Muslims was overwhelmingly Arab and, not surprisingly, some Arabs saw themselves as naturally superior, a ruling class with a proprietary right to interpret Islam. Many of the sectarian divisions of the first two centuries were sharpened by the social division between Arab and non-Arab Muslims. The rapidity of the conquests also gave emphasis to the military interpretation of jihad, "the struggle" for Islam, a term probably meant to denote the inner moral and spiritual struggle as much as the struggle in the outside world.[8] Implicit in a monotheistic system in which revelation has brought a new system of law is the idea that God intends the government applying this legal system to be the government of all mankind. Hence, reinforced by their amazing conquests, early Muslims believed that it was God's intention that Muslims "struggle" to make Islamic government universal, although, as we have said, they had no intention of forcing the conversion of other monotheists like Christians and Jews. From this military interpretation of jihad grew the concept of dividing the world into the *Dār al-Islām* (the Abode of Islam) and *Dār al-Ḥarb* (the Abode of War), the latter the area yet to be conquered.

Early Muslims realized that the military achievement of the Islamic community was little short of miraculous. For some, the "miracle" of

8 See my article, co-authored with Ridwan al-Sayyid, "The Idea of the *Jihād* in Islam before the Crusades" (Article 6 here).

these successes must have been proof of the correctness of their leadership in this period. Even if it were not accepted as confirmation of this leadership, the military achievement seemed to many Muslims too valuable a gain to risk in uncertain struggles for new leadership. Therefore, both for practical reasons and to live within the religious injunction to consensus, they accepted leadership that was not necessarily the "best" that the Islamic community could provide. They felt that unity was more important than purity, and that no leader or other individual could by himself establish the norms of the Islamic community, since they were an extension of the norms of all of the close Companions of Muḥammad. It cannot have been clear to Muslims in the period immediately after Muḥammad's death how they should treat variations in these extensions of the *sunna*. Gradually, however, it became clear that consensus was one way of judging such variation. Interpretations of Islam that did not allow themselves to be judged by consensus could not, of course, be accepted within this framework.

In general, consensus-minded Muslims were more prone to inclusion "of variation" than exclusion, to postponement rather than haste, and remained close to the spirit of the famous saying of Thomas à Kempis that "man proposes but God disposes." In areas not unambiguously discussed in the Qur'ān men would act and suggest how other men should act according to their understanding of Islam; and the long-term judgment of the Islamic community would judge whether their actions and injunctions were appropriate models for future Muslims. The reception of moral principle was similar to the reception of ḥadīth: anyone could elaborate the norms of Islam or transmit ḥadīth, but only the collective judgment of the Islamic community could accept a ḥadīth as genuine or accept that a principle was truly in the spirit of Islam.

For a long time, this attitude of consensus-minded Muslims corresponded with the shared political and economic interests of Muslims. For over two centuries, Muslims were a minority in their new empire. At first, their law and theology were far from being fully elaborated. More particularly, they had, as we have seen, only very general principles to guide them in developing a constitutional theory. Various legal and theological positions did, of course, appear in these early centuries. If factions had succeeded in persuading the majority of Muslims that they must choose a position and fight to impose this position on other Muslims, the Islamic empire might well have shrunk back to the wastes of Arabia from which it had sprung. However, the privileged Muslim minority did in fact recognize its shared interests well enough to stay and prosper.

Moreover, Islam, in the view of most of its followers, was more a religion of correct practice than of correct belief. Four of the five pillars of Islam, often listed as the fundamental principles of the Islamic faith, are things one should do, not ideas one should believe. To preserve a unified Islamic community, consensus-minded Muslims demanded considerable uniformity in the public acts required of Muslims in the Qur'ān, and avoidance of open contradiction to the explicit teachings of the Qur'ān. For the rest, they usually allowed variation and did not seek to anticipate the judgment of history.

Through the collective judgment of the Islamic community, and especially of the ulema, history did—slowly but ineluctably—render its judgment. There was not then, nor has there ever been since, a consensus even on the method for consensus. Did the *ijmāʿ* refer to the consensus among the people of Medina, or among the ulema, or among all Muslims? The emergence of widely accepted views, in spite of the vagueness and variableness in the definition of *ijmāʿ*, shows how strongly Muslims were determined to maintain some degree of unity. Often this consensus was achieved by virtue of allowing that a limited variety of positions was acceptable on certain questions. Accordingly, differing schools of law arose that came (sometimes reluctantly) to accept each other.

The consensus-minded scholars were able to preserve the sense that they were working within a shared tradition only by continual backward glances at the particular strand of the tradition they were elaborating. Hence the strong piety of each school of elaboration toward its founders (often ḥadīth scholars), and toward the Companions of Muḥammad whose practice became a common reference point for these schools. This piety had actually increased as the period of the Companions receded into the remote past, and as the study of ḥadīth became more elaborately systematic in its attempts to link each ḥadīth with a known Companion.

Only after considerable historical experience could *ijmāʿ* create distinctive positions for the consensus-minded Muslims. Agreement on the canonical body of the ḥadīth, the *sunna* in its strictest sense, was an essential element in the evolution of a defined Sunnism; but such agreement was slow in coming. For example, of the six books of ḥadīth that are supposedly canonical to Sunnis, the *Sunan* of Ibn Māja (d. 886 C.E.) began to be accepted as canonical only in the 5th/11th century. North African

Muslims seem never to have accepted it as canonical, yet they remained Sunnis both in their own view and in the view of Middle Eastern Muslims. In its treatment of ḥadīth, as in so many other respects, the more clearly defined and sectarian Sunnism of later generations emerged only gradually.

A LIMITED PLURALISM

Another supposed mark of a defined Sunnism is the doctrine that there were four, and only four, schools of law acceptable to Sunnis. This doctrine is based on the contention that the individual right to bring new ideas into Islamic law by interpreting Qur'ān and ḥadīth ceased in the 3rd/9th century when the founders of the four schools and a handful of their most important followers had died. In the classic phrase of the Muslim lawyers, the "gate" of individual interpretation had closed. While it is true that Muslim lawyers of the 3rd/9th century were increasingly persuaded that there was no more room for individual reasoning on the law, it is also true that they were not agreed as to which of the existing schools were "canonical," and would not agree for centuries.

There were, however, many reasons why there should be a constant movement toward tighter definition of what was or was not acceptable to the Sunnis. With the passage of time, Sunnism became rigid simply because the collective judgment of the Muslim community had established positions on a great number of issues. But the historical circumstances of the Muslim community were an even greater incentive to delimit a Sunni form of Islam. When the Abbasid caliphs lost actual control of vast provinces of the Islamic empire, it became clear that the Muslims could not rely on a central government to preserve a community of belief among Muslims. To confuse matters further, most of the new regimes of the 4th/10th century were Shiʿites. And most of them were founded by men from peripheral areas of the Middle East, nomads or mountain dwellers, who had little interest in the fine points of the religion of their city-dwelling subjects. The Sunnis saw that in the presence of alien and occasionally hostile governments they had to rely largely on themselves to preserve the achievement of earlier consensus-minded Muslims, and to prevent deviant speculation from pulling the community in so many directions that it would be irretrievably rent. An increasing number of scholars therefore sought to find an inclusive but clear definition of the boundaries of Sunnism.

They were spurred on in this effort by the activities of the Isma'ili Shi'ites and the Ḥanbalī Sunnis. Other forms of Shi'ism were, compared with Isma'ilism, ideologically benign. Zaydī Shi'ism was in most respects similar to Sunni Islam, except that it reserved both the "imamate" and the caliphate for descendants of 'Alī. By claiming that its leader had disappeared, Twelver Shi'ism left the confused and dangerous field of 3rd/9th-century caliphal politics. The Isma'ili branch of the Shi'ites, however, refused to bury its claim. A successful Isma'ili rebellion in Tunisia gave a living 'Alid control of an important segment of the Islamic world. In 969 C.E. his descendants conquered Egypt, where the Fatimids, as this 'Alid dynasty came to be known, ruled until the late 6th/12th century.

The Fatimids assumed the title of caliph, and claimed the doctrinal authority granted to the 'Alid imam by most forms of Shi'ism. For the first time, this kind of Shi'ism had the support of a government; and law codes, works of theology, and other expressions of this interpretation of Islam poured forth from the pens of Fatimid supporters in Cairo. The Isma'ili Fatimids also had a carefully organized propaganda service; and their agents were amazingly successful in establishing clandestine groups of Isma'ilis throughout the Islamic Middle East. (The Druze of modern Syria, Lebanon, and Israel are the spiritual descendants of a group of Isma'ilis who were converted by Fatimid missionaries in the 5th/11th century.) The elaborate definition of this form of Shi'ism as well as its successful missionary activity and the direct challenge of its leader's assumption of the title caliph—in open opposition to the Abbasid caliphate, the symbol of consensus-minded Islam—all forced the non-Shi'ites to define their attitude toward the Shi'ites, and so to become, in their own turn, more sectarian.

The Ḥanbalīs were ready to answer this challenge even before the Fatimids appeared. Ḥanbalism is a school of law and of theology. The Ḥanbalīs insisted on finding ḥadīth solutions to questions whenever possible. Correspondingly, they insisted that the close Companions of Muḥammad were all to be respected, and Ḥanbalīs were horrified that the Shi'ites should denounce some of the Companions while over-venerating 'Alī in what was, to their mind, a pagan spirit. In the seat of the caliphate, Baghdad, Ḥanbalism became a genuinely popular movement, in part because it seemed to offer a remedy for the decline of the Sunni caliphate and the related fortunes of its capital. Ḥanbalīs felt that Muslims should take individual action to combat innovations introduced into the Islamic community since the time of the Companions. In 4th/10th-century

Baghdad, the Ḥanbalīs were the most active of all religious groups in mounting popular demonstrations that, since they were often directed against other religious groups, did a great deal to sharpen the boundaries between those groups.

Fear of sharpened boundaries and annoyance at Ḥanbalī agitation drove the Abbasid caliph to compromise the inclusive spirit of consensus-minded Islam. In 934 C.E., because of "their imposing conditions on people" and causing unrest, he issued a rescript declaring that if the Ḥanbalīs persisted, he would use fire and sword against them. Significantly, the decree accuses them of "ascribing unbelief and error to the party of the Prophet's family." The decree implicitly contrasts the Ḥanbalīs with the great majority of Muslims, who called each other unbelievers only in extraordinary circumstances. Ḥanbalī thinkers would probably have rejected the charge that they called Shi'ites unbelievers, but their attitude to anything that they regarded as deviation from Islam was so severe that it may well have seemed to their victims that they had been treated as unbelievers.

In the long run, however, the inclusive spirit of consensus-minded Islam prevailed among most Ḥanbalīs as well as among most of their opponents. The prevalence of consensus-mindedness and the inclusive spirit that accepted a certain pluralism of belief were reinforced by the political circumstances of Muslims after the disintegration of a universal Islamic government. The majority of Muslims, including a majority of the Shi'ites, accepted the necessity of living in societies that were very imperfectly governed, however one interpreted the guidance Muḥammad had offered in his farewell speech during his last pilgrimage to Mecca. Most Muslims understandably refrained from giving deep commitment to these imperfect governments and reserved such commitment for descriptions of ideal Islamic government, which they felt had existed in the past and might again be realized only in a remote, perhaps messianic period in the future.

This devotion to an ideal of Islamic government, together with an allowance of a degree of pluralism within the boundaries of orthodoxy, held the Islamic community as a whole together in the absence of any formal government or structure of state to bind its members. While there was still no clear separation of the sacred and the secular on a theoretical level, most Muslims came to see the utility of a clear distinction between the actual and the ideal. They were willing to live with their actual, very imperfect governments as long as they could cherish their ideal. Devotion to this ideal may have stunted the growth of a political theory that dealt with necessarily imperfect institutions, but it had important practical consequences: it preserved a unified sense of the *umma* based on Islamic law that recognized the sanctity of contracts of all kinds across the borders created by kings and sultans. It had another consequence as well: it preserved a sense of community that could survive repeated changes of governments and conflicts of interest among Muslims. This sense of community, even in the face of the terrifically powerful and divisive force of modern nationalism, is very much alive today.

Does Pre-Modern Islamic Thought Allow for a Secular Realm?

At first the search for any possible analog to the Western dichotomy between the sacred and the secular or profane realms in pre-modern Islamic thought seems unpromising and even, if we are to believe some authorities, totally wrong-headed.[1] Bernard Lewis, the doyen of American specialists on the Islamic Middle East, tells us in an introductory essay published in 1984:

> For a traditional Muslim church and state are one and the same. They are not separate or separable institutions, and there is no way of cutting through the tangled web of human activities and allocating certain things to religion, others to politics, some to the state and some to a specifically religious authority. Such familiar pairs of words as lay and ecclesiastical, sacred and profane, spiritual and temporal, and the like, have no equivalents in classical Arabic and

Author's note: This article was first published as: "Does Pre-Modern Islamic Thought Allow for a Secular Realm?" in Bruce Fudge, Kambiz GhaneaBassiri, Christian Lange and Sarah Bowen Savant (eds.), *Non sola scriptura: Essays on the Qur'an and Islam in Honour of William A. Graham*, Routledge Studies in the Qur'an (London and New York, Routledge: 2022), 215–224. Reproduced by permission of Taylor & Francis Group.

1 A much earlier version of this paper was delivered as a talk at the Harvard Divinity School in the late 1980s, and I revisited the topic for presentation at the September 28, 2018, conference in honor of William Graham's retirement. Three colleagues, Professors Intisar Rabb, Andras Hamori, and Sarah Savant offered valuable comments for this article. Long after this essay was delivered to the editors, I discovered on June 16, 2021, that a recent Harvard Ph.D., Dr. Rushain Abbasi, had written a 2020 dissertation on the religious and the secular. From this he published an article, "Did Premodern Muslims Distinguish the Religious and Secular? The *Dīn-Dunyā* Binary in Medieval Islamic Thought," *Journal of Islamic Studies*, 31:2 (2020) 185–225. This recent work may supersede what I have written here. I congratulate Dr. Abbasi on his work but cannot at this late stage integrate his findings into my own article.

> other Islamic languages, since the dichotomy which they express, deeply rooted in Christendom, was unknown in Islam until comparatively modern times, when its introduction was the result of external influences.[2]

A work in German, the *Lexikon Religiöser Grundbegriffe*, published in 1987 under the general editorship of an excellent Islamicist, Adel Khoury, puts this case even more boldly in its article *Sakral* or the "Sacred" by the learned Dr. S. Balić, the Muslim author of the Islamic section of this article. He states:

> the concept "sacred" is apparently foreign to Islam. This is to be explained by the fact that on the one hand this religion regards the entirety of life—the spiritual as well as the material—as its legitimate field of interest, and on the other hand perhaps takes stronger cognizance of human limits than does, possibly, Christianity. According to the Koran, only God is the holy ruler (*al-malik al-quddūs*).[3]

This essay will argue that such descriptions of the pre-modern intellectual world of Muslims are misleading with respect to some Muslim thinkers. In fact, the widespread view of Western Islamicists that there is a sphere in which, as Bernard Lewis claims, that sacred and profane, or even sacred and secular, are undifferentiated or even undifferentiable, corresponds much more to the assertions of some contemporary Islamic revivalists than to the majority of pre-modern Islamic thought in the Middle East. Here by pre-modern Islamic thought, I mean the thought preserved in the writings of Muslims in the Middle East in the period before the rise of late Muslim empires (the Moghuls, Safavids, and Ottomans) around 1500. Perhaps some of the confusion on this (as on so many other issues) springs from the desire of some Islamicists and some Muslims to offer a reified Islam divorced from historical context.

Before turning to possible analogues of sacred and secular I think we should consider why some contemporary Islamicists have said that no such analogues ever did exist. First, in some sense they correctly see Islam as

2 Bernard Lewis, "Preface," in Gilles Kepel, *Muslim Extremism in Egypt: The Prophet and the Pharaoh* (Berkeley and Los Angeles: 1985) 11.

3 "Sakral," in *Lexikon Religiöser Grundbegriffe*, ed. Adel T. Khoury (Wien and Köln: 1987) 949.

the outcome of one long trend in the history of Western Asia. If the ancient Babylonians carried off each other's gods, and if the Assyrians pretended that they smashed alien gods, and if the new monotheistic religions claimed that their God was not limited to any local place or season or period, wasn't it likely that some form of monotheism would hold that the moral will of the one true God should set the standard for all human conduct in all places and at all times and in all matters? So, it would seem, many Muslims view their own religion. But, not coincidentally, so do many non-Muslim monotheists view theirs as well. Second, many of the specialists in Islamic studies are caught up in Eurocentric considerations that have remained all too common in our field. Only after explaining why Islamic Middle Eastern societies are what they are can we ask why they are not what the West is (or, at least, what we believe the West to be). Instead, however, we have continually approached these societies with topsy-turvy questions: Why didn't the Islamic Middle East produce an industrial revolution? Why didn't it produce representative systems of government? Why didn't the Islamic Middle East grow economically the way that Western Europe has done in modern times? And so on. Such questions are not irrelevant. Anyone who has spent years explaining, as every Islamicist in the West is compelled to do repeatedly, that the Qur'ān is not a Bible, Muḥammad is not a Christ, and that the ulema (or mullahs), the Muslim specialists in religious learning, are not priests, will understand the temptation to dwell on explaining why things are not what they are not, instead of explaining why they are what they are. Incidentally, the point concerning the lack of a priesthood in Islam and of any sacraments that might mark some persons as priestly in function, does largely account for the absence of any distinction between "lay" and "ecclesiastical." Correspondingly, the distinction between a secular and regular clergy would have little meaning in most Islamic settings.[4]

But are we, in pre-modern Islamic Middle Eastern thought, really faced with the vast, flat and undifferentiated terrain as seen by so many specialists? I think not. To begin with, we should look at words from the root of the word mentioned by Dr. Balić above, *al-quddūs*, in the phrase *al-malik al-quddūs*, "The King, the Holy," (a root familiar to many Western readers from the Jewish prayer Kaddish). A word from this root is used

4 Secular clergy do not belong to a monastic order while regular clergy follow the *regulae* of their orders such as the Jesuits or Franciscans or Benedictines.

three times in the Qur'ān to distinguish sacred space which is *muqaddas*, sanctified, from all other worldly space as when we are told that on two different occasions God spoke to Moses in the sacred valley (*al-wādī al-muqaddas*) of Tuwa below Mt. Sinai (LXXIX:16) and as when Moses tells his people to enter the Holy Land (*al-arḍ al-muqaddasa*, V:21). And, to this day Jerusalem is called in Arabic *al-Quds*, the Holy Place. But the words associated most strongly both in the Qur'ān and throughout Islamic tradition with sacred space are *ḥaram* and *ḥarām*, both derived from a root familiar to Westerners in general because it appears in the term "harem" used for private quarters of a house. It is also familiar to Bible scholars in particular because of the Hebrew *ḥērem*, which specialists tell me has the same semantic spectrum as the Arabic *ḥarām*.[5] It is well to remember that in a general way *ḥarām* and *ḥaram* are both terms for places, things and actions that are separated from common use or contact either because they are proscribed as an abomination to God or because they are consecrated to God. *Ḥaram* is most often used for a sacred space and *ḥarām* is most often used as an adjective meaning "forbidden," but both terms have wide application. Both are to some degree concerned with propriety, what is proper and what is not proper. If we think of the harem, a word from the same root usually translated as the women's apartments of a house, in its specific legal sense, as the women's apartments that are allowed only to men within the prohibited degrees of marriage, we understand the relatedness of sanctification and prohibition in those things that have been separated from other things by God's specific injunction.

Not only is the connection of *ḥaram* with sacred space and time amply attested to in the Qur'ān, but it is also amply attested to in the life of Prophet Muḥammad who, according to the traditional accounts of his life, personally supervised the demarcation of the boundaries of the *ḥaramayn*, the two *ḥaram* areas of Arabia, one in Mecca and one in Medina, so that there would be no ambiguity as to the exact areas within which certain ritual laws were to be observed.[6] To my mind we are close to the discussion among students of religion about the sacred and the profane. An interesting feature of the Islamic case is that the sacred and the forbidden are special categories at

5 See Haim H. Cohn, "Ḥerem," *Encyclopaedia Judaica*, VIII (Jerusalem: 1971) 343–355.
6 See R.B. Serjeant, "Haram and Hawtah, The Sacred Enclave in Arabia," in *Mélanges Taha Husayn* (Cairo: 1962) 41–58. Many of the technical terms used in this article such as *ḥarām* and *ḥudūd*, are discussed in greater detail in my article "An Introduction to Islamic Law and Islamic Jurisprudence" (Article 4 here).

the far ends of the spectrum of things and actions, which leaves ordinary things and actions to fill the space between the sacred and the forbidden.

The political life of the Islamic Middle East in the 4th/10th and 5th/11th centuries illustrates a different line along which an analogue to the division of sacred and secular appears, and here I think the word *secular* is more appropriate than *profane*. We need to review the history of the early Muslim community to understand how this came about. Almost unanimously after the death of the Prophet Muḥammad, Muslims accepted that there should be a single political leader for their community, entitled caliph (*khalīfa*) or "successor" and this institution of the caliphate was indivisible. Just as the Universal and All-Powerful God had revealed, through a single prophet, a law meant for all mankind, She/He had intended that all those who accepted that law should participate in a single moral community whose structures of rights and obligations would be made uniform by a single political authority. Hence, in this world which lived in a Neo-Platonic twilight, just as we live in a Neo-Freudian twilight, the One sensibly chose to emanate Itself to the many through a single intelligence as surely in the political world as in the metaphysical world. In many forms of Shiʿite belief theories of the "imamate" (the office of an imam, a religiously chosen leader) continue the system of a single moral authority.

By the 4th/10th century, however, the political unity of the Islamic world was a fond memory. Dozens of independent governments vied with each other. The caliphs, reduced to ceremonial figures, were suffered to continue in part because of the grandiloquent titles they granted to whichever "mayors of the palace," the actual authorities (as in Merovingian times), happened to control them. These titles are eloquent testimony that a sort of de facto recognition of the division between sacred and profane had come into being. At first the Abbasid caliphs gave their mayors of the palace titles such as Helper of the Dynasty, *Nāṣir al-Dawla*, that is, Helper of the Dynasty of caliphs. Caliphs, like the Japanese emperors, possessed a revered lineage even though the caliphs had lost their powers to their mayors of the palace who were Middle Eastern equivalents of Shoguns. Soon, however, the mayors of the palace, the Buyid rulers of Iraq and western Iran in the 4th/10th and 5th/11th centuries, wanted longer and loftier titles. By the second half of the 4th/10th century there are Buyid titles such as Glory of the *Dawla* and Helper of Religion (*Bahā' al-Dawla wa-Nāṣir al-Dīn*).[7] In

7 The title of the Buyid ruler who died in Shiraz in 403/1012.

such a title, *Dawla* is moving away from its reference to a specific dynasty and toward its common late medieval meaning of royal power.[8]

Another step in the evolution of titulature, and associated political ideas, appears with the Seljuks, a powerful Turkish dynasty that entered the Middle East from Central Asia in the 5th/11th century and reunited most of Western Asia under one government. The Seljuks, like the Buyids, controlled the powerless caliphs of Baghdad. The first major ruler of this dynasty was Tughril Beg who took the title *Rukn al-Dunyā wa-l-Dīn*, "Support of the World and Religion." To my understanding, in the use together of "world" and the "religion" we have a reference to something not wholly unlike secular and sacred. Alongside this evolution was an evolution in spiritual thinking which created a stream of piety-minded Muslims who changed their focus from the caliphate to individual morality. As far as they could, these Muslims ignored the formal government of Muslim society. These trends continued until *dunyā* and *dīn* became distinct from each other. It can be argued that this disassociation of political power from religion started earlier when pious early Muslims felt alienated from the Umayyad caliphs of Syria. This attitude among a group of the pious continued to exist more or less throughout the pre-modern period.

Dunyā, the world, is referred to scores of times in the Qur'ān, overwhelmingly to contrast it with the next life, for it means the nearer thing, that is, the nearer life, as contrasted to the final or ultimate thing, *al-Ākhira*, the Next or Ultimate life. *Contemptus mundi*, the despising of the world, is a strong theme in all Islamic thought, which follows the spirit of the Qur'ānic verse (II:86): "These are people who buy this worldly life (*al-ḥayāt al-dunyā*) at the price of the Next (*al-Ākhira*); their penalty shall not be lightened nor shall they be helped." But the world, held at its properly subordinate evaluation, is meant to be used and lived in. Another verse in the Qur'ān (XLIII:32) says: "It is He [God] who apportions their means of livelihood in this worldly life and raises some in position over the others ..." A further verse (XLI:31) explains: "We are your friends in this worldly life and in the Next." Clearly, although the Islamic world produced ascetics second to none in their contempt of the world and mystics second to none in their contention that the world was an illusion, the text of the Qur'ān and a great deal of Islamic homiletic literature offers the world as a place with which a pious man can and probably must come to terms.

8 See E.W. Lane, *An Arabic Lexicon*, I (Cambridge, U.K.: 1984) 935.

In the new political conditions of the 4th/10th and following centuries, Muslim thinkers put the old division of *dīn* and *dunyā* to new use. Muslims recognized that there was a sphere that was probably not run in a righteous manner and almost surely beyond the control of any individual Muslim. This sphere was the *dunyā*. There was another sphere in which a Muslim could work to develop his relation to God and hence his position in the next world/life. This sphere was *dīn*, which I think is rightly translated "religiosity" although here I use the more familiar term "religion." Rulers like Tughril Beg took titles implying that their presence helped people both in *dunyā* and *dīn*. I think the existence of these two spheres, for all that they overlapped and interpenetrated each other, was generally understood. That these rulers never dropped *dīn* (religion) from their titles implied that their support of religion was praiseworthy and part of the reason that their rule might be divinely supported.

Interestingly, the traditional scholastic sciences cultivated among Muslims give considerable theoretical support to this view of two spheres, although the divisions suggested by these scholastic sciences do not exactly correspond to *dīn* and *dunyā*, religion and the world. One such division occurs in the thought of a group of theologians, namely, the followers of the theologian al-Ashʿarī, who died in 324/935. Their argument about the nature of the Creator says that the world has only a possible existence and there is nothing about it in and of itself which requires that it exist. Since it does exist, we must conclude that something other than it has chosen it for existence instead of non-existence, and this something is the divine or numinous world. This argument is called *qiyās al-ghā'ib ʿalā al-shāhid*, usually translated "considering the absent as analogous to the present." Perhaps this argument could also be properly understood as "considering the numinous to be analogous to the phenomenal." The *ʿālam al-ghayb* or "world of absence" is clearly the numinous world in pre-modern Islamic thought.[9]

Islamic jurists and jurisconsults had to face the problem of the two realms/spheres squarely. It was they who had to tell people when and why the law saw actions to be purely matters of the *dunyā*, of this worldly conduct, or matters vital to *dīn*, religion, and hence matters affecting their position in the next world, or a mixture of the two. Another important

---

9 On the translation of the Ashʿarite argument see Bernard G. Weiss, *The Search for God's Law: A Study of the Ethico-Legal Thought of Sayf al-Din al-Amidi* (Salt Lake City: 2010), ch. 1.

consideration in this regard is the distinction between acts of worship (*ʿibādāt*) and transactional matters between people (*muʿāmalāt*). One central tenet that Muslim jurists could bring to bear on these distinctions is contained in the saying attributed to the Prophet: "The central principle in affairs is lawfulness."[10] That is, when anything is neither commanded nor forbidden, it is lawful and therefore open to the free exercise of human wishes. Another central tenet was the distinction between *farḍ al-kifāya* and *farḍ al-ʿayn*. The former, *farḍ al-kifāya*, is the duty incumbent on the community as a whole but not incumbent on each of its members, i.e., a (communal) duty such as the jihad. The latter, *farḍ al-ʿayn*, is the duty incumbent on the individual, such as daily prayers. The distinction between individual and communal obligation made possible a de facto sacred-profane distinction, because many things that are religious—one might even say "sacred" duties—are not essential to an individual's salvation since only the community and not the individual is faulted for failing to fulfill them. According to some Muslims, these two tenets also created space for important distinctions of this world. The existence of concepts such as the lawfulness of all things neither commanded nor forbidden created another axis around which to construct a sacred and profane distinction as with the *ḥarām* and non-*ḥarām* distinction previously discussed.

Yet another relevant consideration of the jurists is the distinction between God's claims and human claims. In the discussion of this distinction many of the previous themes of this chapter are evoked and related to each other. It is important to remember that the word here translated as "claim" (*ḥaqq*, plural *ḥuqūq*) has come to mean "right" or "rights" in modern Arabic. Claims considered as "rights" have also become a central consideration in contemporary Islamic law as in most contemporary legal systems, where the individual is a nexus of rights. Pre-modern Islamic law is indeed interested in rights or, more properly, "claims," but it is *far* more concerned with the classification of actions since, once an action is classified, the claims of those concerned flow from that classification. Declaratory rulings (singular *ḥukm*, plural *aḥkām*) as to the classification of actions are, therefore, much more central to Islamic law. Claims are held to be at least of two kinds, divine and human, *ḥuqūq Allāh* and *ḥuqūq al-nās*. (This last term sometimes becomes *ḥaqq al-ʿabd* or *ḥaqq ādamī*.) Prayer, fasting and the fixed punishments (*ḥudūd*) for certain

10 See *al-Mawsūʿat al-Fiqhīya*, 2nd ed. (Kuwait, Wizārat al-Awqāf: 1983), I:130.

crimes are examples of God's claims against mankind, and as such, cannot be dropped. Their prosecution is a Muslim's duty.[11] In contrast, debt and theft are examples of human claims, in which prosecution can take place only on the demand of the person or persons concerned. Many human claims can be transferred by the human concerned or even transferred involuntarily, as when a creditor's claim is inherited.

The distinction between God's claims and human claims is very important not only for the question of what matters can be prosecuted but also for judicial procedures. An open and still current question in Islamic law is whether a judge can act on his own knowledge in cases before him or must only act according to the evidence presented in court. The majority opinion among the largest Sunni law school, the Ḥanafīs, is that a judge can indeed act according to his knowledge in cases involving God's claims but not in cases in which human claims are involved.[12] There he must operate according to the evidence presented in court. The rationale behind this distinction is, I think, clear. Whereas the judge and only the judge can take on the responsibility for surmising what might be God's ruling (God's *ḥukm*) concerning the fulfillment of God's claims, human claims are all subject to human considerations and even human whims. Hence the judge must defer to the evidence humans *choose* to present to him.[13] Human claims belong to the realm of what Islamic thought (as well as Western thought, in deference to their common Aristotelian heritage) call the realm of "practical reason" (*al-ʿaql al-ʿamalī*) as contrasted to "speculative" or "theoretical reason" (*al-ʿaql al-naẓarī*). (I omit here the very large number of cases in which God's claims and human claims are held to be mixed.)

The brilliant and original 8th/14th-century jurisconsult al-Shāṭibī, brings together many of these themes in his survey of the principles of Islamic law entitled *al-Muwāfaqāt*. Al-Shāṭibī maintains that God's claims by their character are not capable of being rationalized; they are devotional acts. (We should, of course, remember that devotional acts in the context of pre-modern Islamic thought include the prosecution and consequent

11 One exception is the Ḥanafī idea of *qadhf* or false accusation, which is one of God's claims against mankind that can be dropped. See Intisar Rabb, *Doubt in Islamic Law* (Cambridge, U.K.: 2014) 40–94.

12 *Ibid.*

13 David Santillana, *Istituzioni di diritto musulmano malichita con riguardo anche al sistema sciafiita*, I (Rome: 1938) 8.

punishment of people for certain kinds of crime.) Interestingly, al-Shāṭibī discusses the large though not complete overlapping of God's claims with the individual's obligation, the *farḍ al-ʿayn*. As for human claims, their rationality is to be measured in terms of *maṣlaḥa*, a term used in Islamic law to mean something like equity or commonweal but specifically defined by al-Shāṭibī to mean "what concerns the subsistence of human life, the wholeness of a human's way of life, and the acquiring of what man's emotional and intellectual faculties require of him in an absolute sense."[14] At least for this jurisconsult the existence of human claims has created a vast area for the exercise of human judgment.[15]

Let me try to sum up. Of course, in Islamic thought there are no distinctions that neatly fit our distinctions between sacred and secular, sacred and profane, spiritual and temporal, ecclesiastical and lay, or even divine and human. For most of these distinctions, however, analogues exist in the Islamic tradition. Moreover, these distinctions are important in their unexpected difference from the distinctions that Western Christian traditions make.

What precisely are the distinctions that we find in the Islamic tradition of the Middle East? First, there is sacred space and sacred acts and sacred time. The guardians of sacred space in pre-Islamic Arabia were priestly families, and there is some continuity in this tradition in some parts of the Islamic world right up to the present. Of course, in a religion in which religious purity is related to proper access to sacred space, profane space is described using the terms neutral or impure (*nājis*) and similar words. Sacred acts like prayer and the pilgrimage are important concerns for the law. The opposite of sacred acts can be found in the terms sacrilege, blasphemy, profanity and desecration, all of which express reference to rupture with the sacred and/or defilement. With respect to sacred time a common term for sacred time is *al-ayyām al-mutabārika*, "blessed time." The distinction between "blessed" and "unblessed," introduces another aspect of this discussion (that cannot be addressed in this paper due to limitations of space and time).

---

14 Abū Isḥāq Ibrāhīm al-Shāṭibī, *al-Muwaffaqāt fī-Uṣūl al-Sharīʿa*, I (Cairo: n.d.) 160–161 and 291–292. For his definition of *maṣlaḥa*, see Muhammad Khalid Masud, *Legal Philosophy: A Study of Abū Isḥāq al-Shāṭibī's Life and Thought* (Islamabad: 1977) 345.
15 Santillana, (*supra* n. 13), I:11–12; ʿAbd al-Razzāq al-Sanhūrī, *Maṣādir al-Ḥaqq fī-l-Fiqh al-Islāmī*, I (Cairo: 1958) 44–46. See also the discussion and references in Mohammad Jaʿfar Jaʿfari Langarudi, *Dānesh-Nāma-ye Hoquqi* (Tehran: 1352) 6–7.

Interestingly, the two far ends of the spectrum of things, the truly sacrosanct and the truly taboo are described by the two words *ḥaram* and *ḥarām*, and represent, I think, neighboring areas at the beginning and the end of a great circle that gives rulings or classifications for everything available to humans. While purposefully avoiding in this paper the names of Durkheim, Otto, and Eliade, the great Western theorists of the sacred, I do think we have in the idea of *ḥaram* and *ḥarām* a strong element of what Otto calls the *fascinans*, something of powerful and sometimes frightening attraction even if we are commanded to avoid it or approach it only in a special manner.[16] According to some Muslim thinkers the non-sacralized space, time and actions of the world are licit for us to use as we wish but with a divinely-set standard of behavior always before us. Al-Shāṭibī defines this goal as *maṣlaḥa*, equity or commonweal, but others define it differently. Our method of operating within this worldly sphere is practical reason. Man, as the Lord of the Created World, is in effect given a series of moral puzzles to solve by virtue of his right to establish and drop claims in this world. The existence of a partly separate sphere (which encompassed acts of devotion and of individual obligations to God) allowed for this other sphere of practical reason to become in some circumstances a partial analogue to our secular sphere, since it was recognized, usually with regret, but with considerable realism, that it was necessary to compromise with realities of government and communal life. Such compromise did not necessarily affect a person's salvation. In this sense while the distinction between sacred and profane was in some cases accepted de jure, in many cases the distinction between sacred and secular remained overwhelmingly de facto.

Does this mean that sacred and profane are universal categories? Not necessarily. The problem of the apparent dualism of God and the world is common to all monotheistic traditions. One partial solution is, in the words of the very celebrated Karl Rahner and his co-author Herbert Vorgrimler, "the recognition that springs from faith in the independence and comprehensibility of a secular world."[17] Such attitudes have existed among Muslims as well as Christians, but even among Christians they are based precisely on faith, that is, faith that God has *granted* us a secular sphere.

---

16 See Chapter 6, "The Element of Fascination," in Rudolf Otto's, *The Idea of the Holy*, trans. John W. Harvey (New York: 1958) 31–46. I here use the Latin term that Otto uses in the original German text.

17 Karl Rahner and Herbert Vorgrimler, *Dictionary of Theology*, 2nd ed. (New York: 1985) 469.

In the Muslim case the secular sphere is often seen as shot through with references to the numinous sphere. In fact, significant areas of the worldly sphere are under exclusive or partial obligation to God alone. The secular or profane is only a part of this worldly life, albeit a significantly large part.

The different boundaries of these partly analogous distinctions strengthens my conviction that we have spoken all too freely and carelessly of the "disenchantment" of the world, that evocative term that Max Weber brought into currency.[18] Without understanding a fraction of the sophisticated discussion that has developed about "civil religion" (for example, the sacredness that Americans feel towards their Constitution), I believe that some such category has existed among us and must exist, in part to sacralize the rightness of some of the things we do in the worldly sphere, even in an overtly secular society. Consider the confusion among many as to why we punish criminals. This confusion is fostered by the assumption that we can create a desacralized, disenchanted and totally sanitized law. To argue that the punishment fits the crime would be clear in a Biblical context but less clear in a modern secular context.

Even if one does not accept the Islamic approach to the *this-worldly-life* or any other "religious" approach to it, it does seem that the life of this world will always have sacralized *and* profane areas, however variously designated and justified. I do believe as Durkheim believed that we will not remove the sacred completely from the world as long as we share a sense of community. In those monotheistic traditions in which the world is a created thing and not wholly or even partially identical to its Creator, the complete sacralization of the world seems to me difficult to imagine. Correspondingly, the full desacralization and disenchantment of the world has not yet arrived in our supposedly secular tradition. As long as the non-pantheistic monotheisms allow for a sphere in which God's will cannot be fully known and human *this-worldly* principles are applied, these monotheisms allow for a quasi-secular sphere. In this sense some pre-modern Muslim thinkers developed world views through historical experience and the logic of their theology, which allow not just a profane realm but also a partly secular realm.

---

18 See *From Max Weber*, trans. and ed. by H.H. Gerth and C. Wright Mills (New York: 1946) 155.

ISLAMIC LAW AND ETHICS

In the world of Islam the adoption of Arabic as the language of learning aided the transfer of knowledge, the exchange of goods, and freedom of travel in the pre-modern period. Throughout this world a transnational law was created by Muslims that made contracts understandable between merchants of different backgrounds. Remarkably, Armenian merchants in the early modern period are known to have used Islamic contracts within their own communities.

Islamic law (*sharīʿa*) is one of the major legal systems of the world, along with others such as Common law and Roman law. It combines law derived from revelation with a rigorous extension of that law by use of some argument by analogy and some by deductive logic. Corporal punishment is an ancient part of this law and rightly horrifies contemporary people. However, Islamic law allows many sentences to be converted from corporal to lesser punishments. In some parts of the Western world aspects of Islamic law are used to settle cases between Muslims (and corporal punishment is never part of the application of Islamic law in the West). Increasingly, Islamic law has been defined in national contexts, which means that it varies slightly or greatly from country to country. At the time of writing, in late 2021, the Taliban of Afghanistan are threatening to return to *sharīʿa* with corporal punishment, whereas countries like Egypt and Morocco have moved away from corporal punishment.

Both Islamic law and Islamic ethics have a long history in the Middle East, and occasionally medieval and modern Muslim scholars have tried to match ethical considerations with the precepts of Islamic law. To make these matches between law and ethics Muslim scholars turn to jurisprudence, which is the study of the principles behind law. Islamic jurisprudence attempts to present the abstract reasoning behind the law. The famous jurists of the medieval period, such as the celebrated theologian Ghazālī of the 5th/11th century, are still studied in the modern Muslim world. Ghazālī and other jurists tried to extend the understanding of jurisprudence by writing about the relation between law and ethics.

Although I am very much an historian, I realized the importance of Islamic legal history for the understanding of many Islamic societies and therefore studied it with that goal in mind. Islamic jurisprudence aspires to give the reason behind the actual law, and therefore is of great interest. A certain amount of Sunni jurisprudence is available in European languages, but Shi'ite jurisprudence, which has been my interest for many years because it is the principal school of Islamic law in Iran, is comparatively unknown in the West. As Shi'ites began to rely more on rational justification in their religious and legal thought from the eighteenth century on, they sought to use more and more Aristotelian logic in their treatises on jurisprudence. Sometimes they even introduced Greek philosophy as mediated by great Muslim thinkers such as Avicenna (Ibn Sīnā) in the 5th/11th century.

In Shi'ite seminaries today, students use both medieval and modern texts. One of the most widely used modern texts is the first in a series of legal books written by the outstanding madrasa teacher Muhammad Baqir al-Sadr, who was executed by Saddam Hussein in 1980. This book is used in elementary classes, particularly in the seminaries in Qom. Since it had not been previously translated into English, I chose to translate it as *Lessons in Islamic Jurisprudence* (2003). I was fortunate to know some Shi'ite clergymen, above all, Sayyid Hossein Modarressi, now a professor at Princeton University and, since we met at a conference in Hamadan in Iran in 1977, a treasured lifelong friend. He guided me to Muhammad Baqir al-Sadr's first book on jurisprudence, helped me when I was uncertain of my translation, and in general cheered me on. Another friend, the learned Saud Shawwaf, provided intelligent legal comments on my translation.

To Sadr's *Lessons in Islamic Jurisprudence* I added my own explanatory summary of the book and a glossary in the hope that they would help the reader understand the ideas in Islamic law. In my translation of Sadr's text, I worked particularly hard on the technical terms used by Sadr, some of which do not have ready equivalents in English. For my translation of Sadr's book, I wrote an "Introduction to Islamic Jurisprudence," which I have modified and included as the first article in this section.

My article "An Introduction to Islamic Law and Islamic Jurisprudence" is a very general introduction to Islamic law and jurisprudence intended for students in Islamic studies. In it I discuss the formation of Islamic jurisprudence, which began to emerge with the appearance of the great lawyer al-Shāfiʿī (d. 204/820). After al-Shāfiʿī's strong defense of his legal method both Sunnis and Shiʿites adopted aspects of his method of legal reasoning. By the end of the 3rd/9th century, major schools of Islamic law began to appear. In the following century these various schools became more defined. Islamic law has always looked back to the founding jurists. The nineteenth and twentieth centuries have been very active for proposals to modify or reform Islamic law to adapt to modern historical circumstances.

For Muslims jurisprudence is a very important subject and for Islamic clergymen the subject that brings them closest to an abstract discussion of their law. Theology is taught in many Islamic seminaries, but Islamic law and its justification is more central to the mission of these institutions. In the Shiʿite world in particular the claim that everything in the law can be justified by logic places a heavy burden on jurisprudence.

In the years following my publication of Sadr's *Lessons* in English I continued to work on aspects of Islamic law and benefited greatly from discussions of Islamic law with three of my colleagues at Harvard, Baber Johansen, Intisar Rabb, and Kristen Stilt. On several occasions I had the pleasure of addressing the New York Bar Association on such topics as Islamic jurisprudence, the interpretation of jihad, constitutionalism in Islamic countries, and the Islamic law of sale.

The second article in this section, "Consultation and the Political Process in the Middle East of the 9th, 10th and 11th Centuries," was delivered at a symposium at Yarmouk University in Irbid, Jordan, in 1984 and subsequently published in 1989 in *Arabian Studies in Honour of Mahmoud Ghul*, edited by Moawiyah M. Ibrahim. While the text of the Qur'ān is very clear in its strong recommendation of consultation, Muslims have disagreed as to whether the Qur'ān makes consultation compulsory or not, and as to whether the decisions of consultative bodies are binding or not. Liberal democracies in the modern Muslim world have built their legislative bodies on the idea of *shūrā* (consultation) and these bodies have often been named *Majlis al-Shūrā* (the session for consultation) or some close variant. In pre-modern Islamic legal thought the ideal of *shūrā* was preserved, but rulers only rarely gathered such groups and only rarely listened to their advice. The modern literature on *shūrā* is vast, but often not well informed on the role of *shūrā* in earlier Islamic history.

The bigger Qur'ān commentaries feel obliged to quote every opinion known to them on the verses about consultation. When the commentators, like Ṭabarī (d. 310/923), claimed to be comprehensive, they judged that all variant opinion should be cited. This scrupulous devotion to preserving variant opinion makes the Qur'ān commentaries a treasure trove of early Islamic thought. Now that so many commentaries are online, it has become much easier to make comparisons as I tried to do in this early article, which was written long before personal computers and online research were generally available. Opinion on the need for consultation remains unresolved by Muslim thinkers.

Consultation was highly prized in my family and in my Quaker schools. It still exists in some towns in America that are governed by town meetings. From its tribal origins to its redeployment as a justification for democracy in modern Islamic societies, it has been an important ingredient in the political life of the Islamic world. Sometimes the result of consultation has been a sham and preordained, and sometimes it has been real and determined by the participants.

Both as an academic and as a specialist in the history of the Islamic world, I have participated in a number of consultations and found them to be deeply interesting. Before the botched attempt to rescue American hostages in Iran on April 24, 1980, I was invited to a meeting with the Secretary of State, Cyrus Vance. I remember being surprised by the list of questions circulated before the meeting. Most of the questions were essentially on one theme: "How will people respond to the use of force?" The answer was obvious: they would respond badly. I therefore declined to attend the meeting. Secretary Vance got the answer that he wanted and which I had anticipated. After hearing this answer from other scholarly "experts," he added the collective opinion to the papers with which he resigned his post shortly after the meeting. Unfortunately, even confidentiality about the meeting failed and the names of the participants were released to the newspapers a day later. Alas, the hostage crisis dragged on until January 20, 1981, just minutes after Ronald Reagan was sworn in as President.

The third article in this section, "The Idea of the *Jihād* in Islam before the Crusades," was co-authored together with my very learned friend Ridwan al-Sayyid in 2001 for *The Crusades from the Perspective of Byzantium and the Muslim World*, edited by me and my Harvard colleague Angeliki Laiou. I have always been interested in Byzantine history and studied it as one of my fields for my Ph.D. general exams. My teacher Robert Lee Wolf was a very fine historian, and I learned a great deal about the relationship between the orthodox Christian world, including Russia, and the Muslim Middle East. Unfortunately, I never fully developed my Greek and ended up working principally on Arabic and Persian texts for my teaching and research. Angeliki was a good friend and an excellent chair of the Department of History at Harvard, but this book was my only opportunity to work directly with her. Ridwan al-Sayyid was a visiting fellow at Harvard's Center for Middle Eastern Studies more than two decades ago, and we enjoyed collaborating on this article.

Aggressive jihad remains alive among some contemporary Muslim thinkers. Although it is difficult to estimate how many modern Muslims believe in it, I think it is a minority opinion. The overwhelming majority of the Muslim nations belong to the United Nations, which, in its Charter, forbids aggressive warfare. Nevertheless, aggressive warfare has been pursued by many nations—and, for the most part, non-Muslim nations—throughout the history of the U.N. One of the most respected of the ulema in Syria, Shaykh Wahba al-Zuhayli (d. 2015), wrote a book on jihad in 1962 that was frequently republished in which he says: "In modern times we all live in the world of treaty, not in the world of war and Islam." At the end of this very detailed and valuable book, he concludes with the question: "What does *jihād* mean in the modern world? *Jihād* means the struggle against the distortion of Islam." So, for Zuhayli and others, it is jihad by word and by attempts to convert non-believers to Islam.

The Crusades, which began in the 5th/11th century, succeeded in Christian triumph in Spain only in the fifteenth century, and the Islamic jihad in Anatolia, which also began in the 5th/11th century, succeeded in Muslim triumph only in the fifteenth century as well. There was no settled interpretation of jihad in many periods of Islamic history, although the aggressive element remained alive. Interestingly, few modern Muslims know that jihad was interpreted in a variety of ways among Muslims in the first two centuries of Islamic history. It was not always aggressive warfare; it was striving to convert people in conquered lands and extend the reach of Islam. We forget that the Muslims outside Arabia were in the early centuries very much a minority. In later centuries Sufis, who had spread throughout the Islamic world, began to speak of the jihad against the self in their search to find some kind of unity with God.

Ancient fears of the Islamic world live on in many Western cultures just as fears of colonialism and imperialism live on in the Islamic world. Virtually all Islamic countries outside the Ottoman Empire were occupied in the nineteenth and twentieth centuries, which explains to some degree current Muslim thinking about the West. Thank God, holy war now has a bad odor in most of the West and many other parts of the world. In a few places, such as Afghanistan, it is unfortunately still the order of the day.

The fourth article in this section, "Friendship in Islamic Ethical Philosophy," was published in 2016 in *Essays in Islamic Philology, History, and Philosophy*, edited by me and my colleagues Alireza Korangy, Wheeler M. Thackston, and William Granara, in honor of our very learned friend Ahmad Mahdavi-Damghani, who taught for many years at Harvard to everyone's benefit and who embodies so many of the characteristics of a true friend. This article shows the attempts of two outstanding Muslim philosophers to reconcile classical philosophy, in particular Aristotle, with Islam. Miskawayh (d. 421/1030), who is earlier, gives a more purely Aristotelian view, but the later (and more extensive) view of Ṭūsī (d. 672/1274) marries the Greek and Islamic views more easily, in part because by his time the tradition of integrating Greek philosophy with Muslim ethics was better developed. A little realism is introduced by Ṭūsī when we are told to overlook small defects in our friends.

The high value given to friendship between disciple and his/her "master" in Islam is not only in agreement with much ancient philosophy but also with the ideals for teacher and pupil in Islamic thought. Formal friendship was an extremely important topic in pre-modern thought although it has less relevance in the atomized relations of many contemporary societies. Islamic ethical thought offers a great deal to the social historian, not because it gives a realistic picture of society, but because it offers a reading of the ideals that society may support and, occasionally, reflections on how far these ideals are from actual social practices.

The fifth article in this section, "Brother and Brotherhood in the Qur'ān," was published in 2001 in volume 1 of the *Encyclopaedia of the Qur'ān*, edited by Jane Dammen McAuliffe. Searching in the Qur'ān commentaries for Islamic thought often reveals important understandings of theological, legal, and ethical considerations. Muslims understand their common religious bond as analogous to brotherhood or sisterhood. Moses and Aaron, both in the Qur'ān as well as in the Bible, are examples of brothers who closely cooperate. The chapter on Joseph and his brothers is considered one of the most beautiful chapters in the Qur'ān because of its style and language and its comforting reconciliation of brothers at the end. One of the prominent movements in the modern Muslim world is called al-Ikhwān al-Muslimūn, or Muslim Brothers, a group currently banned or suppressed by many governments in Islamic lands which suspect the Muslim Brothers' intention to introduce conservative Muslim ideas into the law and government.

An Introduction to Islamic Law and Islamic Jurisprudence

This introduction to Islamic law and Islamic jurisprudence will discuss the nature of Islamic law, the nature of Islamic jurisprudence and the relation of this system of jurisprudence to Roman and canon law.

THE NATURE OF ISLAMIC LAW

It was by no means inevitable that law should have become so central to higher learning among most Muslims in the pre-modern period. For over a thousand years the great majority of Muslim jurists agreed that out of over six thousand verses in the Qur'ān there were only five hundred verses with legal content. Most of the "legal" verses concern *'ibādāt*, approximately "acts of devotion," such as prayer and the pilgrimage. Out of these five hundred verses, there are about one hundred and ninety that deal with non-ritual aspects of the law; only matters of inheritance are laid out in any detail.

As to why legal culture became central to so many Muslims in subsequent centuries, I can give only a partial answer. The Qur'ān, according to one very widely accepted reading, by its spirit encourages legal culture since it speaks repeatedly of the *ḥudūd*, literally "the limits" or "boundaries." In the Qur'ān this word does not mean "the prescribed punishments," as

Author's note: This article was first published as: "Introduction," in Muḥammad Bāqir aṣ-Ṣadr, *Lessons in Islamic Jurisprudence*, translated, with Introduction, Glossary and Summary by Roy Parviz Mottahedeh (Oxford, U.K., Oneworld: 2003) 1–33. I have modified the title and removed a section about the life of Muhammad Baqir al-Sadr as well as some references to him in order to make this a general introduction to Islamic law and Islamic jurisprudence.

it came to mean in later Islamic law, but "the limits" which circumscribe good behavior; and in almost all instances *ḥudūd* in the Qur'ān is best translated as "laws." For example, in a verse on divorce (and most mentions of "the limits" are in passages on divorce and fasting), the Qur'ān reads, "... these are the laws (*ḥudūd*) of God: do not transgress them. Those who transgress them are unjust (or 'oppressive')" (II:229). Another verse on divorce says, "... these are the laws of God. One who transgresses (literally, 'passes beyond them') has done injustice (or 'acts oppressively') to him or herself ..." (LXV:2). In earlier centuries the study of Islamic law was called "the laws/limits and the knowledge [of them]," *al-ḥudūd wa-l-'ilm*, or simply the "knowledge" (*al-'ilm*). And indeed the Qur'ān connects laws and knowledge, in a verse which ends, "... and these are the laws (*ḥudūd*) of God; he makes them clear (*yubayyinu-hā*) to a people who understand/know (*ya'lamūna*, from the same root as *al-'ilm*)" (II:230).

The Qur'ān also offers a number of statements specifying that certain things are "permitted" (*ḥalāl*) or "forbidden" (*ḥarām*). Therefore, given that there were some "laws" specifically laid down and some things actually classified as "permitted" or "forbidden," and given that Muslims were in touch with three powerful legal systems, the Roman, the Jewish, and the Sasanian Persian, is it surprising that legally minded Muslims felt it necessary to go beyond the brief treatment of the law in the Qur'ān to develop a fully-fledged legal system?

Yet as this system developed it became clear that it was something grander than law: it aspired to classify and categorize all human acts. Later jurists summarized this ambition in a maxim that said, "In the presence of God there is a ruling or 'classification' (*ḥukm*) for every instance of human behavior." The jurists saw it as their responsibility (and, to some extent, that of every human being) to derive, from what they believed to be potential sources of the law, the most likely classification or categorization of any human act in the eyes of God. He is "the Lord of the Day of Reckoning," as the Qur'ān repeatedly says, and it was considered essential to know how He would reckon the deeds of one's life, even when they were neither "forbidden" nor "obligatory." After long dispute the jurists came to agree on five "predicates" appropriate for any legal proposition expressing the ruling (*ḥukm*) which evaluates a human act in moral terms. An act is either "forbidden," "discouraged," "permissible" (meaning free of any moral weight), "recommended," or "mandatory." Normally only the "forbidden" and, in some cases, the "mandatory," could be matters for consideration in an Islamic court, and only these matters would be called "law" according to a widespread Anglo-American tradition. But it should be understood that the so-called manuals of Islamic law would be considerably slighter if they contained only matters enforceable by courts. Islamic law proper is embedded in a moral hermeneutic, or system of interpretation. It can be argued that even in the Anglo-American system we have laws such as tax laws, the object of which is to encourage or discourage certain types of behavior in areas such as personal savings and home ownership, which are of course legally optional. To give another example, "Good Samaritan" laws encourage help to the distressed in cases of emergency by reducing liability to the rescuer.

The jurists understand the middle category, "permissible" or "morally neutral," to be central to the nature of the law. "The legal presumption concerning things is their permissibility (*ibāḥa*)," as the famous maxim says. This word can be translated "license," from which point of view the need for "limits" is clear. It can also be understood as "liberty," and a person's fundamental liberty to act as he/she wishes in the world has been an important concept to many Muslim reformers. Some moral philosophers in the contemporary West consider such a presumption necessary to any system of ethics.

A kindred concept is "the presupposition of innocence," which partly overlaps with the Anglo-American presumption of innocence. When born, every person's legal standing (*dhimma*) is innocent/free of guilt (*barī'*). This presupposition is seen as self-evident; for the accused in a law case is innocent until evidence (*bayyina*) is brought to prove otherwise, and the newborn is not yet responsible for any acts whatsoever.

THE HISTORICAL DEVELOPMENT OF ISLAMIC LAW

The above account of the way in which Islamic law developed is too stylized to be fully historical; it represents the attempts of later jurists to tidy up the history of a very lively intellectual debate which, like any other such formative episode, was filled with disagreement and took place under the pressure of real concerns. Fortunately, a fair amount of material on these early debates survives. (It is one of the merciful aspects of Islamic law that its extended treatments carry the history of virtually all opinions of previous jurists of any importance into later works, a display of learning that allows the author to show that he has considered discarded opinions, as well as—on occasion—to adopt an earlier opinion.)

It would seem both from the Qur'ān and its commentaries that many of these early debates had to do with the way in which Islamic law should understand itself over and against other law or laws. Verses 42 through 50 of Sūra V (al-Mā'ida) are held by most Muslim biographies of the Prophet to relate to an incident (supposed by Muslim commentators to have occurred in the fifth year of the Prophet's authority in Medina) when some of the Medinese Jews came to the Prophet asking him to arbitrate among them. In verse 44 the Prophet is told, "In truth we have revealed the Torah in which is guidance and light, by which the Prophets who submitted to God judged the Jews; and the rabbis and sages judged by such of God's Book as they were bidden to observe ..." Verse 48 goes on to explain that God has revealed laws for each community, "To each of you we have given a law and a way. Had God wished it He would have made you a single [legal] community (*umma*) ..." (This divinely willed legal plurality was, of course, why Muslims generally tolerated religious communities founded before the coming of Islam. They always had the option of considering these communities as "pagans," a category of persons that the Qur'ān and the Prophet did not tolerate within Arabia. Until very recently religions founded after the coming of Islam were not legally recognized.)[1]

The expansion of Muslim rule brought legal questions that had to be sorted out immediately, and the Islamic legal tradition would later consider the decisions on these legal questions to be an exercise in *ijtihād*, the effort to derive rulings from their proper sources. 'Umar, the second caliph (from 13/634 to 23/644) had to choose between precedents. The Prophet had made different arrangements with different Jewish and Christian communities in Arabia. In one instance he arranged for an annual poll tax; in another, the Christian community of Najrān agreed to send two thousand robes to Medina each year. How by extension from such precedents could a ruling be established for the taxation of other Christian and Jewish communities? There was also the problem of the status of the land in the large empire suddenly acquired by the Muslims during the reign of

1 See Wael B. Hallaq, *A History of Islamic Legal Theories*, (Cambridge, U.K., Cambridge University Press: 1999) 4–5, one of the most serious and helpful introductions to Sunni jurisprudence. My introduction leans heavily on the scholarship of others. I do not attempt to cite sources for information well known among specialists in Islamic jurisprudence.

'Umar. The jurist Abū Yūsuf in his book on the land tax tells us that Bilāl, the famous Ethiopian Companion of the Prophet, told 'Umar, "Divide the lands among those who conquer them, just as the spoils of the army are divided [on the battlefield]." But 'Umar refused, saying, "God has given a share in these lands to those who shall come after you." As in the question of taxation there were mixed precedents, and for the next century opposition to 'Umar's decision to give the tax revenue and title of the conquered land to the "treasury of the Muslims" remained controversial and a cause for serious revolts.[2]

While the first four caliphs had an enormous share in making the decisions which would become law, their successors, the dynasty of Umayyad caliphs, continued to promulgate their own rulings as binding legal decisions for matters as various as marriage, the law of sale, and blood-money. The well-known "fiscal rescript" written by 'Umar II (caliph from 99/717 to 101/720), usually counted as the most pious of the Umayyads, shows this caliph ruling on the tax status of converts and kindred matters. Even subordinate Umayyad officials could make rulings which might find subsequent authority in the law. When an Arab general invaded the province of Sind in 93/711, he recognized Hindus as protected people like the Christians and Jews, and the majority of later Muslim jurists of the Ḥanafī school, the Sunni school predominant in South Asia, recognized this ruling.

Gradually the caliphs lost the power to make legal rulings. Yet they retained until the very end the theoretical authority to appoint judges and to hold their own court, the *maẓālim*, or court to judge "contraventions of justice." The jurisdiction of this court was very wide. Although in theory there is no appeal from the ruling of a *qāḍī*, in practice cases were appealed to the *maẓālim* court. Moreover, it functioned as an important court of appeal from decisions in administrative law and against the misbehavior of administrators, matters with which most *qāḍī*s were unwilling to deal. Yet the *maẓālim* jurisdiction never reached out to the masses who lived under the caliph's rule; it did not, for example, develop "delegated" judges, as the *qāḍī*s did in order to have sitting judges in remote towns. The *maẓālim* remained an active but idiosyncratic expression of the ruler's desire to be seen personally as the last resort in the search for justice.

2 N.J. Coulson and R. Le Tourneau, "Bayt al-Māl," *The Encyclopaedia of Islam*, 2nd ed. (hereafter *EI*²), I (Leiden, Brill: 1960) 1141.

The authority of the Umayyad caliphs to make law or even in any way to govern had been challenged from the start, in significant part by the "Partisans" or *Shīʿa*, of ʿAlī ibn Abī Ṭālib, the first cousin and son-in-law of the Prophet, and most of these Shiʿites felt that ʿAlī had been explicitly appointed by the Prophet as his successor. The Khārijīs, in contrast, opposed both ʿAlī and the Umayyads because they had all committed "sins" and the Khārijīs would accept no sinful ruler. (The Ibāḍīs, descended from one branch of the Khārijīs, and now to be found principally in Oman and North Africa, have their own school of law.) The pious opposition to the Umayyads not only shrank the caliph's authority to promulgate legal rulings, it also created a number of circles in which a more intense discussion of religious matters took place, and their members were the forerunners of the ulema, the specialists in religious learning so prominent in the later Islamic Middle East.

Abū Ḥanīfa (d. 150/767) was both prominent in and typical of these circles. He is accounted the founder of the Ḥanafī school of law named after him, although how much Abū Ḥanīfa was a Ḥanafī is far from clear. One story—very possibly a legend—has an Umayyad governor flog him for refusing appointment as a *qāḍī*. It seems without question that he supported the political claims of the family of ʿAlī. He died in prison in Baghdad, the capital of the Abbasids, the dynasty of caliphs that succeeded the Umayyads. The life story of this great early jurist and theologian as constructed from reliable historical accounts and legend shows a suspicion of association with government which would persist among the ulema of the Middle East. It also shows a gap between judges and jurists that would last. Some learned men did become judges, but usually the most learned jurists shunned judgeships. Nevertheless, the practical experience of the judges fed legal thinking in that the decisions of judges were sometimes challenged by the jurists and sometimes ably defended by the judges in circles that met to discuss the law. Ibn Abī Laylā, the judge for Kufa in Abū Ḥanīfa's time, tried—largely unsuccessfully—to establish the legal basis for his judgments against the opinion of his more able contemporary, Abū Ḥanīfa. But the practical nature of Ibn Abī Laylā's opinions is said to have given some of them lasting value as against Abū Ḥanīfa's more theoretical approach, dictated by the latter's search for consistency.[3]

The distance between the "pious opposition" and government also accounts for the development of the independent fatwa, or opinion, so

3 J. Schacht, "Ibn Abī Laylā," *EI*², III (Leiden, Brill: 1971) 687.

similar to the *responsa* which exist in Roman and Jewish law. Conscientious Muslims went to the legally minded among the forerunners of the ulema and got opinions, including opinions on matters not ordinarily dealt with by courts. The Umayyad state, aware of this interest, appointed *muftī*s, givers of fatwas somewhat similar to the jurisconsults in the Roman system. Although later dynasties often appointed *muftī*s, many *muftī*s sought to remain and succeeded in remaining largely independent because people were free to choose their authorities and because a *muftī* who kept his distance from the government gained prestige among ordinary Muslims. The independence of the *muftī* was a significant part of the formation and persistence of a semi-independent community of jurists.

In time these communities of legal thinking developed regional differences. Mālik ibn Anas (d. 179/796), often called simply "the Imam of Medina," was the most able member in his generation among the circles that discussed Islamic law in Medina. The Medinese tradition considered itself continuous with the tradition of the Prophet, who spent the last ten years of his life there. It was assumed, reasonably enough, that the Prophet would have disapproved of Medinese customs not consonant with Islam, and therefore what survived in "the practice of Medina" had been expressly or tacitly approved. Hence, in Medina in Mālik's time, while the quantity and quality of something sold usually had to be known for the sale to be valid, the very practical Medinese custom of exchanging an inexactly known quantity of ripe dates on a tree for dried dates was allowed and became part of the tradition of the Mālikī school of law (and subsequently of other schools). Mālik, by the way, was also very concerned with the classification of rulings and Prophetic sayings and not merely in Medinese traditions. In early books on law Mālik's school is often called "the school of Medina," and Abū Ḥanīfa's school "the school of Kufa," which represents the understanding that these were in fact regional schools although in the homes of all these schools there was a variety of opinion.

It was also in Medina that two of the Imams of the Twelver Shi'ites, Muḥammad al-Bāqir (d. sometime between 114/732 and 118/736) and his son Ja'far al-Ṣādiq (d. 148/765), made a significant contribution to Islamic law in general as well as developing a more specifically Shi'ite school of law. Muḥammad al-Bāqir's disciples included prominent Sunnis such as al-Awzā'ī and Abū Ḥanīfa, both founders of law schools. Muḥammad al-Bāqir's legal views were written down by his circle and passed into Shi'ite law. Ja'far al-Ṣādiq held an even higher position of respect and prominence in legal discussion among Muslims in general and both he and his father are counted as reliable transmitters of ḥadīth among Sunnis. Ja'far al-Ṣādiq gave a very large number of legal rulings which served to orient the Shi'ite tradition.

Another source for regional difference was the pre-Islamic underlay of regional schools. The influence of this underlay is downplayed in many Muslim accounts of the development of Islamic law, but unnecessarily so. The Prophet during his "farewell" pilgrimage in 10/632 carefully went through the rituals of the pilgrimage, understood to have been established by Abraham, and made clear both in action and description what was authentic and what was unacceptable pagan accretion. This method of developing the law is called "confirmation" (*taqrīr*) by the jurists, and it is supported by the first part of one of the verses already cited. Verse 48 of Sūra V of the Qur'ān begins, "We have revealed to you the Book in truth (or, "with the truth"), confirming (*muṣaddiqan*) that Scripture which already exists ..." In a widely respected letter ascribed to 'Alī ibn Abī Ṭālib and written as instructions to Mālik al-Ashtar, his appointee as governor of Egypt, we read, "Abolish no proper custom (*sunna*) which has been enacted by their [the Egyptians'] leaders, through which harmony has been strengthened and because of which the subjects have prospered. Create no new custom which might in any way prejudice the customs of the past, lest reward for them belong to him who originated them, and the burden be upon you to the extent that you have abolished them."[4]

Yet the desire to see Islamic law as a separate system over and against earlier systems outweighed the interest in carefully recording when "confirmation" took place after the Prophet's death. Christians, who at first had little reason to think they should develop a legal system, soon created a whole system of bishops' courts, then took and triumphantly reshaped Roman law to their own ends. A fair number of the axioms which were central to Roman law are to be found in Islamic law. Even if these maxims are present not because of borrowing but because of the common conclusions of developed law, is not their presence a confirmation that other legal systems strove to achieve the same goals as did Islamic law? And yet, unnecessarily, the traditional narrative of Islamic law allowed little place for interest in continuities and parallels.

In any case, it is clear that Islamic law was overwhelmingly jurist made law; and by the second half of the 2nd/8th century full-fledged jurists

4 See my article "Toward an Islamic Theology of Toleration" (Article **28** here).

emerged. In the case of Muḥammad ibn Idrīs al-Shāfiʿī (d. 204/820), usually called by Sunnis al-Imam al-Shāfiʿī, we have not only a powerful jurist but also, according to later Muslim tradition, the founder of jurisprudence, the discipline of deriving law from its proper and appropriate "roots" or sources (*uṣūl al-fiqh*). It should be noted that Shāfiʿī, like Mālik and Abū Ḥanīfa, was at one time a partisan of the ʿAlid cause. In his celebrated *Epistle* he attempted, as an historian of the subject says, "a systematization, a codification, and, up to a point, a rationalization of understanding the Law."[5] It is Shāfiʿī who clarifies that the subject of the law is the legally capable individual considered as someone who is subject to moral obligation (*mukallaf*, legal agent), and that for every act there is a ruling (*ḥukm*). He discusses the need to rank in order of priority the "roots" or foundations of the law and the need to systematize analogical reasoning (*qiyās*). In making the *Sunna* (which means, among other things, the "practice" of the Prophet) a proper source (*aṣl*) alongside the Qur'ān, he stipulated that the jurist is to accept only a properly established account (ḥadīth, *khabar*) about what the Prophet said, did, or gave tacit assent to, to the exclusion of mere local tradition, which his teacher Mālik had accepted. His insistence on a strict study of analogy was a rejection of the freer forms of legal reasons such as commonweal, to which Abū Ḥanīfa had frequent recourse. In short, he sought to rein in the various schools of Islamic law, partly in a traditionalist direction, in that he set scriptural prooftext so far ahead of other sources of law, and partly in an innovative direction, with his demand that legal arguments be justified and (as in the case of analogy) be well developed.

It was too late. The substantive law (that is, the law as written down by specific jurists with the intention that it be generally adopted) was already too developed, and the existing schools too conscious of their tradition, to yield to the challenge of the new rules proposed by Shāfiʿī. For a century Shāfiʿī's *Epistle* remained without progeny. But when jurists turned to writing jurisprudence, the sophistication of Shāfiʿī's program was an overwhelming influence and eventually all the law schools wanted to represent themselves as fitting into some form of Shāfiʿī's system. We will return to the development of jurisprudential writing below.

Shāfiʿī demanded that ḥadīth or *akhbār*, narratives as to what the Prophet did and said and tacitly assented to, be properly accredited. In

5 Eric Chaumont, "Shāfiʿī," *EI*², IX (Leiden, Brill: 1995) 181–184.

this demand he was at the forefront of a movement for ḥadīth criticism which resulted in the writing of "canonical" ḥadīth books in the 3rd/9th century among the Sunnis (and in the 4th/10th and 5th/11th centuries among the Twelver Shi'ites). Although it took centuries to achieve near-consensus as to which ḥadīth collections were canonical, two achieved instant recognition among Sunnis, those of al-Bukhārī (d. 256/870) and Muslim ibn al-Ḥajjāj (d. 261/875). Both aimed to present only such ḥadīth as had a reliable chain of transmitters extending back to the Prophet. (Ḥadīth rather confusingly was used for a single narrative or as a collective plural.) To be reliable, a transmitter had to be known to be of good character and likely to have met both the preceding and succeeding links in the chain. Many early scholars had presented ḥadīth with "imperfect" chains of transmission or even without any chains. Non-Muslim scholars (and recently some Muslim scholars) have suggested that a fair body of ḥadīth acquired its Prophetic pedigree in the century and a half before the "canonical" books appeared. In any case, even the collections of Bukhārī and Muslim ibn al-Ḥajjāj have ḥadīth with incomplete chains of transmitters. By their arrangement of chapters Bukhārī and Muslim show the growing concern of the jurists for reliable legal material, as both use sub-headings somewhat similar to those of the law books.

Throughout the centuries there has been a dispute about the standing of accounts that did not come down through wide-scale transmission, but from a small number—even a single—line of reliable transmitters. Some of these ḥadīth are constantly invoked in the law books. For example, the ḥadīth that says: "The believers must fulfill the lawful conditions [in their contracts] (*al-mu'minūn 'inda shurūṭihim*)" is such a "solitary" or "idiosyncratic" ḥadīth, even though it is continually invoked in the chapters on sale in the law books. Some of the "idiosyncratic" ḥadīth were too important to the law to be shoved overboard. Ibn al-Ṣalāḥ al-Shahrazūrī (d. 643/1245) in his introduction to the ḥadīth sciences, still considered the most authoritative book on this subject, points out that if wide-scale transmission demands transmission from a large number of the Companions of the Prophet as well as multiple transmitters in later generations, then only one ḥadīth of the many hundreds of thousands in existence would qualify.[6]

6 Ibn al-Ṣalāḥ, *Muqaddimat Ibn al-Ṣalāḥ* (Cairo, Dār al-Ma'ārif: 1411/1990) 453–455. I am grateful to Dr. Aron Zysow for this reference.

Ḥadīth came to rank with the Qur'ān as a source of law. The ḥadīth were treated according to the rules developed by the Qur'ān commentators for dealing with the seeming contradictions between Qur'ān verses. Some verses in the Qur'ān, for instance, allow the drinking of wine, but one forbids it. The commentators tried to establish when each verse was revealed. From this chronological framework one could determine that prohibition of wine-drinking came later and "abrogated" the verse permitting wine-drinking. Correspondingly, there were abrogated and abrogating ḥadīth.

The virtually equal status of reliable ḥadīth was a boon to the jurists, who had so little law from the Qur'ān alone; but it created intellectual problems. Whereas the text of the Qur'ān was fixed (except as to minor and clearly established questions such as different pronunciations of certain words), the scholars of ḥadīth accepted as equally sound reliably transmitted ḥadīth with the same meaning but different wording. (Strangely, other textual criticism of the ḥadīth was limited; it was not a subject for concern in ḥadīth criticism that the ḥadīth foretell "heretical" movements such as the Murji'īs and Khārijīs of the early period but do not foretell later heresies.) The standing of sound ḥadīth, which collectively describe the *Sunna*, or practice of the Prophet, was so high that a few jurists held that the *Sunna* could abrogate the Qur'ān.

In the 4th/10th century the book market, agreement within schools of law, and the needs of students and judges called forth manuals of law, some of which have kept their standing until the present. The pressure of the book market deserves more attention among historians of Islamic law. The great polymath al-Mas'ūdī (d. 345/956), for example, released his rambling (but entertaining) world histories in three lengths: a very long everything-I-know version, *Akhbār al-Zamān* (lost but referred to in his other works); a work called the *Kitāb al-Awsaṭ* (*The Middle Book*), an abridgement of the long version, also lost; *Murūj al-Dhahab* (*The Fields of Gold*), also a middle length version, which survives; and *Kitāb al-Tanbīh wa-l-Ishrāf*, an abridgement and summary of the longer works. Books were expensive, and authors often preferred restating their subject at different lengths to revising old works. The same pattern has been followed by some jurists down to our own time.

The need of judges for a quick book to consult, of students for a smallish book to memorize (in what was a highly mnemonic culture) and the achievement of a large degree of agreement within the Mālikī school account for the popularity of the short *Epistle* by Ibn Abī Zayd al-Qayrawānī (d. 386/996), a book still memorized from the author's native Tunisia to Nigeria. Qayrawānī's *Epistle* offers a concrete starting point to consider the way in which law changed. Discussing an important topic, the *ḥubus* or *waqf*, the charitable trust or pious endowment, Qayrawānī in the *Epistle* speaks only of the trust set up for the family and descendants of the founder. The word refers to an institution in Tunisia, where the traditions of the Roman latifundia survived the Arab conquest and were threatened by the complicated divisions of inheritance among relatives required in the Qur'ān and well elaborated by the jurists. The *waqf*, literally the "stopping" of property from circulation, has no Qur'ānic basis except insofar as it fulfills the general exhortations in the Qur'ān to charity. The institution of the "pious trust" founded for non-familial interests exists in Qayrawānī's time even if he thought an elementary book in Mālikī law need not discuss it.

If we turn to a Ḥanafī handbook of the Ottoman period, *al-Durr al-Mukhtār* (*The Chosen Pearl*) by al-Ḥaṣkafī (d. 1088/1677), we find a discussion that has gained sophistication over the centuries. The author tells us that a *waqf* resembles a partnership in that the owner's property is inserted into someone else's property, i.e., God's. The author is aware that Abū Ḥanīfa, the eponym of the Ḥanafī school, thought that any charitable trust was revocable, whereas later Ḥanafīs disagreed. Many aspects of the making and preserving of such trusts are discussed. For example, the objects legally appropriate to be made into charitable trusts are painstakingly defined. Here the author says (contrary to the opinion of most pre-Ottoman jurists) that cash can be the object of a dedication to a charitable trust, the cash-*waqf* that lent money at interest being a widespread institution in the Ottoman Empire. Ḥaṣkafī also raises the interesting point that by the rules of analogy, it would be wrong to dedicate a Qur'ān (since it cannot be the object of a financial transaction, and one cannot dedicate as a *waqf* an object of no market value). However, Ḥaṣkafī says, the ḥadīth tells us, "What the Muslims see as right, is right in the eyes of God." This legal maxim was the justification for *istiḥsān*, "juristic preference," that is to say, a looser method of legal construction which sets aside the results of strict construction in favor of the common good. In many cases, the presence of *'urf* or "custom" is an occasion for the jurist to suspect that this common usage exists for the common good.

Some constant traits of the substantive law can be seen in these law books. By the 4th/10th century it became customary to divide the law into "roots," which I have called jurisprudence, and substantive law, which was called the "branches" or *furūʿ*. The phrase "substantive law" may give the mistaken impression that these law books were "codes." They were not, except for those rare cases in which the government promulgated some area of Islamic law in an official version. Many of these last books stand between an ideal world and a real world over which the jurist has limited influence but nevertheless the jurist wishes the believer to know that there is a practical, yet divinely ordained, path to follow. These books offered legal opinions as to what the law was. They were written within the tradition of a law school and that tradition rests heavily on the writer. By the 5th/11th century it was clear that a certain amount of legal pluralism was here to stay. Some law schools, such as that of Awzāʿī in Syria and Spain, would dwindle. But at least from the perspective of al-Māwardī (d. 450/1058), an extremely influential jurist in Baghdad, there were four legitimate law schools. This view would not find general acceptance until the 7th/13th century when the Mamluk rulers of Egypt made the system of four schools truly and finally canonical. Ideas spread among the four Sunni schools as well as between them and the Twelver Shiʿites, and the revolution started by Shāfiʿī was complete in the sense that Sunni and Shiʿite jurists shared a lot of the scaffolding language of jurisprudence, although this language was comparatively rare in the books on substantive law.

Books on the "differences" among great jurists, among the four law schools, and between Sunnis and Twelver Shiʿites are among the first legal texts preserved for us and this genre has continued to be cultivated right up to the present day. However, after a while this genre became rather stereotyped and seldom acted as a fulcrum by which to raise new discussions in the law. Each law school developed relatively stable subheadings under which things were discussed, most often adhering to the nodes around which legal discussion in that school had developed in the first place. For example, "contract" does not appear in the handbooks as a separate subject in any of the four Sunni schools or in the Twelver Shiʿite traditions, even though it is mentioned in the Qur'ān. The fullest discussion of it comes in the chapters on sales.

The founding of the madrasas or colleges gave a great push to the stabilization of the law. In early times teaching took place in the mosques and by the 4th/10th century lectureships in mosques were endowed. But in the 5th/11th century the institution of the endowed school was brought from the northeastern area of Iran to Baghdad and beyond at the behest of the great vizier Niẓām al-Mulk (d. 485/1092) who served the Seljuks, a dynasty whose empire encompassed almost all of Western Asia. Eventually the institution would spread to Morocco and China. Niẓām al-Mulk gave rich endowments for his madrasas, enough to house and feed their students. He also dictated their curriculum: their principal task was to teach Shāfiʿī law. (Niẓām al-Mulk himself accepted only one other school, the Ḥanafī, as legitimate, and considered it a very distant second.) The madrasas made sure that law was at the center of Islamic learning. Teaching other subjects such as rhetoric and mathematics, and even, in the case of the Shiʿites, philosophy, was allowed in the madrasas, but these subjects were there under the half-true excuse that they aided legal study. In fact, they were kept in a subordinate place. Law's dominance of endowed higher education was a loss for many areas of learning. But the law curricula were similar enough to give a common language to the ulema, in general allowing them to recognize across law schools who were members of their club.

It must be remembered that the ulema were not in any way consecrated and had no sacerdotal function. To maintain their prestige and authority they had to have mastery of something not easily accessible to the average literate person. While accessible elementary legal texts continued to be taught, a whole new class of textbook, including texts on jurisprudence, were written. They aimed at so much concision that they became virtually unintelligible. The student would memorize the passage assigned for the day and possibly read a commentary. In class the teacher would explain the text with examples, and might end the lesson by saying, "And therefore we say: ...," at which time he and the students would recite the dehydrated original, which had by now sprung into its full form in the minds of the students. Later in the student's education these memorized passages were like pegs on which to hang the keys of things learned in further study of the subject. This method accounts in part for the long stability of the order in which chapters were presented in law books and other genres of madrasa books.

THE NATURE OF ISLAMIC JURISPRUDENCE

The history of jurisprudence is narrower and less studied than substantive law and is often more difficult to discover. In a sense the tradition of jurisprudence began in the age of the Prophet when, according to ḥadīth, he was asked questions and sometimes explained his answers, or when, as in the abovementioned ḥadīth given by Ḥaṣkafī, he gave general principles of interpretation. This discussion on these topics continued to flourish after the Prophet and took a great leap forward with the work of Shāfiʿī. But would he have counted his book as jurisprudence, as later scholars did? The *Epistle* of al-Qayrawānī begins with a little theology and jurisprudence but is mostly a book on substantive law. It was only in the course of 4th/10th and 5th/11th centuries that jurisprudence emerged as a genre and its independent position clarified.

Fiqh (literally "discernment") is a human attempt at knowing the *sharīʿa*, the divinely ordained "path" which only God knows perfectly. The word *sharīʿa* shines more brightly and is seen more reverentially than *fiqh*. Nevertheless, it is essential for the *fiqh* to be known on the human plane as accurately as possible. A method of explaining texts gains authority as it gains internal consistency and agrees with theological ideas. Do commonweal arguments, so favored by Abū Ḥanīfa, have as much strength as arguments from scripture or by analogy? What are the presuppositions of the law? How can the linguistic disciplines tell us when commands in the Qur'ān are metaphorical? What were the qualifications for carrying out *ijtihād*, the independent effort at legal reasoning?

To this last question there developed a partial answer: one must be trained in jurisprudence as well as in substantive law. Just as the discipline of jurisprudence was coming into its own, the madrasas were founded, and jurisprudence was adopted into the madrasa curriculum. If one wanted to be a truly first-rate jurist, he/she should have some training in jurisprudence. The books on substantive law reveled in discussing difficult questions and seeming contradictions in the law; jurisprudence provided a means to answer them in an even more subtle way.

Jurisprudence was the threshold between law and theology. Theology was often called *uṣūl al-dīn*, the "roots of religion" just as jurisprudence was "the roots of law." It was assumed that before coming to the law a Muslim had found reasons to believe in God, the Qur'ān, and the exemplary life of the Prophet. Theology, which deals with these issues, also dealt with questions such as free will and predestination, which inevitably occur in a monotheistic system. But Islamic theology also deals with some topics more prominent among Muslim than Christian thinkers. If God speaks to man directly in the second person in the Qur'ān, what is the nature of that speech? On this issue there were many schools of thought, only two of which are discussed here. The speech included "commands," often in the imperative, and "prohibitions." For one school the speech of God was literally true; that is, when the Qur'ān says, "The All-Merciful sat firmly upon the throne," it meant that God literally sat on His throne. Some softened this formula by saying that one should believe without asking "how" (that is, in what sense this language is to be understood). Similarly, the commands and prohibitions in both the Qur'ān and sound ḥadīth were to be literally obeyed. This approach to the text of the Qur'ān existed (with some variation) among Muslims from an early period and still exists; its partisans are sometimes called *ahl al-ḥadīth.* Such literalist views resemble Christian fundamentalism and many (but not all) groups labeled fundamentalist in the Muslim world at present are literalist in this original sense.

An opposing stance was taken by the Mu'tazilī school. This school had almost as many branches as it had members. The branch associated with the Basran Abū al-Hudhayl (d. ca. 227/840) is discussed here. He vehemently opposed anthropomorphism and saw the *literal* acceptance of statements such as "The All-Merciful sat firmly on His throne" as contrary to the absolute transcendence of God above His creatures. God is one; He has no form or limit. God is All-Knowing and All-Seeing, etc., but His knowledge is identical with Himself. A human is responsible for his/her actions. God's speech, including the Qur'ān, is created by God.

The justice of God meant that certain of His laws could be found by reason alone, although the most correct form of these laws and of the way to fulfill them (such as how to worship Him) could be found only through revelation. They therefore adopted the categories "good/beautiful" (*ḥasan*) and "bad/ugly" (*qabīḥ*) as determinable by the "intellect/reason" (*'aql*) whereas the "mandatory" (*wājib*) can be determined by revelation alone. This system resembles Hellenistic theories of natural law with which the Mu'tazilīs were acquainted. The intellectual rigor that Mu'tazilīs introduced into theological discussion commanded respect even among their opponents and influenced all the major schools of theology among Muslims. Its influence on the Karaite "heresy" in Judaism is also well known.

The major school rejecting Mu'tazilism was founded by al-Ash'arī (d. 324/935), who was a former Mu'tazilī, and who, for all his great achievement and undoubted originality, uses many of the techniques of argumentation used by the Mu'tazilīs. Ash'arism formed a more coherent school than Mu'tazilism but its followers were by no means in complete agreement. Of course Ash'arī accepted that God is just, but God's omnipotence cannot be contained. If He is just, it is because He chooses to be just; and we have no business asking whether His commands are just. Ash'arism offered a "strong" theory in that it did not appear to compromise the omnipotence of God in any way. (At times Ash'arism seems close to certain versions of Protestant theology.) It makes Islamic law "positive" law in the sense that God alone, freed of all constraints, posits it. But to strip goodness and continuity of all rational justification had some problems of which the Ash'arites were aware. The perception of the "customary" behavior of things—the Ash'arite formula used to replace natural law in both the physical and moral world—required reason, both inductive and deductive. To carry out analogies—a practice fully accepted by Ash'arītes—required reasoning. Moreover, there had been a broad consensus since the 3rd/9th century that the "right" was "good," a view that the Ash'arītes generally accepted. It was explained by them in ingenious—but to this author not wholly successful—ways.

Eventually Sunnis rejected the theories of the Mu'tazilīs, while the Twelver and Zaydī Shi'ites accepted a large part of them, often in the version developed by Abū al-Hudhayl. Accompanying this parting of ways was a parting of ways in the role given to reason/intellect. For Sunnis there are rational presuppositions such as the use of reason in interpretation of the sources of the law. There is also analogy, one of the four major sources of Sunni law, since analogy requires reasoning in its application (although many Sunnis believe the validity of analogy comes only from its validation by the words of Prophetic ḥadīth).

Shi'ites, on the contrary, embrace reason/intellect as one of their four major sources of law. They reject analogy, however, on the grounds that it sometimes yields too many possibilities. Is smoking prohibited by analogy with the prohibition of wine? It depends on a guess as to what is the explanatory principle for the prohibition of wine: its ability to make someone drunk, or because of some other psychotropic effect. Hence a disagreement on the permissibility of smoking. (One long dead Sunni school said that only what was explicitly forbidden was forbidden; God had forbidden wine, not beer, and we have no business guessing His motives.)

The Shi'ite acceptance of Mu'tazilism was signaled by their adoption of a Mu'tazilī slogan, "Everything that reason ordains, divine law ordains" (and it is understood to be implied, vice-versa). As Muhammad Baqir al-Sadr, the great modern Shi'ite jurist (executed by Saddam Hussein in 1980) said, this program of earlier jurists was never actually carried out by a Shi'ite jurist.[7] But the theoretical and, in some cases, the actual importance of intellect and natural law is everywhere present in Shi'ite jurisprudence. Shi'ites, for example, enthusiastically adopted Aristotelian logic and used the syllogism instead of analogy (although later Sunni jurists came to approve some figures of the syllogism). In the first volume of his *Lessons in Islamic Jurisprudence* Muhammad Baqir al-Sadr also tried, without distorting Shi'ite law, to emphasize its (genuine) scriptural basis, partly to counter the Sunni critique of Shi'ism as too inclined to appeal to reason. It is striking that the theory of obligation which logically should stand at the opening of Sadr's book actually stands two-thirds of the way through it in the discussion of procedural principles.

Shi'ism went through a conservative phase for about two and a half centuries (10th-12th/16th-18th), in which a group of Shi'ite jurists called Akhbārīs insisted on the primacy of the accounts (*akhbār*) of infallible persons. They held that everyone with a good knowledge of: (1) Arabic, (2) the Qur'ān, (3) these accounts, (4) the points of consensus among the Shi'ites, and (5) the proper use of the rational argument (*dalīl 'aqlī*) could find the ruling appropriate to any case. Note that Shi'ite law even in this conservative phase did not completely reject intellect.

In the 13th/19th century the Uṣūlī school in Shi'ite law roundly won the high ground for the claims of intellect (and also for the special position of the jurists). Akhbārīs survive only in a few remote outposts. The decisive blows in this battle were dealt by the saintly Murtaḍā al-Anṣārī (d. 1281/1864), who vastly extended the use of the procedural principles. In the past century and a half the procedural principles have dominated many legal discussions. All of these procedural principles are based on intellect and Shi'ite jurisprudence reflects this change.

Jurisprudence was a threshold which led not only from theology to law but also from law to theology. Modern Shi'ite law with its interest in principles with a rational basis has encouraged the traffic between the two areas. One aspect of Shi'ite jurisprudence has been badly misrepresented in some Western books, which say that Shi'ism rejects the principle of consensus. It is true that Sunni consensus includes all Muslims or all Sunni jurists just as Shi'ite consensus includes either all Muslims or all Shi'ite jurists. Both traditions are concerned with fidelity to the actual

7 Hossein Modarressi-Tabataba'i, *An Introduction to Shi'i Law: A Bibliographical Study* (London, Ithaca Press: 1984) 4 and n. 2, in which Muhammad Baqir al-Sadr is quoted as saying that reason is a potential rather than actual source of law.

general practice of Muslims, presumed, as in the Prophet's confirmation of the pilgrimage, to be preserved in its correct form because of the continuing concern of generation after generation of Muslims. Ritual law in particular is a great river of shared experience that runs down the history of the Muslims. Moreover, within the schools of law there was concern to preserve the integrity of the school tradition. In this sense, although Islamic law did not formally accept the idea of precedent, the law books in practice heavily favored precedents.

How well did jurisprudence account for the substantive law? Jurisprudence made a brave attempt, but when jurisprudence came along, too much substantive law already existed for any theory to account for all of it. In fact, there was a very minor genre of works in which the specialist in jurisprudence attempted to prove the harmony between the "roots" and "branches," but such attempts were curiosities, not fully successful.

Nevertheless, once it was established, jurisprudence disciplined the jurists, and therefore exercised a centripetal influence. I have described the way in which Shāfiʿī wanted to bring both the Kufan and Medinese schools under a common standard, and this impulse remained an important part of jurisprudence. It also, as discussed above, corresponded with the formation of the ulema as a self-conscious group, who would have destroyed their own authority if centrifugal forces had been allowed to operate.

It is a curiosity that jurisprudence did not take on two related topics, the "moral ends" of the law (*maqāṣid*) and the "norms" (*qawāʿid*) of the law. Ḥanafī jurisprudence sometimes discussed a category literally called "cause" (*sabab*) which, if developed, might have constituted a deeper level of rational explanation than did the search for the connecting link of an analogy. A small genre on the moral ends of the law existed but was seldom integrated into jurisprudence. Although the "norms," often given in the form of maxims, seem very central to the way jurists think, and are occasionally cited in the books on jurisprudence before the nineteenth century, they were never, it would seem, central to the construction of any jurisprudential theory. They too were treated in a separate genre. There seem to have been two streams of ethical thinking, one tradition not primarily focused on the law, and another tradition that is a pietistic exposition of the law, often much simplified. Only in a few pre-modern works such as the *Iḥyāʾ* of al-Ghazālī (d. 505/1111) do the traditions of law and ethics meet. (Modern Muslims have given much more attention to this subject.)

In many modern Shiʿite law and theology books the argument for man's obligation to God is that a servant has an obligation to a master. This argument is traditional in Shiʿite jurisprudence and represents the thinking of a hierarchical society. In fact, pre-modern Islamic law represents the pre-modern society of Muslims in the Middle East in that it recognizes three different absolute distinctions of status: between male and female, between Muslim and non-Muslim, and between slave and free. This last distinction was discarded as no longer meaningful by Muslim jurists; and the other two distinctions are no longer universally accepted.

REASON AND CONVENTION

Earlier in this introduction, I referred to reason as a source and method in jurisprudence, but in fact we see a mixture of adherence to inherited conventions with a more rationalist approach. In fact, some such mixture is probably present in most legal systems. The adherence to conventionalism is, however, formally much stronger in a system which wishes to refer to scripture on every possible occasion. When looking for "shared or common elements" as the basis for legal reasoning, the modern Shiʿite jurists are essentially appealing to the authority of the conventions of Islamic jurisprudence, which does not of course exclude the possibility that these conventions might be justified by reason. Sometimes, as in the jurists' acceptance of the single-source account, they in fact give only a scriptural justification, since some jurists believe that this source of law is too uncertain to be trusted on a rational basis alone. Since some modern jurists, including Sadr, consider the guidance given by reason to be more authoritative than that of a weakly attested ḥadīth, the reader may well ask what the methods of reasoning used are. After all, Sadr himself wrote a book trying to establish the importance—some would say, the primacy—of induction in Shiʿite and, more generally, Islamic legal reasoning. Nevertheless, the relations between all modes of reasoning in determining a rational conclusion have never, to my knowledge, been fully elaborated in Shiʿite jurisprudence.

It can be said in defense of conventionalism that the law reflects the long experience of the society in which it exists. This argument applies more fully to areas such as commercial law than to criminal law, which has been very differently enforced in Muslim societies. Moreover, the appeal to the conventions established by great jurists in the past has the virtue of allowing only a limited pluralism when the lack of a formal clerical structure would seem to encourage Islamic law to fly in a thousand directions. In the immediate case of modern Twelver Shiʿites, the obligation for each believer to follow a living authority, a *mujtahid*, has created a formal structure of religious authority perhaps unparalleled in other Muslim communities. The proliferation of internet fatwas by unqualified jurists stands in strong contrast to this Shiʿite system.

There is another type of conventionalism emphasized by later Shiʿite law which is close to the concept of *ius gentium* in Roman law. Many modern Shiʿite jurists speak of common usage (*ʿurf*) and the conduct of reasonable people (*sīra ʿuqalāʾīya*). These two phrases frequently appear together in Shiʿite works on jurisprudence and substantive law. Common usage and the conduct of reasonable people are subject to change. They are therefore not natural law, which exists for the Shiʿites because of their belief in God's justice. They are nevertheless some indication as to what natural law might be, and a guide to the way in which laws should be implemented in practice.

A humane aspect of almost all Islamic law is that it takes into consideration the subjective state of the legal agent when assessing accountability. This consideration includes questions of both capacity and intention. Shiʿite law of the last two centuries has been especially careful in its discussions of assurance in the mind of the legal agent, inspired by, among other things, the great 5th/11th-century philosopher Avicenna's (Ibn Sīnā's) distinction between conceptualization and assent. The increased interest in the subjective state of the legal agent is apparent in recent Twelver Shiʿite thought, and results from two and a half centuries of such discussion in Uṣūlī legal circles.

MEDIEVAL WESTERN LAW AND ISLAMIC LAW

Earlier I referred to the bishops' courts that existed even before the conversion of the Roman emperors to Christianity. In the fifth century C.E. the Roman emperor Theodosius II sought to define a closed body of authoritative jurists, just as Islamic law did retrospectively with its "authoritative" books of ḥadīth. Similarly, the code prepared under Justinian a century later was subsequently regarded as having a privileged standing as the fullest authoritative statement of Roman law.

The New Testament, notwithstanding the harsh words of Jesus against lawyers and the antinomian tone of some passages in the letters of St. Paul, sometimes praises the law, as when Jesus says, "I tell you the truth, until heaven and earth disappear, not the smallest letter nor the least stroke of the pen will by any means disappear from the Law, until everything is accomplished" (Matthew 5:18). It is overwhelmingly likely that Matthew understood Jesus to be speaking of the Jewish law, but as Christianity spread, a more general interpretation became possible. The Church grew in an atmosphere pervaded by Roman law, which became more deeply associated with Christianity after the Roman emperor converted in the early fourth century C.E. Yet the West (as contrasted with Byzantium) had to wait until the revival of Roman law in the twelfth century C.E. for the Church to see the full possibilities that mastery of this sophisticated body of knowledge offered. The greatest figure of this revival, the lawyer Gratian, who wrote in the first half of the twelfth century, said that the Church is both a spiritual and an earthly society. The twelfth century witnessed Western Europe's greatest experiment in religious law. By the thirteenth century, church courts were accepting a great variety of non-ecclesiastical cases. Theologians and canonists were trying to find a firm intellectual connection between the expanding jurisdiction of church-administered Roman law and basic Christian principles.

At some point in the thirteenth century, however, the canonists and the theologians began to part ways. Professor Charles Donahue of the Harvard Law School suggests some contributing reasons for their divergence. First, keeping up with developments in canon law as well as mastering Roman law was a full-time occupation, as was the study of theology. Second, as the Church's legal system had to share jurisdiction with secular law, its lawyers had to be able to talk to secular lawyers. The inevitable result was some secularization of canon law. Third, the greatest canonist of the thirteenth century, Henricus de Segusio, and the greatest canonist of the early fourteenth century, the layman Johannes Andreae, seem to have taken no interest in the new scholastic theology and, like other canonists of the period, adhered to the theology of the twelfth century.[8]

Islamic law may have provided for the theoretical possibility of an adoption of pre-Islamic revealed law that would have paralleled the reception

8 Charles Donahue, Jr., "A Crisis of Law? Reflections on the Church and the Law over the Centuries," *Jurist*, 65:1–2 (2005) 1–30.

of Roman law in Latin Christendom, but in practice Muslim jurists rarely appealed to any previous system. Moreover, the canon lawyers never denied the existence of a secular realm, although they advocated increased Papal oversight of that realm. The de facto separation of the authority of sultans from the authority of the caliph was accepted only as a lesser evil than confrontation and disorder within the Islamic world. Only very rarely was this distinction in the real world defended as an ideal.

Among the Shiʿites the situation was different. They were seldom in power, and since they had to wait for their messianic leader, they could accept sultans with less theoretical difficulty, demanding primarily that they do justice. Furthermore, their belief in divine justice required them to consider the relation between theology and law a permanently open question. At some periods, their discussion of this relationship was repetitive and unoriginal, at others, innovative. One such innovation is the modern interest in the theoretical basis for extended reliance on common usage and the conduct of reasonable people. And like the celebrated thirteenth-century theologian Thomas Aquinas, the Uṣūlīs could not think of law without scholastic philosophy, whereas many Sunni jurists became great specialists in Islamic law without taking any interest in theology or philosophy or even jurisprudence.

The pre-modern tradition of Islamic learning created a monumental body of scholarship as impressive as that of Europe and India and China. It was successful in creating a sophisticated legal system, which in certain areas, such as commercial law, can be and has been, with some adaptation, successfully applied in the contemporary world. Islamic jurisprudence shared the subtlety of the law it described and remains an intellectual achievement which can be studied with benefit.

Consultation and the Political Process in the Middle East of the 9th, 10th, and 11th Centuries

Every student of the pre-modern Islamic Middle East will recognize "consultation" as a familiar friend. Theoretical works, whether mirrors for princes or law books, are replete with advice recommending consultation: *mashwara* or *mashūrā* or *mushāwara* or *shūrā*. Such books urge the prudent ruler to convene consultative assemblies, *majālis al-shūrā* or simply *shūrā*, whenever possible. Belletristic literature also extols consultation. For example, Ibn Qutayba, Ibn 'Abd Rabbih and Abū al-Faraj al-Iṣfāhānī in *al-Aghānī* quote the criticism levelled by Sudayf, a client of the Hāshimīs, against the Abbasids: "By God ... our leadership, which was consultative (*mashwara*), has become arbitrary and our succession hereditary." Furthermore, chronicles represent such consultations and assemblies as actually taking place. If the chroniclers may occasionally have felt obliged to invent some incidences of consultation in order to portray their patrons becomingly, we can feel sure that their patrons invented some unrecorded but real occasions for consultation in order to maintain their self-conception and their image in the eyes of others.[1]

Why was it so important in this world of political values to talk so very much of consultation: and what was actually meant by consultation? Consultation is certainly a respectable activity in modern Western

Author's note: This article was first published as: "Consultation and the Political Process in the Islamic Middle East of the 9th, 10th, and 11th Centuries," in Moawiyah M. Ibrahim (ed.), *Arabian Studies in Honour of Mahmoud Ghul: Symposium at Yarmouk University, December 8–11, 1984*, Yarmouk University Publications, Institute of Archaeology and Anthropology Series 2 (Wiesbaden, Otto Harrassowitz: 1989) 83–88. Reproduced with permission.

1 The criticism of Sudayf and similar sayings are quoted by Bernard Lewis in his excellent article "Meşveret" in *Tarih Enstitüsü Dergisi* (1981–82) 775–782.

governments, but it is an activity that has attracted very little attention on the part of Western social scientists. In the 1968 Macmillan *Encyclopaedia of the Social Sciences* there is no article on or even reference in the index to "consultation." Consultation is, in the political culture of the modern West, a semi-formal or informal process that allows persuasion and the exchange of information without deciding the issue at hand. As the *Grand Larousse* of 1972 says: "consultative" means established in order to give opinions, without powers of decision; and a "consultative voice" is the right to give one's opinion, but not to vote. The powerlessness of consultation seems to have deprived it of some of its interest for us; and we concentrate on those parts of the political process, such as compromise and caucusing, that lead directly toward decision-making and in particular directly toward voting.

In this chapter two major examples of consultation in the Islamic Middle East in the 4th/10th and 5th/11th centuries will be discussed. I believe that they throw some light on the significance of consultation in the political culture of their time.

The first example comes from the beginning of the period of the *amīr al-umarā'*, those "mayors of the palace" who controlled the Abbasid caliphs for a generation at the beginning of the 4th/10th century before the Buyids occupied Baghdad. In 329/940 al-Rāḍī, often called the last independent caliph, died; and it was assumed that the Turkish general Bajkam would choose his successor. Bajkam, however, seems to have had some scruple about doing so directly. Perhaps he felt that the authority of the mayor of the palace was too new to be asserted in such a naked fashion; or perhaps he felt insufficiently familiar with the politics of Baghdad, in which he had arrived recently. Or, perhaps he felt that he would rather follow a political pattern so warmly recommended to serious Muslims. In any case, Bajkam, who was in nearby Wāṣiṭ, sent a letter to Baghdad to al-Kūfī, his chief administrator, ordering a consultation on the choice of the next caliph.

Al-Kūfī was to meet with the dead caliph's vizier (*wazīr*), all former viziers, all heads of *dīwāns* or ministries, the judges, the witness-notaries (*'udūl*), the jurists (*fuqahā'*), members of the family of 'Alī and al-'Abbās, and the leading men of the city (*wujūh al-balad*). This is, incidentally, one of those precious lists of important men which themselves deserve a study. Al-Kūfī was ordered by Bajkam to consult them (*shāwir-hum*) as to who was to be appointed caliph "among those whose principles and conduct were commendable."

On the first occasion that they met some of those present mentioned the name of Ibrāhīm, son of the Abbasid Caliph al-Muqtadir, but they dispersed without taking a decision. On the second day Bajkam's letter was handed to a clerk who read it to those assembled; then he mentioned Ibrāhīm ibn al-Muqtadir. A Hāshimī present asked, "Is it necessary that the man mentioned in the letter be from the descendants of al-Muqtadir, or can he be from another descent?" Al-Kūfī replied: "Whoever has these qualifications is to be appointed whoever he is." The Hāshimī then asked that the matter be discussed privately (*sirran*). So al-Kūfī went into a room and had those assembled brought in two at a time and said to each pair: "The qualities of Ibrāhīm ibn al-Muqtadir have been described to us. What do you say?" When each pair heard this, they had no doubt that the matter had been decided and that Bajkam had ordered his appointment, and they said that Ibrāhīm was worthy of the office. After this process, Ibrāhīm was appointed caliph with the title of al-Muttaqī.[2]

The above account, from the *Tajārib al-Umam* of Miskawayh (d. 421/1030), is slightly different from the account given by al-Ṣūlī, the court poet. Al-Ṣūlī (d. 334–335/946) says that the convocation of notables took place only after al-Kūfī had surveyed the possible candidates and had written Bajkam suggesting Ibrāhīm. Bajkam wrote back instructing al-Kūfī to invest Ibrāhīm with the caliphate only after conferring with an assembly of notables so that there would be unanimity and so that the caliph should not be exclusively the choice of Bajkam.[3] There seem to be no other major sources for this event, and I therefore do not know which to trust—the first account by Miskawayh or the second by al-Ṣūlī. But there is some slight reason to give Miskawayh's account more weight. Miskawayh's informants, written or oral, were usually important clerks while al-Ṣūlī's informants were often mere courtiers; and since al-Kūfī was a clerk, Miskawayh's source may well have been better informed on this matter. In support of this view there are circumstantial details in the account of Miskawayh but not in al-Ṣūlī, such as the consultation with the notables by pairs, that are not likely to be fabrications since some of these notables may well have been still alive when Miskawayh wrote his chronicle.

In this example we see many of the characteristics of one type of consultation between the ruler and the leading men of his realm. First, the ruler

2 Miskawayh, *Tajārib al-Umam*, II (Cairo: 1333/1915) 2–3.

3 Al-Ṣūlī, *Akhbār al-Rāḍī bi-Ilāh wa-al-Muttaqī li-Ilāh*, ed. J. Heyworth Dunne (Cairo: 1354/1935) 187–188.

chooses the participants who will participate in the consultation. Second, if the participants think that the ruler has already made up his mind, their energy is directed principally toward anticipating and supporting his choice. Third, even if the ruler has not chosen beforehand, there is a strictly limited number of candidates or options, chosen sometimes by the ruler or, less often, by those consulted. As in the choice of magistrates in England, it was often understood that only a limited number of people would have the influence, wealth, experience, or whatever, considered necessary to be qualified for the office. One finds examples of this in the choice of men as head of the town, *ra'īs al-balad*, or head of the quarter, *ra'īs al-ḥāra*, or even as judge, *qāḍī*. Fourth, if the group is over a certain size, it usually can function only to give public testimony to the support of the ruler's policy by the leading men assembled. Thus, in the consultation described previously, when the Hāshimī decides that Bajkam really wants the opinions of those assembled, he asks that the matter be discussed "privately," *sirran*, which al-Kūfī understands to mean in smaller groups. Presumably, al-Kūfī knows that when a confidant of the ruler consults with two men at a time, the views of each of the two are relatively safe. Each can deny the other's account of what he has heard, and correspondingly each is in a position to implicate the other, falsely or correctly. The larger the group, the less likely this principle is to work. However, when al-Kūfī states the problem in a way that implies that the ruler has a preference, the second principle—the need to anticipate the ruler's decision—takes precedence. Fifth, it is assumed that at least the public image of the consultation will be one of unanimous agreement: thus, al-Ṣūlī tells us, Bajkam wanted an assembly of notables "so that there would be unanimity."

In Bayhaqi's history of Sultan Mas'ūd we have a somewhat similar consultation. Bayhaqi (d. 470/1077) was a minister of the Ghaznavid court, and in this case we seem to have an eyewitness account, although the eyewitness was strongly partisan in favor of the Ghazanavids. In 421 A.H. letters reached Mas'ūd in western Iran telling him that his father, Maḥmūd of Ghazna, who had conquered most of northern India, had died. The letters advised Mas'ūd to return as quickly as possible since there would be a struggle over succession to the throne. First, Mas'ūd discussed with Bayhaqi, the minister and author, what he should do. Bayhaqi told Mas'ūd that there was no need for consultation (*mushāwara*). Mas'ūd, however, told Bayhaqi: "There is no alternative to consultation" (*mashwara*) and he ordered his own notables, *a'yān*, to assembly, "so that I can speak to them and hear what they have to say and then I will act according to what is decided."

Those assembled advised Mas'ūd to hurry back to the capital to claim the succession, in spite of a certain strategic danger in doing so. As the only three notables named beside Bayhaqi were military commanders, assurance of their support for this course of action was essential to Mas'ūd.

Shortly after this Mas'ūd arranged another consultation in order to deal with a related problem. He wanted to take as many soldiers as possible with him to enforce his claim to the succession, but he did not wish to give up control of central Iran, parts of which he had recently conquered. He was at this moment in Rayy, the key city in this area. His advisers told him to leave a small garrison, which would be sufficient if the people of Rayy remained loyal, while even a large garrison would be insufficient if the people of Rayy decided to be disloyal.

Mas'ūd summoned the notables, *a'yān*, of Rayy, consisting, as Bayhaqi tells us, of the 'Alids, the *qāḍīs*, the *imāms*, the *faqīhs* and "the great ones" and—he adds—some of the *'āmma*, the common people: so we know that he considers the preceding members of the list as *khāṣṣa*, literally "the special people." About fifty or sixty of those who came were admitted into Mas'ūd's immediate presence. First the *a'yān* told Mas'ūd in the most florid terms that they were happy with his rule. Then, Mas'ūd told them in the most unambiguous fashion that if they were loyal to him in his absence, he would reward them well; but if they were disloyal he would feel free to do whatever he liked to them. He demanded a clear and decisive statement from them as to what they would do in his absence.

When he finished this statement, according to Bayhaqi the notables looked at each other, were too amazed to speak, and finally pointed to the *khaṭīb*, the preacher of the Friday sermon. He, an elderly and worthy man, rose and said: "These people are incapable of answering." He suggested that the notables meet with Ṭāhir, a clerk of the king, and give an answer. They withdrew to another place and the *khaṭīb* gave a speech expressing their complete loyalty to Mas'ūd. At the end he turned to the other notables and said, "Are my words also your words?" and all said yes. Mas'ūd went on to gain the succession to the throne, and the majority of the people of Rayy remained loyal.[4]

---

4 Bayhaqi, *Tarikh-e Bayhaqi*, eds. Qasim Ghani and 'Ali Akbar Fayyad (Tehran: 1324) 18–25.

In the two consultations, that of Mas'ūd with his own notables and his consultation with the notables of Rayy, we see some of the traits that we saw in the consultation a hundred years earlier to choose a caliph. The ruler chooses the participants. The participants are eager to anticipate the ruler's mind. It is assumed that the decision will be adopted unanimously. Part of the function of such a consultation is to get renewed expression of commitment to the ruler's policies. But in the story of the notables of Rayy, even more than in the story of the caliph, we see that in such forced consultations those assembled had to be allowed to reach unanimity first or they had trouble expressing any opinion whatsoever. It is possible that the notables of Rayy were partly unable to answer Mas'ūd because they were overawed, but it is very likely that they could not answer also because he had not told them by implication the extent of what he was demanding of them.

Once an ex-minister, who had long served in the cabinet of the former Shah of Iran Mohammad Reza Pahlavi, told me that the members of the cabinet only consulted in earnest and displayed divergence of opinion in meetings before they met with the Shah. In the presence of the Shah, they always displayed unanimity unless one of them wished to make a point while resigning or wished to fight openly in order to destroy someone else's position in the esteem of the Shah.

This same desire to avoid public disagreement can be seen in consultation in which there is no interface with a ruler. Significantly, in this form of discussion, divergent views are expressed. But at the end all present signify their unanimous consent by acclamation. Two examples of this are the famous first *shūrā* at the Saqīfa which chose Abū Bakr as the first caliph and the consultation of the military commanders about the succession after the death of one of Saladin's sons in 595/1198. A somewhat similar consultation is offered by the examples of tribes, especially semi- and fully nomadic tribes. Here, according to the accounts I have read, opinions are offered, but as a consensus seems to be emerging, all those who have expressed opinions divergent from the consensus restate their views so that they agree with the consensus.

These types of consultation seem to conform to certain forms of economic life. Just as consultation between the ruler and notables sometimes represents a covert brokerage, so did the negotiations between the central government and the notables over taxes. The notables were essential to any systematic tax program, but they expected and often got something in exchange for their cooperation as did the notables of Rayy. Within a nomadic tribe, on the other hand, there is extreme interdependence, and the basic unit of the tribe cannot endure if there is sustained disagreement where, for example, to move for new pasture.

In one of his early essays Claude Lévi-Strauss attempts to delineate the universal characteristics of leadership, although he takes as starting place the system of the South American Indian group called the Nambikuara. Among this group, according to Lévi-Strauss, there are several men acknowledged as leaders, who likely acquire this reputation through their behavior during the nomadic life of the Nambikuara over the years. The importance as well as the permanence of the band which they lead depends largely upon the ability of the actual leader to keep his rank and eventually improve on it. Although each lives practically alone during a good part of the year, the existence of other bands is not forgotten. Therefore, it is not enough for the band to do well; the band counts on the chief to try to do better than the others. In significant part to do better means to do economically better. The leader symbolizes and makes actual his role as the coordinator of a policy directed at the common economic welfare of the group by his generosity. His displays of ingenuity, whether in guiding the band to food or in acting as a ceremonial leader, are an intellectual form of ingenuity.[5]

If personal prestige and ingenuity are the foundations of leadership, consent, Lévi-Strauss believed, is the origin of leadership. The leader is chosen through consent and must continue to seek consent. He has no coercive power. When describing the pre-Islamic Arab tribe, H.A.R Gibb used to say that the chief had the right to command but that no one had the duty to obey.

Lévi-Strauss believed that this pattern is found, concealed or unconcealed, in all leadership. How far is that pattern relevant to the vastly more complex society we have been examining, and more specifically, to its use of consultation? At a tribal level I suspect that it is very relevant. All pre-modern Arabic literature emphasizes the importance of the chief's position and the importance of his using *ḥilm*, forbearance, in order to avoid divisions in his group. The Prophet is frequently praised for his masterful use of *ḥilm*, and the *sīra* (the life story of the Prophet) amply

5 Claude Lévi-Strauss, "The Social and Psychological Aspects of Chieftainship," *Transactions of the New York Academy of Sciences* 7 (1944) 16–32.

testifies to its importance. In such a group we expect to find consultation of the third type in which real divergence of opinion is expressed but the leader shapes an emerging consensus and gives a chance for all to restate their opinions in agreement with the emerging consensus.

It is also relevant to the style of consultation in non-tribal society between the *aʿyān* themselves. This is apparent when, for example, wielders of coercive power consult with each other during a power vacuum after the death of a ruler, as in the consultation after the death of Saladin's son. It even appears in those consultations that the *aʿyān* have between themselves before coming face to face with a ruler. The *aʿyān* have a certain measure of economic and even coercive power at their disposal (as Masʿūd knew when he said that even a large garrison could not keep control of a disloyal Rayy). They could make it difficult for the ruler to collect money systematically or to maintain dominance. The ruler had to coordinate the redistribution of surplus wealth that came through the *aʿyān* in a way that did not alienate them in the long run. If they were soldiers or skilled scribes, they could (and did) emigrate to other rulers: for, as among the Nambikuara, the existence of other groups was not forgotten. The generosity of the ruler is as symbolically and practically important to the ruler of the 4th/10th and 5th/11th centuries as to the leader of a Nambikuara band. Hence, by convening a consultation, the ruler initiated a prior consultation that might otherwise not have taken place, as he alone could coordinate the redistribution of the wealth and power that the *aʿyān* shared. In my view these patterns of consultation among the *aʿyān* themselves, both in cases of vacuums of power and prior to meeting with the ruler have close parallels in the lives of modern American corporate executives.

The difference from the tribal consultation lay precisely in this unilateral right of initiative with the ruler. The ruler usually appraised himself informally of the mood of the *aʿyān*; but ultimately if they did not want to accept his proposal they had only the option of emigration or rebellion. Significantly, if they rebelled, it was not in order to set up a collective leadership, but to set up one of their number as a new ruler or to invite someone outside their group to come in as a ruler. Their form of politics by unanimity required a strong figure to take the initiative because they could achieve such unanimity only reactively.

We have evidence that such consultation extended far down into society. It was used to choose and guide the head of the neighborhood; it was used in the relation of the landlord with the village he owned. We are not exactly in the world of the "social contract," yet the element of consent, which Lévi-Strauss thinks universal, is not entirely absent. In these consultations superiors may be unilaterally presenting inferiors with demands, but they are doing that partly to secure a clear understanding as to the negotiating position of the superior. Unlike consultations to choose leaders, such consultations were the beginning of a process of brokerage.

The need for a public display of universal consent stands in contrast to assumption of universal consent that underlays societies which claim as their basis the "volonté générale" and other such impersonal reifications of the social contract. It is not insignificant that voting died out in some of the Middle Eastern Christian churches, especially the Nestorian church. It was inimical to the process of consultation and consensus that was central to the political and social process of Middle Eastern society in this period. In the 3rd/9th, 4th/10th, and 5th/11th centuries Middle Eastern society assumed that the initiative for consensus would come from above and that it would be articulated through consultation. In this system there could be no abstraction, no rectification of the social contract, because the consensus was a reaction to the initiative of a specific ruler.

As a reaction to a personal initiative, it took the form of total collective approval, for an individual's disapproval would have been a challenge to the ruler's right of initiative. In this sense, consultation is praised correctly in the political literature of the time. Besides its function at some levels for exchange of opinion and information, it was the principal ceremonial arena for displaying the consensus without which, in the view of the *a'yān* and, possibly, even their inferiors, the social fabric would be torn apart.

The Idea of the *Jihād* in Islam before the Crusades

The "jihad," often loosely translated as "holy war on behalf of Islam," is usually understood to be a fairly stable idea in Islamic law. In that standard reference book, *The Encyclopaedia of Islam,* the very considerable scholar Émile Tyan tells us that the notion of jihad stems from the principle that Islam, "along with the temporal power which it implies, ought to embrace the whole universe, if necessary by force." Moreover, according to Tyan the jihad is "a religious duty" and "has a perpetual character." Tyan mentions only one major pre-modern figure of the Sunni tradition, Sufyān al-Thawrī, who disagreed with this view. Sufyān al-Thawrī, a thinker of the 2nd/8th century, regarded the jihad as an obligation only as a defensive war.[1]

In fact, differences about the status and nature of jihad are a marked feature of early Islamic law, and details about the conduct of jihad continue to reflect historical circumstance throughout the history of Islamic law in the Middle East. It is important to remember that there is no authoritatively codified Islamic law before the nineteenth century C.E. Therefore, we have an accretional body of law (or more accurately, of legal thinking) in which minority opinions are preserved and in which there may be more than one widely held or "normative" position. This article attempts to give some idea of the divergence of opinion on the "universal" and "perpetual" nature of the jihad in the first Islamic century in Syria and the Hijaz, the province

---

Author's note: This article, co-authored with Ridwan al-Sayyid, was originally published as: "The Idea of the *Jihād* in Islam Before the Crusades," in Angeliki E. Laiou and Roy Parviz Mottahedeh (eds.), *The Crusades from the Perspective of Byzantium and the Muslim World* (Washington, D.C., Dumbarton Oaks Research Library and Collection: 2001) 23–29. Reproduced with permission.

1 É. Tyan, "Djihād," *The Encyclopaedia of Islam,* 2nd ed. (hereafter EI^2), II (Leiden, Brill: 1965) 538–540. We wish to thank Michael Bonner, Fred Donner, and Hossein Modarressi for their very useful comments.

of western Arabia that contains Mecca and Medina. It then tries to show how, in Iraq in the second half of the 2nd/8th century, certain normative theories of jihad were accepted which continued to have widespread acceptance through and beyond the period of the Crusades. However, as there are literally hundreds of legal books and other genres of literature that deal with the jihad in the centuries before the Crusades, well over half of which exist only in manuscript, this essay in no way attempts to give a full survey of the normative theories of jihad in the pre-crusading period or to weigh the comparative importance of these theories at different periods.

We start with a review of the primary sources available to reconstruct the earliest discussions of jihad. The first half of the second Islamic century (which ends in 766 C.E.) saw the emergence of two genres of writing about jihad which either mixed history and legal thought or attempted to set down rulings for war that relied upon historical precedents. The first were the books on the military expeditions organized by the Prophet in the Medinan period, and some of these books also included the military expeditions of the early caliphs. The second were the books on the conduct of state, or *siyar*. The books on military expeditions—most of which, unfortunately, are no longer extant—were written by such important figures as 'Urwa ibn al-Zubayr (d. 94/714), al-Zuhrī (d. 124/741), and Mūsā ibn 'Uqba (d. 141/758). In fact, the late Martin Hinds suggests that before Ibn Hishām (d. 213/828 or 218/833), all transmitters of biographical accounts of the Prophet were primarily concerned with this genre, including Ibn Hishām's primary source, Ibn Isḥāq (d. 150/767), who is usually regarded as the first major biographer of the Prophet.[2] While the concern in this genre on military expeditions appears to be historical, these works were undoubtedly also seen as sources for the Islamic rules of war, as we understand from the advice of the jurist Mālik ibn Anas (d. 172/795) to his students to refer to the *maghāzī*, or accounts of exemplary early campaigns, by Mūsā ibn 'Uqba and not to those of Ibn Isḥāq.

Among the books on the conduct of state (*siyar*) from the second Islamic century there is a lost book by the very celebrated Syrian jurist al-Awzā'ī (d. 157/773), of which parts are preserved in a refutation written by Abū Yūsuf (d. 182/798)[3] and long extracts in the above-mentioned Ibn Isḥāq. There is also a lost book by Muḥammad al-Nafs al-Zakīya (d. 145/762)

2 M. Hinds, "al-Maghāzī," *EI*², V (Leiden, Brill: 1986) 1161.
3 Abū Yūsuf Ya'qūb ibn Ibrāhīm, *Al-Radd 'alā Siyar al-Awzā'ī*, ed. Abu al-Wafa' al-Afghani (Cairo: n.d.).

of which many fragments survive in the writing of later Zaydī authors.[4] Another book of this genre is ascribed to the celebrated jurist Abū Ḥanīfa (d. 150/767), which we also know through the above-mentioned treatise of Abū Yūsuf refuting al-Awzāʿī. In fact, Abū Yūsuf represents his own work as completing the groundwork laid by Abū Ḥanīfa. A yet further work of this genre is the *Siyar* of Abū Isḥāq al-Fazārī (d. ca. 185/801), of which a section has been found in Morocco.[5] While this survey is far from complete, it shows that we know, in fragmentary or occasionally in full-form, literature of the second half of the 2nd/8th century, much of which is in dialogue with the opinions of authors or "authorities" of the early 2nd/8th century, the end of the Umayyad period. These early surviving books on the conduct of state are united by two concerns: first, their discussion of the virtues of jihad and, second, their discussion of legal rulings related to jihad, a subject that often occupies by far the largest part of such texts.

At the end of the second half of the second Islamic century (which ends in 820 C.E.), a new genre of writing on the legal aspects of war appears, namely, the books on the *kharāj*, or land tax, and on *amwāl*, the public finances of the Islamic community. The earliest example of this genre appears to be a composition written by a vizier of the caliph al-Mahdī (r. 158/774–169/785).[6] The earliest extant book is the well-known treatise on *kharāj* by a famous pupil of Abū Ḥanīfa who became supreme judge in the period of the caliph Hārūn al-Rashīd, namely the Abū Yūsuf mentioned above. Other such works of the third Islamic century were written by Yaḥyā ibn Ādam (d. 206/821) and by Abū ʿUbayd al-Qāsim ibn Sallām (d. 224/838). This genre continued to exist for many centuries; and the *Kitāb al-Istikhrāj fī Aḥkām al-Kharāj* by the Ḥanbalī author Abū al-Faraj ʿAbd al-Raḥmān Ibn Rajab (d. 795/1392) is, perhaps, the last book of this type to achieve prominence among Sunni jurists in the Arab world.

It should be noted that after the appearance of books on the land tax and public finances, the books on the conduct of state and on the military expeditions of the Prophet appear to dwindle. However, books specifically on the jihad increased. These, by and large, fall into two categories. One

4 al-Nafs al-Zakīya Muḥammad ibn ʿAbd Allāh ibn al-Ḥasan ibn al-Ḥasan ibn ʿAlī ibn Abī Ṭālib, *Kitāb al-Siyar wa-mā Baqiya min Rasāʾil al-Daʿwa wa-l-Thawra*, ed. Ridwan al-Sayyid (Beirut: 2021). F. Buhl, "Muḥammad b. ʿAbd Allah, called al-Nafs al-Zakīya," *EI²*, VII (Leiden, Brill: 1991) 388–389.

5 Al-Fazārī, *Kitāb al-Siyar*, ed. F. Hamada (Beirut: 1986).

6 See A. Ben-Shemesh, *Taxation in Islam* (Leiden: 1969) 8–9.

category consists of specific sections of the collections of Prophetic tradition, or separate books, on the "virtues of the jihad." The *Kitāb al-Jihād* by 'Abd Allāh ibn al-Mubārak al-Marwazī (d. 181/797) must surely be one of the earliest examples of such individual books.[7] Another category consists of the chapters on jihad in the law books.

This early literature raises many questions, only a few of which are addressed here. The view of Sufyān al-Thawrī (d. 161/778), who, as we mentioned above, believed that only the defensive jihad[8] was obligatory, is not as idiosyncratic as Tyan has led us to believe. It has already been noted by Jacqueline Chabbi that there is some divergence between the Ḥijāzī and the Syrian schools on this question. She points out that the *Muwaṭṭa'*, written by the Medinan Mālik ibn Anas (d. 179/795), seems in the version compiled by al-Shaybānī (d. 189/804) to lack any endorsement of warfare on the frontier in a context of jihad. She concludes:

> It is thus possible to suppose that in the mid second/eighth century, the Medinan editor (or, at least, his Ḥanafī editor, a generation later) may have belonged to a tendency which was skeptical about warfare on the frontier; particularly with regard to the purity of the intentions of the fighters ... In the Cordovan recension (but not that of al-Shaybānī) there is furthermore attributed to Mālik the transmission of a Ḥadīth, according to which the most scrupulous piety (ablutions, attendance at the mosque, continued observance of prayer) would be the true *ribāṭ* ... This does indeed seem to represent a position which would effectively have been professed by Mālik ... It may be wondered whether these traditions do not allow the supposition of a conflict of representation between traditionalists at the end of the second/eighth century. These indications could permit the fixing of the time when the ideology of *jihād*, professed by circles yet to be identified, began to stress the meritorious aspect of military service on the frontier, while in other circles there was manifest opposition to this new point of view (possibly from the people of Arabia, i.e., of Iraq ...). If such was the case, it could be said that this conflict would, as if symbolically, have divided those who, of quietist tendency, aspired to make *mujāwara* ["living close to the

7 'Abd Allāh ibn al-Mubārak, *Kitāb al-Jihād*, ed. N. Hammad (Beirut: 1977).
8 Al-Sarakhsī, *Sharḥ al-Siyar al-Kabīr*, ed. Salah al-Din al-Munajjid, I (Cairo: 1958) 187.

> Ka'ba"] ... from those who aspired to make *ribāṭ* (... "dwelling on the frontier"). This latter would have professed a new type of activism.[9]

There is a fair amount of evidence to support Chabbi's hypothesis. Chabbi has already noticed that Ibn Qutayba (d. 276/889) tells us that al-Fuḍayl ibn 'Iyāḍ (d. 187/863), who died as a *mujāwir*, told an anecdote unfavorable to the destiny of frontier warriors,[10] and al-Dhahabī confirms this account.[11] In fact, Chabbi's supposition that the very early Mālikī school, usually understood to express the majority opinion in the Hijaz, did not believe in the obligatory nature of certain kinds of aggressive war, seems borne out by statements from Mālik himself quoted in the extremely important foundational text of Mālikī law, *al-Mudawwana*, compiled from Mālik's teachings by Saḥnūn (d. 240/854). These passages indicate that, in whatever circumstances Mālik did approve of jihad, he was extremely cautious—even doubtful—about the legitimacy of a Muslim offering his services in border warfare led by the Syrian Umayyads, presumably because of questions on the legitimacy of their rule. Mālik is asked several times: Do you see any harm in fighting the jihad against the Byzantines alongside these rulers (*wulāt*)? He repeatedly says, "There is no harm in doing so," twice justifying his stand by mentioning the Byzantine success at Mar'ash (Germanikeia), presumably referring to its destruction by Constantine V in 129/746. The implication of the passage is that for this major Ḥijāzī jurist, fighting the jihad with the Syrian Umayyads was in no sense a duty of a Muslim, only a permissible act that was to some degree meritorious, especially because of the general danger to Islamic territory.[12]

A neglected but extremely valuable source for this subject is *al-Muṣannaf*, a book composed by 'Abd al-Razzāq al-Ṣan'ānī (d. 211/826), which consists of materials he gathered from his teachers in the Hijaz and in Syria. An analysis of this material allows us to understand how jihad as obligatory aggressive war came to be the prevalent opinion in the second half of the 2nd/8th century. 'Abd al-Razzāq mentions a group of highly respected Ḥijāzī jurists in the circle of Ibn Jurayj (d. 150/762), who rejected the idea

---

9 J. Chabbi, "Ribāṭ," *EI²*, VIII (Leiden, Brill: 1995) 495.
10 *Ibid.*, VIII:496.
11 Al-Dhahabī, *Siyar A'lām al-Nubalā'*, VIII (Beirut: 1990) 421–422.
12 *Al-Mudawwana*, III (Cairo: 1326) 5. Michael Bonner suggests that the polemical tone in some verses ascribed to Fuḍayl ibn 'Iyāḍ reflects their disagreement over this matter; see Ibn Taghribirdī, *Al-Nujūm al-Ẓāhira*, II (Cairo, n.d.) 103–104.

that the jihad was obligatory for all; and they seem, moreover, to have given primacy to other religious acts.[13]

Yet the Syrian jurists quoted by ʿAbd al-Razzāq, perhaps reflecting the determination to make progress on the Byzantine frontier in the first half of the second Islamic century, were quite naturally attracted to the idea that aggressive war was obligatory. So, in the *Muṣannaf* we see that in Syrian circles pious stories circulated about the importance of being a frontier warrior in Syria, and of warfare by sea as well as by land.[14]

A jurist of this period, the above-mentioned ʿAbd Allāh ibn al-Mubārak, was alarmed by what he considered to be the bad conditions of the Muslims on the Syrian frontier and its critical points (*thughūr*). He wrote, as already mentioned, a book on jihad, and he also devoted a section of his still extant book on asceticism to the jihad, which he considered an ascetic practice.[15] He was a Khorasanian from Marw who came to Syria to study with the "jurist of Syria" par excellence, as al-Awzāʿī was called; and he supported al-Awzāʿī in his dispute with the jurists of the Hijaz about the virtues of jihad. It should be remembered that, because of the troubled internal state of the Islamic empire at the end of the Umayyad period, the central government of the caliphate neglected the frontier. It is in this context that al-Awzāʿī and ʿAbd Allāh ibn al-Mubārak wrote. Several of the key jurists of the next generation, especially al-Shāfiʿī (d. 204/820), wrote on this subject and proved to be in most respects followers of al-Awzāʿī and ʿAbd Allāh ibn al-Mubārak. Hence the Syrian doctrine of jihad was transformed into the normative doctrine of the majority of Iraqis.

The more general acceptance of the Syrian school reached its peak in the thought of al-Shāfiʿī, who elevates the destruction of unbelief to be the primary justification for jihad.[16] Nevertheless, as we have seen, the

13 ʿAbd al-Razzāq, *Al-Muṣannaf*, V (Beirut: 1983) 171–172. It might be argued that the "pietist" jurists are merely supporting the later normative view that jihad is an obligation of the community as a whole and not of individuals; but their tone and emphasis on other religious duties seem to make a further point. It should not, however, be imagined that they in any way whatsoever opposed all jihad.

14 *Ibid.*

15 *Kitāb al-Zuhd wa-l-Raqāʾiq* (Mālīkāwan, al-Hind, Majlis Iḥyāʾ al-Maʿārif: 1966).

16 M. Khadduri, *The Islamic Law of Nations: Shaybani's Siyar* (Baltimore, MD: 1966), "Translator's Introduction," 58. While Khadduri's contention that Shāfiʿī was the "first" to formulate this doctrine that, "the *jihād* had for its intent the waging of war on unbelievers for their disbelief," is open to doubt, Shāfiʿī's stamp of approval for this doctrine seems to have made this additional motivation for jihad much more commonly accepted.

opinions of the pre-Shāfiʿī jurists continued; at least up to the seventies of the second Islamic century, it is clear that some of the jurists did not see jihad as an individual or communal duty.

This essay considers jihad and its justifications among early jurists. We have tried to show that there is evidence that a belief in the defensive jihad existed in the Hijaz, more especially in Medina, where at least an earlier generation had reason to resent the removal of the capital from that city. Furthermore, even if they accepted an offensive jihad, they had objections to participating in it if it were led by the Syrian Umayyads, who were illegitimate leaders of the Muslims in the eyes of many Ḥijāzī jurists. Varieties of this earlier Ḥijāzī attitude continue to reappear in Islamic thought when circumstances favored it. For example, Rashīd al-Din Faḍl Allāh, the famous early 8th/14th-century vizier to the Mongolian Ilkhanid government of the Middle East, argues that the so-called Verse of the Sword (IX:29) is specifically directed toward Arab polytheists,[17] a view in accord with much contemporary scholarship; for, as Tyan says, "according to a view held by modern orientalist scholarship, Muḥammad's conception of the *jihād* as attack applied only in relation to the peoples of Arabia."[18]

Yet this legal context must be related to wider contexts that have been suggested by more recent studies of jihad. First, it is now clear that in their earliest examples the *siyar*, or books on the conduct of state, and *maghāzī*, or literature on exemplary early campaigns, were mixed. Only in their later examples, when law and history became more distinct disciplines, did *siyar* and *maghāzī* become distinct genres.[19] Furthermore, in the process of the development of law, although there was probably a great deal of common ground in the very earliest period because of the close interaction of the original Muslim community, local schools developed, and the differences of at least some members of the early Ḥijāzī school with Syrian schools become apparent in this study. Nevertheless, in this early period, as in later periods, the schools interact; and when a normative view was formed in Iraq, "minority" opinions continued to be transmitted by the tradition.

Second, the gradual emergence of normative jihad theory must also be seen as a function of the adjustment of the early Islamic world to an

17 D. Krawulsky, "Fī al-Ḥarakīya al-Taʾrīkhīya al-Īdiyūlūjīya li-l-Jihād fī al-Islām," in *Al-Ijtihād* 12 (1991) 127–131.
18 Tyan, (*supra* n. 1), 538.
19 M. Bonner, "Some Observations Concerning the Early Development of Jihad on the Arab-Byzantine Frontier," in *Studia Islamica* 75 (1992) 5–31.

apocalypse that never conclusively happened. Roman and Sasanian traditions of war already had established the idea of victory as divine confirmation; and, given the apocalyptic atmosphere that pervades much of the Qur'ān, the early Islamic conquests seemed to confirm that Islam was destined to create a universal state. Yet Constantinople and a significant part of the Byzantine Empire remained unconquerable. Muslim jurists became more interested in fiscal problems—in particular, the status of land—as determined by the earlier conquests. In this way the genres on "land tax" and "state finances" came into existence and were more cultivated than was the literature on campaigns, which passed into biographies and histories, while the genre on "the conduct of state" became a relatively (though not uniformly) static section of general law books. We believe, though it cannot be demonstrated here, that the transition to a formal legal theory of war changed jihad from a theory primarily based on historical memories of the battles fought in the time of the Prophet and the early Islamic period to a more precisely defined and normative theory rooted in very specific events in the life of the Prophet and very specific interpretation of Qur'ānic verses. In the theory based on Qur'ānic verses, an attempt was made to organize the relevant verses in chronological order so that the so-called Verse (or verses, according to some) of the Sword, which made war perpetual and a permanent obligation of the Islamic community, came last and therefore abrogated verses that could clearly have allowed a different development of the law. Incidentally, Ṭabarī, who opens his work on *The Divergences of the Jurists* with a careful list of which Qur'ānic verses supersede which others, when he comes to the so-called Verse of the Sword in this Qur'ānic commentary gives no indication that it supersedes other verses.[20]

Third, as a state of relative equilibrium is established on the Byzantine frontier, the concept of the "realm of Islam" and the "realm of war" comes into being, which recognizes the temporary failure of the Islamic conquests to become universal. The division is found as early as the first half of the 2nd/8th century in Muḥammad al-Nafs al-Zakīya.[21] The division appears by its nature to be more an expression of something that jurists had to deal with after it had occurred and not as an expression of what

20 Ṭabarī, *Ikhtilāf al-Fuqahā'* (Cairo: 1933) 1–21, and *Jāmi' al-Bayān 'an Ta'wīl al-Qur'ān*, III (Cairo: 1968) 109–110.

21 al-Nafs al-Zakīya, (*supra* n. 4). Ṭabarī, *Ta'rīkh al-Rusul wa-l-Mulūk*, ed. M.J. de Goeje *et al.*, III (Leiden: 1879–80) 208–215 records the letters between al-Nafs al-Zakīya and the caliph al-Manṣūr discussing their entitlement to the caliphate.

they thought should happen.[22] By the long reign of the Umayyad Caliph Hishām (105/724–125/743), Muslim armies suffered setbacks in Western Europe and Central Asia as well as on the Byzantine frontier. At the same time, the relative stabilization of the frontier led to a truce and arrangements for furtherance of trade. By the time of al-Shāfiʿī a juridical theory of a third abode, "the realm of treaty relations," had emerged.[23] These juridical developments had become necessary to deal with a new situation and seem to reflect rather than precede the appearance of this situation.

Fourth, jihad had become an element of formalized piety, in part to keep alive the momentum lost by the caliphate as an instrument of conquest and in part as an attempt to "spiritualize" a deferred apocalyptic event. The Syrian tradition of al-Awzāʿī had seen a continuous line of leaders from the Prophet through the Umayyads whose rule was justified by their active expansion of the realm of Islam, thereby fulfilling injunctions and prophecies of the earliest Islamic period. These leaders represent a continuous tradition of the uninterrupted practice of the Muslims, which in one view should be a major basis for law. But the apocalypse had not come. In contrast to al-Awzāʿī, his equally belligerent Khorasanian contemporary ʿAbd Allāh ibn al-Mubārak emphasized the spiritual discipline and merits of jihad. Quotations directly from the Prophet take pride of place in his work, and his interest in asceticism (on which he wrote a separate book) is never far away. No wonder that, during the Second Crusade, Ibn ʿAsākir gave public readings of ʿAbd Allāh ibn al-Mubārak's *Kitāb al-Jihād* in Damascus, which inspired Abū al-Ḥasan ibn Munqidh, brother of the famous Usāma, to volunteer to help raise the siege of Ascalon.[24]

While ʿAbd Allāh ibn al-Mubārak tried to integrate the role of government, society, and the individual in jihad, the subsequent propagation of a popular jihad literature created a strangely balanced problem for later Islamic leaders. The majority of jurists regarded jihad as lawful only if led by a legitimate Muslim ruler,[25] in particular a legitimate caliph/imam, on

22 F.M. Donner, in his fundamentally important and innovative essay on the jihad: "Sources of Islamic Conceptions of War," in J.M. Kelsay and J.T. Johnson (eds.), *Just War and Jihad* (New York: 1991) 50 and n. 88, p. 67, dates the appearance of the two abodes to the late 2nd/8th century, a point that he promises to develop in a further publication.

23 H. Inalcık, "Dar al-ʿAhd," *EI²*, II (Leiden, Brill: 1965) 116.

24 E. Sivan, *L'Islam et la croisade* (Paris: 1968) 75, cited in Bonner (*supra* n. 19) 20.

25 Donner, (*supra* n. 22), 41. Other important recent literature on jihad in European languages includes P. Crone, "The First-Century Concept of *Higra*," *Arabica* 41 (1994) 352–387; K. Yahya Blankinship, *The End of the Jihad State: The Reign of Hisham ibn Abd*

whose exact identity fewer and fewer of the jurists were willing to pronounce in any decisive way. Yet many military leaders exploited the image of jihad in popular piety by saying that they owed their legitimacy, at least in part, to their successful pursuit of jihad. At some point such a leader, if successful enough, might try to imply that he was sanctioned by some caliph or even, either obliquely or directly, to imply that he was a caliph. In this way he might win the overt support of some of the jurists. Jihad had become an unpredictable variable in the internal politics of Islamic lands just as it had become in their relations with non-Islamic lands.

---

al-Malik and the Collapse of the Umayyads (Albany, N.Y.: 1994); M. Bonner, *Aristocratic Violence and Holy War: Studies in the Jihad and the Arab Byzantine Frontier* (New Haven, CT: 1996); A. Morabia, *Le Gihad dans l'Islam médiéval: Le "combat sacré" des origines au XIIe siècle* (Paris: 1993); A. Noth, *Heiliger Krieg und heiliger Kampf in Islam und Christentum* (Bonn: 1966); and Reuven Firestone, *Jihād: The Origin of Holy War in Islam* (New York: 1999).

Friendship in Islamic Ethical Philosophy

Matthew Arnold, the great Victorian social and literary critic, offers us a valuable context in which to interpret much pre-modern Islamic philosophy. In 1869 he wrote: "Hebraism and Hellenism—between these two points of influence moves our world."[1] By Hebraism he meant the Bible, by Hellenism he meant classical Greek thought, and by "our world" he meant the world of Western civilization. Significantly, the civilization of most educated Muslim thinkers of the pre-modern era was also under the influence of Hebraism and Hellenism, to which they added the enormously powerful influence of the Qur'ān. The Qur'ān, of course, sees itself as a continuation and perfection of the revelations of Jesus and the Prophets.

A word that symbolizes this rich heritage is *sa'āda*, sometimes misleadingly translated as "happiness." The Qur'ān uses the root of this word to explain the condition of the saved. We read in Sūrat Hūd, verse 105 that:

> On that Day [of Judgment] when it comes no soul will speak except by His permission; then some among them will be wretched and some will be blessed.

Author's note: This article was first published as "Friendship in Islamic Ethical Philosophy," in Alireza Korangy, Wheeler M. Thackston, Roy P. Mottahedeh and William Granara (eds.), *Essays in Islamic Philology, History, and Philosophy*, Studies in the History and Culture of the Middle East 31, A Festschrift in Celebration and Honor of Professor Ahmad Mahdavi Damghani's 90th Birthday (Berlin and Boston, De Gruyter: 2016) 229–239. It is reproduced here with permission of Walter de Gruyter and Company. I would like to thank Professors Thomas Scanlon and Robert Wisnovsky for their invaluable comments on a draft of this article, which was originally given as a lecture at Oberlin College at the kind invitation of Jafar Mahallati in 2011. I hope this article on friendship is received as a true token of my friendship for Ostad Mahdavi-Damghani.

1 Matthew Arnold, *Culture and Anarchy* (New York: 1910) 110.

The word for blessed in this verse, *saʿīd*, does indeed mean "happy," but here it is associated with divine blessedness or bliss. This approach is fully consonant with the Bible where, for example, the eleventh verse of Psalm 16 reads:

> Thou dost show me the path of life; in Thy presence there is fullness of joy, in Thy right hand are pleasures for everyone.

Strong confirmation that "blessedness" and "fullness of joy" were the moral goal of life was found in the translation of Aristotle's term *eudaimonia* as *saʿāda*. For the classical philosophers this state is one in which all possible human virtues are realized and come to flourish; hence some modern translators render it as "flourishing." The understanding of *saʿāda* as the realization of a person's virtues and the fulfillment of his/her possibilities was strong in pre-modern Islamic philosophy. It was combined with a view of the afterlife in which the "blessedness" or "bliss" continued for the virtuous. Henceforth, the word *saʿāda* is translated in this essay as "virtuous well-being."[2]

Yet the classical Greek and pre-modern Muslim philosophers agreed that it would be nearly impossible to achieve this state alone and that one of the essential ingredients for the full flourishing of the virtues was friendship, which indeed was itself one of the virtues. Friendship was one of the ties that prevented the pursuit of "virtuous well-being" from becoming a solitary and self-absorbed preoccupation. On this account both of the Muslim ethical philosophers discussed in this essay devote a chapter to friendship.[3]

The first philosopher considered is the great 4th/10th-century polymath Miskawayh, whose full name was Aḥmad Abū ʿAlī ibn Muḥammad Miskawayh (d. 421/1030).[4] He was born in Rayy, an important city near modern Tehran, and lived much of his life there as well as in Baghdad.

2 Professor Wisnovsky has pointed out to me that there are inclusivist and exclusivist interpretations of Aristotle. According to the inclusivist view, *eudaimonia* consists in the sum of all activities that are in accordance with virtue. According to the exclusivist view, *eudaimonia* consists in one activity, contemplation. The authors discussed here belong to the inclusivist view.

3 This essay considers only two books: Aḥmad Abū ʿAlī ibn Muḥammad Miskawayh, *Tahdhīb al-Akhlāq*, ed. C. Zurayk (Beirut, American University of Beirut: 1966) and Naṣīr al-Dīn al-Ṭūsī, *Akhlāq-e Nāṣeri*, (Tehran, Enteshārāt-e ʿElmiya-ye Eslāmi: n.d.). What both authors have written elsewhere is not discussed. Both texts on friendship are so rich that they deserve much longer separate treatment, especially the *Akhlāq-e Nāṣeri*.

4 There are several good accounts of Miskawayh's life, including the excellent chapters in Mohammed Arkoun, *L'humanisme arabe au IVe/Xe siècle* (Paris, Libr. Philosophique J. Vrins: 1982).

He was a member of the intellectual elite of his time and his works on ethics and history had a very significant influence on the Islamic tradition right through to the nineteenth century when Muhammad ʿAbduh taught Miskawayh's ethics as a fundamental text. Although Iranian (Miskawayh's name in Persian means "smelling of musk"), he wrote exclusively in an elegant and economical Arabic. Miskawayh's belief in the autonomous authority of reason infuses the later chapters of his outstanding "world history," which are analytical and sophisticated in a way that few premodern Muslim historians are—a feature from which I greatly benefited in my book *Loyalty and Leadership*. In his ethical text *Tahdhīb al-Akhlāq* (*The Refinement of Character*), Miskawayh begins by quoting Aristotle's famous maxim "Man is communal by nature."[5] Both in Greek and in Arabic this maxim is often translated "political by nature," but the Arabic word employed by Miskawayh and by Islamic philosophers in general—*madanī*—means, more exactly, "belonging to a *madīna*, a city or community."

That "communal" is the meaning here is confirmed by Miskawayh's and Aristotle's references to bees and ants, which we would call communal or social animals. Miskawayh goes on to explain that consequently the perfection of human virtuous well-being can only be realized with friends. Miskawayh believes this is so even at the most basic level because of shared needs among friends. The man of virtuous well-being obtains friends and strives to give goods to them in order that he receive from them goods which he is unable to obtain himself. Moreover, on a higher level, the man of virtuous well-being enjoys the days of his life through his friends and so do they through him.

Miskawayh distinguishes this "unchanging and indissoluble" pleasure, which is had by few, with the "animal pleasures" of the majority. So refined is true friendship that it can only subsist with one person. In contrast, the good and virtuous man will approach everyone with good comradeship (*ʿishra*) and try to behave toward everyone with the approach of a true friend.[6] This immediately raises a question to which I shall return. As mutuality of friendship is necessary for the material and moral exchange within a community, can friendship based on mutuality be feigned or superficial

5 Miskawayh, *Tahdhīb al-Akhlāq*, ed. C. Zurayk (Beirut: American University of Beirut, 1966), trans. C. Zurayk, *The Refinement of Character* (Beirut, American University of Beirut: 1968). Hereafter, page numbers for the Arabic are followed by those for English. Zurayk's edition and translation are excellent, and, by and large, I accept his translation without revision. Here, however, he translates *madanī* as "civic" (155/139)—whereas I prefer "communal."

6 Miskawayh, 153–155/138–139.

or merely limited? According to Miskawayh, it can be all of these because it falls short of deep or true friendship. Sincere gratitude, lack of greed, and a comparative disinterest in domination and praise are essential in the character of a true friend. Yet a human without defects does not exist and if one does not overlook small defects, one will have no friends.[7] Miskawayh plainly states that if you achieve "good fortune," you should share it with friends. Furthermore, the sharing of "bad fortune" is even more incumbent and the effect of doing so on the friend who has bad fortune is much deeper. Miskawayh writes: "Do not wait until he asks you either explicitly or implicitly ... [rather] share with him the pain of what has befallen him."[8]

Miskawayh strongly supports the duty to contradict any backbiting or slanderous comment about one's friend that has been made in the absence of the other friend. If one becomes aware of a defect in his friend, he should show it to his friend in a gentle manner "because the tactful doctor may accomplish with a delicate treatment what others do by cutting, amputation and cauterizing."[9] In two different passages Miskawayh emphasizes the importance of teaching the value of friendship. Miskawayh quotes a Greek author of the fourth century B.C.E. who says, "I am greatly astonished at those who teach their children the tales of kings and the fighting between them, and the stories of wars, hatred, revenge, and rebellion, who forget the subject of affection, the accounts of concord, and the benefits which all people gain through love and fellowship (*al-maḥabba wa-l-'uns*). For no man can live without affection (*al-muwadda*) even though the world may favor him with all its attractions."[10] In another passage he recommends the wisdom conveyed by the famous book of animal fables, *Kalīla wa-Dimna*. He draws attention to "the parable about the powerful lions which are killed and destroyed by the weak but cunning fox that gets into their midst."[11]

Miskawayh relates all the ethics of friendship to a basic Islamic theme. He says, "We have chosen concord, sought and praised it, and have said that God—Mighty and Exalted is He—has summoned us to it by the prescription [of] the upright Divine Law (*sharī'a*)."[12] And indeed it is in man's relation with God that friendship reaches its apotheosis. Miskawayh writes:

7 Miskawayh, 160/143.
8 Miskawayh, 162/145.
9 Miskawayh, 165/147.
10 Miskawayh, 156/140.
11 Miskawayh, 166/148.
12 Miskawayh, 163/146.

> It is the necessary truth which admits of no doubt that [God] is loved only by the person of virtuous well-being (*saʿīd*) and goodness who knows true virtuous well-being and the real good (*al-saʿāda wa-l-khayr*). That is why he endeavors to seek His favor through both [virtuous well-being and good], strives to the utmost of his ability to please Him, and imitates His acts to the extent of his capacity. And he who shows such love of God—Exalted is He—such interest in seeking His favor and such obedience to Him will be loved, favored and gratified by God and will become worthy of His friendship—that friendship to some men by the Law wherein Abraham is called "the friend (*khalīl*) of God" and Muḥammad "the Beloved (*ḥabīb*) of God."[13]

One would expect that in a strongly monotheistic system—and it is difficult to think of a more strongly monotheistic system than Islam—God would be too remote to be a friend. Yet both the Bible and the Qur'ān call Abraham the friend of God. Excepting love affairs, friendship with God or gods would have been unusual in the classical Greek context before Christianity. Despite the strong influence of Greek philosophy, such friendship between God and man is a persistent theme in the Islamic tradition. In later Islamic tradition saintly Sufi mystics are called the *awliyā'*, the friends of God.

The second moral philosopher we consider is Naṣīr al-Dīn al-Ṭūsī, a giant in the intellectual tradition of the Islamic Middle East. Ṭūsī, who was born in Khorasan in northeast Iran and who lived from 597/1201 to 672/1274, was an outstanding astronomer, philosopher, and theologian. His prolific output includes works on astronomy, mathematics, physics, mineralogy, medicine, jurisprudence, logic, mysticism, and theology. Significantly, for his discussion of patronage and friendship, Ṭūsī made his peace with the non-Muslim Mongols who conquered most of southwestern Asia in the 7th/13th century and became the official astronomer to the conquering Mongol ruler. In this capacity he dispensed patronage to many other leading scholars of his day.[14] Ṭūsī wrote in both Arabic and Persian, and his ethical work *Akhlāq-e Nāṣeri* (a book on morals dedicated to his patron Nāṣer), abundantly copied in the age before printing, was written in a stiff and occasionally difficult Persian. In this text Ṭūsī draws a large-scale picture of the sociological and emotional need for affection: "Since

13 Miskawayh, 170/151–152.
14 See the excellent sketch of Ṭūsī's life and work by H. Daiber and F.J. Ragep, "Ṭūsī," in *The Encyclopaedia of Islam*, 2nd ed., X (Leiden, Brill: 2000) 746–752.

people need each other and the perfection and completion of each one lies with others of the human species ... hence the necessity to combine in a way so that all individuals help each other as do the limbs of a single person ... This yearning for this combination is [called] love (*maḥabba*)."[15]

Ṭūsī sees several motives for friendship. Friendship (*ṣadāqat*) among young men and people of like nature is the quest for pleasure (*lizzat*). The motive for friendship among old men and personages of like nature is the quest for benefit (*manfa'at*). Such friendships endure as the link of profit or benefit endures. As for the friendship of the good (*ahl-e khayr*), when it is purely good that binds them, and good is something constant and unchanging, such friendship does not change or decline.[16]

Ṭūsī says that the friendship of the good is made possible by "the simple [i.e., noncompound] divine substance (*jawhar-e baṣīṭ-e elāhi*)" which exists in men. This substance opens man to an entirely new kind of pleasure unlike other pleasures. This new pleasure is the product of an "utter passion and divine love" (*'eshq-e tāmm va-maḥabbat-e elāhi*).[17] Interestingly, Ṭūsī relates all forms of love to the communal nature of man, which he further relates to religion.

> The principle of love calls forth communal life and social combination (*tamaddon va-ta'allof*) ... For this reason, mankind has been urged to share (*eshterāk*) in both their acts of worship (*'ebādāt*) [Arabic *'ibādāt*] and entertainments (*żiyāfāt*), for it is in their coming together that feeling of fellowship (*'ons*) is developed from a potential to an actual act. It may be too that this is the reason the Divine Law of Islam (*shari'at-e Eslām*) has given preference to communal prayer over praying alone ... It may even be that [those who engage in the communal prayer] progress from the degree of fellowship (*'ons*) to that of love (*maḥabbat*).[18]

Ṭūsī recommends restricting the number of one's friends: "As for the [category of the] true friend one cannot find them in large numbers, for he

15 Ṭūsī, *Akhlāq-e Nāṣeri*, (*supra* n. 3), trans. G.M. Wickens, *The Nasirean Ethics* (London: Allen and Unwin: 1964). Hereafter page numbers are given first for the Persian then for the outstanding English translation, which I have only rarely revised, except to insert key words in Persian. The passage here is Ṭūsī, 216–217/195.

16 Ṭūsī, 220/198.

17 Ṭūsī, 220/198.

18 Ṭūsī, 222/199–200.

[the true friend] is noble and hard to find ... However, good companionship (*ḥosn-e ʿeshrat*) and liberality of spirit in encounters (*karam-e leqāʾ*) should be shown to all. For without the blessings of love (*maḥabbat*) and companionship (*moʾānasat*) living would be impossible."[19]

Ṭūsī discusses the criteria for picking a friend in much the same way as Miskawayh. He emphasizes the need to avoid any discrepancy among possible friends insofar as they love authority (*reyāsat*), since a person who likes domination and superiority (*ghalabat va-tavaffoq*) "will not employ equity in affection (*mavaddat*) or be satisfied with equal giving and taking. On the contrary, haughtiness and arrogance will lead him to despise friends and to behave disdainfully towards them."[20]

Yet Ṭūsī is explicit in encouraging friends to overlook minor shortcomings in each other: "It is incumbent to overlook trifling faults of friends (*ṣeghār-e ʿoyub-e yārān*) ... No person will survive unscathed [from such an examination] ... As the law-giver [Muḥammad] has said: 'Happy is the person whose preoccupation is his own faults rather than the faults of other people.'"[21] Near the end of his treatment of friendship Ṭūsī gives a stirring summing up of the virtues: "The farthest of men from virtue are those who depart from communal life and social combination and incline to solitude and loneliness. Thus, the virtue of love and friendship (*mavaddat o ṣadāqat*) is the greatest of virtues, and its preservation the most important of tasks. This is why we have spoken at length on this matter, for this is the noblest topic in the present discourse."[22]

There are broad areas of agreement between these two ethical philosophers, which have been partly determined by the similarity of their sources. Their goal is to describe the virtuous well-being and flourishing of humans. For those who believe in the afterlife this virtuous well-being continues as a state of blessedness after death. Friendship is essential for such human development and man is by nature communal. While the deepest friendship may be restricted to one or two people, good companionship and sociability are necessary for the material economy in matters such as the division of labor and for the moral economy in matters such as the customary expectation of good faith in obligations. According to the Muslim

---

19 Ṭūsī, 278–279/243.
20 Ṭūsī, 282/246.
21 Ṭūsī, 282/246.
22 Ṭūsi, 291/252.

philosophers discussed here, there is a third category of friendship, which the Greeks did not believe in, namely friendship between man and God.

Ṭūsī is in some ways the more religiously inclined of the two authors. He speaks of the "noncompound divine substance" in each person. In this expression we see not only the influence of Neo-Platonic views but also of Sufi philosophy, which by Ṭūsī's time had become part of the mainstream of Islamic thought.

A relatively important theme in both writers is mutuality or, as Ṭūsī expresses it, "equity in affection" (*enṣāf dar mavaddat*).[23] True friends overlook each other's defects. True friends defend each other from slander and backbiting and correct each other gently. Even love with God is mutual although not engaged in by beings on an equal level. Rather striking is the mutuality implied in the insistence upon a true friend sharing the pain that has befallen another friend.

Both authors are interested in the types of lesser friendships, which are classified as "for pleasure" or "for profit." Ṭūsī acknowledges that there are composite types of friendship as well as friendship held on different sides for different reasons: "The causes of some loves are diverse ... An instance is that between a singer and a listener, where the singer loves the listener by reason of profit while the listener loves the singer for pleasure."[24]

Indeed, in the case of the teacher and the student the higher love exists, but so does the love motivated by profit. It seems to me reasonable to consider most cases of friendship in the actual world as mixed and/or weighted differently on the two sides of the friendship.

Many questions are not directly answered by the text. Is friendship between a man and a woman possible, and is a marriage also a friendship? Both Miskawayh and Ṭūsī quote Artistotle's sentiment that the virtue of friendship causes people to meet for exercise, hunting and banquets, which give a rather masculine cast to friendship.[25] According to Ṭūsī, among the bad behavior that arises from contention among friends is "attacking each other's manhood."[26] Nevertheless, Ṭūsī takes serious interest in the growth of friendship between husband and wife. He says: "[As to] the benefits common to wife and husband in respect of domestic goods: if both cooperate therein, these become a reason for common love (*maḥabbat-e*

23 Ṭūsī, 282/246.
24 Ṭūsī, 224/201.
25 Miskawayh, 156/140.
26 Ṭūsī, 287/249.

yak-degar)."[27] While not a ringing endorsement of marital love, a kind of friendship between husband and wife is acknowledged.

Another question arises about the ability of friendship to extend across social levels. Ṭūsī answers this question more directly: "Let a man be careful not to act stingily with friends over the science or the accomplishment by which he is adorned, or in respect of the trade or craft in which he is skilled."[28] I have the impression that Miskawayh would disapprove of friendship between a craftsman and a man of learning, a possibility that Ṭūsī's statement on generosity among friends seems to allow.

Interestingly, both these highly learned men, who no doubt taught students in some fashion or other, acknowledge friendship between teacher and student. Ṭūsī, who is particularly fulsome on the subject, places "the love of the teacher in the student's heart" between the love of God—the strongest love—and love of children for parents. Parents nurture the bodies of their children whereas teachers nurture their souls. "Likewise," adds Ṭūsī, "the love by the teacher for the student in a good way is superior to the love of the father for the son, for the teacher nurtures [the student] with complete virtue and sustains [him] with pure wisdom."[29]

There seems no doubt that both our thinkers endorse patronage by friends in power for (the benefit of) their less fortunate friends, a system called clientelism or, more negatively, cronyism, and indeed disputes continue to our day as to the need for and the harm done by these systems. Miskawayh is fully aware of the possibility that love and justice might be in conflict. He states that good judgment based on sound religious beliefs must be exercised before the benefit of love is realized: "This desirable and coveted type of union [of people through love] can be accomplished only by means of sound opinions on which sane minds will be expected to agree, and by means of strong beliefs which result only from religions directed toward the Face of God."[30] Ṭūsī, somewhat confusingly, calls both love in one passage and justice in another the primary virtue.[31]

Modern sentiments are strongly on the side of meritocracy. Yet in the highly personalized world of politics in the time of Miskawayh and Ṭūsī, patronage was essential to maintaining a coherent government and to

27 Ṭūsī, 224/201.
28 Ṭūsī, 287/250.
29 Ṭūsī, 228–229/204–205.
30 Miskawayh, 134/118.
31 Ṭūsī, 73/80 (here, perhaps *'adālat* is to be translated as "justice"), 291/252.

fostering an ongoing cultural world. Both authors point out that the ruler is the most needy of friends because he has only two ears and two eyes. Ṭūsī writes: "The need of great emperors (*pādeshāhān*) for those worthy of nurture and care is as the need of poor men for those who will show them kindness and favor."[32] Patronage survives today in the arts and, to some extent, in the world of learning. Clearly, a new field in which one can reject patrons is suggested by Samuel Johnson's celebrated letter of 1755 to Lord Chesterfield: "Is not a patron, my lord, one who looks with unconcern on a man struggling for life in the water, and, when he has reached ground, encumbers him with help?"[33]

The great and unwavering message of both authors is that friendship is an aspect of that cardinal virtue, love. It is through friendship that association of people is turned into community. In its deepest form friendship is the strongest bond that can exist between human beings. It is also a human capacity that can be focused on God and God welcomes that focus. Without friendship we would have no society and no spiritually deep relation with the Divine.

APPENDIX

The vocabulary of *friend*, *friends*, and *friendship* tells us something of what our texts are trying to convey. The variety of words is sanctioned by the Arabic translation of Aristotle's *Nicomachean Ethics*. The translation used by Miskawayh may well correspond with the Fez manuscript edited by Anna A. Akasoy and Alexander Fidora.[34]

The unknown translator of Aristotle, attributed by the editors to "the school of Ḥunayn ibn Isḥāq" (d. 260/873) frequently uses *aṣdiqā'*, the most common word for "friends," but seldom uses *ṣadāqa* the abstract noun for "friendship" from the same root. Thus, in part 3 of book VIII we read:

> Since these [grounds for friendship] differ from one another in form, the affections (*iḥbābāt*) and friendships (*maḥabbāt*) differ

32 Ṭūsī, 289/243.

33 James Boswell, *The Life of Samuel Johnson, LL.D.*, 4 vols. (London: Routledge, Warne, and Routledge: 1865).

34 Aristotle, *The Arabic Version of the Nicomachean Ethics*, eds. Anna A. Akasoy and Alexander Fidora, trans. Douglas M. Dunlop (Leiden, Brill: 2005); see p. 31 on the relation of this manuscript found in Fez to Miskawayh's sources.

> accordingly. Thus, the kinds of friendship (*maḥabba*) are three, equal in number to the lovable things. In each one of them there is reciprocity in friendship ... and those who love each other (*yuḥibbūna baʿḍuhum baʿḍan*) wish for good things for each other, for this very friendship (*maḥabba*) which they have. For those who love each other for advantage, do not love for themselves but because they have some mutual good from each other. Similarly, those who love for some pleasure do not love [those who easily] change because of their possessing a quality, but because they are pleased with them ... These friendships are accidental, for they are not loved for what the person is loved for, but because they provide, the one of them a certain good, the other pleasure ... So, when the cause of their being friends is dissolved, the friendship (*maḥabba*) is dissolved also, since the friendship was something superadded on that account.

Here we have the Greek word for friendship, *philía*—which specialists say can "sometimes rise to the meaning of affection or love, but also includes any sort of kindly feeling"[35]—consistently translated as "love." Yet shortly after this passage the Arabic translates "the best friendship" (*tōn agathōn philía*) as "*al-ṣadāqa al-tāmma,*" using the same root as *ṣadīq*.[36] In other cases "beloveds" (*maḥbūbīn*) and "friends" (*aṣḍiqāʾ*) seem nearly interchangeable in the same sentence.[37]

As for *agape*, the celebrated virtue of Christian thinking (and often in Christian contexts understood as "selfless love" or "charity"), in the Arabic version of the *Nicomachean Ethics* (book IX, part 12), it is translated with a word derived from *ʿishq*, which is a generic word for love, particularly physical love.[38] Interestingly, another Persian word for friendship, *dūstī*, does occur in Ṭūsī[39] but is not as common as the Arabic equivalents.

35 See Aristotle, *Nicomachean Ethics*, trans. H. Rackham, Loeb Classical Library (Cambridge, MA, Harvard University Press: 1934) 45 note a.

36 Aristotle, *Arabic Version*, (*supra* n. 34), 434–35.

37 Aristotle, *Arabic Version*, 436, lines 5–8.

38 Aristotle, *Arabic Version*, 525. The Greek context is a discussion of *eros*, also translated as *ʿishq*. The outstanding glossary by Manfred Ullmann, *Die Nikomachische Ethik des Artistoteles in arabischer Übersetzung* (Wiesbaden, Harrassowitz: 2011) gives more guidance on the Arabic terms for "friends" and "friendship," a subject which would require a separate essay.

39 Ṭūsī (Pers.) 229, line 6.

Brother and Brotherhood in the Qur'ān

The term brother (*akh*) is used in the Qur'ān in several senses: in its strict biological sense; in several partly metaphorical senses, especially to indicate membership in a genealogical group; and, in a more extended metaphorical sense, to indicate membership in a group united by a shared belief. There are verses in the Qur'ān that indicate that the sense of community and mutual respect, concern and aid implied by brotherhood in this extended, metaphorical sense can unite not only Muslims but any humans who do virtuous acts in response to God's expectations of them.

Brother, in its literal sense, a male who shares one or both parents with another sibling, is the object of several verses with legal implications. A brother is within the closer degrees of kinship and therefore forbidden to marry the daughter of his brother[1] and allowed to see his sisters dressed less formally than would be proper before men not in close kin relation or considered likely to see them as sexually desirable.[2] Since Qur'ān IV:23 also forbids a "milk sister" to marry a biologically unrelated male suckled by the same mother, specialists in Islamic law have usually included the milk brother as well as the milk sister and milk mother in most of the legal rulings that regulate marriageability and acceptable private associations. The brother also has a fixed position in entitlement to inheritance.[3] The brother is referred to as the archetype of the *walī al-dam*, the next of kin

Author's note: This article first appeared as: "Brother and Brotherhood," in Jane Dammen McAuliffe (gen. ed.), *Encyclopaedia of the Qur'ān*, 1 (Leiden, Brill: 2001) 259–263. Reproduced with permission. Here Qur'ān and other references that were originally in the text have been placed in footnotes.

1 Qur'ān IV:23.

2 Qur'ān XXIV:31; compare XXXIII:55 on the Prophet's wives.

3 Qur'ān IV:176 and IV:11, in which "brothers" (*ikhwa*) is generally understood to mean both brothers and sisters.

with the right to demand retaliation for a deliberately slain kinsman or to settle for blood money.[4]

The most important "blood" brothers who figure in the Qur'ān are Cain and Abel, (who are referred to but not mentioned by name), the brothers of Joseph (Yūsuf), and Moses (Mūsā) and Aaron (Hārūn). It is interesting that a figure so centrally important as Moses has a brother who is specifically called both a "prophet" (*nabī*)[5] and a messenger (*rasūl*)[6] of the Lord and who could, like his brother, receive divine inspiration (*waḥy*)[7] as well as miraculous signs (*āyāt*)[8]. Moses, whose speech is hard to understand, has asked God to give him Aaron, his brother, as a "helper" (*wazīr*) from his family.[9] Moreover, both Moses and Aaron are given *sulṭān*, a word usually understood to mean authority, power and authoritative proof, in which the phrase is *sulṭān mubīn*, "clear authority."[10]

The simultaneous appearance of two prophet brothers among one people raised, for later generations, questions about the nature of prophethood. The Qur'ān seems to contain a two-fold explanation of the need for both prophets, namely, the rebelliousness of the Israelites towards Moses and his resultant need of Aaron's help, and the assistance Moses needs in circumventing his difficulty in speech. Thus, when Moses orders them to enter the Holy Land and they refuse, Moses prays: "My Lord, I control only myself and my brother. Distinguish us (or "distance us") from such perverse people."[11] Yet one might argue that God could have given Moses the gifts of speech and authority that would have freed him from the need of a prophet-brother.

A further problem is raised by Aaron's presence when the calf was made to be an object of worship while Moses was absent and receiving the law on Mount Sinai, especially as Moses told Aaron, "Be my deputy among my people, act righteously and do not follow the path of the perverse."[12] That Moses on his return at least pretends to hold his brother responsible is shown by the words: "He [Moses] took his brother by the head, pulling

4 Qur'ān II:178.
5 Qur'ān XIX:53.
6 Qur'ān XX:47.
7 Qur'ān X:87.
8 Qur'ān XXIII:45 and XX:42.
9 Qur'ān XX:29–30, XXV:35, XXVIII:35.
10 Qur'ān XXVIII:35 and XXIII:45.
11 Qur'ān V:25.
12 Qur'ān VII:142.

him toward himself."[13] Hence Aaron says in explanation: "O son of my mother, the people have humiliated me [or, "thought me to be weak"] and almost killed me. So do not let my enemies gloat over me nor place me among the wrongdoers."[14] Moses then prays for both himself and his brother: "O Lord, forgive me and my brother and cause us to enter in your mercy."[15] Alongside all of these problems was the problem of the apparent sin of Moses in killing a man."[16] These verses offered rich material for the speculation of later Muslim thinkers on the sinlessness, the degree of foreknowledge (or reasons for withholding foreknowledge) and the timing of divinely ordained persuasive miracles that God might grant his prophets.

The commentators by and large avoid this discussion. Ṭabarī (d. 310/923) explains that "From our mercy we gave [Moses] his brother Aaron as a prophet (*nabī*)" (Qur'ān XIX:53) means: "We supported and helped him [Moses] through his [Aaron's] prophethood."[17] Ṭabarī also implies[18] that Aaron's station is in answer to Moses' prayers (which, perhaps, God anticipated) when Moses asks God to give him his brother Aaron as a vizier (*wazīr*) and says: "Let him share in my mission (*amrī*)."[19] Moses is saying, Ṭabarī explains, "Make him a prophet just as you made me a prophet." Bayḍāwī (d. ca. 716/1316–17) seems to be explaining Aaron's inability to stop the worship of the calf—and also, perhaps to be justifying Aaron as a second prophet—when he says that Aaron was three years older than Moses and was "a mild-tempered and tractable person, better loved by the people of Israel."[20] Yet often, even when the verse refers to prophetic traits possessed by both brothers, the commentators remain principally interested in Moses. Thus, in discussing the "miraculous signs" mentioned in Qur'ān XXIII:45, *Tafsīr al-Jalālayn* [21] only refers to the miracles of Moses since Aaron plays such a subordinate role in the

13 Qur'ān VII:150.
14 Qur'ān VII:150.
15 Qur'ān VII:151.
16 Qur'ān XX:40, XXVI:14, XXVI:19.
17 Abū Ja'far Muḥammad ibn Jarīr al-Ṭabarī, *Jāmi' al-Bayān 'an Ta'wīl āy al-Qur'ān* (hereafter *Tafsīr*), XVI, (Cairo, Muṣṭafā al-bābī al-Ḥalabī, 3rd printing: 1388/1968) 94–95.
18 Ṭabarī, *Tafsīr*, XVI:160.
19 Qur'ān XX:32.
20 'Abdallāh ibn 'Umar al-Bayḍāwī, *Anwār al-Tanzīl wa-Asrār al-Ta'wīl* (hereafter *Anwār*), ed. H.O. Fleischer, I (Leipzig: 1846; Beirut: 1988) 345.
21 Jalāl al-Dīn Muḥammad ibn Aḥmad al-Maḥallī and Jalāl al-Dīn al-Suyūṭī, *Tafsīr al-Jalālayn* (hereafter *Jalālayn*), (Damascus: 1385/1965) 450.

narrative of their lives. Nevertheless, as Ṭūsī (d. 460/1067) explains,[22] when Moses went up to Mount Sinai, he was able to order Aaron to be his deputy even though God had sent Aaron as a prophet with a mission (*nabī mursal*) because Moses had leadership (*riyāsa*) over Aaron as well as over all of the rest of the religious community (*umma*) to whom Moses brought revelation. Interestingly, the *sulṭān* given to Moses and Aaron is understood by several commentators to mean *ḥujja*, "argument (for a case)."[23] Bayḍāwī interprets *sulṭān mubīn* (Qur'ān XXIII:45), in which *mubīn* would ordinarily be understood to mean "manifestly clear," as "a manifestly clear argument, compelling to the one who opposes it" and says that it may mean such miraculous signs as Moses' staff which turned into a snake.[24] Incidentally, the use of terms such as *sulṭān* and *wazīr*, later to become political terms frequently used in the Islamic world, caused the verses on Moses and Aaron to be examined in the light of this use. The example of Aaron as an "infallible" aide sent to help Moses was of importance to some Shi'ites in understanding the role of 'Alī and other Imams.

Very common in the Qur'ān is the largely metaphorical use of "brother" to mean members of a tribe or people especially (though not exclusively) in connection with three of the so-called "Arabian" prophets sent by God to their people. Hūd is the "brother" of the 'Ād,[25] Ṣāliḥ is the "brother" of the Thamūd[26] and Shu'ayb is the "brother" of Midyan.[27] Similarly, Noah (Nūḥ) is the brother of the "people" or "tribe" (*qawm*) of Noah.[28] Lot is the brother of the *qawm* of Lot (Lūṭ);[29] and, correspondingly, "the brothers (*ikhwān*) of Lot" (meaning the people of Lot) are listed among those people who rejected messengers sent by God.[30] Al-Rāghib al-Iṣfahānī (d. early 5th/11th century)[31] says that brother is used in these verses to convey that the compassion that such a messenger has for his people is

22 Muḥammad ibn al-Ḥasan al-Ṭūsī, *al-Tibyān fī Tafsīr al-Qur'ān*, ed. Ahmad Habib Qusayr al-'Amili, IV, (Najaf, Maktab al-I'lām al-Islāmī: 1409/1988–89) 532.
23 Ṭabarī, *Tafsīr*, XX, 76.
24 Bayḍāwī, *Anwār*, (*supra* n. 20).
25 Qur'ān VII:65, XI:50, XXVI:124, XLVI:21.
26 Qur'ān VII:73, XI:61, XXVI:142, XXVII:45.
27 Qur'ān VII:85, XI:84, XXIX:36.
28 Qur'ān XXVI:105–6.
29 Qur'ān XXVI:160–1.
30 Qur'ān L:13.
31 al-Rāghib al-Iṣfahānī, *Mufradāt* (Beirut: 1412/1992) 68, under the heading "*akh.*"

just as that which a brother has for his brother. In a parallel usage the kin of Mary address her as "sister of Aaron."[32]

There are a few verses that bridge or partially indicate the transference of "brother" from its literal or partly metaphorical use (as when it means kinsman) to its full metaphorical sense. A striking example of the use of the emotional closeness implied by brotherhood is the simile which warns the believers to avoid suspicion, spying and speaking ill of each other, for: "Would one of you like to eat the flesh of his dead brother? For you would have a horror of such things."[33] The believers are told if they "become mixed" with orphans, "they become your brothers (*ikhwānukum*)."[34] *Tafsīr al-Jalālayn*[35] echoes many commentaries in saying that "brothers" here means "brothers in religion"; but, like many other commentaries it implies that such acceptance means acceptance in a quasi-familial relationship, "For it is customary for a brother to mingle his expenses with his brothers, so you should act in this way [with such orphans]." Similarly, it is said of adoptive children that they should keep the names of their fathers "but if you do not know their fathers, then they are your brothers (*ikhwānukum*) in religion (*dīn*) and your friends/clients/protégés (*mawālī*)."[36]

While several verses attest that biological kinship, including brotherhood, is less important than spiritual kinship, the verse following the discussion of adoption shows that for legal purposes real brotherhood is still the measure relevant to inheritance and kindred matters: "Blood relatives are closer to each other in God's book than to the believers and the Emigrants. If (nevertheless) you act with goodness toward those affiliated with you (*awliyā'ikum*), that is set down in the Book."[37] This verse is said by virtually all the commentators to confirm the abrogation of the *mu'ākhāt*, the adoption of each other as brothers by the Meccan Emigrants (*muhājirūn*) and certain members of the Helpers (*anṣār*), the sincere believers among the Medinans, at the time that the Prophet settled in Medina.

Nevertheless, in the larger scheme of things, the ties created by religion are more meaningful in the eyes of God and should be a more significant source of motivation. If your kin and your wealth are dearer to you than

32 Qur'ān XIX:28.
33 Qur'ān XLIX:12.
34 Qur'ān II:220.
35 *Jalālayn*, 46.
36 Qur'ān XXXIII:5.
37 Qur'ān XXXIII:6.

the Prophet, God and the struggle in His path, "Then lie in wait until God brings His command to pass."[38] "Those who believe in God and the last day will not show love to those who oppose God and His Prophet whether they be fathers or sons or brothers or members of their clan (*'ashīra*)."[39] This Sūra belongs to the Medinan period and may refer to the attempts by the Prophet to make the sincere converts among the Medinans place their loyalty to Islam above their feelings of kinship to their relatives who were not real converts, the "hypocrites."

Several verses affirm the brotherhood of the verses. The Qur'ān reminds Muslims that before accepting Islam they were enemies, "Then he unified your hearts so that through his bounty you became brothers (*ikhwān*)."[40] The believers must take care to preserve this condition for they "are but brothers (*ikhwa*); therefore, make peace between (any) two of your brothers."[41] Correspondingly, those who share in some form of sinful behavior can be considered members of a "brotherhood" so that "those who squander money [or are prodigal] are the brothers of the devils (*shayāṭīn*)."[42] Ṭabarī adds: "In this way the Arabs speak of anyone who adheres to a habit of a people and follows their tradition: [he is] their brother."[43]

Other verses show that the brotherhood of the believers entails a feeling of mutual affection and interdependence regardless of gender. Thus Qur'ān III:195 reads: "And their Lord answers them, 'I do not/will not cause the action of anyone of you to be lost, male or female; you depend on/belong to/proceed from each other (*ba'ḍukum min ba'ḍin*)." Similarly, Qur'ān IX:71 reads: "The believers, male and female, are friends/guardians of each other (*ba'ḍuhum awliyā' ba'ḍin*)." Indeed, Qur'ān LIX:9, which refers to the Emigrants from Mecca and the Helpers in Medina but may be generalized to indicate the degree to which all true believers prefer the interests of other believers to their own, reads: "They do not find envy in their hearts for that which has been given [to the Emigrants] but prefer them to themselves even if there be poverty amongst themselves. Whoever guards himself from the avarice of his own soul, those are the truly fortunate."[44]

---

38 Qur'ān IX:24.

39 Qur'ān LVIII:22.

40 Qur'ān III:103.

41 Qur'ān XLIX:10.

42 Qur'ān XVII:27

43 Ṭabarī, *Tafsīr*, XV:74.

44 See also the next verse, Qur'ān LIX:10, and compare LXIV:16.

According to some modernists all humans are believers by nature, and only by willful commitment to evil leave that state. Some verses might be seen to support this view. There are those who associate others with God (*mushrikūn*); "but"—adds a verse which need not be read as exclusively designating Muslims—"if they repent and establish worship and pay the alms-tax (*zakāt*), they are your brothers (*ikhwān*) in religion."[45] And in a verse which seems from its context to be addressed to the righteous (*al-muttaqīn*). they are promised that in heaven: "We shall root out whatever [remains] of hatred in their hearts; [they shall be] as brothers (*ikhwān*) on raised couches, face to face."[46] If this verse is addressed to the righteous, both Muslim and non-Muslim, it conceives of brotherhood as their universal reward and ideal condition in the future life.

Elaboration of the concept of brotherhood as a heightened form of religious identification became prominent in medieval Islam. Literary examples of this would include the writings of the Brotherhood of Purity (Ikhwān al-Ṣafā')[47] and of Ibn Abī al-Dunyā (d. 281/894),[48] whose ideas on "brotherhood" in God are often quoted by al-Ghazālī (d. 505/1111) in book 15 of his *Iḥyā' 'Ulūm al-Dīn*.[49] Historical formulations, especially those associated with Sufism, are a prominent feature of religious life in virtually every Islamic century.

45 Qur'ān IX:11.
46 Qur'ān XV:47.
47 Y. Marquet, "Ikhwān al-Ṣafā," *The Encyclopaedia of Islam*, 2nd ed., III (Leiden, Brill: 1971) 1071–1076.
48 Ibn Abī Dunyā, *Kitāb al- Ikhwān*, ed. M. Tawliba, rev. M. 'A. Khalaf (Cairo: 1988).
49 Abū Ḥāmid Muḥammad al-Ghazālī, *Iḥyā' 'Ulūm al-Dīn*, II (Būlaq: 1289/1872) 139–197.

ISLAMIC SOCIETIES

Islamic societies, that is societies dominated by Muslims, have been one of my interests throughout my career. My grandfather first owned a caravanserai in Kashan and then one in the Caspian port of Rasht, and I have always been fascinated by the warp and woof of Middle Eastern city life.

In the 1960s I lived for some years on a Harvard fellowship that required me to learn more about the social sciences. I read a lot of Max Weber, Clifford Geertz, and other worthies. However, I remained a stalwart historian, although somewhat improved by sociology and, especially, anthropology. I also gained insights by reading extensively in early modern English history. I chose to work principally on the 4th/10th and 5th/11th centuries not only because they were a formative period for the Islamic Middle East but also because I admired the cultural production of that period.

The first society I studied in great detail was that of the Iranian city of Qazvin (Qazwīn in Arabic) for my dissertation, discussed here in the section on Islamic cities. Afterward I looked at several provincial societies surrounding a central city to develop my understanding of the social organizations of these places, particularly in the 4th/10th and 5th/11th centuries. This research resulted in 1980 in my first book, *Loyalty and Leadership in an Early Islamic Society*, in which I tried to analyze and translate the social categories mentioned in the primary sources, such as chronicles, city histories, biographical dictionaries, etc. I believe that understanding the categories used in these primary sources to classify people in their own time is invaluable. Modern categories such as "class" can sometimes be equated with the medieval categories but at other times they do not fit. Medieval categories often have to be understood in the first instance in the terms with which contemporaries describe them.

The first article in this section, "The *Shuʿūbīya* Controversy and the Social History of Early Islamic Iran," was begun as a graduate student and only published in 1976 when I was teaching at Princeton University.[1] The *Shuʿūbīya* movement arose as a comparatively early attempt at ranking Muslims according to the honor due to their ancestors. The pro-Iranian Shuʿūbīs believed that greater honor was due to their Persian ancestors who had lived civilized life when the Arabs (in their view) had a primitive culture. This disagreement as to whom the greater honor was due, to Arabs or Persians (and, secondarily, in Spain, to Arabs or non-Arab Spanish converts), created a literature both in the Middle East and in Spain and remained a live controversy for centuries.

My revered teacher H.A.R. Gibb wrote an influential article on the subject, but for all his very great talent he had a slight moral disapproval of the Persian Islamic world. Gibb wrote that the "Sasanian [i.e., Persian] strands which had been woven into the fabric of Muslim thought were, and remained, foreign to its native constitution."[2] This anti-Persian sentiment has a long history in Western (and particularly English) political thought. After all, was not Greek victory in the Greco-Persian wars a victory of democracy against authoritarianism? Was not the egalitarianism of early Islam in contrast to the monarchical style of Sasanian Persian rule and the hierarchical structure of Iranian society?

Yes, there was an Iranian tradition of monarchy, just as there was a Greco-Roman, a Mesopotamian, and a Visigothic tradition of monarchy, conquered by the early Muslims. Yes, the Syrian rulers of the Umayyad dynasty created de facto a monarchy a generation after Muḥammad. Yes, the next line of rulers in Baghdad was de facto a monarchy. At the same time in the medieval Western world the heirs to the semi-democratic traditions of the classical world resolved themselves into monarchies without any Persian influence. It is true, however, that certain aspects of Persian royalty, such as the *farr* (nimbus of light said to cover the head of a king) made their way into Islamic art and literature.

The second article in this section, "Bureaucracy and the Patrimonial State in Early Islamic Iran and Iraq," was written at the request of a friend at the American University of Beirut for the journal *al-Abḥāth*, published by

1 Subsequent work on the "*shuʿūbīya*" is too numerous to mention here. James T. Monroe, *The Shuʿūbiyya in al-Andalus: the Risāla of Ibn García and Five Refutations* (Berkeley, University of California: 1970) and H.T. Norr, "Shuʿubiyyah in Arabic Literature," in Julia Ashtiany, *et al.* (eds.) *Abbasid Belles-Lettres* (Cambridge, U.K., Cambridge University Press: 1990) 31–47.

2 H.A.R. Gibb, "Social Significance of the Shuubiya," *Studies in the Civilization of Islam* (Boston: 1962) 72.

the Faculty of Arts and Sciences at AUB. This 1981 article meant a return to the pre-Seljuk Middle East where I was somewhat well read because my doctoral dissertation was written on the Buyids of the 4th/10th and 5th/11th centuries, and I had recently written on the Abbasids for the *Cambridge History of Iran*. The accidental preservation of bureaucratic documents from that period was another reason to study the medieval Islamic bureaucracy. Those centuries were a high period in Arabic composition, and some of the great viziers wrote model letters that were copied by bureaucrats for centuries. Later generations considered this period the pinnacle of Arabic prose writing.

Bureaucracy is a large subject for historians of the West. Documents produced by bureaucrats in European and American settings have a good chance of surviving. The more casual attitude of earlier Middle Eastern bureaucrats was illustrated to me when I went to Afghanistan in the spring of 1961. As I hoped to stay for two months in that beautiful country, I had to give my passport over to an official of the government. In an effort to retrieve my passport I returned to that official three times on successive weeks, and each time I was given a cup of tea and a biscuit. Finally, I screwed up the courage to ask to see my passport. The official to whom I was speaking got up from the lidded box on which he was sitting and revealed hundreds of passports. After a few minutes we found my passport, which had not been processed. I asked why my passport had been kept so long and was told by the Afghan official that he enjoyed our conversations (in spite of my feeble Persian). He immediately offered to process my passport. Sadly, I never saw him again. Sixty years later I still treasure the memory of what seemed a nineteenth-century Islamic country, and I grieve for the suffering that Afghans have experienced since then.

The third article in this section, "Some Attitudes towards Monarchy and Absolutism in the Eastern Islamic World of the 11th and 12th Centuries," was delivered in a colloquium in Tel Aviv in 1979. The colloquium proceedings were edited by my friends Joel Kraemer and Ilai Alon and published the following year in *Israel Oriental Studies*. This article discusses the idea of kingship in the Islamic world. One of the consequences of the shift from rulers called "caliphs" to rulers called "kings" was a new political standing for the idea of kingship. Somehow the justification for kingship comes close to saying whatever rule does not violate Islam is to be endured. However, alongside this brutal equation there was the belief that God removed unjust kings. This idea in turn not only encouraged kings to portray themselves as just but also provided a right to rebellion against kings understood to be unjust. A continuing loyalty to the larger idea of the caliphate was yet another way by which many Muslims qualified their loyalty to the many dynasties of kings they had to endure.

The initial revival of the tradition of Iranian kingship under the Buyids in the 4th/10th century can be explained by the inheritance of pre-Islamic Iranian kings. In later times this explanation would be repeated in the Eastern Islamic world again and again. The early Islamic dislike of kingship was not completely forgotten but lived on in scholarly books. Most later kings embraced the title "king," as did the pious Ayyubids, the dynasty of Saladin. The Ottomans adopted the title "caliph" somewhat casually but when they abandoned the title in the 1920s, it had repercussions throughout the Islamic world. This interest in kingship was encouraged by the difficulty of claiming the title "caliph." Attempts to identify a new line of caliphs came to nothing.

The fourth article in this section, "Oaths and Public Vows in the Middle East of the 10th and 11th Centuries," was written for a conference entitled "Oralité et lien social (Occident, Byzance, Islam)" in 2007. The conference was organized by Marie-France Auzépy, who had read my first book, *Loyalty and Leadership in an Early Islamic Society*, and asked me to readdress the subject of oaths and vows at her conference. In my book I tried to show the frequency and strong implications of oaths and vows in public life. This article looks at oaths and public vows from a more legalistic angle. I chose new examples for the Paris conference and laid emphasis on the way in which oaths represented commitment in a somewhat individualistic society. The inclusion of oaths and vows in Islamic law shows the heavy weight given to both subjects in pre-modern Islamic societies.

The fifth article in this section, "Qur'ānic commentary on the verse of *Khums* (al-Anfāl VIII:41)," was presented at an international conference in Tokyo in 2009 on "The Role and Position of Sayyid/Sharīfs in Muslim Societies," which was organized by Kazuo Morimoto. It was published in 2012 in *Sayyids and Sharifs in Muslim Societies: The Living Links to the Prophet*, edited by Kazuo Morimoto. Many modern Muslim societies have adapted to the prominent emphasis on the equality of male believers on the one hand and the preferential treatment owed, on the other hand, to some who are the descendants of the Prophet Muḥammad. At the heart of the problem is the interpretation of the Qur'ānic passage quoted here. This article illustrates the variety of opinion about the tax called *khums* available through reading Qur'ān commentaries. Some issues, such as the objects of this tax and its beneficiaries, remain open to the present day.

Recently there has been a strong call for the revival of Islamic law. With respect to the *khums* tax, the implications for actual economies of such revival are different from one nation to another. This occurs because there are differences (sometimes large) in historic practice. Islamic law is not univocal, and in pre-Ottoman times there were competing versions of Islamic law. A modern state needs an established version of the law, and the strains of finding such a version is evident in many contexts in Muslim societies.

The *Shuʿūbīya* Controversy and the Social History of Early Islamic Iran

And We have made you into peoples and tribes.

Qur'ān (XLIX:13)

"In a state of *rude* nature," wrote Edmund Burke, "there is no such thing as a people ... The idea of a people is the idea of a corporation. It is wholly artificial; and made, like all other legal fictions, by common agreement. What the particular nature of that agreement was, is collected from the form into which the particular society has been cast."[1] Whether the Iranians in the early Islamic period—that is, the period from the 1st/7th to the 6th/12th century—were in Burke's sense a "people" is a question that the cautious scholar would be eager to disregard and loath to handle. After all, those specialists on early Islamic Iran who have directly or indirectly, expressed opinions on this subject have all too often projected events from the life of their own nation and times back to these earlier centuries. In no case is this projection more obvious than in the many essays written in the late nineteenth and early twentieth centuries which see this question only as a question of "national liberation": did the Iranians hate the Arabs, and did they hope to regain their empire by destroying, or profoundly reshaping, the empire of the Muslim caliphs?

To describe in what sense the early Islamic Iranians were a people, scholars have quite naturally looked at the fairly generous literary remains of the *shuʿūbīya* controversy, a controversy over the position of the Arabs

Author's note: This article was first published as: "The *Shuʿūbīyah* Controversy and the Social History of Early Islamic Iran," *International Journal of Middle East Studies* 7:2 (1976) 161–182. Reproduced with permission.

1 "An Appeal from the New to the Old Whigs," *The Writings and Speeches of the Right Honorable Edmund Burke*, IV (Boston: 1901) 169.

and the non-Arab peoples, especially the Iranians, in Islam. At first sight the evidence has an exciting familiarity. The Arabs, Persians, and other participants insult one another's customs and pretensions with a vigor that would warm the heart of any modern ethnic nationalist. Moreover, the *shuʿūbīs*, those who claimed the equality or superiority of their group to the Arabs, took on the coloring of many different movements of their period. Since not all the subjects of early Muslim governments admired the Arabs, there is evidence in the literature of the *shuʿūbīya* that for some few *shuʿūbīs* the movement was, in fact, an expression of political aspirations—one could almost say political fantasies—that so-called Arab rule would be judged a mistake before the bar of history and that Arabs would be sent back to their deserts where they could practice their loathsome customs away from their betters. Certainly, many anti-*shuʿūbīs* (or, loosely, pro-Arabs) tried to tar all the *shuʿūbīs* with the same brush by claiming that rejection of Islamic government was the secret motivation of all *shuʿūbī* writers, since it was natural to assume that anyone with such a low opinion of the historical rule of the Arabs must have a low opinion of Islam itself.

At second sight, however, the remains of the *shuʿūbīya* controversy provide very little evidence of any overt political aspirations on the part of the *shuʿūbīs*. The *shuʿūbīya* was primarily a literary controversy, and if it was used on rare occasions by political movements with a noticeable "ethnic" (or regional) character like the Ṣaffārids, most *shuʿūbīs* were not political and were, as often as not, faithful servants of the caliphate. Political movements against the established caliphate were regularly accused of religious heresy; such charges were so diffuse that they had some chance of sticking to any opponent. Even the Abbasids had, at first, faced such charges, as when the Umayyad general Naṣr ibn al-Sayyār said in his well-known poem: "If one should ask me the basis of their [the Abbasids'] religious belief, [I answer] their religion is to kill Arabs."[2] The charge was hardly fair to the Abbasids. But, in any case, most *shuʿūbī* and anti-*shuʿūbī* polemic was concerned not with activist Islamic movements like the Abbasid *daʿwa*; rather, it was concerned with points of honor and dishonor in the customs and past of the Arabs and of the peoples they had conquered. Such polemics are a treasure trove of information on the curiosities of pre-Islamic life such as the nature of the *miswāk*, the proto-toothbrush

2 Al-Dīnawarī, *al-Akhbār al-Ṭiwāl*, ed. V.F. Guirgass (Leiden, Brill: 1888) 360; Ibn ʿAbd Rabbih, *al-ʿIqd al-Farīd*, ed. ʿAbd al-Majid al-Rahini, V (Beirut, Dār al-Kutub al-ʿIlmīya: 1983, 3rd printing, 1987) 221 (with slight differences).

used by the pre-Islamic Arabs and Persians, since issues of this kind gave writers a good chance to display a lifetime of miscellaneous learning. But anyone who hopes to find in a tract on the *shu'ūbīya* sentiments like, "I regret that I have but one life to give for my country," will, I think, be severely disappointed. After reading countless discussions as to whether lizards were a food of choice to the ancient Arabs, or whether ancient Persians relished the brother-sister or mother-son marriages which were sanctioned by Zoroastrianism, it becomes clear that the central issues for the *shu'ūbīs* were not overtly political; that is, they were not primarily concerned with the creation of new governments.

Some scholars, having found that the *shu'ūbīya* controversy says so little about the questions that scholars have traditionally associated with it, have chosen to demote and dismiss it as an issue peripheral to the great intellectual and social struggles of the early Islamic world. As G. Lecomte has said in his masterful book on Ibn Qutayba: "One is persuaded that too much importance has been given to the phenomenon of the *Shu'ūbīya.* One cannot properly speak of a concerted movement with leaders, a program and spokesmen. Rather, in our opinion it is a question of a diffuse tendency among the non-Arabs, often coinciding with heterodox religious and intellectual aspirations."[3] Yet, somehow, we have to account for the strong emotion produced by the *shu'ūbīya* controversy in the third, fourth, and fifth centuries of Islam; if the controversy seems unimportant to us, why did it seem very important to Muslims of that period? We have, for example, five heated replies extant to the extremely short *shu'ūbī* tract of Ibn García (Garshīya). All five replies were written in or before the 6th/12th century, and all are framed in violent language. The tone of the reply of Ibn al-Dūdīn al-Balansī is representative of the tone of all the replies, as when he addresses Ibn García as a "very ignorant apostate and depraved religious hypocrite ... may your mother be bereft of you ...! True justice in answering you ... would consist of stripping you of your skin and crucifying you on your gate."[4] Clearly, if the *shu'ūbīya* was not a concerted movement with a clear program, it nonetheless involved matters that were even more sensitive to Muslims than the diets and marriage laws of their non-Muslim ancestors.

3 G. Lecomte, *Ibn Qutayba* (Damascus: 1965) p. x.

4 James T. Monroe, *The Shu'ubiyya in al-Andalus; the Risāla of Ibn García and Five Refutations* (Berkeley, University of California Press: 1970) 69.

The more substantive issues between the *shu'ūbīs* and their opponents, and the motivations that these issues betray, have been the subject of two essays which will long remain classics in Middle Eastern studies, one by Ignaz Goldziher and another by H.A.R. Gibb. Goldziher was, in a sense, studying the *shu'ūbīya* for evidence of nationalist movements, and as a subject of the Austro-Hungarian Empire, may have given more political significance to expressions of ethnic pride than they deserved. But in examining these expressions of ethnic pride, Goldziher demonstrated with a wonderful abundance of detail the cultural conflicts caused by the assimilation of diverse people into the Islamic community and the traces of these conflicts in ethnical precepts ascribed to Muḥammad. Gibb sought to analyze more closely the motivations of the *shu'ūbīs* and their opponents and believed that the issue at stake was the "whole cultural orientation of the new Islamic society" since the *shu'ūbīs* wanted to remold the political and social institutions of the Islamic empire and inner spirit of Islamic culture on the model of Sasanian institutions and values.[5]

Neither of these summaries does justice to these two brilliant essays which illuminate many areas of Islamic history beside the *shu'ūbīya* controversy. Yet, surprisingly, neither Gibb nor Goldziher looked for evidence in one of the most obvious places—the Qur'ān commentaries which provide a copious and almost untouched source of information for the opinions of Muslims in every age on social and political ideas. Virtually all Muslim controversialists tried to find proof texts in the Qur'ān; and since Qur'ān commentaries are one of the largest and best distributed branches of Arabic prose literature, they give a fairly continuous and geographically broad view of the ideas considered important enough to need Qur'ānic proof.

The very name of the *shu'ūbīya* comes from a proof text. Verse 13 of Sūra XLIX (al-Ḥujurāt) reads: "Oh men, We have created you from a male and a female, and We have made you into groups (*shu'ūb*) and tribes (*qabā'il*) that you may come to know one another; truly, the noblest (*akram*) among you before God is the most righteous (*atqā*) among you; truly God is the All-Knowing, the All-Seeing." (I have deliberately chosen the colorless translation "groups" for *shu'ūb*, singular *sha'b*, to avoid prejudicing the interpretations of the commentators.) Why did the *shu'ūbīya* take its name from this verse? In his essay on "The Arabic Tribes and Islam," Goldziher

5 Ignaz Goldziher, *Muslim Studies*, I (London: 1967) 137–163; H.A.R. Gibb, "The Social Significance of the Shuubiya," *Studies on the Civilization of Islam* (Boston: 1962) 62–73.

does, in fact, briefly discuss use of this verse by early Muslims. He makes an important point: The last part of this verse, "the noblest among you before God is the most righteous among you," was used to combat the tribal pride which was such a danger to the early Islamic community.[6] Although Goldziher is not here speaking of the *shu'ūbīya*, what he says is germane to the self-conceptions of many *shu'ūbīs*. The *shu'ūbīs* were often called the *ahl al-taswīya*,[7] "the people [who advocate] equality," and sometimes used the Qur'ānic phrase, "Truly the noblest among you before God is the most righteous." as a cornerstone of their argument. The *shu'ūbīs* say, according to Ibn 'Abd Rabbih (d. 328/940):

> The believers are brothers, whose lives are equal in value before the law (*tatakāfa'u dimā'uhum*). As [Muḥammad] said in the farewell pilgrimage in the speech in which he bade farewell to his community and with which he set a seal on his prophecy: "O man, God has removed from you the baseless pride of the period of ignorance (*nakhwat al-jāhilīya*) and its glorying in ancestors. You are all from Adam, and Adam was from the dust. The Arab has no superiority to the non-Arab (*'ajamī*) except by virtue of righteousness (*taqwā*)." These words of the Prophet [add the *shu'ūbīs*] are in agreement with the words of God: "Truly the noblest among you before God is the most righteous."[8]

6 Goldziher, (*supra* n. 5), 55.

7 See S. Enderwitz, "Shu'ūbiyya," *The Encyclopaedia of Islam*, 2nd ed., (hereafter *EI*²), IX (Leiden, Brill: 1998) 513–516. Cf. Ibn 'Abd Rabbih, (*supra* n. 2), III:356.

8 Ibn 'Abd Rabbih, (*supra* n. 2), III:356. Actually, Muḥammad's speech during the farewell pilgrimage occurs in several versions. The most egalitarian version, and the version most often quoted in Qur'ān commentaries on verse XLIX:13, reads: "Oh men, your Lord is one and your ancestors are one. You are all from Adam and Adam was from the dust. Behold, neither the Arab has superiority to the non-Arab, nor the red to the black, nor the black to the red except by virtue of righteousness. Truly, the noblest among you before God is the most righteous." (A roughly similar version is found in several of the classic books of ḥadīth, including the *Musnad* of Ibn Ḥanbal.) This version is quoted, for example, without the Qur'ānic phrase, by al-Qurṭubī (d. 671/1273), *Jāmi' li-Aḥkām al-Qur'ān*, XVI (Cairo: 1387/1967) 342. "Black" and "Red" were common terms for the Arabs and the Persians respectively; cf. Goldziher, (*supra* n. 5), 243–244. The earliest biographer of Muḥammad, Ibn Isḥāq (d. ca. 150/767), quotes a similar speech of Muḥammad, which is almost as egalitarian in tone. He places this speech in the context of the conquest of Mecca, not of the farewell pilgrimage. This version, unlike the preceding versions, includes a full (and not partial) quotation of XLIX:13; *The Life of Muḥammad*, trans. A. Guillaume (London: 1955) 553.

Yet the egalitarianism of this verse is not enough to explain its great interest for both the *shuʿūbīs* and their opponents. There are other egalitarian verses in the Qur'ān; one is partly quoted at the beginning of Ibn ʿAbd Rabbih's summary of *shuʿūbī* arguments, for in the very same Sūra, verse 10 reads: "The believers are but brothers. So, make peace between your two brothers and be pious toward God; perhaps He will have mercy on you." The 7th/13th-century commentator al-Bayḍāwī, with the elegant conciseness that has made his commentary a favorite for later generations of Sunni Muslims, explains: "'The believers are brothers' since they claim common descent (*muntasibūn*) from a single source which is belief (*al-īmān*)."[9] An even clearer summons to equality could be found in III:195 which reads: "And their Lord has hearkened to them [saying], 'I will not allow the [pious] work performed by anyone among you, whether male or female, to be lost. The one of you is of the other.'" This last sentence (*baʿḍukum min baʿḍin*), permitted more than one interpretation, but the verse provided an ideal opportunity for those commentators who were interested in finding Qur'ānic warrants for equality. In his Persian commentary Abū al-Futūḥ al-Rāzī (d. 538/1144) paraphrased the verse as follows: "'All men are one in respect to their inborn characteristics (*khilqat*) in My sight'; as [Muḥammad]—Peace be upon him—said, 'Men are like the teeth of a comb,' that is, in respect to their inborn characteristics."[10]

Admittedly, the question of nobility is directly discussed in XLIX:13; yet, if this verse was quoted only because it equates the "most noble" (*akram*) with the "most righteous" (*atqā*), why was an earlier word in the verse, *shuʿūb*, or groups, chosen as the badge by which these supposed "egalitarians" came to be described? Very simply, because a dispute over the nature of *shuʿūb* constituted one of the fundamental issues dividing the *shuʿūbīs* and their opponents, an issue that has somehow gone unnoticed by modern historians. It is sometimes said that the egalitarianism of Islam gives no standing for—or theoretical basis to—any social unit smaller than the *umma*, or total community of Believers, except for the "family," which has a standing in Islamic personal law.[11] It is true that few social units other

9 Al-Bayḍāwī, *Anwār al-Tanzīl*, II (Leipzig: 1848) 274–275.

10 Abū al-Futūḥ al-Rāzī, *Rawḍ al-Jinān*, III (Teheran: 1383/1963–64) 291. "Inborn characteristics" can, of course, have a very limited meaning. The oneness of mankind is not unambiguously defined in this passage.

11 The neighborhood also has a very limited juridical standing since its inhabitants are collectively liable for the blood money of a murdered man found in the neighborhood whose murderer cannot be identified.

than the *umma* and the family are specifically mentioned with approval in the Qur'ān. Yet most Muslims believed that some such units rightfully existed; and it was precisely for this reason that verse 13 of Sūra XLIX became so well known and widely disputed. This verse states that the division of men into *shu'ūb* and *qabā'il* is a division created by God Himself, and implies that men must be mindful of what division(s) they belong to so that they can identify themselves when they come to know each other. In interpreting this verse, early Muslims had to express opinions on the "common agreement" which, in Burke's phrase, established the idea of a people. From their disputes as to the nature of agreements we can discern the various forms into which their society was actually cast, even if these forms were often imperfectly achieved. One such dispute was the *shu'ūbīya.*

The first school of interpretation—a school that was, as we shall see, unacceptable to the *shu'ūbīs*—felt that XLIX:13 by itself sanctioned only genealogical divisions of society, and therefore only larger groupings based on genealogy. For these commentators, *sha'b* meant something like "tribal confederacy" or super-tribe, the next largest genealogical unit after the *qabā'il* which were mentioned alongside *shu'ūb* in this context. This interpretation has a strong philological basis since *sha'b* is also a verbal noun meaning "a collecting" or "a separating" and had come by extension to be used for genealogical units that resulted from the gathering or branching off of earlier units. This genealogical interpretation is well represented by the Arabic Qur'ān commentary of Ṭabarī, the great historian and lawyer who died in 310/923. He paraphrases XLIX:13 as follows:

> We have caused you to be related in genealogy. Some of you are related to others remotely and some are related closely ... For example, when an Arab is asked "Of what *sha'b* are you?" he says: "Of Muḍar," or "Of Rabī'a" ... When it says "That you may come to know one another," it means, "That you may know each other in respect of genealogy ... not because you have any superiority to others in that respect, nor any nearness which will bring you nearer to God"; rather "The noblest among you is the most righteous among you."[12]

12 Al-Ṭabarī, *Jāmi' al-Bayān 'an Ta'wīl al-Qur'ān*, XXVI (Cairo: 1373/1954) 138–140. "Nearness" or *qurba* in the last phrase can imply both kinship and "spiritual" nearness as in Qur'ān IV:172. "Genealogy" in this last sentence is a translation for *qarāba*, which is relationship through the male line; in most contexts of this essay, genealogical ties through the female line are of minor importance.

Ṭabarī cites three pages of traditions which support this interpretation, and many Qur'ān commentaries repeat the basic ideas which he presents.

His interpretation agrees with several of the very earliest commentaries on the Qur'ān; for example, Sufyān al-Thawrī, who died in 161/778, states very simply that: "The *shu'ūb* are like [the tribes] Tamīm and Bakr and the *qabā'il* are sub-tribes (*afkhādh*)."[13] Abū 'Ubayda (d. 209/824–25), the great Basran philologist who is sometimes called a *shu'ūbī*, writes in his commentary *Majāz al-Qur'ān*, "One is asked 'Of what *sha'b* are you?' and you say 'Of Muḍar' [or] 'Of Rabī'a'; and *qabā'il* are lesser divisions."[14] Many later commentaries follow this tradition and give no other interpretation of this verse.[15] I understand these passages to imply that a genealogical framework is natural to society; that a *sha'b* is a larger (or, very occasionally, a smaller) genealogical division than a *qabīla* (pl. *qabā'il*); and that the Qur'ān says that men should know their genealogies in order that they may recognize how they are related to one another. To claim a false ancestry is an act of criminality, just as it is criminally wrong to make a false claim that someone is your father; and the commentators sometimes quote from the ample ḥadīth literature on this subject. Furthermore, as several of the commentators point out, if men ignored genealogies they would be unable to follow the divine law, the *sharī'a*, in distributing inheritance and avoiding marriage within the forbidden degrees; they would even be unable to study the authenticity of ḥadīth, traditions of the sayings and deeds of the Prophet, since it would be impossible to place the transmitters. That knowledge of one's ancestry is a positive good with important benefits is supported in several commentaries by a ḥadīth from the collection of al-Tirmidhī: "Know concerning your genealogies that by which you may make your ties of blood kinship close; for the close tie of

13 *Tafsīr al-Qur'ān al-Karīm*, ed. Imtiyaz Ali Arshi (Rampur: 1385/1965) 240. The editor makes a strong case for the authenticity of this work.

14 Cited from the unedited MS of *al-Waraqa* by Abū 'Ubayda in Ṭabarī, (*supra* n. 12), XXVI:139 n. 1.

15 E.g., al-Farrā' (d. 207/882), *Ma'ānī al-Qur'ān*, III (Cairo: 1972) 72; al-Nasafī (d. 710/1311), *Tafsīr*, IV (Cairo: 1387/1968) 167; al-Ṭūsī ("Shaykh al-Ṭā'ifa") (d. 460/1067), *al-Tibyān*, IX (Najaf: 1382/1963) 352; al-Suyūṭī (d. 855/1451), *Tafsīr al-Jalālayn* (Beirut: 1971) 684; al-Wāḥidī (d. 468/1075), "al-Wajīz," MS Princeton University Library, Yahuda Coll. 3771, f. 126 B; Abū al-Layth al-Samarqandī (d. 383/993), MS Yahuda Coll. 2567, no pagination, under XLIX:13; al-Zamakhsharī (d. 538/1144), *al-Kashshāf*, IV (Beirut: 1366) 374–375. It is appropriate that al-Zamakhsharī, a strong anti-*shu'ūbī*, should identify with the school of Ṭabarī.

kinship is a cause of love among family, a creator of wealth and a means to prolong one's life."[16]

There exists, however, a tradition of interpreting this verse which is significantly different from the tradition of Ṭabarī. The so-called "Cambridge *Tafsīr*," an early Persian Qur'ān commentary in the library of Cambridge University, translates and explains this verse as follows:

> Oh men, know that We have created you all, white and black, rich and poor, great and small, Arab and client (*mawlā*) from one man and one woman. We have made you one city (*shahr*) after another and one tribe after another so that when you asked "Do you know each other ?"—so that people may know where you are from—you say "such-and-such city from such-and-such village (*dih*) of such-and-such locality (*maḥallat*)" and "of such-and-such tribe, son of so-and-so," so that you may know each other. It is for this reason that We have given names (*nām-hā*) [designating relationships], not so that you should assert pride in this respect over one another.[17]

The author of this work is unknown but was probably from Khorasan, the great northeast province of Iran, and almost certainly lived not later than the first half of the 5th/11th century.[18]

The interpretation given in the Cambridge *Tafsīr* is not an aberrant interpretation, the idle invention of some backwoods Iranian who felt

---

16 E.g., Ibn Kathīr, *Tafsīr*, VI (Beirut: 1966) 387. Cf. al-Tirmidhī, with the commentary of Muḥammad al-Mubārakfūrī, *Tuḥfat al-Aḥwadhī*, VI (Cairo: 1965) 113, where the above ḥadīth is explained with this meaning, although the meaning "as a means to prolong one's line of descent" is given as a less likely explanation of the last phrase. This ḥadīth is also found in the *Musnad* of Ibn Ḥanbal.

17 Anon., *Tafsir-e Qor'ān-e Majd*, ed. Jalal Matini, II (Tehran: 1349 A.H. solar/1970–71) 256. *Shahr* can, of course, mean region; and since Persians of this period usually used the *nisba* for the largest city in their region, a translation like city-region would be appropriate. Some early Persian commentaries translate *shaʿb* as *shākh* or *shākha*, "branch," presumably because *shaʿaba* (or, much more commonly, *tashaʿʿaba*) can also mean to branch off; *shākh* is also a common equivalent of *shuʿba*, "branch" or "division, portion" in Persian. In Maybudī's *Kashf al-Asrār* (written ca. 520/1126), IX (Tehran: 1339 solar/1960–61) 256, *shuʿūban wa-qabāʾila* is translated *shākh shākh ... va khānidān khānidān*, "branch after branch ... and family after family." *Shākh shākh* can mean torn or piece by piece or divided into branches; cf. ʿAli Akbar Dehkhoda, *Loghat-Nāma*, VIII (Tehran: 1373 solar) 12310.

18 Anon., *Tafsīr*, (*supra* n. 17), editor's introduction, xxiii–xxvi. The Cambridge MS was copied in 628/1230–31.

unconstrained by the traditions established by the great scholars who wrote in Arabic. It is an interpretation frequently mentioned in the Qur'ān commentaries and, as we shall see, an interpretation of deep importance to the *shuʿūbīya*. This tradition of interpretation is traced back in part to ʿAbd Allāh ibn ʿAbbās (d. ca. A.H. 69) one of the greatest scholars of the second generation of Muslims and, in the opinion of many Muslims, the father of Qur'ānic exegesis. Although Ibn ʿAbbās seems to have, in fact, written or dictated some work on Qur'ānic exegesis, none of the works or the frequent quotations ascribed to him can be unhesitatingly accepted as authentic. Nevertheless, his position at the origin of the Qur'ānic sciences and his distinction as the ancestor of the Abbasid caliphs guaranteed him a conspicuous place in later Qur'ān commentaries. It is not surprising, therefore, to find that Ibn ʿAbbās is quoted as an authority on the meaning of *shaʿb*. ʿAtā' (presumably ʿAtā' ibn Abī Rabāḥ, a Nubian *mawlā* and a prominent "lawyer" who died in 114/732 or 115/733)[19] is supposed to have related that Ibn ʿAbbās said, "The *shuʿab* are the *mawālī* (non-Arab clients) and the *qabā'il* are the Arabs."[20] Those who follow this interpretation often add (without the authority of Ibn ʿAbbās) that the *shuʿūb* are the *ʿajam* (non-Arabs, principally—in the eastern Islamic world—the Iranians), while the *qabā'il* are the Arabs and the *asbāṭ* are (the divisions of) the Jews.[21]

It is more important for our purposes, however, to notice that several commentators are aware of the territorial interpretation of *shaʿb* which the Cambridge *Tafsīr* assumes to be the only interpretation. As al-Qushayrī,

19 On ʿAṭā' cf. J. Schacht, "ʿAṭā' ibn Abī Rabāḥ," *EI²*, I (Leiden, Brill: 1960) 730.
20 E.g., (pseudo-) Ibn ʿAbbās (as edited from one version by al-Suyūṭī, *Tanwīr al-Miqbās* (Cairo: 1951) 323; al-Wāḥidī (d. 468/1076), "al-Wasīṭ," MS 1260, Garrett Coll., Princeton University Library, under XLIX:13 (no pagination); al-Thaʿlabī al-Nīṣābūrī (d. 427/1035) "Kitāb al-Kashf wa-l-Bayān," MS 1255, Garrett Coll., Princeton, under XLIX:13 (no pagination); al-Qurṭubī, (*supra* n. 8), XVI:344. A different version of Ibn ʿAbbās is quoted by Ṭabarī, (*supra* n. 12), XXVI:139, from Saʿīd ibn Jubayr: that the *shuʿūb* are *jummāʿ*, a word which means "clusters." Ibn Manẓūr, *Lisān al-ʿArab* (Beirut: n.d.), under *shaʿaba* quotes Ibn ʿAbbās as interpreting *shuʿūb* as *jummāʿ* and *qabā'il* as *buṭūn*, which would indicate that the somewhat neutral *jummāʿ* is here understood in the sense of "super-tribe" given in some dictionaries. Still other sources quote Ibn ʿAbbās as giving the interpretation characteristic of al-Ṭabarī's tradition.
21 Al-Ṭabarsī (more correctly pronounced Ṭabrisī), (d. mid-6th/12th century) *Majmaʿ al-Bayān*, XVI (Beirut: 1955) 97; al-Baghawī (d. 510/1117 or 516/1122) *Maʿālim al-Tanzīl*, IV (Bombay: 1273) 88; Maybudī, (*supra* n. 17), IX:264; al-Isfarāyinī, called "Shāhfūr" (d. 471/1078–79), "Tāj al-Tarājim," Bodleian MS under XLIX:13. I am grateful to Donald Richards of Oxford for sending me photostats of the relevant pages of this manuscript.

a Khorasanian scholar who died in 465/1072, said: "The *shu'ūb* are those the origin (*aṣl*) of whose genealogy (*nasab*) is not known like the Indians and the Iranians and the Turks."[22] A similar view is ascribed to Abū Rawq in the commentary of al-Baghawī: "The *shu'ūb* are those who do not trace their descent back to any one person; rather, they trace themselves (*yantasibūna*) to cities (*madā'in*) and villages. The *qabā'il* are the Arabs who trace themselves to their ancestors (*ābā'*)."[23] The Persian commentary by Abū al-Futūḥ al-Rāzī, a Shi'ite who died in 538/1144, elegantly summarizes this group of interpretations: "Abū Rāzī and Abū Rawq said, "*Shu'ūb* are those whose relations are not described in terms of a person; rather, they are described in terms of a city (*shahr*) or land (*zamīn*). Tribes are those who describe their relations in terms of ancestors (*pedarān*)."[24] This interpretation has been favored by many Persian commentators ever since.[25]

22 Quoted in al-Qurṭubī, (*supra* n. 8), XVI:344, who also quotes al-Māwardī (pp. 344–345) as saying "It is possible that *shu'ūb* are those associated with (*al-muḍāfūna*) regions and valleys, while the *qabā'il* are those who share in genealogies." The word "Iranians" after "Indians" in the quote from al-Qushayrī is uncertain. The editor of al-Qurṭubī has *jibilla* since this last word is used in the Qur'ān to mean "a people": I have used the reading *jīl* since the editor admits that the word is unclear in the manuscript. The context requires some word like *'ajam* or *furs*; the phrase *jīl al-'ajam* is commonly used, e.g., Ibn Manẓūr, (*supra* n. 20), II:321. Ibn al-Jawzī (d. 597/1201) also seems to have been confused by the word since he writes that Abū Razīn said that "the *shu'ūb* are the men of the mountains (*jibāl*) who do not trace their origin to any one person": *Zād al-Masīr*, VII (Damascus: 1965) 474. Al-Wāḥidī, "al-Wasīṭ," gives (among several interpretations of XLIX:13) an explanation of *shu'ūb* identical with al-Qushayrī, his close contemporary, but the word *jibilla/jīl/jabal* is unpointed in the manuscript.

23 Al-Baghawī, (*supra* n. 21), IV:88. Abū Rawq is presumably Abū Rawq 'Aṭīya ibn al-Hārith al-Hamdānī (d. ca. 140/757). This interpretation is given in almost identical words in Maybudī, (*supra* n. 17), IX:264, who adds after "villages," "and to lands (*'arāḍīn*)." A summary of this interpretation is given in Shāhfūr, (*supra* n. 21), who says under XLIX:13: "Some have said that *shu'ūb* are groups which one traces to cities (*bi-shahr-hā bāz-khwānand*) and *qabā'il* are groups which one traces back to ancestors (*pedarān*)."

24 *Rawḍ al-Jinān*, X (Tehran: 1389/1969–70) 261. The short tradition quoted in note 22 from Abū Razīn has apparently been seen in some version by Abū al-Futūḥ al-Rāzī. Abū Razīn is probably Abū Razīn Mas'ūd ibn Mālik al-Kūfī, ca. 90/708.

25 The slightly later commentary of another Rāzī, the brilliant polymath Fakhr al-Dīn (d. 606/1209), *al-Tafsīr al-Kabīr*, XXVIII (Cairo: n.d.) 138, gives the non-genealogical explanation first (unlike most of the sources quoted so far, who give it as an alternative to the genealogical explanation): the *shu'ūb* are groups "not knowing who joins them, like the *'ajam*; the *qabā'il* are groups joined by a single known [ancestor] like the Arabs and Israelites." The only interpretation in the *Tafsīr* of the celebrated Lāhijī (Tehran: 1340 solar/1961–62), IX:223, is that the *shu'ūb* are the *'ajam*, perhaps because he attributes this interpretation not to Ibn 'Abbās but to Ja'far al-Ṣādiq, as does Ṭabarsī, an earlier Shi'ite. The nineteenth-century commentary of Sulṭān 'Alī Shāh Gunābādī,

In this second group of Qur'ān commentaries a distinction is made between *sha'b* understood as a people related by a common place of residence or birth, and *qabīla* understood as a people related through a common ancestor. The residential or territorial concept is specifically associated with the *'ajam*, the non-Arabs, while the genealogical concept is associated with the Arabs. I think, therefore, it is fair to say that we have an interpretation which was favored by one group of Iranian (and especially Khorasanian) commentators, whatever early Arab authorities they may quote to support their interpretations. Though this interpretation is mentioned very briefly by a number of commentators, among the commentaries I have consulted only those by Iranians give it in such detail. A few Iranians (and only Iranians) give it preference over the interpretation of Ṭabarī. In the Cambridge *Tafsīr* it is given as the sole interpretation of this verse. I do not mean to imply that Iranian commentators automatically accepted this view; Ṭabarī, for example, who left Iran only in late adolescence, does not even hint at any of the ideas in the Cambridge *Tafsīr*.

It is not surprising that *sha'b* had taken on a special coloring for some Muslims; *sha'b*, even if it had originally meant "super-tribe," had always been a vague word. Already in the time of 'Umar (d. 23/644), if we can accept early traditions, the word was being used in a loose sense without connection to vast tribal entities like Muḍar. One tradition about 'Umar, reported on the authority of Masrūq, begins: "A man of the *shu'ūb* became a Muslim, and the *jizya* (a head tax) was being taken from him"; the philologists explain that *shu'ūb* in this context means *'ajam* (non-Arabs).[26] According to the *Musnad* of Ibn Ḥanbal, when 'Umar on his deathbed was asked to give testamentary instructions he said, among other things: "I commend to you the Anṣār, for they are the *sha'b* of Islam."[27] As the Arabs come into contact with many nontribal peoples, and members of these communities became Muslim, the word *sha'b* was naturally asked to do new work. Ibn Sīdah (d. 458/1066), a famous Spanish Arab philologist who was himself accused of being a *shu'ūbī*,[28] says in his dictionary "every

Bayān al-Sa'āda, IX (Tehran: 1344 solar/1965–66) 135, gives this same interpretation preference over any other.

26 Al-Jawharī (d. ca. 400/1010). *al-Ṣiḥāḥ*, I (Cairo: n.d.) 155.

27 Aḥmad ibn Ḥanbal, *al-Musnad*, ed. Ahmad M. Shakir, I (Cairo: 1949) 363.

28 Al-Dhahabī in his *Siyar al-Nubalā'* says that Ibn Sīdah "was a *shu'ūbī* who considered the *'ajam* superior to the Arabs"; quoted from a MS by A.M. Harun, *Nawādir al-Makhṭūṭāt* (Cairo: 1954) 233.

people (*jīl*) is a *sha'b*" and later in the same entry says: "*Shu'ūb* in the plural has come to be used predominantly of the *jīl al-'ajam*."[29]

Still, a strong school of opinion refused to acknowledge that any group not related by traceable genealogies could be properly called a people. The well-known saying ascribed to 'Umar expressed the incomprehension of the early Arabs that peoples could be organized on principles other than genealogy: "Learn your genealogies," said 'Umar, "so that you may make your ties of blood-kinship close; and do not be like the Nabataeans of the plains of Iraq who, when asked 'From whom are you?,' say 'From such and such a village.' For, by God, there would be something between a man and his brother, if he only knew the tie of affection through blood kinship (*dikhlat al-raḥim*) between them, which would restrain one from abusing the other."[30] The *shu'ūbīs*, however, found in the Qur'ān itself a warrant for the nontribal and nongenealogical organization of the societies to which they belonged. They did so by interpreting *sha'b* as a people united by a territorial principle, and it is largely for this reason that their movement continued to be called after *shu'ūb*, a single word in XLIX:13.

The association of the *shu'ūbīya* with this understanding of XLIX:13 does not rest only on the inference that such an interpretation was appropriate to the *shu'ūbīs* and is most often invoked by Iranians. Some authors made the association explicit. Ibn Ya'īsh (d. 643/1245), for example, says that the *shu'ūbīya* are said to have this name "because of their attachment to the external meaning" of this verse.[31] Ṭabarsī, a Khorasanian who died in 548/1153, writes in his commentary on the verse: "The *shu'ūbīs* are those who belittle the importance of the Arabs and do not consider them superior to others. They are called that because they have interpreted (*ta'awwalū*) 'And we have made you *shu'ūb*' on the understanding that the *shu'ūb* are [the divisions] of the *'ajam* just as 'tribes' are the Arabs."[32] Yet a large school of opinion refused to allow the *shu'ūbīs* this Qur'ānic

29 Ibn Sīdah, *al-Muḥkam*, I (Cairo: 1958) 235; quoted by Ibn Manẓūr, (*supra* n. 20), II:320–321, without reference to his source; quoted word for word by Ibn Ya'īsh, *Sharḥ Mufaṣṣal al-Zamakhsharī*, ed. G. Jahn (Leipzig: 1882) 4, wherein it is ascribed somewhat mysteriously to the *Muḥkam* of Ibn Hubayra.

30 Ibn 'Abd al-Barr, *al-Inbāh*, (Cairo: 1350/1931–32) 43. I owe this reference to a footnote in Franz Rosenthal's translation of Ibn Khaldūn, *The Muqaddimah*, I (Princeton, N.J., Princeton University Press: 1967) 266 n. 55.

31 Ibn Ya'īsh, (*supra* n 29), 4.

32 Al-Ṭabarsī, (*supra* n. 21), XVI:91. Al-Ṭabarsī adds "Abū 'Ubayda said: 'The *shu'ūb* are the *'ajam*.'" Al-Ṭabarsī also uses *shu'ūb* as the plural of *shu'ūbī*, a usage sanctioned by Ibn Manẓūr, (*supra* n. 20), II:321, on the analogy of Yahūd and Majūs.

warrant. No wonder Ibn Mas'ada, in his refutation of Ibn García's *shu'ūbī* tract, considered it a withering insult to call the Slavic Muslim ruler of Spanish Denia who was the patron of both Ibn García and Ibn Sīdah: "he of the forged genealogy ... Is he not but one of the pieces of refuse of the tracts of towns and cultivated lands, and of the shores of the sea ...?"[33] For Ibn Mas'ada, as for a large school of early Muslim thought, men who traced their origin to a region and not a person virtually had no recognizable origin.

The Qur'ān commentaries therefore give us a partial explanation of the common agreement according to which the Iranians considered themselves to be a people; for Iranian *shu'ūbī*s (and probably for the majority of Iranians) the agreement was based in large part on ties to the land. But the *shu'ūbīs*, like most polemicists, are too closely preoccupied with refuting their opponents. They are only defending a minimal definition of their differences with the Arabs; and in the fragments of *shu'ūbī* literature which still exist, they seldom elaborate on the specific nature of this territorial understanding of peoplehood among the non-Arabs. We find indications of the specific nature of this understanding in the Persian epic, the *Shāhnāma* of Firdausi (Ferdawsi), which was completed in 400/1010. The *Shāhnāma* has always been used as evidence for some kind of Iranian "national" feeling; but again, scholars have too often been exclusively concerned to look in this vast work for evidence of Firdausi's contempt for Arabs and Central Asians. They have too seldom asked how the *Shāhnāma* describes the ties which the Iranians had with each other and which made them a distinct group. I have neither the long acquaintance with, nor the thorough knowledge of, the *Shāhnāma* which would be necessary to answer this last question; but the remarkable glossary to the *Shāhnāma* prepared by Fritz Wolff makes it possible to get some idea of the vocabulary which Firdausi uses to describe a long persisting group or people. Several modern Persian words for nation, *millat*, *qawm*, and *vaṭan* (all, incidentally, from the Arabic) do not occur in the *Shāhnāma*; nor does *umma*, an Arabic word used in the Qur'ān to designate (among other things) a group who were the special object of a divine revelation. The word *mihan*, a word used in contemporary Persian for "native land," occurs three times, twice in the sense of house, and once in the sense of extended family. As one would expect, neither *sha'b* nor *qabā'il* appears.

33 Monroe, (*supra* n. 4), 35.

Keshvar occurs but is often used in the sense of region or zone as it is often used later in the phrase *haft-keshvar*, the seven regions (which is parallel to the common phrase *haft-eqlim*, the seven climes). The territorial concept of Iran, as we would expect from the Persian Qur'ān commentaries, is very important in the *Shāhnāma*; and the terms *Irān-zamin* (or "the land of Iran") and *shahr-e Irān* ("the city, i.e., land of Iran") occur with great frequency. Correspondingly, the distinction between Iran and Anirān (literally, "non-Iran," describing the territories beyond the boundaries of Iran proper), a distinction well known in Pahlavi inscriptions,[34] survives in Firdausi as Iran and Nirān. Genealogical distinctions are by no means disregarded in the *Shāhnāma* and the term *nezhād*, meaning something like "descent" or even "race," is very frequently used in the earlier parts of the *Shāhnāma* where a system of group descent from common ancestors is described. For this reason, we are sometimes reminded that the Ṭūrānians—the Central Asian opponents of the Iranians—are *ze tokhm-e Ṭur* ("from the seed of Ṭūr) or, simply *Ṭurān-nezhād* ("of Ṭūrānian descent"). Questions of *nezhād* also play an important part in relations among Iranians and in certain circumstances *nezhād* can even mean "well-born" (among the Iranians).

The *Shāhnāma*, therefore, offers genealogical explanations to account for both the differences among Iranians and the differences between Iranians and non-Iranians. But Firdausi seems to consider those people who live in Iran proper, *shahr-e Irān*, and who accept that they share a common ancestry with each other, as almost automatically part of the Iranian people even if they cannot trace their genealogies person by person. Iranians of royal or princely birth can trace their genealogies back in such a way, though Iranian nobles and especially the petty nobility of the *dehqān*s are usually satisfied with a vague claim that they are descended from some great Iranian of the past. While it is almost impossible for those Iranians who are not of gentle birth to acquire such gentility in one generation, they remain Iranians all the same.

An anecdote about the great *shu'ūbī* poet, Bashshār ibn Burd (d. 167/783–84), illustrates some of the characteristics of the Iranian *shu'ūbīya* which we have discussed. Bashshār said:

34 E.g., K.Z. Kartir, quoted in Richard N. Frye, *The Heritage of Persia* (New York: 1966) 244.

> When I entered the presence of [the caliph] al-Mahdī, he said to me: "Of whom do you reckon yourself, Bashshār?" I said, "As for my language and dress, they are Arab; but as for my origin, it is non-Arab (*'ajamī*). As I said in my poem, Oh Commander of the Faithful: "I am told of a people who have an inveterate hatred—they would say, 'Who is that?' when I was the distinguished person present. Oh, you who stupidly question [me], I am unsurpassed in nobility (*anf al-karam*) ... I am of the Quraysh of the *'ajam*."
>
> [Then Bashshār argued with another man present, and finally al-Mahdī asked him:] "From which of the *'ajam* is your origin?" And I said, "From those most prolific in cavalry men, fiercest to their opponents, the people of Ṭukhāristān." Someone present said, "Those are the Soghdians," and I said, "No, the Soghdians are merchants."[35]

Here, in miniature, we see many of the traits of the *shu'ūbīya* among the poets, and these traits are consonant with the features we have already noticed in the Qur'ān commentaries and the *Shāhnāma*. While the literary *shu'ūbī* wrote mostly in Arabic, the terms of self-description used by the Arabs were irrelevant to them; the Iranians described themselves according to their town and locality, not according to their tribe. Furthermore, as we have seen, noble Iranians wanted to be recognized as noble, not just as Iranians. In many parts of Iran these nobles continued under the caliphate to be great landed proprietors as they had been before the Islamic conquest; but they also wanted to keep the esteem which their gentle birth had won them under the Sasanians, and, in some cases, long before the Sasanians. Even Bashshār, who comes from an area not directly ruled by the Sasanians for a long time before the Arab conquests, in some of his poems takes pride in the Sasanian royal past. As in many aristocratic systems, the glory of the ruling family sanctified and was emblematic of the social order which gave the aristocrats their position in society. Yet Bashshār's pride in the ancient Persian kings as a shared symbol does not overshadow his pride in his particular region, Ṭukhāristān. Local divisions among Iranian peoples remained of the greatest importance, and consequently Bashshār spoke of the Soghdians with a certain contempt. Similarly, there is ample evidence that southwestern Iranians, when they

35 Abū al-Faraj al-Iṣfahānī, *Kitāb al-Aghānī*, III (Cairo: 1929) 138.

were ruled by the Daylamīs, a people from the Caspian provinces of Iran, in many circumstances regarded their Caspian cousins as outsiders.[36]

The *shu'ūbīya* movement among clerks can, I think, be shown to have a similar character. The clerks not only rejected much in the Arab humanities, as H.A.R. Gibb has shown in his essay on the *shu'ūbīya*, but they also resented the low opinion which the Arab rulers in general had of their non-Arab secretaries. Clerks were not the equals of the landed aristocracy under the Sasanians, but they were a powerful and respected group who had a certain hereditary position in society. They did not retain this position under the Umayyads and early Abbasids. The early Abbasids regarded their non-Arab clerks as servants to be used as skillfully as possible to centralize and control their vast empire. Only under the later Abbasids, and especially in the reign of al-Muqtadir (r. 295/908–320/932) did the clerks acquire a status which they considered worthy of themselves; earlier, many Arabs probably shared the contempt of al-Jāḥiẓ who said that clerks were more subservient to the will of their masters than men of any other profession, and therefore more contemptible. "What proves that the profession of the clerks is detestable," writes al-Jāḥiẓ, "is that only subordinates or people of—so to speak—servile condition practice it ... In spite of all this, they attain the pinnacle of boasting, the summit of vanity, swimming on an ocean swelled with pride and self-conceit."[37] Doubtless, al-Jāḥiẓ saw some of this conceit in the *shu'ūbī* literature of the clerks which portrayed the ideal ruler as one who gave the greatest positions of honor and privilege to his clerks.

The Iranian landlords and Iranian (or, more often, Iranized Aramean) clerks had survived into the Islamic period as a concealed and subsidiary ruling class who were collectively indispensable to the new Arab Islamic government but, at first, individually of little account. A central prop of their self-respect, their relation to the king, had been removed; and their vague genealogical claims to be descendants of kings seemed laughable to the genealogically minded Arabs who felt that, in any case, the success of Islam had proved that the Divine Hand intended to cancel the warrants

36 See, for example, the references to the Buyids in Maḥmūd ibn 'Uthmān, *Die Vita des Scheich Abū Isḥāq al-Kāzarūnī* (Leipzig: 1948).

37 Al-Jāḥiẓ, "Dhamm al-kuttāb," trans. Ch. Pellat, "Une charge contre les secretaires d'état attribuée à Ǧāḥiẓ," *Hespéris* 43 (1956) 34. The struggle of the clerks to get the recognition and authority they wanted is a central theme of D. Sourdel's *Le Vizirat 'Abbāside* (Damascus: 1959–1960); cf. particularly pp. 718–720 on the contrast with the Sasanian model.

of earlier systems of rule. There can be little doubt that some Arabs in the Umayyad period openly advocated the preservation of this two-tiered ruling system without mixture of the old and new ruling classes. When the Umayyad governor of Mecca in the 2nd/8th century discovered that a non-Arab client had married a woman of the Arab tribe Banū Sulaym, he ordered the husband and wife separated, had the husband whipped two hundred strokes, and had his hair, beard, and eyebrows shaved off. An Arab poet congratulated him on this judgment, saying:

> Since you have judged them as permissibly equal for marriage (*kāfa'ta*) with the daughters of Chosroes, can the *mawālī* (non-Arab clients) [hope to] find anything further?
> For what right is more just for the *mawālī* than the right of slave to join in marriage with a slave?"[38]

I think it is fair to say that if such violent contempt was rare, mild contempt for even the *mawālī* administrative class was common among the Arabs.

Since Arab indifference or contempt for the past of the *'ajam* and particularly of the Iranians had implications for the respect owed landlord and/or secretarial Iranians in the Islamic period, these classes were obliged to produce arguments supporting the importance of their pre-Islamic past. Sometimes these arguments are mere assertions as when Ibn García says: "Lo, we the company of the *mawālī*, give friendship only to those who show friendship for our greatness."[39] A more sophisticated argument tries to equate the value of the pre-Islamic past of the Iranians with that of the Arabs. This argument, of course, had direct implication for the "corpus of humane learning" which Gibb has discussed; for a vast literature on pre-Islamic Arabia had developed, and this literature claimed (sometimes with little reason) that its ultimate purpose was to facilitate the explanation of ḥadīth and the Qur'ān. The *shu'ūbī* poet al-Khurramī discusses the relation of the Arab and non-Arab past when he says: "It does not harm me that the tribes Yuḥābir are not my ancestors, nor that the tribes Jarm and 'Ukl do not count me as one of them. If you do not preserve former glory

38 Abū al-Faraj al-Iṣfahānī, (*supra* n. 35), XVI:107. The *mawālī* (non-Arab clients) are, of course, Muslims.
39 Monroe, (*supra* n. 4), 28.

with the new, what has gone before has not benefited you."[40] Al-Khurramī is saying that if the past does not count, the pre-Islamic Arab past does not count either; but insofar as the pre-Islamic past was a point of honor for anyone, it was equally a point of honor for the Iranians and the Arabs. The idea is carried even further in the lines of Bashshār quoted above; if he has become a client of an Arab tribe, they have acquired nobility by this association, since Bashshār is of the Quraysh—that is, of the very best group—of the *'ajam*. This argument (which has received little attention) quite naturally produced a mushrooming literature on the *miswāk*s, the carnal and culinary appetites and the sins of the ancestors of each side. The enthusiasts for pre-Islamic Arabia had a certain advantage, in that their study of the Arab past did at times provide the explanation of passages in religious literature which might otherwise have remained obscure. In the long run this advantage told, and the so-called "Islamic humanities" included more material on the pre-Islamic past of the Arabs than on that of the Persians. Yet the *shu'ūbī* argument is in no way anti-Islamic, since the Arab and Iranian pasts were both "pagan."

These arguments are a long way from the sentiments concerning equality of men which were discussed at the beginning of this article; the *shu'ūbī* poets we have quoted are arguing, at most, for a parity of honor among the upper classes of two distinct peoples. The *shu'ūbīya* had its origin as a movement with egalitarian tendencies among the Khārijīs, the most egalitarian of early Islamic sects. Since, however, it was reinterpreted by the landlords and clerks for their own purposes, in most (though not all) cases it lost its egalitarian tenor. The *shu'ūbī*s and some of their opponents continued to use a rhetoric that has been mistaken for egalitarianism, but on closer examination has no such meaning. Verse 13 of Sūra XLIX, as we would expect, acts as a sort of magnetic attractor for discussions of equality. The interpretation of the well-known Iranian Shi'ite scholar Muḥammad ibn al-Ḥasan al-Ṭūsī (called by the Shi'ites "Shaykh al-Ṭā'ifa") is worth quoting at length because it is representative of a widespread opinion on the possible egalitarian implications of XLIX:13. Ṭūsī (d. 460/1067) writes:

---

40 Yāqūt, *Mu'jam al-Buldān*, III (Leipzig: 1868) 395, where the editor, Ferdinand Wüstenfeld, vocalizes the poet's name as al-Khurramī. One of these two lines is also quoted by Ibn Qutayba, *Kitāb al-Shi'r*, II (Cairo: 1967) 857, where the poet is given his usual *nisba*, al-Khuraymī.

Al-Balkhī has said: "Men have differed on the virtue (*faḍīla*) of genealogy (*nasab*). Some have denied it, others have affirmed it. Our opinion is that no one is more excellent (*afḍal*) than the righteous (*taqī*) believer, for distinction (*ḥasab*) and genealogy (*nasab*) are no substitute for religiosity (*dīn*) in any way, because the two of them have [at most] an excellence (*faḍl*) like that of fur over canvas ... and like the superiority of the elder (*shaykh*) over the youth [i.e., a superiority only over comparable things, not over religiosity]. Men are in agreement (*al-ijmāʿ wāqiʿ*) that if an elderly man and a youth be equal in excellence and religiosity, the elderly man is given preference to the youth and is more revered and honored. The same is the case with the father and the son ... and the master and his slave. This is a matter about which intelligent men have no dispute. Similarly, if two men should be equal in religiosity and one of them had male-kinship (*qarāba*) with the Messenger of God ... it would be necessary to give precedence to the one related to the Messenger of God ... Similarly, if one of two people had ancestors (*ābāʾ*) known for excellence and good character and noble deeds and dignity (*waqār*) and bravery (*najda*) and cultivation (*adab*) and learning (*ʿilm*) it would be according to men's natures (*ṭabāʾiʿ*) to give him precedence over the other. If it is said: It is according to human nature to give precedence to men of wealth, in which case [if your argument is correct] wealth and riches would have to be considered nobility (*sharaf*), we answer: Just so; we do not deny or reject this ... though the poorer man who spends his money appropriately is better than the man who does not spend his money ... Similarly, as for a man who has distinction (*ḥasab*) and nobility through his ancestors, yet is himself immoral, foolish and vulgar, a pious, noble-minded man without distinctions [through the deeds of his ancestors] (*ḥasab*) would be better than he in those characteristics (*awṣāf*) which are evident. The distinction (*ḥasab*) of that foolish man would be something which increases the bad consequences of his deeds.[41]

41 Ṭūṣī, *al-Tibyān fī Tafsīr al-Qurʾān*, ed. Ahmad Habib Qusayr al-ʿAmili (Najaf, Maktab al-Iʿlām al-Islāmī: 1409/1988–89) IX:352–353. Respect for wealth is not an unusual sentiment in this context. Two commentaries on XLIX:13 quote the ḥadīth from the collection of al-Tirmidhī: "*Ḥasab* is wealth (*māl*) and nobility (*karam*) is righteousness"; al-Qurṭubī, (*supra* n. 8), XVI: 345, and al-Baghawī, (*supra* n. 21), IX:88. *Ḥasab* means

Many of the commentaries make this point and they often add a well-known ḥadīth which, in fact, seems to refer directly to XLIX:13:

> Abū Hurayra related that, when the Messenger of God was asked who among men was noblest (*akram*), He replied: "The noblest among men is the most righteous (*atqā*)." "Oh Prophet, this is not what we are asking," they said. Muḥammad then said, "The noblest of men is Joseph, God's Prophet, son of God's Prophet, son of God's Prophet, son of God's Prophet, son of [Abraham] the Friend of God." "This is not what we are asking you," they said. So He said, "Then are you asking me about the origins [from which nobility was derived] among the Arabs?" When they replied that they were, He said, "The best (*khiyār*) of you in the pre-Islamic period are the best of you in Islam if they truly understand the law (of Islam)."[42]

The message of the commentators who quote this ḥadīth is not very different from the message in the long quote from Ṭūsī; the commentators believe that this verse justifies only a very limited degree of egalitarianism in our present worldly life. All commentators are agreed that the nobility of piety outweighs all other forms of nobility; but many commentators remark on the practical and theological difficulties in deciding who is most righteous. In discussing part of an earlier verse in the same Sūra (XLIX:11), "Oh believers, do not let one group mock another, who may perhaps be better than they, or let some women [mock other] women, who may perhaps be better than they," al-Qurṭubī follows the main trend among commentators when he says that however a man may seem outwardly, he may be pure of heart—in which case the man who ridicules him "would do himself an injustice by belittling one whom God honors (*ʿazzama*)."[43]

A society of degrees, a hierarchy in which points of honor gave each man a rank on the ladder which extended from the lowest to the noblest of men, was an idea that many Iranians (and Arabs), whether *shuʿūbī* or anti-*shuʿūbī*, strongly supported. When al-Rūdhrāwarī tells us that ʿAḍud

---

the total accumulation of distinctions acquired by a man's own deeds and the deeds of his ancestors.

42 Al-Bukhārī, *al-Jāmiʿ al-Ṣaghīr*, ed. M.L. Krehl, II (Leiden: 1864) 348. Slightly different versions of this ḥadīth are found in other chapters of al-Bukhārī and in almost all the major early collections of ḥadīth.

43 Al-Qurṭubī, (*supra* n. 8), XVI:318.

al-Dawla (d. 372/983) was a great ruler because he did not give to any of his followers more than his "station" (*manzila*) required, he is echoing a central theme in the tradition of early Islamic (and particularly Iranian Islamic) social thought.[44] Although the *shu'ūbīya* has sometimes been loosely labeled an egalitarian movement (as it was at its origin and in some of its rarer manifestations) we have seen that the *shu'ūbīya* controversy soon reflected rival principles of social hierarchy. As the Qur'ān commentaries show, neither the *shu'ūbīs* nor the anti-*shu'ūbīs* had difficulty in interpreting the apparent egalitarian tenor of XLIX:13 to allow a division of society into a hierarchy of degrees (which, incidentally, should not be confused with the modern divisions of social class). The social form into which Iranian society was cast by what Burke has called the common agreement, was, therefore, not egalitarian—as the verses of Bashshār and other *shu'ūbī* poets show. It was, instead, elaborately hierarchical.

In fact, the seeming egalitarianism found in religious contexts in medieval Islamic literature is egalitarian only in its other-worldly implications. It is a condemnation of pride, that sinful attitude of the soul before the Almighty rather than an encouragement for men to cast off or disregard the differences of rank which separated them in their present life. The sentiment expressed is akin to the sentiment which Huizinga describes among Western Europeans of the later Middle Ages—a contemplation of the approaching equality of men in death which consoles men for the inequities of this world, in short, a kind of *memento mori*.[45] This further permutation in the understanding of XLIX:13 is also found in the Qur'ān commentaries, where Ibn 'Abbās is quoted as saying, "The nobility (*karam*) of this world is wealth (*ghinā'*) and of the next is righteousness (*taqwā*)."[46] But the fullest discussions of the equality of men in death are to be found in the commentaries on verse 101 of Sūra XXIII of the Qur'ān: "When the trumpet [of Resurrection and judgment] will be sounded, there will no longer be genealogies (*ansāb*) among them on that day, nor will they question each other." The commentators dwell with fascination on the astonishment that will so overcome men at the trumpet blast that they will forget the affections caused by family ties and stand isolated, stripped of worldly distinctions, before their Creator. This theme, with its strong implication of the futility of human pretensions—that the spider would

44 Al-Rūdhrāwarī, *Dhayl Tajārib al-'Umam* (Cairo: 1916) 74.

45 J. Huizinga, *The Waning of the Middle Ages* (London: 1952) 53–54.

46 Al-Baghawī, (*supra* n. 21), IV:88.

become chamberlain in the palace of the Caesars, that the mighty should look on and despair—was always a favorite theme of Persian writers. As a theme that combined both fear of loss and consolation for the inequities of this world, it was well designed to produce a shudder of both pleasure and dread in those who contemplated it. Rūdakī (d. 329/940), standing at the very origins of modern Persian literature, refers to XXIII:101 for this effect: "All these things on the day of death will be the same; you will not be able to distinguish them one from the other."[47] This sentiment could be given secular meaning as the Jacqueries did in fourteenth-century Europe and as the Khārijīs did on occasion in the Islamic world; but in the Islamic contexts of the centuries we are examining, it seems usually to have been only an exhortation to men of privilege to use that privilege with justice and piety.

If the *shu'ūbīya* controversy touched on such important issues of self-conception, why did the controversy disappear after the 6th/12th century? Part of the answer is given by H.A.R. Gibb when he points out that the great Arabic prose writers from al-Jāḥiẓ to Ibn Qutayba admitted a limited part of the Persian materials admired by the *shu'ūbīs* after which no later (or excluded) Persian works "entered into Arabic literature or the standard Islamic works on Ethics." Gibb suggests that the canon was closed because the "Sasanian strands which had been woven into the fabric of Muslim thought were, and remained, foreign to its native constitution."[48] But then many of the later works of Persian ethics and literature did enter the canon of Turkish and Indian Muslim humanities. Were the Turks and Indians less aware of the foreignness of these works to their Islamic beliefs?

Again, the commentaries on XLIX:13 are of some help. The mid-4th/10th-century commentator, 'Ali ibn Ibrāhīm al-Qumī (or al-Qomi, from western Iran as his name indicates) understands XLIX:13 strictly according to the interpretation ascribed by some to Ibn 'Abbās and by

---

47 *Ganj-e Sokhan*, ed. Dh. Safa, I (Tehran: 1339 solar/1960–61) 9. In his essay, "Manāqib al-Turk," in *Rasā'il*, ed. 'Abd al-Salam M. Harun (Cairo: 1963) 35, Al-Jāḥiẓ describes with stunning effect how the scores between men will be made equal only in death: "It is not possible for this world (*al-dunyā*) to be purified and cleansed of corruption and misfortune until all created beings die, and the world becomes equable for its inhabitants (*tastawīya li-ahlihā*) ... for that [purity] is a characteristic of the world of reward (*dār al-jazā'*) [heaven], not of the world of [striving to do worthy] deeds (*dār al-'amal*)." Compare the sentiment of a late 4th/10th- or early 5th/11th-century poet who is quoted by Tha'ālibī, *Yatīma*, IV (Cairo: 1377/1957–58) 159: "When hope is lost among men, then all men are equals (*akfā'*)."

48 Gibb, (*supra* n. 5), 72.

others to Ja'far al-Ṣādiq; the *shu'ūb* are the *'ajam* and the *qabā'il* are the Arabs. He adds that the verse is a refutation of pride in *ḥasab* and *nasab*, for as Muḥammad said on the day he conquered Mecca, "God has removed from you the baseless pride of the period of ignorance and its rivalry of boasting of ancestry. The Arabic language (*al-'arabīya*) is not a father and a mother; it is an understandable speech (*lisānun nāṭiqun*) and whoever speaks in it is an Arab."[49] Al-Qumī may have also been referring to the spiritual aspect of speech, that is, whoever has meaningful converse with God; but the exoteric meaning of his words is supported by other passages.[50]

To offer men who spoke Arabic recognition as Arabs was an acknowledgment that it was highly desirable to be an Arab; but it was also an invitation to men to vote with their tongues. Much of the Middle East chose to speak Arabic, and by this token they came to assume that they were descended from the ancient Arabs even if they had lost the intermediate genealogical steps that would explain this descent. Most of the people of the Iranian plateau spoke Persian or some related language. Now that the Iranians of the plateau were writing popular literature in their own language, they were no longer closely engaged in a dialogue with the genealogically minded Arabs—who had, in any case, through sedentarization and assimilation, become much less genealogically minded. But even more important, outside of Spain the *shu'ūbīya* controversy had been a controversy largely among the *'ajam* themselves; it is remarkable how many of the anti- *shu'ūbīs* like Ibn Qutayba and al-Zamakhsharī were non-Arabs. Eventually, the Aramean clerks of southern Iraq had become Arab clerks. Similarly, numerous Arabs had been broadcast throughout Iran as landowners by the original conquest and had held onto their Arab genealogies tenaciously for three or four hundred years. Eventually, they ceased to identify themselves with the Arabic-speaking peoples who were their Western neighbors, and—as local histories testify—they became increasingly identified with the pretensions of the Iranian landlord and administrative classes. For them, as for all Persian-speaking peoples, the canon remained open and even ethical thinkers felt free to add new "Sasanian" stories to their works, as Ghazālī (d. 505/1111) did in his *Nasīḥat al-Mulūk*.

Ibn Qutayba had already advocated the assimilation of the upper classes in that humane and intelligent book *Kitāb al-'Arab aw al-Radd*

49 Al-Qumī, *Tafsīr al-Qumī*, II (Najaf: 1387/1967–68) 322, ending: *fa-man takallama bihī fa-huwa 'arabī*.

50 Cf. Goldziher, (*supra* n. 5), 111–112.

'alā al-Shu'ūbīya. Ibn Qutayba begins by claiming that the most ardent *shu'ūbīs* were the refuse from the lower orders of the *'ajam*. "Now the noblemen (*ashrāf*) of the *'ajam*, their men of importance and their men of religion understand what is to their advantage and disadvantage; and they consider a proven genealogy to be a sign of nobility."[51] Many of the most ardent *shu'ūbīs* like the Sāmānid vizier al-Jayhānī, were anything but men of the lower orders; nevertheless Ibn Qutayba, who wants to encourage the upper classes of the *'ajam* to identify with the Arabs, tries to win these upper classes over by assuming they are not *shu'ūbīs* and that they have genealogies as reliable as those of the Arabs. As for pride in the Persian past, Ibn Qutayba continues:

> only the sons of their kings and of their high officials and clerks and chamberlains and their mounted warriors have a point of pride in the kingship (*mulk*) of Persia. But as for a man from the masses (*'urḍ*) of the *'ajam* and from their common people (*'awāmm*) for whom no *nasab* (genealogy) is known, and who has no celebrated ancestor, what then is his share in the thrones and crown of Chosroes ...? If he were to say, [I have a share] since I am one of the *'ajam* and Chosroes was one of the *'ajam*, then welcome to the common proverb: "Every mixed breed camel has the traits of all its ancestors," [i.e., can be ascribed to any one of its purebred ancestors].[52]

Ibn Qutayba then points out that *'ajam* once ruled the greater part of the earth; "then are all of these (*'ajam* who ruled) noblemen (*ashrāf*)? Where are the base and lowly, the sweepers and the cuppers? ... Did they all become extinct so that not one of [their issue] survived, while the sons of kings and of the noblemen survived ?"[53] The *shu'ūbīya* was, as we have said, a diffuse movement which evoked a wide variety of responses; there is no canonical *shu'ūbī* or anti-*shu'ūbī* program. Ibn Qutayba, unlike some anti-*shu'ūbīs*, goes part way to meet the objection of the *shu'ūbīs*. Ibn Qutayba who, in this same treatise affirms his own Persian origin, in effect

51 Ibn Qutayba, *Kitāb al-'Arab*, in *Rasā'il al-Bulaghā*, ed. Kurd Ali (Cairo: 1946) 345.
52 Ibn Qutayba, (*supra* n. 51), 350. The proverb in Kurd Ali's text is given as "*ibn jār al-nijār*," which seems to be a misreading of the proverb "*kullu nijār (ibilin) nijāruhā*," given with the meaning as translated above by Jawharī, (*supra* n. 26), I:823, and quoted from Jawharī by Ibn Manẓūr, (*supra* n. 20), III:585.
53 Ibn Qutayba, *Kitāb al-Shi'r* (*supra* n. 40), 351.

believes that the new Arab ruling class and the older Iranian ruling class can enjoy shared genealogical prejudice against their "rootless" subordinates. In Iran, the assimilation of the two ruling classes eventually took place; but it took place because both classes accepted a mixed territorial and genealogical self-definition, and because they found themselves united by a community of language (and its shared literature) which was distinct from the community of the Arabs. As the Iranian and Arab worlds drew apart, and the Arab and non-Arab ruling classes in Iran became one, the *shuʿūbīya* controversy no longer had any reason to exist.

In the light of these passages, I want to suggest an answer to the question implicit in the quotation from Burke—that is, in what sense did the Iranians have a common agreement as to the ties which made them a people? In answering this question, we should, as suggested, pay attention to the form into which this society cast itself, since this form expresses the nature of the agreement. I would emphasize that we are talking only about educated Iranians who could record their opinions, not about peasants whose feelings of group identity are lost to history. Literate Iranians saw themselves as a people joined by their shared tie to *Irān-zamin*, the heartland of Iran. Correspondingly they assumed that those accepting a special tie to this land were of common ancestry, even though they could not recount their genealogies person by person back to a fictive ancestor, as even the non-noble Arab did to Ishmael or Qaḥṭān. In the opinion of many Iranians, the warrant for the continued existence of such a people in the Islamic period was to be found in the Qur'ān, where it was explicitly stated that God Himself made tribes and peoples. Yet if the division between the Iranians as a people—between their *shaʿb* and other *shuʿūb*—was acceptable to God, regional and social divisions among Iranians continued to be just as important. Some of these divisions were geographical, which was natural enough among a people who identified themselves in terms of the city or *shahr* and region or *maḥallat* from which they came. Doubtless the inhabitants of each region considered themselves for some purposes to constitute a people. Alongside these geographical divisions there existed an elaborate horizontal division of Iranian society into a hierarchy of degrees. Privileged Iranians, especially landlords and clerks, shared a pride in their Iranian past and resented the derogation of this past. They did so partly because such derogation also called into question their claim to be men who ranked in the upper levels of this hierarchy.

If the description of these Iranians was not overtly political, it nonetheless had important implications for the shape of Iranian politics in this period. There is very little evidence that Iranians felt their political life to be deficient if they could not express their group feeling by having their own national state—what we would call self-determination. A government that protected their portion of *Irān-zamin* and kept men in the stations that were proper to them was an acceptable government. Government was personal, and therefore dynastic concepts of government had been adapted to the Iranian style of self-identification which we have described. In this respect medieval Iran partially resembled early modern Europe. Many historians have remarked on what seems at first a paradox: that in the sixteenth century when nationalism came into full flower the policy of European rulers was, as Huizinga characterizes it, "above all a dynastic policy."[54] Iranian group feeling in the 4th/10th and 5th/11th centuries is hardly a mirror image of the nationalism of sixteenth-century Europe. For one thing, Iranians of that period were ready to see *Irān-zamin* divided among different rulers, and many Iranians were probably indifferent to such divisions, while most Europeans of the sixteenth century could not easily contemplate the redivision of their national states into independent political units for any long period. Yet there is a certain resemblance. Just as the Hapsburgs could succeed to the throne of Spain and become acceptable rulers because they supported the prevailing social values of the society they ruled, so the Seljuk Turks could rule part or all of Iran without contradiction to Iranian group feeling, insofar as their rule was consonant with the territorial and cultural responsibility which educated Iranians expected to be fulfilled by a ruler of *Irān-zamin*. Like early modern Europeans, Iranians of the early Islamic period had a dynastic and territorial understanding of the relation of political power to group feeling. In both societies, the power of the government was mediated through an elite of local administrators and men of influence whose group identification was territorial and cultural. For this elite, questions of racial ancestry were secondary justifications of the established territorial and cultural unity of the area for which they were spokesmen. Yet kingship was still highly

54 J. Huizinga, "Patriotism and Nationalism in European History," in *Men and Ideas: History, the Middle Ages, the Renaissance, Essays*, trans. J.S. Holmes and Hans van Marle (New York, Meriden Books: 1959) 128. In this essay and in his *Erasmus of Rotterdam* (London: 1952) Huizinga argues very persuasively that it is appropriate to speak of certain limited kinds of nationalism in the context of medieval Europe.

personal, and the king ruled not because he was the "fullest expression" of the character of these elites, but because he had established himself as the personal master of the members of these elites. Within their understanding of Islam, the Iranians had found a self-definition which was strong enough to survive a long succession of non-Iranian masters.

Bureaucracy and the Patrimonial State in Early Islamic Iran and Iraq

History is often written in terms of heroes and villains; but in the case I wish to raise for consideration in this essay, the heroes and villains are the same people—those men who, because of their talent in writing documents, were called in Arabic "men of the pen," and who are usually referred to as clerks or secretaries by Western scholars of Islamic history. The prominence of these "hero-villains" emerged at the end of the Abbasid period in the late 3rd/9th and early 4th/10th centuries, when bureaucrats or clerks were encouraged to try, and *did* try, to become a surrogate ruling class of a vast empire, evolving in the following hundred years from a surrogate ruling class into a group of indispensable specialists acting as a buffer between the actual ruling classes and the subject population. In this process, bureaucrats were transformed from a group dependent on the sovereign for most of its power and prestige, into an order of society which drew its support from other social groups as much as from the sovereign's will.

As a consequence of this change, bureaucracy itself in this second stage changed from a relatively hierarchical method of administration to a much less hierarchical method. In light of this transformation, we can consider the relation of both varieties of bureaucracy to the idea of patrimonialism, the category most often evoked in studies of the administration of stable, extensive, and literate pre-modern states.

We all know, or at least we think we know, why bureaucrats, in every period and in every part of the world, are villains. We automatically suppose

Author's note: This article was first published as: "Bureaucracy and the Patrimonial State in Early Islamic Iran and Iraq," in Ihsan Abbas (ed.), *al-Abḥāth* 29 (1981) 25–36, Journal of the Center for Arab and Middle East Studies, Faculty of Arts and Sciences, American University of Beirut. It is based on a paper read at the conference held in Hamadan in 1977 on the history of administration in Iran. Reproduced with permission.

the bureaucrat to be small-minded, inefficient and ill-mannered. The early Muslims often felt the same way. The Islamic empire had been created by warriors who looked down on the people they had conquered. These soldiers, much as they may have disagreed on some matters, agreed to recognize their common ties in the new government. After all, an Arab in Spain at first had more in common in culture, language and religion with an Arab in Central Asia, than did either Arab with the subject populations of these areas, who were as yet overwhelmingly non-Muslim. Clerks were the petty functionaries left over from the defeated regimes who, after the great battles had been fought, emerged from hiding ready to collect taxes and keep accounts for the new conquerors. This contempt for clerks continued even after the Abbasids came to power. True, the Abbasids employed non-Arab clerks, who were increasingly often converts to Islam, in all sorts of positions hitherto reserved for Arabs. But they did so at least in part because these non-Arabs could make no sensible claim to descent from the religiously prestigious families which had surrounded Muḥammad. These non-Arab clerks, therefore, could not conceivably aspire to replace the Abbasids as rulers. The non-Arab clerks were, in one view, very simply the "creatures" of the caliph.[1]

This contempt for clerks is nowhere expressed more eloquently than in the treatise *Dhamm Akhlāq al-Kuttāb* by al-Jāḥiẓ, who died in 255/868. "What proves that the profession of clerk is detestable," wrote al-Jāḥiẓ, "is that only subordinates or people of, so to speak, servile condition practice it. We have never seen a great man assume this profession, or even share the labor of his own secretary. Any secretary is condemned to a constant loyalty and is expected to suffer [in such loyalty] ... [yet] he himself has no right to impose any condition [on his employer]; on the contrary, he is blamed for his slowness at the slightest failure, even if it is not his fault ... The slave has at least the right to complain to his master, and to ask to have his situation changed; but a clerk cannot demand back pay, or even leave his master if his master is slow to pay him. A clerk has the situation of a slave; and among slaves, they occupy the rank of idiots. In spite of all this, they attain the pinnacle of boasting, the summit of vanity, swimming on an ocean swelled with pride and self-conceit!"[2]

1 See my book *Loyalty and Leadership in an Early Islamic Society* (Princeton, N.J., Princeton University Press: 1980) 82–93.

2 Al-Jāḥiẓ, *Āthār al-Jāḥiẓ*, ed. 'Umar Abu al-Nasr (Beirut: 1969) 53–54; see also Charles Pellat, "Une charge contre les secrétaires d'état attribuée à Ğāḥiẓ," *Hespéris* 43 (1956) 34.

We possess an extensive and contrasting description of these clerks and of administration in general, composed just fifty years after this passage was written, at a time when the clerks were swollen not only with pride but also with real power—a rare and possibly unique moment in the history of the early Islamic Middle East—and when the clerks came close to occupying a position which corresponded with their own high opinion of themselves. But first, let us consider the background to these events. The Abbasid Empire had been founded by an army from Khorasan and had introduced into the administration officials from this province, the most notable of which were the famous Barmakids. But the caliph we associate with the Barmakids, Hārūn al-Rashīd, actually did everything possible, albeit unintentionally, to destroy the cooperation between Khorasan and the seat of the empire, Iraq—a cooperation which had been the cornerstone of Abbasid power. First, he disgraced all the Barmakids and destroyed the tradition of administrative cooperation. Then he gave Iraq and the title of caliph to one son, al-Amīn, and full control of Khorasan and the heir-apparency to another, al-Ma'mūn. In the inevitable civil war that broke out after Hārūn's death, al-Ma'mūn and the army of Khorasan conquered Iraq. But the breach between the two provinces could not be healed, and Khorasan began its gradual drift toward independence.

The Abbasid caliphs thus had to seek alternatives to Khorasanian military and administrative skills; they found these alternatives in the corps of Turkish slave soldiers and the Iranized Aramean clerks of southern Iraq. In the Samarra period the Turkish soldiers had everything their way. But ultimately the Turkish generals realized that in their infighting they were killing each other off even more rapidly than they were killing off caliphs, and that the badly administered empire not only could no longer pay their salaries but threatened to disappear altogether before the spectacularly successful rebellions of the Zanj and the Ṣaffārids. Al-Muwaffaq, the brother of the Abbasid caliph, actually won the full support of the Turks, defeated the Zanj and the Ṣaffārids, and restored Abbasid rule to the heartlands of the empire.

Al-Muwaffaq, however, did much more than this. He set in motion the process of administrative reform which was completed by his son, the caliph al-Mu'taḍid, and his grandson, the caliph al-Muktafī. These three men created entirely new ministries for auditing the existing financial bureaus of the government and tried in general to make the chain of command in the bureaucracy much clearer than it had been before. The greatest handiwork of this reform was the post of vizier (*wazīr* in Arabic).

We are so used to thinking that the vizier was the greatest official under the monarch in pre-modern Islamic government that it is important to emphasize that the vizier acquired this position on a regular basis only in the reign of al-Muʿtaḍid, who ruled from 279/892 to 289/902. Up to this time most, though not all, of the Abbasid caliphs had had viziers. But some of these viziers had had quite restricted functions, and almost none of them had had full control of all parts of the administration. From the reign of al-Muʿtaḍid, the vizier was the voice of the caliph in the day-to-day affairs of government. He had control of virtually everything, including matters related to the army; and as the stand-in for the caliph, he was so respected by the army that he often led them on campaigns. He was first after princes of the blood in court ceremonial; and he maintained his new dignity by an elaborate style of life. But at no moment did the caliph give up his personal surveillance of the vizier. Having created a more hierarchical administration, the caliph needed a technical expert at its top to keep the administrative instrument finely tuned; but the caliph did not need a rival and did not allow the vizier to overestimate his place.[3]

It is against this background that we should consider the remarkable events of 295/908, during the final illness of the third of these reforming caliphs, al-Muktafī. His vizier, riding home with the heads of the most important ministries (*dīwāns*) of the government, consulted with them on the succession to the caliphate. We have at least three accounts of this conversation, and all three agree in most essential respects. While there is no reason to believe any of them to be accurate, they are all written by historians who were clerks and lived close to the period of the events, so these accounts represent the shrewdest possible guess as to what was likely to have been said. When asked whom the vizier should support as the successor to the dying caliph, who could not speak, the head of the *dīwān al-kharāj* (Ministry of Land Tax) said to the vizier, "Do not nominate somebody who has been in society and has practical experience, who knows how things go in this world and has too shrewd ideas as to who is the real owner of what." "Whom do you suggest?" the vizier asked. He replied, "Al-Muʿtaḍid's son, Jaʿfar." "What," said the vizier, "Jaʿfar is only a child!" "True enough," replied the other, "but he is the son of al-Muʿtaḍid [who was generally admired as the ideal caliph] ... Why bring in a man who will really govern, a man who knows how much property we clerks own,

3 See Dominique Sourdel, *Le Vizirat ʿabbāside de 749 à 936* (Damascus: 1959–60).

who will take the administration into his own hands and regard himself as independent of us? Why not deliver the empire to a person who will leave you to administer it?" The argument seemed irresistible. The vizier chose the thirteen-year-old Ja'far, who became the next caliph with the throne title al-Muqtadir.[4]

His long reign from 295/908 to 320/932 was the apogee of the power of the clerks in the early Islamic period. The clerks held control of the government not only during al-Muqtadir's childhood but also in subsequent years, since he grew up to be a weak and frivolous ruler who did not care to follow the affairs of government closely. During their period of control, the clerks squandered the resources of the state and showed little concern for the interests of most other important parties. Their leaders, the viziers of the Jarrāḥid and Furātid families, took turns in office, each squeezing the state for as much as he could get, and using the enormous patronage which was allowed by the vizier's full control of the administrative hierarchy to get bribes from his inferiors. The vizier was encouraged to make a fortune during his tenure of office by the certainty that the rival team of clerks, who were languishing in disgrace, would eventually return to power and would be allowed to fine, and often torture, their predecessors. The army, though at first loyal, was inefficient and expensive and was therefore often not sent on campaigns; consequently, provincial governors withheld revenues. Within a period of about twelve years the caliph sold the crown lands and the viziers reduced the pay year to ten, then eight months; but nothing could make the government solvent. At the beginning of the fiscal year of 932 no revenues for 931 remained; the vizier had previously sold a large part of the anticipated revenue of 932 for cash, and the government already had a deficit. In 936 the government abandoned a whole province, Diyār Muḍar, as too expensive to handle.[5]

At first the inefficient and swollen army was loyal to the caliph, in part because it was commanded by men like al-Mu'nis who had been trained under the great reforming caliphs of the three preceding reigns. Then, gradually, the army became conscious of its power; and al-Muqtadir, encouraged by one faction of clerks, decided on a direct contest of strength with the army. The caliph was defeated and killed. With the death of al-Muqtadir, the heyday of the bureaucrats was at an end, and the caliphal

4 Hilāl al-Ṣābī, *Kitāb al-Wuzarā'*, ed. 'Abd al-Sattar Ahmad Farraj (Cairo: 1958) 131.
5 Miskawayh, *Tajārib al-Umam*, ed. H.F. Amedroz, I (Cairo: 1332/1914) 367.

army was in control of Baghdad. Five years later the vizier, who no longer had effective control of the administration, found that the government was, very simply, bankrupt. The vizier went into hiding and the caliph invited the governor of a rich neighboring province to control the army and bureaucracy in exchange for defraying the expenses of the court. So, in 324/936 Abbasid administration, in the sense of administration created and maintained by the Abbasid caliphs, ceased. Rival military regimes fought to be the caliph's keeper until, in 336/945, the relatively stable regime of the Buyids (or Buwayhids) gained and kept this position until the arrival of the Seljuk Turks in the mid-5th/11th century.

With this picture of later Abbasid administration in mind, we can consider in some detail the kind of administration that existed in the following period and, in particular, in the governments of the Buyids. In this discussion it is important to remember that almost all of the regimes which succeeded the Abbasid in the next few hundred years were based on armies of some shared ethnic descent, and that the *amīr*, who owed his position in the first place to his military power, was usually of the same ethnic group as the army. At first, such rulers feared that the solidarity of their armies might somehow be compromised by administrative arrangements which gave the impression that the sovereign and his soldiers were individual employees of some government bureau. Describing the very first *amīrs* of the Buyids, Miskawayh (himself a clerk) wrote:

> The utmost that the vizier or administrator could do [for the earliest Buyids] was to find each day some provision for the *amīr*'s daily expenditure by fining the humble or borrowing from the great, or scheming against someone, whoever he might be, who was suspected of affluence. Often for a day or even two days they were unable to provide barley for the horses. The expenses of the *amīr*'s dependents, their salaries, even their bare maintenance had often to be replaced or even left in abeyance for days ... The administrators used to get out of the way [of importuning soldiers], making appointments for nightly gatherings in hidden places, and sometimes going out into the country to hold their meetings on horseback.[6]

6 Miskawayh, *Tajārib al-Umam*, ed. H.F. Amedroz, II (Cairo: 1332/1915) 280.

The new military regimes soon realized that they needed bureaucrats—not because of any sympathy with their subjects, but because clerks were needed to guarantee a steady income for their armies. These armies needed sizable numbers of bureaucrats directly attached to them as paymasters, quartermasters, currency experts, and so forth; and indirectly, as revenue-collecting agents of the state. Eventually, the soldiers even came to recognize that it would *not* be in their long-term interest to destroy commerce and cultivation by arbitrarily extracting money from any person who fell into their hands. Their commander, therefore, usually tried to tax according to some principle understood by the subject population. When a clerk was not available to explain such a principle and put it into effect, the soldiers were at a great disadvantage. For example, the repeated expeditions by the Buyids of Iraq against their northern neighbors, the Ḥamdānids of Mosul, were failures because, though the Ḥamdānids always fled from the Buyids, they also took every local clerk (*kātib baladī*) out of Mosul with them. The Buyids, too poor to occupy Mosul for a long period, were thereby left without the local bureaucratic help needed even to collect the cost of their campaigns.[7]

A bureaucracy was also needed to help preserve order in the cities. All the tribes which founded states in this period had lived fairly near to great cities for generations and apparently felt the awe which the organization and luxury of cities can inspire. They were also aware of the strategic and psychological importance of cities. When an Arab chieftain of the Banū 'Uqayl, a group which founded a relatively long-lived dynasty in northern Syria at the end of the 4th/10th century, heard that his younger brother had taken Mosul and was ruling it, he insisted that his younger brother recognize his suzerainty over Mosul. The older brother did so because an adviser had warned him, "If the town becomes your [younger] brother's, he will be the *amīr* and you will be the bandit."[8]

The need for clerks and administrators accounts for the elements of continuity between the great imperial administrative apparatus of the Abbasid civilian regime and the smaller regimes which followed. First, there was a continuity of the categories of administrative life. Government was still arranged in *dīwāns*, or ministries, which were subdivided into *majālis*, or committees. There was also a continuity in the categories of

7 Miskawayh, (*supra* n. 6), II:382.
8 Al-Rūdhrāwarī, *Dhayl Tajārib al-Umam*, ed. H.F. Amedroz (Cairo, 1334/1916) 281.

administrative personnel. Clerks still had the special styles of handwriting, of composition, and even of dress which they had developed in the Abbasid period, and which made clear their distinctive status in life. This feeling of distinction was preserved in the later period. I will quote only one of the many examples which could be brought forward to show this. In 362/973 the Buyid *amīr* of Baghdad chose as his vizier the master of the king's kitchens, an important post which included control of the customs houses on the Tigris. Miskawayh, who was a Buyid clerk as well as an historian and a philosopher, says that this new vizier, who had not been trained as a clerk, still tried to present himself before the *amīr* girt with a large greasy napkin, and was only persuaded by the *amīr* himself not to do so. The episode is almost certainly an invention of the envious clerks, for it seems very unlikely that an official who had previously held a relatively high position in the court and administration should be so ignorant of court ceremonial.[9] Alongside the clerks we also still find the *jahbadh*s, the experts in currency, in writing receipts and in money matters in general, who continue to dominate certain financial aspects of the administration.

Another element of continuity, even more striking than the continuity in categories, is the continuity of much of the membership of the administration. The upper ranks of the administration changed rapidly, as we would expect, with the changes of regimes and rulers; and the personnel of the lower ranks remain largely unknown to us. Yet from the information available to us it seems that much of the personnel of the middle ranks of administration remained in office in spite of all the changes which took place in this period. Such continuity is not surprising if we remember the need for the special skills and knowledge of local financial affairs which the clerks possessed. The career of Aḥmad ibn Muḥammad ibn Jaʿfar ibn Thawāba provides only one of several examples of this continuity. Ibn Thawāba succeeded his father as head of the *dīwān al-rasāʾil* in 312, at the height of the bureaucratic domination of Abbasid government. He remained in charge of that office until 349, fifteen years after the Buyids had established themselves in Baghdad. He was the very type of the colorless, faceless bureaucrat suited to survive the tumult of the eight changes of regime which took place in Baghdad during his tenure of office. He is

9 Miskawayh, (*supra* n. 6), II:313.

so faceless, in fact, that we would probably not even know of his existence if his eloquent style had not earned him a place in Yāqūt's *Irshād al-Arīb*.[10]

A third element of continuity was the vizierate. At first, the title vizier was not granted by the new regimes, especially the Buyids, to anyone, even their leading secretaries. The vizierate in the Abbasid period had originally been a semi-religious office, inspired by the example of Aaron as described in the Qur'ān.[11] The caliph, as a figure of religious authority, was to have a spokesman called vizier (*wazīr*) just as Moses, the Prophet, had had a spokesman/helper called *wazīr*. It was, therefore, a strange idea that any ruler except a caliph should have a vizier. The new regimes were also reluctant to grant anyone the title vizier because they did not want to recreate an office which might rival their own office in practice, and certainly did rival it in Islamic political thought, which explained this new crop of rulers as special kinds of viziers. These rulers, according to this theory, had *wizārat al-tafwīḍ*, the vizierate of delegated authority, since the caliph had supposedly wearied of affairs of state and delegated to them all the practical business of government. As a consequence of their fear of a rival, these rulers did not even allow their first secretaries control of all the bureaus of government; for, after all, while an Abbasid vizier could never by any stretch of the imagination become an Abbasid caliph, why could a vizier, who was more generous and efficient than his master, not replace his master as ruler?[12]

Eventually, however, the force of circumstances and the increasing stability of the Buyids and similar regimes encouraged the new rulers to put their secretaries in full charge of the government and to restore the title vizier. The first viziers of the Buyids kept themselves scrupulously separate socially and in style of life from the army, and so reassured their masters that they had no intention of winning the favor of their soldiers. Furthermore, as time passed the new regimes were seen as stable regimes of Daylamīs, Kurds, and so forth, and not as soldiers of fortune who were here today and gone tomorrow. Consequently, ethnic identity was understood by the troops and by the rest of the population to be a somewhat more important qualification for rulership. For example, in a regime which Kurds had established and maintained, the army no longer regarded themselves

---

10 Yāqūt, *Irshād al-Arīb fī Ma'rifat al-Adīb*, ed. D.S. Margoliouth, 2nd ed., 5 vols, (London, Luzac: 1923–31), II:80.

11 Sūrat Ṭāhā XX:29; Sūrat al-Furqān XXV:35.

12 Cf. 'Abd al-'Aziz al-Duri, *Al-Nuẓum al-Islāmīya* (Baghdad: 1950) 229.

as temporarily fortunate Kurds, but as a governing order in society which thought it natural to have a fellow Kurd as ruler. Judged on this basis, most clerks did not qualify to become rulers.

Yet, if many of the categories of administration and their middle-ranking members were preserved from the late Abbasid period, the style of bureaucracy had changed. The vast bureaucracy of the late Abbasids, which included over twenty *dīwāns*, had been drastically reduced. Very often we find that a function performed by a whole *dīwān* in Abbasid times was now performed by a single official, usually called *nāẓir*, or inspector. This reduction was, of course, the result of the reduction in the size of states; but it was also the result of the assignment of revenue-collecting rights to individuals in the form of *iqṭāʿ* and of the very common but little-studied *tasbīb*.[13] Assignment of government revenues to individuals was part of a general internal fragmentation of the state which changed the style of administration for hundreds of years. The government also assigned to tribes the task of protecting certain strategic roads in exchange for subsidies; and these tribal areas were often only loosely controlled by the central government.[14]

Furthermore, while viziers were careful not to behave too much like army officers, all sorts of middle and lower clerks in the administration developed special ties of mutual help with army officers who got better *iqṭāʿ*s, prompter pay and all sorts of favors in exchange for the support these officers gave to the helpful clerk. The general fragmentation in power also allowed local clerks to create closer ties with the local landlords and merchants, so that a local clerk was more essential than ever for implementation of orders from the central administration. Therefore, clerks, with their assignments of *iqṭāʿ*s and *tasbīb*s in place of salaries, with their special associations with tribal leaders, landlords, merchants and—above all—army officers, were no longer members of enormous factions which the vizier, at the pinnacle of a hierarchical administration, could move into office. Administrative tasks were also less clearly defined and discrete. Many officials were assigned to overlapping responsibilities, because a clerk was doing a little bit of everything for a few people. One astonishing result of this change was that bribes no longer flowed uniformly upward; often viziers had to bribe their subordinates, i.e., middle-ranking bureaucrats,

13 On this, see my article "A Note on the *Tasbīb*" (Article 17 here).

14 See the letter of a Kurdish leader to a Buyid general, quoted in Ibn al-Athīr, *Al-Kāmil fī l-Taʾrīkh*, ed, C.J. Tornberg, IX (Leiden: 1867) 138–139.

even to attain the vizierate, because these middle-ranking bureaucrats had backers whom the ruler respected.[15]

Just as astonishing, in light of the former history of the vizierate, was the appearance of joint vizierates, and the extremely common appointment of a deputy vizier. The first joint vizierate that I know of was appointed in 366/976; thereafter, many are mentioned. Formerly, just as in the Neo-Platonic system God, or the One, could create the many only by first producing a Logos which might be interested in (and willing to be tainted by) creating many lesser creatures, so the caliph, who conceived of himself as God's vice regent on earth, created a single proxy who would be willing to create lesser officials. This attitude explains why a single official, instead, for example, of a cabinet, usually carried out the orders of the caliph in early Islamic government. It also provided an elegant means of changing policy without changing regimes or killing too many people—the ruler or caliph could always claim that he had been uninvolved in the misdoings of his vizier, and therefore had himself remained untainted, like the Platonic One, by the acts of his single creation.

This conception had been partly, though not completely, weakened by the collapse of the Abbasid caliphate. The Abbasids, more than most successor states, based their right to rule on a divine mandate. The vizierate, hitherto indivisible, became a divisible office; and this arrangement corresponded with the fragmented and less hierarchical nature of administration. It also corresponded with a general change in attitude, throughout the Middle East, to status acquired through appointment. Gradually, in the late 3rd/9th century, and increasingly in the next three centuries, there appeared dynasties of officials; for, increasingly, people believed that the son of a *qāḍī* was more likely to be a good *qāḍī* than was, for example, the son of a saddler. Consonant with this change, and with the new fragmented sources of support for bureaucrats, was the conception that titles and official status in life were inherited and not achieved. A man through heredity was born of "vizieral" quality; or, at least, once a man had been vizier, his "vizierable" quality had been proved and could not be disregarded. Formerly, a vizier who was dependent for his prestige on appointment by a caliph, on dismissal retained none of his standing as a vizier. In contrast, in the Buyid period, Miskawayh reports that when one ex-vizier met another, the distinguished al-Ḍabbī, in a refuge area in central

15 See, for example, al-Rūdhrāwarī, (*supra* n. 8), 181, 240, 257.

Iran, the one "determined by addressing the other as vizier to teach him that loss of office did not remove the title vizier."[16]

How does all this fit in with the concept of patrimonialism? Many students of bureaucracy distinguish a form of bureaucracy associated with patrimonialism, in which bureaucracy is an expansion of the household of the king. This view is in agreement with the work of several distinguished historians of late medieval and early modern Europe. For example, Professor G.R. Elton in his monumental book, *The Tudor Revolution in Government* (1953), explicitly states that the reign of Henry VIII saw the transition from a household to a national administration. Undoubtedly, in a certain sense the bureaucracies we are describing conform to the type described by Elton and others as household bureaucracies. When the king relaxed his grasp on the apparatus of the state, under the Abbasids or Buyids or Plantagenets, the bureaucracy lost its direction and the state foundered. But this is partly a negative description; it tells us that a concept of the "state," which one served regardless of the personality of the ruler, had not yet appeared. It does not tell us about the character of the medieval bureaucracies of the Middle East. In a sense, Abbasid bureaucracy, especially in its final period, does come close to being an extension of the caliph's household. However, bureaucrats in the post-Abbasid period, while happy to bow down before any ruler, were not really the "king's men" in the European sense. They were an order in society, almost a caste, of technical experts. They were men of some inherited status and of long apprenticeship, who tied together networks of local interest with the passing parade of military regimes. This relationship can, I believe, be shown even more convincingly in a description of local government, as I have attempted to do elsewhere.[17]

The bureaucrats described in the first part of this paper qualified to be called "villains." The Abbasid regime, having lost its original basis of power, temporarily revived when the caliphs created a strange alliance between a slave army and a surrogate ruling class of hierarchically arranged bureaucrats. But the alliance was doomed to failure. The bureaucrats not only acted irresponsibly and bankrupted the state; they also lacked the instruments of power necessary to maintain effective control of the central government.

16 Hilāl al-Ṣābī, *Ta'rīkh*, ed. H.F. Amedroz (Cairo: 1337/1919) 455.
17 See my article "Administration in Buyid Qazvin" (Article **19** here).

When, then, do the bureaucrats assume their guise as "heroes"? Under the new military regimes, the bureaucrats regained some of the importance they had possessed under the Abbasids. There were still *dīwāns*, but they were now manned by bureaucrats who saw themselves as buffers between the various regimes of rapacious soldiers and the people they ruled. Bureaucrats were now part of both worlds, the world of the sovereign's court and the world of his subjects. Let us take as the type of this "hero" a bureaucrat named Ibn Haṣṣūl, who was born in Rayy and served first the Buyids of Rayy, then the Ghaznavids after they conquered the city, and finally the Seljuks, who took Rayy about ten years after the Ghaznavids. With each conquest he was sent to the central court to be watched and examined so as to determine his loyalty and competence. Apparently, he satisfied his new masters on each occasion. Consequently, he was returned to Rayy each time, and to no other city in Iran. Presumably, he knew the finances of Rayy and the surrounding region better than any other living man. He obligingly wrote a book for his last set of masters, the Seljuks, entitled *The Superiority of Turks over Other Ethnic Armies*. In the course of the book he told the Seljuks that part of their superiority over others lay in their willingness to preserve and perpetuate Islamic learning and Islamic kingly tradition, something of which the Seljuks may not yet have been aware.[18] For this is the last—and perhaps the greatest—contribution of the bureaucrats: through their intermediacy between ruler and ruled, they helped to preserve a great deal of the learning and high culture of the Islamic Middle East.

---

18 "*Risāla fī Tafḍīl al-Atrāk*," in *Belleten* 4 (1940) 1–51.

Some Attitudes towards Monarchy and Absolutism in the Eastern Islamic World of the 11th and 12th Centuries

Secular kingship is not an office of great distinction in the early Islamic world. Kingship, or *mulk*, is the quality of Umayyad rule for which this first dynasty of caliphs is most often blamed in the Islamic tradition. Islam, in the view of the overwhelming majority of its early adherents, was meant not to create kingdoms but to bring a divinely appointed polity, based on a Divine Law which would last until the Day of Judgment. The word for king in Arabic, *malik*, was associated with the verb *malaka*, "to possess," and the word is therefore most frequently used in the Qur'ān for God who is, as the Qur'ān repeatedly says, "The King, The Truth" and has *mulk*, "Possession of" (or Sovereignty over) the Heavens and the Earth," just as he is "Possessor (*mālik*) of the Day of Judgment" when He will test men to see how far they have conformed to his revelation. Since the world and its divinely appointed laws belong to God, temporal kings are not really possessors or sovereigns over anything; for, as the Qur'ān says, "Say, oh God, Possessor of Sovereignty (*mālik al-mulk*), You give sovereignty to whomever You choose and take it from whomever You choose" (III:26). The fault of the Umayyads was precisely this, that they acted as if their family collectively possessed sovereignty, instead of acting as "stewards," who administered their trust in full knowledge that they possessed nothing; for the world, and judgment of our conduct in it, belong exclusively to God.

Author's note: This article was first published as: "Some Attitudes towards Monarchy and Absolutism in the Eastern Islamic World of the Eleventh and Twelfth Centuries A.D." in Joel L. Kraemer, Ilai Alon (eds.), *Religion and Government in the World of Islam*, Proceedings of the Colloquium held at Tel-Aviv University 3–5 June 1979, Israel Oriental Studies, X (Tel-Aviv, Tel Aviv University: 1980) 86–91.

Nevertheless, a form of kingship with many of those far-reaching prerogatives which are associated with absolutism became a common and largely accepted feature of Islamic political life by the end of the 6th/12th century. The purpose of this paper is to examine some of the justifications given by Muslim authors in the 5th/11th and 6th/12th centuries for this style of rule, and also to examine some of the limitations on absolute monarchy implied by these justifications. These justifications, however, can only be understood as attempts at creating a political theory congruent with or separate from the political theory developed in the Islamic world in the 1st/7th through 4th/10th centuries, and this paper begins with a brief review of such earlier developments.

The first form of government to appear in the Islamic world after Muḥammad's death was the caliphate; but the exact nature of the caliph's authority and the manner in which he was to be chosen was always strongly disputed. The majority of Muslims accepted that Muḥammad should have a single *khalīfa*, or successor, as leader of the Islamic polity though at first, as we can see from the account of Abū Bakr's election, some Muslims disputed even this principle. As a Medinese tribesman said, "One ruler for us, and one for you, oh men of Quraysh." While this attitude did not die out immediately, the concept that the Islamic state had a single head was almost universally and permanently accepted. Collegial rule was relatively rare in the pre-modern Islamic Middle East—the Qarmaṭī state of the 4th/10th century is one of these rare exceptions—and the only association of collegiality with the caliph was a sentiment among some Muslims that a *shūrā*, or consultative assembly, should choose the caliph, though how such a *shūrā* should itself be chosen, or how it should proceed, was never agreed upon. Although some of the smaller movements in Islam, the Zaydīs and the Khārijīs, accepted that the leaders of two Zaydī or Khārijī states remote from each other might call themselves caliphs, such an arrangement was viewed only as a temporary expedient to allow Zaydīs or Khārijīs to live under the guidance of such a caliph; when such states grew close to one another, the caliphal power was presumably supposed to reside in one individual only.

The caliphate, therefore, unlike the Roman *imperium*, was an indivisible distinction, and established a strong precedence for monocratic rule in Islam. But the function of the caliph was nowhere near as quickly decided. The caliphs themselves tried to extend their sphere of authority by representing themselves not simply as the "successor of Muḥammad," but also as the *Khalīfat Allāh*, "the vice regent of God," a use of the word *khalīfa* which drew some of its strength from the Qur'ānic designation of Adam as God's *khalīfa* on earth. In the actual exercise of government, the caliphs not only appointed judges but they also maintained courts of appeal against oppressive acts, or *maẓālim*, which gave the caliph a judicial function; and some caliphs, like al-Ma'mūn, who ruled from 813 to 833, actually tried to dictate theology to the Islamic community.

By and large, the efforts of the caliph to acquire a "priestly" function failed, and their control of the judiciary in Islam remained limited. Did they de facto exercise absolute power in the state? Certainly, whatever obligation the caliph may have felt to God for the gift of sovereignty in the Islamic community, he felt no such obligation to any of those whom he ruled. Abū al-'Abbās, the first caliph of the Abbasid line, the longest and most important of the medieval dynasties of caliphs, is supposed to have said in his inaugural address in Kufa in 749 C.E.: "Praise be to God who has placed us in respect to Islam and its people in an exalted position. He has informed them of our excellence and made it obligatory for them to render us our right and to love us."[1] If, therefore, the Abbasids disdained any mandate for their rule except that mandate given by God, they also showed that they intended that no class of people in the Islamic world should be exempt from the orders that they would issue. Like any long-lived government, they were loath to alienate major groups under their rule. But the executioner, with his black bag to carry away the head of anyone who incurred the caliph's anger, was a fixture of the Abbasid court meant to warn all his subjects that nobody's life was inviolate.

The whole style of the caliph's life was changed correspondingly. By the end of the Abbasid period the caliph was no longer a sort of paramount chief, coordinating the conquests of the Arab armies, but a remote figure claiming divine sanction and hidden from his subjects by chamberlains and an elaborate court procedure. Such a figure would almost naturally be more feared than loved; and it is therefore not surprising that hardly a single one of his subjects raised a hand to restore the caliph's temporal power during the period in which his governors and generals, while respecting him in name, transformed him into a puppet.

---

1 Al-Ṭabarī, *Ta'rīkh al-Rusul wa-l-Mulūk*, ed. M.J. de Goeje *et al.*, III (Leiden: 1879–1880) 29–33.

By the second quarter of the 4th/10th century this process was complete, and the caliph was stripped of his temporal power; but Islamic thought, as we indicated above, had for at least three centuries been firmly decided that there should be only a single head for the Islamic polity and that his rule should be universal. The new regimes therefore had to justify themselves as something other than caliphs; for it was obvious that they had received authority neither through some mandate from the Islamic community—by a *shūrā*, for example—nor through Muḥammad's designation of their family as a charismatic line of descent.

The justifications actually given for two of the most important of these dynasties, the Ghaznavids and the Seljuks, are fairly typical of the justifications for monarchy used in the Middle East from the 5th/11th to the 7th/13th century—as well as in some later centuries. Bayhaqi, a former vizier of the Ghaznavids, includes in his history of one king of that dynasty a very telling apology for Ghaznavid rule. The Ghaznavids were descended from a Turkish slave soldier who had become a semi-independent governor of a small state in what is presently Afghanistan. The son of this soldier, Maḥmūd, had been famous both for his extremely successful campaigns into Northern India, and for his ostentatious concern for the dignity of the puppet Abbasid caliph and his consequent persecution of those suspected of supporting the counter-caliph in Cairo. The Ghaznavid kings could hardly claim royal descent; but, says Bayhaqi:

> If any defamer or jealous person says that this great house has come from humble or unknown origins, the answer is that God, since the creation of Adam, has decreed that kingship be transferred from one religious polity (*umma*) to another and from one group to another. The greatest testimony to what I am saying is the words of the Creator: "Say, oh God, Possessor of Sovereignty, You give sovereignty to whomever You choose and take it from whomever You choose ..." So, it should be realized that God's removal of the shirt of kingship from one group and His putting it on another group is in that sense divine wisdom and for the commonweal of mankind, [wisdom] which surpasses human understanding ... [Thus, one] must be satisfied with God's decision ... [After all, God knows] that in such and such a spot a man will appear through whom men will obtain happiness and good fortune.[2]

2 *Tārikh-e Bayhaqi*, ed. A.A. Fayyad and Q. Ghani (Tehran: 1324/1945–46) 97–98.

Therefore, says Bayhaqi, having chosen this future ruler God also raises up a group of supporters for him. Notice that in Bayhaqi we have the passage of the Qur'ān which we quoted earlier used not as a derogation of kingship but as a justification for it; and the parallel to prophethood, implied by Bayhaqi's mention of the transfer of power among religious polities, is made explicit in the succeeding paragraphs. Kingship is a natural part of political life, and its possession by one or another family is to be accepted fatalistically as part of God's decree. This passage implies—though other sections of Bayhaqi do not support this—that might is right since it masks the working out of a divine wisdom.

A less passive justification of kingship is given by the historians of the Seljuks, the dynasty of Central Asian Turks who defeated the Ghaznavids and reunited most of Western Asia in one loosely knit kingdom. Al-Rāvandī, writing under the patronage of a cadet line of this family at the very beginning of the 7th/13th century, says of his patron: "His kingship and sultanate are based on the satisfaction of God; the flags and emblems of his luck and good fortune are protected by God."[3] This is so because "his royal attention is limited to exalting the word (i.e., the cause) of God, and he has devoted his incomparable self to the aid of religion and the welfare of the Muslims. The sun of Muḥammad's religion is shining throughout the world from the boss on top of the battle standard of this potent ruler."[4] The apologists for the Seljuks, therefore, accept that kingship is always granted only with the agreement or satisfaction of God. But these apologists view God's satisfaction in the same way as some Christian predestinarians view God's grace. Just as salvation is only through God's grace and we cannot be certain who will receive this grace—yet, just as there are important presumptive signs of that grace—so, there are certain signs as to why God in his unfathomable wisdom has chosen certain dynasties to rule.

A rightful king is, in the phrase used repeatedly by al-Rāvandī's contemporaries, a king "by heredity and merit" (*be-erṣ o-esteḥqāq*). If it is impossible to connect the Ghaznavids with a former kingly line, such connections are made whenever possible for other rulers, especially after the appearance of Ghengis Khan established yet another dispensation of dynastic families in addition to the dispensation of Muḥammad's descendants and that of the descendants of the ancient Persian kings. But descent

3 Al-Rāvandī, *Rāḥat al-Ṣudūr*, ed. M. Iqbal (London: 1921) 149. Persian authors often adopt Arabic titles even when the text is in Persian.

4 *Ibid.*, 137.

is only a sign of possible royal capacity; merit, which principally means defense of Islam, and especially its sacred law, and which is rewarded by divine assistance, is the real touchstone of rightful rule.

The Islamic concept of kingship in the Middle East never lost the coloring given to it by each of the stages we have described. The belief that the world was God's and that man only had its temporary usufruct remained strong in the Islamic world, though tempered by the idea that kings have received this usufruct as a divine gift. Their kingship was not only divinely ordained, a shirt—as Bayhaqi says—in which God has clothed them, but also a garment of the greatest resplendence because they are emblematic on a human level of God's kingship throughout his creation. They did not possess the Day of Judgment and therefore, in theory, did not have God's authority to create laws or even to judge men; but some of the absolutism of divinity hung about them all the same. The monocratic concept of the caliphate colored all future Islamic political thought, not only because it was reinforced by very important social forces, but also because it fitted so intelligently with the inner logic of a universal monotheistic religion—the Universal and All-Powerful God had revealed through a single Prophet a law meant for all mankind, and that law required all those who accepted it to participate in a single religious community. But the kings who succeeded the caliphs as rulers of the Middle East, even if they were inspired by the example of monocratic caliphal rule, could not enmesh themselves in the system of belief of their subjects as the caliphs had done; they therefore had to pose as defenders of these beliefs and as champions of Islam, thereby meriting their kingship. In line with the general belief of Middle Eastern society that most abilities were hereditary, just as the son of a *qāḍī* was more likely to inherit judicial ability, the descendant of a great royal line was more likely to inherit royal abilities, though there were, of course, exceptions like the Ghaznavids.

In this paper, I have only discussed the powers and limitations of a king according to the theory of kingship in the Islamic Middle East. But the implied limitations on the theoretical powers of kings are important and explain why kings in the Islamic Middle East were nowhere near as absolute in practice as has been supposed. Kings received their mandate from God and not from their subjects; they were, moreover, emblematic of God's kingship. But God might take away their kingship at any moment, and they had continually to justify their position, which no principle of primogeniture, no anointment, nothing except the presumptive satisfaction of God had allowed them. This uncertainty also meant that Islamic Middle Eastern kings reacted to any threat to their rule with an arbitrary ferocity which might have surprised their European royal brothers; but their absolutism was in theory and in practice modified by a continual need to justify their rule, both to their subjects and to themselves, in terms of Islam. Correspondingly, their subjects never allowed any dynasty of kings a permanent place in their system of belief. The caliphs had had a real chance to combine the theory with the practice of absolutism; but their attempts to do so had been unsuccessful. Nevertheless, once kingship, though accepted only very conditionally and with qualifications, became the important political form of rule, many Muslims, unwilling to give full-hearted support to such kingship, clung all the more tenaciously to the idea of the caliphate which—now that it was removed from the ugliness of practical politics—was the one political office consonant with the universalism inherent in their religion. Commitment to the idea of the caliphate was in one sense a way of withholding full commitment to kings.

Oaths and Public Vows in the Middle East of the 10th and 11th Centuries

Middle Eastern histories and collections of literary anecdotalists from the 4th/10th and 5th/11th centuries bristle with accounts of oaths and publicly sworn vows. For example, the chronicler Hilāl al-Ṣābī tells us (as I paraphrase him) that Abū ʿAlī ibn Ismāʿīl, the talented minister of Bahā' al-Dawla whom that king had disgraced, escaped from prison in 392/1002 and then, after a while on the run, wanted to return to the capital city of Shiraz in safety. He therefore sent an emissary to ask that Bahā' al-Dawla grant him a guarantee of safety attested by a leading ʿAlid, Abū Aḥmad al-Mūsawī. Bahā' al-Dawla agreed, though he requested that the document not be "exhaustive." The emissary, however, turned up with a long, written oath (*yamīn*, literally "right hand"), and Bahā' al-Dawla immediately noticed that it was, in fact, intended to be exhaustive. He started to read it out loud, then stopped in the middle to ask a question. The emissary kissed the ground before the king and asked his gracious favor in reading straight through from the beginning again without interruption. Bahā' al-Dawla was angry but did reread the document without interruption, and at the end of the document, he wrote: "I have sworn to this oath (*yamīn*) and undertake to observe its stipulations."

To me, this story illustrates the seriousness with which people of this period took even the oath of a comparatively unscrupulous ruler like Bahā' al-Dawla. Abū ʿAlī's emissary doubtless knew that the king was treacherous,

---

Author's note: This article was first published as: "Oaths and Public Vows in the Middle East of the Tenth and Eleventh Centuries," in Marie-France Auzépy and Guillaume Saint-Guillain (eds.), *Oralité et lien social au Moyen Âge (Occident, Byzance, Islam): parole donnée, foi jurée, serment*, College de France-CNRS, Centre de recherche d'histoire et civilisation de Byzance, Monographies 29 (Paris, ACHCByz: 2008) 117–122. Reproduced with permission.

but still thought it worth risking the king's anger to make sure that the oath was technically sound because read without interruption. He also knew the seriousness with which Abū Aḥmad al-Mūsawī would take the oath, and that Bahā' al-Dawla might be restrained from treachery by fear of future embarrassment before this revered leader of the family of 'Alī. It was precisely the grave importance of oaths to such prestigious men that allowed the oath to remain a central form of political action, in spite of dishonorable kings like Bahā' al-Dawla.[1]

The Islamic legal tradition fully recognizes the importance of oaths and vows, which are almost always treated together in a single chapter of the law books.[2] Wahba al-Zuhayli, widely respected as the foremost modern authority on the Sunni tradition of Islamic law, says that oaths (*aymān*, pl. of *yamīn*) and vows (*nudhūr*, pl. of *nadhr*) lexically and legally signify the formation of a sincere commitment and the act of creating a contractually binding obligation (*'aqd*). He who swears voluntarily and deliberately binds himself to sincere commitment and firm resolve either to do a thing or abstain from doing it. Vows are acts whereby the agent obligates himself to seek to accomplish a specific goal. For failure to keep certain oaths and vows, i.e., to forswear oneself or commit perjury (*ḥinth*), there are acts of atonement or expiation (*kaffāra*). Oaths, vows and expiations are considered to belong to that part of the law called *'ibāda*, "worship and obedience to God," because they create obligations and commitments to which God is a party. The Shāfi'ī school of law said that no oath is valid without explicit mention of God. In this essay, private vows will not be considered, since they do not constitute a public contract.[3]

It is hard to imagine any language in which there is no way to signal the presence of solemnly committing speech. Even the Quaker and Mennonite traditions, which take seriously the commandment not to swear and believe that all speech should be truthful and therefore that there need

1 See my book *Loyalty and Leadership in an Early Islamic Society* (Princeton, N.J., Princeton University Press: 1980, reprinted London: 2001) 48–49.

2 See C. Melchert, "The History of the Judicial Oath in Islamic Law," in Marie-France Auzépy and Guillaume Saint-Guillain (eds.), *Oralité et lien social au Moyen Âge (Occident, Byzance, Islam): parole donnée, foi jurée, serment*, College de France-CNRS, Centre de recherche d'histoire et civilisation de Byzance, Monographies 29 (Paris, ACHCByz: 2008) 309–326.

3 Wahba al-Zuhayli, *Al-Fiqh al-Islāmī wa-Adillatuhu*, III (Damascus: 1409/1989) 357–359; on the Shāfi'īs, p. 383.

be no distinction between plain speech and sworn speech, have accepted the need to say "I affirm" before testimony in a legal setting.

Chronicles and belles-lettres from the period that I study, namely from 900 to 1100 C.E., are filled with instances of oath-taking (and oath breaking). In this period formal oaths were the most prominent feature of all discussions about duties and obligations that could be enforced without physical coercion. Undoubtedly oaths carried only a comparatively small part of the weight of that sense of obligation and loyalty which held society together. Nevertheless, they were universally acceptable, and other forms of social obligation were to some extent adapted to the pattern of oaths. The Caliph al-Muqtadir (r. 908–932 C.E.) said to those who rebelled against him, "Whoever has sworn allegiance to me has sworn allegiance to God; so that whoever violates that oath, violates the compact with God (*'ahd Allāh*)."[4]

In the understanding of Muslims, this compact with God was formed or reaffirmed at the dawn of history. The primary acknowledgment of all moral responsibility by mankind was symbolized by an oath taken from all humans *in posse*. According to the Qur'ān, this event happened as follows:

> And when your Lord drew the descendants of Adam from the loins of Adam and called them to bear witness: "Am I not your Lord?" They answered, "Yes, truly; we bear witness to this." [We called on them to bear witness] lest you should say on the Day of Resurrection, "We were unaware of this [allegiance owed to God]" or lest you should say "Our ancestors before us have given partners [to God]. We are their descendants after them; will You then destroy us, for what was done by the upholders of falsehood?"
>
> (al-A'rāf, VII:172–173)

According to these verses, it is no excuse for a person to claim that he is "unaware" (whether this means, as some commentators believe, that people pretend they have forgotten, or—as others believe—that people pretend never to have been told of this covenant). It is not even an excuse that one is born to parents who have turned from God, and who might therefore be held responsible for the heedlessness of their children. All future humanity was in some sense present at this primal covenant, and they have individually "borne witness" and thereby entered into an agreement

4 *Loyalty and Leadership*, (*supra* n. 1), 43–45.

with God that makes them responsible to God. Many Muslim thinkers have said that God holds people responsible regardless of their commitment through a covenant, and that this covenant merely confirmed a responsibility inherent in man's situation. For our purposes, it is only important to notice that the Islamic tradition considered this solemn primal covenant between man and God to be a powerful and widely quoted argument for the fundamental moral responsibility of every human being.

The reader will notice that in this Qur'ānic passage the oath is oral. The preference for oral testimony remains strong in Islamic law at a theoretical level, although actual practice often seems to have differed. In judicial procedure oral testimony is in most cases more powerful (*aqwā*) than other forms of testimony, although testimony in respect to oneself has more value than that in respect to third parties. Theoretically an evident clear statement (*bayyina*) does not need to be reinforced in court by an oath. In early Islamic law there were attempts to rule out oaths in support of the plaintiff's case as called for in the Qur'ānic verses al-Baqara II:282–286. Later practice, however, supported the use of the oath by the plaintiff, a good indication of the importance of oaths in many Islamic cultures.[5] Court testimony aside, most of the schools of law agreed that a letter containing an oath does not constitute an oath unless it is spoken.[6] At the same time we find that sworn copies of the charters of pious trusts (*waqfīyāt*) were placed in the archives of the judge in towns important enough to have such an official in every generation by interested parties so that there could be no doubt as to the original terms.[7] This procedure may not have been strictly necessary, but its repeated use demonstrates the power of oral swearing even to support written documents.

Arabic has an unusually rich vocabulary for oaths. The most generic word is *qasam*, which literally means swearing by something, as in the common phrase "I swear by God." When the verb from this word is used with the conjunction *'an*, it means "to swear that one will do such and such a thing." A near synonym is *ḥilf*, to swear (for example, by God). Another very common synonym, which supplants the preceding words

5 R. Brunschvig, "Bayyina," in *Encyclopaedia of Islam*, 2nd ed., I (Leiden, Brill: 1960) 1150–1151. This brief account is still one of the most important discussions on the subject. See now Melchert, (*supra* n. 2).

6 Zuhayli, (*supra* n. 3), 422.

7 L.E. Fernandes, *The Evolution of the Sufi Institution in Mamluk Egypt: The Khanqah* (Berlin: 1988).

in the medieval period, is *yamīn*, which literally means the right hand, but also frequently refers to the oath, as in the phrase "He made us swear oaths." The word *ʿahd* is often used for making a sworn agreement as is the slightly more modern *ʿaqd* (contract). There is also the *bayʿa*, which was originally an oath associated with a contract of sale, but came to be an oath of allegiance. Many of these words produce secondary meanings such as compact, alliance, covenant, contract. Most law books have a chapter on oaths and vows, as they can have considerable legal significance.

Every age knows hardy rogues who openly disregard the central moral principles of their age and there are perjurers and perjuries aplenty in this period. Nonetheless, in 944, when the chief general who had taken repeated oaths of good conduct towards the reigning caliph, had him arrested and blinded, the historian Miskawayh writes, "The world trembled with shock." Another chronicle tells us that, when someone first suggested to the general that he arrest the caliph, he replied, "How could I do such a thing, when he has made a formal agreement with us, and I have had all the people of the court testify to my compliance, and this matter is well known in other regions?"

Although oaths could be broken, there were issues of the judgment of God, personal honor, and the opinion of society which could and did prevent perjury. The chronicler continues, "When in this manner, the general blinded the caliph and betrayed him, broke his oaths to him (*ḥanitha aymānahu*) and violated his covenants (*ʿuhūd*) which he had taken before God to support and obey him, [this act] deeply troubled men both high and low and they thought it a momentous event. Everyone who had believed and had faith in His promise and warning [knew] that God—He is powerful and glorious—would grant him no respite or enjoyment of life hereafter." The chronicle then turns the story into a morality tale. The general, bitterly regretting what he had done, "asked for wine to drink; and when the wine came, he had a stroke ... his sight went before he died [in the following year]."[8] The accuracy of such anecdotes is not at issue, although it is hard to imagine a chronicler and government clerk like Miskawayh inventing large parts of his narrative. The anecdotes represent common forms of social action that are attested in a wide range of sources including documents quoted in chronicles and collections of official correspondence.

8 *Loyalty and Leadership*, (*supra* n. 1), 46–48.

Kings attempted to bind their officials and their prominent subjects by oaths. When the Buyid ruler of Iraq was confronted with fighting between his Turkish and Iranian soldiers in 971, he had officers from each side swear oaths of reconciliation to one another. We are told on several occasions that a town, presumably represented by its leading men, swore oaths to a ruler. Ḥarrān in northern Mesopotamia swore (*ḥalafū*) to fight with a Syrian prince against anybody who might oppose him and to make peace with whomever he made peace with. The townsmen stuck by their oath at great risk.[9]

The importance of public witnessing to treaty-oaths is shown by the instruction given by the ever-astute ʿAḍud al-Dawla to the three judges whom he sent as envoys to the Sāmānids in 371/981. He told them that if they succeeded in making peace with the Sāmānid general in Nishapur, they should then go to Bukhara, the Sāmānid capital, and conclude the agreement with a deposition (*maḥḍar*) from the *qāḍīs*, witness-notaries, leading courtiers, officers, *ghāzīs* (volunteer fighters against non-Muslim governments), and great men of the region witnessing that the Sāmānid ruler had actually agreed to the peace. When such agreements were prepared, apparently two copies of them were made, each of which concluded with the oath by one of the rulers, contingent on the taking of a similar oath by the other ruler.

All the oaths described above were between real persons. They were, moreover, between real persons present in this world (including, of course, God). None of these oaths was sworn, for example, between two men on behalf of their descendants; and none of them was between a man and an artificial person like a municipality or clan or school. When people expected a city to be carried along by the oaths of its notables, it was not because those notables could legally obligate their followers by their oaths, but because these notables could deliver the cooperation of their followers, who were bound to them by other loyalties. The oaths that the notables took were not oaths to the "state"—no such artificial entity existed with whom one might exchange oaths. Even the first generation of men, the sons of Adam, in the primal oath that was the example and guarantee that overshadowed all later oaths, could not swear on behalf of all his

9 *Loyalty and Leadership*, (*supra* n. 1), 59–60.

descendants to recognize God's eternal sovereignty; all future men had to be brought forth in the form of seed so that they could individually swear.[10]

Public vows served a function similar to oaths. The vow follows the style of the oath and is usually treated in the same chapter of Islamic law books. It differs in that it is a unilateral swearing by a person to God, rather than a transaction between two persons with God as witness. The Arabic word for vow, *nadhr*, in its root sense means "to consecrate something to God." Public vows were a symbolic action by which the ruler could commit himself before his subjects. For example, a Kurdish ruler of the earlier 5th/11th century, gave a vow in public to conquer the neighboring district of Shāhrazūr. His father, who was overlord of the city, instructed him to desist. The son replied, "I have sworn not to stop in this matter nor turn back until I have entered the city." So, his father said, "Go to the city with a few men, and I will order [the governor] to open the gate and then you will be freed from your oath (*yamīn*)." Incidentally, this transition between oath and vow reveals how closely they were associated.

From the discussion of oaths and vows we see that the issue of public and private, a fairly well-established distinction in the Islamic law of the market, is as important as the distinction between the categories of oath and vow.[11] Islamic law prescribes elaborate rules for the expiation of unfulfilled "private" oaths and vows, but these remain largely a matter between the believer and his Creator. Oaths and vows made in the presence of at least one other party, whether they be contracts or public acts, are another matter. Failure to perform is good cause to bring a case before a judge.

We can classify the emotions seen to be working in fidelity to oaths and vows or lack thereof as follows: honor, shame, guilt and fear of retribution. In the examples given above, we may say that the Kurdish chief offered to allow his son a token of fulfillment of his vow in order to save his honor. Similarly, the people of Ḥarrān seemed to maintain their oath as a matter of honor. We may also say that the chroniclers wish the ʿAbbasid general's betrayal of his caliph to live on as a story of shame and this-worldly retribution. The Buyid king ʿAḍud al-Dawla wishes to guarantee a treaty with a powerful rival kingdom by committing its great men in a way that will both shame and dishonor the rival king, should he repudiate the treaty.

10 The preceding two paragraphs closely follow my account in *Loyalty and Leadership*, (*supra* n. 1), 61–62.

11 R.P. Mottahedeh and K. Stilt, "Public and Private as Viewed through the Work of the *Muḥtasib*," *Social Research* 70 (2003) 683–686.

Presumably the Turkish and Iranian troops were made to swear friendship with each other because of potential shame in this world and retribution in the next consequent upon breaking their oath. In all these cases, the initiator of the oath or vow may have hoped that guilt would ensure fulfillment.

In fact, to discern the roles of honor and shame we must move away from modern ideas on the subject and accept a world in which shame at the Day of Judgment is as present to a person in this world as is shame before any immediate audience. Similarly, conflicts of honor will often force the historical character to judge what action is least dishonorable. The strong contextualization of each of these anecdotes, that is consideration of the audiences, present and future, that the actors may have had in mind, will show the interplay of shame and honor throughout. In a society in which very few stable institutional elements existed, impersonal commitment is more difficult to visualize and sustain. A more lively agonistic discussion of obligation should be expected. The personalistic character of the obligations individuals create, not only through oaths and vows but more generally, made the open expression of oaths and public vows an even more essential part of the creation of a moral order. The public oath might even symbolize the ruler's commitment to the moral order, as in the case of Mu'izz al-Dawla, the Buyid king who conquered Iraq in 334/945. When he interviewed the most senior and distinguished of the former administrators of Iraq, the latter said, "One of the matters most worthy of receiving the attention of the emir and of priority in his regard is the repair of these breaches [in the irrigation canals of central Iraq], which are the root of the ruin and devastation of the Sawād." Mu'izz al-Dawla said, "I take a vow to God (*nadhartu li-llāh*) in the presence of those here that I will give precedence over this matter, even if I must spend all I possess on it."

The chronicles tell us that the king's subjects knew he was sincere in his vow, and when he re-entered Baghdad after defeating a rebel in 345/957, "the people gathered on the banks and invoked blessings (*da'ā*) on him, and curses on [the defeated rebel] Rūzbehān. For indeed the populace (*'āmma*) were attached to the reign (*muḥibbūn li-ayyām*) of Mu'izz al-Dawla because of what he had done to repair the breach of the Nahr Rūm and that of Bādūrīya. For he had himself gone out to repair this breach and himself carried earth in the bosom of his cloak, to set an example to his whole army. When he had repaired the breaches, Baghdad became prosperous, fine bread being at twenty *ratl*s the dirham. Hence the populace was attached to his reign and loved him."[12] In large political undertakings as well as everyday transactions, oaths and public vows were among the most powerful social formulae to convey commitment.

Islamic law is fully aware of perjury (*ḥinth*). The written sources of the 4th/10th and 5th/11th centuries in the Middle East are rife with examples of perjury. Nonetheless the "public" oath was seen as the best instrument of commitment before society. Perjury in no way discouraged the frequent and continuing use of oaths and vows as an important means to shape social behavior.

It was difficult for members of such a highly individualistic society to reckon a calculus of obligation. The linguistic formalism of oaths and public vows was extremely frequently used to establish an obligation or evoke compliance with it. Naturally, force, monetary patronage and other incentives were used to create and perpetuate obligations. In the absence of so many institutions such as the Church and the feudal order which figure prominently in later medieval European history, the more loosely woven, yet resilient, social and moral world of the Middle East in the 4th/10th and 5th/11th centuries was in particular need of formulae rendered in the presence of God that signaled commitment between two parties. In some cases vast chains of such dyadic oath-taking created what amounted to temporary institutions. By the end of this period the vast Sufi brotherhoods—also entered into individually by taking an oath—were beginning to appear and showed the possibility of society organizing itself from within on the basis of oaths.

12 Al-Hamadhānī, *Takmila Ta'rīkh al-Ṭabarī* (Beirut: 1961) 156, quoted in *Loyalty and Leadership*, (*supra* n. 1), 69 and n. 31.

Qur'ānic Commentary on the Verse of *Khums* (al-Anfāl VIII:41)

A famous Qur'ānic verse grants an economic benefit in the form of the *khums* or one-fifth to *sayyids* and *sharīfs*. This essay surveys the interpretation of this verse in Qur'ān commentaries, a task which, as far as I know, has not been done before. The verse in question, verse 41 of Sūra VIII, al-Anfāl, is very often called "The verse of *khums*."[1]

An English understanding of this verse is:

> Know that anything in the way of booty/benefit you have taken, one-fifth of it belongs to God and to His Messenger and to the relatives and the orphans and the poor and the wayfarer, if you have believed in God and what We have revealed to Our servant on the Day of Separation, the day in which the two gatherings will meet. And God is Mighty over all things.

THE DIMENSIONS OF INTERPRETATION

As with so many questions concerning entitlements to money and, perhaps, honor, the breadth of disagreement is astonishing. The problems in interpreting this verse are laid out elegantly and succinctly by al-Māwardī, a very celebrated Sunni jurist of the Shāfi'ī school who died

---

Author's note: This article was first published as: "Qur'ānic Commentary on the Verse of *khums* (al-Anfāl VIII:41)," in Kazuo Morimoto (ed.), *Sayyids and Sharifs in Muslim Societies: The Living Links to the Prophet* (London and New York, Routledge: 2012) 37–48. Reproduced by permission of Taylor & Francis Group.

1 Some material from Qur'ānic commentaries is given in the excellent article "Khums" by A. Zysow and R. Gleave in *The Encyclopaedia of Islam*, 2nd ed. (hereafter *EI²*), Supplement XII:7–8 (Leiden, Brill: 2003) 531–535.

in 450/1058. There are, he says, three theories as to the relationship of the word *ghanīma*, which means "booty/benefit" to *fay'*, a word implied by the verb used in verse 7 of Sūra LIX, al-Ḥashr, which begins: "What God granted as *fay'* from the people of the towns belongs to God and His Messenger and the relatives and the orphans and the poor and the wayfarers."

The first theory is that the *ghanīma* and *fay'* are the same thing, and that the verse in Sūrat al-Anfāl abrogated the verse in Sūrat al-Ḥashr.

The second theory is that *ghanīma* is booty taken by force, whereas property taken by treaty is *fay'*. This theory is supported by the early jurists Sufyān al-Thawrī (d. 161/778) and al-Shāfi'ī (d. 204/820).

The third theory is that *ghanīma* represents the movable property (*māl*) of the nonbelievers and *fay'* represents their landed property.

Furthermore, people disagree as to whether the verse specifies a share for God. Some believe the phrase "belongs to God" is a prologue to the five categories of people mentioned subsequently. This is the opinion of several early Sunni jurists, including al-Shāfi'ī.

A second opinion, attributed to Abū 'Alīya al-Riyāḥī, a Basran Qur'ān expert of the end of the first Islamic century, is that the portion belonging to God is a separate sixth category and should be given to the Ka'ba.

Yet another issue concerns the understanding of what happens to the Prophet's share after his death. One view gives it to the caliphs. A second view, which believes that the Prophet could have heirs, assigned his share to his kin group. A third view adds the Prophet's share to the four categories mentioned subsequently. A fourth view holds that it should be used for the common good of the Muslims. Al-Māwardī mentions that this is the view of al-Shāfi'ī, the founder of al-Māwardī's own legal school. Finally, some say the share should be used for weapons and horses.

There are three different understandings as to who the Prophet's "relatives" are. The first is that they are the Banū Hāshim, descendants of Muḥammad's great-grandfather. The second makes them the Banū Hāshim and the Banū Muṭṭalib, descendants of Muḥammad's great-granduncle, Muṭṭalib. This is the view of al-Shāfi'ī and al-Ṭabarī (d. 310/923). A third opinion is that they are the entirety of the Quraysh, the tribe at Mecca to which the Prophet belonged.

Al-Māwardī offers four opinions about use of the relatives' share after the Prophet's death. Al-Shāfi'ī believes that it belongs to the relatives of Muḥammad forever. A second school holds that it belongs to the relatives of the ruling caliph. A third school believes that the Imam, the leader of the Muslim community, can use it as he wishes. A fourth view, followed by the Ḥanafīs, adds the relatives' share and the Prophet's share to the three categories mentioned subsequently, namely, the orphans, the poor and the wayfarers.[2]

EARLY QUR'ĀN COMMENTARIES

This rather legalistic presentation of al-Māwardī opens most of the questions that are considered in earlier and later commentaries. A very early Qur'ān commentary by Muqātil ibn Sulaymān (d. 150/767) explains "relatives" as the "kin (*qarāba*) of the Prophet," without further discussion.[3] Two other early commentaries, one by Mujāhid (d. 104/722) and another ascribed to Zayd ibn 'Alī (d. 122/740) have nothing to say about the verse.

Ṭabarī in his classic *tafsīr*, written a century and a half before al-Māwardī, adds many traditions to the opinions. In refuting the views that the share of the relatives can go to the ruler (*walī al-amr*), he recites a ḥadīth which becomes a standard frequently cited by later commentators:

> I [Jubayr ibn Muṭ'im] and 'Uthmān ibn 'Affān saw the Prophet giving the share of the relatives to the Banū Hāshim and the Banū Muṭṭalib after the victory at Khaybar and we said, "O Messenger of God, these are our brothers, the Banū Hāshim. We do not deny their excellence because of the place God has given you amongst them. Do you think it right for the Banū Muṭṭalib [to get a share]? You give it to them and leave us out! We [as descendants of Nawfal and 'Abd al-Shams, Hāshim's brothers] and they [the Banū Muṭṭalib, also descending from a brother of Hāshim's] are in the same position in regard to [genealogical closeness to] yourself!" [Muḥammad] said, "They [the Banū Muṭṭalib] did not separate themselves from us either in the Jāhilīya or in Islam. The Banū Hāshim and Banū Muṭṭalib are one and the same."

2 'Alī ibn Muḥammad al-Māwardī, *al-Nukat wa-l-'Uyūn*, ed. al-Sayyid ibn 'Abd al-Maqsud ibn 'Abd al-Rahim, II (Beirut, Dār al-Kutub al-'Ilmīya and Mu'assāt al-Kutub al-Thaqāfīya: 1413/1992) 318–321.

3 Muqātil ibn Sulaymān, *Tafsīr Muqātil ibn Sulaymān*, 5 vols., ed. 'Abd Allah Mahmud Shihata (Cairo, al-Hay'a al-Miṣrīya al-'Āmma li-l-Kitāb: 1399–1410/1979–1989), II:116.

Ṭabarī says:

> The most correct view, in my opinion, is that the share of the relatives belongs to the relatives of Banū Hāshim and their allies (*ḥulafā'*, sing. *ḥālif*), the Banū Muṭṭalib—because this ḥadīth is sound and because the sworn allies of a people belong to that people.

Ṭabarī mentions a Prophetic ḥadīth, "Nobody inherits from us! What we leave behind will be *ṣadaqa* (voluntary alms)." He also mentions the contrary opinion, namely, the opinion of the Shi'ites. Ṭabarī tells us that Zayn al-'Ābidīn 'Alī ibn al-Ḥusayn (d. 94/712 or 95/713) was asked about the *khums* and 'Alī said, "It belongs to us." And the questioner said to 'Alī, "God speaks of orphans and poor and wayfarers." 'Alī said, "Our orphans and our poor." Ṭabarī also reports that Ibn 'Abbās wrote to Najda: "We are them [the relatives]; and our people have done this [act of deprivation] to us and have said, 'All the Quraysh are the relatives.'"

Ṭabarī strongly supports Sunni opinion that *ghanīma*, the booty/benefit referred to in the verse is battlefield booty and not, as Shi'ites believed, immoveable property of non-Muslims or the income from it. He mentions several times the strong statist opinion which he ascribes to "a group of Iraqis" (meaning the proto-Ḥanafīs) who say that after Muḥammad's death the *khums* was divided only among the orphans, poor and wayfarers. A similar statist opinion states that the share of the relatives goes to the "guardian of the affairs of the Muslims" (*walī amr al-Muslimīn*).

Ṭabarī, who was the founder of his own law school, believed that the Prophet's share goes back into the divisible booty, which is then divided four ways, with one for the relatives. He did not think it permissible "for persons [explicitly] mentioned in the Book not to get their share," though of booty only.[4]

Hūd ibn Muḥakkam al-Huwwārī, an 'Ibaḍī commentator approximately contemporaneous with Ṭabarī, has fewer disagreements with the Sunni tradition than might have been anticipated. Like Ṭabarī, he says that Abū Bakr and 'Umar transferred the share of the relatives to "the Path of God." We get a slight taste of Khārijī egalitarianism and piety when Hūd gives a ḥadīth about a man asking the Prophet, "Is any one person entitled to

4 Al-Ṭabarī, *Jāmi' al-Bayān 'an Ta'wīl āy al-Qur'ān* (hereafter *Tafsīr*), 3rd printing, X (Cairo, Muṣṭafā al-Bābī al-Ḥalabī: 1388/1968) 1–9.

more booty (*ghanā'im*) than another?" Muḥammad answered, "No, even the portion he takes personally is not something that he has a special right to."[5] To jump many centuries forward, the commentary of Muḥammad ibn Yūsuf Aṭṭafayyish, an 'Ibāḍī who died in 1332/1913, also does not differ much from the Sunni accounts. It agrees with those Sunnis, principally Shāfi'īs, who feel that one-fifth of the *khums* should be given to relatives of the Prophet, whether they be rich or poor.[6]

A Shi'ite contemporary of Ṭabarī is Muḥammad ibn Mas'ūd al-'Ayyāshī. His death date is unknown, but his works can be dated to the late 3rd/9th century. He lived at Samarqand and belonged to an Eastern school of Shi'ism, which preserves many traditions attributed to the Prophet and the Imams not to be found in the Iraqi and Qumī (Qomī) schools. Some of these traditions are not picked up by the central Twelver Shi'ite tradition until the enormous seventeenth-century collection called *Biḥār al-Anwār*. Al-'Ayyāshī quotes Muḥammad al-Bāqir, the Fifth Imam, as saying, "We have a scriptural right to the *khums*. Even if some were to crush it, or claim it is not from God, or claim that they do not know about it, that would make no difference." He quotes the same Imam as explaining, "['Alī, the First Imam] said that God has forbidden the Family the *ṣadaqa* and revealed the *khums* for their benefit, an obligation owed to them, a mark of their nobility, and a matter lawful for them." Al-'Ayyāshī also anticipates the later Twelver Shi'ite position in that he believes the Imam has a claim to the *khums* over everything classified as *fay'* (immoveable property) and *anfāl* (booty). He adds that the Family has a claim to everything in this world but mentions a contrary ḥadīth to the effect that *khums* is payable only on booty (*ghanā'im*). He does not define the sources of wealth subject to *khums*.[7]

The Iraqi and western Iranian Twelver Shi'ite tradition is represented by 'Alī ibn Ibrāhīm al-Qumī, who flourished around the beginning of the 4th/10th century. Al-Qumī tells us that the *khums* is divided into six parts, a standard Twelver Shi'ite position thereafter. He explains that it is the

---

5 Hūd ibn Muḥakkam al-Huwwārī, *Tafsīr Kitāb Allāh al-'Azīz*, ed. Balhajj ibn Sa'id Sharifi, II (Beirut, Dār al-Gharb al-Islāmī: 1411/1990) 90–94. It is very hard to determine the authenticity of the work ascribed to Hūd and many scholars consider the material in this commentary may not belong to Hūd.

6 Muḥammad ibn Yūsuf Aṭṭafayyish, *Tafsīr Himyān al-Zād ilā Dār al-Ma'ād*. www.altafsir.com (accessed June 25, 2011).

7 Muḥammad ibn Mas'ūd al-'Ayyāshī, *al-Tafsīr*, ed. Qism al-Dirāsāt al-Islāmīya, II (Qom, Mu'assasat al-Ba'tha: 1421/2000) 199–203.

Imam's duty to act as a father for the community, just as the Prophet did. As a consequence, the Imam acts as the Prophet's trustee or executor and receives three parts of the six because of his position. Therefore, he collects the monies to be distributed among the categories assigned by the Qur'ān.[8]

If we turn to the later Shi'ite commentary by Ṭūsī, who was a contemporary of al-Māwardī and died in 460/1067, we find a more developed treatment of the Twelver Shi'ite tradition. Ṭūsī's eminent position in the development of Twelver Shi'ite law is so great that he is called "*Shaykh al-Ṭā'ifa*" ("Leader of the Sect," i.e., Shi'ites). Ṭūsī says that immoveable property (*fay'*) is subject to *khums*, which the Imam is free to distribute as he pleases. He distinguished it from booty from battle, *ghanīma*, three-sixths of which (must) go to the Imam and the rest to the orphans and poor and wayfarers of the House of the Prophet. Again, he tells us that the Banū Hāshim are forbidden *ṣadaqa*, and that the *khums* replaces this benefit. He notes that some Twelver Shi'ites disagree about this but says that they are wrong. He holds what will become the standard Twelver Shi'ite position hereafter, that the *khums* is an obligatory 20 percent tax on every legitimate source of profit, whether made through trade, treasure trove, mines, diving and the like.[9]

Al-Ṭabarānī (d. 360/971), of Syrian origin, and supposedly a pupil of Ṭabarī, wrote his "Great Commentary" (*al-Tafsīr al-Kabīr*) about a half century after his teacher. He explicitly names the Ḥanafīs as believing that the Prophet's share died with him because the Prophets do not have heirs. This principle also rules out the relatives, which leaves three categories that deserve the *khums*. Al-Ṭabarānī quotes Shāfi'ī as saying that there are still five categories, the share of the Prophet going to the most urgent needs of the Muslims, and the other shares as specified, in the case of the relatives, both the rich and poor.[10]

A commentator of the eastern Ḥanafī school, Abū al-Layth Naṣr ibn Muḥammad al-Samarqandī, is a near contemporary of al-Ṭabarānī (d. between 373/983 and 393/1002–3). His work continued to have wide currency, as Joseph Schacht has said, "from Morocco to Indonesia." He

8 'Alī ibn Ibrāhīm al-Qumī, *Tafsīr al-Qumī*, ed. Tayyib al-Musawi al-Jaza'iri, I (Beirut, Dār al-Surūr: 1412/1991) 204–205.

9 Muḥammad ibn al-Ḥasan al-Ṭūsī, *al-Tibyān fī Tafsīr al-Qur'ān*, ed. Ahmad Habib Qusayr al-'Amili, V (Najaf, Maktab al-I'lām al-Islāmī: 1409/1988–89) 143–146.

10 Sulaymān ibn Aḥmad al-Ṭabarānī, *al-Tafsīr al-Kabīr*, ed. Hisham ibn 'Abd al-Karim al-Badrani al-Mawsili, III (Irbid, Dār al-Kitāb al-Thaqāfī and Dār al-Mutanabbī: 1429/2008) 260–261.

follows the opinion of Abū Ḥanīfa (d. 150/767) and his school that the *khums* after the Prophet's death is to be divided in three portions, the relatives only benefiting if they can be classified as poor.[11]

An Eastern commentator of slightly later date is Aḥmad ibn Muḥammad al-Thaʿlabī al-Nīsābūrī (d. 427/1035) whose enormous *al-Kashf wa-l-Bayān* has only recently been published. Although many of his sources are similar to al-Ṭabarī, he quotes Ibn ʿAbbās as saying that the Prophet never took his share and that the *khums* in Muḥammad's time was divided among the remaining four categories.

Al-Thaʿlabī relates on the authority of al-Zuhrī (d. 124/742) the well-known account that Fāṭima and ʿAbbās went to Abū Bakr requesting their inheritance in Khaybar and Fadak. Abū Bakr told them that he had heard the Prophet say: "We stand in the company of Prophets and do not have heirs. What we have left as inheritance is *ṣadaqa*." Yet he quotes ʿAlī's contrary opinion: "Every person should be given his [proper] share of the *khums* which does not go to anyone else; and the Imam is in charge of the portion belonging to God and His Messenger." He even quotes the opinion—presumably Shiʿite—that all of the *khums* is for the relatives (*qarāba*) of the Prophet.[12] A student of al-Thaʿlabī, ʿAlī ibn Aḥmad al-Wāḥidī al-Nīsābūrī (d. 468/1076), perhaps the most famous pre-modern expert on "occasions of revelation," follows his Shāfiʿī law school in giving a fifth of the fifth for relatives to Banū Hāshim and Banū Muṭṭalib.[13]

The outstanding philologist and commentator, al-Zamakhsharī, died 538/1144, is often said to be the last Sunni Muʿtazilī. The extremely widely used commentary of al-Bayḍāwī (d. 685/1286) is essentially the commentary of al-Zamakhsharī with the Muʿtazilī and some rhetorical discussions removed. Al-Zamakhsharī repeats much of the material in al-Ṭabarī, including the three schools of thought on the distinction between *ghanīma* and *fay'*—either they are identical or *fay'* implies real estate or *fay'* implies wealth taken under a treaty. He explicitly gives a ḥadīth attested in much

11 Abū al-Layth al-Samarqandī, *Tafsīr al-Samarqandī*, eds. ʿAli Muhammad Muʿawwad, ʿAdil Ahmad ʿAbd al-Mawjud, and Zakariya ʿAbd al-Majid al-Nawuti, II (Beirut, Dār al-Kutub al-ʿIlmīya: 1414/1993) 18–19. See J. Schacht, "Abū al-Layth al-Samarḳandī," in *EI²*, I (Leiden, Brill: 1960) 137.

12 Aḥmad ibn Muḥammad al-Thaʿlabī, *Al-Kashf wa-l-Bayān al-Maʿrūf bi-Tafsīr al-Thaʿlabī*, ed. by Abu Muhammad ibn ʿAshur and Nazir al-Saʿidi, IV (Beirut, Dār Iḥyāʾ al-Turāth al-ʿArabī: 1423/2002) 357–361.

13 ʿAlī ibn Aḥmad al-Wāḥidī, *al-Wasīṭ fī Tafsīr al-Qurʾān al-Majīd*, ed. by ʿAdil Ahmad Abd al-Mawjud *et al.*, II (Beirut, Dār al-Kutub al-ʿIlmīya: 1415/1994) 460–463.

earlier sources that, "It is not legal to give *ṣadaqa* to the people of the House, when God has allotted them one-fifth of the *khums*." Interestingly, he acknowledges that the Twelver Shiʿite position exists and records that "some say the whole of the *khums* belongs to the relatives of the Apostle of God." He even quotes the saying of Zayn al-ʿĀbidīn ʿAlī mentioned above, but he himself supports the view that "orphans and poor and wayfarers" applies to all Muslims.[14]

Another Eastern commentator is Abū al-Muẓaffar Manṣūr ibn Muḥammad al-Samʿānī (d. 489/1096) of Marv. He puts forward the standard Shāfiʿī view that, of the booty, the share of the Prophet is spent on the welfare of the Muslims, and the share of the relatives goes to them whether they are poor or wealthy. He mentions the opinion of the Ḥanafīs, that the relatives' share is added to the last three categories, and of Mālik, that the Imam has discretion over all shares and can or cannot distribute them, as the groups mentioned are permitted to have these shares but do not have them "by entitlement." There is no mention of the Ḥanbalī school, which was not strongly represented in Khorasan and Transoxiana at this time.[15]

A later scholar, Abū Muḥammad al-Ḥusayn ibn Masʿūd al-Baghawī (d. 510/1117 or 516/1122), author of one of the most admired works on ḥadith, wrote an extensive commentary. Surprisingly, he believes that Mālik and al-Shāfiʿī agree that the share of the booty for the relatives still is an established right down to the present. Al-Baghawī adds:

> The Book [the Qur'ān] and the Sunna both indicate the permanence [of the right of the relatives to a share of the *khums*] and the caliphs succeeding the Prophet used to distribute it, and the poor were not given preference over the rich because the Prophet and the caliphs gave a share to ʿAbbās ibn ʿAbd al-Muṭṭalib in spite of his abundant wealth.[16]

14 Al-Zamakhsharī, *al-Kashshāf ʿan Ḥaqā'iq Ghawāmiḍ al-Tanzīl*, II (Beirut, Dār al-Kitāb al-ʿArabī: 1366/1947) 221–223.
15 Abū al-Muẓaffar al-Samʿānī, *Tafsīr al-Qur'ān*, ed. Abu Tamim Yasir ibn Ibrahim and Abu Bilal Ghanim ibn ʿAbbas ibn Ghanim, II (Riyadh, Dār al-Waṭan: 1418/1997) 265–266.
16 Abū Muḥammad al-Ḥusayn ibn Masʿūd al-Baghawī, *Tafsīr al-Baghawī*, ed. Muhammad ʿAbd Allah al-Nimr, ʿUthman Jumʿa Dumayriya, and Sulayman Muslim al-Harash, III (Riyadh, Dār al-Ṭibah: 1418/1997) 357–359.

A near contemporary of al-Baghawī is the scholar al-Maybudī who flourished around 520/1126. His commentary is one of the largest pre-modern works in Persian. Al-Maybudī, somewhat surprisingly, says that *khums* comes out of both wealth acquired as booty and wealth in immoveable property acquired from non-Muslims through conquest or treaty, including the categories of *jizya* and *kharāj*. He describes the Prophet's share as going to the treasury for the welfare of the Muslims for such purposes as securing the frontier posts and the salaries of judges and muezzins.[17]

COMMENTARIES OF THE MIDDLE PERIOD

The seventh century of the Hijra (thirteenth century C.E.) was a rich period for Islamic scholarship, and one of the great commentators of this period was the Spanish jurist al-Qurṭubī (d. 671/1272), who was of the Mālikī school. He begins with an interesting philological discussion: *ghanīma* is "that which a man or a group attains by an effort from the unbelievers." *Fay'* is all wealth or property that comes to Muslims without war, such as the canonical taxes of *kharāj* and *jizya*. Characteristically of the Mālikīs, Qurṭubī says, "portions under the *khums* are at the discretion of the leader of the Muslims." He holds that the four first caliphs acted in this way.[18]

In the following century, one of the most important and respected commentaries is by the conservative scholar Ibn Kathīr, who died in 775/1373. As a specialist in the biography of the Prophet, he is particularly concerned with the occasion of revelation. He holds that the verse of *khums* was revealed after the battle of Badr, while the verse of *fay'* was revealed after the occupation of the quarter of Banū Naḍīr. But the verses do not really contradict one another. He quotes in several different forms letters from the Prophet to groups submitting to Islam. For example, there is a letter that reads "To Banū Zuhayr ibn Qays: If you bear witness that there is no god but God, and establish the prayer, and pay the *zakāt*, and separate from the heathen and pay the *khums* of the *ghanā'im* and the *ṣafī* [i.e., the object or objects which the leader of the victorious army may select for himself], then you are protected by the safe-conduct of God and of the Apostle!"

17 Al-Maybudī, *Kashf al-Asrār wa-'Uddat al-Abrār*, 10 vols. (Tehran, Dāneshgāh-e Tehrān: 1331–1339/1952–3–1960–1), IV:49–64.

18 Al-Qurṭubī, *al-Jāmi' li-Aḥkām al-Qur'ān*. www.altafsir.com (accessed March 5, 2011).

Ibn Kathīr judges this ḥadīth to be sound. Interestingly, in the context of the early Mamluk state, he says the *walī al-amr*, the general legatee of the Prophet, has the right of disposal over the *khums*. He judges another ḥadīth sound in which the Apostle of God said to the Banū Hāshim, "I wish you to be free from washing other people's hands, because you have a fifth of the fifth, which will make you rich, or at least self-sufficient."[19]

The major Twelver Shi'ite commentary of the 6th/12th century was written by al-Ṭabarsī—or, more correctly, al-Ṭabrisī (d. 548/1154). He says that the tradition transmitted from the Imams agrees with al-Shāfi'ī that *ghanīma* is what is taken in battle and *fay'* is what is taken without fighting. This verse therefore does not abrogate a similar verse in Sūrat al-Ḥashr (LIX:7) that specifies *fay'* for the relatives (among other categories). Al-Ṭabrisī says that according to his school (Shi'ism), *khums* is to be divided into six categories, of which the first three, God's share, the share of the Prophet and the share of the relatives goes to the Imam who stands in the place of the Prophet. The last three categories, the orphans, the poor and the wayfarer, all refer to the Family of the Prophet, as God has forbidden them the *ṣadaqāt*. The Twelvers agree with Ibn 'Abbās and Mujāhid that the Banū Hāshim alone are intended, to the exclusion of the Banū Muṭṭalib. The Twelvers also believe that the *khums* is to be paid on any profit made from transactions, profits of trade, treasure trove, mines, diving and the like. Al-Ṭabarsī quotes two opinions that agree with his own, namely that three of the six shares go to the Imam arising after the Prophet. Finally, he quotes Ibn 'Abbās as saying: "The *khums* is licit for us and the mark of honor (*karāma*) is licit for us."[20]

In his commentary, the Ḥanbalī polymath Ibn al-Jawzī (d. 597/1201) says that one of the three opinions on the fifth not distributed to the fighting men is that the share of God and of the Prophet is added to that of the relatives. This opinion is transmitted by the Companion Ibn Abī Ṭalḥa from Ibn 'Abbās. Ibn al-Jawzī then discusses opinions about the Prophet's share, and says that the founder of his school, Aḥmad ibn Ḥanbal (d. 241/855), agreed with al-Shāfi'ī that the Prophet's share after his death went to the welfare of the Muslims. He also understands Aḥmad ibn Ḥanbal to be

---

19 Ibn Kathīr, *Tafsīr Ibn Kathīr*, ed. by Salh 'Abd al-Fattah al-Khalidi, III (Amman, Dār al-Fārūq: 1429/2008) 1483–1487.

20 Faḍl ibn al-Ḥasan al-Ṭabrisī, *Majma' al-Bayān*, II (Qom, Maktabat al- Mar'ashī: 1403/1983) 543–545.

supporting the view of al-Shāfiʿī that the relatives are the Banū Hāshim and the Banū Muṭṭalib, even if they are rich.[21]

The commentator al-Nasafī (d. 710/1310) is a typical member of the Central Asian Ḥanafī school from far off Soghd. He flatly states as most Ḥanafīs do that the shares of the Prophet and the relatives are canceled with the Prophet's death. Yet he adds that a share goes to the poor relatives, not the rich relatives of the Prophet. It is not clear whether he considers their entitlement to come from this verse or from the share of the poor, although as a Ḥanafī he probably means the latter.[22]

THE SUFI COMMENTATORS

A separate strand of interpretation is found among the Sufi commentators. Al-Qushayrī (d. 465/1072), one of the most important mystics of the Islamic tradition, in his commentary relates the verse to the greater jihad in which the *ghanīma* is the recapture of the self or soul from desire and Satan. Inwardly, the place of seeking one's desires becomes the place of seeking God's satisfaction. In this way the servant of God is freed from the slavery of owning any share.[23]

Sufi commentary by ʿAbd al-Razzāq al-Kāshānī (d. 736/1336), often attributed to the great Ibn al-ʿArabī (d. 638/1240), discusses the verse in the same spirit. The five portions mentioned in the verse are the elements in the "comprehensive unicity [of man]" (*al-tawḥīd al-jamʿī*). The heart belongs to the Prophet; the share of the relatives means "the secret" (*al-sirr*) (which is given to them). The orphans are the theoretical and practical rational faculties. The poor are the faculty of sense perception, and the wayfarer is the inner traveling self in exile, traveling far from its original place.[24]

---

21 Abū al-Faraj ʿAbd al-Raḥmān ibn ʿAlī ibn al-Jawzī, *Zād al-Masīr fī ʿIlm al-Tafsīr*, ed. ʿAbd al-Razzaq al-Mahdi, II (Beirut, Dār al-Kitāb al-ʿArabī: 1422/2001) 211–212.

22 ʿAbd Allāh ibn Aḥmad al-Nasafī, *Tafsīr al-Nasafī: Madārik al-Tanzīl*, ed. Marwan Muhammad al-Shaʿar, II (Beirut, Dār al-Nafāʾis: 1417/1996) 41.

23 ʿAbd al-Karīm ibn Hawāzin al-Qushayrī, *Laṭāʾif al-Ishārāt*, ed. Ibrahim Basyuni, 2nd printing, I (Cairo, al-Hayʾa al-Miṣrīya al-ʿĀmma li-l-Kitāb: 1401/1981) 625.

24 Ibn al-ʿArabī (attr.), *Tafsir al-Qurʾān al-Karīm*, ed. by Mustafa Ghalib, 2nd printing, I (Beirut, Dār al-Andalus: 1398/1978) 477. Another important commentary in the Sufi tradition is by Ibn ʿAjība (d. 1224/1809): *al-Baḥr al-Madīd fī Tafsīr al-Qurʾān al-Majīd*, ed. ʿUmar Ahmad al-Rawi (Beirut: 2002); *The Immense Ocean*, trans. Mohamed Fouad Aresmouk and Michael Abdurrahman Fitzgerald (Louisville, KY, Fons Vitae: 2009).

THE LATER COMMENTATORS

The Ottoman commentator Abū al-Su'ūd, who died in 982/1574, served as Shaykh al-Islām under Süleyman the Magnificent. He was a Ḥanafī, like all holders of that office. He believed that the Imam has the right to do as he likes with prisoners as well as with land seized as plunder. This theory was important for Ottoman rule because it sanctioned the *devşirme*, a levy of the Christian youths of the Balkans, to form the elite army corps called Janissaries. On the issue of the rights of the House of the Apostle, he quotes Zayd ibn 'Alī (d. 122/740), who is supposed to have said, "We ['Alids] do not have the right to build forts or buy mounts from [the *khums*]." Doubtless the Ottomans, who saw themselves faced with the Safavid Twelver Shi'ite movement to their east, which championed the rights of the Family of the Prophet, wished to hear that defending their lands had priority over the claims of the Family.[25]

A Safavid commentator, al-Fayḍ al-Kāshānī, died 1091/1680, is one of the great intellects of the Shi'ite tradition. His commentary on this verse, however, is completely traditional and shows strong continuity with the commentary of Ṭūsī. He writes, "I say that *ghanīma* means the income from wealth (*māl*) of any sort whatever." He quotes not only Ṭūsī but also al-'Ayyāshī, who by this time had been integrated into the mainstream Twelver Shi'ite tradition. He makes it clear that payment of the *khums* is necessary for the individual believer's salvation, writing, "If you have believed in God, know that the *khums* is obligatory in order to draw near to Him, and be satisfied with the four-fifths [that remain for you]."[26]

CONCLUSION

It will be no surprise to any specialist in Qur'ān commentary that the commentators draw heavily on each other, particularly as the tradition develops. Nevertheless, some of the later commentators go back to collections of ḥadīth as does Ibn Kathīr whose commentary stands as one of the most extensive *tafsīrs bi-l-ma'thūr* or "commentary explicated by

25 Abū al-Su'ūd Muḥammad ibn Muḥammad, *Tafsīr Abī al-Su'ūd*. www.altafsir.com (accessed March 15, 2011).

26 Al-Fayḍ al-Kāshānī, *Kitāb al-Ṣāfī fī Tafsīr al-Qur'ān*, ed. by Muhsin al-Husayni al-Amini, III (Tehran, Dār al-Kutub al-Islāmīya: 1419/1998–9) 340–342.

tradition." In the commentaries less exhaustive of ḥadīth, there continues to be a difference in the choice of ḥadīth used as proof text. Only the longer commentaries are interested in preserving established points of *ikhtilāf*, "difference," such as whether the phrase "for God" implies a sixth portion—a view nearly universally rejected by the Sunnis and nearly universally adopted by the Shi'ites.

The adhesion of commentators to their respective Islamic law school dominates the commentaries from the middle Islamic period almost to the present, but this adhesion is not absolute. The insistence of the Shāfi'ī al-Baghawī that the Mālikī position agrees with the Shāfi'ī position is both contradicted by some scholars (e.g., al-Qurṭubī, a Mālikī, and Ibn Kathīr, a Shāfi'ī). Among Ḥanafīs the most important modification of the original opinion of that school is offered by Abū al-Su'ūd who adds to the Imam's rights the land seized as plunder.

Among Twelver Shi'ites there is general agreement although with some modifications. Al-'Ayyāshī, except for affirming the Imam's right to *khums*, does not describe the sources of wealth to which it applies. Al-Qumī states the Twelver Shi'ite case more plainly: there are six parts to the *khums*, three of which go to the Imam. The Imam also collects the other three parts to give to those named in the Qur'ān. In the commentary written over a hundred years later by Ṭūsī, we are given a presentation of subsequent Twelver belief without, however, explaining to whom *khums* is paid in the absence of the Imam. The seventeenth-century commentary by al-Fayḍ al-Kāshānī is also silent on this point.[27]

The Sufi commentaries are remarkable for the largely individual ways in which they interpret the inner meaning of the verse. Not one of the three Sufi commentators draws on another.

Modern Shi'ite scholars point out that none of the schools restrict *khums* to the spoils of battle. All law schools recognize that buried treasure is *ghanīma*, and Ḥanafīs and Twelver Shi'ites agree that mines are subject to *khums*.[28] But the Ḥanafīs regard wealth from mines not fully exploited as well as buried treasure to be plunder abandoned by pre-Muslim peoples.

---

27 For the discussion of *khums* among the Shi'ite jurists, see the learned appendix on the subject by Abdulaziz Sachedina, *The Just Ruler in Shi'ite Islam* (New York, Oxford University Press: 1988), esp. 239–243.

28 See, e.g., Sayyid Muhammad Rizvi, *Khums: An Islamic Tax* (Qom, Ansariyan Publications: 1992).

An interesting discussion in many commentaries bears on the reasons that the Qur'ān gives the relatives a claim to the *khums*. No commentary known to me says that all the *sayyids* or *sharīfs* have inherently better inherited characteristics (or, to use contemporary language, better genetic material). Clearly, for many authors, it is a mark of respect for the Prophet that his heirs should have special rights. Both Sunni and Shi'ite commentaries say that it replaces the *ṣadaqa*, which is forbidden for the descendants of the Prophet. It is significant that only the *ṣadaqa* and not the *zakāt* is mentioned in these contexts and, because when the two terms are not used interchangeably, *ṣadaqa* means voluntary alms.

Al-'Ayyāshī quotes Ja'far al-Ṣādiq, the sixth of the twelve Imams, as saying: "The *khums* for us is a duty (*farīḍa*), and the mark of honor/grace (*karāma*) bestowed on us is a licit matter."[29]

Al-Ṭabrisī, as mentioned above, repeats this sentiment, again referring to the mark of honor/grace that the payment of the *khums* embodies. As al-Maybudī observes above, this right of the relatives has nothing to do with the poverty or wealth of the recipients. Yet Ibn Kathīr quotes the Prophet as saying that he wished the Banū Hāshim "to be free of washing other people's hands," because the *khums* will make them rich or at least self-sufficient.

Is the *khums*, even that minor *khums* granted by Ḥanafīs out of treasure trove, meant to keep the relatives of the Prophet from poverty? Is it meant to honor the Prophet by honoring his kinsmen, regardless of their need? Is it a privilege to pay the kinsmen of the Prophet? Or, is it all or some or none of these? This question is in part addressed by the commentaries as well as other sources. It is a distinct question but related to the question of the sociological function of *sayyids*/*sharīfs*. These respected kinsmen of the Prophet wished to maintain their collective right to some sort of income and also to preserve their role as sanctified members of the societies in which they lived. A fuller answer to the questions as to why they "deserve" this distinction will provide insight into the presence of this privileged category in Muslim societies.

29 Al-'Ayyāshī, (*supra* n. 7), II:202.

ISLAMIC EDUCATION

My interest in medieval Islamic education grew in the 1980s after the Iranian Revolution. I began to see Khomeini in part as a product of his education and experience in the somewhat vague hierarchy of Iranian religious leaders, the mullahs. I was fortunate enough to make the acquaintance and take lessons from the teacher of Islamic jurisprudence Ali Gomaa at the Azhar, which is the premier university of Islamic learning in Cairo. My teacher subsequently became the Grand Mufti of Egypt (2003–2013). He, of course, taught me Sunni jurisprudence, which is the law followed by the majority of Muslims.

My central interest, however, remained Shi'ite jurisprudence, which is the school of law for the Twelver Shi'ites living principally in Iran and southern Iraq. I made the acquaintance of several Iranian mullahs living in Iran and in exile as well as others trained in Islamic *ḥawzas*, or Shi'ite seminaries, in Iraq, Lebanon, Oman, and even in South Asia. The conversations we had about Islamic education, together with a great interest in Iran, the country of my father's birth, were the two factors that led me to write *The Mantle of the Prophet* in 1985, which attempted to explain Iran and its people to the Western world. That attempt, which discussed two thousand years of history, focused heavily on education as it developed in the Islamic seminaries and survived alongside the introduction of secular education in the modern Muslim world. To understand the Iranian clergy of the present day it is important to understand the style and content of Islamic religious education in Iran.

Islamic education from Morocco to Indonesia used to begin in simple Qur'ān schools which usually taught through rote learning. Before World War II some children went to both state and Qur'ān schools at the same time. In Iran secular state education has been required for elementary education since the 1930s (but only achieved on a national level in the late 1940s), and Qur'ān schools have mostly disappeared. Qur'ān schools continue to give elementary education in many Muslim countries. Children who have finished Qur'ān school or a secular elementary school may go on to study at madrasas, or seminaries for higher Islamic religious education, which are collectively called *ḥawza*s by Shi'ites.

The first article in this section, "The Transmission of Learning: The Role of the Islamic Northeast," was delivered at a roundtable discussion on madrasas at the Centre d'études pédagogiques à Sévres in Paris in 1992 and published in 1997 in *Madrasa: la transmission du savoir dans le monde musulman*, edited by Nicole Grandin and Marc Gaborieau. This article discusses the rise of the madrasas in the 4th/10th and 5th/11th centuries in the Islamic Northeast, which comprises the area of Khorasan in Iran and the adjacent part of Central Asia (made up of parts of Afghanistan and Turkmenistan). As the curricula of the madrasas developed, they strongly reflected the central ideas of Islamic clergymen in their times.

The second article in this section, "Traditional Shi'ite Education in Qom," was published in 1995 in the *Harvard Middle Eastern and Islamic Review*. It focuses on both the textbooks and the method of learning in the nineteenth and twentieth centuries. Many of the texts are from earlier centuries, both from the medieval and pre-modern periods. New texts are introduced very slowly, and there is a slight variation from the curricula taught at Najaf and Kerbala in Iraq. Very few of these texts are available in English. One, which I translated and on which I wrote copious comments, is *Lessons in Islamic Jurisprudence*, by Muhammad Baqir al-Sadr, published in 2003. Disputation is strongly encouraged in the classes of the *ḥawza*s. To some extent the elementary levels of this education resemble the *trivium* (that is, grammar, rhetoric, and logic) used in Latin education in the medieval European world.

The third article in this section, "The Najaf *Ḥawza* Curriculum," was published in the *Journal of the Royal Asiatic Society* in 2016. This article views the curriculum used in the *ḥawza*s of Najaf through an historical lens focusing on curricula published in 1913 and 2007. Both of these curricular lists contained many pre-modern texts but also introduced new works written in the nineteenth and twentieth centuries. A somewhat similar style of education still exists in some theological seminaries in the West. It would be interesting to compare *ḥawza* education with yeshiva education, but I am not knowledgeable enough to discuss yeshiva curricula.

Najaf owes its importance to its being the site of the burial of the Prophet's cousin and son-in-law 'Alī. By its own reckoning the Najaf *ḥawza* is one of the oldest institutions of learning in the world, having been created in the 5th/11th century. From the nineteenth century to the present day it has been the residence of one of the most powerful mullahs among the Shiʿite clergy. I visited Najaf twice in my life, most recently in 2014, and was deeply fascinated by the city. I read parts of the curriculum in the original Arabic and translated into English one of the standard elementary texts (that of Muhammad Baqir al-Sadr mentioned earlier) written in the twentieth century. The Najaf *ḥawza* seemed in its methods of teaching to represent a tradition of teaching through disputation that stretched back to antiquity. The dialogic presentation of texts, in particular, seems to have a long tradition.

The study of the curricula of *ḥawzas* is not much in vogue in the West. However, to me it seems central to a deeper understanding of the scholars produced in this system, including Khomeini and his contemporaries and successors, from at least the 11th/17th century to the present. In spite of its age, *An Introduction to the History of Education in Modern Egypt* (1968) by J. Heyworth Dunne retains its value for the information it gathers. George Makdisi's *The Rise of Colleges* (1981) is a useful guide to the rise of madrasas in the Islamic Middle East. About the style of learning, one of the best introductions is still the relevant chapter in Ibn Khaldūn's *Muqaddima* of the late 8th/14th century. The biographies of the ulema (mullahs) can be important sources for what was (and is) taught across the centuries.

If this kind of scholarship seems marginal or antiquated today, one need only remind oneself about modern-day struggles in the United States to teach evolution rather than creationism in our elementary and high schools and even the very contemporary struggles to teach so-called "critical race theory" in our colleges or to promote "replacement theory" conspiracies in our politics. The ongoing attempts in the U.S. to pack school boards across the country with partisans of fake historical views unfortunately mirrors attempts in third-world countries to sideline minorities and tighten authoritarian control of society through religion and ethnocentric policies,

The Transmission of Learning: The Role of the Islamic Northeast

This essay attempts to clarify certain points about the history of the transmission of knowledge among Muslims in the eastern Islamic world, especially Khorasan and Transoxiana. I hope to rectify a history of Islamic education that in my view has been excessively Baghdad-centered. This Baghdad-centeredness is largely the result of the loss of chronicles written in the eastern Islamic world before the *Tārikh-e Mas'udi* by al-Bayhaqi (d. 470/1077). Even a glance at V.V. Barthold's monumental historical survey, *Turkestan Down to the Mongol Invasion* (London: 1968), will reveal how overwhelmingly modern historians have had to rely on universal histories such as those of Ṭabarī and Ibn al-Athīr for the eastern Islamic world of this earlier period.

First, we would do well to try and recall some of the recurrent features and themes in the self-representation of the transmission of learning in the Islamic Middle East. There is, of course, no reified Islamic education and no "necessary" connection between these themes and Islam, although some of these themes have strong affinities with Islam as it was generally understood in the milieux that are discussed here. The place of medicine in the madrasa is symptomatic of the variable content of Islamic education; generally accepted as part of the curriculum in India and Turkey, medicine was generally rejected in the madrasas of the Middle East. Nevertheless, some themes do recur.

One such theme is the tension between the desire to transmit learning and the questionableness of being paid for it. A second such theme is the

---

Author's note: This article was first published as: "The Transmission of Learning: The Role of the Islamic Northeast," in Nicole Grandin and Marc Gaborieau (eds.), *Madrasa: la transmission du savoir dans le monde musulman* (Paris, αρ éditions Arguments: 1997) 63–72.

permissibility of accepting money from governments. A third theme is the permissibility for a scholar of having any association with people of power.

A fourth theme is the relation between piety and learning. There seems to be an overwhelming agreement that learning cannot take place without piety[1] and a fair number of voices that claim that learning enhances the status of a pious person.[2] Concurrent with this theme is a fifth theme that emphasizes the "ordeal"—abstinence, sleepless nights of study and the like—without which the truly learned would never have obtained learning.[3] Yet a sixth theme is the loose boundaries of the ulema in the pre-Ottoman Middle East, which allowed dictionaries listing local ulema to include scholars only marginally involved in the transmission of learning.[4]

A seventh theme is the tension between the essentialism of most definitions of knowledge[5] and the conventionalism of the theory of language accepted by most Islamic Middle Eastern scholars, namely, that words considered as sounds are arbitrarily associated with meanings.[6] An eighth theme is, perhaps, related: namely, the essentialist character of the message of a scholar in his/her maturity. There is a consciousness that there may have been a maturation of a scholar's thought but little interest in dividing his/her thought into early, middle, and later periods. While *juvenalia* may be separated, there is comparatively little interest in the early, middle, and later phases of the mature Mutanabbī or Ibn Sīnā or Aristotle: rather, the emphasis was on harmonization of the thoughts of an author such as Aristotle. This model may have been based in part on Galen, who wrote a guide on how to read his own books, which suggested that they were a united body of work. Another reason to see the works of

1 On this last theme, see Franz Rosenthal, *Knowledge Triumphant* (Leiden: 1970) 330–331.

2 See, for example, the 6th/12th-century scholar from the eastern Islamic world: al-Zarnūjī, *Taʿlīm al-Mutaʿllim*, with the commentary of Ibrāhīm ibn Ismāʿīl (Cairo, Muṣṭafā al-Bābī al-Ḥalabī: n.d.) 39–41, his "Chapter on Piety/Abstinence (*Waraʿ*)." Cf. Zarnūjī, *Taʿlīm al-Mutaʿllim*, trans. G.E. von Grunebaum and Theodora M. Abel, *Instruction of the Student* (New York: 1947) 64–66 for this chapter.

3 See my article "Traditional Shiʿite Education in Qom" (Article 15 here).

4 See my book *Loyalty and Leadership in an Early Islamic Society* (Princeton, N.J., Princeton University Press: 1980) 135–150.

5 Franz Rosenthal, "Muslim Definitions of Knowledge," in Carl Leiden (ed.), *The Conflict of Traditionalism and Modernism in the Muslim Middle East* (Austin, TX: 1966) 117–133.

6 For a beautifully clear exposition of conventionalism, see Muhammad Baqir al-Sadr, *Durūs fī ʿIlm al-Uṣūl*, I (Beirut: 1397) 84ff and also my translation, *Lessons in Islamic Jurisprudence* (London, Oneworld: 2003) 34–35.

a specific author as homogenized was the tendency of authors to present their works as expositions of the same message for different audiences. Thus, Mas'ūdī composed extended works such as the *Murūj al-Dhahab*, summaries such as the *al-Tanbīh wa-l-Ishrāf*, and middle works such as the appropriately named *Kitab al-Awsaṭ*.

A ninth and partly related feature of education in this milieu is that it is centripetal to texts. Texts are only properly assimilated when studied with a teacher, preferably a teacher who can trace his understanding of the text back through a line of teachers to a disciple taught the text by the author himself. The text is in some sense a distillation of the author's thought which must be rehydrated; hence the authors are often referred to with the shorthand of their most famous text, as the great Shi'ite jurisconsult (*faqīh*) Murtaḍā al-Anṣārī is most commonly called simply *ṣāḥib al-makāsib*, the author or master of the book *al-Makāsib*. This view of the transmission of learning is consonant with a general visualization of professions and, indeed, institutions, as vertically integrated through chains of transmission across time.[7]

The tenth and last feature to be mentioned here is the "personalistic" character of the transmission of learning. This feature is, of course, related to the personal guarantee of a teacher that the text is correctly transmitted, as we have discussed above. Even after the madrasa was founded, the biographical dictionaries for the pre-Ottoman Islamic Middle East seldom mention the madrasa at which a scholar studied, although they frequently mention by name the teachers with whom he studied at these madrasas.[8] This personalistic character is clear for other fields, such as medicine (even though there are "teaching" hospitals), the art of the government clerk/scribe and so forth. Ibn Khaldūn describes teaching and, indeed, scholarship/learning (*'ilm*) as a "craft" (*ṣinā'a*), and in this sense teaching was seen in these milieux as one part of the spectrum of "crafts" taught by masters to apprentices.[9] Anyone who has tried to understand *siyāqat*,

7 See my article "Some Islamic Views of the Pre-Islamic Past" (Article 32 here).
8 See Daphna Ephrat, *A Learned Society in a Period of Transition: The Sunni 'Ulama' of Eleventh-Century Baghdad* (Albany, State University of New York: 2000) 59. This book comments on how infrequently madrasas are mentioned in biographical entries for scholars who live in Baghdad in the 5th/11th and 6th/12th centuries. This infrequency, as Ephrat says, is noticed for the Mamluk period by Jonathan Berkey, *The Transmission of Knowledge in Medieval Cairo* (Princeton, N.J., Princeton University Press: 1992) 18.
9 Ibn Khaldūn, *Muqaddimat, Prolégomènes d'Ebn Khaldoun*, ed. E. Quatremère, III (Paris: 1858) 171–173.

the number system and preferred bookkeeping technique of officials and great merchants in the Ottoman, Safavid, and Moghul empires would understand the apprenticeship necessary to enter these spheres of life. Hence madrasa teaching, while better endowed and more written about than these parallel and/or alternative paths of learning, may not have been radically different from them in style.

The stages of development of the madrasa system are described with a wealth of important detail by George Makdisi in his magisterial book, *The Rise of Colleges,* sure to remain for generations the classic treatment of this subject.[10] Makdisi sees an evolution from teaching in the mosque to teaching in the mosque-*khān* complex under the Ḥasanwayhids to teaching in the madrasa proper. While this overall picture seems hard to challenge, it is difficult for me to accept Makdisi's contention that the mosque-*khān* complex was popularized by Badr ibn Ḥasanwayh, a ruler of part of western Iran who died in 405/1014. I do not understand the critical passage of Ibn al-Jawzī to state that Badr "established throughout the realm of his administration three thousand *masjid-khān* complexes: these were *masjid*-colleges, with adjacent *khāns* for out-of-town students." To my understanding the passage reads: "He created/rebuilt (*istaḥdatha*) in his territories three thousand mosques and caravanserais (*khān*) for strangers."[11] I am not acquainted with any reference that proves that these thousands of mosques were teaching institutions, or that the caravanserais mentioned were attached to them.

The arrangements for endowment and for lodging students in madrasas that existed before Niẓām al-Mulk are not clear, although it seems certain that the word madrasa was more common in Khorasan than elsewhere in this earlier period. In Richard Bulliet's very useful list of the madrasas of Nishapur there are four madrasas that a local history describes as built in the first half of the 4th/10th century. Some later madrasas were built by government officials such as the Madrasa Ibn Fūrak founded by Nāṣir al-Dawla Abū al-Ḥasan Muḥammad, a governor of the semi-independent Simjūrid family of governors of that city some time before his ouster in 372 A.H. In 390 A.H. Naṣr ibn Sabuktagīn, the brother of Maḥmūd of Ghazna, founded the Madrasat al-Ṣaʿīdī, which Bulliet tells us, "was first

10 George Makdisi, *The Rise of Colleges: Institutions of Learning in Islam and the West* (Edinburgh: 1981) 29–30.

11 *Ibid.*, 29–30, quoting from Ibn al-Jawzī, *Muntaẓam*, VII (Hyderabad: 1357) 272.

and foremost a school of law. It seems quite likely that this madrasa was the pattern for the later Nizamiya ..."[12]

A great deal of this activity can be ascribed to the involvement of local leaders (and governments) in the factional struggles of the region which in Khorasan so often took religious coloring, as in the case of the Shāfi'ī-Ḥanafī struggle which the Seljuk dynasty would import into their central administration. The geographer al-Muqaddasī, who wrote circa 380/990 and visited Khorasan in 374/984, writes that in Khorasan, "there is no *qāḍī* except from the two groups" (i.e., the Ḥanafīs and Shāfi'īs).[13]

Factional strife was not the only reason that this northeastern region of the Islamic world had so many institutions of learning. Khorasan, the nearby cities of Transoxiana, and Rayy in north-central Iran, which had become integrated into the scholarly network of Khorasan, were areas that had developed strong traditions of learning from the 2nd/8th century. (Al-Muqaddasī says of Rayy, as he says of Khorasan, that it is a place of madrasas).[14] A wealthy man of the town of Bayhaq in Khorasan, Khwāja Abū al-Qāsim 'Alī ibn Muḥammad ibn al-Ḥusayn ibn 'Amr, offers us an example of a patron who rose above faction. Sometime before the death of Maḥmūd of Ghazna in 421/1030, Khwāja Abū al-Qāsim built four madrasas in that town, each differently oriented. One was for the Ḥanafīs and another for the Shafi'īs and both were still operating in 563/1168. He also built one for the Karrāmīya. The fourth was built for the "Sayyids, the Mu'tazilīs and the Zaydīs." This interesting list of four schools proposed by these foundations as in some sense "orthodox" did not please Sultan Maḥmūd, who had Khwāja Abū al-Qāsim brought to his capital in 414/1022. Maḥmūd scolded the hapless donor and asked, "Why do you not aid the one *madhhab* in which you believe and build a madrasa [just] for the leading scholars of that group (*ṭā'ifa*)? When a person builds a madrasa and fosters education for all groups, that person has acted against his/her belief. A person who has acted against his/her belief, does so for the sake of hypocrisy and fame, not for the sake of drawing near to Almighty God." Fortunately, vigorous intercession persuaded Maḥmūd to let Khwāja Abū al-Qāsim go.[15]

12 Richard Bulliet, *The Patricians of Nishapur: A Study in Medieval Islamic Social History* (Cambridge, MA: 1972) 249–251.

13 Al-Muqaddasī, *Aḥsan al-Taqāsīm*, ed. M.J. de Goeje (Leiden, Brill: 1906) 323.

14 *Ibid.*, 390.

15 Ebn Fondoq, *Tārikh-e Bayhaq* (Tehran: 1938) 194–195. I am grateful to the book of Husayn Sultanzadah, *Tārikh-e Madāres-e-Irān* (Tehran: 1364) 106, for calling my attention to this passage.

If factional strife is not a sufficient reason for the rise of the madrasa in the northeastern Islamic world, another plausible reason is the extraordinary development of study in this area. It has been noticed in passing, but nowhere, to my knowledge, discussed in detail, that four of the six ḥadīth books considered "canonical" by the majority of the Sunni tradition are from Khorasan and the immediately neighboring parts of Transoxiana, namely: al Bukhārī (d. 256 A.H.), Muslim ibn al-Ḥajjāj al-Nīsābūrī (d. 261 A.H.), al-Nasā'ī (d. 303 A.H.) and Tirmidhī (d. 270 or 275 or 279 A.H.).[16] The other two are from provinces immediately neighboring Khorasan: Abū Dā'ūd al-Sijistānī (d. 275 A.H.) and Ibn Mājah al-Qazwīnī (d. 273 A.H.), if we understand Qazwīn/Qazvin, as most geographers do, to be part of al-Jibāl. It should be remembered that many of the chapters of ḥadīth books, at least from the time of *al-Muwaṭṭa'* of Mālik (d. 179 A.H.), are organized around legal topics, and these headings are taken over directly by the early law books and show that such ḥadīth books are proto-lawbooks. It is, therefore, no surprise that the development of legal studies and the madrasa oriented to a specific jurist or law school should immediately follow the flowering of ḥadīth studies in this eastern Islamic area. I here offer a sketch—albeit much too brief—of the development of ḥadīth study.

The study of ḥadīth began relatively late in the Islamic East. Its founder is usually said to have been 'Abd Allāh ibn al-Mubārak (d. 181 A.H.), born in Hamadan to a Turkish slave father and a Khwārazmian mother. Ibn al-Mubārak traveled and taught widely in the central and eastern Islamic world. In Marw (Marv) one of his pupils was Ibrāhīm ibn Naṣr al-Sūrīnī (or Sūryānī) from Nishapur who died in 210 A.H. Ibrāhīm's list of pupils includes some of the most distinguished ḥadīth specialists of the next generation in Khorasan and Rayy, including Abū Zur'a 'Ubayd Allāh ibn 'Abd al-Karīm al-Rāzī (d. 264 A.H.) and Abū Ḥātim Muḥammad ibn Idrīs ibn al-Mundhir al-Ḥanẓalī al-Rāzī (d. 277 A.H.). According to Yāqūt, the son of the second Rāzī, 'Abd al-Raḥmān ibn Abī Ḥātim, said, "I heard my father and Abū Zur'a placing Ibrāhīm ibn Naṣr al-Sūrīnī Nīsābūrī ahead of others in preserving knowledge of ḥadīth organized according to informants (*musnad*) ... Abū 'Abd Allāh [Muḥammad ibn 'Alī] al-Ḥākim al-Nīsābūrī [d. 404] said, I read in the handwriting of Abū 'Amr, the professional speaker of ḥadīth (*mustamlī*): Abū Aḥmad Muḥammad ibn 'Abd

16 See, for example, Berthold Spuler, *Iran in früh-islamischer Zeit* (Wiesbaden: 1952) 151.

al-Wahhāb said to me, 'The very learned, religious and pious Ibrāhīm ibn Naṣr [al-Sūrīnī] was the first to expound the science/knowledge (*'ilm*) *of* ḥadīth in Nishapur.'"[17]

The two Rāzīs mentioned above are critical to the development of the discipline of critiquing ḥadīth transmitters, called in its widest sense *'ilm al-rijāl* also called, sometimes in a slightly narrower sense, *al-jarḥ wa-l-ta'dīl*. There is no question that the intellectual conflict between adherents of *ra'y* (individual reasoning) on the one hand, and the adherents of ḥadīth as primary sources of law on the other, was at its most vigorous in Iraq and areas to the east of Iraq. The development of a rigorous discipline of ḥadīth was in some measure a response to this conflict. Goldziher identifies the beginnings of the stricter criticism of the authorities cited in *isnāds* with the abovementioned 'Abd Allāh ibn al-Mubārak and the two Basrans, Shu'ba ibn al-Ḥajjāj (d. 160 A.H) and Abū 'Awn 'Abd Allāh ibn 'Awn (d. 151 A.H.).[18] (This criticism spread to Khorasan and Transoxiana not only through 'Abd Allāh ibn Mubārak but to Marv through al-Nadr ibn Shumayl who died in 204 A.H. and to Samarqand through 'Abd Allāh al-Dārimī who died in 255 A.H.)[19]

'Abd Allāh ibn Aḥmad ibn Ḥanbal is quoted as saying of his father, the author of the greatest *Musnad*, that when Abū Zur'a al-Rāzī stayed with him, "I only prayed the obligatory prayer; I preferred our sessions reciting hadīth to one another (*al-mudhākara*)[20] over my supererogatory devotions. 'Abd Allāh ibn Aḥmad ibn Ḥanbal said on his own authority, 'No one has crossed the bridge [that connects the two sides of Baghdad] who is better in *fiqh* than Isḥāq ibn Rāhawayh, and no one greater in memory of ḥadīth than Abū Zur'a.' He once said to his father, Aḥmad ibn Ḥanbal, 'Who are the masters (*ḥuffāẓ*) of ḥadīth? He (Aḥmad) said, 'My son, young men from Khorasan who were with us and have dispersed.' I said, 'Who are they, father?' He said, Muḥammad ibn Ismā'īl, that man of Bukhāra, [Abū Zur'a] 'Ubayd Allāh ibn 'Abd al-Karīm, that man of Rayy, 'Ubayd Allāh ibn 'Abd

17 Yāqūt, *Kitāb Mu'jam al-Buldān*, III (Leipzig: 1868) 187. This passage was called to my attention by a short but useful notice by J. Fueck, "The Role of Traditionalism in Islam," reprinted in *Studies on Islam*, trans. and ed. by Merlin L. Swartz (New York: 1981) 103–104.

18 Ignaz Goldziher, *Muslim Studies*, II (London: 1971) 135.

19 *Ibid.*, 76 to which Spuler, (*supra* n. 16) 151, adds small details; an examination of the ḥadīth activity of these two ḥadīth experts goes beyond the present essay.

20 On *mudhākara*, see Ḥasan ibn 'Abd al-Raḥmān al-Rāmhurmuzī, *al-Muḥaddith. al-Fāṣil* (Beirut: 1391/1971) 545–548.

al-Raḥmān, that man of Samarqand, and al-Ḥasan ibn Shujā', that man of Balkh.'"[21] Noteworthy here is not only that an explicit recognition of the Khorasanian connection is made by Aḥmad ibn Ḥanbal and included by a Baghdadi in a history of Baghdad, but also that Rayy and Samarqand are included in Khorasan.

Most of the writings of Abū Ḥātim Muḥammad ibn Idrīs ibn al-Mundhir al-Ḥanẓalī al-Rāzī.) are lost; but one of his books is *Kitāb al-Du'āfa' wa-l-Kadhdhābīn*; "The Book on Weak/Unreliable and Lying (Transmitters) [of ḥadīth]," which confirms the reports of the short biographies about him that he was centrally interested in the criticism of the chains of transmission of ḥadīth.[22] His son Abū Muḥammad 'Abd al-Raḥmān (commonly called Ibn Abī Ḥātim), born in 240 in Rayy (where he died in 327 A.H.) advanced and codified the ḥadīth criticism of his father and Abū Zur'a and preserves very many of the fragments of the writings of both scholars in his monumental *al-Jarḥ wa-l-Ta'dīl*.

Another important intermediary between 'Abd Allāh ibn al-Mubārak and the authors of the "Six Books" of the ḥadīth of the Sunnis is Abū Ya'qūb Isḥāq ibn Ibrāhīm ibn Makhlad, called Ibn Rāhawayh (mentioned above), who was born in Marw/Marv in 161 or 166 and died in Nishapur in 238 A.H. One of his principal teachers was 'Abd Allāh ibn al-Mubārak (who was, like Abū Ḥātim, a Ḥanẓalī, i.e., a descendant of the tribe Ḥanẓala or one of its clients). Ibn Rāhawayh was the teacher of all the authors of the "Six Books" except Ibn Māja.[23] Ibn Rāhawayh's respect for the tradition of Rayy is attested by his remark: "Any ḥadīth that Abū Zur'a al-Rāzī does not know has no basis (*aṣl*)."[24]

The connection of all of these six authors with the above-mentioned earlier or contemporaneous members of the "Khorasanian" school is direct, and in most cases is intimate. The prominent Shāfi'ī scholar 'Abd al-Karīm ibn Abī Sa'īd Muḥammad al-Rāfi'ī al-Qazwīnī, in his authoritative history of the ḥadīth transmitters of Qazvin, says, "I heard my father, may he rest in peace, say, 'The *Sunan* of Ibn Māja was presented to Abū Zur'a al-Rāzī and he approved it.'"[25] Al-Dhahabī says that it was reported on

21 Abū Bakr Aḥmad ibn 'Alī al-Khatīb al-Baghdādī, *Ta'rīkh Baghdād*, X (Beirut: n.d.) 327–328.

22 Fuat Sezgin, *Geschichte des arabischen Schriftums*, I (Leiden: 1967) 153.

23 J Schacht, "Ibn Rahawayh," *The Encyclopaedia of Islam*, 2nd ed. (hereafter *EI²*), III (Leiden, Brill: 1971) 902.

24 Al-Baghdādī, (*supra* n. 21), X:331.

25 Al-Rafi'ī, *Kitāb al-Tadwīn fī Dhikr Ahl al-'Ilm bi-Qazwīn*, II (Beirut: 1408) 49.

the authority of Ibn Māja himself that he said, "I presented this *Sunan* to Abū Zur'a and he examined it, and said, 'I believe that if this [collection] falls into people's hands those [other] collections, or [at least] most of them, will fall out of use.' He added, 'Perhaps there is not a total of thirty ḥadīth in it in which there is weakness in the chains of transmission.'"[26] Similarly, Muslim, born in 202/817 or 206/821 in Nishapur (where he died in 261/875) submitted his *Ṣaḥīḥ* to Abū Zur'a al-Rāzī and retained only those traditions that Abū Zur'a considered genuine.[27] The two Rāzīs seemed to have returned the compliment, for we are told that, "Aḥmad ibn Salama said, 'I saw Abū Zur'a and Abū Ḥātim giving preference to Muslim ibn al-Ḥajjāj in knowledge of sound (*ṣaḥīḥ*) ḥadīth over other learned specialists (*mashāyikh*) of their time.'"[28]

The case of al-Bukhārī, the author of the other *Ṣaḥīḥ*, is more complicated. Al-Bukhārī was born in 194 and died in 256, and he is therefore approximately eight years older than Muslim. Al-Dhahabī mentions as his first important accomplishment that al-Bukhārī "memorized the writings of ['Abd Allāh] ibn al-Mubārak as a boy."[29] Bukhārī's interest in compiling the *Ṣaḥīḥ* is said to owe its origins to a remark by Ibn Rāhawayh that he wished that some specialist in ḥadīth would compile a comprehensive book containing only genuine traditions.[30] He is part of this tradition in that he was a student of Aḥmad ibn Ḥanbal who refined his *isnāds* by more exacting standards.

Abū Dā'ūd of Sijistān (modern Sistan) stands a little apart from this tradition. He did not visit or hear ḥadīth from Ibn Rāhawayh. His most important teacher was Aḥmad ibn Ḥanbal, and it is said that he presented his book to Ibn Ḥanbal who thought well of it.[31] Unlike the other five authors, he died in Iraq (to be exact, in Basra). Not lacking in self-confidence, Abū Dā'ūd places his book second only to the Qur'ān as a book for Muslims to study. More importantly, he extended the style of Muslim, who offered an introductory discussion of his principles of ḥadīth criticism. Abū Dā'ūd is the first to give fairly frequent detailed notes in the text itself, in which, for example, he indicates that a certain tradition might

26 Al-Dhahabī, *Tadhkirat al-Huffāẓ*, (Hyderabad: 1914–5) 636.

27 Muhammad Zubayr Siddiqi, *Hadith Literature* (Calcutta: 1961) 101, quoting from Abū Zakarīya Yaḥyā al-Nawawī's commentary on *Ṣaḥīḥ Muslim*.

28 Al-Dhahabī, (*supra* n. 26), 589.

29 Al-Dhahabī, (*supra* n. 26), 555.

30 Siddiqi, (*supra* n. 27), 93.

31 Al-Baghdādī, (*supra* n. 21), IX:56.

be considered continuously transmitted from the Prophet or might stop short of the Prophet. He deliberately includes some "nearly sound" or even "weak" ḥadīth when they are the sole testimony for certain questions.[32] In this sense he continues and strengthens the tradition of making ḥadīth books as useful as possible for the *faqīh* or lawyer while showing the critical attitude necessary for a ḥadīth book to claim a higher moral ground than that occupied by the adherents of *ra'y* (opinion).

Tirmidhī, the pupil of Abū Dā'ūd (and, to a lesser extent, of al-Bukhārī) makes the critical approach of Abū Dā'ūd more systematic. (Tirmidhī as well as Ibn Māja, Muslim, Abū Dā'ūd, and Nasā'ī, soon to be mentioned, heard ḥadīth from Abū Zur'a al-Rāzī.[33]) Tirmidhī is concerned both with the rigorous criticism of *isnāds* and with the difference between the schools of law.[34] Therefore, even though Tirmidhī includes a great deal of theological material he is particularly useful to lawyers and ḥadīth scholars. Al-Nasā'ī, who died well after the other five authors, draws on all of them. He is connected to the methods of his predecessors in that he had "two abiding interests": criticism of the transmitters mentioned in the *isnāds* and comparisons of the difficult wordings in the texts of the ḥadīth.[35]

What are the common characteristics of the "Six Books"? They are arranged by topic, not by the original transmitter, and are therefore much more readily useful to the lawyer and theologian. In this they followed (among others) 'Abd Allāh ibn al-Mubārak who "set down knowledge [of ḥadīth] in topical chapters (*abwāb*)."[36] Secondly, they are all concerned with the discipline of *rijāl*, the examination of the aspects of the lives of transmitters considered relevant to their acceptability as transmitters. Al-Bukhārī, earliest of the six, wrote separate from his *Ṣaḥīḥ*, a many-volume work, *al-Ta'rīkh al-Kabīr*, on transmitters. In this sense the six authors were in part heirs to several figures of the "greater Khorasanian" tradition, and in particular to the two Rāzīs, Abū Ḥātim and Abū Zur'a, who advanced this discipline most significantly in the middle of the third century A.H.

---

32 J. Robson, "Abū Dā'ūd al-Sidjistanī," *EI²*, I (Leiden, Brill: 1960) 114, and John Burton, *An Introduction to the Hadith* (Edinburgh: 1994) 126–128.

33 Al-Dhahabī, (*supra* n. 26), 557.

34 A.J. Wensinck, "Al-Tirmidhī," *First Encyclopaedia of Islam*, VIII (reprint, Leiden: 1987) 796–797. and G.H.A. Juynboll, "Al-Tirmidhī," *EI²*, X (Leiden, Brill: 1999) 546.

35 Burton, (*supra* n. 32), 129.

36 Al-Dhahabī, (*supra* n. 26), 274.

Thirdly, the authors seek to make their ḥadīth "Prophetic," i.e., traced directly back to the Prophet, whenever possible. It is true that many ḥadīth in Bukhārī do not have complete *isnāds*. Whether this lack is because the ḥadīth involved were considered essential on points of law and belief and confirmed by *ijmāʿ*, or because, as Fuat Sezgin says, they were adapted from authentic books, all recognizable as quotations by the special terminology with which Bukhārī introduces them and therefore derived from reliable written sources which contained full *isnād*s, the present author is unqualified to judge.[37] But that the six authors strove to make the ḥadīth they quoted "Prophetic" whenever possible seems certain. Moreover, they were generally clear as to where their material stood, even if, as in the case of Abū Dā'ūd, they quoted ḥadīth that they considered "weak." Goldziher suggests that the *Sunan* of al-Dārimī (a man of Samarqand) did not qualify for "canonicity" partly because it was much shorter than the four "canonical" *Sunan* and partly "owing to [the] hesitant attitude of the author toward his material" (of which Goldziher offers several examples).[38]

More puzzling is the failure of any Iraqi author to qualify, if we consider the size and prestige of the scholarly community of Iraq and, above all, of Baghdad. There is some evidence that Iraqi ḥadīth scholars were not trusted. Both Ibn Abī Ḥātim al-Rāzī and Abū Zurʿa al-Dimashqī quote a conversation between the Caliph al-Manṣūr and Mālik ibn Anas in which the caliph said that in the Umayyad period he had investigated the state of religious learning and discovered that, "The transmitters of Iraq are liars and forgers."[39] Certainly the organization of the ḥadīth books of great Baghdadi scholars such as Aḥmad ibn Ḥanbal and Yaḥyā ibn Maʿīn (d. 233) in the form of *musnad*s made them more cumbersome to use (even though Yaḥyā ibn Maʿīn was a pioneer in the discipline of *rijāl*).

Yet surely one of the most important elements in the victory of the ḥadīth of "greater Khorasan" was a Seljuk political success. Seljuk orthodoxy was fairly strict. Niẓām al-Mulk says, "In all the world there are only two schools (*madhhab*) that are good and on the right path. One is that of Abū Ḥanīfa and the other that of al-Shāfiʿī (may God have mercy on them

37 Sezgin, (*supra* n. 22), 79.
38 Goldziher, (*supra* n. 18), 239.
39 Quoted in G.H.A. Juynboll, *Muslim Tradition: Studies in Chronology, Provenance and Authorship of Early Hadith*, Cambridge Studies in Islamic Civilization (Cambridge, U.K., and New York, Cambridge University Press: 1983) 63.

both). All the rest is vanity (*havā*) and heresy (*bid'at*)."[40] These two great schools accounted for the better part of the population of Khorasan. With the Seljuk conquest, they were given the lion's share of royal and vizieral patronage in Iraq, and many Eastern scholars emigrated to partake of this lion's share.

Of the immigrant and transient ulema of 5th/11th-century Baghdad whose geographical origins we can trace, seventeen percent came from eastern Iran and Transoxiana, and twenty-eight percent came from western Iran.[41] Interestingly, a fair number of the ulema of 5th/11th-century Baghdad emigrated eastwards; but only five percent to western Iran, and twenty-five percent to Khorasan and Transoxiana.[42] These movements are easier to understand if we remember that Niẓām al-Mulk founded Shāfi'ī institutions (such as his Niẓāmīya madrasa) in Baghdad where Shāfi'īs had not previously been as important. Perhaps the best-known example of this patronage is al-Ghazālī, who, after studying law in eastern Iran, was sent by Niẓām al-Mulk to teach at the Niẓāmīya in Baghdad. It would be interesting to see whether the adoption of the "Six Books" by Shāfi'īs (and, possibly, Ḥanafīs) established the model for their general (though by no means universal) adoption by Sunni Muslims.

It is important to remember that alternate lists were put forward. In the Maghrib the third Almohad ruler, Abū Yūsuf Ya'qūb, put forward a list of ten books, including five of the "Six Books" and omitting Ibn Māja who continues to be considered "non-canonical" by Maghribī Mālikīs up to the present.[43] In the long run, however, the weight of the East was greater and, as Goldziher says, "it cannot be overlooked that the canonical bracketing together of the 'six books' was the work of Eastern Islam."[44]

Makdịsi warns us that, "One should not attach undue importance to the fact that the *madrasa* developed especially in the eastern lands of the caliphate, in 'Irāḳ, Persia and Transoxiana; this does not imply a cultural swing away from Arab Baghdad towards Persian Khorasan, especially towards Naysābūr (Nishapur), which would be a misreading of cultural history due to anachronistic nationalist sentiment."[45] Surely, insofar as anyone

40 *Siyar al-Mulūk* or *Siyāsat-Nāma*, (Tehran: 1340) 122; *The Book of Government or Rules for Kings*, trans. Hubert Darke (London: 1960) 99 (here slightly adapted).

41 Ephrat, (*supra* n. 8), 36.

42 Ephrat, (*supra* n. 8), 37.

43 Goldziher, (*supra* n. 18), 243.

44 Goldziher, (*supra* n. 18), 243.

45 "Madrasa," *EI*², V, (Leiden, Brill: 1986) 1128.

attempts to disassociate the Arab world and—most particularly—Baghdad from these intellectual activities, they deserve this censure. It should be noted that for all of the six authors their Arab "tribal" affiliation is preserved in their *nisbas*, although almost all of these affiliations are known to be acquired by clientage and not by descent. But when al-Muqaddasī says of Khorasan, "It is the province with the most learning (*'ilm*) [probably, concerning ḥadīth] and the most law (*fiqh*)," he is not motivated by nationalist sentiment.[46] The area of which he speaks is principally northeastern Iran and the remark is no general compliment to Iranians. Hamadan in western Iran and Damascus Syria produced important scholars, but later Islamic learning did not give them a role as important as the leading scholars of "greater Khorasan."

In short, the northeast Islamic lands were especially prominent for a more rigorous discipline in ḥadīth studies that was motivated in large part by the attempts of its scholars to base Islamic law on ḥadīth rather than *ra'y* (opinion). It was also prominent because a large number of early madrasas arose in its cities. The two developments are related. The cultivation of ḥadīth disciplines, centered around legal and theological topics, was an essential tool for teaching and disputation and led to the foundation of schools for specific teachers. These schools eventually became madrasas as they have traditionally functioned in the Middle East. The Seljuks and their viziers spread this Khorasanian system, including its preferred ḥadīth books, to the central lands of Western Asia. Because the madrasa and the Middle Eastern Islamic style of learning revolved to such a degree around the central teacher rather than the madrasa, education continued to have a highly personalistic character. And because the Ottomans—through the Seljuks of Anatolia—and the Moghuls of India inherited so much in their traditions of learning from this northwest area, its influence continued to expand in the later history of many Islamic lands.

---

46 Al-Muqaddasī, (*supra* n. 13), 323.

Traditional Shi'ite Education in Qom

Before describing traditional education in Qom it is important to remember the likely path of education and socialization of the students who subsequently studied there. [Traditional education in Qom in Iran closely resembles religious education in other centers of Shi'ite learning, most particularly in Najaf in Iraq, even though these two centers are in different countries with different languages. Iran and southern Iraq are strongly Shi'ite and have similar cultural traditions, which determine how and when education begins and proceeds. Moreover, Twelver Shi'ite centers such as these have exchanged teachers and students for over two centuries.]

In traditional Iranian households the upbringing of a young Muslim boy rests firmly with his mother until about the age of six, when he starts to go to the public bath with his father instead of his mother. (Among the Shi'ites circumcision, often performed at birth, can be performed even as late as the sixth year.) At about the same age as a Muslim boy begins to accompany his father to the public bath he also begins to sit with his father and other male relations when male visitors are received at home. And, in Iranian society before the spread of universal primary state education after the Second World War, many children also entered Qur'ān schools in their sixth year. Although ties with mothers remained strong, the sudden introduction of Muslim boys into the world of men during their sixth year may have formed a model for the sense of sudden mastery of different levels of knowledge which characterizes much of the traditional Shi'ite system of education.

Author's note: This article was first published as: "Traditional Shi'ite Education in Qom," in *Harvard Middle Eastern and Islamic Review* 2:1 (1995) 89–98. Reproduced with permission. It is my pleasure to thank Sayyid Muhammad Husain Jalali, Sayyid Reza Borqe'i, Shaykh Reza Ostadi, Ayatollah Majd ad-Din Mahallati, Dr. Abbas Zaryab, and—above all—Professor Hossein Modarressi for their unstinting generosity in discussing their education at Qom with me.

In the case of the older generation of students at Qom, such as Ayatollah Khomeini, this sense of abrupt change would be reinforced by their experience at Qur'ān schools. (Such schools virtually ceased to exist in Iran after the Second World War, unlike other Islamic countries such as Morocco where they continue to exist in great numbers even today.) In a Qur'ān school this sacred text was taught word by word in the original Arabic with little more than word-by-word glosses in Persian and not much grammatical explanation, even though Arabic grammar is far from easy and very different from Persian. Students who have gone through this system have described to me their initial sense of being completely at sea, and then their experience of a sudden leap in understanding. Incidentally, a fair number of the teachers at Qur'ān schools for both boys and girls were women, and in village and tribal settings, boys and girls might be taught together.

Education at one of the seminaries or colleges (in Arabic and Persian madrasas) at Qom begins at about twelve to fourteen years of age, roughly the age of puberty, an association not without significance. There are a few separate seminaries for women, but there the students are taught by women, and female students can only listen to male teachers behind a curtain or similar barrier. Although the archetypal student in Qom will be represented as masculine throughout the rest of this essay, many of the statements about men also apply to women in their separate but parallel educational track. Qom is one of the two most prestigious centers of Twelver Shi'ite education, the other being Najaf in Iraq. Therefore, students trained at less prestigious centers consider a period of study at Qom and/or Najaf essential to their accreditation in the higher stages of their education, and so new students of all ages arrive at Qom every year.

The first level of education is called "preliminaries" (*muqaddamāt*).[1] Grammar, rhetoric, and logic are the three subjects studied. These are, of course, identical with the *trivium*, the first stage of education in late antiquity and the European Middle Ages. Eton, in fact, was called a "trivial" school up into the eighteenth century. A connection between the seven "liberal arts" in the medieval Western tradition and the present system practiced at Qom is hard to establish but there is a basic similarity between the two systems. Both systems consider it appropriate that students be

1 Mahdi Zavabiti, *Pazhuheshi dar Nezām-e Ṭalabegi* (Tehran: 1359/1940) gives an overview of the methods and curriculum, although my informants have corrected several points of detail in this work.

given fairly uniform training in the three basic "arts" or "sciences," because these subjects, which offer basic methods of textual analysis, necessarily precede exposure to more serious textbooks.

The texts for this first level of education are gathered in a single volume called *Jāmiʿ al-Muqaddamāt*, and the edition used is an offprint of a very old lithographic edition, and is therefore handwritten. Hence the very appearance of this volume suggests its continuity with the training of teachers for many generations past. The explanations of the basic texts that are printed between the handwritten lines and in the margins emphasize the fact that the transmission of the text has always required teachers.

In the pre-modern Middle Eastern educational system, a pupil usually needed the written permission of a teacher before he in turn could teach the book to others. While this system is no longer as prevalent as it once was, there still remains among students and teachers at Qom a conviction that a great deal of knowledge is passed "from chest to chest," that is, passed in the explanation and commentary offered by the teacher during the reading of the book.[2] Therefore, a book not studied with a master is not likely to have been properly assimilated by a student. For non-Arabic speaking students (the overwhelming majority in Qom), this need for a teacher is reinforced at the first level because all but two of the texts—the exceptions are a text in logic and a short Persian grammar of Arabic—are written in Arabic.

Already at the first level one encounters some of the pervasive features of the school texts used at all levels in traditional Shiʿite education. In Aristotelian logic (as modified by later thinkers) mutually exclusive statements are either contraries, such as "This man is blue-eyed" and "This man is brown-eyed," which are exclusive but do not exhaust all the possibilities of eye color; or contradictories, such as "Socrates existed" or "Socrates did not exist," which do exhaust all possibilities. Even the presentation of the morphology of the Arabic verb is given in schemata that show this basic understanding of the way an argument is conducted. The student therefore learns to construct solutions to problems into what we would call "decision trees." In cases where there are many contraries the students would necessarily have to memorize these contraries in order to master the subject. Consonant with this vision of knowledge as organized

---

2 While many works have been written on pre-modern Islamic education, the most comprehensive work on the transmission of text remains Franz Rosenthal, *The Technique and Approach of Muslim Scholarship* (Rome: 1947).

into decision trees is the view that items of knowledge are divided into "roots" (*uṣūl*) and "branches" (*furū'*). This distinction is already applied in the study of grammar; it is frequently repeated, especially in the later study of law and theology.

It is interesting to note that, in contrast with many Sunni systems of education, the Qur'ān is not taught as such in the required curriculum (although there are classes in which the teacher offers a commentary on the Qur'ān); nor is memorization of the Qur'ān a formal prerequisite for entry into the Shi'ite system of education, as it once was in the most celebrated Sunni center of traditional education, the Azhar in Cairo. In fact, the Shi'ite system does not consciously regard itself as mnemonic, in contrast to most Sunni systems, although most serious Shi'ite students do memorize the Qur'ān; and often, because of the slow and thorough way in which they proceed through their textbooks, students retain all or parts of some of these texts for life. Since misquotation of the Qur'ān or any basic text is tantamount to losing an argument, memorization is very often a necessity, even if not overtly valued.

Talent in disputation or "dialectic" (*jadal*) is the most respected achievement of students, and is key in understanding classroom techniques, and, indeed, an important aspect of the intellectual approach that traditional Shi'ite education fosters in its pupils. The study of rhetoric and logic are seen as contributing to dialectic, although their primary importance is to train students to reason properly about the derivation of substantive law, or "the branches" (*furū'*) of law from its "roots" (*uṣūl*). Students are encouraged to dispute points whether made in the textbook, or by other students, even by the teacher himself. Here the student learns that by analyzing the text into contraries and contradictories he can demonstrate that certain positions can be refuted by showing that an opponent's argument leads to an infinite regress or a vicious cycle. Of course, more mundane items of information also count in such disputations.

To prepare himself for class a student chooses a study partner called a "fellow discussant" (*ham-mobāhese*) with whom he practices disputing the meaning of the text. The students also read commentaries, some of which are written in a style reminiscent of disputation, that is, the commentary offers the original text with the words: "He says," and then adds after the quotation from the original: "But I say," followed by the remarks of the commentator. After classes the best student may hold a review session in which he reads his notes on the teacher's remarks; and, for more advanced textbooks or the highest stage of learning, which involves disputations outside the texts, these lecture notes or "reports" (*taqrīrāt*) are published with the teacher's permission, although with the name of this most favored student listed as the author on the title page.

The image of education as disputation is so powerful that in theory when a student wins a disputation with the teacher, the teacher should cede his place to another teacher. While this seldom happens, and while there are limits beyond which challenges to the teacher might amount to unacceptable behavior and/or an unacceptable denial of fundamental precepts of Islam, teachers are likely to teach only those texts over which they feel they have complete mastery. This self-selection more or less decides what level teachers achieve in the system. And, since students can shop around and find which teacher teaches the set textbooks in a way most congenial to them, there is a natural selection that "retires" unpopular teachers to provincial seminaries or other tasks in the Shi'ite religious establishment.

The middle level of education is called merely "texts" or, more literally, "surfaces" (*suṭūḥ*) of the texts, although the same analytical and dialectical approach employed in the first level is applied even more rigorously on this level, and the students are expected to go well below the surface. The textbooks for this level are on theology, law and—above all—jurisprudence, or as it is called in Arabic, "The roots of juridical understanding" (*uṣūl al-fiqh*). Whereas the colleges of Najaf claim superiority in understanding the Holy Law itself, the colleges of Qom claim superiority in understanding the more theoretical discipline of jurisprudence. At this stage the homogenization of the various branches of Islamic learning becomes yet clearer to the student because the techniques of the various disciplines are carried more fully across disciplinary lines.

A fairly homogeneous vocabulary is used in the different branches of learning, in part because a substantial number of the texts were written in the 6th/12th to the 9th/15th centuries, a period in which Islamic learning was homogenized by great teachers such as Sa'd al-Dīn al-Taftāzānī (d. 793/1390) in a newly established form of Islamic institution, the endowed college or madrasa. (The Shi'ite colleges of Qom are, as we have said earlier, called madrasas.) For example, the word *ḥukm*, from an Arabic verb which means "to decide," is used for the grammatical governance of one word over another, for a general precept, for an actual law, for a sentence given in court, for jurisdiction, for legal provision, etc. The repeated discovery of a *ḥukm* or "ruling" in a variety of disciplines, as well as the repeated occurrence of such a word in the disciplines, suggests to the student that knowledge is governed by certain universal principles, an idea explicitly espoused by Shiʿite theology.

The third and highest level of education, called "outside the texts" (*khārij al-suṭūh*), is the level of pure disputation in which students exhibit all the information and dialectical skills acquired previously. A master teacher announces a subject of study and, usually without any books or notes, will cite key passages and contested areas in well-known works on this subject which he introduces by declaring, "It has been said ..." Then he will introduce his own reflections on the subject by adding, "But I say ...," after which the student can respond, "But it can be said ..." At this final level it becomes clear who has the capacity to become a *mujtahid*, a doctor of the law authorized by some previous doctor of the law to issue an authoritative opinion on Islamic law. Nowadays it is customary for a student who has shown skill at several classes at the third level to write a treatise on some area of the law before being accepted as *mujtahid*. To receive recognition from another *mujtahid* has always been sufficient to make someone a *mujtahid*, but such recognition is given exceedingly sparingly; there are only about two hundred *mujtahid*s in the world.

Certain subjects considered slightly suspect according to the most orthodox scholars, yet highly esteemed by a great number of students and teachers, are taught in circles outside the madrasa. One such subject is philosophy, rejected as a subject by almost all Sunni madrasas but often (though not uniformly) accepted in Shiʿite circles, in part because Shiʿites, in contrast with many Sunnis, consider that *ʿaql*, "reason," is one of the sources of the law. Philosophical methods have influenced jurisprudence, the queen of the sciences in this system of education, and vice versa; so, philosophy can be important to a student's understanding of advanced texts as well as to his ability to produce new texts himself. It should be noted, however, that all philosophy taught is of the school of Avicenna (Ibn Sīnā), as modified by major Shiʿite thinkers such as Mullā Ṣadrā, who died in 1640.

The other highly important subject studied outside the madrasas is *ʿirfān*, or gnostic mysticism, which is often associated with philosophy insofar as it draws on a strong tradition of Neo-Platonism in Islamic thought. This subject is taught privately with only teacher and pupil present and involves the assignment and practice of mystical exercises meant to open the doors of perceptions and to purify the inner self. These private sessions establish a strong bond between teacher and pupil, and the world of the mullahs in Qom is honeycombed with ties created by mystical training. Such training reinforces the paradigm of learning as a long struggle with sudden leaps of understanding. It also creates a great self-confidence in those who feel that they have made this kind of "leap" in mystical development. As the ability to project self-confidence and to answer objections quickly and confidently is a sign of mastery in the world of the madrasa, mysticism, like philosophy, can bring an added strength to its devotees in their careers as mullahs. Ayatollah Khomeini, incidentally, was perceived to be a master of gnostic mysticism and was a good example of the kind of extraordinary self-confidence it can produce.

Economic resources, traditional status (as, for example, that enjoyed by sons of prominent *mujtahid*s and/or descendants of the Prophet Muḥammad), patronage, provincial loyalties, and the like, prevent this, like every other, educational system from being the pure meritocracy it imagines itself to be. Nevertheless, one of the significant aspects of the system is that it offers a clever boy as good a chance of advancement as the secular systems of education do.

This meritocracy is very much at work in the efforts of the mullahs in Qom to reach out for new pupils through networks in their province of origin. At the provincial levels the mullahs of the "small" community, the neighborhood and the village mullah, will actively recruit local young men with a serious interest in religion. Once these young recruits have arrived in Qom, the teacher from that province will often assume the responsibility for seeing to it that they receive some kind of very minimal stipend. If they remain in the system for a while most of them will return to their province to become mullahs and will maintain a connection with successful teachers in Qom from their province. They will also direct contributions to these teachers, who will be able to distribute further basic stipends. Such provincial ties, based both on economic redistribution and differences in provincial culture still strongly felt in Iran, were shown in, for example, the continuing loyalty of the Isfahan area to Ayatollah Montazeri (from Najafabad, a town in that area) in spite of the coolness of the central government toward him.

Another characteristic of traditional education at Qom, as in so many systems of education, notably the English public school, is a puberty rite, in an entirely male environment in which there is a sense of ordeal and a great sense of accomplishment for those who survive the ordeal. Madrasa students feel that ordinary people, lacking the dedication to pass sleepless nights in study, would not have achieved what these madrasa students have achieved. A contemporary mullah, Yusuf Ghulami, has given us a portrait of his student years which conforms closely to the accounts of other former students. On first seeing the rooms or *ḥujras* which line the upper stories of the residential colleges—and the great majority of the students are boarders—he says: "My head began to hurt from looking at the rooms of this prison ... Rooms two, three- or four-square meters in which two, three, and four people lived! [Nothing was to be seen in the students' rooms except] a mat, damp and colorless walls, a handful of books on one side, a few bowls and grains and an oil lamp on another, in the comer a bed and blanket." Their food is similarly modest, a typical dinner being bread, yoghurt, cucumber, salt, onion, and, occasionally, meatless meat soup. While some students were more privileged, most, even from well-to-do families, were made to live in such conditions as an essential part of their training. Such an ordeal must have made fellow sufferers close to each other and given them a heightened sense of their "heroism" and their "distinctiveness."[3]

A third characteristic of this education is that it is highly speculative about the formal relations of agreed sources of knowledge, but not necessarily about uncertain knowledge. In part, this is so because traditional Shi'ite education is textually centripetal, and, of course (as is the case for virtually all Islamic systems of education), ultimately centripetal to the text of revelation itself. The logic studied is deductive; induction, needed for dealing with necessarily uncertain matters, is not formally studied, although it is used to some extent in legal reasoning. Probabilistic thinking, and the sort of statistical orientation it supposes, is only involved when commonweal questions are raised, and commonweal is in the last resort a source of law when conclusions from the usual sources of jurisprudence must be suspended.

A fourth characteristic of this system is that, while encouraging disputation in class, outside the classroom students are very much bound to their teachers by feelings of deference and loyalty. Students believe they have a lifelong debt to their teachers and are cautious about issuing controversial opinions as long as there are senior scholars who are widely

3 Yusuf Ghulami, *Āyā Kasi Sargozasht-e mā (Ṭalabeh-hā) rā Bāvar Mikonad?* (Qom: 1403/1982) 9–10. This title significantly asks, "Does Anyone Believe our Past as Students?"

accepted as being learned. The genealogical view of knowledge—tracing one's teachers' teachers back to the early centuries of Islam—goes along with an ahistorical view of knowledge. Although intellectually very rigorous, this training develops little in the way of historical consciousness and little impulse to understand the thinking of past scholars of the tradition in the context of their time.

In this age in which many things are indiscriminately labeled "fundamentalist," it is important to notice that most aspects of the Shi'ite madrasa education described here would best be characterized as "traditional." There may be other aspects that would lead observers to characterize the system differently. But most teachers and students in pre-revolutionary Qom represented a very real continuity of intellectual approach in their teaching with teachers of a century ago. It remains to be seen which of the traditional features of this system of education will survive the political changes that Ayatollah Khomeini and his followers have wrought.

The Najaf *Ḥawza* Curriculum

Najaf has been the cradle of Shiʿite learning for many centuries. According to Najaf tradition, it has been so ever since the prominent scholar Muḥammad ibn al-Ḥasan al-Ṭūsī, called Shaykh al-Ṭāʾifa or "senior scholar of the sect," migrated there shortly after the Seljuk conquest of Baghdad in 447/1055.

We have very little information about the teaching system and curriculum in Najaf before the nineteenth century. In this essay, I will try to present the basic elements of a Najaf *ḥawza* education as they exist in contemporary Iraq and compare it with a Najaf curriculum of 1913. Quite remarkably, the curriculum, teaching methods and patronage networks have been remarkably stable over the last century. Politics and reform movements have, however, had their effects on the curriculum too, as I shall explain in the course of this essay.[1] [Some information in this article about the general organization of the Najaf educational system is very similar to the information in my article on "Traditional Education in Qom," written twenty years earlier. The systems of education in both madrasa cities closely resemble each other despite being in different countries with different languages. The exchange in students and teachers between the two centers of religious learning has aided their similarity. Traditional learning changes slowly, although urgent questions of the day influence

---

Author's note: This article was first published as: "The Najaf Ḥawzah Curriculum," in the *Journal of the Royal Asiastic Society*, 3rd series, 26:1–2 (2016) 341–351. Reproduced with permission. As indicated in the Preface, the names of authors and editors from the late nineteenth century to the present in this article are not transliterated although they retain ʿ*ayn*s and internal *hamza*s. Four sentences in brackets have been added to the paragraph above to explain some similarities between this article and the previous article about traditional education in Qom.

1 The first version of this paper was a lecture delivered in 2009 at the British Academy through the kind offices of Professor Robert Gleave of Exeter University. The version given here was prepared in January 2011 and does not discuss developments after that date. I thank my colleague Professor Intisar Rabb for her very thorough proofreading of this article.

some teachers and students, such as the past challenge of communism and the present challenge to democratic governance.]

The contemporary curriculum given below is well described in an excellent book by 'Abd al-Hadi al-Hakim published in 2007.[2] Some preference may be shown to the curriculum of the Madrasat al-Ḥakīm, as the author belongs to the family of the founder of this madrasa. Over twenty madrasas are part of al-Ḥawza al-'Ilmīya at Najaf. (See Appendix C.)

The curriculum begins with the study of Arabic grammar. The *Alfīya* by Ibn Mālik who died in 672/1274, which usually gets memorized from intensive study, remains the primary text. The slightly easier *Ājurrūmīya* of the North African scholar Ibn Ājurrūm (d. 723/1323), is also studied at Najaf (though seldom, if ever, used at Qom).

At the first level, *al-muqaddamāt*, two rhetoric works of the great Eastern scholar al-Taftāzānī (d. 793/1390), *Mukhtaṣar al-Ma'ānī* and his *Muṭawwal* are occasionally used. One innovation in the curriculum is the addition of the very popular work on logic of Muhammad Rida al-Muzaffar (d. 1383/1964), commonly called *al-Manṭiq*. Some go on to study commentaries on the long favored traditional logic called *al-Risāla al-Shamsīya* by Najm al-Dīn 'Alī al-Kātibī (d. 693/1276).

Another area of elementary study is theology, using *Sharḥ al-Bāb al-Ḥādī 'Ashar*, which is the commentary of Miqdād al-Suyūrī (d. 826/1423) on a work by 'Allāma al-Ḥillī (d. 726/1325), itself a commentary on a part of the brilliant *Tajrīd al-Aqā'id* of Naṣīr al-Dīn al-Ṭūsī (d. 672/1274).

These works are called *muqaddamāt*, which means "preliminary" disciplines for the study of subsequent subjects. The more difficult of these books, however, might not be studied in the preliminary phase of study. The middle level of study, rather unusually called *suṭūḥ* "surfaces," meaning the word-by-word study of set texts, begins with one of the practical manuals of law issued by one of the *marāji'*, the highest Shi'ite authorities on the law. Teaching such works has long been the custom in Najaf, perhaps to guarantee the correctness of advice given by ulema who do not continue their education to higher levels. It has recently been introduced in Iran. A useful traditional book for introducing *fiqh* is *al-Mukhtaṣar al-Nāfi'* by al-Muḥaqqiq al-Ḥillī (d. 676/1277). After that, the student is introduced to the *Sharā'i' al-Islām* by the same al-Ḥillī, one of the first compendious

2 'Abd al-Hadi al-Hakim, *Ḥawzat al-Najaf al-Ashraf: al-Niẓām wa-Mashārī' al-Iṣlāh* ([Baghdad?], Mu'assasat Āfāq li-l-Dirāsāt wa-al-Abḥāth al-'Irāqīya: 1428/2007).

works on Shi'ite *fiqh*. It established the basic divisions of Shi'ite law, most of which have stood the test of time. The great and voluminous commentary on this work, much consulted by students and teachers, is the *Jawāhir al-Kalām* by Muḥammad Ḥasan al-Najafī (d. 1266/1849), the forty-six volumes of which are sometimes considered the greatest published work on Shi'ite *fiqh*. The author is known to students as Ṣāḥib al-Jawāhir, the "master of the *Jawāhir*," and the great twentieth-century Iraqi poet al-Jawahiri is one of his descendants.

The first book in *uṣūl al-fiqh* (the roots or principles of jurisprudence) used to be *Ma'ālim al-Dīn* by Shaykh Ḥasan (d. 1011/1602), son of Zayn al-Dīn ibn 'Alī, called al-Shahīd al-Thānī (d. 965/1558), a scholar from Jabal 'Āmil in Lebanon. Muhammad Baqir al-Sadr, the famous twentieth-century Najafī jurist-scholar, tried twice to replace this book. His first attempt, *al-Ma'ālim al-Jadīda*, is still worth study, but was never widely adopted as a textbook. His second attempt, *Durūs fī Uṣūl al-Fiqh*, is a brilliant book. Strangely, while it has come to dominate the elementary teaching of *uṣūl* in Qom, the teachers of Najaf have preferred the *Uṣūl al-Fiqh* of Muhammad Rida al-Muzaffar, first published in 1966, because of its extreme clarity. The *Ḥawza* in Qom believes that the work of Muhammad Baqir al-Sadr raises subtle points missed by al-Muzaffar. In general, the *Ḥawza* in Najaf considers itself deeper in *fiqh*, while that of Qom considers itself deeper in jurisprudence proper (*uṣūl*). The rivalry between the two institutions is somewhat reminiscent of the rivalry between Harvard and Yale, or Oxford and Cambridge.

At this level of study, students gain some acquaintance with arithmetic, which is considered essential to mastering inheritance law. They also acquire a very considerable knowledge of the science of verifying transmitters and transmission of the ḥadīth of the Prophet and the Imams, in particular through study of the vast work of ḥadīth called *Wasā'il al-Shī'a* written by al-Ḥurr al-'Āmilī (d. 1112/1700). Another *fiqh* book that is carefully studied is *al-Rawḍa al-Bahīya fī Sharḥ al-Lum'a al-Dimashqīya* by al-Shahīd al-Thānī previously mentioned. This work is characterized by its careful use of inference from the sources of law and the variety of opinions it gives on disputed points of law.

After the *Rawḍa*, the students begin *al-Makāsib*, the epoch-making work of nineteenth-century Shi'ite jurisprudence by Murtaḍā al-Anṣārī (d. 1281/1864) which, while containing a great deal of practical law, is extremely innovative in its use of jurisprudential theory. This work was so widely influential that we can speak of "the school of al-Anṣārī" which dominates the Najaf *Ḥawza* right down to the present. His expansion of jurisprudence dealt mostly with the procedural principles, *al-uṣūl al-'amalīya*, and led to a restructuring of the law in the area of transactions. A number of other works may be studied along with, or after, *al-Makāsib*. By far the most important of these is the masterwork on jurisprudence proper, *Kifāyat al-Uṣūl* by Akhund-e Khorasani (d. 1329/1911).

For those interested in philosophy and *kalām*—an interest not much encouraged by some past *marāji'* in Najaf—the works of Mullā Ṣadrā (Ṣadr al-Dīn al-Shīrāzī, d. 1050/1641) are sometimes read. Philosophically inclined students nowadays often read *Bidāyat al-Ḥikma* and *Nihāyat al-Ḥikma* of the great Qur'ān commentator Allama al-Tabataba'i (d. 1981).[3]

We have a survey of the set texts used in Najaf in 1913 (See Appendix A).[4] Two-thirds of the books I have mentioned were in use at that time, although a different set of texts was more favored in 1913 than at present. It will be noticed that many of the more advanced books of 1913 were written in the nineteenth century when Shi'ite jurisprudence underwent a great transformation. It is interesting to note that several of these works were written in the Arab world in the period from the 6th/12th through the 10th/16th centuries, when among Shi'ites *ijtihād*—the effort to derive rulings from their proper sources—came more into favor. Such works include books of the al-Ḥillīs and of Fāḍil al-Miqdād and of both al-Shahīd al-Thānī and his son Shaykh Ḥasan. The rise of the popularity of the books of Muhammad Rida al-Muzaffar and the overwhelming influence of Akhund-e Khorasani stand out as major changes in the Najaf curriculum.

Two autobiographical accounts from the end of the nineteenth and beginning of the twentieth century give us an idea of the texts and the methods of teaching in use at that time. One of these accounts is by the Lebanese Shi'ite scholar, Muhsin al-Amin, who arrived in Najaf in 1891. There he studied the following books:

3 *Ḥawzat al-Najaf*, (*supra* n. 2) 89–100, although on pp. 449–451 are listed the statistics for students registering and students actually taking exams in the major texts. For example, for the *Kifāya* of Khorasani, perhaps the most difficult advanced set text, in 1427 A.H., 54 registered for the exam and 31 actually sat the exam (p. 452). See Appendix B for a 2010 version of an abstract Shi'ite *Ḥawza* curriculum, not specific to Najaf.

4 Sabrina Mervin includes the 1913 book list in her outstanding article, "La quête du savoir à Najaf," *Studia Islamica* 81 (1995) 179–180, without, however, fully identifying the dates of the authors and the full titles of the books.

- a commentary [presumably *al-Rawḍa al-Bahīyaḥ*, mentioned above] on the *Lum'a*
- *al-Qawānīn* by Mīrzā Abū al-Qāsim Ḥasan ibn Muḥammad al-Jīlānī
- *al-Rāsā'il* of Murtaḍā al-Anṣārī
- *al-Kifāya* by Akhund-e Khorasani
- *Miṣbāḥ al-Faqīh* by Rida ibn Muhammad al-Hamadhani (d. 1322/1904).[5]

Interestingly, all of these books except the last, which was never completed, are still in use.

At approximately the same time, the Iranian scholar Aqa-Najafi Quchani went to Najaf. He mentions many teachers but few books. These books are:

- *al-Rāsā'il* of Murtaḍā al-Anṣārī
- *al-Kifāya* by Akhund-e Khorasani
- *Sharḥ Maṭāli' al-Anwār fī 'Ilm al-Manṭiq* by Quṭb al-Dīn Muḥammad al-Rāzī al-Taḥtānī (d. 766/1364).[6]

This third book, which is on logic, is no longer in general use.

To some extent these books form part of the shared intellectual endeavor of madrasa learning in the Ottoman, Safavid, and Moghul empires. All three empires were heirs to the Timurid "renaissance," in which Taftāzānī (d. 793/1390) and Sayyid Sharīf Jurjānī (d. 816/1413) played important roles. As Francis Robinson has pointed out, not only did they contribute books to the curriculum, but they also wrote commentaries on earlier books of grammar, rhetoric, and logic, such as the *Shamsīya*, which encouraged the canonization of these books among later generations.[7]

After the set texts, students begin the stage called *al-baḥth al-khārij*. In this stage the teacher speaks from a raised bench and pursues for several weeks or months a subject not necessarily treated in the textbooks. He gives a survey of views that support or contradict his own, which he

---

5 Muhsin al-Amin has been the subject of several very fine studies by Sabrina Mervin, including an outstanding translation along with Haytham al-Amin, of his autobiography: *Autobiographique d'un clerc chiite du Jabal 'Āmil* (Damascus: 1998). See pp. 179–180 for the books he studied in Najaf.

6 Aqa-Najafi Quchani, *Siyāḥat-e Sharq o Gharb* (Qom: 1377) 201, 225, 227, 234.

7 Francis Robinson, "Ottomans-Safavids-Mughals: Shared knowledge and connective systems," *Journal of Islamic Studies* 8:2 (1997) 151–184 (especially p. 155). Many of these texts are also met with in Khaled El-Rouayheb, "Opening the gate of verification: The forgotten Arab-Islamic florescence of the 17th century," *International Journal of Middle Eastern Studies* 38 (2006) 263–281.

presents last, with the arguments and proofs that he considers decisive. After his talk, students question him, and the discussion can become so heated that the professor has to demand quiet. Some few teachers did not encourage much disputation, such as Ayatollah al-Khoei, who taught *al-baḥth al-khārij* for sixty years with four to five hundred students at his lectures.[8] An interesting anecdote of an earlier period concerns the leading Sunni authority of the Ottoman Empire, the Shaykh al-Islām of Istanbul. He went to visit the *Ḥawza* sometime before al-Khorasani's death in 1911. Although al-Khorasani's lectures were thronged by up to two thousand listeners, the students made way for the Shaykh al-Islām to sit in front. Khorasani took a maxim from Abū Ḥanīfa, the great Sunni jurist whose tomb in Baghdad the Shaykh al-Islām had just visited. He offered the visitor the lecturer's bench, but the offer was declined.[9] The anecdote illustrates the freedom of the teacher of *al-khārij* to choose his approach to the general topic of his lectures.

METHODS OF TEACHING

The methods of teaching throughout the nineteenth and twentieth centuries in Najaf have remained largely traditional, although outside influences, principally from the civil educational system, have caused significant changes. Many contemporary madrasas offer hourly classes for the elementary and intermediate texts, in a model clearly taken from civil education. The *ḥalqa* or "circle" which surrounds the teacher is still the usual method for teaching set texts. Sometimes the most favored students sit nearest the teacher, and in theory any of the students can raise objections at any point. When the lesson is finished and the teacher has left, the students often pair up to review the explanations offered by the teacher. Serious students write down the lesson every day and may carry it to the professor for review. If the teacher finds such study notes outstanding, he may authorize their publication.

In the nineteenth century and the first half of the twentieth, many of the stages of education coincided with stages in recognition of the adulthood of the student. The upbringing of a young Muslim boy rested with his mother up to age six, when he started to go to the public bath with his father

8 *Ḥawzat al-Najaf*, (*supra* n. 2), 120–121.
9 *Ḥawzat al-Najaf*, (*supra* n. 2), 155

instead of his mother. At about the same age, he begins to accompany his father to visit male relatives and receive them at home. It was also around the sixth year that Muslim boys were introduced to the traditional system of education. Such education took place in Qur'ān schools, in which the sacred text was taught word by word with little grammatical explanation. Children brought up in this system have described to me their initial sense of being at sea and then experiencing a sudden leap of understanding. When the student went on to the *Ḥawza* at age ten to fourteen, roughly the age of puberty, a somewhat similar situation obtained: again, a sense of being at sea with extraordinarily abstruse texts, and, for the more able students, a sudden leap of understanding about the subject matter.

Incidentally, a fair number of teachers in Qur'ān schools were women both for pre-pubescent boys and girls. In villages boys and girls were sometimes even taught together in the same school. In contrast, the *Ḥawza* corresponds to a period in which men and women (who are not related) are kept strictly divided from each other. Many *Ḥawza* students who formerly lived at home would now live in the all-male or all-female atmosphere of *Ḥawza* dormitories.

Students had comparative freedom in choosing with whom to study the set texts and, in agreement with the pre-modern educational system of the Middle East, a pupil usually needed written permission, the *ijāza*, before he could teach a book to others. Unlike the secular system in both the Middle East and in the West, the *Ḥawza* system recognizes achievements text by text and, in this way, allows middle-level students many opportunities to teach and therefore to support themselves as madrasa teachers while continuing their education.

In both past and present great respect is shown to the teacher. Sometime lifelong bonds of affection join pupil and teacher. Although the subject matters of the books vary considerably, there is a fairly consistent use of technical terminology. To give a very simple example: grammar, law, and theology all organize their subject into "roots" (*uṣūl*) and "branches" (*furū'*). Many of the subjects studied present the material in schemata which lead the student up decision trees to the branch which determines the solution to a problem. This technique is much used in *uṣūl al-fiqh* or jurisprudence proper.

Nowadays almost all Iraqi students have received some degree of state-sponsored education before they arrive at the *Ḥawza*. There is also some accommodation to the difficulty in understanding the set texts.

The very much simplified and clear exposition of *Ḥawza* subjects offered by contemporary writers such as the Saudi Shiʿite author Shaykh ʿAbd al-Hadi Fadli eases the path of students. Nevertheless, the traditional set texts can be extremely difficult. The *Ḥawza* atmosphere continues to be all male or all female.

It is interesting to note that in contrast with many Sunni systems of education, memorization is not formally required, although many basic texts will in the end be thoroughly committed to memory. Another contrast with most living Sunni traditions of education is the strong emphasis on dialectic and disputation (*jadal* and *munāẓara*) in class as the most respected achievement of students. In the most elegant uses of disputation, one shows that the opponent's position leads to an infinite regress or a vicious circle. There are many stories of teachers ceding their position to more able students. The famous Shaykh Waḥīd al-Bihbahānī, considered by Shiʿites to be the *mujaddid* or "renewer" of the thirteenth Hijrī century, retired from the *marjaʿīya* in his later years and referred questions to his leading students. The prominent mullah Saʿīd al-ʿUlamāʾ al-Māzandarānī, even though he had many followers, wrote to Murtaḍā al-Anṣārī: "What makes you different from me is your preoccupation with research (*baḥth*) and writing. I have given that up! Therefore, you are more learned than I and it is religiously incumbent upon the *ṭāʾifa* to emulate you and entrust you with *marjaʿīya* in their affairs."[10]

This passage brings us to the question of the *marjaʿ al-taqlīd*, a term usually translated as "source of imitation" but most correctly understood as "point of authoritative reference in matters of behavior and belief." Murtaḍā al-Anṣārī is usually considered the first *marjaʿ* accepted by the great majority of the Shiʿite world, although lists of *marjaʿ*s going back to Ṭūsī (d. 1067), founder of the Najaf *Ḥawza*, are often met with. The informality by which a person is recognized as "the most learned" and therefore the *marjaʿīya* has concerned many reformers of the Najaf *Ḥawza*. Pre-eminent among these is Muhammad Baqir al-Sadr (d. 1980), who called for a council of *marjaʿ*s, a point of view also supported by the Iranian mullah Mortaza Motahhari. This proposal failed. However, Sadr did succeed in making some of his books, such as *Iqtiṣādunā* ("Our Economy"), the subject of study circles and in this sense achieved his goal of making the teaching of the *Ḥawza* more relevant to contemporary life.

10 *Ḥawzat al-Najaf*, (*supra* n. 2) 268–270.

An earlier and more modest effort was begun by Shaykh Muhammad Rida al-Muzaffar, who favored a partial integration of the *Ḥawza* into the national university system by establishment of the Kullīyat al-Fiqh. In 1935 he and several like-minded mullahs established the Club for Publication (*Muntadā al-Nashr*). Interestingly, this group included Muhammad Sadiq al-Sadr. Its aim was to publish works in a style less archaic than that used in the textbooks at the *Ḥawza*. Towards the end of the 1930s Muzaffar established a religious college called Kullīyat al-Fiqh, which in 1957 was recognized by the Ministry of Education in Iraq. Overt opposition to this institution among the ulema of the *Ḥawza* ceased when Ayatollah al-Isfahani (d. 1946) indicated his acceptance of it.[11]

Another dramatic change in the life of the *Ḥawza* took place when Muhammad Sadiq al-Sadr, a graduate of the Kullīyat al-Fiqh and son of the founder mentioned above, was allowed limited access to the Iraqi media to publish and broadcast his sermons in the 1980s. At the time the *marjaʿīya* of Ayatollah Abu al-Qasim al-Khoei was powerful and widespread in Iraq. Nevertheless, Muhammad Sadr put himself forward as a *marjaʿ*, and a nationalistic element in the regime of Saddam Hussein welcomed the presence of an "Iraqi *marjaʿ* in contrast with the so-called "Persian" *marjaʿ*s in Iraq in the past, including Khoei. On the death of Khoei in 1992, although Khoei had clearly recognized the Iranian-born Ali al-Sistani as his successor and the majority of *Ḥawza* teachers had accepted him, a large popular element began to follow Sadr, who revived the practice of preaching sermons at the Friday prayer, a custom strictly forbidden by the senior Shiʿite clergy of Iraq for centuries. Sadr's Friday sermons on the radio with their admixture of colloquial Arabic and repeated chanting of slogans by his congregations were broadcast in Shiʿite mosques throughout Iraq. This success brought him accusations of being an agent of the government, which had already given him supervision of the *Ḥawza*. These activities also brought him both a reputation for theological naiveté and fame as a renewer of Shiʿite spirituality in the face of the "reactionary" *Ḥawza* of Najaf. In the end his demand that Shiʿite processions be performed in the traditional way convinced the government to kill him and his two sons in 1999. A third son, Muqtada al-Sadr, survived and claims to be the heir

11 See Yitzhak Nakash, *The Shiʿis of Iraq* (Princeton, N.J.: 2003) 265–266.

of both his populist father and his cousin Muhammad Baqir al-Sadr, the highly respected jurist.[12]

The *Ḥawza*, whose members had dwindled to less than two thousand in the last years of Saddam Hussein, has more than doubled its numbers since the fall of the Ba'ath and continues to attract students from most parts of the Shi'ite world. One of the great ironies of the recent upheavals in the *Ḥawza* is that Ayatollah Kazim al-Ha'iri (Kazem al-Haeri), who was an outstanding student of Muhammad Baqir al-Sadr and was recognized by Muhammad Sadr as his successor in religious matters, has steadfastly refused to return to the *Ḥawza* in Najaf and remains at his own madrasa in Qom. Hence there is a vacuum of senior religious leadership in the Ṣadrist movement led by Muqtada al-Sadr. Likewise, in the Islamic Da'wa Party, which is devoted to the memory of Muhammad Baqir al-Sadr, there is internal disagreement as to which living religious authority should be recognized.

Sistani has grown in stature both within Iraq and beyond while moving from a cautious to a bolder position toward politics. Whenever possible, he had his important fatwas co-signed by Muhammad Bashir al-Najafi, Muhammad Ishaq al-Fayyad and Muhammad Sa'id al-Hakim (when they were still alive). The Hakim family has never overcome their loss of the *marja'īya* at the death of Ayatollah Muhsin al-Hakim in 1970 and continued to champion Ayatollah Muhammad Sa'id al-Hakim (until his death in 2021). Meanwhile, Sistani's international recognition has made him the most important source of funds for the Iraqi *Ḥawza*. Perhaps the time will come for reconsideration of the model of collective leadership by the *marāji'* proposed by the most brilliant Iraqi Shi'ite clergyman of the twentieth century, Muhammad Baqir al-Sadr.

The eternal value and authority of a *ḥawza* education is brought home by a florid passage in Ayatollah Khoei's *ijāzat al-ijtihād* (permission to issue fatwas) which he granted to Sistani:

> The nobility of knowledge cannot be overestimated, nor its virtue reckoned. Inheritors of [knowledge] are the heirs of the Prophets. By it they attain deputyship to the Seal of the Prophets so long as earth and sky endure! Among those who followed the path of

12 Among the large number of books defending Muhammad Sadr, the earliest by Adil Ra'uf, *Muḥammad Muḥammad Ṣādiq al-Ṣadr, Marja'īyat al-Maydān* (Damascus: 1999), gives a good general overview.

> virtue to seek Him is ... Ḥujjat al-Islām Sayyid Ali al-Sistani. (May God prolong the days of his effusion of learning and excellence and multiply his like among the active scholars!) For he has expended in this path a sizable portion of his noble life, devoting himself to living in the vicinity of ʿAlī ... at noblest Najaf.[13]

Few systems of knowledge can have been more self-confident, and even fewer can have claimed more inherited authority than the *Ḥawza* system. Yet, in spite of all this self-confidence, the emergence of Shakespeare, who according to Ben Jonson had "small Latin and less Greek" shows that some creative advantage can be acquired by escaping too many set texts. In contrast, the great Iraqi poet Jawahiri, who started in the *Ḥawza* system, shows that a deep knowledge of classical Arabic acquired while learning set texts can also inspire memorable modern poetry written in the classical style.

APPENDIX A: CURRICULUM IN NAJAF IN 1913[14]

The first grammar book used was the *al-Ājurrūmīya*,[15] followed by *Sharḥ Qaṭr al-Badā* [*wa-Ball al-Ṣadā*].[16] Some deepened their knowledge of Arabic grammar by studying Ibn Hishām's *al-Mughnī* [*al-Labīb*] and a commentary on the *al-Alfīya*.[17] To learn syntax students often studied *al-Nukat*,[18] the *Lumʿa* [*fī al-Naḥw*], [19] and the *Kitāb* [*Sībawayhi*].[20]

Persian students followed a somewhat different curriculum which included the books printed in the *Jāmiʿ al-Muqaddamāt* such as the grammar

13 *Ḥawzat al-Najaf*, (*supra* n. 2), 159.

14 Anon., "Le programme des études chez les chiites et principalement ceux de Nedjef," *Revue du Monde Musulman* 23 (June 1913) 268–279.

15 Abū ʿAbd Allāh Muḥammad ibn Dāʾūd al-Ṣanhājī, also known as Ibn Ājarrūm, 672–723 A.H.

16 Jamāl al-Dīn Abū Muḥammad ʿAbd Allāh ibn Yūsuf, also known as Ibn Hishām, 708–761 A.H. The work consists of a basic text with the author's own commentary included.

17 Abū ʿAbd Allāh Jamāl al-Dīn Muḥammad, also known as Ibn Mālik, 600 or 601–672 A.H. The *Alfīya*, his thousand-verse poem, was a standard textbook. Although it was commonly known as the *Alfīya*, its proper title is *Kitāb al-Khulāṣa fī-l-Naḥw*.

18 Probably the *Nukat* written by Jalāl al-Dīn ʿAbd al-Raḥmān al-Suyūṭī, 849–911 A.H.

19 Abū al-Fatḥ ʿUthmān ibn Jinnī, 330–392 A.H.

20 Abū Bishr ʿAmr ibn ʿUthmān ibn Qanbar Sībawayh, d. ca. 177 A.H.

books, the *'Awāmil*,[21] *al-Namūdhaj*,[22] and *al-Fawā'id al-Ṣamadīya*.[23] They also studied the *Sharḥ al-Jāmī* [*al-Fawā'id al-Diyā'īya*][24] and a commentary on the *al-Alfīya* [*al-Bahja al-Marḍīya*].[25]

In the study of logic the students turned to the Ḥāshīya of Mullā 'Abd Allāh[26] and the *Sharḥ al-Shamsīya*.[27] Many also read *al-Jawhar al-Baḍīd*.[28]

In *fiqh* a wide range of books were studied, including *al-Tabṣira* [29] as well as the manual of the *mujtahid* that the student followed. The students then progressed to *Kitāb Sharā'i'* [*al-Islām*].[30]

In rhetoric the well-known works were *al-Fawā'id al-Diyā'īya*,[31] *Sharḥ* [*Talkhīṣ*] *al-Miftāḥ*,[32] and *al-Muṭawwal* [33]with the commentaries of Muḥammad ibn 'Alī ibn Abī Jumhūr al-Aḥsā'ī[34] and Shaykh Yūsuf ibn Aḥmad al-Baḥrānī.[35]

In the study of jurisprudence proper, the students began with *al-Ma'ālim* [*al-Dīn wa-Malādh al-Mujtahidīn*][36] although some read beforehand *al-Mabādi' wa-l-Ma'ārif*.[37] After these books, students moved on to *al-Qawānīn* [*al-Muḥkama*][38] which was usually read alongside the

---

21 The author attributes the *'Awāmil* to Mullā Ḥusayn, but the correct name is Mullā Muḥsin, better known as Fayḍ al-Kāshānī, d. *circa* 1090 A.H.

22 Abū al-Qāsim Maḥmūd ibn 'Umar al-Zamakhsharī, 467–538 A.H.

23 Muḥammad ibn Ḥusayn Bahā' al-Dīn al-'Āmilī, 953–1030 A.H.

24 This commentary on the *Kāfīya*, written by Ibn al-Ḥājib, d. 646 A.H., is by the celebrated Persian poet 'Abd al-Raḥmān Jāmī, d. 898 A.H.

25 This commentary of the *Alfīya* was written by al-Suyūṭī; see n. 5.

26 This book is most likely the *Ḥāshiya 'alā Tahdhīb al-Manṭiq* written by 'Abd Allāh ibn al-Ḥusayn Yazdī, d. 981 A.H., a commentary on the *Tahdhīb al-Manṭiq* by Mas'ūd ibn 'Umar Taftazānī, d. 793 A.H.

27 Quṭb al-Dīn Maḥmūd ibn Muḥammad al-Rāzī, d. 766 A.H.

28 al-Ḥasan ibn Yūsuf ibn al-Muṭahhar al-Ḥillī (generally known as 'Allāma al-Ḥillī), d. 726 A.H.

29 *Ibid.*

30 Ja'far ibn al-Ḥasan Muḥaqqiq al-Ḥillī, d. 726 A.H.

31 See n. 10.

32 This is a commentary by 'Alī ibn Muḥammad al-Sayyid al-Sharīf Jurjānī, 740–816 A.H., on the *Talkhīṣ al-Miftāḥ* by Jalāl al-Dīn Muḥammad ibn 'Abd al-Raḥmān Qazwīnī, 666–739 A.H.

33 Mas'ūd ibn 'Umar Taftāzānī, d. 793 A.H.

34 d. 901 A.H.

35 d. 1186 A.H.

36 Shaykh Ḥasan ibn al-Shahīd al-Thānī, d. 1011 A.H.

37 [author still unidentified]

38 Abū al-Qāsim ibn Ḥasan al-Qumī, d. 1231 A.H.

al-Lum'a al-Dimashqīya[39] studied with the commentary by al-Shahīd al-Thānī.[40] At a yet higher level, the students read two classics, *al-Rasā'il*[41] on the principles of jurisprudence and *al-Makāsib*,[42] applying these principles to a specific area of law.

In the author's time, the work "most in vogue" was the *Kifāyat* [*al-Uṣūl*],[43] which for many had replaced *al-Qawānīn* [*al-Muḥkama*]. The author adds that students interested in theology read the commentary on *Tajrīd al-'Aqā'id*[44] by ['Alī ibn Muḥammad] al-Qūshjī[45] or by 'Allāma [Ḥasan ibn Yūsuf ibn al-Muṭahhar al-Ḥillī].[46] Two books formerly popular in Najaf, the *Majma' al-Bayān* [*fī Tafsīr al-Qur'ān*][47] and *al-Shāṭibīya* [on Qur'ān readings],[48] were completely neglected by the author's time.

APPENDIX B: STANDARD *ḤAWZA* CURRICULUM

1. Logic

While the *Sharḥ al-Manẓūma fī al-Manṭiq* by Sabzawārī is still used, the most popular work on this subject is the *Uṣūl al-Manṭiq* by Shaykh al-Muzaffar. Some *Ḥawza*s begin with the simpler *Khulāsat al-Manṭiq* of Shaykh 'Abd al-Hādī Faḍlī.

2. Uṣūl al-Fiqh

Some students begin with *Mabādi' Uṣūl al-Fiqh* by Shaykh Faḍlī or the second volume of *al-Mūjaz fī Uṣūl al-Fiqh* by Ayatollah Ja'far Subḥānī. After finishing these preliminary books, the most widely used works are *Durūs fī Uṣūl al-Fiqh* (or *Durūs fī 'Ilm al-Uṣūl*) by Muhammad Baqir al-Sadr and *Uṣūl al-Fiqh* by Shaykh al-Muzaffar. At a higher stage, students advance to the *Ma'ālim* by Shaykh Ḥasan ibn al-Shahīd al-Thānī, *al-Rasā'il* by Murtaḍā al-Anṣārī, and the *Kifāya* of Akhund-e Khorasani.

39 Shams al-Dīn Muḥammad ibn Makkī al-'Āmilī al-Shahīd al-Awwal, d. 786 A.H.
40 See n. 22.
41 Shaykh Murtaḍā al-Anṣārī, d. 1281 A.H.
42 *Ibid.*
43 Muhammad Kazim Akhund-e Khorasani, d. 1329 A.H.
44 Naṣīr al-Dīn al-Ṭūsī, d. 673 A.H.
45 d. 879 A.H. The author misspells his *nisba*.
46 d. 726 A.H.
47 al-Faḍl ibn al-Ḥasan al-Ṭabarsī [or Ṭabrisī], d. 548 A.H.
48 al-Qāsim ibn Farrukh al-Shāṭibī, d. 590 A.H.

3. Fiqh
Students usually begin with *Mukhtaṣar al-Nāfi‘* by Muḥaqqiq al-Ḥillī, although this book is fast being replaced by *al-Durūs fī-l-Fiqh al-Istidlālī* of Muhammad al-Baqir al-Irawani. The next book is *al-Lum‘a al-Dimashqīya* by al-Shahīd al-Awwal Shams al-Dīn Muḥammad ibn Makkī al-‘Āmilī, usually studied with the commentary by al-Shahīd al-Thānī, which is commonly called *Sharḥ al-Lum‘a.* At the same stage, some students study *Sharā’i‘ al-Islām* by al-Muḥaqqiq al-Ḥillī and the *Āyāt al-Aḥkām* of al-Irawani.

4. Tafsīr al-Qur’ān
The most popular book in this category is *al-Mīzān* by al-Tabataba’i.

5. ‘Ulūm al-Qur’ān
The most popular work in this category is *al-Tamhīd fī ‘Ulūm al-Qur’ān* by Muhammad Hadi Ma‘rifat.

6. ‘Ilm al-Ḥadīth
The most used reference book in this field is *Wasā’il al-Shī‘a* by al-Ḥurr al-‘Āmilī.

7. ‘Ilm al-Rijāl
A popular book in this category is *Mu‘jam al-Rijāl* by Abu al-Qasim al-Khoei.

8. ‘Aqā’id
Widely used works include the *Tajrīd al-‘Aqā’id* by Naṣīr al-Dīn al-Ṭūsī and the *al-Bāb al-Ḥādī ‘Ashar* by ‘Allāma al-Ḥillī. The *Tajrīd* is often read with a commentary by ‘Allāma al-Ḥillī.

9. Arabic Language
The *Alfīya* of Ibn Mālik is read with the commentary of Ibn ‘Aqīl and/or of al-Suyūṭī.

10. Philosophy
This subject is usually broached with the *Bidāyat al-Ḥikma* and the *Nihāyat al-Ḥikma* by ‘Allama Tabataba’i.

11. ‘Irfān
[Since this subject is not publicly taught in most *Ḥawza*s the curriculum is idiosyncratic and not given here.]

Sources:
al-Islam.org (accessed December 2010)
imamreza.net (accessed December 2010)
[The information on these sites reflects a mixture of the practice in Najaf and Qum.]

APPENDIX C: LIST OF MADRASAS IN NAJAF IN 2010

1 Jāmiʿat al-Najaf (Madrasat al-Kalāntar)
2 Madrasat ʿAbd al-ʿAzīz al-Baghdādī
3 Madrasat al-Mahdī
4 Madrasat al-Yazdī
5 al-Madrasa al-Lubnānīya
6 al-Madrasa al-Shīrāzīya (Buzurg)
7 Madrasat Imām ʿAlī
8 al-Madrasa al-Afghānīya (founded by ʿAllāma Mudarris al-Afghānī)
9 al-Madrasa al-Kāẓimīya (founded by Ṣadr al-Aʿẓam)
10 Madrasat Burūjirdī al-Kubrā (founded by Ayatollah Boroujerdi)
11 Madrasat Ākhūnd al-Kubrā
12 Madrasat Ākhūnd al-Ṣughrā (like no. 11, founded by Akhund-e Khorasani)
13 Madrasat Imām Ṣādiq (al-Madrasa al-Shubarīya)
14 Madrasat Qiwām
15 al-Madrasa al-Hindīya
16 al-Madrasa al-Mahdīya (li-Kāshif al-Ghiṭā)
17 Madrasat Kāshif al-Ghiṭā
18 Madrasat al-Qazwīnī
19 Madrasat Dār al-Abrār
20 Madrasat Dār al-Muttaqīn
21 al-Madrasa al-Ḥusaynīya al-Shīrāzīya

ISLAMIC ECONOMICS

In many parts of the contemporary Muslim world there is a search for an economic system that agrees with the ethics of Islam. Some of these attempts start from reading the Qur'ān and ḥadīth. Some other attempts start with socialist or capitalist ideas and try to work back to scripture. Ideas about Islamic economics are many, but their authors are far from agreement. There is a body of medieval Muslim speculation about economic matters to which many modern scholars of the Islamic world might turn. Some of this speculation appears in the literature on Islamic ethics; some appears in Islamic law; and some appears in the literature for marketplace inspectors.

There is a general prejudice against fixed interest on loans in Islamic law. There is also a general sentiment in favor of partnership in loans between the lender and the borrower, which disallows fixed interest. The law of sale was highly developed, and the idea of "market price" in terms of time and place was clear. In most Islamic societies fluctuations in price are accepted except in times of famine or other disasters. The pre-modern Islamic economic tradition is strongly against hoarding to achieve profit.

Modern interest in socialism in many Muslim countries has resulted in varied attempts to associate public ownership with the Qur'ān, although the Islamic legal system has been strongly in favor of private ownership from the beginning. A principle of commonweal in Islam fosters not only charity but a strong belief in giving ownership of pious endowments, such as mosques, schools, shrines, and hospitals, to God and the community.

While studying European medieval history, I realized that for some periods and places the best documented history involved feudal relations or taxes. The same is true for parts of the medieval Middle East. The late Abbasid period and the following period saw administrative practices somewhat similar to Western European feudalism but also significantly different. There was no subinfeudation and no hereditary class of "nobles."

The dominant class (often called *ashrāf*) were partly but certainly not entirely a hereditary group.

The two articles in this section address two aspects of economic life allowed in the medieval Islamic world without religious objection. One deals with the assignment of revenue from tax to individuals (*tasbīb*), and the other deals with a medieval text that partly foreshadows real economic thinking of the modern period.

The first article in this section, "A Note on the *Tasbīb*," was published in 1981 in the Festschrift for my admired friend the late Ihsan 'Abbas, edited by my friend Wadad al-Qadi (Wadad Kadi). This article describes a neglected part of the system, namely *tasbīb*, for paying soldiers and bureaucrats in the time of the Buyids, the 4th/10th and 5th/11th centuries. In this system some of the revenue collection rights of the government were assigned to individuals, who had to collect the revenue themselves. One reason for the assignment of these rights to collect taxes was the debasement of the currency. Consequently, the army officers and bureaucrats would not have cause to argue with the ruler but only with the landowner from whom they were collecting taxes.

The second article in this section, "The Economic Thought of al-Rāghib al-Iṣfahānī," was finished in 2016 and submitted at that time for the Festschrift planned in honor of my close friend and colleague Roger Owen (d. 2018), who specialized in the economic history of the Middle East. This Festschrift has remained unpublished for six years, which is why I am including the article here. Al-Rāghib was a prominent theologian and moralist of the 5th/11th century who wrote a very respected Qur'ān commentary and an important book on Arabic grammar. He also wrote a work on Islamic ethics that discusses economic ideas. In this work on ethics, which remained influential for centuries, al-Rāghib offered an explanation of the economic motives that drive people to seek gain. While far from a modern economist, he shows some insight into the psychology of medieval Islamic workers, merchants, and governments. As a moralist he disapproves of some aspects of economic life, but he warmly approves of the desire for gain as an important driver of the economic world.

A Note on the *Tasbīb*

The sources for Middle Eastern history of the 4th/10th century frequently mention a form of payment called the *tasbīb* (plural: *tasbībāt*); but, to the best of my knowledge, this financial institution and its importance have been only briefly discussed by modern historians. As both the *iqṭāʿ* and the *tasbīb* became widespread at the same period and owed some of their popularity to the same causes, the study of the *tasbīb* is not only important for the administrative history of this period but also has significance for any comparison of European feudalism with the *iqṭāʿ* system.

The *Mafātīḥ al-ʿUlūm*, written circa 367/977, gives a valuable definition of the *tasbīb*. In C.E. Bosworth's very helpful translation of the relevant chapter of this work, we read: "*At-tasbīb* means that the salary of a man is diverted on to a source of taxation which it has so far proved impossible to collect, so that the assignee may help the *ʿāmil* extract this money. From the point of view of bookkeeping it will be considered one of the *ʿāmil*'s receipts and as an item of expenditure assigned to the one drawing the salary." Bosworth states that the necessity for *tasbīb* arose either when the central treasury could not meet the demands on it, and so authorized the claimants to take direct action to procure the money, or when the central government itself no longer had sufficient authority to collect the taxes; and he refers to two mentions of *tasbīb* in the chronicle of Miskawayh.[1]

Bosworth also refers to the discussion of *tasbīb* by Frede Løkkegaard, who says that both the *ḥawāla* and the *tasbīb* or *tasabbub* "belong to the darker sections of Abbasid administration." Løkkegaard suggests that the

---

Author's note: This article was first published as: "A Note on the '*Ṭasbīb*,'" in Wadad al-Qadi (ed.), *Studia Arabica et Islamica: Festschrift for Ihsān ʿAbbās on his Sixtieth Birthday* (Beirut, American University in Beirut: 1981) 347–352. Reproduced with permission.

1 Al-Khwārizmī, *Mafātīḥ al-ʿUlūm*. ed. G. van Vloten (Leiden: 1895) 62; C.E. Bosworth, "Abū ʿAbdallāh al-Khwārizmī on the Technical Terms of the Secretary's Art," *Journal of the Economic and Social History of the Orient* 12 (1969) 139–140.

tasbīb was "apt to bring about the ruin of the province concerned in the long run." He observes that the *tasabbub* was held not only by soldiers but also by others who had some claim due from the government, while the *ḥawāla* was "simply the commercial technical term for a money assignation" and might "be drawn upon any of the debtors of the government."[2] While both of these useful notices of the *tasbīb* are in general correct, I hope to show that this financial institution was more flexible than they imply and fitted into a particular niche in the structure of government finances in Islamic Middle Eastern states of the 4th/10th century.

Even in the best of times, when powerful governments could, in general, guarantee the security of the principal arteries of communication in their territories, the transportation of tax monies was dangerous and expensive. In 303 A.H., for example, a shipment of 300,000 dinars of tax money to Baghdad was attacked on the Tigris in an area that was normally under full Abbasid control; and if the money had not been transported in three *shadhawāt*, the strongly defensible ships used for this purpose, it might well have been lost. In the Buyid period, when central governments frequently lost control of important routes, the dangers to such shipments increased. Thus in 344 A.H. the ruler of the marshes of southern Iraq, ʿImrān ibn Shāhīn, having heard that the Buyid ruler of Baghdad was dead, seized a shipment of 100,000 dinars on its way to Baghdad from al-Ahwāz. No wonder the assignment of government revenue rights to individuals, i.e., *iqṭāʿāt* and the assignment to individuals of specific sums to be collected on provincial tax centers, *tasbībāt*, became more widespread under the Buyids.[3]

Like the *iqṭāʿ*, the *tasbīb* had been well known before the Buyid period. As Løkkegaard points out, in 307 A.H. when Abbasid officials are discussing the size of the average tax yield of a large district, they divide the income into revenues to be transmitted (*maḥmūl*), i.e., to Baghdad, and revenues assigned, *musabbab*.[4] Løkkegaard's presumption that "assigned" means "assigned to the provinces" is borne out by a passage about the same period in which a member of the powerful Mādharāʾī family of officials got

2 Frede Løkkegaard, *Islamic Taxation in the Classic Period* (Copenhagen: 1950) 63–64.
3 ʿArīb, *Ṣila*, ed. M.J. de Goeje (Leiden: 1897), 55 (shipment of 303). Miskawayh, *Tajārib al-Umam*, II (Cairo: 1915) 158 (ʿImrān). My translations of Miskawayh are in most cases my own but influenced by the translation of D.S. Margoliouth, *The Eclipse of the Abbasid Caliphate: Classical Writings of the Medieval Islamic World* (London, I.B. Tauris: 2015).
4 Løkkegaard, (*supra* n. 2), 63.

Egypt as a tax farm for one million dinars a year after "running expenses," *al-nafaqāt al-rātiba*, a standard phrase in budgets of the period. It is further explained that this million was *khāliṣa li-ḥaml ilā bayt al-māl*, "a net sum to be transmitted to the central treasure" without, as the text goes on to explain, any reductions whatsoever. Mādharā'ī also had to sign a separate deed with the details of the payments expected of him for running expenses and for the army, district by district. Local running expenses and the cost of local troops are probably the equivalent of the "assigned" revenues in the other passage. It is likely that one of the reductions that the contract intended to preclude was any charge by the Mādharā'ī for the cost of transmitting the million dinars to Baghdad.[5]

Similarly, al-Tanūkhī in his *Nishwār al-Muḥāḍara* tells us that in the year 299 A.H. the Abbasid vizier assigned (*sabbaba*) the expense of maintaining the pilgrimage road to Mecca to the *'āmil* of Kufa. Since the road started in southern Iraq, it was reasonable that the tax office of some important southern Iraqi center bear the expense, rather than the treasury in Baghdad farther to the north.[6] Since the *'āmil* had to be instructed to make these disbursements, we can presume that the expense of the pilgrimage road was previously not part of "running expenses." It is to these special assignments that 'Alī ibn 'Īsā referred in the circular letter he wrote to the *'āmil*s of the Abbasid Empire when he was appointed vizier in 301 A.H. He said that the *'āmil*s should delay "the execution of *tasbībāt* and the like until my letters and rescripts come to you." It is unlikely that he would instruct them to delay disbursements for standard running expenses.[7]

An incident in 315 A.H. during a later vizierate of 'Alī ibn 'Īsā gives us further insight into the accounting procedures associated with the *tasbīb*. Hārūn, a commander, had lent money to al-Khāqānī when the latter was vizier in return for allocations assigned to him (*tasbībāt*). Hārūn put before 'Alī ibn 'Īsā the charge that according to a ledger (*daftar*) in the office of Ibn Shīrzād, the secretary of Hārūn, Ibn Shīrzād had received fifteen thousand dinars of these assigned allocations, but the money was not in the receipts (*khatamāt*) of the *jahbadh* (accountant-collector) recording monies received at Ibn Shīrzād's office. Therefore, said Hārūn, Ibn Shīrzād had kept the payments from the *tasbībāt* for himself. Eventually the correct receipt book was produced and Ibn Shīrzād was cleared. As this incident

5 Miskawayh, *Tajārib al-Umam*, I (Cairo: 1914) 107.
6 Al-Tanūkhī, *Nishwār al-Muḥāḍara*, II (Beirut: 1971–72) 283.
7 Miskawayh, (*supra* n. 5), I:27.

shows, there were at least two records made out when a *tasbīb* was paid in: one in the receipt book of the collector, and one in each office's central ledger.[8] Despite such safeguards, the *tasbīb* offered great opportunities to defraud the government for anyone with full authority over bookkeeping. Thus in 319 A.H. another vizier of the Abbasids, al-Kalwadhānī, included in the accounts *tasbībāt* to non-existent people which he paid to himself.[9]

As we have seen, there were probably two forms of *tasbīb* in the Abbasid period. The passage cited by Løkkegaard seems to show that provincial revenues which, for whatever reason, were not sent to the capital, were called *musabbab* (assigned to someone as a *tasbīb*). Many other passages establish that specific "extraordinary" assignments of revenues to individuals, often on provincial tax offices but also on tax offices in the capital, were called *tasbībāt*. While the first form of *tasbīb* was, under whatever name, a normal practice of pre-modern governments in all periods, the second form of *tasbībāt* became extremely widespread in the Buyid period.

While the Abbasids were strong, the *tasbīb* was a financial instrument over which the government had control. When a foolish vizier, al-Khaṣībī, hired the semi-independent Iranian condottiere Ibn Abī al-Sāj to fight the dreaded Qarmaṭī soldiers of northeast Arabia, he assigned the financial administration of several provinces to Ibn Abī al-Sāj to pay him for his troubles. 'Alī ibn 'Īsā later upbraided al-Khaṣībī for this unprofessional handling of the situation and asked him why he had not been satisfied to have Ibn Abī al-Sāj's army paid on the same principle as the army of Mu'nis, the regular commander-in-chief, "because certain revenues are assigned (*yusabbab*) to him and disbursed on behalf of the government through paymasters who have to render their accounts to the ministries of the army (*dawāwīn al-jaysh*) ...? Why not leave the provinces in the hands of the government's *'āmils*?"[10]

Soon, however, as the Abbasid government lost control of even nearby territories, it lost control of *tasbībāt*. When, for example, an Abbasid commander fled to Fars in 321 A.H. because the caliph was likely to arrest him for participating in an abortive plot, he was fortunate enough to be carrying *tasbībāt* on Fars which he redeemed when he got there. Shortly after, in 321, the Abbasid government tried to stop another rebel general

8 Miskawayh, (*supra* n. 5), I:164.
9 Miskawayh, (*supra* n. 5), I:213.
10 Miskawayh, (*supra* n. 5), I:153–154, translation slightly adapted from that of D.S. Margoliouth (*supra* n. 3).

by having the *tasbībāt* of the general and his men called in; but, increasingly, such efforts were futile. The *tasbīb* had always had something of the character of a government-issued bill of exchange. Now that the central government had a more shadowy control over its administration, this character became more marked.[11]

Under the Buyids, not only were *tasbībāt* less under the control of the central ministries of the government, but their assignees were less easily controlled, especially as many of these assignees were the soldiers who founded and/or maintained the Buyid governments. For example, in 347 A.H. the Buyid ruler of Baghdad said that the Turkish soldiers, whom he was heavily favoring at the time, should go to centers in southern Iraq to collect the *tasbībāt* which had been given to them. As the *tasbībāt* could not be paid immediately, the Turks drew maintenance pay from these provincial centers and, according to the historian Miskawayh, some of them remained for two or three years. Similarly, we read that in 356 A.H., under the even more lax administration of the next Buyid ruler of Iraq, the Turkish soldiers were dispersed to the provinces to realize their *tasbībāt*.[12]

Another historian, al-Rūdhrāwarī, does mention one instance in which one of the very few strong Buyid rulers, ʿAḍud al-Dawla, actually used *tasbībāt* as a method of control. He would allow his officials to take advances on their salaries from a financial official in Basra on whom these advances would be assigned (*yusabbab*). But the *tasbībāt* were paid in dates or something similar (and, presumably, as plentiful in Basra as dates were) valued somewhat above the market price. By this means the *tasbībāt* yielded a profit to the government.[13]

Al-Rūdhrāwarī also makes clear how common *tasbībāt* were as an element of pay in the middle Buyid period when he writes that a Buyid vizier in about 373 A.H. originated the practice of levying the tithe (*ʿushr*) on all *tasbībāt* given to men of the regime for their salaries. Obviously, if *tasbībāt* were still truly an "extraordinary" grant of funds, this practice would not have been established.[14]

As has been mentioned above, the Buyid period marked the extension of another form of payment to men of the regime, the well-known *iqṭāʿ*. The *iqṭāʿ* was an assignment of government revenue rights, most particularly to

11 Miskawayh, (*supra* n. 5), I:265 (Fars); 274 (recall).
12 Miskawayh, (*supra* n. 3), II:174 (347 A.H.) and 237 (356 A.H.).
13 al-Rūdhrāwarī, *Dhayl Kitāb Tajārib al-Umam* (Cairo: 1916) 67.
14 al-Rūdhrāwarī, (*supra* n. 13), 85.

high officials and the great majority of trusted soldiers of the regime. The relation of the *tasbīb* to the *iqṭāʿ* is clarified by a very important passage in the fragmentary history of Hilāl al-Ṣābī. He writes that after a Buyid official reconquered the province of Kerman for his king, he offered the defeated soldiers there an opportunity to stay on as part of the garrison of the province on the understanding that they would receive no *iqṭāʿāt*, only salaries and *tasbībāt*. They were to be treated financially as were the Iranians who were freshly arrived from Daylam, the province from which the Buyid ruling family, and half their armies, came. *Tasbīb*, therefore, was a common form of payment, but did not imply the same trust by and involvement in the regime as did *iqṭāʿ*.[15]

Doubtless other historians will find further references to the *tasbīb*, both in the Buyid period and in other periods.[16] The references gathered in this article are, I think, sufficient to provide a general picture of its evolution in Iraq and surrounding areas from the end of the 3rd/9th to the end of the 4th/10th century. When the Abbasids were powerful, the *tasbīb*, far from being one of "the darker sections of Abbasid administration," was a normal bookkeeping practice of the central government to account for monies not transferred to the capital. The *tasbīb* was also an assignment to an individual of a specific sum of money to be collected at a local or, occasionally, central tax office. While the Abbasid government was strong, the payment of such assignments or drafts was prompt, and the *tasbīb* could be recalled if the government wished to cancel it.

Under the weaker governments of the late Abbasid and Buyid periods, the *tasbīb* became a sort of bill of exchange, often issued without the expectation that it would be paid promptly or could be easily recalled. As some *tasbībāt* were not redeemed for a considerable period, they could exchange hands several times. Increasingly, the recipients of these *tasbībāt* were privileged soldiers. Hence, as al-Khwārizmī's *Mafātīḥ al-ʿUlūm* says, they were often assigned to "a source of taxation which has proved impossible to collect," since a privileged army officer might have a better chance of collecting such taxes than had the central government or its local representatives.

15 Hilāl al-Ṣābī, *Ta'rīkh* (Cairo: 1919) 362.
16 See the references to *taṣbīb* in the Ghaznavid period in Hasan Anvari, *Eṣṭelāḥat-e Divāni* (Tehran: 1355 solar/1976–77) 85–86; and the references collected by M.J. de Goeje for his glossary to al-Ṭabarī, *Annales*, XV (Leiden, Brill: 1901) cclxxxiv.

Both the *tasbīb* and the *iqṭāʿ* owed some of their popularity to the new situation of these weaker and more decentralized governments. Transportation of money was more dangerous than ever before, and it was easier to let government employees collect their pay for themselves. These weaker governments were usually on the verge of bankruptcy, and they were both glad to be spared the extra cost of transporting revenues, and happy to send their creditors to the provinces where they would be out of sight. Moreover, the traditional monetary system went totally haywire in the 4th/10th century with wildly fluctuating ratios of gold and silver exchange, periodic shortages of specie, and drastic debasements of coinage. Not unexpectedly, troops frequently revolted when they were paid in debased coin. Hence, it became easier to assign the government's revenue collecting powers to officials and soldiers than to pay them in coin. Sometimes there was a direct assignment of such powers, in the case of an *iqṭāʿ*, which, typically, would be the assignment of the land tax of an estate or area for a year. At other times, there was an assignment of the central government's powers to collect sums from its lower or local tax collectors—this was the *tasbīb*.

However, although these assignments in some respects resemble the benefice of medieval Europe, they were also significantly different. The *iqṭāʿ* and the *tasbīb* always kept their character as bookkeeping procedures, and no one had a claim to an *iqṭāʿ* or a *tasbīb* unless they had received the proper warrant from the central government, which also had to record these assignments in its general registers of the allocations of each year's expected revenues. This maintenance of central registers through weakness and strength is one of the most surprising features of governments of the pre-modern Islamic Middle East, and it was one of the important reasons that certain features of European feudalism, like vassalage, appeared in only very attenuated forms in this region of the world. As long as the central government insisted (and often succeeded) in treating *iqṭāʿāt* and *tasbībāt* in this way, it was hard to transform the ties between the king and even his trusted subjects into the kinds of ties that bound a medieval European to his liege lord.

The Economic Thought of al-Rāghib al-Iṣfahānī

"Islamic economics": it is one of the catchwords of our time, like "globalization" or "commoditization."[1] How newly born and innocent of history it sounds in the mouths of many of its contemporary advocates, a subject that springs across fourteen hundred years of history, from the time of the Qur'ān to our time, without encountering any of the centuries in between. Of course, as long as there has been Islam there has been Islamic economics. All ethical systems have prescriptions that seek to influence economic behavior, and Islam is no exception. My purpose here is to present one of the many forgotten thinkers on Islamic economics, al-Rāghib al-Iṣfahānī, and to discuss the relation of his ideas to the time in which he lived.

Al-Rāghib was an author of the first importance. His largest work *Muḥāḍarāt al-Udabā'*, ranks among the most important works of Arabic literature. His dictionary of the Qur'ān, *Mufradāt fī Gharīb al-Qur'ān*, is still widely used by Muslim scholars and is said to be one of the principal philological sources for the widely admired Qur'ān commentary of Bayḍāwī. Al-Rāghib's book on ethics, *al-Dharī'a ilā Makārim al-Sharī'a*, which will be the focus of this essay, has been printed many times and exists in many dozens of manuscripts in public collections. According to one anecdote, the very prominent theologian al-Ghazālī, who died in 505/1111, is supposed to have always kept a copy of al-Rāghib's *al-Dharī'a* with him. As Professor Wilferd Madelung has masterfully shown, Ghazālī's

Author's note: This article was submitted in 2016 to the planned but as yet unpublished Festschrift in honor of Roger Owen. It is being published for the first time here.

1 It is a pleasure to acknowledge the wonderfully helpful comments of Don Babai, Alexander Key, Louise Marlow and Emma Rothschild.

Mīzān al-'Amal, is an enlarged version of *al-Dharī'a*. The *Mīzān* of Ghazālī in turn forms the basis of his masterwork, the *Iḥyā'*.[2]

Reliable biographical information on al-Rāghib al-Iṣfahānī is relatively scarce, however great his later influence. From a manuscript we know that al-Rāghib was alive in or before 409/1018. Al-Rāghib mentions his connection with the court of the great and very literarily pretentious vizier Ṣāḥib ibn 'Abbād (d. 385/995). This court was in Rayy near modern Tehran although Ibn 'Abbād did travel around the Buyid kingdom of western Iran which existed from 331/943 until 420/1027. Al-Rāghib, therefore, was active in the late 4th/10th and early 5th/11th centuries. Yet the scarcity of material about al-Rāghib suggests that he was retiring and uninterested in society, perhaps in accordance with his Sufi beliefs.

The sixth section (*faṣl*) of al-Rāghib's book on ethics, *al-Dharī'a*, is entitled, "Concerning those things which pertain to productive occupations, means of acquiring gain, expenditure, generosity and avarice." The pages that follow are a treatise on economic morality of exceptional interest. Al-Rāghib begins:

> Know, that since it is difficult for anyone to furnish for himself the least of his needs except through the help of a number of men—so that, were we to list the labors of farmers, millers and makers of implements needed to furnish one mouthful of food, it would be difficult to enumerate them. Therefore, men need to gather in groups and support each other—for this reason it is said that man is by nature social; that is, he is not able to subsist singly apart from society. Rather, humans need each other for their religious and worldly interests.[3]

---

2 Wilferd Madelung, "Ar-Rāġib al-Iṣfahānī und die Ethik al-Ghazālīs," in R. Gramlich (ed.), *Islamwissenschaftliche Abhandlungen* (Wiesbaden: 1974) 152–153. Carl Brockelmann writes, "a book that Ghazālī is supposed to have always carried with him," *Geschichte der arabischen Literatur*, I (Leiden: 1943) 343. See the very informative overview of al-Rāghib's work by Alexander Key, "al-Rāghib al-Isfahānī," in Terri de Young and Mary St. Germain, (eds.), *Essays in Arabic Literary Biography 925–1350* (Wiesbaden: 2011) 298–306.

3 Al-Rāghib, *al-Dharī'a ilā Makārim al-Sharī'a*, ed. 'Ali Mirlawhi (Isfahan: 1996) 381. I translate *madanī* as "social" and not "political" as one would translate Aristotle, an obvious source for this passage, because Muslim thinkers in this vein refer to swarming creatures such as bees and birds as *madanī*. See my article "Friendship in Islamic Ethical Philosophy" (Article 7 here). Louise Marlow in her outstanding book, *Hierarchy and*

Division of labor is a theme that continues at least from classical Greek thought to modern times. In pre-modern Islamic thought (as in some classical predecessors) it is strongly associated with the communal (or social) needs of mankind. In his examination of pin-making, Adam Smith notes that "about eighteen distinct operations" are involved.[4] Ghazālī observes that "even the small needle becomes useful only after passing through hands of the needle maker about twenty-five times." Although it might have been self-evident to Ghazālī, he did not go on to estimate (as Adam Smith did) the benefit to productivity of separating the tasks among more individuals.[5]

After a number of Qur'ānic and ḥadīth proof texts al-Rāghib continues:

> Since men are in need of each other, God has determined each one of them without exception for some productive occupation which he can follow and has created hidden correspondences and divine conformities between their own natures and their productive occupations, so that each one in his turn prefers a certain profession, delighting in being associated with it, and devoting his powers to its pursuit. Thus, if he were entrusted with another productive occupation, he might be found dull-witted or easily annoyed in practicing it. For this reason, God has determined their interests lest they all choose a single productive occupation, and food stuffs and services would cease. Were it not so, men would have chosen only the best things for themselves, only the most pleasant places to live in, only the cleanest productive occupations, and only the most exalted tasks to work on, and on this account would fight each other.[6]

Egalitarianism in Islamic Thought (Cambridge, U.K., and New York: 1997) 152 n. 39, which uses my translation of this section.

4 See Book One, Chapter One of Adam Smith, *An Inquiry into the Nature and Causes of the Wealth of Nations*, first published in 1776. Specialists in Adam Smith trace his comments in part to the article "Épingle" in the French *Encyclopédie* (1755). See J.-L. Peaucelle, "Adam Smith's Use of Multiple References for his pin-making examples," *European Journal of the History of Economic Thought* 13:4 (2006) 480–512.

5 This passage on the needle was brought to my attention by Profs. S.M. Ghazanfar and A. Azim Islahi, *Economic Thought of Ghazali (450–505 A.H./1058–1111 A.D.)*, (Jiddah: 2011) 34. These two scholars very kindly guided me to the subheading in Ghazālī under which I found the passage available to me in the *Ihyā'*, ed. 'Ahd al-'Aziz 'Izz al-Din Sirwan, IV (Beirut, n.d.) 113. These two scholars translate "needle maker" as "needle makers," which may be correctly translated "needle makers" if the singular is understood as a generic. The passage does not make clear the number of people involved in the needle-making.

6 Al-Rāghib, (*supra* n. 3), 382.

Many proof texts follow this statement, after which al-Rāghib moves onto his third subsection, which has the striking title: "The Existence of Poverty and Fear of It Are a Cause of Order in Human Affairs." He explains:

> The occurrence of poverty and fear of it are the two stimulants which make men want things. They are the two causes that make men strive, endure hard work to the benefit of people in general, whether by choice or necessity. For this reason it is said: "How many run for each one who sits." This is so since, if each man could meet his needs by himself, it would lead to the corruption of the world. For then no one would take care of any job for another, as he would for this reason be unable to accomplish all his personal interests, and such a state of affairs would lead to the impoverishment of all. Perhaps it can be said that the world's subsistence is based more on poverty than on wealth, because the occupations subsisting through wealth are three: kingship, trade and landlordism. All the rest subsist through poverty; and if it were not for poverty and fear of it, who would take care of weaving and cupping and dyeing and sweeping? Who would transport provisions and clothes from East to West and from South to North?[7]

Some of these ideas are as old and persistent as the belief in private property. In rejecting the proposal of the much-admired Enlightenment thinker, Nicolas de Condorcet (d. 1794), for a form of social security, Thomas Malthus (d. 1834) wrote that Condorcet wrongly believed that labor would be performed "without the goad of necessity." "If by establishments of this kind, this spur to industry be removed ... can we expect to see men exert that animated activity in bettering their condition ...?"[8]

According to al-Rāghib, the unseen hand of God's economic planning can be glimpsed everywhere. Poverty and fear of it maintain the division of labor; otherwise, all would be impoverished. Only a few professions, basically government, gathering the yield from agriculture, and large scale

7 Al-Rāghib (*supra* n. 3), 384. The word translated as "landlordism" is *tināya*, which means "possessing much land or other immoveable property." See E.W. Lane, *Arabic English Lexicon*, I (London: 1863) 318.

8 See the elegant essay by Emma Rothschild, *The Debate on Economic and Social Security in the late Eighteenth Century: Lessons of a Road not Taken* (Geneva, United Nations Research Institute for Social Development: 1995) 11.

trade subsist on economic surplus. He mentions an old (but disputed) Islamic (and possibly pre-Islamic) tradition of ranking professions according to prestige with bloodletting (by cupping) at the bottom.[9]

Next, al-Rāghīb turns to a very familiar theme among Islamic thinkers, namely that "To earn wealth is religiously obligatory." He then explains:

> This is so because a man cannot himself turn to the worship of God without taking care of the basic necessities of his life. And to take care of these basic necessities is a religious obligation, for anything which is essential to the accomplishment of a religious obligation by this same token is itself a religious obligation. Since there is no way to take care of these necessities except by taking people's labor, these people must necessarily be repaid.[10]

Interestingly enough, al-Rāghib includes in this subsection an attack on:

> ... the one who claims to be a Sufi and withdraws from means of gain while possessing no religious knowledge that might be learned from him or pious conduct that might be imitated.[11]

Of such a man, al-Rāghib says:

> On the contrary his belly and his crotch are the center of his interest. For, he takes the gains of others and decreases the amount of their livelihood and gives them nothing beneficial in return. People like them are of no use except to muddy the waters with confusion and to inflate prices.[12]

Al-Rāghib then strikes a pose that looks at first glance somewhat vaguely like the pose commonly associated with Calvinists of the sixteenth and seventeenth centuries. He writes:

---

9 On this subject see the excellent discussion in Louise Marlow's *Hierarchy*, (*supra* n. 3) 156–173.

10 Al-Rāghib, (*supra* n. 3), 387.

11 Al-Rāghib, (*supra* n. 3), 388. Alexander Key in his thesis makes clear al-Rāghib's sympathy for Sufi thought.

12 Al-Rāghib, (*supra* n. 3), 388. "Muddying waters and inflating prices" is a cliché frequently used in ethical literature.

> The Prophet thought well of the delegations from the tribe of 'Abd Qays when he asked them, "What is manliness/valor (*murūwa*)?" and they answered, "Chastity (*'iffa*) and the pursuit of a profession (*ḥirfa*)."[13]

This seeming resemblance to an early Calvinist pose is strengthened in the next subsection, a condemnation of sloth:

> He who remains idle and unemployed has stripped himself of his humanity and even of his animality and entered the category of the dead. This is so because man was endowed with three faculties in order that he may strive for the virtue(s) they offer. For, the appetitive faculty (*al-quwwa al-shahwīya*) demands that he acquire gainful occupations which increase him in wealth ... One should realize that one's inner agitation (*iḍṭirāb*) is the cause of one's ascending from powerlessness to might, from poverty to wealth, from lowliness to glory, and from obscurity to fame.[14]

With proper publicity al-Rāghib might join the brilliant Arab philosopher of history, Ibn Khaldūn (d. 1406 C.E.), already honored by Arthur Laffer, Ronald Reagan and Margaret Thatcher as the discoverer of the Laffer curve, as one of the Islamic forerunners of neo-liberal/neo-conservative economics.[15] Certainly, al-Rāghib would have had nothing to quarrel with in the famous statement of Benjamin Franklin made in 1766 in a pamphlet addressed to the British public on the Corn Laws and Poor Laws: "[Y]ou offered a premium for the encouragement of idleness, and you should not now wonder that it has had its effect in the increase of poverty."[16] But how much is al-Rāghib really like those early modern European thinkers who began the change (so beautifully laid out in Albert Hirschman's book,

---

13 Al-Rāghib, (*supra* n. 3), 388.

14 Al-Rāghib, (*supra* n. 3), 390. My colleague, Emma Rothschild, has pointed out that Adam Smith believed that the "inner agitation" could be satisfied by conditions other than wealth; see Adam Smith, *The Theory of Moral Sentiment*, 2nd ed. (London: 1761), Bk. 1, Ch. 3.

15 Arthur B. Laffer, "The Laffer Curve: Past, Present, and future," *Backgrounder* 1765 (The Heritage Foundation, June 1, 2004).

16 Benjamin Franklin, *Arator*, viewed on "Franklinpapers.org" on July 24, 2015.

The Passions and the Interests)[17] through which the desire for gain was transformed from one of the seven deadly sins to that wonderfully useful passion that was implanted in men by divine design for the common good?

Certainly, there are real resemblances, as when al-Rāghib claims that the appetitive faculty exists to impel men toward gain and that all good forms of advancement, including advancement from poverty to wealth, comes from a desire to scratch an obviously beneficent universal itch, the *iḍṭirāb* or "agitation" mentioned above. This brings us to one of the richest historical debates on the relation of ideology to action, the discussion of the relation of Protestantism to the rise of capitalism, a debate which we associate with Max Weber and R.H. Tawney, but which continues to be waged among historians at present with increasing sophistication.

Right away I should confess that I have omitted some passages that show al-Rāghib to be decidedly different from the forerunners of capitalist thought. When discussing the division of labor, he quotes the ḥadīth, "each is enabled to do what he was created for," as Rāghib says in a quote above. Such a belief would work against the vigilance for new roles and professions that would characterize the entrepreneur who is always eager to maximize his wealth. Similarly, when al-Rāghib explains how all of us must to some extent avail each other of each other's labor, he adds that "if someone is satisfied with a small portion of the worldly things of others, he will take only this small portion and be satisfied with doing a small amount of work."[18] This sentiment is not anti-capitalist but does not agree with the conventional idea of the Protestant ethic. At some point al-Rāghib, who is, after all, a Sufi, even contradicts the thrust of his argument in favor of the appetitive faculty as when he writes: "It is the duty of each person who is obliged to earn wealth to confine him or herself to acquire that which will for the moment avert poverty without transferring his anxiety for tomorrow to today."[19] In agreement with this last statement there is no mention of reinvestment of wealth.

Al-Rāghib, in his work on theology, reasserts his ideas in a more religious framework. In his discussion of "good and evil" he plainly states that "worldly ease" is good. One of the treasures in sound intellects is bearing up well under hardships "in traveling to seek profit (*ribḥ*)." Since everything

17 Albert Hirschman, *The Passions and the Interests: Political Arguments for Capitalism Before Its Triumph* (Princeton, N.J.: 1977).
18 Al-Rāghib, (*supra* n. 3), 6.
19 Al-Rāghib, (*supra* n. 3), 7.

is created for a purpose, hence "the differences in their professions and businesses (*matjarāt*)." "God made poverty, ignorance and heedlessness as a mercy (*raḥma*)." Although Rāghib is trying to explain a theological point, namely, that seeming evils have benefits, his belief in the social necessity of poverty and hierarchy stands out. Rāghib is not altogether consistent, but his theology supports his ideas on the ethics of economics.[20]

Let us very briefly consider the actual social and economic world of al-Rāghib. Al-Rāghib said that the "occupations subsisting through wealth were three: kingship, trade and landlordism." If we understand by "king" a military ruler *and* the army that maintains him, we would certainly agree that kingship and the military elite it requires subsist through wealth. Merchants and landlords were certainly elites that subsisted through wealth, although landlords were a group in some disarray by the late Buyid period when al-Rāghib lived. The *Shīrāz-Nāma*, with some exaggeration, states that:

> [I]n the time of the Daylamīs [Buyids] the affairs of the country were thrown into confusion. Disorders and acts of sedition followed one after another, so much that estates were forsaken and abandoned ... Most of the land became state land (*divāni*). Before most of the lands were private property (*melk*)."[21]

The ulema, or clergy, was a group that was to be professionalized largely in the following period, the early Seljuk period, when endowments of the Seljuks and their high officials established madrasas and similar institutions.

By and large there was no question that honestly gained wealth gave honor. A contemporary of al-Rāghib, the very learned Abū Ja'far al-Ṭūsī (d. 460/1067), writes that just as preference is given to well-born people and to the elderly, so it should be given to the wealthy:

> If it be said: Is it according to human nature to give precedence to men of wealth, in which case wealth and riches would be considered

20 Al-Rāghib, *Al-I'tiqādāt*, ed. Shamra al-'Ajali (Beirut: 1988) 255–258.

21 A.K.S. Lambton, *Landlord and Peasant in Persia* (London: 1991) 51. Lambton quotes another source to the same effect but both sources are post-Buyid and may have been intended to please the Seljuks.

> nobility (*sharaf*)? We answer: Just so, we do not deny or reject [such a claim].[22]

At the same time the society of al-Rāghib's time continued to have a complex system of rank that mitigated the difference between rich and poor. In discussing points of honor, a matter that decided, among other things, who led the prayer in a caravan, it continued to be assumed that all members of any group could be ranked in sequence from the presumptive "Best" (*afḍal*) on down. We have, then, a system of relational and not absolute hierarchy in which wealth was only one of many signs of excellence. Certainly, for many pietists wealth was the lowest mark of honor. In al-Rāghib's discussion of poverty, however, we see one of the changing ideals of his time.[23]

The virtue of poverty among the *ṣaḥāba*, the Companions of the Prophet, seems never to have been open to question among Muslim thinkers, although—as with apostolic and evangelical poverty among Christians—it was not always held up as an ideal to be imitated in the present. But a certain kind of Sufi poverty, in which lack of possessions left the seeker unencumbered in his inward spiritual search, was just becoming a popular ideal in the early 5th/11th century, although, I believe that it would be correct to say that it was still largely opposed by the ulema in part because of the firm belief in property shown in classical Islamic law.[24]

Islamic law of this period shows a great deal of sophistication about economic matters. It discusses the determination of market prices, the nature of "consideration" in exchange, credit, commoditization and a host of other economic issues. It has a sophisticated discussion of contracts, partnerships and leases. Of all aspects of traditional Islamic law, commercial law has passed most easily into modern national codes in Muslim-majority countries.

---

22 See Ṭūsī, *Al-Tibyān fī Tafsīr al-Qur'ān*, IX, ed. Ahmad Habib Qusayr al-'Amili (Tehran: 1409/1988–89) 251 (commentary on verse XLIX:13).

23 See the discussion of relational hierarchy in my book, *Loyalty and Leadership in an Early Islamic Society* (Princeton, N.J., Princeton University Press: 1980) 98 ff.

24 See the excellent articles by Michael Bonner, "Poverty and Charity in the Rise of Islam," in M. Bonner, M. Ener and A. Singer (eds.), *Poverty and Charity in Middle Eastern Contexts* (Albany: 2003) 13–30 and "The Kitāb al-Kasb," *Journal of the American Oriental Society* 121:3 (2001) 410–427. See also the very fine work by Adam Sabra, *Poverty and Charity in Medieval Islam* (Cambridge, U.K., Cambridge University Press: 2000) and Amy Singer, *Constructing Ottoman Beneficence* (Albany: 2002).

While, strictly speaking, there was no word for "economics" in medieval Islamic thought, there is a phrase for "economic thought." *Tadbīr al-manzil*, or "organization of the household," a literal translation of the Greek *oikonomia* (which is in turn the origin of our word "economy") was frequently used. The inclusion of this subject in the philosophical tradition in the category of "practical ethics" is fairly continuously attested at least from the time of the philosopher al-Fārābī (d. 339/951) on. The extension of the term to a wider meaning, the management of economic affairs, is fairly common and the word *siyāsa* (management) is a common substitute for *tadbīr*.[25]

The relation of al-Rāghib to earlier and later writers is a vast subject far beyond the scope of this essay. Aristotole's discussion of economic thought, especially in *The Nicomachean Ethics*, influenced many writers, sometimes through the interpretation of *The Nicomachean Ethics* by Ibn Miskawayh (d. 421/1030) in his book on ethics, *The Refinement of Character*. Another book that was influential in forming Middle Eastern economic thought is the treatise by a Neo-Pythagorean thinker, Bryson, possibly of the first century C.E.[26] This treatise survives only in Arabic translation (as well as in later Hebrew and Latin translations). Bryson describes the diversification of labor, the need for money to facilitate exchange, and economic management of the family. Bryson is not as rich in speculation as Aristotle. As they both begin with a patriarchal view of the family, most of the authors in this tradition, whether classical Greek, Muslim or Christian, have a patriarchal view of society.

Discussions of *tadbīr al-manzil* in the Islamic Middle East continued after Miskawayh and were joined by al-Rāghib and other Muslim authors with a great many Qur'ānic and Prophetic proof texts. It is a tribute to al-Rāghib's success in marrying the Islamic and Hellenic elements in economic thought that Ghazālī, the Muslim Aquinas, followed him so closely. As part of the ethical tradition, al-Rāghib's influence stretches to Naṣīr al-Dīn al-Ṭūsī (d. 673/1274), whose *Akhlāq-e Nāṣeri* is the apotheosis

25 Of the many surveys of the *tadbīr al-manzil* literature the fullest and most recent is: Simon Swain, *Economy, Family and Society from Rome to Islam* (Cambridge, U.K., Cambridge University Press: 2013). A good short survey in Persian is offered by Reza Pourjavady, "Tadbīr," *Dānesh-Nāma-ye Jahān-e Eslām*,VI (Tehran: 2002) 737–742.

26 Simon Swain is preceded as an interpreter of Bryson. See Martin Plessner, *Der Oikonomikos des Neupythagoreers 'Bryson'* (Heidelberg: 1928) 47, who raises the question of Weberian categories.

of the tradition of Islamic Middle Eastern books on ethics. Ṭūsī's work continued to influence Islamic ethical thought to the nineteenth century.[27]

Yet none of the discussions that I know about economic matters directly ask about the overall economy, "the state of a country or region in terms of the production and consumption of goods and services and the supply of money," as the Oxford Dictionary defines the word "economy."[28] The nearest we come to it are fairly abstract discussions of prosperity. Scholars have discovered two Abbasid budgets, which show estimates of the productivity of the land since the tax is a percentage of either the actual harvest or of an estimate of the harvest based on the size of arable land.[29] Theoretically, in addition to the land tax, there was an income tax based on the net increase of wealth, which would be a slightly better barometer of regional wealth, but the income tax seems to have been seldom or irregularly enforced.[30]

If "economics" had a shadowy existence in al-Rāghib's time, "economic man" existed in the 4th/10th and 5th/11th centuries as certainly as he/she does in the twenty-first century. The judge and anecdotalist al-Tanūkhī (d. 384/994) tells us that the celebrated vizier of the Buyid kingdom of Iraq, al-Muhallabī (d. 352/963), on his way through the streets of Baghdad felt an urgent need to relieve himself. After accomplishing this task in a "dwelling of some humble people," he summoned the owner of the house, a maker of jugs. The vizier then:

> ... asked the man if it was his property. The man said it was hired. The vizier asked what rent he paid. Five dirhams a month, he replied. What is its value? the vizier asked. Five hundred dirhams was the answer. What, the vizier asked, is your capital as jug-manufacturer? A hundred dirhams, he answered. The vizier at once gave him a

27 Naṣīr al-Dīn al-Ṭūsī's work is available in an excellent English translation by G.W. Wickens, *The Nasirean Ethic* (London: 1964).

28 *Oxford Dictionary of English*, (3rd ed.), ed. Angus Stevenson (Oxford: 2010) under "economy," viewed online July 28, 2015.

29 A. von Kremer, "Über das Einnahmebudget des Abbasiden-Reiches," *Denkschriften der kaiserlichen Akademie des Wissenschaften* (Wien: 1887); Makoto Shimizu, "Les finances publiques de l'état abbaside," *Der Islam* 42 (1966) 1–24.

30 See A. Zysow, "Zakāt," *The Encyclopaedia of Islam*, 2nd ed., XI (Leiden, Brill: 2001) 406–422. As Emma Rothschild has pointed out to me, the concept of "national economy" may have arisen in France and England in the eighteenth century along with the emergence of a national state with its system of transport and communications.

> thousand dirhams, bidding him purchase the house and increase his capital with the remainder. He then mounted.[31]

The very sophisticated bureaucratic class that al-Muhallabī represented would have loved to know the size and extent of the economy of the region that they supervised. But the physical limits of the time and place prevented them from having any larger picture of the economy. The "economy" was beyond their reach statistically and, perhaps, conceptually.[32]

Al-Rāghib's Islamic economics fits well into his early 5th/11th-century setting. He believes in an industrious population that by its surplus will allow for elites whose occupations subsist through the wealth of others. People should accept their place in an economic rank-ordering system because such rank-ordering corresponds to their innate professional ability, and no matter how feeble this ability may be, they are better off in a system of economic cooperation than outside such a system. Al-Rāghib's ideas, not surprisingly, work for the preservation of the world in which he lived.

One point of this exercise is to discredit a question that was implicit in what I have previously said. It is no use asking how medieval or modern a thinker al-Rāghib is within the history of economic thought. The meaning of such thought must in the first instance be taken from its context, both in its own time and in its own textual tradition. However, once we have taken its meaning in these contexts, there is no end of significant questions that can be raised by comparing and contrasting it with the thought not only of any other period and place but also with the other thinkers of the same period. I do, for example, think that some of the resemblance of al-Rāghib's economic thought to early modern European economic thought is due to admiration for profit and commercial ideals in many Islamic societies. This proposition, however, would be extraordinarily difficult to demonstrate.[33]

Here I cite only two examples of this admiration for profit. The Persian equivalent of the eighteenth-century Lord Chesterfield, Kay Kāvus ibn

---

31 Muḥassin ibn 'Alī al-Tanūkhī, *The Table-Talk of a Mesopotamian Judge*, translated by D.S. Margoliouth (London: 1922) 42.

32 Perhaps one might consider al-Rāghīb more contemporary in that he shows interest in "prosperity" and does so in a transregional context.

33 See Abū al-Faḍl al-Dimashqī, *Kitāb al-Ishāra ilā Maḥāsin al-Tijāra* (Cairo: 1397); French translation *Éloge du Commerce* (Tunis: 1995); also A.K.S. Lambton, "The Merchant in Medieval Islam," in W.B. Henning and E. Yarshater (eds.), *A Locust's Leg: Studies in Honour of S.H. Taqizadeh* (London: 1962) 121–130.

Eskandar, who composed a general book of advice to his son, wrote in 475/1082: "Look for profit and do not account it as a fault ... Whatever you buy must be bought with profit-and-loss in mind ... And never, in anything that you do, lose sight of your own interest—to do so is superfluous folly."[34]

Another hearty defender of gain is Jalāl al-Din Davāni (d. 908/1502), whose treatise on ethics was vastly popular in the Ottoman Empire and South Asia from his time through the nineteenth century. He wrote: "One should know that no ornament is better in this worldly life than prosperity ... Whatever is acquired through beautiful (*jamīl*, perhaps meaning "lawful") gain, be it ever so little, is auspicious and a blessing."[35]

A second point of this exercise is to remember that the great Ibn Khaldūn, while remaining a highly original thinker, had an important body of earlier speculation on which to draw. It was the common assumption of this body of speculation that there were certain "natural" features to human dispositions and human situations. This meant, of course, that there could be predictability in human society and therefore a science of society.

A third point which does not, admittedly, arise from the discussion of al-Rāghib is that that there is, in fact, no invariable relation between theory and practice, between ideology and action. Islamic economics, however construed, can at certain times be a powerful force. At other times it can be utopian and intended more for edification than for action, as in the large literature, pre-modern and modern, that sees avarice and generosity as the central questions of economic thought. No simple statement of theory, only an examination of each theory in its historical context (or contexts) can yield any guess as to the relation of theory to practice.

It is not surprising that some of the ayatollahs involved in the debate on Iranian land reform in the 1980s and 90s were closer in spirit to al-Rāghib than to most contemporary thinkers on Islamic economics who assume a world of abundance instead of al-Rāghib's world of scarcity. These ayatollahs also were oriented by classical Islamic law, which ardently defends private ownership, in contrast with Islamic socialism which flourished in the fifties, sixties and seventies of the twentieth century.

I think that as the current discussions on Islamic economics continue, more and more of the preceding fourteen centuries of this debate will be

34 Kaykāvus ibn Iskandar ibn Qābūs, *A Mirror for Princes: the Qābūs Nāma*, trans. Reuben Levy (New York, Dutton: 1951) 109.

35 Jalāl al-Din Davāni, *Akhlāq-e Jalāli*, ed. 'Abd al-Mas'ud Arani (Tehran: 1391) 184.

discovered and used by those interested in Islamic economics. And, God willing, a few scholars will discover that there is a large and important pre-modern literature on this subject. Perhaps the present century will see contextualized histories of economic thought in the Islamic world worthy to sit beside Albert Hirschman's *The Passions and the Interests.*

ISLAMIC CITIES

American anxiety at the decay of our inner cities encouraged a generation of scholars to devote themselves to city history in the Middle East. Ira Lapidus, my senior, wrote a path-breaking study of Syrian cities and for six weeks I, as a Harvard graduate student, worked for Ira earning money to buy books while discussing the development of Islamic cities with him.

To the great good fortune of scholars of the Middle East, medieval Muslims liked to write biographical dictionaries of the prominent men associated with their cities—occasionally, even their prominent women. These biographical dictionaries were organized according to generations and usually included death dates, so they became the best source available to scholars for understanding the social history of the medieval Islamic world.

The first article here, "Administration in Buyid Qazvin," is actually a chapter drawn from my 1970 Harvard Ph.D. dissertation, which I never published. I found an unedited biographical dictionary in Arabic for the small Iranian city of Qazvin (Qazwīn in Arabic) which covered the period from the Arab conquest to the 6th/12th century. I used this dictionary along with the invaluable letters of a vizier of the Buyid period to create a picture of the administration and social history of Qazvin in the 4th/10th and early 5th/11th centuries. The dissertation was respectable but not, in my view, ready for publication, so I only published this article from it on the history of Qazvin. About the same time, Richard Bulliet, my near contemporary and fellow graduate student at Harvard, published his important study of Nishapur.

All three of us, Lapidus, Bulliet, and myself, were concerned with the internal government of Islamic cities of the Middle East from the mosque cleaner to the "head" (*raʾīs*) of the city, and the cities' dependence or independence from the "central" governance of the time.

The second article in this section, "Medieval Kashan: Crossroads of Commerce and Culture," discusses the Iranian city of my father's birth, and his ancestors reaching back several centuries. It was written for a conference on medieval Iranian cities, which I organized in 2015 at Harvard. The article was written together with a friend, Mehrdad Amanat, whose ancestors also come from this city. I particularly enjoyed my research on Kashan both because of my ancestry and because of my long-term interest in medieval Islamic art. Kashan was famous in the medieval and early modern period for its lusterware pottery and its luxurious silk brocades. Large amounts of Kashan's prized lusterware have survived in museums around the world and even some of its silk fabrics survive, though to a much lesser extent due to their fragility as a textile. Kashan's artisanal skills allowed it to have a lively economic life from the medieval period through the nineteenth century.

Throughout the medieval period Kashan was a largely Shi'ite city in Sunni-controlled Iranian kingdoms. Its relation to its absent ruler in Rayy (Tehran) or Isfahan was complicated by its heterodoxy. However, in the early sixteenth century Iran became overwhelming Shi'ite, and Kashan became well integrated with the rest of Iran and continued to prosper.

My father's deep interest in Islamic art was passed on to me, and I have often thought that I would have enjoyed a career as a curator or teacher of Islamic art. Such a career would have avoided the pitfalls and problems of being an historian of the Middle East.

The third article in this section, "Faith and Practice: Muslims in Historic Cairo," was written for the lavishly illustrated volume commemorating the Agha Khan's restoration of parts of historic Cairo. The Agha Khan recognized the decay in certain neighborhoods built in the Middle Ages when his ancestors ruled Egypt. Thanks to his restorations, some of the ancient parts of Cairo have been rebuilt and preserved for future generations. In addition, the Agha Khan built the large and beautiful al-Azhar Park for the residents of this area.

My article focuses on historic festivals and celebrations that are still observed today. I was fortunate enough to live in Cairo during the month of the Muslim fast for Ramadan. The liveliness of the evenings during Ramadan was a pleasure to watch. A few of the festivals, such as the Inundation of the Nile, have Pharaonic antecedents. However, these civic or non-religious festivals are now celebrated with Muslim overtones such as the inclusion of Qur'ān readers.

The final article in this section, "Medieval Lexicography on Arabic and Persian Terms for City and Countryside," was written, like the Kashan article above, for inclusion in the publication of the proceedings of the Iranian Cities conference mentioned earlier. It attempts to show the range of information available in bilingual medieval dictionaries. For this article I used the original Arabic-to-Persian and Persian-to-Arabic dictionaries from pre-modern times. Most of these dictionaries exist to help Persian speakers in Iran who regarded Arabic as a sacred language because of the Qur'ān. For many centuries, educated Iranians had to deal with Arabic-speaking religious figures and a religious culture centered on Arabic. Just as Latin became a second language for the Western medieval world, Arabic became a second language for many Muslims, including Iranians, who wrote some of the earliest Arab grammars. (In the early twentieth century my father won a prize in his intermediate school in Iran as the best student of Arabic.)

There is a lot to be discovered in these dictionaries about many aspects of medieval Islamic society. By using a simple but painstaking method of comparison and analysis, one can reveal shades of meaning in the written work of different periods in both Arabic and Persian. The use of modern historically oriented lexicographical works such as Dehkhoda's Persian dictionary, the *Loghat-Nāma*, can help in this effort. With the digitization of many historical texts the possibility of using such methods increases.

Administration in Buyid Qazvin

The collapse of Abbasid government during the early 4th/10th century forced many local Islamic communities to work out ways of dealing with the near anarchy which accompanied this collapse. This essay will describe the adjustment of the people of Qazvin (Qazwīn in Arabic) to new conditions, compare their history with the history of other communities in the Jibāl (western Iran), and discuss the possible relevance of such local history to the question: can we consider the 4th/10th and 5th/11th centuries a turning point in Islamic history?

Qazvin offers an unusually favorable subject for such a study. The unedited biographical dictionary *Kitāb al-Tadwīn fī Dhikr Ahl al-ʻIlm bi-Qazwīn* by al-Rāfiʻī[1] gives approximately three thousand biographies of Qazvinis for the period from the Islamic conquest to the end of the 6th/12th century—a surprisingly large number of entries for a relatively small town. The author mentions—along with the relators of ḥadīth who are his principal interest—several local officials, especially local *ru'asā'* or headmen. When the biographies of these officials are set in the context of the administrative history of the Buyid kingdom of Rayy, they show

---

Author's note: This article was first published as: "Administration in Būyid Qazwīn," in D.S. Richards (ed.), *Islamic Civilisation 950–1150*, Papers in Islamic History, III (Oxford, U.K., Cassirer: 1973) 33–45.

1 Abū al-Qāsim ʻAbd al-Karīm ibn Muḥammad al-Rāfiʻī; Istanbul Ms., Koğuşlar 1007, 311 folios. This manuscript was written in 676 A.H., about a half century after the death of the author. Al-Rāfiʻī's information on the 3rd/9th and 4th/10th centuries is largely based on the lost *Irshād* of al-Khalīl ibn ʻAbd Allāh al-Ḥāfiẓ. Subsequent to writing this article, the manuscript was printed three times, in Tehran (1374/1995 or 1996), Beirut (1987) and Hyderabad (1984).

Al-Rāfiʻī includes many scholars from villages near Qazvin, and since this essay deals with the people in and near the town who considered themselves and were considered by others to be Qazvinis, I have frequently used the word "community" instead of town to make clear that I am not referring to a narrowly defined administrative unit.

that relations between the local and the central government were more complex than the chronicles written in Baghdad or Rayy imply.

From the middle of the 3rd/9th century, when 'Alid rulers established governments in the Caspian provinces of Iran, Qazvin was in the path of the march and countermarch of caliphal, Daylamī, and eastern Iranian armies. In less than a century the Qazvinis were ruled in turn by the 'Alids of Ṭabaristān, the Ṭāhirids, the Ṣaffārids, the Sāmānids and finally the Buyids, as well as by occasional caliphal governors and passing Daylamī generals like Asfār ibn Shīrūya. The period was made even more confusing by the different land and taxation policies of these conquerors, some of whom seem to have deliberately favored either large or small landowners.[2]

It is probably not an accident that the first hereditary headmanship or *riyāsa* emerged in Qazvin in the middle of the 3rd/9th century. The wealthy family of the 'Ijlīs, who provided *wālīs* (governors) for Qazvin in the first half of the 3rd/9th century, held the office of *ra'īs* from this time down to the fall of the Buyids of Rayy with the conquest of that city by Maḥmūd of Ghazna in 420 A.H. The 'Ijlīs in the late 3rd/9th and early 4th/10th centuries were sometimes *wālīs* as well as headmen. Their prestige with their fellow townsmen was enormous. The learned men of the town helped them to keep their wealth when one conqueror wanted to confiscate it, and the Abbasids took an 'Ijlī to Baghdad at one time as a guarantee of good behavior on the part of the Qazvinis. The town needed a spokesman and a focus of loyalty in this troubled period, and the 'Ijlī headmen served as both.[3]

---

2 Ismā'īl ibn Aḥmad, the Sāmānid, "appropriated the possessions of some landowners and repaid them with money"; al-Rāfi'ī, fol. 149a. In nearby Ṭabaristān the 'Alids are said to have redistributed land and the Sāmānids to have given the land back to its original owners; cf. A.K.S. Lambton, *Landlord and Peasant in Persia* (London: 1953) 49, n. 1. Several transfers of districts to and from Qazvin took place in this period; cf. al-Rāfi'ī, fol. 10b.

3 Abū Dulaf al-Qāsim ibn 'Īsā al-'Ijlī, who died in 225 A.H., was *wālī* of Qazvin under al-Ma'mūn: al-Rāfi'ī, (*supra* n. 1), fol. 284a. At least part of his family settled there, for his lineage had the *imāma* in one of the mosques of the city: *ibid.*, fol. 30b. Al-'Abbās ibn Muḥammad ibn Sinān al-'Ijlī, not a close relative of al-Qāsim, was *wālī* and *ra'īs*; he died in 251 A.H.: *ibid.*, fol. 240a. His nephew Muḥammad was a *ra'īs* and a *wālī*; when arrested by a passing conqueror, the local notables and *qāḍī* arranged that his property become a *waqf* for his descendants. The conqueror, unable to break the trust, killed him: *ibid.*, fols. 10b and 96a. His son Aḥmad was *ra'īs*, and also a *wālī* under the Sāmānids and died in 303 A.H.: *ibid.*, fol. 142. Ma'qil ibn Aḥmad succeeded his father as *ra'īs* and was held as a hostage (*rahn*) in Baghdad during the campaigns against the 'Alids of Ṭabaristān; his income from his huge estates allowed him to give generous

Near the beginning of Buyid rule a *sharīf* descended from Ja'far ibn Abī Ṭālib moved to Qazvin and through marriage acquired a large estate. The two sons of this *sharīf* seem to have been favored by the Buyids, for although they were only second generation Qazvinis, they had the *riyāsa* "over all groups" (*'alā al-ṭawā'if kullihā*). Under Buyid government, their fortunes steadily improved and they were shown special marks of favor by Ṣāḥib ibn 'Abbād, the great vizier of Mu'ayyid al-Dawla and Fakhr al-Dawla.[4] The Ja'farī *ru'asā'* (headmen) continued to grow in prestige after the Buyid period, and by the Seljuk period they had such wealth that one Ja'farī *ra'īs*, Sharafshāh, was said to have a yearly income of 66,300 dinars and was appointed *wālī* of Qazvin by the Seljuks.[5]

Al-Rāfi'ī mentions a third *riyāsa* which was not as politically important as that of the 'Ijlīs and Ja'farīs. Ibrāhīm ibn 'Alī al-'Aqīlī (or al-'Uqaylī) was "headman of the large cultivators" (*ra'īs al-tunnā'*), and his considerable wealth allowed him to build the first *qaṣr* in Qazvin.[6] He died in 375 A.H. and was therefore a contemporary of the Ja'farī as well as the 'Ijlī headmen. Since most of the wealth of the Ja'farīs and 'Ijlīs was in land, it is interesting that the *tunnā'* were seen as separate from these families and had their own headmen. *Ra'īs*, of course, is a flexible term and could be used for any leading figure from a tribal chieftain to the head of the carpet trade in Baghdad.[7]

Al-Rāfi'ī includes a considerable number of judges in his biographical dictionary and their short biographies give some idea of the office of *qāḍī* and its appointees in Buyid Qazvin. At first, *qāḍīs* changed fairly rapidly,

gifts to caliphs and viziers: *ibid.*, fol. 301b. Al-Faḍl ibn Ma'qil, who was also a *ra'īs*, died in 352 A.H. Muḥammad ibn al-Faḍl ibn Ma'qil, though generous, "did not treat the headmanship (*riyāsa*) with proper dignity and was excessive in his spending," and lost most of his wealth. He died in 425 A.H.: *ibid.* fol. 115a.

4 Al-Rāfi'ī, (*supra* n. 1), fol. 245b; cf. also fol. 35a. One brother died in 383 A.H. and the other in 385 A.H. It is not clear whether the two *sharīfs* held the office jointly or in succession. The office would not necessarily be ill-defined or unofficial if held jointly because joint appointments, including joint vizierates, were frequent under the Buyids. Neither brother left any male heirs and the next Ja'farī *ra'īs* was a son-in-law, Aḥmad, who in turn was succeeded by his sons, Muḥammad and Abū Ṭayyib, both of whom had the *riyāsa*: *ibid.*, fols.143 and 41a. Aḥmad is the Abū 'Alī Ja'farī who, according to Mustawfī (Mostawfi), *Nuzhat al-Qulūb* (London: 1919) 63, repaired the walls of Qazvin after they were destroyed in an insurrection in 411 A.H.

5 Al-Rāfi'ī, (*supra* n. 1), fol. 201a.

6 Al-Rāfi'ī, (*supra* n. 1), fol. 119a. I do not know whether a *qaṣr* here means a fortified enclosure or a palace or both.

7 Al-Tanūkhī, *Nishwār al-Muḥāḍara* (London: 1921) 150.

for different *qāḍīs* are mentioned in 347, 351, 362, 376, and 379.[8] Three of these *qāḍīs* are explicitly said to be representatives (*niyābatan ʿan*) of the Chief Judge (*qāḍī al-quḍāt*) in Rayy, and almost certainly all the judges of Qazvin were so regarded. The beginning of the term of the *qāḍī* appointed in 376 A.H. coincides with the appointment of a new Chief Judge and some of the *qāḍīs* of Qazvin may have been appointed when their "patron" came to power in the capital.[9]

It is significant that during the troubled first decades of the 5th/11th century the *qāḍī* in Qazvin was not changed. Muḥammad ibn Ibrāhīm held this position from 398 A.H. until his death in 431 A.H. Possibly the different rulers of Qazvin in this period were not interested in who was *qāḍī*, and Muḥammad ibn Ibrāhīm, who was famous for his loyal opinions, may have had the support of local notables who were grateful for legal continuity under quickly changing governments.[10] Although witnesses (*shuhūd*) are not dealt with in this essay, it should be mentioned that they provided another element of continuity in the legal system. For example, al-Ḥasan ibn Aḥmad served the *qāḍīs* of Qazvin as a witness for sixty years before his death in 383.[11]

At least one military governor of Qazvin is mentioned by al-Rāfiʿī: Isfahsalār ibn Kūrankīj (Gūrangīj?), who from his name seems to have been a Daylamī soldier. We are fortunate to have Isfahsalār's patent of investiture (*ʿahd*) which is preserved in the letters of Ṣāḥib ibn ʿAbbād.[12] Although most of the language of this and similar documents is formulaic, the formulae were chosen to cover real conditions, and therefore tell something of what the government expected of its appointee. He was given charge of prayer, war, *al-aḥdāth*[13] and police (*maʿāwin*), as well as all principal sources of

8 Al-Rāfiʿī, (*supra* n. 1), fols. 272a, 271b, 240b, 89a and 218b.

9 Al-Rāfiʿī, (*supra* n. 1), fol. 208a. Though a new Chief Judge may have customarily appointed a new *qāḍī* in Qazvin, a new appointment as *qāḍī* in Qazvin was not the result of a change of Chief Judges. ʿAbd al-Jabbār, in the middle of his long term, appointed a new *qāḍī* in Qazvin in 379 A.H.: *ibid.*, fol. 272a.

10 Al-Rāfiʿī, (*supra* n. 1), fol. 27b.

11 Al-Rāfiʿī, (*supra* n. 1), fol. 168b.

12 Al-Ṣāḥib Ismāʿīl ibn ʿAbbād, *Rasāʾil* (Cairo: 1366 A.H.) 46–49 (patent of investiture). This leading Daylamī soldier was captured by the Ziyārid Qābūs in a victory over Majd al-Dawla in 388 A.H.; cf. Marʿashi, *Tārikh-e Ṭabarestān* (Tehran: 1333 solar) 139.

13 The term *al-aḥdāth* may mean "troubles," as R. Dozy suggests: *Supplément aux dictionnaires arabes*, 2nd ed., I (Paris: 1927) 257–258; or it may mean "the youth," as was the case in Syria. One of the few explicit references to groups like the Syrian *aḥdāth* in the Jibāl in this period is the mention of *ʿayyārūn* who killed the *qāḍī* of

taxes in Qazvin and its districts. As he was a soldier, he probably did not personally direct the assessment and collection of taxes, and this clause may indicate that he was superior to the *ʿāmil* or financial governor. The relative standing of these two officials was always a delicate question in the Abbasid period, but during the continued military emergency of late Abbasid rule the financial governor seems generally to have been subordinate to the military governor. Isfahsalār was also charged with seeing that proper weights and measures were used and that the slave market was properly run. These clauses seem to have given him some authority over the *muḥtasib* (market inspector). He was to oversee the work of the head of the mint as well as that of the assayer (*al-manṣūb li-l-ʿiyār*), from the text, clearly a separate official who tested coins for their fineness. He was supposed to support the local judge (*al-manṣūb li-l-ḥukm*). The patent also gave Isfahsalār some general instructions:

> "He [the King] orders him [Isfahsalār] to encompass the common people (*al-ʿawāmm*) in the shadow of awe of him, in order to keep them from extreme partisanship (*taʿaṣṣub*) and to prevent them from being opposed to each other and from attaining—through difference of [religious or legal] schools (*madhāhib*)—to extreme positions and mutual aversion. He should do this in order that each person may apply himself to cultivate what he chooses for his life to come and may occupy himself with undertaking what he prefers for his sustenance, except for the person who says something that goes outside of the agreement of the Muslim community (*iṭbāq al-umma*) and rends apart the consensus of competent authority. The government (*al-sulṭān*)—and not its subjects (*dūna al-raʿīya*)—is the investigator of what comes to its attention, and the punisher of what it observes."

Emphasis on avoiding religious factionalism is found over and over again in Ibn ʿAbbād's letters and in the words of other Buyid administrators,

---

Dīnāwar, Yūsuf ibn Aḥmad ibn Kajj, in 405 A.H. Cf. Ibn Khallikān, *Wafayāt al-Aʿyān*, VI (Cairo: 1948) 63; al-Dhahabī quoted in n. 1 to Abū Shujāʿ al-Rūdhrāwarī, *Dhayl Tajārib al-Umam* (Cairo: 1916) 305; and Ibn al-Jawzī, *al-Muntaẓam*, VII (Hyderabad: 1358 A.H.) 275–276. Ibn al-Athīr, *al-Kāmil*, IX (Leiden: 1851) 176, says only that he was killed by the *ʿāmm*.

though nowhere is it stated more clearly that the government alone has the right to punish heresy.

Riots and threats of riots repeatedly appear in the history of Buyid Qazvin and show that the government had good reason to instruct officials to discourage factionalism. In 352 A.H. a *fitna* broke out and a delegation, made up principally of ulema went to Rayy to appease the anger of the central government.[14] Though the government's reaction to this *fitna* is not known, another *fitna* was sufficiently serious that Abū al-Fatḥ—the son of the famous vizier Abū al-Faḍl ibn al-ʿAmīd and himself a future vizier—was sent with a large army in 358 A.H. Abū al-Fatḥ fined the people of Qazvin 1,200,000 dirhams as "disciplinary money" (*māl al-taʾdīb*). Al-Rāfiʿī quotes a letter of instruction to Abū al-Fatḥ by Abū al-Faḍl ibn al-ʿAmīd; and, if, as is likely, it is genuine, the letter was almost certainly meant for circulation to the Qazvinis. It is significant that Abū al-Faḍl uses a conciliatory tone: "Do not be neglectful of [the Qazvinis'] rights and do not forget to recognize what is their due. Be eager to calm the community and to win over the spirits of the majority ... The people are not inured in wrong-doing. Their leader is well known, and the sources of their wickedness are [also] known ... If there is an intercessor for someone who is punished, then do not punish; and remedy the loss of someone fined and do not fine [him further]."[15]

This was far from the last internal disorder of the Buyid period in Qazvin. Two letters of Ibn ʿAbbād deal with disorders, or most likely with the same disorder. One letter, sent to someone who is addressed as "brother," discusses the continued enmity which has "blazed forth" among the people of Qazvin. One of the reasons for the trouble, according to Ibn ʿAbbād, is that the leaders of the common people (*zuʿamāʾ li-l-awāmm*) thought that their positions would be preserved with the help of the foolish (*sufahāʾ*). Horrifying things have been recounted by the messenger of the ʿAlid *sharīfs*; it has even been said that these *sharīfs* have been forbidden from trading in the market and earning a living. They have been persecuted and have had to protect their private property (*amlāk*) from plunder (*ghāra*) and their houses from destruction. The recipient is ordered to arrange a meeting (*majmaʿ*) to which the leading people (*al-wujūh wa-l-aʿyān wa-l-amāthil wa-l-ṣudūr wa-l-afāḍil*) and not their lower adherents (*adhnāb*)

14 Al-Rāfiʿī, (*supra* n. 1), fol. 96.
15 Al-Rāfiʿī, (*supra* n. 1), fol. 260a.

come. He should read the letter to them, and it should be understood that the purpose of the letter is the common good; its purpose is not that any party (*ṭā'ifa*) should be required to turn from the school [of religious and legal belief] (*madhhab*) and doctrine (*'aqīda*) which it chooses (and this point is repeated several times by Ibn 'Abbād). The *sharīfs* should respect the leading ulema and religious lawyers (*fuqahā'*) and keep away from the rabble (*adnās*). The 'Alids should be protected from the rabble.[16]

The other letter addressed to "the two *sharīfs*," discusses "the hatred (*shaḥnā'*) between the 'Alid *sharīfs* of Qazvin and other groups (*ṭawā'if*) whose coals can hardly die down and whose outpourings cannot be removed. I [Ibn 'Abbād] have written concerning that subject a letter which I had hoped would unite [all] on the basis of amity, would guard against faction, and would arrange the abandonment of the quarrel and the turning to reconciliation. For a truce is deemed proper between two religious communities (*millatayn*); how much more so between two sects (*niḥlatayn*)!" This disorder has broken out within the Banū Ṭālib and led to the spilling of blood. The two *sharīfs* should undertake to stop the fighting among the Banū Ṭālib.[17]

These letters seem to refer to the same or closely similar events. A long-standing enmity had flared up and brought the leaders and the common people of the town to use violence and unlawful constraint. Al-Muqaddasī, who wrote in about 375 A.H., said that Qazvin was divided into two factions (*farīqayn*) by religious questions. There were Ḥanafis, Shāfi'īs and Shi'ites in Qazvin.[18] Of course, not all 'Alids were Shi'ites and therefore the quarrel was not necessarily a conflict between Shi'ites and Sunnis. The struggle was reflected, or possibly even originated, among the Banū Ṭālib; and the two *sharīfs* addressed by Ibn 'Abbād are almost certainly the Ja'farīs Muḥammad and 'Alī. These two *sharīfs*, as we mentioned above, were headmen in Qazvin and were members of the Banū Ṭālib because they were descendants of Ja'far ibn Abī Ṭālib. These brothers may well have been on the side opposed to the 'Alid *sharīfs*, for there were few members of the Banū Ṭālib beside the descendants of 'Alī and of Ja'far, the ancestor of the two brothers.

This short survey of provincial government in Qazvin shows that, as one might have expected, officials had two sources of support, their position in

16 Ibn 'Abbād, (*supra* n. 12), 92–94.
17 Ibn 'Abbād, (*supra* n. 12), 91.
18 Al-Rāfi'ī, (*supra* n. 1), fol. 10b.

the local community and the backing of the central government. The *ra'īs* was the official most dependent on local support, while the *amīr* (or *'āmil li-l-ḥarb*) was most dependent on support from the central government; but neither official was solely supported by one or the other. Unfortunately, it is not clear to what extent the *riyāsa* was a formal office. It seems likely, however, that if the Ja'farīs could replace the 'Ijlīs as leading *ru'asā'* in one generation, the leading *riyāsa* was formally conferred by the government, perhaps through a patent of investiture as in the Seljuk period.[19] If the *aḥdāth* represented some sort of militia, the government apparently hoped that they would accept military leadership from the *amīr*. The financial governor also owed his position to the backing of the central government. Other offices were not so clearly dependent on either the community or the central government. The *muḥtasib*, though often a native of the city or region of his jurisdiction, drew at least some of his authority from official appointment by the central government.[20] The *qāḍī* was appointed and deposed by the central government but seems always to have been a local man and sometimes a wealthy local man,[21] for the government did well to pick a man who had enough local prestige to be effective in his office. Although the *qaḍī* Muḥammad ibn Ibrāhīm was initially appointed to his office, his ability to keep it under such different regimes as the Buyids, Buyid rebels, the Ghaznavids and the Sallārids distinguishes him from any more purely appointive official like the *amīr*.

The history of Qazvin, other local histories and the letters of Ibn 'Abbād make clear the great importance of local rights in the thinking of local notables and of the central government. Local variation was very real and affected many aspects of life. The people of Qom, for example, had their own unit of measurement, their own calendar, and their own system of taxes. They wanted their tax year to begin in the solar month Bahman, not one month earlier, or at Nowruz, or at any other time, because their climate and choice of crops made that month the time of harvest.[22] The people of Qom, like the people of other areas, wanted their traditional tax status

19 Heribert Horst, *Die Staatsverwaltung der Grosselǧūqen und Ḫōrazmšāhs* (Wiesbaden: 1964) 54–66 and 130–133.

20 A patent of investiture for the *muḥtasib* of Rayy is given in Ibn 'Abbād, (*supra* n. 12), 39–41.

21 For example, Muḥammad ibn Yaḥyā, *qāḍī* from 323 to 327 A.H., was wealthy enough to build a section of the mosque: al-Rāfi'ī, (*supra* n. 1), fol. 106a.

22 Ḥasan ibn Moḥammad ibn Ḥasan al-Qomi, *Tārikh-e Qom* (Tehran: 1934) 28–31 and 144–146.

clearly recognized even if the tax was burdensome; for the government was more likely to increase taxes than to remove burdensome taxes, and likely to tax arbitrarily if not held to established tax customs. Naturally, they were pleased to have their taxes reduced; but they were eager, even when taxes were not reduced, to have their taxes clearly defined (as Ibn ʿAbbād defined them in Qom), and to have the near permanent *aṣl* or tax-basis, on which first estimates were made, clearly distinguished from supplementary taxes in all documents.[23]

The Buyid government of Rayy, especially during the vizierate of Ibn ʿAbbād, largely accepted local claims to traditional local rights. The government was forced to accept at least some portion of these traditions because it did not have the enormous and mobile military force necessary to challenge all local rights. A few officials were killed in local riots and many other officials were threatened.[24] The government could not have survived such disorders if they had occurred simultaneously in many cities.

The government gained a positive advantage by showing some respect for local rights, as local cooperation was extremely important in attaining the two principal objectives of the central government in its local administration: to collect taxes and to ensure order. Although the former system of collecting taxes in Qom through the agency of ten local men as "guarantors" did not continue under the Buyids, many taxes there, and probably elsewhere, were paid through a personal guarantee; and if the guarantor defaulted on his obligation, his fellow townsmen were expected to coerce him into paying.[25] Furthermore, in gratitude for the recognition of local rights, for gifts of privileges, and for public works, the notables of a town were expected to take an active role in discouraging and stopping disorders.[26] The vizier enlisted their help in keeping the peace by ordering

23 Al-Qomi, (*supra* n. 22), 142–143 and 166.

24 The Qomis even had the audacity to attack important army officers who were passing through their town. Even if the officers had greatly provoked the townsmen, one would expect the town to be fined or the ringleaders to be punished; but apparently Ibn ʿAbbād only warned the Qomis; cf. Ibn ʿAbbād, (*supra* n. 12), 177–179. Riots were sometimes effective, as in 375 A.H. when the Baghdadis forced the Buyid government of Iraq to cancel a new duty on cloth; al-Rūdhrāwarī, (*supra* n. 13), 118.

25 Ibn ʿAbbād, (*supra* n. 12), 211, on methods of tax collection.

26 Ibn ʿAbbād, (*supra* n. 12), 177–179, says that the men of learning and descendants of Muḥammad in Qom should have come forward to reprove the rioters in their city even if they did not take part in the riots. The vizier claims that he interceded with the king on behalf of Qom by mentioning "those gifts which he had deposited as security with them."

them to convey his instructions to the assembled notables or by writing to the *ra'īs* personally. Local notables were able to help the central government to some effect because, as we have said, their authority was partially derived from the social structure of the town, and they were respected independently of any connection with the government.

Offices like the headmanship tended to become hereditary in Qazvin, and in some towns the judgeship was also hereditary. This was also true of many local religious offices. Several local administrative offices, like the custodianship of the Divan of Water by one group of Arab settlers of Qom, were hereditary.[27] The social system in at least some of the communities in the Jibāl favored corporate responsibility and the tax system reflected this principle. In Qom, one department of government, the mint, managed in three generations to become both strictly hereditary and corporate, each son inheriting a share in the mint as a birthright.[28] Certainly this tendency to the hereditary and corporate exercise of authority must have been aided in Qom and Qazvin by the concentration of large amounts of wealth in a few families.[29] Local communities were to some degree self-governing, and it was with the help of the *ra'īs* and notables that the central government sought to gain its objectives.

Within this system it was possible for either side, the central government or the local notables, to gain more of what it wanted than the other side. It was easier to impose an arbitrary fine on most towns than on the warlike Qazvins; at the same time, the headmanship in Qazvin meant so much that it was possible for a pre-Buyid ruler to use the *ra'īs* of that city as a hostage for the cooperation of his fellow townsmen. Although the central government opposed disorder, the factionalism that divided many communities must have weakened the position of the notables in relation to the central government, for in such circumstances not only did they desire recognition of local rights and of their social and economic privileges, but they also desired recognition of their faction instead of the opposing faction. The Buyids seem to have fostered the Ja'farīs, a new family of headmen

27 Al-Qomi, (*supra* n. 22), 53.

28 Al-Qomi, (*supra* n. 22), 39.

29 Of twenty-one *qanāts* in Qom, fourteen belonged to a single owner and the other seven to two owners, although a certain portion of the flow, usually one quarter, was for general use: Al-Qomi, (*supra* n. 22), 44. It is very likely, therefore, that much of the cultivable land in Qom belonged to a few owners, and that their estates were continuous and not divided into scattered parcels. According to al-Rāfi'ī, (*supra* n. 1), fol. 301b, one of the 'Ijlīs employed twenty thousand (tenant) farmers (*'akkār*).

in Qazvin, and it is possible that the Jaʿfarīs were so heavily fined by the Sāmānids when they briefly reconquered the Jibāl in 339–40 A.H. because the Jaʿfarīs were Buyid proteges.[30] It is interesting that while there were ʿIjlī governors (*wālīs*) in the century before the Buyids and Jaʿfarī governors after the Buyids, neither family seems to have supplied governors under the Buyids who usually appointed Daylamī soldiers to this post. Possibly the factionalism in Qazvin found the Jaʿfarīs and ʿIjlīs on opposite sides and thus allowed the Buyids to gain sufficient cooperation from the Qazvinis by giving each side lesser rewards than the governorship.

When we speak of the desire of a community to preserve its traditional rights, we mean, of course, the desire of its notables, for the common people, whatever their opinions and wishes, did not benefit from the preservation of these traditional rights nearly as much as the notables did. Ibn ʿAbbād's long and very successful administration was based on an open recognition of the importance of both traditional rights and privileged classes. Not only does he frequently repeat the theme that the local government should observe "the permanent rules of the region"[31] but also, as the *History of Qom* says, "he kept [people] established in their duties and customs according to the former determination [of such matters]."[32] In one of his letters Ibn ʿAbbād says that the king grants the recipients' requests "because the basis of his noble policy is the honoring of members of old distinguished houses."[33] It is doubtful, however, that an astute politician like Ibn ʿAbbād would allow such important families any more privileges than he considered necessary to gain his own ends.

Ibn ʿAbbād's policy of local administration seems to have been fairly successful. As far as we know he never had to send the army to restore order after any of the frequent local riots, but instead successfully used the local notables and local representatives of the central government to restore order. His great problem in preventing local disorder seems to have been in obtaining early information about such disorders. Repeatedly he told his correspondent to keep the capital informed, and when he received early information that "false rumors" were circulating among the people

30 Al-Rāfiʿī, (*supra* n. 1), fol. 22a.
31 E.g., Ibn ʿAbbād, (*supra* n. 12), 53.
32 Al-Qomi, (*supra* n. 22), 5.
33 Ibn ʿAbbād, (*supra* n. 12), 53. Many Islamic writers and administrators spoke in this vein, but Ibn ʿAbbād's actions and appointments show a genuine policy of supporting "old families."

concerning the officials who governed them, he wrote warning the people in the strongest terms to desist from spreading such rumors.[34] In handling religious quarrels, he managed to make himself sound like a supporter of the dominant Sunnis while defining orthodoxy so broadly that it included at least the Twelver Shiʿites.

The scanty sources for the period after Ibn ʿAbbād's death give the impression that the great vizier's success was not equaled by later Buyid viziers.[35] Ibn ʿAbbād's manner of administration, like that of most other administrators of the period, was based on a network of personal relationships. In his letters he often encouraged officials, notables and whole communities to feel indebted to him personally for his protection and generosity. He claimed that only his personal intervention had preserved the people of a certain region from punishment by the king. In an earlier period, it was the personal visit of the caliph which won Qazvin the position of *kūra* (independent province).[36]

Because they recognized this personal element in the central government local notables sought to get as high a standing as possible both for themselves and for their province in the eyes of the central government so that they could get the vizier himself to recognize their local customs. To be able to deal with the highest officials of the government meant, among other things, that the caliph might forgive your town for killing a tax collector, or the vizier might listen to complaints from the town about the corruption of the governor.[37]

---

34 Ibn ʿAbbād, (*supra* n. 12), 176–177; cf. also 122–123.

35 Fakhr al-Dawla gave Ibn ʿAbbād, to whom he owed his throne, almost full control of the administration. However, on Ibn ʿAbbād's death, the king ordered that the new vizier collect 30,000,000 dirhams from the provinces and the officials. This sum was supposed to represent the arrears which Ibn ʿAbbād had neglected to collect: Al-Rūdhrāwarī, (*supra* n. 13), 263–264; Yaqūt, *Kitāb Irshād al-Arīb*, I (Leiden: 1907) 73.

36 Al-Rāfiʿī, (*supra* n. 1), fol. 183b. Ibn al-ʿAmīd made skillful use of his personal attachment to Qazvin in the letter cited above. He claimed family ties with the city and expressed great solicitude for the city's ancient rights. He ingeniously suggested that he favored the Qazvinis when in fact he was sending a large army to collect a very burdensome fine.

37 The Qomis praised Ibn ʿAbbād for fulfilling their wishes so that an intermediary or intercessor was not needed, and time was not lost: al-Qomi, (*supra* n. 22), 5. Members of an administrative unit sought a higher rank for their unit so that they could deal directly with the top of the central government. The recognition of Qom and Qazvin as *kūras*, therefore, is given a very central place in their histories. The same consideration, aided by the smaller size of the Buyid kingdoms, probably explains the upgrading of units smaller than the *kūra*. In 189 A.H, Qom had been composed of four *rustāqs* divided

The personal element also affected the scope of the authority of important local representatives of the central government, all of whom were, in a sense, personal representatives of the vizier. These officials were given overlapping spheres of authority because they were supposed to watch each other on behalf of the vizier.[38] While this system could provide a very useful control over provincial administration in the vizier's lifetime, it was not guaranteed to continue to work after the vizier's death.

After emphasizing the personal element in government and the uniqueness of different communities in the Jibāl it may seem strange to argue that the 4th/10th and 5th/11th centuries were in fact a turning-point which affected all or the majority of Islamic communities. I would suggest, however, that a permanent turning-point had been passed not in the actual situation of such communities, but in the possible ways in which such communities could be integrated into an extensive Islamic state.

The Abbasid caliphate sought to base its right to rule over its vast empire on legitimist religious claims based on widely accepted Islamic principles. It hoped that the popular acceptance of these claims—along with its professional army and its extensive bureaucracy—would form a lasting support for its rule. The majority of the ulema rejected the Abbasids' efforts to legislate doctrine and weakened their religious claim. The army and bureaucracy squandered the resources of the state, and often acted in such an overbearing manner that the dynasty's claim to be a source of justice was seriously compromised. Bankrupt and discredited, the dynasty lost all real power.

The Buyid regime was more clearly based on naked force than the Abbasid regime had been. The Buyids posed as defenders of their captive caliph and patronized Shiʿite ulema who were favorable to the continuance of Buyid rule; but these efforts were irrelevant to the beliefs of most of their subjects and consequently failed to create any deep-seated loyalty to their regime. The Qazvinis may never have been greatly impressed by Abbasid claims, but with the Buyids no similar religiously based claims arose or could arise. Under the Buyids, the only positive contributions which the

into *tassūjs*. By 378 A.H. all of the former *tassūjs* had become *rustāqs*, the number of rustāqs having increased to twenty-one. This was not just a change in nomenclature, for the new *rustāqs* continued to be divided into *tassūjs*: al-Qomi, (*supra* n. 22), 158.

38 The mint, for example, was under the supervision not only of the military governor but also of the *qāḍī*, the postmaster, and possibly also of the financial governor and the *muḥtasib*.

Qazvinis could hope to receive from the central government were protection against the external and internal enemies of Islam, protection against nomads, occasional public works, and maintenance of the *sharīʿa* through the appointment and support of a qualified judiciary. But they probably hoped even more eagerly for a negative contribution—non-interference in their traditional rights.

It can be argued that the Abbasids never had any real chance of establishing a religiously based universal empire and that their attempts are not very different from the makeshift attempts of the Buyids to appear as Sasanians. But, unlike the Buyids, the Arabs had brought a new and unifying system of beliefs which justified their rule. By adopting Islam, their subjects could participate in their rule. In contrast, the Buyids had little or no exportable culture, and they could not convincingly integrate their rule into the existing Islamic framework. Their rule was based on an ethnic group—an army of Daylamī descent—and their subjects, however successful or deserving they might be, could never become Daylamīs. Under the Abbasids, many provinces remained only loosely related to the central government, and provincial communities often felt indifference or hostility to the central government in the Abbasid as well as in the Buyid period. But the Abbasids reasonably could and did try to establish their rule as an integral part of Islam, and their collapse marked the failure of the only really promising attempt to make the whole of Islam effective as a political community before the Seljuks.

Medieval Kashan: Crossroads of Commerce and Culture

This article first attempts to explain why the Iranian city of Kashan is where it is and then how it came to grow. Extensive use of irrigation allowed an adequate and perhaps abundant agriculture in the surrounding region. The arrival of substantial numbers of Arab immigrants in Kashan in the early Islamic period played an important role in the city's development and its continuation as a center of Shiʿism. A strong educational tradition produced many talented Kashani officials, who served in the Seljuk and later administrations and sent some of their wealth back to Kashan.

It was also in the Seljuk period that Kashan gained a reputation for its production of luxury ceramics. Artisanal traditions were passed from generation to generation and contributed to exports of brass, and especially of textiles, which continued for centuries. Wealthy Kashanis (probably including a fair number of *sayyids*) invested heavily in charitable endowments, which served the poor and furthered learning in general. In the Timurid period, investments in mathematical education produced several

---

Author's note: This article, co-authored with Mehrdad Amanat, was first published as: "Medieval Kashan: Crossroads of Commerce and Culture," in David Durand-Guédy, Roy P. Mottahedeh and Jürgen Paul (eds.), *Cities of Medieval Iran, Eurasian Studies* 16 (Leiden, Brill: 2018) 395–429. Reproduced with permission. Here I have used Arabic transliteration in general for authors and titles but use Persian transliteration for some Persian authors and most Persian terms and titles. However, this choice is somewhat arbitrary.

Both authors regard Kashan as their ancestral home and are greatly interested in the history and culture of the city. We wish to thank Hossein Modarressi, Ali Mousavi, and Heidi Walcher. Persian place names are used throughout the article, but the Arabic versions of these names are shown in parentheses at the first occurrence and on Fig. 1. Medieval Persian proper names are given in either Arabic or Persian form (the choice is somewhat arbitrary); however, Arabic book titles are given in Arabic transliteration even if the texts themselves are in Persian.

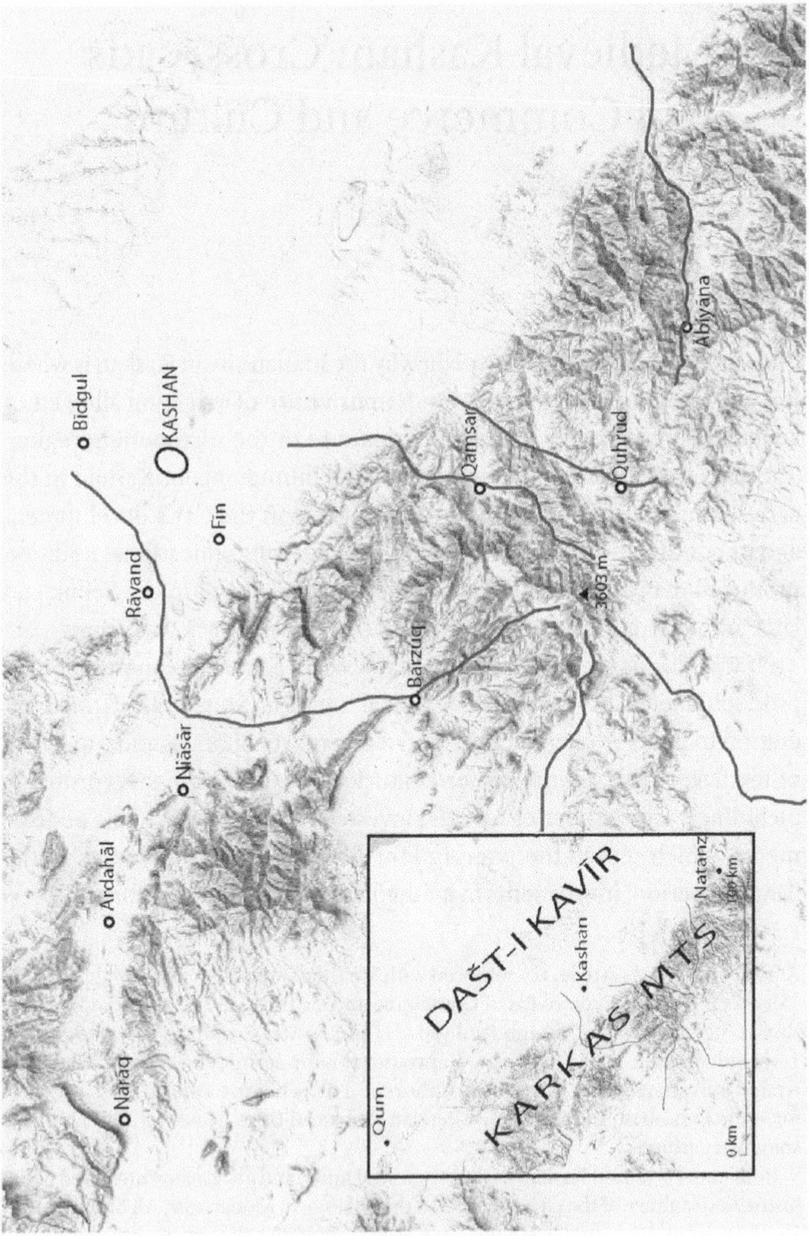

Figure 1: Map of Kashan and nearby villages. (Drawing by D. Durand-Guédy.)

outstanding mathematicians and astronomers. Tax yields from the medieval period may indicate the increasing prosperity of Kashan.

No city history of Kashan survives from the Middle Ages, and it is possible that no such history was written. The *Mir'āt al-Qāsān* is an extraordinarily fine example of local history produced in the nineteenth century, incorporating a fair amount of previous history and further amplified by very rich appendices, assembled by the late Iraj Afshar.[1] Kashan served only rarely as a seat of government, and most dynastic histories offer only passing references. Yet Kashan was an important artisanal center, and for this we have significant material evidence, which we can only hint at in the present essay. The history of smaller yet important centers such as Kashan represents a new frontier in city histories for Iran. Although smaller cities did not always escape sack and pillage, such settlements survived as alternate centers towards which displaced people could move. They could also serve as sites for refuge of minority beliefs, as is the case for Shiʿism in Kashan.

WHY KASHAN IS WHERE IT IS

Kashan arose at the center of the fan of an alluvial plain, approximately halfway between a plentiful spring at Fin (Fīn) and the distant town of Bidgol (Bīdgul), at the end of the plain (Fig. 1). Beyond Bidgol lies the Kavir (Kavīr),[2] one of Iran's extremely arid interior deserts. Kashan has its own seasonal river, the Shāhāb, known upstream as the Qohrud (Quhrūd). An elaborate system of underground water channels (sing. *qanāt* or *kāriz*),

1 The main appendix consists of the notes of Allah-yar Saleḥ.

2 Habibollah Zanjani, s.v. "Kashan i. Geography," *Encyclopaedia Iranica*, XVI/1 (2012) 1–2, available online at https://www.iranicaonline.org/articles/kashan-i-geography, (viewed December 11, 2016). Xavier de Planhol, s.v. "Kashan ii. Historical Geography," *Encyclopaedia Iranica*, XVI/1 (2012) 2–5, available online at https://www.iranicaonline.org/articles/kashan-ii-historical-geography, (viewed December 11, 2016). De Planhol offers several strong arguments for the existence of Kashan at its present location. On surface channels see Xavier de Planhol, s.v. "Kārīz i. Terminology," *Encyclopaedia Iranica*, XV/6 (2012) 564–565, available online at https://iranicaonline.org/articles/kariz_1, (viewed December 11, 2016). We were unable to obtain a copy of the geological thesis by Mehdi Nadji-Esfahani, *Geologie und Hydrogeologie des Gebietes von Kashan*, (Aachen, Technische Hochschule, Fakultät für Bergbau und Hüttenwesen: 1971); however, his 1972 article is available, published under the name Mehdi Nadji: Mehdi Nadji, "Luftbild: Kanate in der Ebene von Kashan, Iran," *Die Erde* 103 (1972) 209–215.

fed by the higher water table in the Karkas Mountains and streams in the foothills as well as waters from the spring at Fin, distributes this asset to farms and towns on the alluvial plain. The primary components of this system are the underground channels. However, there are also surface channels, often the extension of the underground channels as they reach the settlements. The *qanāts* are oriented in the same directions as the groundwater flows and at intervals are provided with air holes. The underground channels minimize losses to evaporation and aid in balancing the salinity of the waters. We can immediately understand that any upstream irrigation drawn from the *qanāts* would decrease the downstream supplies of water, and in fact the *History of Qom*, written in 378/988–89, reports the elaborate attempts to calculate the fractions of water that landholders in Qom (Qum) would be entitled to take from the channels passing by their various properties.[3] These agreements, as well as the extensive social cooperation necessary for construction and maintenance of the channels, indicate the levels of organization required to irrigate such arid lands, where the alluvial plain abuts the desert.[4] In more recent centuries the underground system is known to have included large rooms called *saypak* or *u'i*, which probably served as refuges from both invaders and heatwaves,[5] and may have existed in pre-Safavid times.

Kashan itself became a city only after the arrival of Islam in the seventh century C.E. although the general area has been a site of cities since at the least the third millennium B.C.E. In the pre-Islamic period Kashan was at most a village or small town near the spring of Fin; it did not merit a mention in the geographical works surviving from the Sasanian period.[6]

---

3 Ḥasan ibn Muḥammad Qomi, *Tārikh-e Qom*, ed. Mohammad Reza Ansari Qomi, (Qom, Markaz-e Qomshenāsi: 2006) 26–43. See also the outstanding study by Hossein Modarressi Tabataba'i, *Torbat-e pākān: āṯār va banāhā-ye qadimi*, 2 vols, (Qom, Chāpkhāna-ye Mehr: 1976) includes considerable reference to Kashan.

4 See Mahmoud Jomehpour, "Qanat Irrigation Systems as Important and Ingenious Agricultural Heritage: Case Study of the *qanats* of Kashan, Iran," *International Journal of Environmental Studies* 66:3 (June 2009) 297–315, who has a good discussion of the social organization necessary to maintain *qanāts*; Nadji, "Luftbild," (*supra* n. 2), 209–215. On the classification of *qanāts*, see M. Mahdavi and E.W. Anderson, "The Water-Supply System in the Margin of Dasht-e-Kavir," *Bulletin: British Society for Middle Eastern Studies* 10:2 (1983) 131–147.

5 Mahmud Sadat Bidgoli, and Zahra Sarukhani, "Bar-rasi-ye 'elal-e tārikh-e eqlimi-ye ijād-e u'i-hā dar manṭaqa-ye Kāshān," *Ganjina-ye asnād* 71 (Fall 1387 solar/1967) 25–36.

6 See Shahrestān-e Irānshahr or *A Catalogue of the Provincial Capitals of Eranshahr*, ed. and trans. J.A. Markwart (Rome, Pontificio Istituto Biblico: 1931); see also Bidgoli and Sarukhani, "Bar-rasi" (*supra* n. 5), 28.

WHEN DID KASHAN EMERGE AS A CITY?

Al-Yaʿqūbī, who wrote his geography in 278/891, mentioned only the surrounding villages and completely omitted Kashan.[7] Ibn Rosta, probably writing in the period 290–300/903–13, also fails to mention Kashan.[8] One of the earliest references to Kashan is in the geography of Ibn Khurradādhbih, who served as a postmaster for much of western Iran in the late 3rd/9th century. Ibn Khurradādhbih refers to two adjacent regions, *rustāq Ṣard-Qāshān* (the sub-province of cold Kashan) and *rustāq Jarm Qāshān* (the sub-province of warm Kashan) but does not mention Kashan as a city.[9] (The district of Kashan continues to be divided into "cold climate" and "warm climate" zones up to the present day.)

Other 3rd/9th-century references are set in the context of the Muslim conquest of Kashan, almost invariably attached to references to the prior conquest of Qom. We believe these references were added to the conquest narratives of Qom after Kashan emerged in the 3rd/9th century, at one hundred kilometers distance from Qom. Many of these colorful narratives have fanciful details as to how the attackers and defenders of Kashan rained scorpions on each other.[10]

A small town called Kāshān (or, in its earlier spellings, Qāshān or Qāsān) may well have existed near the present site of Kashan. A fundamental factor in its development would have been the flight of proto-Shiʿite Arabs from anti-Shiʿite governors of Iraq to central Iran, especially to Qom and Kashan. (Twelver Shiʿism was not fully formed until the 5th/11th century.) A history by al-Ṭabarī (d. 310/923) mentions that an anti-Umayyad leader from Iraq, Muṭrif ibn al-Mughīra, entered into open opposition with al-Ḥajjāj, the ferocious governor of Iraq, in 77/696–97. Muṭrif was killed but, according

7 Yaʿqūbī, *Kitāb al-Buldān*, ed. M.J. de Goeje (Leiden, Brill: 1892) 275.

8 However, he does mention a "wondrous spring" (Fin?), and an antimony mine. Ibn Rosta, *Kitāb al-aʿlāq al-nafīsa*, ed. M.J. de Goeje (Leiden, Brill: 1892) 156.

9 Ibn Khurradādhbih, *Kitāb al-Masālik wa-l-Mamālik*, ed. M.J. de Goeje (Leiden, Brill: 1889) 21.

10 For example, Qudāma ibn Jaʿfar (fl. 320/922), a learned and generally reliable source, tells the story that after conquering Qom, Abū Mūsā al-Ashʿarī sent al-Aḥnaf ibn Qays to conquer Qāshān (Kāshān), which he succeeded in doing "by force": Qudāma ibn Jaʿfar, *al-Kharāj wa-Ṣināʿat al-Kitāba*, ed. Muhammad Husayn Zabidi (Baghdad, Dār al-Rashīd li-l-nashr: 1981) 373. This last detail is probably meant to establish the status of the Kashan area as owing the heavier *kharāj* tax levied on conquered areas. Many similar accounts exist, as in the earlier work by al-Balādhuri (d. 279/892): Balādhurī, *Futūḥ al-Buldān*, ed. M.J. de Goeje (Leiden, Brill: 1866) 312.

to al-Ṭabarī, his followers fled to Qom and Qāshān.[11] If al-Ṭabarī is not adding Kashan because of the customary habit of mentioning it after Qom, this would be a genuine early reference to the developing town of Kashan.

Another early mention of Kashan in the geographical literature is in the *al-Masālik wa-l-Mamālik* of al-Iṣṭakhrī (d. 346/957). The only comments from this author are that Kashan is three stages (*marḥala*) or twelve *farsakhs* beyond Qom, that it is a part of Quhistān, the Persian name for the province al-Jibāl, and that it is "a small city in which the houses are built of clay."[12] A geographer of the same century writing in Persian, the unknown author of *Ḥudūd al-ʿĀlam* (begun in 372/982–83) says that Kashan is "a city with excellences, in which there are numerous Arabs. It has produced many scribes (*dabirān*) and literati (*adibān*)."[13] This important passage anticipates the role that sophistication in Arabic and scribal talents will play in Kashani history. It also testifies to the importance of the Arab element in Kashan, where the Arabs were proto-Shiʿites largely of the Ashʿarī tribe, as were the Arabs in Qom.

THE GROWING IMPORTANCE OF SHIʿITE ORIENTATION

During the ninth and tenth centuries C.E. many proto-Shiʿites gradually became Twelver Shiʿites, which as many geographers testify remained the dominant religious community in Kashan. However, some towns in the Kashan district were and continued to be Sunni, throughout this period.[14]

---

11 Ṭabarī, *Ta'rīkh al-Umam wa-l-Mulūk*, ed. M.J. de Goeje, 15 vols., (Leiden, Brill: 1879ff.) VI:293; see also VII:405. Some early references to Qāshān could relate to the town of that name in Central Asia. Ṭabarī, *Ta'rīkh*, IX:186 also mentions Kashan after Qom, in his description of the arrangements of 235/850 regarding which sons of Hārūn al-Rashīd would inherit governorship in the Abbasid Empire. This is clearly not a reference to the Kashan in Central Asia but to the Kashan in central Iran discussed here.

12 Iṣṭakhrī, *Kitāb al-Masālik wa-l-Mamālik*, ed. M.J. de Goeje (Leiden, Brill: 1870) 201 (*madīna ṣaghīra*). See also the early Persian translation: Iṣṭakhrī, *al-Masālik wa-al-Māmālik*, ed. Iraj Afshar (Tehran, Bungāh-e tarjama va-nashr-e ketāb: 1340 solar/1961) 166, where Kashan is called *shahrak*, "a small city."

13 Anon., *Ḥudūd al-ʿĀlam min al-Mashriq ilā al-Maghrib*, ed. Manuchehr Sotuda (Tehran, Dāneshgāh-e Tehrān: 1962) 143. Could this sentence be a later interpolation?

14 A few Ẓāhirīs may have come from Kashan. See Ibn al-Nadīm, *The Fihrist of al-Nadim: A Tenth-Century Survey of Islamic Culture*, trans. Bayard Dodge, I (New York, Columbia University Press: 1970) 523, concerning a Muḥammad ibn Isḥāq al-Qāshānī. There was also an Ismaʿili presence; see Shafique Virani, *The Ismailis in the Middle Ages* (Oxford, Oxford University Press: 2007) 107, 112, 117.

Like many other central Iranian cities, Kashan changed hands several times until the Shi'ite dynasty of the Buyids took control in the 4th/10th century. The Buyids showed favor to Qom because of their Shi'ite orientation and presumably did so to nearby Kashan,[15] until the conquest of central Iran by the Ghaznavids in 420/1029. In this period the legend grew that Kashan was founded by Zubayda bint Ja'far, wife of the Abbasid caliph Hārūn al-Rashīd, and the story of her secret Shi'ism developed correspondingly.[16]

It was no secret that Shi'ites favored *sayyids*, so many descendants of 'Alī emigrated to Shi'ite cities such as Kashan. The 4th/10th-century history of Qom says that the first of the descendants of Imam al-Riḍā (d. 203/819) to arrive in Qom from Kufa was Abū Ja'far Mūsā ibn Muḥammad ibn 'Alī al-Riḍā. But because of the disrespect shown him by some of his fellow Arabs in Qom he then went to Kashan, and the Shi'ites of that city honored his coming. Eventually he returned to Qom and was provided with a handsome stipend.[17]

THE SELJUK PERIOD

The conquest by the Seljuks in 443/1051 ushered in a long period of prosperity for the people of Kashan. The city flourished, in part for economic and in part for political reasons. One of the political reasons was the success of the people of Kashan and the surrounding district in acquiring positions in the Seljuk bureaucracy. A Kashani clerk of the very late Seljuk period, Muḥammad ibn 'Alī al-Rāvandī, writes in his *Rāḥat al-Ṣudūr*:

> Holders of senior positions such as vizier and chief-treasurer and the majority of clerks in the government of the *sulṭān* were Kāshīs. Our origin and place of birth has been the district of Kashan [...] In Iraq [western Iran] whenever they see good handwriting, they say it is the writing of a Kāshānī.[18]

---

15 The destruction caused by an earthquake in the Buyid period may have left evidence in the form of the rubble of the original mosque. See Fatema Karimi, "Kāshān," in *Shahr-hā-ye Irān*, ed. Muhammad Yusuf Kiyani, III (Tehran, Vezārat-e Farhang: 1989) 211.

16 Guy Le Strange, *The Lands of the Eastern Caliphate* (London, Cass: 1966) 209.

17 Qomi, *Tārikh-e Qom*, (*supra* n. 3), 575–580.

18 Muḥammad ibn 'Alī Rāvandī, *Rāḥat al-Ṣudūr*, ed. Muhammad Iqbal (Leiden, Brill: 1921) 51. It is significant that local patriotism outweighs the very Ḥanafī (and anti-Shi'ite) sentiments of this Rāvandī.

The eminence of Kashani (often shortened to "Kāshī") administrators arose in large part from their excellent education, including in calligraphy. Scholarly excellence can also be a useful defense against charges of heresy, which Shiʿites in Iran continually encountered in the pre-Safavid period.

The Seljuk period was the golden age for the founding of madrasas or seminaries, and in Kashan several such schools were established. Two generations of scholarship have associated the founding of such seminaries with the "Sunni Revival." However, the fact that these foundations took place simultaneously in Shiʿite Kashan suggests that they were also expressions of more general advancement in teaching and scholarship. Ṣafī al-Dīn Abū Ṭāher Ismāʿīl Kāshī was a high clerk in the service of Malik-Shāh (r. 465–85/1072–92), whose famous vizier, Niẓām al-Mulk, hated everything Shiʿite. Ṣafī al-Dīn founded the Ṣafīya Madrasa along with a worthy library in his native Kashan. In spite of his known Shiʿite adherence, Ṣafī al-Dīn was granted great favor in the Seljuk court.[19] His nephew, Mukhtaṣṣ al-Mulūk Muʿīn al-Dīn Aḥmad ibn ʿAbd Allāh al-Kāshī, again a high official, also founded a much frequented madrasa in Kashan (this madrasa was still functioning in the 9th/15th century).[20]

A generation later, Majd al-Dīn Abū al-Qāsim ʿUbayd Allāh ibn Faḍl ibn Maḥmūd al-Qāshānī[21] (d. 535/1141) founded the Madrasa Majdīya. He was very rich and famous for his benefactions of every kind, including building a city wall and hospitals, and the provision of a fund for dowries of poor women. Urban notables played significant roles in the public works of many Islamic Iranian cities, and this may have been even more important in smaller centers such as Kashan, which did not become capital cities. Their works could include militarily and politically important structures, including city walls. The Shiʿite Kashani vizier Sharaf al-Dīn Anūshīrvān ibn Khālid (d. 532–3/1137–39), whose significant career is described below, founded a madrasa and library, the Sharafīya, in his native town. Hindūshāh Nakhjavānī, a prominent official and author of the Ilkhanid period, writes:

19 See Mahmud Tayyar Maraghi, "Madāres-e ʿelmiya-ye Kāshān," *Mirāṣ-e jāvidān* 6:2 (1377 solar/1999) 69.

20 *Ibid.*, 69–70.

21 *Ibid.*, 70–71. See also Ḍiyāʾ al-Dīn Abū Riḍā Faḍl Allāh Rāvandī, *Dīwān*, ed. Jalal al-Din Mohaddith Ormavi (Tehran, Maṭba ʿat al-Majlis: 1334 solar/1955) 60 and 87 on the benefactions of Majd al-Dīn.

> In the year 674 [1275–6] when this humble man governed Kashan on behalf of his brother, that madrasa and library [founded by Anūshīrvān] was prospering (*ma'mūr*) but now in Muḥarram 724 [January 1323] I have heard that the madrasa is ruined.[22]

Another madrasa of the Seljuk era was the 'Azīzīya, founded in the second half of the 6th/12th century by yet another vizier, 'Azīz al-Dīn ibn Raḍī al-Dīn As'ad Kāshānī (d. 588/1192), who served the Sultan Ṭughril ibn Arslān. The *Nasā'im al-Asḥār* says of 'Azīz al-Dīn that: "He was one of the heads of department who were extremely skilled and one of the masters among scribes of financial administration for the two Iraqs [meaning Arab Iraq, modern central Iraq, and Persian Iraq, the Iranian lands between Fars and Azerbaijan]." Not surprisingly, the madrasa curriculum was said to involve deep study of varieties of accounting (*istīfā'*) as well as "multiplication, division, algebra, and other forms (*ashkāl*) [to be understood through mathematics]."[23] It is a measure of the excellence of Kashani education that the future Sunni chronicler of the Seljuks, 'Imād al-Dīn al-Iṣfahānī, as a talented boy, was sent to study in Kashan, along with his brother.[24]

Niẓām al-Mulk was fully aware that these well-educated Shi'ite clerks with "excellent handwriting" were penetrating the Seljuk bureaucracy. He writes:

> In the days of Mahmud, Mas'ud, Toghril and Alp Arslan (may Allāh have mercy on them) no Zoroastrian or Jew or Rafidi [i.e., Shi'ite] would have had the audacity to appear in a public place or to present himself before a great man. Those who administered the affairs of the Turks were all professional civil servants and

22 Maraghi, "Madāres," (*supra* n. 19), 70. There is a half century between these dates, which is not impossible but slightly suspicious.

23 *Ibid.*, 71. Nāṣir al-Dīn Kirmānī, *Nasā'im al-asḥār min Laṭā'im al-Akhbār dar Tārīkh al-Vuzarā'*, ed. Mir Jalal ad-Din Urmavi (Tehran, Chāpkhāna-ye Dāneshgāh: 1364 solar/1985) 91. *Ashkāl* in mathematical texts is usually translated as "figures," but this translation does not work here. Perhaps *ashkāl* should be translated as "operations." In his very full article on education in Kashan Maraghi, (*supra* n. 19), lists over thirty madrasas in Kashan, up to and including those of the Safavid period; only two of these were Sunni in orientation.

24 Carla L. Klausner, *The Seljuk Vezirate: A Study of Civil Administration, 1055–1194* (Cambridge, MA, Harvard University Press: 1973) 66. See also the outstanding recent study of the Seljuks by Andrew C.S. Peacock, *The Great Seljuk Empire* (Edinburgh, Edinburgh University Press: 2015) 214.

> secretaries from Khurasan, who belonged to the orthodox Hanafi or Shafi'i sects. The heretics of Iraq [i.e., western Iran] were never admitted as secretaries and tax-collectors; in fact, the Turks never used to employ them at all; they said, "These men are of the same religion as the Dailamites [i.e., Buyids] and their supporters; if they get a firm footing, they will injure the interests of the Turks and cause distress to the Muslims. It is better that enemies should not be in our midst." Consequently, they lived free from disaster. Now things have reached such a state that the court and divan are full of them, and every Turk has ten or twenty of these individuals running after him, and their object is to prevent even a few Khurasanis from entering the service of this court and earning a living here. In former times if a man offered himself for service to a Turk as an administrator or in any other capacity, and said that he was of the Hanafi or Shafi'i sect and from a Sunni city, he was accepted; but if he said that he was a Shi'i from Qum, Kashan or Āba [Āva] he was refused and told, "Be gone; we kill snakes not nourish them."[25]

Early Seljuk rulers and viziers such as Niẓām al-Mulk, and their largely Khorasanian ministers, allowed comparatively few Shi'ites into government. However, the later rulers of this dynasty were lax, and even the sons and grandsons of Niẓām al-Mulk hired Shi'ites.

The Twelver Shi'ite scholar 'Abd al-Jalil Qazvini, in writing a long and rambling defense of Twelvers, circa 560/1165, offers a picture that is partially complementary to the comments of Niẓām al-Mulk. Throughout his book, Qazvini quotes a Sunni opponent (who had recently written a refutation of Shi'ism) as saying that under the sultans Malik-Shāh and Muḥammad, Shi'ites were not allowed to open schools; Qazvini counters with examples, including that of the schools opened by ministers from Kashan.[26] The Sunni opponent says: "In the ministries (*dīvānhā*) the clerks

---

25 Niẓām al-Mulk, *Siyar al-Mulūk* (*Siyāsat-Nāma*), ed. Hubert Darke (Tehran, Bongāh-e tarjama va-nashr-e ketāb: 1962) 203–204: *The Book of Government or Rules for Kings*, trans. Hubert Darke (London, Routledge & Kegan Paul: 1960) 164–166. For a similar quote, see David Durand-Guédy, *Iranian Elites and Turkish Rulers. A History of Iṣfahān in the Saljūq Period* (London, Routledge: 2010) 189. This book is the most important study of the rivalry between Khorasanian secretaries and those from central and western Iran.

26 'Abd al-Jalil Qazvini Rāzi, *Ketāb-e naqż*, ed. Jalal al-Din Mohaddeth (Tehran, Anjoman-e Āṣār-e Melli: 1358 solar/1980) 34.

are all [Shi'ites] and things now are exactly as under [the Sunni Abbasid caliph] al-Muqtadir [who had Shi'ite viziers]." Qazvini replies that since God has given Turks rule of the world they are free to foster whomever they like.[27] Of course Twelver Shi'ites had ceased their political claims in 260/874 and were free to support any ruler until the return of the Twelfth Imam. Qazvini also mentions other Shi'ite clerks who were good viziers to the Seljuks, including 'Alī ibn 'Imrān al-Kāshī and Anūshīrvān ibn Khālid (discussed below), both from Kashan.

Qazvini devotes a passage to Kashan, its excellent schools (naming all four of them) and charitable endowments, with teachers like Ḍiyā' al-Dīn (the author of the *Dīwān*) who "is without rival in all the lands of the world for knowledge and religious devotion." He also mentions that the judges in Kashan are Shi'ite, which the government may have allowed because only a prominent Shi'ite could command obedience. He refers to the benefactions of Majd al-Dīn to the magnificent shrine of 'Alī ibn Muḥammad al-Bāqir at Ardahāl.[28]

The success of Kashani bureaucrats in the late Seljuk administration is well illustrated by the career of Anūshīrvān ibn Khālid, founder of the Sharafīya madrasa mentioned above. Anūshīrvān, supposedly a descendant of the Sasanian monarch, was one of the clerks who worked for the staunchly Sunni vizier Niẓām al-Mulk despite the vizier's extreme disdain for Shi'ites.[29] He was especially close to Niẓām al-Mulk's son, Mu'ayyid al-Mulk, a vizier to the Seljuk sultan Barkyāruq (r. 485–498/1092–1105). Anūshīrvān was treasurer in Isfahan for a time; subsequently, another son of Niẓām placed him in charge of the budget for the army. Under the Seljuk ruler Sultan Maḥmūd he was appointed vizier (518/1124–25), but Anūshīrvān could accomplish little under this greatly enfeebled sultan. Very surprisingly, this Shi'ite clerk was then appointed vizier to al-Mustarshid, an Abbasid caliph and a symbol of Sunnism. As noted above, there had previously been crypto-Shi'ite viziers to the Abbasid caliphs, such as the Banū Furāt under the caliph Muqtadir (reg. 295–320/908–932), but Anūshīrvān's Shi'ism was no secret. Anūshīrvān died in Baghdad in 532

27 *Ibid.*, 78–79. See also p. 114, quoting the Sunni opponent as saying that everyone in the service of the Turks is Shi'ite, down to the cooks and cleaners.

28 *Ibid.*, 198–199.

29 Niẓām al-Mulk, (*supra* n. 25), *The Book of Government or Rules for Kings*, 214, 238, and *Siyar al-Mulūk* (*Siyāsat-Nāma*), 263, 289, mentions Kashan twice for its Shi'ism, along with Qom.

or 523/1137–39 and was buried near the tomb of ʿAlī in Najaf.[30] Besides a madrasa and a library he also had other important structures built in Kashan, such as a hospital (*dār al-shifāʾ*) and a caravanserai.

Two families of Kashani scholars of the Seljuk period had the place-name Rāvandī. Rāvand is a small town a few miles from Kashan. One set of Rāvandīs consisted of the Ḥanafī family related to Muḥammad ibn ʿAlī al-Rāvandī, author of *Rāḥat al-Ṣudūr*.[31] Although Muḥammad ibn ʿAlī offered high praise to the Kashanis' education and handwriting, he distanced himself strenuously from their Shiʿism. He rebukes them for "rejecting the *ijtihād* of the [Sunni] schools of law, for praying only three times a day, for refusing to pay the *zakāt* [alms tax] and for going on pilgrimage to Ṭūs [near where Imam al-Riḍā is buried]".[32] The second family, who were *sayyids* and Shiʿites, included the very wealthy Majd al-Dīn Rāvandī, founder of the Madrasa Majdīya noted above, and nephew of Anūshīrvān ibn Khālid. Ḍiyāʾ al-Dīn Abū Riḍā Faḍl Allāh, another member of this Shiʿite family, was the director of a madrasa and a prolific poet in the Arabic language. His *Dīwān* is filled with references to contemporaries, and to Kashan, where his relative Majd al-Dīn founded "schools (*madāris*) and caravanserais (*khānāt*) and a hospital (*māristān*)."[33] In another poem

30 ʿAbbas Iqbal, *Vezārat dar ʿAhd-e Salātin-e Bozorg-e Saljuqi* (Tehran, Chāpkhāna-ye dāneshgāh: 1959) 254–262. Another prominent Shiʿite family in Seljuk employ was that of Mukhtaṣṣ al-Mulūk, a vizier to Sultan Sanjar, and the vizier's son Fakhr al-Mulk, vizier to Sulaymānshāh, as well as the vizier's grandson, vizier to Ṭughril III. Peacock, *Great Seljuk Empire*, (*supra* n. 24), 263. Among several short sketches of Anūshīrvān's life, see C.E. Bosworth, s.v. "Anūšervān Kāšānī," in *Encyclopaedia Iranica*, II:2 (1987) 139. For the benefaction of the Seljuk governor Abū Naṣr al-Kāshī to Kashan, see Hasan Naraqi, *Tārikh-e Ejtemāʿi-ye Kāshān* (Tehran, Institut d'Études et de Recherches sociales: 1345 solar/1967) 57–58.

31 Muḥammad ibn ʿAlī was first helped by his maternal uncle, a member of the court of a Seljuk *atabeg* who ruled Hamadan. He was then fostered by another uncle, Zayn al-Dīn Maḥmūd Kāshī. He acknowledges the patronage of a Shihāb al-Dīn Aḥmad al-Qāshī. See Julie Scott Meisami, "Rāvandī's *Rāḥat aṣ-Ṣudūr*," *Edebiyat* V (1994) 183–215, especially 183–184.

32 All of these actions or misperceptions apply to Twelver Shiʿites. Rāvandī, *Rāḥat al-Sudūr* (*supra* n. 18), 394–395.

33 Ḍiyāʾ al-Dīn Rāvandī, *Dīwān*, (*supra* n. 21), 33. On the prominent Rāvandī families, see Mustafa Sadiqi, "Didgāh-e tārikhi-ye Rāvandīyān," *Nāma-ye Tārikh-Pazhuheshān*, X (1386 solar/2008) 115–138. A deed of pious endowment by Majd al-Dīn dated Rabīʿ II 565 (January 1170) survives. Husayn Vatheqi, "Barā-ye tārikh-e Kāshān," *Mirāṣ-e Shahāb*, 84–85 (1395 solar) 147–151.

Ḍiyā' al-Dīn also praises his relative for building mosques, water channels and bridges/aqueducts (*qanāṭir*).[34]

Perhaps the most dramatic of Ḍiyā' al-Dīn's poems is his description of the siege of Kashan in 532/1137–38. The work offers the names of forty nearby towns and villages that had been attacked and despoiled by the besiegers but praises Majd al-Dīn for paying forty thousand dinars to have them lift the siege of Kashan itself. (Later, in 595/1198–99, the Khwarazmshah laid siege to Kashan and sacked it savagely after a resistance lasting four months.[35]

The list of those praised in this *Dīwān* also shows the connections of these learned men of Kashan with other regions. We have a poem in praise of the vizier Qiwām al-Dīn Abū al-Qāsim al-Nāṣir, delivered in his vizieral palace in Isfahan in 524/1129–30.[36] Ḍiyā' al-Dīn also wrote a poem to Qiwām al-Dīn, said to be a crypto-Nizārī Isma'ili, on the occasion of this vizier's visit to Kashan. The same Ḍiyā' al-Dīn also wrote an elegy on the vizier's death and dedicated a further poem to his son.[37]

KASHAN AS A CENTER OF CERAMIC PRODUCTION

The Seljuk period saw the rise of Kashan as a major center of ceramic production. Writing around 380/990, al-Muqaddasī twice mentions Qāshān and praises its "long-necked bottles."[38] By the time of Yāqūt (d. 626/1229),

34 Ḍiyā' al-Dīn Rāvandī, *Dīwān*, (*supra* n. 21), 52.

35 On the sack of 595 A.H., see Rāvandī, *Rāḥat al-Ṣudūr*, (*supra* n. 18), 493–494. Mehrdad Amanat, "Kashan iii. History to the Pahlavi Period," *Encyclopaedia Iranica* online, http://www.iranicaonline.org/kashan-iii-history.

36 Ḍiyā' al-Dīn Rāvandī, *Dīwān*, (*supra* n. 21), 1.

37 *Ibid.*, 74–90.

38 See Muqaddasī, *Aḥsan al-Taqāsīm fī Ma'rifat al-Aqālīm*, ed. M.J. de Goeje (Leiden, Brill: 1906) 390 and 396. The Arabic word, *qamāqim* (sing. *qumqum* or *qumquma*), is hard to interpret. As in later Persian, it could mean "brass vessels." In later Arabic it often refers to a flask of glass or pottery. The great lexicographer Ibn Manẓūr (d. 711/1311) offers "jar" and "a kind of vessel" but also mentions the interpretation of "copper/brass" vessels and says that it can mean a vessel for water "of copper, or otherwise, narrow of neck": Ibn Manẓūr, *Lisān al-'Arab*, XII (Beirut, Dār Ṣādir: 1990) 495. Paul Schwarz, *Iran im Mittelalter nach den arabischen Geographen* (Reprint, Hildesheim, Olms: 1969) 568, translates the bottles as "Tonkrüge," clay ewers. On ancient copper mining in the Kashan area, see J.H. Harrison, "Minerals," in W.B. Fisher (ed.), *Cambridge History of Iran*, I (Cambridge, U.K., Cambridge University Press: 1968) 487–516: here p. 502.

Kashan was famed for its pottery dishes or platters (*ghaḍā'ir*).[39] Some fifty years later, Zakarīyā' al-Qazwīnī (d. 682/1283) writes:

> From [Kashan] come shiny pottery utensils (*ālāt*). They [the Kashanis] have an outstanding gift in this, which other lands do not have. The utensils (*ālāt*) and vessels (*ẓurūf*) from Kashan are transported from Kashan to other lands.[40]

Pottery is both heavy and breakable, meaning that exportability required high artistic standards and strong fabric. The pottery of Kashan offered both attributes, from the 6th/12th to the 9th/15th century. The body was of a density achieved only much later in European stone-paste earthenware, though not yet to the standard of porcelain. The use of a mixture of ground quartz and white clay had survived from ancient Egyptian pottery techniques, which art historians often call "faience."[41] The earliest appearances of enamel overglaze painting (*minā'i* or, in earlier usage, *haft rang*) probably coincided with the invention of this technique in Kashan.[42] In both lusterware and *minā'i* forms (Figs. 2 and 3) the decorative patterns and illustrative painting is of such high quality that these works are widely regarded as related to the art of miniature illustration in books.[43]

It could have been in the 6th/12th and 7th/13th centuries that the adjective *qāshī*, which means "things belonging to Kashan," passed into other languages such as Arabic, with the meaning of "tiles."[44] Some of the ingredients of Kashan pottery could be found nearby, such as quartz pebbles which are "white, clear and shiny, not as clear (*ṣafā*) as rock crystal but more clear than white marble,"[45] and finely-divided white stone from

---

39 Yāqūt, *Mu'jam al-Buldān*, ed. F. Wüstenfeld, IV (Leipzig: Brockhaus, 1869) 15.

40 Zakarīyā' Qazwīnī, *Āthār al-Bilād wa-Akhbār al-'Ibād* (Beirut, Dār Ṣādir: 1988) 433.

41 Oliver Watson, *Persian Lustre Ware* (London, Faber & Faber: 1985) 23.

42 *Ibid.*, 24.

43 See Sheila Blair, "A Brief Biography of Abū Zayd," *Muqarnas* 25 (2008) 155–176, here p. 157, who states that the second style of Kashan lusterware "was clearly inspired by book painting." For ample literature on the relation of Kashan pottery to miniatures, see Robert H. Hillenbrand, "The Relationship between Book Painting and Luxury Ceramics of 13th Century Iran," in Robert H. Hillenbrand (ed.), *The Art of the Saljuqs in Iran and Anatolia* (Costa Mesa, C.A., Mazda: 1994) 134–141.

44 R. Dozy, *Supplément aux dictionnaires arabes*, II (Paris, Maisonneuve: 1927) 295–296.

45 Abu al-Qāsem 'Abd Allāh Kāshāni, *'Arāyis al-Jawāhir wa-Nafāyis al-Aṭāyib*, ed. Iraj Afshar (Tehran, Almā'i: 1386 solar/2007) 339–348, trans. in J.W. Allan, "Abū 'l-Qāsim's

the villages near Fin. From nearby Qamṣar there was a stone "like white sugar" and the famous cobalt called *lājvard*. Some white clays also come from the Kashan district.[46]

A relatively neglected text written in 592/1195–6 by a jeweler from Nishapur, Moḥammad ibn Abi al-Barakāt Jawhari, contains some of the earliest references to lusterware. He discusses a formula for putting "golden marcasite and other ingredients on pottery and glass" so that when these vessels emerge from the kiln (*dāsh*), they have "a color like gold," and he also reports on enameling techniques on pottery, but the procedures described may fall short of the more elaborate techniques of the Kashan potters. The text offers numerous formulas that require analysis by chemists, but among these is one which Jawhari says is used for "Syrian glass" and "Kashan pottery."[47]

Signed works by four generations of Kashani lusterware potters, all of the Abu Ṭāher family, testify to the development and preservation of the many in-house skills and trade secrets that went into the production of these wares.[48] In the very early 7th/13th century a master ceramicist at the head of another family of Kashani potters, Abu Zayd, collaborated

Treatise on Ceramics," *Iran* 11 (1973) 111–120.

46 The line between porcelain and pottery is fairly clear: porcelain usually contains a great deal of kaolin and is fired at temperatures above 2500 centigrade. However, there is some confusion between various kinds of pottery, including fritware (often containing ground glass), stone paste (often containing crushed quartz), faience and soft paste porcelain (terms that are even more loosely defined). Both Kashan lusterware and *minā'i* are best called stone paste. Cf. Oliver Watson, *Ceramics from Islamic Lands* (London, Thames & Hudson: 2004) 54–55 for a somewhat different view.

47 Moḥammad Jawharī Nishāpuri, *Javāher-Nāma-ye Neẓāmi*, ed. Iraj Afshar (Tehran, Mirāṣ-e Maktub: 2004) 265 (like gold), 350 (enamel), 354 (Syrian glass). Sayyed Mohammad Mir-Shafi'i, and Mas'ud Baqer-zada Kathiri, "Moṭāla'a-ye sākht-e lo'āb-e zarrin-fām," *Pazhuhesh-hā-ye 'olum va-fannāvari rang* (2016) 71–78 report using one of Jawharī's formulas for lusterware pottery with success.

48 Given that the techniques used were so complicated and expensive and were only handed down in a very small number of families, the Kashani potters in some ways resemble the great Italian Della Robbia family. See Fatima Karimi, s.v. "Abū Ṭāhir (Family)," trans. Rahim Gholami and Farzin Negahban, in W. Madelung and F. Daftary (eds.), *Encyclopaedia Islamica* (2008): www.referenceworks.brillonline.com/entries/encyclopedia-islamica/abu-tahir-family, viewed 4/24/2017; Oliver Watson, "Abū Ṭāher," in *Encyclopaedia Iranica*, I:4 (2011) 385–387 and *Persian Lustre Ware*, (*supra* n. 41), 177. The vast literature on Kashan lusterware includes Watson's *Persian Lustre Ware* and his *Ceramics from Islamic Lands*, (*supra* n. 46); Alan Caiger-Smith, *Lustre Pottery: Technique, Tradition, and Innovation in Islam and the Western World* (London, Faber & Faber: 1985); and Jean Soustiel, *La céramique islamique* (Fribourg, Suisse, Office du livre: 1985).

with the head of the Abu Ṭāher family on the tile-work in shrines in Qom and Mashhad.[49] Abu Zayd worked in both *minā'i* and luster, and left more signed works than any other potter, the earliest of which is a *minā'i* bowl of 582/1186.[50] He identifies himself as a Ḥasanī *sayyid* on a fine luster plate of 607/1210 (Fig. 2).[51] On other works he not only says that he made the piece but also that he wrote the inscription, perhaps a reflection of Kashani pride in handwriting.[52] Manijeh Bayani, a great expert on medieval Persian inscriptions, says that "the inscriptions of Persian luster-painted, *mīnā'ī* and underglaze-painted wares of the late twelfth to the thirteenth century have no precedent or parallel in other medieval wares."[53] Bayani discusses the various styles of handwriting on Kashan pottery of this period, noting that the cursive style used for the popular poetry on luster-painted wares is closest to *ta'līq*, a style in which hanging and joining of letters are used. Bayani does not regard the cursive style on lusterware as crude, rather as competent and consistent.[54] Certainly it is tempting to connect this type of handwriting to that of the Kashani clerks trained in the madrasas of Kashan.

We have a treatise on the methods of fabrication for both lusterware and *minā'i* pottery, written by a later member of the Abu Ṭāher family, Abu al-Qāsem 'Abd Allāh Kāshāni, in 700/1300–1.[55] Although the treatise

---

49 Sheila Blair, and Jonathan Bloom, "Signatures on Works of Islamic Art and Architecture," *Damaszener Mitteilungen* XI (1999) 49ff. Blair, "A Brief Biography," (*supra* n. 43). Interestingly, Abu Zayd is the only Kashani potter known to have produced both vessels and tiles: Blair, "A Brief Biography," (*supra* n. 43), 161.

50 Blair, "A Brief Biography," (*supra* n. 43), 156. The survival of dated pieces and signatures of potters such as Abu Zayd, from the late 6th/12th century, together with the group of pieces displaying both *minā'i* and luster techniques, proves that these different products were made in the same workshops: Watson, *Persian Lustre Ware* (*supra* n. 41), 84 n. 11.

51 Blair and Bloom, "Signatures," (*supra* n. 49), 54–55 and Blair, "A Brief Biography, (*supra* n. 43)."

52 Blair and Bloom, "Signatures," 55. See also Blair, "A Brief Biography," and Fatima Karimi, "Abū Zayd Kāshānī,", trans. Farzin Negahban, in W. Madelung and F. Daftary (eds.), *Encyclopaedia Islamica* (2008): www.referenceworks.brillonline.com/entries/encyclopedia-islamica/abu-zayd-kashani, viewed February 21, 2017.

53 Oya Pancaroghlu, *Perpetual Glory: Medieval Islamic Ceramics from the Harvey B. Plotnick Collection*, with transcriptions and translations of inscriptions by Manijeh Bayani (New Haven, Yale University Press: 2007) 155.

54 *Ibid.*, 154–155 for Bayani's excellent account of the inscriptions, entitled "A Note on the Content and Style of Inscriptions."

55 For a good discussion of Abu al-Qāsem himself, see Caiger-Smith, (*supra* n. 48), 73–76. See also Priscilla P. Soucek, "Abu 'l-Qāsem 'Abdallāh Kāšānī", in *Encyclopaedia Iranica*, I:4 (2011) 362–363.

Figure 2: Luster plate signed by Abu Zayd, Kashan, 607/1210. (Freer Gallery, Smithsonian Institution, Washington, D.C.: Purchase—Charles Lang Freer Endowment, F1941.11.)

is in part drawn from earlier works on stones and gems by Jawharī and Naṣīr al-Dīn al-Ṭūsī, who were in turn inspired by Bīrūnī (and ultimately by Aristotle), it contains an original section about the manufacture of Kashan luster and *minā'i* pottery. Abu al-Qāsem also wrote a history of an Ilkhanid ruler, and his brother wrote a treatise on Sufism, all of which testifies to the high literary achievements of these later members of the Abu Ṭāher family.[56] The family had clearly benefitted and prospered, thanks

56 Soucek, "Abu al-Qāsem." Margaret S. Graves, s.v. "Kashan vii. Kashan Ware," *Encyclopaedia Iranica*, online edition, 2014, available at https://www.iranicaonline.org/articles/kashan-ware (viewed April 27, 2017).

to the excellent education available in Kashan, and had risen to become authors and scholars.

In the nearby town of Qohrud (Quhrūd) we have the last recorded member of the Abu Ṭāher potter family, who signs: "the work of Yūsuf [...] 'Alī ibn Muḥammad [...] the Kāshānī potter (al-Ghaḍā'irī al-Qāshānī)." In this case the work is not in luster but in blue and white ware, a type of production that would soon dominate.[57] Thanks to this and other individual signatures we can distinguish four different families of potters, and at least seven other potters.[58]

It has been suggested that some of the inspiration for Kashan pottery of this period was due to the arrival of artisans migrating from Fatimid Egypt, or Raqqa in eastern Syria.[59] In any case, given that they were firm Shi'ites, the potters of Kashan (including several families of *sayyids*) travelled to the shrine cities such as Qom, Mashhad and Najaf. There is also evidence of their activity in centers not connected with Shi'ism, such as Varamin, Damghan and Baku.[60] We know of the specific case of a potter in the 7th/13th century who migrated to Kashan, as seen in the signature to his work: Muḥammad ibn Muḥammad Nīshāpūrī "residing in (*muqīm*) in Kashan".[61]

Some of the themes illustrated on Kashan lusterware are specifically Shi'ite, such as the circular tile with a "horseshoe-shaped" imprint on a foundation plaque bearing the date 711/1312, intended to commemorate a dream visit by Imam 'Alī on his famous mount, which left a hoof-print.[62]

---

57 Oliver Watson, "The Masjid-i 'Ali, Quhrūd: An Architectural and Epigraphic Survey," *Iran* 13 (1975) 59–74, here p. 63 and Watson, *Persian Lustre Ware*, (*supra* n. 41), 179. Blair, "A Brief Biography," (*supra* n. 43), 160. Although the date has been differently read, all readings put the piece in the early 8th/14th century.

58 Watson, *Persian Lustre Ware*, (*supra* n. 41), 178.

59 See Arthur Lane, *Early Islamic Pottery. Mesopotamia, Egypt and Persia* (London, Faber & Faber: 1947) 37–38. See also T. Pradell. *et al.*, "The Invention of Lustre: Iraq 9th and 10th Centuries AD," *Journal of Archaeological Science*, 35:5 (2008) 1201–1215.

60 We have families of Ḥasanī *sayyids* (Abu Zayd) and Ḥusaynī *sayyids* (Abu Ṭāher family) and some other individual *sayyids* signing Kashan ceramics. Examples of collaboration between individuals and families are well documented. Cf. Watson, *Persian Lustre Ware*, (*supra* n. 41), 176–182 and Blair, "A Brief Biography," (*supra* n. 43), 159–160.

61 M. Bahrami, *Gurgan Faiences* (Cairo, Le Scribe Egyptien: 1949) 92 (Victoria and Albert Museum, C. 162–1977). Cf. Sheila Blair, *Islamic Inscriptions* (Edinburgh, Edinburgh University Press: 1998) 148–159, whose chapter on ceramics of the early and middle periods provides a useful summary of the inscriptions and signed and dated pieces in their historical contexts.

62 Watson, *Persian Lustre Ware*, (*supra* n. 41), 146–149, fig. 124.

It also appears that many buyers of Kashan *minā'i* and lusterware pottery preferred themes from the *Shāhnāma,* such as that of Bahrām Gur and Āzāda (Fig. 3). Complementary themes are the enthroned monarch, musicians, female figures and male-female couples. Most large installations of Kashani lusterware tiles are at mausolea, such as the Tomb of 'Alī in Najaf, yet even in these sacred settings, some "secular themed" tiles have been used to fill in spaces.[63]

Figure 3: Minā'i *bowl with Bahrām Gur and Āzāda, Kashan, late 6th/12th—early 7th/13th century. (Metropolitan Museum of Art: Purchase—Rogers Fund, and Gift of the Schiff Foundation, 1957, 57.36.2. Image copyright © The Metropolitan Museum of Art, Image source: Art Resource, N.Y. (ART433912).)*

Some tiles spell Kashan in a more Persian style using a "K" rather than "Q," as in a star-shaped tile dated 738/1338, for which the full wording is "in the place (*maqām*) of Kashan, may God the Exalted protect it from

63 Watson, *Persian Lustre Ware,* (*supra* n. 41), 154.

the accidents of time."[64] The Kashan pride in calligraphy is reflected in the numerous inscriptions in which the potter says that the writing is "in his [own] handwriting (*bi-khaṭṭihī*)."[65]

The learned 'Abd Allāh Quchani shows that the majority of verses shown on the ceramics of Kashan are quatrains, some of which are attributed to Kashan's Sufi poet, Afḍal al-Dīn. Quchani estimates that the works of some one hundred different poets are recorded on ceramics, although some quatrains are used repeatedly. Some of the poetry is quite difficult, which would be evidence suggesting the production of some pieces on commission and for a fairly literate audience.[66]

The earliest dated Kashan lusterware is from 575/1179[67] and the last dated piece is from 739/1339.[68] One reason for the cessation of production could be that the tastes for this elaborate ware waned, although as noted above, the less expensive blue and white Kashan tiles continued to be popular. The shift of interest from expensive tiles for building interiors to less expensive production for coverage of exteriors, as seen in Timurid architecture, may be another reason for the decline of traditional Kashan pottery. It seems that prior to the waning of lusterware, the production of *haft rang* or *minā'i* had already declined. In this case it could be that the flourishing of painting in book illustration would account for part of the change in taste. Another important reason for cessation of this production could have been the difficulty and cost of obtaining the necessary ingredients for the many colors used in *minā'i* ware.[69] We have a tile that reads:

> It was written in the place Kashan on the 10th of Rabī' II 738 [1337] in the workshop (*kārkhāna*) of the sayyid of sayyids, Sayyid Rukn al-Dīn Muḥammad, son of the late Sayyid Zayn al-Dīn 'Alī, the

---

64 Richard Ettinghausen, "Evidence for the Identification of Kashan Pottery," *Ars Islamica* III:1 (1936) 44–75, here p. 59.

65 See Graves, (*supra* n. 56).

66 'Abd Allāh Quchani, "Sofālgarān-e Kāshān va-She'r-e Fārsi", *Nashr-e Dānesh* 84 (1373 solar) 31–40.

67 See Graves, (*supra* n. 56), and Yves Porter, "Lustres fatimides et potiers de Kâshân: Historiographie et obscurs transferts," *Keramik-Freunde der Schweiz* 129 (2015) 12–14.

68 See Graves, (*supra* n. 56).

69 Abu al-Qāsem, writing when lusterware was still in production, comments that *minā'i* or *haft rang* pottery has "passed into oblivion in this time": Allan, (*supra* n. 45), 115. Cf. Soustiel, (*supra* n. 48), 193.

> potter [...] The work of the revered and respected Master (*ustād*) Jamāl the designer (*naqqāsh*).[70]

The mention of the workshop indicates the significant scale of labor involved. The manufacturers needed not only to produce the pottery but also to build the kilns and fire the pieces.[71] The separate and very respectful mention of the "designer" tells us that the manufacture of high-quality Kashan pottery likely included the presence of such a personage, which in this case probably meant a painter.

AGRICULTURE IN THE KASHAN DISTRICT

As we would expect in any largely agrarian society, the prosperity of Kashan during and subsequent to the Seljuk period would have been based more on agricultural production than on artisanal or scribal patronage. The geographers mention tarragon, plums, peaches, apricots, apricot leather and vegetables.[72] However, the range of crops and food products was surely far greater. A government "order" (*farmān*) dated 869/1464–65 lists the production of Kashan as including wheat, barley, cotton, cotton-pods (*koluza*), beans (*bāqalā*), sorghum (*ẕorra*), millet (*kāvors*), cumin seed, sesame (*konjed*), chickpea (*nokhwod*), almonds, raisins (*maviz*), grape syrup (*dushāb*) and other vegetables (*khożrāviyāt*, literally "greens").[73]

---

70 Watson, *Persian Lustre Ware*, (*supra* n. 41), 142. Watson also refers here to another inscription in which the artist called himself "the builder" (*al-bannā'*).

71 Some of the best descriptions of the techniques and labor involved in Kashan pottery come from scholars who are themselves potters or who work closely with experienced potters. See Caiger-Smith, (*supra* n. 48), 73–75, who discusses the man-hours involved in producing Kashan pottery and Soustiel, (*supra* n. 48), 193, who states "*la fabrication des céramiques de prestige en Orient ne relevait pas de l'artisanat, mais bien d'une entreprise rigoureuse faisant appel à des chimistes expérimentés et dotée d'une infrastructure stable destinée à promouvoir son exploitation.*"

72 Schwarz, *Iran im Mittelalter*, (*supra* n. 38), 568–569.

73 Hasan Naraqi, *Āṣār-e Tārikhi-ye Shahrestānhā-ye Kāshān va-Naṭanz* (Tehran, Anjoman-e Āṣār-e Melli: 1348 solar/1969) 220, quoting the *farmān* of Jahānshāh, written on stone and installed in the Masjed-e Maydān in Kashan. It is unclear as to why a secondary product, "grape syrup," enters in this list. A slightly different reading of the list is given in Nosrat Allah Meshkati, "Naẓari be-Tārikh-e Bāstān-shenāsi-ye Kāshān," *Honar va-Mardom*, series 5, 53–54 (1345 solar/1966) 7–14 and 55 (1346 solar/1967) 8–13, here pp. 8–9.

This document confirms that thanks to its extensive *qanāt* irrigation, the Kashan district was engaged in a wide range of agricultural production.

MONUMENTS OF THE SELJUK PERIOD

Several buildings of the Seljuk period still survive in Kashan and its surroundings. A minaret of the Old Friday mosque (generally known as Masjed-e Maydān, because of its closeness to the central square) bears an inscription—unfortunately somewhat repaired—that reads: "The glorious *qāḍī* Majd ... ordered it to be built in 466 [1073–74]" (see Fig. 4).[74] Could this be an indication of Majd al-Dīn Rāvandī, who is known for founding the Madrasa Majdīya and so many other benefactions? A different member of the Rāvandī family, the abovementioned Ḍiyā' al-Dīn Abū Riḍā, who was known for his poetry, celebrates Majd al-Dīn's construction of the famous shrine of "Sulṭān 'Alī," son of the Imam Muḥammad al-Bāqir, in nearby Ardahāl.[75] Another Seljuk building is the fortress to the west of Kashan called Qal'a-ye Jalāli, ascribed to Malik-Shāh (r. 465/1072–485/1092), a surprisingly large structure for a small city like Kashan.[76]

KASHAN UNDER THE ILKHANIDS

The extent of Kashan's suffering under the Mongol invasion is still a matter of debate.[77] However, it is clear that Kashan thrived in the subsequent

74 Naraqi, (*supra* n. 73), 115.

75 Naraqi, (*supra* n. 73), 126. There was a great deal of repair and new building work at this shrine in a further period of prosperity in the 9th/15th century; see *Ibid.*, 136–137, 172, 184–185. "Sulṭān" is, of course, a purely fictive epithet added to the name of this *sayyid.*

76 Naraqi, (*supra* n. 73), 120ff. 'Abd al-Raḥim Kalantar Żarrābi, *Tārikh-e Kāshān*, ed. Iraj Afshar (Tehran, Ibn Sinā: 1962) 469 discusses the dimensions of this castle and the remnant of a town wall attached to it, but given that this is an account, completed in 1288/1871, it may not represent the size in the Seljuk period. See also Mohammad-Reza Haeri, s.v. "Kashan v. Architecture (2) Historical Monument," in *Encyclopaedia Iranica*, XVI/1 (2012) 12–21.

77 Ibn al-Athīr, *al-Kāmil fī al-Ta'rīkh,* ed. Muhammad Yusuf al-Daqqaq, 13 vols. (Beirut, Dār Ṣādir: 2003): sub anno 621. There seems to have been a Mongol raid in 620–21/1223–25. Two manuscripts of Juvayni say: "And part of the army laid siege to Kashan, which they took [...] with much slaughter and pillage," but the translator, Boyle, takes this to be a later interpolation. See John A. Boyle, *The History of the*

Figure 4: Location of the Old Friday Mosque in Kashan; its minaret with an inscription dated 466/1073–74. (Photo courtesy of Wikisource.)

Ilkhanid period. Perhaps the Mongol sack of larger cities such as Rayy and Isfahan permitted a temporary advantage for smaller cities like Kashan. The trade in lusterware platters continued, but artisanal production at Kashan increasingly centered on other wares. Kashan was a major supplier of star and cross tiles for architectural ornamentation, beginning in the heyday of lusterware production and continuing with "blue and white" technologies.

In the late Mongol and post-Mongol period the potters of Kashan also specialized in blue and white tiles showing decorative patterns with dedicatory or pious inscriptions, used in mosques and tombs. There were also multi-colored tiles forming scenes of hunting, feasting and fighting, for display in private settings.[78] The excellent cobalt blue mined at the nearby village of Qamṣar gave the coloring of these tiles a unique character. The

World Conqueror, II (Manchester, Manchester University Press: 1958) 437, n. 46, and ʿAṭā Malek Jovayni, *Tārikh-e Jahān-Goshā*, ed. M.M. Qazvini, 3 vols. (Leiden, Brill: 1912–37) II:169 n. 3.

78 The shrine of Sulaymān ibn Mūsā offers evidence of continuation of the local tile industry: the tile *miḥrāb* bears the inscription "work of Sayyid Quṭb al-Dīn, a descendant of Ḥusayn, the potter (*Ghaḍā'irī*) in the year 902 [1496–97]. Naraqi, (*supra* n. 73), 174.

cobalt itself was exported as far as China, where it played a role in the development of the famous blue and white porcelain of that country.[79]

The *pax mongolica* favored trade, and Kashan benefited due to its location on several major routes. Until the nineteenth century it was an important stop on the road from Rayy/Tehran to Isfahan and beyond to Shiraz and the Persian Gulf, as well as on the route from Yazd to Rayy. Through Simnan, Kashan communicated with Khorasan and Central Asia. The *pax mongolica* attracted European merchant travelers such as Marco Polo, who seems to have stayed at the famous Zoroastrian town of Gabrābād, near Kashan. Marco Polo reported that one of the three Wise Men came from Kashan itself,[80] and his account is partly confirmed by the travel narrative of Friar Odoric of Pordenone, who in approximately 1320 "halted at the city of the three Magi, which is called Cassan, a royal city and of great repute."[81] Another traveler of the late Ilkhanid period was the Moroccan Ibn Baṭṭūṭa, who reported seeing "Qāshānī" tiles on madrasas and [Sufi] convents, as well as on the Tomb of ʿAlī in Najaf and the bath in Isfahan. He compares these tiles to the faience tiles of North Africa, the *zalīj* or *zulayj*.[82]

The reforming Ilkhanid ruler, Ghāzān Khān (r. 694/1295–703/1304) established "alms houses for *sayyids*" (sing. *dār al-siyāda*), and it is a mark of the importance of Kashan that the city is mentioned in this respect. The historian Ḥāfeẓ-e Abru writes "A number of "alms houses for *sayyids*" were constructed in large cities (*shahr-hā-ye bozorg*) like Kashan, Isfahan and Sivas [in Anatolia]."[83] (It is unusual for Kashan to be called a large city.) These "houses" seem to have been charitable foundations, since they

79 Rose Kerr and Nigel Wood, "Ceramic Technology," *Science and Civilisation in China* 5:12 (Cambridge, U.K., Cambridge University Press: 2004) 628–692.

80 A.V. Williams Jackson, "The Magi in Marco Polo," *Journal of the American Oriental Society* 26 (1905) 79–83. See also Marco Polo, *The Travels of Marco Polo*, trans. Ronald Latham (Harmondsworth, U.K., Penguin: 1958) 27–29, which identifies Gabrābād as "Kala Atashparastan," meaning "Castle of the Fire-Worshippers." Jackson is surely correct in identifying this as reference to a town in the Kashan district.

81 Odoric of Pordenone, *Cathay and the Way Thither*, trans. Henry Yule, 2 vols. (London, Hakluyt Society: 1866), I:50–51. We do not know why Odoric says "royal" city.

82 Ibn Baṭṭūṭa, *The Travels of Ibn Battuta, 1325–1354*, trans. H.A.R. Gibb, 5 vols. (reprint, New Delhi, Munshiram Manoharlal: 1993), I:256 and II:296. *Zalīj* is the term from which Spanish "azulejo" is derived.

83 Hasan Naraqi, *Tārikh-e Ejtemāʿi-ye Kāshān*, (Tehran, Institut d'Études et de Recherches sociales: 1345 solar/1967) 90.

typically included buildings for a mosque, a school, and a place for travelers to rest. Their roles included fostering orphans and housing the indigent. The expenses were to be paid from income on the endowments left in the nearby towns of Bidgol, Mokhtaṣṣābād, and Harāskān. Money was also given for shrouds and burial expenses. Supervision of the establishment and the endowment at Kashan was given to Jalāl al-Dīn Murtaḍā, a grandson of Ḍiyā' al-Dīn Abū Riḍā al-Rāvandī. This grandson was called the "model" (*qudwa*) for great men, and supreme marshal (*naqīb al-nuqabā'*) of the descendants of the Prophet.[84]

The Shi'ite Rāvāndī family was still in strong form at the beginning of the 8th/14th century,[85] as demonstrated by the marriage of a daughter into the ruling family of the Muzaffarids.[86] In his history of this period, Nāṣer al-Din Kermāni (fl. 725/1324) mentions that Abu Ṭāher Ṣafi al-Din Esmā'il, who held Kashan as a kind of fief (*soyurghāl*), showed kindness to "the members of ancient houses" (*boyutāt-e qadim*).[87] As in neighboring Qom, these "ancient houses" very likely included both descendants of long-term Iranian landowners and Arab elites, especially *sayyids*.

With the breakup of the Ilkhanid Empire, Kashan passed briefly under the Īnjū'id ruler of Shiraz, Abū Isḥāq Jamāl al-Dīn, who was in turn defeated and executed by the Muzaffarids in 758/1357. (Both dynasties were patrons of the poet Ḥāfeẓ.) The post-Mongol period continued as a time of prosperity for Kashan. We know that there was a fair amount of building under Muzaffarid patronage.[88] Muzaffarid rule was dispersed among several members of the family, some of whom seem to have resided in Kashan.

TOMB SHRINES

Just as the Zoroastrians had sacralized the landscape before the coming of Islam (a *chahār-tāq* fire temple still survives in the area[89]), the city of

84 This endowment deed of 703/1304 was published by Iraj Afshar, "Vaqf-nāma-ye seh dih dar Kāshān," *Farhang-e Irānzamin*, IV (1335 solar) 122–138.

85 Naraqi, *Tārikh-e Ejtemā'i*, (*supra* n. 83), 90–91 quoting *Ẕayl-e Jāme' al-Tavārikh-e Rashidi* and the *Vaqf-nāma*.

86 Parviz Rajabi, *Kāshān: Negin-e Angoshtari-ye Tārikh-e Irān* (Tehran, Nashr-e Pezhvāk-e Kayrān: 2011) 131.

87 Naraqi, *Tārikh-e Ejtemā'i*, (*supra* n. 83), 56 quoting Kermāni.

88 Naraqi, *Tārikh-e Ejtemā'i*, (*supra* n. 83), *passim*.

89 Naraqi, *Tārikh-e Ejtemā'i*, (*supra* n. 83), 46–47.

Kashan and surrounding lands were re-sacralized through Shiʿism and Sufism, particularly in the 6th/12th through 9th/15th centuries. The prime Sufi example is the Tomb of Bābā Afżal Kāshāni with its handsome conical dome, situated in nearby Maraq.[90] Bābā Afżal lived in the second half of the 6th/12th and first half of the 7th/13th centuries.[91] He was a gifted poet (some of his quatrains were later ascribed to Omar Khayyam) and an outstanding figure in the Sufi philosophical tradition.

The hostility between Shiʿism and Sufism, so strongly developed in later Twelver thought, is not evident in pre-Safavid Kashan.[92] Given the city's loyalty to Shiʿism, tomb shrines of descendants of the Prophet called *imāmzādas* (Persian *emāmzādas*), have always been important in the area. The most prominent of these is the Tomb of ʿAlī, son of Imām Muḥammad al-Bāqir,[93] which as we have noted is situated in the nearby town of Ardahāl. ʿAlī is said to have migrated to this town in 113/731, at the request of the early Shiʿites of Fin (or the Chehel Ḥeṣārān), but he was then martyred by the hostile "governor" of the Umayyads in 116/734. The circumstance that ʿAlī is not buried in the city itself reflects the assumption of Kashan to the role of regional center only through gradual growth.

The tomb had become important at least as early as the Seljuk period, and Ḍiyā' al-Dīn Rāvandī mentions ʿAlī in several poems. Very surprisingly, the shrine is now the setting for a broadly diffused pre-Islamic custom. The ceremony of "carpet washing" in a "healing spring," associated with the story of the "Sulṭān" ʿAlī, said to be buried at this location, takes place on the second Friday of the Persian month of Mehr (September–October). The calculation by non-Islamic date suggests that this widely celebrated event is associated with the Zoroastrian festival of Tirgān, in which water plays a central role.[94]

---

90 Naraqi, *Tārikh-e Ejtemāʿi*, (*supra* n. 83), 351–355.

91 His *terminus ante quem* is 644/1246. Mortaza Qara'i Gorgani, s.v. "Bābā Afżal Kāshānī," in *Dāyerat al-Maʿāref-e Bozorg-e Eslāmi* (*The Great Islamic Encyclopaedia*), X (2001) 735–739, here p. 735.

92 A Sufi treatise by Kamāl al-Dīn ʿAbd al-Razzāq ibn Jalāl al-Dīn Kāshānī shows that the tradition was thriving in the 8th/14th century: *Tuḥfat al-Ikhwān fī Khaṣā'iṣ al-Fityān*, ed. Mohammad Damadi (Tehran, Sherkat-e Enteshārāt-e ʿElmi va-Farhangi: 1991).

93 Naraqi, *Tārikh-e Ejtemāʿi* (*supra* n. 83), 125–145.

94 See Habib Borjian, s.v. "Mašhad-e Ardahāl," *Encyclopaedia Iranica* online edition, 2016, available at http://www.iranicaonline.org/articles/mashad-e-ardahal, viewed 12/11/2016. See Muqaddasī's description of the festival of Tir, reporting that the people of the Kashan area carry receptacles and go to a mountain exuding water where they say, "Water us with thy water because of such and such [reason to be supplied] and

The violent irruption of Timur (Tamerlane) brought about dramatic change in the Iranian dynastic landscape. Kashan in fact submitted to Timur in about 787/1387, and so escaped the horrendous slaughter that befell the inhabitants of nearby Isfahan. After Timur's death (807/1405), his enlightened successors drew on Kashani traditions for the blue and white tile work that became such an important feature of Timurid architecture.

MATHEMATICIANS AND ASTRONOMERS

Timur's grandson Ulugh Beg (governor and subsequently ruler, 811–850/1409–1449) invited the mathematician-astronomers of Kashan to his capital, Samarqand. The development of such talents among Kashanis was at least in part due to the curriculum of the madrasa founded by 'Azīz al-Dīn Kāshī (d. 588/1192). From the same family "the most 'judgely' of judges," 'Imād al-Dīn Yaḥyā ibn Aḥmad al-Kāshī (d. 766/1364–65), was a highly respected author who wrote several treatises on mathematics, a tradition that continued among his descendants.[95]

The practical benefits of mathematical knowledge would have been evident to medieval Kashanis, who, like their neighbors in central Iran, faced challenging tasks in areas such as land surveying, water distribution and tile design.[96] Ghiyāṣ (Ghiyāth in Arabic) al-Din Jamshid Kāshāni (d. 832/1429) was the most brilliant mathematician of the period, having studied in the Madrasa Khān, which was founded in Kashan by Sayyid Laṭif ibn Rokn al-Din, a fifth-generation descendant of the poet Ḍiyā' al-Dīn al-Rāvandī. Here, the rational sciences, including mathematics

they carry away water": *Aḥsan al-Taqāsīm*, (*supra* n. 38), 396–397. A similar practice, Ābrizān or Ābpāshān, observed on the same day of the year was customary among Kashan's coppersmiths until recently: Rajabi, *Kāshān*, (*supra* n. 86), 98 note 3. For a vigorous defense of the historicity of Sulṭān 'Alī, see Ahmad Sajjadi, "Qāli Shuyān," *Dāyerat al-ma'āref-e tashayyu'*, XII (Tehran, Ḥekmat: 1386 solar/2007) 531–533.

95 Naraqi, *Tārikh-e Ejtemā'i*, (*supra* n. 83), 82; Rajabi, *Kāshān*, (*supra* n. 86), 193.

96 The potential connections between irrigation works and mathematics are shown by Moḥammad Karaji, an Iranian mathematician of the early 5th/11th century, in his treatise on math and hydrology; see Mehdi Nadji and Rudolf Voigt, "'Exploration for Hidden Water' by Mohammad Karaji—the Oldest Textbook on Hydrology," *Ground Water* X:5 (1972) 43–46. Nevertheless, the relations between artisans and scientists remain problematic; see George Saliba, "Book review: Artisans and Mathematicians in Islamic Architecture by Gulru Necipoğlu," *Journal of the American Oriental Society* 119 (1999) 637–645.

and astronomy, were an important part of the curriculum.[97] Early in his career Jamshid, also known as al-Kāshi, was invited to the Timurid capital of Samarqand, under the patronage of Timur's grandson, Ulugh Beg, one of most mathematically gifted rulers of the medieval era. Jamshid's enormous talent had supposedly been immediately recognized by another astronomer, on discovering him in an astrolabe shop in Kashan.[98] An entire chapter of Jamshid's treatise on calculation (*ḥisāb*) is devoted to architectural problems, such as the design of *muqarnas* patterns.[99] He seems to have been in Samarqand at the same time as his nephew, Mo'in al-Din. The latter was another Kashani mathematician-astronomer who worked for the Timurids, as did his astronomer son, Manṣur al-Kāshi.[100]

We have a letter from Jamshid to his father, who remained in Kashan, showing that the latter also understood mathematics and astronomy. Applying the characteristic mix of flattery and self-promotion, in correct manner for the times, Jamshid writes:

> Thanks to divine guidance, to the solicitude of His Majesty who uttered the words "You can solve it," and by the blessing of the good wishes of the master [my father], which are always with me, the whole content of that book including [that] difficult problem ... was solved.[101]

We know that Jamshid travelled back and forth between Kashan and Samarqand and that he completed a book in Kashan on 10 Dhū al-Ḥijja

97 Naraqi, *Tārikh-e Ejtemā'i*, (*supra* n. 83), 94. On *Sayyid* Laṭīf, see Maraghi, "Madāres," (*supra* n. 19), 73–74.
98 See, among others, Jafar Taheri, "Mathematical Knowledge of Architecture in the Works of Kâshânî," *Nexus Network Journal* 11 (2009) 77–88, here p. 82.
99 Jamshid Kāshāni, *Miftāḥ al-Ḥisāb*, ed. Nadir al-Nabulsi (Damascus, Wizārat al-Ta'līm al-'Alī: 1977) 353–391.
100 V.V. Barthold, *Four Studies in the History of Central Asia* (Leiden, Brill: 1956); Rajabi, *Kāshān*, (*supra* n. 86), 193. [I have chosen to use Persian transliteration for the names of the famous mathematician Jamshid al-Kāshi and his relatives as well as for the madrasa founder who was a fifth-generation descendant of Ḍiyā' al-Dīn, the poet of Arabic verse.]
101 Mohammad Bagheri, "A Newly Found Letter of al-Kashi on Scientific Life in Samarqand," *Historia Mathematica* 24:3 (1997) 241–256, here p. 250.

818/10 February 1416, under the patronage of Sultan Iskandar, a different Timurid ruler.[102]

TURCOMAN PERIOD

After Timurid rule, Kashan entered under control of the Turcoman dynasties, first the Qara-Qoyunlu and subsequently the Aq-Qoyunlu. The Qara-Qoyunlu ruled Isfahan on and off until their defeat in 874/1469. The wife of Jahān-Shāh Qara-Qoyunlu seems to have been particularly generous to Kashan, both in constructing buildings and endowing charities.[103] Documents and inscriptions from the 9th/15th century provide excellent insight into the city in this period. The foundation deed (*vaqf-nāma*) of the Mir ʿEmād Mosque (or Masjed-e Maydān) is the longest of these documents. The surviving copy is written on 23 Rajab 877/January 1472, following the death of the mosque founder. ʿEmād al-Din Shirvāni (d. 872/1467), a minister of Jahān-Shāh, endows the mosque, a Sufi convent (*khāneqāh*) and a bath house situated next to a school (Madrasa-ye Khān), with two of the eighty-eight portions of the *qanāt* named Esfidābād, of the village of Fin; the endowment includes further properties, among which are an oil-press, blacksmith shop and bakery. This document details a fair amount of agricultural property (one hundred and eleven *jarībs*), including farms (sing. *mazraʿa*) with accompanying water rights in Muhadhdhabābād and Naṣrābād.[104] The salaries of the ulema and staff are specified, down to the sweeper, as well as the stipends of the teacher and students in the school to be held at the mosque. The students are to be examined every six months to see if they are worthy of their stipends.[105]

102 Edward S. Kennedy, "A Letter of Jamshid al-Kāshi to His Father: Scientific Research and Personalities at a Fifteenth Century Court," *Orientalia* 29:2 (1960) 191–213, here p. 206. Jamshid also completed the further work *Sollam al-samā'* in Kashan, in March 1407, before travelling to Samarqand; see Petra G. Schmidl, s.v. "Kāshī," in Thomas Hockey *et al.*, (eds.), *The Biographical Encyclopedia of Astronomers*, I (Springer, New York: 2007) 613–615.

103 Naraqi, *Tārikh-e Ejtemāʿi*, (*supra* n. 83), 74.

104 A "small" *jarīb* was sixty cubits by fifty cubits. The Iranian *jarīb* varied locally from 400 to 1450 square meters. See C.E. Bosworth, s.v. "Misāḥa (measurement of plane surfaces), 1. In the central Islamic lands," *The Encyclopaedia of Islam*, 2nd ed., VII (1993) 137–138.

105 Żarrābi, (*supra* n. 76), 507–521; Husayn Shahshahani, "Kholāṣa-e az Vaqfnāma-ye Masjed-e Mir ʿEmād," *Farhang-e Irānzamin* V (1336 solar) 23–50.

Another deed dated 877/1473 establishes an endowment for a *khāniqāh* situated opposite and to the right side of the mosque, facing "a building for time and hour," which would appear to be a type of clock or astronomical tower. The new building is to be a residence for the ulema, "the poor" [Sufis], the pious, and "the pure." The endower awards both the *khāniqāh* and the clock tower with both water rights and properties "in the neighborhood of Kashan," and some on the road to Bidgol. There is mention of a hospital (*dār al-shefā'*) and salary and equipment for the "astronomer," Fakhr al-Din 'Ali, who worked in the tower.[106] Many positions, including those for upkeep of the tower, are to be continued by inheritance.

By the time Giosafat Barbaro, Venetian ambassador to Uzun Ḥasan (r. 871–883/1466–1478), visited Kashan, the major exports were in textiles. This would remain true until the early twentieth century. Barbaro wrote:

> We found a well inhabited city called Cassan, where for the most part they make silks and cotton in so great quantity that he who would spend ten thousand ducats in a day may find enough of that merchandise to spend it on.[107]

Other important textile exports included rugs and felt.

MINT CITY

Kashan's nearly continuous status as a mint for silver dirhams and gold dinars is testimony to the robustness of its economy throughout the medieval era. The written sources record large issues of gold coins in the 5th/11th century under the Buyids.[108] Shortly after that came an issue of gold coins under the Great Seljuk, Alp Arslān, in 457/1064–65.[109] There are

106 Shahshahani, "Kholāṣa," 39–50. Żarrābi, (*supra* n. 76), 523–529. Fifteenth-century Italian clocks are common in North Africa; it is unclear what kind of clock is meant here.
107 Giosafat Barbaro, *Travels to Tana and Persia by Josafa (Giosafat) Barbaro and Ambrogio Contarini*, trans. William Thomas and S.A. Roy (London, Franklin: 1873 [reprint 1963]) 72 (adapted to contemporary English).
108 Luke Treadwell, *Buyid Coinage: A Die Corpus* (Oxford, Ashmolean Museum: 2001), does not list any Buyid coins from Kashan/Qashan. However, Ibn al-Athīr, *al-Kāmil*, (*supra* n. 77), VIII:153 and 254, under the years 416 and 428 (1025–26 and 1036–37), mentions Qāshāni dinars, both in his accounts of a wheat price of 200 dinars (in Baghdad, considered extremely high) and a (royal) dowry of 50,000 dinars.
109 N.M. Lowick, "Seljuk Coins," *The Numismatic Chronicle*, 7th series, X (1970) 241–251.

also Kashan coins from the times of the Ilkhanids, Jalayirids, Muzaffarids, Timurids, the Qara-Qoyunlu and Aq-Qoyunlu.[110] Coins of the Ilkhanid Abū Sa'īd (r. 716–36/1316–35) survive in abundance,[111] among them a double dirham of 726. The Abū Sa'īd coins could all be from a single trove, perhaps discovered in the nineteenth century. Nevertheless, the variety of dates testify to a city that thrived under several of the later Ilkhanids. The presence of a mint continued through the Safavid period.

TAX INCOME

The sources offer scarce but valuable information on the tax income from Kashan. However, it is difficult to know the true buying power of the incomes reported, the fineness of the coinage metals, or the underlying principles of tax collection.[112] *The History of Qom* (378/988–89) reports two different surveys, describing the estimated taxes for Kashan as 158,192 dirhams or 181,092 dirhams.[113] Ibn Khurradādhbih gives the combined average annual tax revenues from Qom and Kashan as three million dirhams (compared to the four and a half million dirhams from Azerbaijan).[114] Al-Muqaddasī (who is somewhat careless with figures) gives the land tax of Kashan as one million dirhams.[115] In 740/1346 the learned polymath Ḥamd-Allāh Mostawfi Qazvini says that the revenue of Kashan and its district was 117,000 dinars (compared to 275,000 dinars for Tabriz), which at the rate of ten dirhams to a dinar would make 1,170,000 dirhams: an income considerably greater than that indicated in the citations from the 4th/10th-century *History of Qom*.[116]

---

110 Eduard von Zambaur, *Die Münzprägungen des Islams*, I (Wiesbaden, Steiner: 1968). This very dated but valuable book lists Kashan coins for the dynasties mentioned.

111 See Judith Kolbas, *The Mongols in Iran* (London, Routledge: 2006) 276, n. 47. Many of the Abū Sa'īd coins were struck in 729 A.H., which suggests that they came from a hoard. See Zambaur, (*supra* n. 110), I:202. There are also numerous Muzaffarid coins from Kashan. On a hoard of Kashan coins minted by Abū Isḥāq, see Rajabi, *Kāshān*, (*supra* n. 86), 130, note 3.

112 Ibn Ḥawqal, *al-Masālik wa-l-Mamālik*, ed. M.J. de Goeje (Leiden, Brill: 1872) 259, who flourished 331–378/943–988, says that Kashan is a city that "brings in high tax income."

113 Qomi, (*supra* n. 3), 349. The repetition of ninety-two in both estimates is suspicious.

114 Ibn Khurradādhbih, (*supra* n. 9), 244.

115 Muqaddasī, (*supra* n. 38), 400.

116 Ḥamd-Allāh Mostawfi Qazvini, *The Geographical Part of the Nuzhat al-Qulūb*, trans. Guy Le Strange (London, Luzac and Leiden, Brill: 1919) 72. The non-Islamic *tamgha* tax imposed on commerce in the Ilkhanid period remained in place until the

CONCLUSION

Kashan emerged as a small city in part because of the shift in wealth brought about by the Arab conquests. Arabs acquired capital during these events and created new cities or enlarged existing cities, thereby expanding urban life in early Islamic Iran. The long period of stability between the Arab conquest in the seventh century and the invasion by the Ghuzz Turks in the late Seljuk period allowed cities to flourish. This was the case for Kashan, which in some senses was a new city. When there was strong central rule such as under the Ilkhanids, Kashan and other cities with primary resources and artisanal skills could participate advantageously in intercity trade.

Historians of Iran usually consider mountainous territories as areas of refuge. Although not in a mountainous area, Kashan served as a refuge by virtue of its small size and distance from major cities. Military occupations of smaller cities would have been hard to sustain, due to limitations of both food and plunder. It was thanks to its relative remoteness that Kashan was able to have Shiʿite madrasas and judges. The Shiʿite families who largely controlled Kashan benefited the resident population by promoting extensive public works, such as the construction of city walls and maintenance of irrigation systems. Kashan sometimes fell under the sway of the rulers of Rayy, but more continuously under those of Isfahan. The Shiʿite elites of Kashan strove for good relations with the Sunni elites who dominated in these capital cities.

Kashan's comparative prosperity depended on its *qanāt*-based agriculture, a location on important routes, the continual nurturing of artisanal traditions, and an emphasis on education. It was fortunate to have leaders, and sometimes rulers, who invested in trusts for the support of institutions such as schools and charities. Education enabled Kashanis to acquire patronage as bureaucrats and astronomers. These individuals then often patronized their home city. Non-educational charitable institutions sustained the social fabric of a society with highly disparate levels of income. The continuity of elites, reinforced in Kashan by the presence of *sayyids*, fostered stability (and surely stifled some talents) across turbulent centuries of changes of regime. Kashan was considerably smaller than Isfahan and somewhat smaller than its Shiʿite neighbor, Qom. However, diverse sources indicate that Kashan maintained a relatively robust civic and regional life from the 4th/10th century through the 9th/15th century.

---

early Safavid period and may be one reason that later tax income is higher. We are assuming that dinar here means a gold coin and dirham means a silver coin.

Faith and Practice: Muslims in Historic Cairo

The main body of this essay is devoted to a discussion of the Muslim liturgical year, the annual cycle of public religious observance. This will involve the private and public devotional lives of Muslims, [more specifically in historic Cairo]. In addition, some of the changes in religious observances [in Cairo] over the years will be discussed, and those observances described in both the past and the present.

The Islamic revelation sees itself as Adamic, since God's kindness has provided man with spiritual guidance from the time of the first man. This recurrent revelation was monotheistic from the start but became more dramatically so from the time of the Prophet Abraham, who smashed idols and openly defied polytheism. With the coming of Islam, revelation is perfected for mankind. This perfected revelation is largely contained in the Qur'ān, the full body of the formal revelations received by the Prophet Muḥammad. The great majority of Muslims accept the Qur'ān as the stable center of their belief. In time, the behavior of the Prophet, presumably because he was the best qualified to understand the revelation, became a supplement to the Qur'ān as a source of correct Islamic behavior. The general word for correct behavior became *sharīʿa*, or "way," which included many precepts concerning reward or punishment not in this world but in the next. *Sharīʿa* eventually became the term for Islamic law.

Before turning to Muslim devotional life, its possible and actual relations to its legitimating sources should be mentioned. The broad agreement on the centrality of the Qur'ān left some important questions

---

Author's note: This article was first published as: "Faith and Practice: Muslims in Historic Cairo," in Farhad Daftary, Elizabeth W. Fernea and Azim Nanji (eds.), *Living in Historic Cairo: Past and Present in an Islamic City* (Seattle, WA, Azimuth Editions, London, in association with the Institute of Ismaili Studies; University of Washington Press: 2010) 104–116. Reproduced with permission.

unresolved. Does it correspond to the "Guarded Tablet" referred to in the Qur'ān, apparently an archetype of perfect revelation that exists in heaven? If this archetype is something beyond any specific language, does the interpretation of it into a specific human language such as Arabic deprive it of some of its clarity? Such disputes, with their various strategies intended to interpret scripture, are characteristic of great scriptural traditions. To make an analogy, in the study of the United States Constitution, for example, we see, on the one hand, those who regard the historically determined specific intent of the framers as the paramount criterion for interpretation and, on the other hand, those who believe that the widely expressed intent of the framers is "justice" as the paramount criterion. For the latter group provisions should be interpreted in a sense most likely to result in the doing of justice.

In a broad sense two streams of interpretation exist in the Islamic tradition, a scholastic tradition and an anti-scholastic tradition. Both would agree that it is sometimes important to know the specific circumstances of revelation; is a passage in the Qur'ān addressed to a limited group, or to an individual, or to all mankind or to all Creation? Both would also agree that it is important to recover the lexical and grammatical world of the time of revelation. But the anti-scholastic would feel that at this point he/she could immediately apprehend the meaning and implication of revelation, whereas the scholastic would have many more questions: is the language metamorphic, hortatory, etc.

In any case, in pre-modern times the general Muslim understanding of religion was continuous and it has enveloped such figures so important to Christians as Jesus, Mary and John the Baptist. This places Muslims in the mainstream of the Abrahamic tradition of Jews and Christians that sees the Creation as the beginning of things and judgment leading to heaven or hell as the end of things. Many modern believers, in all three Abrahamic faiths, have tried to reinterpret these beliefs. Islam shared with other Abrahamic monotheisms the dilemmas that seem to be created by belief in an almighty God: is there free will or predestination; could God's omnipotence create objects beyond His control, and the like. The radical monotheism of the Qur'ān, as generally understood, made some of these problems easier and some harder to resolve. Rejection of the Trinity removed the Christian problem of the status of Jesus as an intermediary but posed a dramatic problem regarding how to know God, since many Muslims felt that God was only describable by His entire difference from worldly things. A rich literature of Muslim devotional works makes clear that such philosophical problems did not affect the devotional life. The extraordinary presence and influence of Sufism, the mystical orientation among Muslims, from the eleventh to the twenty-first century show that the individual's striving to find the divine within themselves remained a vital part of the life of many Muslims.

For all the different interpretative and theological strategies of Muslims, the vast majority agreed on the basic forms of worship expected of them. Many Qur'an commentaries on IV:94 assert in various words that people who pray to the *qibla* [i.e., in the direction of the house of Abraham constructed in Mecca and the focus of Muslim pilgrimage] do not call each other unbelievers. When asked to define Islam, many Muslims will quote the saying ascribed to the Prophet in which he sets out the five principal duties of Muslims: to perform the daily prayers, to give alms, to fast in the month of Ramadan, to perform the pilgrimage to Mecca, and to bear witness there is no god save God and that Muḥammad is the Messenger of God. All of these fundamentals of religion are acts, even though the last act is a testimony to a belief. This essay describes these acts and the way in which they explain the life of the believer. It should be remembered that Muslims use a lunar calendar of twelve months, which is approximately eleven days shorter than the solar year, and therefore "annual events" in this lunar calendar move over time through all four seasons.

The obligatory prayers are said five times a day, once at dawn, once at noon, once halfway to sunset, once at sunset, and once when night has closed in. As can be seen, these times are determined by observation; the time for the mid-afternoon prayer is the moment when a stick casts a shadow half its length. The act of obligatory prayer consists mainly of a prescribed number of "bowings," which include recitation both of the Qur'ān and of pious formulas, as well as movements which include the worshipper placing his hands, nose and forehead on the ground. Such prostration is understood to engender humility before God. A ḥadīth relates that God states: "I accept the Worship only of him who humbles himself before My Greatness and does not exalt himself over Me, and feeds the needy for the sake of [the vision of] My Face."[1] Worship in the obligatory prayers is an aspect of *dhikr*, "mindfulness," of God, frequently

1 E.E. Calverley, *Worship in Islam, Being a Translation with Commentary and Introduction of al-Ghazzālī* (Cairo: 1957) 55.

mentioned in the Qur'ān and with the implication that one should both keep God present in the mind and make mention of God.

On Fridays (except among certain Shi'ites) an extra congregational prayer of two "bowings" replaces the usual noon prayer. All Muslims who are able should attend; hence specific mosques (*masjid*, literally, place of prostration) like the Cairene Mosque of 'Amr ibn al-'Āṣ, founded by this conqueror of Egypt, are given the appellation of *masjid jāmi'* or congregational mosque. In these mosques, after the Friday prayer has been said a sermon is preached. (Some Muslims reverse the order and put the sermon before the prayer.) The preacher customarily stands on a high place; hence the beautiful pulpits that adorn most Cairo mosques. The sermon consists of two parts with a brief pause between, and it was an established element of the second part to offer a prayer on behalf of all Muslims. It became customary to mention the ruler's name in the sermon, an important act recognizing a claim to sovereignty. When the Fatimid general Jawhar entered Egypt in 969 C.E., he immediately went to the Mosque of 'Amr and had the Friday sermon preached in the name of the Fatimid caliph, then still in Ifrīqīya.[2]

Alongside this daily and weekly schedule of obligatory prayers there are the prayers at the festivals and the non-obligatory or supererogatory prayers which are so prominent in the life of Muslims. The liturgical year of feast and fasts, especially among Egyptians who have grown so fond of the birthdays of their "saints," is as full of solemnity and celebration for the Muslim as one could desire.

The tenth day of Muḥarram, the first month of the year, was a voluntary day of fasting, and celebrated as such by the Sunni Muslims. For Shi'ite Muslims, however, it is the day of the martyrdom of Ḥusayn, the grandson of the Prophet, whose killing is seen by Shi'ites as history's blackest betrayal of a saintly figure, one who was the rightful and divinely guided leader of the Muslims. The tragic events leading up to and following Ḥusayn's martyrdom make all of the first twelve days of Muḥarram occasions for mourning. In Fatimid times the head of Ḥusayn was transferred to Cairo where a special section of the caliphal palace was devoted to it. Although Egyptians have for centuries been Sunnis and no longer have public mourning ceremonies like the Shi'ites on 'Āshūrā', anyone who has visited the Mosque of "Our Master" Ḥusayn knows the intensity of

2 Paula Sanders, *Ritual, Politics and the City in Fatimid Cairo* (Albany, N.Y.: 1994) 44.

emotion that surrounds it. Its importance as a congregational mosque is such that overflowing crowds are to be found on adjacent streets praying on mats and rugs every Friday at noon. Even today the highest Muslim officials come to it to pray on the days of the great festivals.

The twelfth day of the third month, Rabīʿ I, is the great *mawlid al-Nabī*, the celebration of the Prophet's birthday, and is in some ways the model for the "birthdays" of holy men and women that fill the Egyptian religious calendar. In Cairo the popular celebration of this birthday dates back at least to the 7th/13th century.[3]

The great English scholar E.W. Lane, describing the Prophet's birthday in 1834, tells of the enormous tents erected, mostly for the Sufis, the devotees of the mystical interpretation of Islam, whose ceremonies are called *dhikr*, the mindfulness and mention of God discussed above. Many lanterns, some of them in fanciful shapes, illuminated the festival which went on night and day for nine days. Swings for children, rope dancers, sweet sellers, storytellers, all added to the semi-carnival atmosphere that surrounded this and many lesser *mawlid*s. Professional reciters sang poems that use the language of love as an expression of religious longing. For many years, on the actual day the master of the Saʿdī Sufis rode his horse over the backs of devotees, but legal scholars disliked this public "miracle," and it has long been abandoned. Similarly, there were ecstatic Sufi-inspired women dancers, whose presence in public was sometimes tolerated and sometimes not.[4]

The emergence of the Prophet's birthday as a major festival reflected an increasing interest in personal devotion to the Prophet. Most learned Muslims accept accounts of the Prophet which emphasize his claim to be a man like other men, principally distinguished by his mission to receive and transmit revelation, and hence called "the Messenger" (*rasūl*). The greatest (some would say only) "miracle" he performed was to pass on the Qur'ān to humankind. Yet, in time, most popular and even some learned believers openly identified the "light of Muḥammad" with the "principal light" which was the first thing created. To tell stories of the Prophet or sing poems in his honor came to be meritorious acts in themselves and were the model of much other literature not of the high tradition. And yet the

3 H. Fuchs and F. de Jong, "*Mawlid*," *The Encyclopaedia of Islam*, 2nd ed. (hereafter *EI*²), VI (Leiden, Brill: 1991) 895–897.

4 E.W. Lane, *An Account of the Manners and Customs of Modern Egyptians* (New York: 1973) 442ff.

antagonism of those who believed in a more austere version of Islam and rejected these celebrations never died away. Occasionally, governments even supported this austere view.

The next month, Rabīʿ II, is witness to what used to be the second most celebrated *mawlid* in Egypt, named after "the two Ḥasans," Ḥasan and Ḥusayn, the grandsons of the Prophet, of whom Ḥusayn is by far the more important, in part because of his martyrdom referred to above. This *mawlid* was widely celebrated in and around al-Darb al-Aḥmar district, so close to the Mosque of Our Master Ḥusayn, and where many shops stayed open all night. The day after the event Qur'ān readers could still be seen in the area, for many visitors paid for the entire Qur'ān to be recited (or, more accurately, to be cantillated), which would take four reciters, relieving each other at intervals, about nine hours. The actual recital of the revealed book, itself a miracle in part because of the unique beauty of its language, is a pious act whether performed in private or in public; and the proper cantillation of the text by professional reciters can have variations that delight the listener and enhance what is seen to be the majesty of the text.

The festival of Sayyida Zaynab, or Our Mistress Zaynab, the sister of Ḥusayn and the granddaughter of the Prophet, which takes place in the middle of the seventh month, or Rajab, is one of several festivals commemorating a saintly woman. It is a measure of the intensity of popular feeling that her mosque is the only mosque other than that of Ḥusayn at which non-Muslims are not welcome. At those times when women visitors are numerous in the inner sanctuary it is considered out of bounds to men.

The night of 27 Rajab commemorates the *miʿrāj*, the Prophet's miraculous ascension to Heaven, usually understood to be the topic of the Qur'ānic verse: "Glory be to He who has carried His servant by night from the sacred mosque to *al-Masjid al-Aqṣā* (the farthest mosque) which We have surrounded by blessings (or "whose enclosure We have blessed"), in order that We might show him certain of our signs; He is the All-Hearing, the All-Seeing (XVII:50)." That such an event was an occasion for story and legend is no surprise. On the night of the *miʿrāj* the Cairene Sufis until recently carried out the same variety of ceremonies as they had at the *mawlid al-Nabī*. Storytelling was strongly associated with this festival, especially stories of the Prophet's Night Journey. These stories sometimes grew in popular telling to encompass a glamorous journey through the seven heavens with descriptions of all parts of the cosmos. For the pious, the Night Journey became symbolic of the journey of the deceased to the presence of the Throne of the Divine judge. For Sufis it was also the archetype of the journey of the soul from its attachment to the physical world to its release into the world of pure consciousness of God.[5]

The *mawlid* of the very great jurist, al-Shāfiʿī, (d. 820), is commemorated near the beginning of the eighth month, Shaʿbān. This descendant of the Prophet's tribe, Quraysh, was born in Ascalon and died in Cairo at the age of forty-seven. A brilliant student of lslamic learning, he gave system to the young science of Islamic law and in the process may have helped the legal disciplines to gain precedence over theology. After two centuries of rule by the Shiʿite Fatimids, the Sunni dynasty of Saladin, who had conquered Egypt in 1171, sought to make the tomb of al-Shāfiʿī, an intellectual hero of the Sunnis, as popular as the Holy Shrines of the Shiʿites, such as the mosque of Ḥusayn. Al-Shāfiʿī's resting place is the largest freestanding mausoleum in Egypt, built in Cairo in 1211. The shrine is not only filled at the time of the *mawlid* but also daily by many visitors, including the ill, who are borne in litters around the cenotaph. For those who seek Shāfiʿī's spiritual guidance and/or intercession there is even a place to post letters to him.

Two weeks later comes the night of the middle of Shaʿban, which has some of the character of a New Year's Day in that it is felt to be the turning point of the year. It is often called the night of the *barāʾa*, the Absolution. A special prayer is recited after the evening prayer and the 36th chapter of the Qurʾān, Sūrat Yāsīn, is recited, after which the believers offer their personal prayers. In Egypt this night is associated with the *sidrat al-muntahā*, the lote tree that sits at that point which is the closest a person can come to God and beyond which no one can pass. Legend has claimed that this tree has as many leaves as there are people. The tree is shaken on this night and the leaves inscribed with the names of those destined to die in the coming year fall off. The awe felt at the boundary between divine knowledge and human knowledge (which is limited by ignorance of the time of one's end) made this popular story a favorite theme of Muslim poets.

With the sighting of the new moon at the end of Shaʿbān, the ninth month, Ramaḍān, begins. In this month, believers fast from sunrise to sunset. (Muslim days and dates run from sunset to sunset.) Many Egyptians

5 B. Schrieke, *et al.*, "*Miʿradj*,", *EI*², VII (Leiden, Brill: 1993) 97–105.

who observe the daily prayers indifferently feel the Fast to be an iron obligation. The ill, the infirm, pregnant or nursing women and children are exempt, as are travelers who make a journey of more than three days, but these latter must make up the fast days missed at some other time of the year.

For most Muslims this is a time of heroism and inner purification. This month of fasting is not seen as a hardship (although when it falls in summer it is a considerable feat). Yet anyone who has fasted knows the sense of surprise that one feels afterwards when one allows oneself to drink or eat. And the denial of other sensual pleasures, including sex, during the daytime gives the one who fasts the sense of mastery over the "lower self." The Prophet is reported to have said that in this way fasting becomes the "gateway to divine service." It is also one of the main duties of Muslims, the fulfillment of which is visible to God alone.[6]

The great Sunni theologian al-Ghazālī explains that there is a higher stage of observance of the Fast since the Prophet is reported to have said five things annul it: lying, backbiting, slander, a false oath and a "glance of passion." Concentration on the name of God and recitation of the Qur'ān is the fast of the tongue; refraining from listening to evil the fast of the ears. But at its highest level: "The fruit of hunger is contemplation of God, of which the forerunner is mortification. Contemplation is the battlefield of humans, whereas mortification is the playground of children."[7]

For the ordinary Muslims of Cairo, however, the Ramadan fast has the excitement of a world half turned upside down. In Cairo, families eat a glorious pre-dawn brunch which may include specialties prescribed in family tradition. After the dawn prayer, work and even schools begin earlier to accommodate the early start of daily life. By the noon prayer some of the festive spirit of the pre-dawn brunch has worn thin. The working day ceases for most Muslims in the early afternoon, and by late afternoon many Muslims are at home resting (which often turns into sleep). Immediately after sunset the believer prays, then eats lightly, smokes if so inclined, then sits down to a serious meal, which includes meat for those who can afford it.

This schedule implies a shift of emphasis from day to night, when the most emotionally resonant events take place. The pious spend much of the night in supererogatory prayers called *tarāwīḥ*, in which many of

---

6 G.E. von Grunebaum, *Muhammadan Festivals* (Ottawa: 1976) 57.

7 *Ibid.*, 58–59.

the "bowings" that are the essential units of the obligatory prayers are performed. These may be interspersed or followed by readings from the Qur'ān, and the larger mosques are open all night for prayer. In Cairo many go home to sleep a few hours before the early brunch preceding the "daybreak prayer." But many also go to coffee shops or to the numerous tents put up for the month, both to meet friends and to listen to the musicians and, especially, the reciters of tales who come into their own more on these nights than on other occasions. In shops nowadays, which are often gaudily strung with "Christmas tree" lights, and where thin, newly baked pastries with a pleasing but never filling taste of honey are served, reciters tell the exploits of figures such as 'Antara. This son of a black slave girl, who in history and in legend was already a hero before the Prophet appeared in the 1st/7th century, lives on for several centuries among the storytellers to fight for the good, even dealing the Crusaders heavy blows in the 5th/11th century. It is no surprise that older texts of *The Thousand and One Nights* seem to be prompt texts for reciters of this ingenious collection of stories. As the Ramadan fast obliges the believer to feel that normal daytime pleasures are not to be taken for granted, Cairene Ramadan nights give a sense of the wondrous world that ordinary nights of sleep so lack.

The crown of Ramadan is the night of the twenty-seventh, called *Laylat al-Qadr*, "The Night of Power (or Destiny or Decree)." This night is discussed in the Qur'ān, where it is declared "better than a thousand months. The Angels and the Spirit descended with the permission of their Lord to regulate everything. It is Peace until the rising of the dawn" (XCVII:3–5). It is understood that the "Angels" and "the Spirit" are free from their usual charges and engaged in blessing mankind. Moreover, tradition relates, as the gates of heaven have been opened, prayer enters freely and is more certain of success; and many Muslims pray fervently on this night. It is said that on this night all animal and vegetable kind bow down to God in adoration, thereby assuring the universal peace that envelops Creation on this occasion.

The first day of the next month, Shawwāl, is one of the two days properly designated "festival" (*'īd*) in the Islamic liturgical calendar. It is called the "Festival of Breaking the Fast," or, simply, the "Lesser Festival." While giving alms is an important part of the preceding month of fasting, this Lesser Festival is above all about almsgiving. It is felt fitting that after a month of restraint and self-purification, those believers able to do so should give whatever they might still owe morally to others in order to complete the "change" that the Fast has effected. After a special prayer of two "bowings," a sermon, and spontaneous prayer, the congregants, usually dressed in their finest, visit their friends, warmly greeting even remote acquaintances, affirming the ties strengthened by the Fast. On this festival, which continues for a few days, Cairenes go out to the City of the Dead at Qarāfa carrying branches of palm and sweet basil to put on the tombs. While women were the majority of visitors to the dead a century ago, such visits are (now) occasions when men and women associate with each other fairly freely, as they do in the *mawlids*.[8]

Egyptian control of the Hijaz, the province that contains Mecca, Medina and all the places essential to the Pilgrimage proper, was effective during much of the Fatimid (969–1171), Ayyubid (1171–1250), and Mamluk (1250–1517) periods. Egyptian domination meant that the Pilgrimage caravan from Egypt with its government-appointed "Commander of the Pilgrimage" had precedence over other caravans. At some time in this period Egypt acquired the honor of providing the "covering" (*kiswa*) for the Ka'ba, the rectangular structure called "the house of God," said to have been built first by Adam and rebuilt by Abraham, which pilgrims must circumambulate. For most of the past eight hundred years the "covering" has been designed and constructed in Egypt, and it was long the custom for the "covering" to be put on display on the sixth day of Shawwāl in the mosque of Ḥusayn until the departure of the Pilgrimage. In 1834 Lane, witnessing the parade of military bands and Sufi dervishes that accompanied the "covering" to its place of display, mentions a mounted man "fantastically dressed in sheepskins" and wearing "a high skin cap and a grotesque false beard" who occasionally pretended to write legal opinions with a stick.[9] Clearly an element of mockery of high authority, not only of great legal authorities but of the sultan himself, made a sly appearance in some of these great public events.

In the latter part of Shawwāl the principal officials of the Pilgrimage used to pass from the Citadel, which dominates the city visually, along a procession route, accompanied by the *maḥmal,* which is a square frame of wood covered with richly embroidered panels and silver crescents that is carried on the back of a tall camel. On one of the front panels is a representation

8 Lane, (*supra* n. 4), 480; see also Louis Massignon, *Opera Minora*, 3 (Beirut: 1963) 237. Due to the demolition of many shrines in recent years, this practice is no longer the same in 2022.

9 Lane, (*supra* n. 4), 483.

of the enclosure of the Ka'ba together with the sultan's cartouche. Until 1952 the *maḥmal* was a symbol both of the holy and communal nature of the Pilgrimage and of the sultanic authority that supervised and patronized the Pilgrimage caravan.

It seems not at all inappropriate that in the Islamic tradition, usually so opposed to physical representations of divine things, the "clothing" of the most holy building and of the beast that accompanied the pilgrims in their journey to this most holy place, should be a focus of such loving care. To walk in procession to see off and then to welcome home this caravan (for the *maḥmal* returned) was one way in which Cairene Muslims as a community indirectly participated in the Pilgrimage.

The twelfth and final month of the year is literally called Dhū al-Hijja, the "Month of the Pilgrimage" (to Mecca). Pious tradition makes the site of the Ka'ba the first place devoted to the One God, and the Black Stone, embedded in the walls of the Ka'ba, the object which holds the covenant between man and God. It is moreover of cosmological significance, as it was and sometimes still is seen as the spiritual axis of the world, the most central place on the earth, the first spot at which dry land appeared over the waters and the place at which the upper and lower worlds communicate. It is, in terms of place, what *Laylat al-Qadr* or the Night of Power is in terms of time.

The pilgrim approaching the Hijaz must at certain set points put him or herself in a state of *iḥrām*, "consecration," which is not only a state of ritual cleanliness but also of dress in a simple cloak-like garment. Like the Fast, a state of consecration will be broken by certain acts such as sexual relations, and Muslim thinkers notice and speculate on the similarity.[10]

Throughout the Pilgrimage the pilgrim must form the "intention" to do an act before performance of the act. Many Muslims feel this pattern should fill their lives, for God judges humankind by intentions and not acts; circumstance can intervene in all sorts of ways that prevent the fulfillment of a sincere intention.

The actual rites of the Pilgrimage are rather complicated, and groups of pilgrims generally have a guide. On the tenth day of the Month of the Pilgrimage the pilgrim (or group of pilgrims) must slaughter a sheep, goat, a bovine or a camel in commemoration of God's substitution of an animal for Abraham's son (identified as Ismā'īl, Ishmael, by most contemporary

10 Von Grunebaum, (*supra* n. 6), 27.

Muslims, but as Isaac in the Old Testament). At present, great care is taken that this food be given to the poor. This festival is celebrated on the same day by Muslims everywhere in the world and is called the Great Festival or the Festival of Sacrifice. In discussing this sacrifice, the Qur'ān specifically discusses the relation between ritual and belief: "For every religious community we have established a rite (or, 'place to perform a rite')" (XXII:34); and: "Neither their flesh or their blood will ever reach to God; but the reverential fear/piety from you will reach Him" (XXII:37). Just as the repeated refrain in the obligatory prayer is: "God is Great," so the repeated refrain of the pilgrim is *labbayka*, "I heed Thy call/I am at Thy service."

According to a popular etymology a much-used word for sacrifice, *qurbān*, reflects the effort to grow close to God; and, indeed, the repeated explanation of much pious behavior is that it is "seeking closeness to God." The longing for the Beatific Vision, seeing the Face of God, is an honorable goal in the eyes of most Muslims (even if some hold that, strictly speaking, God is "unseeable"). The Sufi mystics see Abraham's willingness to sacrifice his son as an understanding that obedience to God will slay the "lower self," which is the true sacrifice at the Great Festival.

The great periodic celebrations of the Muslim community described above by no means include the full devotional life of the believer.[11] It is hard to imagine a Muslim community that celebrated more *mawlid*s than Egypt. The growing acceptance of the *mawlid* or birthday of the Prophet led to increasing numbers of yearly *mawlid*s honoring "saints," often leading Sufis but sometimes persons adopted as saints by Sufis, and sometimes persons of a sanctity more diffusely defined. In Egypt in the past there were more *mawlid*s than days in the year; *mawlid*s are still so numerous that there is a category of people, *mawlidīya*, who travel throughout the year from *mawlid* to *mawlid* selling "sugar dollies" (a specialty of *mawlids*) or accommodation in tents with bedding and the like. Some advocates of an austere form of Islam detest these *mawlid*s altogether; others dislike only the entertainments that accompany them: the feasting and shopping at the fairs that spring up at most *mawlid*s, the sword-swallowing and glass-eating "miracle" workers, etc.

11 "Periodic" is the term used by William A. Graham in his brilliant essay, "Islam in the Mirror of Ritual," in Richard G. Hovannisian and Speros Vyronis Jr. (eds.), *Islam's Understanding of Itself* (Malibu, CA: 1983) 62.

Rituals are multivalent, capable of encompassing several different types of significance at the same time. Feasting is as often a companion to piety as is fasting. One reason is that feasting is communal. Many of the lesser *mawlids* in some sense constitute the largest possible versions of the face-to-face communities to which villagers and inhabitants of small towns could belong. And this sense of belonging, particularly in the period before the modern system of universal elementary education (and sometimes even now), provided a possible path by which to bring talented local people into the wider community. The village teacher would send his promising student to continue his religious education at the local town of the *mawlid*, and the teacher there would send students on to the city. In the *mawlid* town and the city were pious endowments that would give a modest living to students who had been recommended. Since such schools were once the only means of education except for private tutoring, some students would leave the system at some middle level and work for the government. Others, of modest ability, would be sent back to be teachers in their original *mawlid* district. Others with more learning (and, possibly, more political skill) would pass to the top of the ladder as well-paid judges, professors at *madrasas* (colleges), etc. The local *mawlid* not only defines a community, but also defines ways to enter the wider community of Egypt.

The emphasis in this essay on communitarian religious rituals should not obscure the importance of more private rituals. Some of these more private practices coincide with public rituals. For example, the practice of *i'tikāf*, a vow to retreat to the mosque and more or less withdraw from society in order to fast and recite the Qur'ān can be observed for any number of days at almost any time of the year. Yet it is most observed for the last ten days of Ramadan, in part because the exact day of the Night of Power is uncertain but must surely fall in these ten days and the one who withdraws for this period is therefore constantly spiritually ready to participate in the blessings of this wondrous night.

Many other practices of private piety exist, from saying the rosary (older in the Muslim than in the Christian world) to observing the many supererogatory fasts recommended for the truly devout. Yet even in Muslim ritual matters which were usually public, a strong emphasis on the privacy of the home meant that a Muslim might absent him or herself from public ceremony or even flout such private duties as fasting. A much-repeated story is told of the second caliph, 'Umar, who scaled the walls of a house and saw the owner in a reprehensible state. When 'Umar reproved him, he replied, "I have sinned once, you have sinned three times." "How so?" asked 'Umar. "The Qur'ān says 'Do not spy' and you have done so. The Qur'ān says 'Come into houses through their doors' and you have entered over the roof. And the Qur'ān says 'Do not enter the houses of others until you have made yourself known and greeted the inhabitants,' and you have not greeted me." Totally "out-lawyered," 'Umar retreated.[12]

Some of the rituals already discussed helped to create a larger community in a different way. The Coptic Christian holiday (possibly of Pharaonic origin), "Smelling the Breeze," is celebrated on the Monday after Easter by virtually all Egyptians. A fair number of *mawlid*s are interconfessional; in Upper Egypt Christian *mawlids* are very popular with Muslims. The *mawlid* of a Jewish saint, Abū Ḥaṣīra, in the Delta province of Beheira still attracts both Muslim and Jewish devotees. In 1940 an astute observer of *mawlid*s wrote that the Feast of Saint Teresa, celebrated by the comparatively small Catholic community of Egypt, was attended by many Muslims and Jews.[13]

Rites de passage, like supererogatory piety, do not fit into the formal liturgical year, as people are not born, married or buried according to schedule. Women can play special functions at these occasions. Egyptian women use the high-pitched trill, called "ululation" (*zaghārīd*) at the emotional climax of such rituals, even the burial of a distinguished man of learning.[14] More surprising (and often condemned) is the appearance of the *ghazīya*, "dancing women," at weddings and other events, including the *mawlids*. Popularly believed to be from a tribe of gypsies, their numbers probably included non-gypsies who adopted the gypsy style. Some say their performances inspired the Western belief (to which Egyptians have adapted) that Egypt was the home of an established type of dance called the "belly dance."

Egyptian festivals such as the "Smelling of the Breeze" mentioned above, and the Inundation of the Nile, have no overt connection with the Muslim liturgical year. But this last festival was and is a major event that all Egyptians celebrate. Like many other festivals, it was also an occasion for the caliph or sultan to participate in a *mawkib*, a procession or cavalcade. In the time of the Fatimid caliphs (969–1171) the caliph, surrounded by

12 See R. Mottahedeh, and K. Stilt, "Public and Private as Viewed Through the Work of the *Muhtasib*," *Social Research* 70:3 (2003) 735–748.

13 J.W. McPherson, *The Moulids of Egypt (Egyptian Saints-Days)* (Cairo: 1941) 322.

14 Lane, (*supra* n. 4), 517.

finely dressed soldiers and courtiers, and heralded by drums and trumpets, would set out from the palace to the place of the festival or ritual. The procession would move to the point where the canal which ran through Cairo was cut open to the flooding Nile.[15] The presence of Qur'ān readers at this ceremony shows that no one ever felt that a Jeffersonian high wall should separate civic and religious ceremonies. The caliph (and later the sultan) would also lead processions to the great gatherings where prayer was conducted on the two *'īds*.

The Shi'ite Fatimid caliphs led a major procession on the great festival of al-Ghadīr on 18 Dhū al-Ḥijja. This procession ceased to take place with the fall of the Fatimids. Such a festival gives us some understanding of the ruler's motives for participating in selected rituals and festivals of the capital. The ruler could foster a ritual which reinforced the ideological and emotional claims of the dynasty, as did the festival of al-Ghadīr when Shi'ites commemorate the occasion on which the Prophet publicly designated 'Alī as his successor. On Muslim festivals already established, the ruler could show that he commanded not only the final source of coercive power but also decided at what time and at what places ceremonies began. Some degree of acceptance of the ruler was shown by the popular and learned participation in these events.

The position of the ruler in ritual reminds us how futile it is to import the modern Anglican Church concepts of "high" and "low" into the analysis of pre-modern Muslim Egypt. "High church" implies a ritual-prone, priestly-oriented church as contrasted with "low church," which minimizes these things in favor of a looser organization of liturgical patterns and a declared intent to focus on the message of Christianity rather than its external forms. In contrast, a Muslim learned man opposed to *mawlid*s might well be an enthusiastic devotee of a Sufi *dhikr*. Designations like "high" and "low" culture also do not fit well on the medieval Egyptian versions of Islamic culture. The court and the circles of learned men might be considered the focuses of high cultural life (and courtiers did indeed help to define "elegance"). But if one asks who did or did not believe in the efficacy of magic squares, no "high" and "low" distinctions emerge.

The appearance of the ruler at two kinds of rituals, one based on the solar and the other based on the Muslim lunar year, created a dissonance. Urban rents were often fixed against the lunar calendar; agricultural rents

15 Sanders, (*supra* n. 2), 114–117.

were fixed against the solar calendar. Living through a year calculated two ways does cause some confusion. But it also puts the more religious nature of the liturgical year in the foreground. One is obeying God whether the Fast be in December or July. There is both wonder at the change of circumstances and fascination in one's ability to obey regardless of the length or the harshness of the climate.

In all discussions of the ritual year there are important distinctions that the learned consider but others may not. Since *dhikr*, "mindfulness/ mention" is important, a great emphasis is put on speaking or reading out loud. Of course, one can read the Qur'ān silently, but it is more common to read it out loud. There are obligatory and prohibited acts in Islamic legal thinking, but there are also recommended, not recommended, and morally neutral acts. In the case of worship, there are obligatory things but also acts of common usage in worship, such as saying "Amen." And, as mentioned above, in performing the obligatory elements in worship, an act can only be properly performed if the believer has first formed the intention to perform the act. How well people adhered to these prescriptions of the schoolmen is another question.

Was there a consciously constituted category of religious rituals? The ceremonies of the Pilgrimage are called *manāsik*, a term which may at first have referred to the place of sacrifice. The day of sacrifice and the day of the end of the fast are called *'īd*, which comes close in meaning to "festival." A *du'ā* is a calling upon God, sometimes required as in the Pilgrimage, sometimes spontaneous. Many other terms are used for specific "rituals." "Ritual" is a useful category, but it does not seem to have existed as an overt category in pre-modern Muslim Egypt.

One key to understanding the category that these and similar words might constitute is given in a saying ascribed to the Prophet: "Whoever performs a prayer in congregation has filled his chest with divine service" (*'ibāda*). The category of "divine worship" (*'ibādāt*) is well known to every student of Islamic law but covers a wider category than the words "rituals," "ceremonies," "prayers," and so forth. It covers all things that "express the relationship and attitude" of an individual to God.[16] Therefore, vows might be part of a book on *'ibādāt*.

This understanding of ritual as a part of the direct interaction of a single person with God is shaped in the eyes of the learned by the radical

16 Calverley, (*supra* n. 1), 37 (a saying of the Prophet), p. 3 on *'ibādāt*.

monotheism of Islam. According to a frequently repeated story: ʿUmar said, when he kissed the Black Stone, "By God, I know that you are only a stone, and had I not seen the Messenger of God kiss you, I would not kiss you."[17] It is God who chooses to sacralize the Black Stone and the Kaʿba in Mecca. Nothing is sacred in its own right: it becomes sacred only through God's designation. Of course, to many Muslims living near a shrine associated with the local *mawlid*, the sanctity of the shrine may have seemed stronger than a spot with some revocable license.

If, however, Divine license is so important for the learned, then the specific moment that God granted that license becomes significant. In this sense Divine history becomes an anchor for the believer's understanding of rituals. Adam, Abraham and Muḥammad created the Pilgrimage to Mecca at God's behest. (The widespread agreement among Muslims as to how to perform the Pilgrimage argues that this and many similar rituals do genuinely go back to the time of the Prophet.) Rituals can also offer the possibility of reenacting events of sacred history. The theme of the reenactment of the sacrifice of Abraham is very strongly present in the Festival of Sacrifice, but commemoration, as in the *mawlids*, is more often a theme than is reenactment. Yet as the case of the *mawlids* shows, for many Muslims the book of ritual possibilities was not shut at the death of the Prophet. The distinguished scholar-jurist, al-Suyūṭī, said that there was no evidence that early Muslims celebrated the Prophet's birthday, but that this festival is a "praiseworthy innovation" (*bidʿa ḥasana*).[18]

Rituals force us to think about the relation between what people do in a ritual, what they say (or are supposed to say or think) while performing it, and what they think or say afterwards as to what happened in the ritual. Let me first suggest that too much difference has been created between thinking and doing; thinking is a physiological activity which is "action," while "doing," such as speaking in the context of supplication in prayer, may be a means to formulate a "thought," such as the form in which God may answer the prayer. Some scholars speak of the "meaning" of ritual: for example, as we have said above, it creates community, whether at the local *mawlid* or, among all Egyptians, at the rising of the Nile. Yet it is unlikely that this interpretation of the "meaning" of these rituals would be held by many of the participants. Moreover, Islam is necessarily a flexible religion,

17 Graham, (*supra* n. 11), 67.
18 Von Grunebaum, (*supra* n. 6), 76.

in that it encourages congregation, especially for rituals, yet admits the possibility of a person stranded on a desert island living a morally perfect life and being saved.

It is misleading to speak about the "meanings" of ritual since there is nothing approaching the lexical correspondence between "word" or "utterance" and "definition" or "meaning." Perhaps we can only search for the various forms of "significance" of ritual, a word that better comprehends implied or unstated meanings. The term "significance" also allows for unintended meanings and meanings of which the participants are not fully aware. Moreover, the significance of ritual can shift.

The significance of ritual often includes the affirmation of continuity, not only because of the largely fixed order in which they are carried out but also because of the language, often the same in different rituals. This makes the worshippers sense that they are related to each other. One powerful way in which rituals in the Egyptian context are significant is that they unite the seen world and the unseen world (and in the Qur'ān God is frequently called "the Knower of the Unseen World," e.g., VI:73). The significance of the ritual will almost always be modified both by context and by that inward configuration (based on prior experience or disposition) of the worshipper that leads him or her to interpret context.

This very brief list of aspects of the significance of ritual omits one element of ritual that is very often present. In the Abrahamic faiths, ritual signifies doing and saying things because one believes. It may never be possible completely to deconstruct "belief." The believer acts for the sake of "God's Face." We have mentioned the claim that Muslims disagree over theology more than over certain central religious practices. The other side of this coin is the inner freedom of the believers to weave interpretation into their rituals, for who can pretend to say definitively to another what is the "Face of God"?

Medieval Lexicography on Arabic and Persian Terms for City and Countryside

Medieval Arabic to Persian dictionaries are a relatively untapped source for the conceptual world in the time of their authors. This article closely examines four such dictionaries from the late 5th/11th century to the 7th/13th century written in eastern Iran. These dictionaries are quite rich in terminology for cities, towns, farmland, pasture and desert. They also describe architectural features of buildings. They offer scant but valuable information on markets and social structure. The information from these dictionaries combined with the rich detail available in the Islamic geographers of the 3rd/9th and 4th/10th century allows us to form a more perfect picture of medieval Iranian society.

The Arabic-Persian dictionaries of the period from the 4th/10th to the 7th/13th century offer a rich and relatively unused source for the cultural history of that period. For this article, I consider the terms for city and countryside and the characteristic elements of each of these divisions as found in Arabic-Persian dictionaries supplemented by lexicographical evidence found elsewhere.[1]

Author's note: This article was first published as: "Medieval Lexicography on Arabic and Persian Terms for City and Countryside," in David Durand-Guédy, Roy P. Mottahedeh and Jürgen Paul (eds.), *Cities of Medieval Iran, Eurasian Studies* 16 (Leiden, Brill: 2018) 465–478. Reproduced with permission. Here I have used Arabic transliteration in general for authors and titles but use Persian transliteration for some Persian authors and most Persian terms and titles. However, this choice is somewhat arbitrary.

1 Solomon I. Baevskij, *Persian Lexicography: Farhangs of the Eleventh to the Fifteenth Centuries*, trans. N. Killian, revised and updated by John R. Perry (Folkestone, U.K., Global Oriental: 2007), offers a good survey of the pre-modern Persian dictionaries. However, the author omits several of the Arabic to Persian dictionaries which I discuss here, including Karamīnī, Naṭanzī, and Zamakhsharī. A very useful list of such

One of the early Arabic to Persian dictionaries of this nature is the *Takmilat al-Aṣnāf* by ʿAlī ibn Muḥammad al-Adīb al-Karamīnī (also vocalized Karmaynī), dated to the 5th/11th or 6th/12th century.[2] Another lexicographer, securely dated to the late 5th/11th century is Ḥusayn ibn Ibrāhīm Naṭanzī (d. 497/1103), whose *Mirqāt* is one of the earliest extant Arabic to Persian dictionaries.[3] In the same Seljuk era, in 474/1082, Yaʿqūb Kurdī Nīshāpūrī wrote *Kitāb al-Bulgha*, which like many early dictionaries is organized by topic.[4] In this period the very prominent philologist Zamakhsharī (d. 538/1144) wrote the *Pishraw-e Adab* (*Muqaddimat*, or *Muqaddamat al-Adab* in Arabic).[5] Additional clarifying materials can be found in the earliest extant Persian dictionary by Asadi-Ṭusi (d. 465/1072–3).[6]

The outstanding geographical literature in Arabic and Persian from the 3rd/9th century onward contains many references to the terms discussed in this essay. This material is so large that it would require a separate book to evaluate the use of various geographical words. The limited geographical

---

dictionaries can be found in Charles A. Storey, *Persian Literature: A Bio-bibliographical Survey*, III:1 (Leiden, Brill: 1984) 78–110. For an important Persian discussion of such material, see ʿAli-Naqi Monzavi, *Farhang-Nāma-hā-ye ʿArabi ba-Fārsi* (Tehran, Tehran University Press: 1959).

2 ʿAlī ibn Muḥammad al-Adīb Karamīnī, *Takmilat al-Aṣnāf*, 2 vols., ed. ʿAli Ravaqi (Tehran, Anjomān-e Āṣār-o Mafākher-e Farhangi: 1385 solar/2006); the pagination in these two volumes runs consecutively. Karamīnī was known as "al-Adīb" because of his literary writing and learning. Some sources now give an exact death date, 13 Ṣafar 554 A.H. ʿAli Navidi Malati, "Āgāhi-hā-ye tāza dar bāra-ye Karamini," *Farhang-nevisi*, 98 (1393 solar) 69–76, dates this author to the 6th/12th century. John Perry, "Lexicography: ii Alphabetical dictionaries," in *Encyclopaedia Iranica online*: www.iranicaonline.org/articles/lexicography (viewed 9/27/2017), dates Karamīnī to the eleventh century C.E.

3 Naṭanzī, *al-Mirqāt* (*al-Mirqā* in Arabic), ed. Jaʿfar Sajjadi (Tehran, Bonyād-e Farhang,: 1346 solar) p. "w" for death date. This dictionary is organized by subject matter, such as "food," "clothing," "categories of people," and "discussion of professions," etc.

4 Nīshāpūrī, *Kitāb al-Bulgha*, ed. Mujtaba Minuvi and Firuz Harirchi (Tehran: Bonyād-e Farhang-e Irān: 2535 in the calendar of Mohammad Reza Shah). Some of the topics are "artisans and craftsmen" and "springs and canals." In contrast, Karamīnī's *Takmilat* is primarily alphabetical. Both the topical and alphabetical schemes are used in Arabic to Arabic dictionaries.

5 Zamakhsharī, *Pishraw-e Adab*, ed. Mohammad Kazem Imam (Tehran, Enteshārāt-e Dāneshgāh-e Tehrān: 1342 solar/1963).

6 Asadi-Ṭusi, *Loghat-e Fors*, ed. Fath Allah Mojtabaʾi (Tehran, Khwārazmi: 1365 solar). This article does not consider dictionaries of the fourteenth and fifteenth century C.E. in any detail.

analogs I offer here are derived in part from the magisterial four-volume work on Islamic geography by André Miquel.[7]

The selection of dictionaries I have used are mostly of the middle to late Seljuk era. This closeness in period gives them some coherence in their focus. With the exception of Naṭanzī, these lexicographers come from eastern Iran where New Persian first appeared. The Seljuk Empire was one of the last political entities to have real presence in both the Arab-speaking and Persian-speaking worlds. Arabic words entered Persian rapidly, although their survival was not assured. The highly Arabicized style of Naṣīr al-Dīn al-Ṭūsī (d. 672/1274), who wrote toward the end of this period, is barely comprehensible to a contemporary Persian speaker. Similarly, some Persianized versions of Arabic words, like *mezgit* for mosque, are no longer used in modern Persian. When reading these dictionaries, it is important to understand that Persian explanations of Arabic terms are offered as well as exact equivalents. Considerations as to how much these dictionaries copy each other are not discussed here.

The greatest modern Persian dictionary, the fourteen-volume *Loghat-Nāma* compiled under the supervision of 'Ali-Akbar Dehkhoda, is of great assistance in interpreting these early dictionaries, in large part because of its many citations from early poetry and prose.[8] Some of the pre-modern purely Arabic dictionaries, such as the *Lisān al-'Arab*, written by Ibn Manẓūr (d. 711/1311–12), are also cited for their enlargement on the meanings of words, often tersely defined in the Arabic to Persian dictionaries.[9] There are very few extant Persian to Persian dictionaries from the Seljuk period, rendering these Arabic to Persian dictionaries all the more valuable.

Within any language there are words for reading the land that are very strongly defined by culture, period and location—English is no exception. "Landscape" is originally an old Frisian term for "shoveled land" (particularly between land and sea). From this it has evolved to mean anything from

7 André Miquel, *La géographie humaine du monde musulman* (Paris, École des Hautes Études en Sciences Sociales: 1973–1988). I have been unable to consult Negin Miri, "Administrative and historical geography of Fars province during the Sasanian and early Islamic period (3rd–12th century)," Ph.D. dissertation, University of Sydney, 2007, which deals with administrative divisions of Fars province.

8 'Ali-Akbar Dehkhoda, *Loghat-Nāma*, 14 vols. (Tehran, Tehran University Publications: 1372 solar). The numbering of pages in this dictionary is continuous throughout the volumes and therefore only page numbers will be given.

9 Ibn Manẓūr, *Lisān al-'Arab* (Beirut, Dār Ṣādir: 1410/1990).

a "view from a particular place" to a "category of painting." It has inspired "seascape" and "cityscape" and continues to evolve. This article surveys four centuries of reading the land, both the city and the countryside, from the 4th/10th to the 7th/13th century. However, due to the paucity of secondary literature on these dictionaries, I can only cursorily describe the terms used. Also of enormous interest, but beyond the purview of this essay, are the different attitudes toward these terms, as demonstrated by the European "Romantic" attachment to landscape that emerged in the later years of the eighteenth century.

THE CITY

The basic Arabic word for city, *al-madīna*, is rendered by the basic Persian word, *shahr*.[10] However, *balad* (town or district) is also translated as *shahr*.[11] Surprisingly, *baladī* (belonging to the city) is translated as *hamshahri* (fellow city dweller).[12] Why the lexicographers offer the Persian word *hamshahri*, which is narrower in meaning than the Arabic *baladī*, is unclear to me. *Kūra*, usually understood as "province," is translated as *shahr-e bozorg* or "large city," in which the earlier larger sense of *shahr* as an area, as in *Irānshahr*, is preserved. However, in contrast, *kūra* is understood by Zamakhsharī as "little city, city and *shahristān*."[13] In Naṭanzī *miṣr*, *madīna*, and *fusṭāṭ* are translated as "large city" or *shahr-e bozorg*. *Fusṭāṭ* is also translated by Naṭanzī as *shahr-e jāmi'*, a city with a Friday mosque (or city where it is appropriate to congregate on Friday).[14]

---

10 E.g., Naṭanzī, (*supra* n. 3), 153.

11 Yet in Zamakhsharī, (*supra* n. 5), 111, *balda* is translated "small city."

12 See Dehkhoda, (*supra* n. 8), 20820 on *hamshahri*, which is only understood as "fellow citizen." See also Nīshāpūrī, (*supra* n. 4), 61.

13 Zamakhsharī, (*supra* n. 5), 111, adds: "large road." Yāqūt, *Mu'jam al-Buldān*, 6 vols., ed. M.J. de Goeje (Leiden, Brill: 1866–69), I:39 presents the classical geographers' understanding that *kūra* is the subdivision of a province consisting of villages with either a city or a *qaṣaba*. Ibn al-Faqīh, *Kitāb al-Buldān*, ed. M.J. de Goeje (Leiden, Brill: 1885) 105, explains *kūra* as an *iqlīm* (clime), which over time gains currency as a word for "province"; see Miquel, (*supra* n. 7), IV:126. Although this essay hints at the analogs to the words discussed in the early Islamic geographical literature, a thorough treatment of this literature is far beyond the scope of this essay.

14 Naṭanzī, (*supra* n. 3), 153.

STREETS

One of the various words for a smaller street is the Arabic *darb*, translated as *darvāza* or "gate" in Persian, an understanding supported by other texts, (as is the translation *darband* meaning "barrier" or "bar of a door").[15] *Shāri'* and *shāri'a*, the basic modern Arabic words for street, are rendered in Persian as *shāhrāh* or "principal thoroughfare," while for *fūhat al-ṭarīq* (literally "mouth of the road") we have the Persian *sar-e rāh* ("roadside opening").[16] *Zuqāq*, "alley," is appropriately translated as *kucha* (or in the alternate spelling *kuzha*).[17] According to Nīshāpūrī, *al-bayḍa wa-l-qaṣaba*, "the heart and township" is "the center of the city," *miyan-e shahr*.[18] *Sikka*, meaning "lane" or "road," is translated *kuy* by Zamakhsharī.[19]

SUBURBS

The suburbs of the city, *rabaḍ* (an Arabic word which Persian adopted early) is translated idiosyncratically by Karamīnī as *divār-e pirāsta*, "a wall embellished" [by outside gardens?].[20] Naṭanzī explains it more understandably as *gerdā-gerd-e shahr*, "the surroundings of the city," which Zamakhsharī repeats and adds "a wall surrounding the city."[21] The importance of the *rabaḍ* is shown by the great Central Asianist, V.V. Barthold, who states that the cities of the Sāmānid realm in greater Khorasan consisted of a citadel, a *shahrestān* or city proper and the suburb or *rabaḍ*.[22]

---

15 Naṭanzī, (*supra* n. 3), 154.

16 Nīshāpūrī, (*supra* n. 4), 282; Zamakhsharī, (*supra* n. 5), 57; perhaps also to be vocalized as *fuwwahat*.

17 Nīshāpūrī, (*supra* n. 4), 318.

18 Nīshāpūrī, (*supra* n. 4), 317.

19 Zamakhsharī, (*supra* n. 5), 118.

20 Karamīnī, (*supra* n. 2), 243. All further references have only a page number because pagination in this edition runs consecutively through two volumes.

21 Naṭanzī, (*supra* n. 3), 153; Zamakhsharī, (*supra* n. 5), 112.

22 V.V. Barthold, *An Historical Geography of Iran*, trans. Svat Soucek (Princeton, N.J., Princeton University Press: 1984) 13–14, 97. Barthold, who had an outstanding mastery of the primary sources, says of Balkh that it is divided into three elements "like all large towns," and adds that the Persian term for *rabaḍ*, *birun*, is not used in the historians and geographers: see V.V. Barthold, *Turkestan down to the Mongol Invasion*, E.J.W. Gibb Memorial Series (London, Luzac: 1968) 78. See also Miquel, (*supra* n. 7), IV:218 on this theme.

Al-Muqaddasī (writing ca. 375/985) says of Kabul, "it has a prosperous *rabaḍ* in which merchants gather as well as a well-fortified citadel (*quhandiz*)."[23] In addition, speaking of Bost, in the province of Sistan next to contemporary Lashkar-Gah in Afghanistan, he says that the city has a *rabaḍ* in which there are markets (*aswāq*), a theme echoed in descriptions by many of the contemporary and later geographers.[24] Ibn Ḥawqal describes proto-Tashkent as a city (*madīna*) outside which is a citadel (*quhandiz*), and adds that the wall encompasses both citadel and city. It also has a suburb (*rabaḍ*) with its own wall, outside which is another suburb with gardens and dwellings surrounded by yet another wall.[25] The pattern of extension of the city from one suburb to another can be seen elsewhere, as can the presence of agriculture (particularly orchards) within the walls. Ibn al-Faqīh, writing in the late 3rd/9th century, says the *rabaḍ* of Samarqand extended for thousands of *jarīb*s and included fields, gardens and farms.[26] In some cases the suburb and outer wall seem to be identical. A local history tells us that the people of Bukhara asked the Ṭāhirid Muḥammad ibn ʿAbd Allāh to build a *rabaḍ*, "so that we can close the gates at night and be safe from thieves and highwaymen. He ordered that a *rabaḍ* be built, which was excellent and strong with towers."[27]

FORTRESS AND PALACE

The Arabic *quhandiz* (citadel or fortress) is a loan-word from the Persian word for citadel (*kohan-dez* or "old fort"), encountered during the Arab conquests. *Quhandiz* seems to have been used more in greater Khorasan than elsewhere.[28] Yaʿqūbī says that after the conquest of Samarqand, the

23 Muqaddasī, *Aḥsan al-Taqāsim fī Maʿrifat al-Aqālīm*, ed. M.J. de Goeje (Leiden, Brill: 1906) 304.

24 Muqaddasī, *Aḥsan al-Taqāsīm*, 304. See also Ibn al-Faqīh, (*supra* n. 13), 326 on Samarqand.

25 Ibn Ḥawqal, *Ṣūrat al-Arḍ*, ed. M.J. de Goeje, (Leiden, Brill: 1873), II:508.

26 Ibn al-Faqīh, (*supra* n. 13), 326. Several readings of the text disagree as to how many thousands of *jarīb*s there were. The Iranian *jarīb* varied locally from 400 to 1450 square meters; see C.E. Bosworth, "Misāḥa," in *The Encyclopaedia of Islam*, 2nd ed., viewed online 12/21/2017.

27 Narshakhī, *Tārikh-e Bokhārā*, ed. Modarres Razavi (Tehran, Bonyād-e Farhang: 1366 solar) 48.

28 According to Ḍehkhoda it was used for Bukhara, Samarqand, Balkh, Nishapur and Marv. The entry on *arg*/*ark* (p. 1591) in this dictionary particularly associates

Muslims had to capture the *quhandiz* separately.[29] Narshakhī in his *History of Bukhara*, reports that Qutayba ibn Muslim took the city of Paykend but had a far greater struggle to take the citadel/castle keep (*burj*).[30]

The Persian word *kushk*, meaning "pavilion" and "palace" in modern Persian, is the translation of a number of different words in medieval Arabic, such as *qaṣr* (fortress), *burj* (tower), and *jawsaq* (an Arabization of *kushk*).[31] Durand-Guédy has established that *kushk* in some instances means "tent."[32] *Ḥiṣn*, another Arabic word for fortress is translated as "a secure refuge" (*panāh* and *dezh*, an alternate form of *dez*).[33] Palace, in Arabic *īwān* (literally "high arch" or "portico"), used to create settings for enthronement, is translated as *dargāh* and *kāshāna* (which in modern Persian is a humble dwelling).[34] For the well-known Persian word for palace *kākh* we have *kūshak*, an Arabization of *kushk*.[35] *Kushk* in the meaning of "palace pavilion" is used quite frequently. Nāṣer-e Khosraw (d. ca. 470/1077) in his Persian account of his travels explains that the palace (*qaṣr*) of the Fatimid caliphs in Cairo consists of twelve *kushks*.[36] *Kushk* is also well attested in the meaning of "garden pavilion." It is uncertain which meaning Nāṣer-e Khosraw intends here, "tent" or "garden pavilion," but a castle in Cairo is more likely to consist of pavilions.

---

this word with Sistan. Yāqūt, (*supra* n. 13), IV:210 says that *quhandiz* is a word used in Khorasan and Transoxiana. However, the geographers use it for other parts of Iran. *Ḥudūd al-ʿĀlam* uses it for Qā'in in Central Iran, and Iṣṭakhrī in his discussion of Fars in southwest Iran says that many large and small cities such as Shiraz and Fasā have a *quhandiz*. *Ḥudūd al-ʿĀlam min al-Mashriq ilā al-Maghrib*, ed. Manuchehr Setuda (Tehran, Enteshārāt-e Dāneshgāh-e Tehrān: 1340 solar) 90; Iṣṭakhrī, *Kitāb al-Masālik wa-l-Mamālik*, ed. M.J. de Goeje (Brill, Leiden: 1870) 116.

29 Yaʿqūbī, *Ta'rīkh*, ed. M.T. Houtsma, (Leiden., Brill: 1883), II:282.

30 Narshakhī, (*supra* n. 27), 61.

31 Naṭanzī, (*supra* n. 3), 155 for *burj* and *qaṣr*. Zamakhsharī, (*supra* n. 5), 114. Karamīnī, (*supra* n. 2), 530. Edward Lane, *Arabic-English Lexicon*, II (Cambridge, U.K., Islamic Texts Society Trust: 1984) 486, gives *jawsaq* an extended definition, emphasizing the building's position above others as a belvedere with views. Nīshāpūrī, (*supra* n. 4), 323.

32 David Durand-Guédy, "The Tents of the Saljuqs," in David Durand-Guédy (ed.), *Turko-Mongol Rulers, Cities and City Life* (Leiden, Brill: 2013) 149–189, esp. 172–174.

33 Zamakhsharī, (*supra* n. 5), 112; on p. 113, he gives a similar definition for *qalʿa*, but adds "road between two mountains," perhaps meaning "palisade." Miquel, (*supra* n. 7), IV:25 suggests that *ḥiṣn* is more than a wall (*sūr*) because it has defensive features in it.

34 Karamīnī, (*supra* n. 2), 16.

35 Asadi-Ṭusi, (*supra* n. 6), 64 has *kākh* as equivalent to *kushk* but adds *qaṣr*.

36 Nāṣer-e Khosraw, *Safar-nāma*, ed. Muhammad Dabir Siyaqi (Tehran, Zavvār: 1381 solar) 77.

MOSQUE

For the Friday mosque, *al-masjid al-jāmi'*, one finds *mazgit-e ādina.*[37] *Mazgit* (also spelled *mazkid, mizkid,* and *mazkit*) is found as early as *Ḥudūd al-'Ālam* and Bal'amī.[38] The courtyard (*raḥba*) of the mosque is explained in Persian as *farākhnā-ye mazgit.*[39]

MARKET

The market (Ar. *sūq*, Pers. *bāzār*) receives more thorough coverage than the mosque. *Kārvānsarāy*, caravanserai, is translated as *tim* in Persian, for which we also have the Arabic *khān.*[40] In a more expansive explanation, Zamakhsharī says: "the place where merchants (*bāzārgānān*) and traders (*sawdāgārān*) come together for exchange."[41] The Arabic word for "drain," *bālū'a*, is translated as "well/hole in the midst of a caravanserai."[42] Shop (*ḥānūt* in Arabic) is translated as Persian *dukkān.*[43] Arabic *ḥujra*, (still fully usable in modern Persian), literally "room" or assigned space in the market, is translated *sarācha*, small caravanserai.[44] One dictionary explains the Arabic *ma'riḍ* (showroom) as a place for selling slaves (*barda* in Persian).[45] A "moveable shop," *dikka* (literally "bench") in Arabic is defined in Persian as "a shop at the gate of the caravanserai wherever that shop might be."[46]

37 Karamīnī, (*supra* n. 2), 101.

38 Bal'amī, *Tārikh-e Bal'ami* (adapted translation of Ṭabarī's *Ta'rīkh* or *History*), ed. M.T. Bahar and M.P. Gonabadi (Tehran, Zavvār: 1353 solar/1974), which was begun in 352/963, is the oldest extensive prose work in New Persian. See Dehkhoda, (*supra* n. 8), 8333.

39 Nīshāpūrī, (*supra* n. 4), 75. Naṭanzī, (*supra* n. 3), 160. Dehkhoda, (*supra* n. 8), suggests that *mazgit* has an Aramaic origin. Prof. Andras Hamori of Princeton University informs me that "masgeda" means mosque in Syriac.

40 Karamīnī, (*supra* n. 2), 189. See also Asadi-Ṭusi, (*supra* n. 6), 186. Muqaddasī, (*supra* n. 23), 272, in his description of Esbijāb (often spelled Asfijāb, which is on the middle course of the Syr Darya) says that it has *timāt.*

41 Zamakhsharī, (*supra* n. 5), 115 and for the word *tim*, plural *timāt.*

42 Nīshāpūrī, (*supra* n. 4), 325.

43 Naṭanzī, (*supra* n. 3), 154; Zamakhsharī, (*supra* n. 5), 115, spells this word *dukkān.*

44 Naṭanzī, (*supra* n. 3), 155. The Arabic word *ḥujra* is also used for rooms or cells for students in a madrasa.

45 Zamakhsharī, (*supra* n. 5), 118.

46 Nīshāpūrī, (*supra* n. 4), 326.

WITHIN THE CITY

The center of the city is *bayḍa* in Arabic, *miyān-e shahr* in Persian.[47] The crossroads (often at the center of the city) in Persian is *chahār-su-i gāh*, or *murabba'* (literally "quadrangular meeting of roads") in Arabic.[48] The town or city dump is referred to in several dictionaries as the place "where they throw *khāshāk* (refuse) or *khāk* (dust)".[49]

A fair number of other institutions in the city are mentioned. Somewhat surprising is the mention of the *nādī*, the Qur'ānic and the modern Arabic word for "club," as meaning a "society (*anjoman*) for talking (*jā-ye ḥadiṣ goftan*)".[50] Less surprising is the presence of the *maktab*, the Arabic word for a Qur'ān school, translated as *dabestān* and *dabirestān*, the modern words for secular schools.[51] Another somewhat institutionalized space is suggested by the translation of the Arabic word for a long and wide bench (*maṣṭaba*) which is translated as "place for strangers, place for beggars, place for the impoverished."[52] Some words suggest the layout of the city. Neighborhood, in Arabic *nāḥiya*, is translated as "one side of the city," *yak-su-ye shahr*.[53] The well-known Arabic word for quarter (*ḥāra*) is translated as "the market place (*sarāygāh*), the old market (*sarāy-e kohan*)".[54] Arabic *janāb* is translated as "around the caravanserai," *gerdā gerd-e sarāy*.[55] The Arabic word for "plaza," *finā'*, is translated as "opposite the market," *barābar-e sarāy*.[56] *Maydān*, the word for "square" used in both Persian and in Arabic, is mostly absent from these dictionaries, perhaps because it was so well known in both languages.[57]

47 Naṭanzī, (*supra* n. 3), 153.

48 An equivalent already explained by Jāḥiẓ in the 3rd/9th century. See Dehkhoda, (*supra* n. 8), 7340.

49 Zamakhsharī, (*supra* n. 5), 122.

50 Nīshāpūrī, (*supra* n. 4), 319.

51 Naṭanzī, (*supra* n. 3), 162. Witness to the long use of these words is found in Dehkhoda, (*supra* n. 8), 9189 and 9199–9200. In this last entry one finds a quote from Bal'amī that "I memorized this book for children in *dabirestān*."

52 Zamakhsharī, (*supra* n. 5), 116. This Arabic word preserves the meaning "refuge for the poor" in later Persian.

53 Naṭanzī, *Mirqāt*, (*supra* n. 3), 153. Nīshāpūrī, (*supra* n. 4), 317, gives the Arabic *khāfiq* as "one side (*kenāra*) of the city."

54 Zamakhsharī, (*supra* n. 5), 122.

55 Naṭanzī, (*supra* n. 3), 155.

56 Naṭanzī, (*supra* n. 3), 155.

57 Nīshāpūrī, (*supra* n. 4), 318 for *maydān* gives "s.p.r.y.s" which I understand as a rendering of *sepris* or *asbris* or *aspris* meaning "place for running horses," but I welcome

LOCAL HIERARCHY

A range of words point to the hierarchy of inhabitants in the city. The headman (or mayor), *ra'īs* in Arabic and as a loan word in Persian, is explained as the "superior of the city," *mehtar-e shahr*, and the Arabic term for leader, *za'īm*, is explained in the same way in Persian.[58] *Ra'īs* (with the office called *riyāsat*) has eclipsed *mehtar* in Persian usage but there are echoes of *mehtar* in early Persian literature, such as the *Garshāsp-Nāma* by Asadi-Ṭusi, written in the 5th/11th century. Asadi-Ṭūsi says: *hamī mehtar-e shahr guyad ke man to-rā banda-am va-in bozorg anjoman* ..., or "The mayor of the city (*mehtar-e shahr*) kept on saying 'I am your servant. This great assembly ...'"[59]

'Arīf, an "expert," "master craftsman," "head person," or "master of a guild," is translated as a "chosen" or "excellent person" (*gozida*).[60] The Arabic term *a'yān*, notables, is translated as "respected or celebrated people," *ruy-shenāsān* (literally, "those whose faces are known"). This word, more often in the form *ru-shenās* (*-ān*), is well attested in Persian literature.[61] A vast literature on the internal organization of the city exists in the secondary literature: I confine myself to mentioning the appearance of such words in these medieval dictionaries.[62]

TOWN AND VILLAGE

No generally agreed term for "town" seems to have emerged in pre-modern times, but the modern Persian term *qaṣaba* (a loan word from Arabic)

---

other suggestions.

58 Naṭanzī, (*supra* n. 3), 27.

59 In the chapter: "The emperor of China (*faghfur*) becomes aware of the killing of his son," viewed online 6/27/2018: www.ganjoor.net/asadi/garshaspname/sh/120. According to Dehkhoda, (*supra* n. 8), 19325, s.v. "*mehtar*," *Ḥudūd* says that every tribe (*qabīla*) or group (*goruh*) has a *mehtar*. Cf. Asadi de Tous, *Le livre de Gerchâsp*, trans. Henri Massé, II (Paris, Imprimerie Nationale: 1951) 203, where the mayoral title is translated "le chef de la cité."

60 Naṭanzī, (*supra* n. 3), 17. In this edition it is vocalized *'errif*, but *'arīf* in this meaning is well known.

61 Dehkhoda, (*supra* n. 8), 10908; Naṭanzī, (*supra* n. 3), 27.

62 My first article on a city deals with the negotiation in the Buyid period between the ruler and the local community about the appointment of the "head" or mayor of the city; see "Administration in Buyid Qazvin" (Article 19 here).

corresponds to this meaning. In medieval usage *qaṣaba* is used to designate a provincial capital.[63] The Arabic word for village, *qarya*, is *deh* (often spelled *dih*) in Persian. *Qarawī*, Arabic for villager, is translated into Persian as *rustā'i*, (countryman) or *ham-dehi* (fellow-villager).[64] One sub-category of village is *daskara*, attested in both Persian and Arabic, and sometimes translated as Persian *kalāt*, all of which are explained as habitation on a high place. Naṭanzī glosses it as "a small village which has been built in a high place."[65] Karamīnī adds to his definition of *daskara/kalāt*, "it is like a castle (*qaṣr*) around which are houses (*buyūt*) belonging to the kings."[66]

André Miquel shows that 4th/10th- and 5th/11th-century Muslim geographers had some idea as to what was the smallest size that could be called a "city" and the largest size of "village." Ibn Ḥawqal describes Sūq Ibrāhīm in the Maghrib as "a city but small with a bath and marketplace."[67] He describes some cities in the Middle Euphrates as "the smallest [possible] cities" (*aṣāghir al-mudun*).[68] This issue becomes confused through the differing interpretations of entitlement to a Friday mosque (*jāmi'*) in the different schools of law. The Ḥanafī attitude is that only the capital of a province is entitled to such a mosque, and Ḥanafism was dominant in many eastern Iranian cities such as Balkh, Bukhara and Samarqand.[69]

URBAN AND RURAL

The distinction between urban and rural is fairly clear, *rustā* being the common Persian word for cultivated countryside, which was adopted into Arabic as *rūstāq* or *rustāq*. Yāqūt gives a very clear explanation of the standard use of *rustāq* by geographers. Fars, the large province of southwest Iran, is divided into five *ustāns*. These are divided into *rustāqs*, which in

63 Reinhart Dozy, *Supplément aux dictionnaires arabes*, II (Paris, Maisonneuve Frères: 1927) 354, *kursī al-kūra*. It is also understood as "the center of the city" (*miyān-e shahr*) in Zamakhsharī, (*supra* n. 5), 114.

64 Nīshāpūrī, (*supra* n. 4), 61.

65 Naṭanzī, (*supra* n. 3), 154. Nīshāpūrī, (*supra* n. 4), 317.

66 Karamīnī, (*supra* n. 2), 219. This reference may be to royal fortifications in southwestern Iran.

67 Miquel, (*supra* n. 7), IV:207.

68 Miquel, (*supra* n. 7), IV:207 and note.

69 Baber Johansen, in his excellent essay, "The All-Embracing Town and its Mosques," deals with Ḥanafī law on city and Friday worship, reprinted in his *Contingency in a Sacred Law* (Leiden, Brill: 1998) esp. pp. 89–106.

turn are divided into *ṭassūjs*, in turn composed of villages. Thus, the *ustān* of Iṣṭakhr (Eṣṭakhr) contains the *rustāq* of Nā'īn, which contains the village of Niyāstāna. Yāqūt adds that in his time among the Iranians (*Furs*) *rustāq* means a place in which there are farms (*mazāri'*) and villages, but the term is not applied to cities like Basra and is similar in meaning to the Iraqi word *sawād* (cultivated land).[70] The Arabic word for farm (*mazra'a*), which in the plural *mazāri'* is the modern Persian term for cultivated countryside, is defined in Persian as *kesht-zār*, "a cultivated area."[71]

Very general terms for "urban" exist, such as *ḥaḍarī*, translated into Persian as *shahri*.[72] *'Umrān*, the "culture" of habitation, a well-known term in Ibn Khaldūn, is appropriately rendered into Persian as *ābādāni*.[73] Some definitions suggest that the later Persian distinction between winter house (*qeshlāq*) and summer house (*yaylāq*) existed before these words were adopted from Turkish. For example, Asadi-Ṭusi defines *kāshāna* explicitly as a "winter house."[74]

The words for "country" do not have the broad general sense of this word as we know it in modern English but instead show distinctions. *Rīf* in Arabic is explained in Persian as "the embellished green area on the edge of the plain/desert (*dasht*)," *sabzibar-kenāra-ye dasht va-pirāsta*.[75] (*Pirāsta* can mean a pleasure ground outside a town.) Zamakhsharī explains *rīf* as "cultivated land" (*zamin-e ābādān*) and "green and watered land" (*zamin-e sabz va āb-gāh*).[76] *Barr*, meaning "open country" in Arabic but also in some instances meaning "outside the city," is translated as *dasht* or "plain," "steppe" and "desert" in Persian.[77] *Sawād*, the Arabic word for "black" is explained as "cultivated area outside the city or surrounding the city."[78] *Mazlafa* is defined as "country between green open country (*rīf*) and the outback (*barr*)."[79]

70 Yāqūt, (*supra* n. 13), I:20–21.
71 Naṭanzī, (*supra* n. 3), 140.
72 Karamīnī, (*supra* n. 2), 166. Dozy, (*supra* n. 63), II:298 translates *ḥaḍarī* as "bourgeois, citoyen d'une ville."
73 Karamīnī, (*supra* n. 2), 476.
74 Asadi-Ṭusi, (*supra* n. 6), 217.
75 Karamīnī, (*supra* n. 2), 248.
76 Zamakhsharī, (*supra* n. 5), 38. Dozy, (*supra* n. 63), I:575–576, who reflects Spanish and Maghrebi Arabic, translates *rīfī* as "villageois, rustique."
77 Karamīnī, (*supra* n. 2), 35.
78 Zamakhsharī, (*supra* n. 5),112.
79 Karamīnī, (*supra* n. 2), 44.

IRRIGATION

Irrigation receives some attention in all these dictionaries. The equivalence of the general Arabic word for water channels, *qanāt*, with the Persian *kāriz* is mentioned. Curiously, Nīshāpūrī translates Arabic *al-ʿidd* (fountain, well) as "that which gives it (water) assistance like the water of a spring and irrigation canal (*kāriz*)."[80] The Arabic word for cistern, *ṣahrīj*, is translated as *ḥawz-e bozorg*,[81] a large reservoir. *Al-faqīr*, Arabic for a watercourse, is explained in Persian as "a place where water comes out of the canal (*kāriz*)."[82] Arabic *jisr* is correctly translated as "small bridge," while *qanṭara* (which often means aqueduct) is translated as "large bridge."[83]

CONCLUSION

These dictionaries offer insights into the cities and countryside of medieval Iran. They make clear that the land of both city and town could be used for commerce, habitation and even agriculture. Walls (many of which may have appeared with Abbasid decline) gained an important secondary use as points of toll collections useful to rulers who had very limited means to tax trade. Some of the major features of most cities were the Friday (or congregational) mosque, the central marketplace with its caravanserais (probably including places both for display and storage of goods), a large plaza often filled with small traders, a citadel for the garrison in or next to the walls, and a town dump.

There is no universal word for countryside. Deserts compose a category in themselves, to be distinguished from pasture and cultivable land, and cultivable land is further divided into several categories. It seems that generally people do not live on farms scattered over the land; by and large they are together in villages from which they go out to the land. The comparative absence of words for meadow and pasture could be related to the urban origins of the lexicographers.

80 Nīshāpūrī, (*supra* n. 4), 285. This is probably to be understood as an analogy: "just as spring is to an irrigation canal."
81 Naṭanzī, (*supra* n. 3), 154.
82 Nīshāpūrī, (*supra* n. 4), 289.
83 Zamakhsharī, (*supra* n. 5), 62. See also on *qanṭara*, Karamīnī, (*supra* n. 2), 549.

The limited but very significant evidence of hierarchy in the city tells us that while there was appointment to position from forces outside the community there were also external forces creating hierarchy within the community. Evidence from elsewhere seems to show that at least in some periods, the head of the city, the "mayor," was chosen by negotiation between city and ruler.[84]

---

84 For a discussion of the *ra'īs* or mayor, see my article "Administration in Buyid Qazvin" (Article 19 here).

SHI‘ISM

Americans began to learn about Shi'ism during the Iranian Revolution of 1978–79. Despite the Iran–Iraq war of 1980–88, Americans in general remained confused by sectarian differences among Muslims. Basic misconceptions persisted about Iran and Iraq, their people, and their different versions of Islam, not only among the general public but also among journalists and politicians. As a result, I was often asked to explain who Shi'ites and Sunnis were and what they believed.

Iran is principally Shi'ite but Iraq is split between a Shi'ite south and a Sunni north from which Saddam Hussein came. Shi'ites represent only ten to fifteen percent of the Muslim population of the world. They are concentrated principally in Iran, southern Iraq, and Bahrain where they are the majority, but significant minorities of Shi'ites exist in Afghanistan, India, Pakistan, Lebanon, eastern Turkey, and Yemen. Most of these Shi'ites are called Twelvers because they believe in Twelve Imams as infallible early interpreters of Islam, but the followers of the Agha Khan believe in a continuing line of Imams right up to the present. The word "imam" means the person who stands in front, and, consequently, Muslims defer to the most prestigious person present the right to stand in front and lead the prayer. The term imam has been and still is used in a broad sense for someone who claims leadership, even if only in his local mosque. The Nation of Islam in the United States, led in its early years by Elijah Muhammad, has sought to avoid classification as Sunni or Shi'ite. There has been conflict between the majority sect of Islam, the Sunnis, and the Shi'ite minority from the seventh century C.E. to the present. The current hostility between Iran and Saudi Arabia is still clouded by religious sectarian differences.

The first article in this section, "Keeping the Shi'ites Straight," was published in 2003, the year the U.S.-led coalition invaded Iraq. It grew out of a public lecture on Shi'ites given at the invitation of the Center for the Study of Religion in Public Life at Trinity College in Connecticut, which published the article in its journal *Religion in the News*. This journal was interested in the way in which news about religion was presented in the press and its accuracy. This article has no footnotes as it was intended for the general public. Nevertheless, I decided to include it here because so many non-Muslims still do not fully understand the important divisions among Muslims. The article tries to explain, in very concise terms, the relevant historical background to the formation of Shi'ism and its basic tenets of belief. Some of the article is devoted to the treatment of Shi'ites in the American press, where even the best sources obviously needed clarification. Despite the Iranian Revolution and subsequent hostage crisis of 1979–81, the Iran–Iraq War of 1980–88, and the Gulf War of 1990–91, the Shi'ite version of Islam was not well understood among the general public. Since then, the press has become much better informed and more accurate on these subjects, although most Americans still know very little about Islam (as well as about Shi'ites). The unceasing sectarian violence seen in Afghanistan, Bahrain, Iraq, Lebanon, Pakistan, and Yemen tells us, sadly, that we are still a fair distance from Sunni–Shi'ite understanding, although a number of enlightened leaders from both sides have tried to promote toleration and even acceptance. The dissolution of the old Yugoslavia and the civil war in Lebanon have shown where sectarian violence can lead. One can only hope that a willingness to share political power among religious and ethnic groups develops in the near future.

The second article in this section, "Shi'ite Political Thought and the Destiny of the Iranian Revolution," was written for a conference on Iran and the Gulf held in Abu Dhabi, the proceedings of which were published in 1996 in *Iran and the Gulf: A Search for Stability*, edited by Jamal S. al-Suwaidi. The encounter between Iran's Shi'ite clergy and the government changed the nature of clerical leadership. Before the Iranian Revolution pious Shi'ites taxed themselves and paid this tax to the "highest" clergyman. The identification of this person was the result of an informal consensus among the clergy as to who was the most learned. The clergymen of the shrine city of Najaf in southern Iraq produced many such "highest" clergymen in the past two centuries as did the shrine city of Mashhad in Iran and, more recently, the shrine city of Qom, also in Iran.

The clerical hierarchy was wrenched by political realities after the Iranian Revolution when the Iranian mullahs took over the state. Khamenei, the mullah who was appointed head of state after Khomeini's death in 1989, was politically prominent but not recognized by most other mullahs as learned. How Khamenei raised himself up to be considered "learned" is part of the subject of this article. The vast wealth available to a modern government like that of Iran helped him pacify the rest of the clergy.

The last article in this section, "The Quandaries of Emulation: The Theory and Politics of Shiʿi Manuals of Practice," was written for The Ninth Farhat J. Ziadeh Distinguished Lecture in Arab and Islamic Studies, May 2, 2011, which was published separately by the University of Washington in Seattle in 2014. Serious illness prevented me from delivering the article for several years after my lecture in May 2011. The article was therefore updated to include relevant subsequent events and material which I learned in 2014 during a conference at the University of Kufa, immediately adjacent to Najaf in Iraq.

After the publication of my translation, introduction and lengthy analysis of the *Lessons in Islamic Jurisprudence* by Muhammad Baqir al-Sadr in 2003, I started working on a book about the Shiʿite clergy of the nineteenth and twentieth centuries. I was fascinated by the number of Muslim reformers coming to the fore and interested in how they developed a following. I read extensively in Arabic and Persian, but at no point did I feel that I had acquired mastery of the vast amount of material that would qualify me to write a book on the modern and contemporary reformers or the Shiʿite clergy. My failure to write either of these books can be laid against my lifelong enemy, perfectionism. This article on the quandaries of emulation, written in 2014, was the fruit of my research on the Shiʿite clergy and should be understood as a précis of a book I never wrote.

The question of leadership among the Shiʿite clergy remains open and vitally important today, years after the death of Ayatollah Khomeini. Before I wrote this article, I followed the websites of the major clerics and political figures in the Shiʿite world for a considerable time. It became clear that their encounter with real political authority had changed the semi-hierarchical system that had existed before the Iranian Revolution of 1978–79. Many Americans do not understand the pre-revolutionary or the post-revolutionary system of Shiʿite hierarchy that determines which groups of Muslims follow a certain cleric or adhere to his set of beliefs. This article was written to clarify these questions.

Keeping the Shiʿites Straight

No story has been more confusing for the Western news media to cover in postwar Iraq than the politics of the country's Shiʿite majority. That the Shiʿites would be a central story was universally expected. They had suffered systematic repression under Saddam Hussein, especially after the first Gulf War (of 1990–91), when they staged a revolt in the South. If anyone required liberation in Iraq, it was the Shiʿites. After they failed to welcome their liberators with rapturous joy following the Second Gulf War in 2003, and one of their religious leaders was brutally murdered by followers of another one of their religious leaders, the rosy storyline of liberation collapsed amid a host of unanswered questions.

Were the Shiʿites pro-American ("grateful") or anti-American ("ungrateful")? Did they look for direction to the Shiʿite religious leaders in neighboring Iran?[1] What did they want? And why did they have so many leaders?

There were, of course, the normal orthographical problems associated with transliterating a strange alphabet, and some of these had more than merely orthographic significance. For example, after some floundering the *New York Times* (followed by most other papers) decided to identify the leader of the Shiʿite Supreme Council of the Islamic Revolution in Iraq as Muhammad Bakr al-Hakim (d. August 2003), not realizing that "Bakr" is conventionally used by Sunni Muslims, "Baqir" by Shiʿites.

Observing such linguistic niceties mattered less than making readers aware of the basic outlines of Shiʿite religious history. At best, the news media offered brief accounts of the figures of ʿAlī and Ḥusayn,

Author's note: This article was first published as: "Keeping the Shiʿites Straight," in Mark Silk (ed.) *Religion in the News* 6:2 (2003) 4–6, 27. Reproduced with permission. This article has been modified slightly to bring it up to the present (2022).

1 For a longer treatment of the history of Shiʿites in Iraq and Iran, see my book *The Mantle of the Prophet: Religion and Politics in Iran* (New York, Simon & Shuster: 1985).

but that, while useful, was not enough to make Shiʿite behavior in Iraq understandable.

ʿAlī was the first cousin of the Prophet Muḥammad and the husband of his eldest surviving child, Fāṭima. According to Shiʿite belief, ʿAlī was designated by the Prophet as his successor and endowed with divine guidance so that the community of Muslims would not go astray.

In 661 C.E. ʿAlī was murdered—an event that for Shiʿites represents the rejection by the Muslim majority of the opportunity for a truly godly government. His burial at Najaf, now an Iraqi city with a population of 585,000 [in 2003], established a religious center for Shiʿism. Shiʿites believe that a succession of Twelve Imams, each appointed by his predecessor from the line of ʿAlī, possesses the same infallibility that ʿAlī possessed.

After ʿAlī, only the third of these Imams, ʿAlī's son Ḥusayn (through Fāṭima a grandson of the Prophet) made a bid to be an actual political ruler, and he was brutally murdered in 680. (To their eternal shame, his followers, afraid of the anti-Shiʿite government of the time, failed to come to his aid.) It was not long before some Shiʿites began to flagellate themselves on the anniversary of Ḥusayn's death, and his martyrdom is still commemorated on that date.

Ḥusayn is buried at Kerbala in Iraq, which became the second most important Shiʿite shrine city and boasts a population of 572,000 [in 2003, but 929,00 in 2022]. Reliving his passion is, for Shiʿites, what reliving the passion of Jesus is for many Christians.

Some newspapers did get the bare bones—if not the emotional significance—of this early Shiʿite history right, but they almost universally skipped everything between 680 and the twenty-first century. For present purposes, the crucial issues in subsequent Shiʿite history are: the absence of a current Imam; the establishment of a madrasa, or seminary, at Najaf; and the change in the structure of Shiʿite leadership in the nineteenth century.[2]

In 941 Shiʿite leaders declared that the Twelfth Imam had disappeared to return as the Messiah at the end of time. Those Shiʿites who accept this disappearance are often called Twelvers. This left the Shiʿites—the overwhelming majority of whom are Twelvers—with the same dilemma faced by the Jews in the absence of their Messiah. Many Shiʿites chose to withdraw from politics and quietly await his coming.

---

2 For a discussion of Shiʿite education, including the *Ḥawza* of Najaf, see my article "The Najaf *Ḥawza* Curriculum" (Article 16 here) and other articles in the section on "Islamic Education" here.

Around 1057 C.E. a man named Ṭūsī, the leading Shi'ite scholar of his day, migrated from Baghdad, where Sunnis had burned his house and books, to Najaf, where he began the systematic teaching of Shi'ite learning. Shi'ites understand this to be the parent of all their madrasas down to the present.

Already by the end of the 4th/10th century Shi'ite scholars had developed full systems of theology and jurisprudence that—like Catholic but unlike Sunni thought—were based on natural law. In the nineteenth century Shi'ite teaching underwent a dramatic transformation when, after much controversy, the majority of madrasas accepted that only the most qualified jurists could establish norms of behavior for ordinary Shi'ite believers. Each of these few jurists, who seldom numbered as many as ten, was called a "Source of Imitation" (*marja' al-taqlīd*). Consequently, unlike most other Muslim groups, the Twelver Shi'ites have a semi-hierarchy with figures roughly equivalent to Catholic bishops or the Grand Rabbi of Vilna.

Knowing this history would have saved English-speaking reporters from many mistakes. Take, for example, the *Ḥawza* of Najaf, identified by the *Los Angeles Times'* Megan K. Stack, April 29, 2003, as a "council of scholars" and by the *Washington Post's* William Booth, May 15, 2003, as an "open university." Abbreviated from *al-Ḥawza al-'Ilmīya* ("the learned area"), the *Ḥawza* was supposedly established by Ṭūsī and is now used to designate that part of the city where the madrasas are located—and, metaphorically, the seminary community as a whole.

Western reporters sniffed but could not identify the Shi'ite hierarchy. By far the most important Source currently on the scene [still in 2022] in Najaf is Ayatollah Sistani, and this is what makes him, as many reporters did say, the "senior" cleric. In fact, no other Iraqi mullah possesses his learning or piety, and he has more followers in the Twelver Shi'ite world than any other Source alive.

Also confusing to reporters were the Sadrs, an important clerical family that has provided at least two Sources in recent history. Muhammad Baqir al-Sadr (d. 1980) was the most innovative Iraqi Shi'ite thinker of the twentieth century. Aware that the Communists had a disproportionate appeal to Shi'ites in Iraq, Sadr studied Marxist thought with a view to fighting back. He believed in "Islamic government" but thought the time was not ripe for it, and his exposition of the principles of Shi'ite jurisprudence has replaced older books in Iran as well as Iraq.

In the 1970s Sadr's followers founded a political party and, excited by the success of the Iranian Revolution in 1978–79, attempted to assassinate the foreign minister Tariq Aziz. The shock was enormous when Saddam Hussein had Sadr and his sister killed in 1980, because Sadr seemed destined to head Iraqi (and possibly Iranian) Shi'ites. When the Shi'ites in the South revolted in 1991 after the First Gulf War it was Muhammad Baqir al-Sadr's portrait that was seen everywhere.

After the revolt, the Baathist government asked the leading member of the Kelidar family in Najaf to suggest, as the Kelidars had done for generations, an official head of the Shi'ite community. Rather than consult the living Sources or their close associates, the Kelidar put forward a list of clergymen considered to be politically pliant and of strong Arab identity. One of these was a remote cousin of Muhammad Baqir al-Sadr's named Ayatollah Muhammad Sadiq al-Sadr. Muhammad Sadiq was pious, and he had written on morality and the history of Shi'ism, but he was not a great legal expert. Nevertheless his "pastoral" ability gained him increasing favor with the ordinary Shi'ites, and he was accepted as a Source.

Eventually, Muhammad Sadiq's piety and pastoralism led him to voice the desires of his flock, and he became his own man to an extent intolerable to Saddam. In 1999 he was killed along with two of his sons.

But another son, Muqtada al-Sadr, was not killed, and now [in 2022 in his late forties,] he is playing an important role in post-Saddam Iraq. While the press caught the essence of this father-son story, the relationships were often jumbled. For example, on May 14, 2003, Peter Ford of the *Christian Science Monitor* wrote that Muqtada "derived most of his popularity from his relationship with his grandfather, Muhammad Bakr Sadr, and his uncle, Mohamed Sadeq Sadr."

The semi-hierarchical system means that no one but a Source can give an answer (or fatwa) to a question on a disputed point of law. A local mullah might tell a member of his flock that a strange species of fish was or was not kosher, but he would be ashamed to issue a fatwa on how to behave toward the central government as long as superiors were available. (It was thus embarrassing to discover, in a good *New York Times* article by Douglas Jehl and David E. Sanger on April 24, 2003, that U.S. special forces troops and intelligence officers were "identifying friendly clerics in small towns and cities and encouraging them to issue fatwas in support of the post-war American administrations.")

For his part, the young Muqtada al-Sadr, who may not have passed even the intermediate stage of Shi'ite seminary study, would have been at sea early on without the advice and counsel of Ayatollah Sayyid Kazem

Haeri, an Iraqi who lived in Iran. Indeed, the interaction of Shi'ites in Iraq and Iran explains a great deal about Shi'ite politics in both countries [even now in 2022].

Shortly after Muhammad Baqir al-Sadr was executed, Saddam put Ayatollah Khoei (d. 1992), the senior Source at the time, under house arrest and expelled the so-called "Iranian" Shi'ites, many of whom were so Arabized that they could not speak Persian. About 40,000 left in 1980, more in succeeding years, and their property was confiscated and auctioned off.

Out of fellow Shi'ite feeling, Iranian clergymen got government jobs for some of these refugees. One, the highly conservative Sayyid Mahmud Hashimi Shahrudi (d. 2018), headed the Iranian judiciary from 1999 to 2009. (He and Haeri were Muhammad Baqir al-Sadr's closest pupils.) As the mood in Iran turned against the conservatives, the Iraqi clerics in Iran, who had long been seen by Iranians as more hard-line, became less and less welcome, particularly in positions of authority. [However, in 2022, the Iraqi clerics, led by Sistani, seem more liberal than their Iranian counterparts.]

Something of an exception was Muhammad Baqir al-Hakim (d. 2003), an Iraqi who mirrored the views of more moderate Iranian clergymen. Like Muqtada al-Sadr he was the son of a Source but unlike Sadr he had more than his lineage to rely upon.

Al-Hakim completed the higher level of seminary study with Muhammad Baqir al-Sadr and went on to run the office of his father and, eventually, the office of Sadr himself. (Every popular Source has an office in order to supervise, among other things, the payments of religious taxes.) Somewhat before Sadr's death in 1980, al-Hakim fled to Iran where he became the head of the Supreme Council for Islamic Revolutions in Iraq (SCIRI), which commanded the 10,000 to 15,000–member Badr Brigades of Iranian-trained Iraqi exiles.

Aware of the limitations of trying to establish a place for himself in Iraq from an office in Tehran, al-Hakim sought to enhance SCIRI's standing by diplomatic efforts. These ranged from meeting with Crown Prince Abdullah of Saudi Arabia to serving as a member (not always active) of the Iraqi National Congress, the organization led by the late indefatigable and unquestionably liberal secularist Shi'ite Ahmed Chalabi (d. 2015).

Al-Hakim's well-orchestrated return to Iraq was covered extensively on May 12, 2003, by the London *Times*' Stephen Farrell, who traveled a considerable distance with al-Hakim and paid close attention. The cleric's line had been fairly consistent. As Farrell reported, the motifs throughout his speeches were "Islam, democracy, Islamic law, unity, freedom and tolerance of other religions"—and, one might add, Iraqi nationalism.

Of course, some of this was accommodationist: The Americans were listening. But everywhere al-Hakim was greeted by large crowds. He was a real politician, and he understood the need to pay a political price for what he wanted to get.

The Americans were suspicious of al-Hakim. After all, the conservative "Supreme Leader" of Iran, Ayatollah Khamenei, had accompanied him to the airport as he left Iran. He received Iranian financial support during his long years in Iran. Yet the Americans needed him as much as he needed them. As a Shi'ite vegetable and fruit merchant in Nasiriya told the *New York Times'* Craig S. Smith, April 12, 2003, "If Hakim is shut out, the Iraqi people, especially in the South, will not accept this." [Alas, al-Hakim's untimely death in 2003 in a bomb blast as he left the Shrine of 'Alī in Najaf shortly after his return to Iraq unfortunately raised the question of succession as the senior Source for Iraq.][3]

Unlike al-Hakim, Ayatollah Abd al-Majid Khoei, the Shi'ite cleric favored by the U.S. and Britain, was a known quantity to the West. A respected cleric in his own right as well as the son of a Source, Khoei made the Khoei Foundation in London into a center for devout but liberal Iraqi Shi'ites. But when he returned to Iraq in May 2003 he was murdered by thuggish followers of Muqtada al-Sadr as he was about to enter the Shrine of 'Alī in Najaf—an event well narrated in an interesting detail in the May 19, 2003, issue of *Newsweek*.

The most telling event in Shi'ite clerical affairs in post-Saddam Iraq may have been the siege of Ayatollah Sistani's house in Najaf. The thugs that killed Khoei besieged the house and asked Sistani to leave. After a few days Shi'ite tribesmen arrived and the besiegers departed. The tribes from which so many settled Iraqi Shi'ites trace their origin have always looked for guidance to that Source whose authority has been recognized by the consensus of the teachers at the *Ḥawza* in Najaf, and Sistani [91 or 92 in 2022] is the genuine article. While he detests politics, his circle has repeatedly asserted that Iraq should be ruled by Iraqis. [It took Americans

---

3 For a detailed discussion of the problems of succession among the Shi'ite hierarchy of Iran and Iraq, see my article "Quandaries of Emulation: The Theory and Politics of Shi'ite Manuals of Practice" (Article 25 here).

some years to understand how important Sistani was and is for the future of Iraq. Sistani realized that Prime Minister Nouri al-Maliki (whom he blamed for the rise of ISIS) had to go if democracy was to be maintained in Iraq. Sistani's opinion carried great weight, and in short order in 2014 Nouri al-Maliki resigned. Even Pope Francis understands Sistani's importance and recently visited him in his garden in Najaf in 2021.]

Only William Booth, writing in the *Washington Post*, May 15, 2003, demonstrated early on a grasp of the importance of national origins when it came to the leading figures in the *Ḥawza*. Sistani is from Mashhad in Iran but has spent most of his life in Iraq and was the leading pupil of Ayatollah Abu al-Qasim al-Khoei, the previous Najaf senior Source and father of the Ayatollah Abd al-Majid Khoei who was killed. [Sistani was in 2003 and still is in 2022 accepted by some Iranians and most Arab Shi'ites as the pre-eminent Source.] But the Afghan Shi'ite community looks to their own Ayatollah in Najaf, Fayyad [91 or 92 in 2022]. The South Asian Shi'ites look to Bashir Najafi [79–80 in 2022], who is of Pakistani origin. [Great age is a positive aspect to leadership among Shi'ite clerics.] And the complexities of ethnic allegiance in the *Ḥawza* only begin here.

The difficulty of reporting on the Iraqi Shi'ites has at times been physically dangerous. [During my own trip to Najaf in 2014 I was advised not to visit the nearby countryside to see the site of ancient Babylon because it was too unsafe. How I miss the beautiful and peaceful Iraq that I visited in 1961! Americans have so much invested in Iraq in blood and treasure that it behooves us to maintain a close and helpful relationship with our ally. Unfortunately, these days American news sources report very little news from Iraq.]

[Back in 2003,] it would have been a service if someone had tried to move beyond the issues of what the Shi'ites think of the United States and actually told us what the Shi'ites believe. The *New York Times*' Daniel J. Wakin filed a characteristically interesting story on Shi'ite self-flagellation in metropolitan New York on April 25, 2003, which must have been shocking to many. However, might the shock at seeing self-flagellation among Iraqis (forbidden by the great Ayatollahs but so far unstoppable) have been tempered for both the reporter and the reader by the realization that Jesuits flagellated themselves until recently, and that members of Opus Dei and Native American Christians in the Southwest still do?

When it comes to the [Iranian and] Iraqi Shi'ites, the U.S. government would do well to cooperate with moderate Shi'ite clerics, when possible. Their pragmatic approach to their flocks suggests that they are accomplished at adjusting to political realities if they have a say in matters vital to them.

It will be very hard, and possibly very unwise, to build a new Iraq without allowing some of the Shi'ite clergy to participate. [Americans, like] President George W. Bush, might feel comfortable with calling them "faith-based political leaders."

Shi'ite Political Thought and the Destiny of the Iranian Revolution

Even those who have little sympathy with Hegel have been drawn to his stunningly evocative phrase, "the cunning of reason," for we have no more concise way of saying that unintended consequences appear as an idea enters the arena of events, some following from the logic of the idea itself and some from the interaction of the idea with its surroundings. This chapter examines the evolution—in which reason's cunning is dramatically at work—of two key ideas in the making of the Iranian Revolution, the ideas of the "source of imitation" or *marja'īya* and "the guardianship of the jurist" or *wilāyat al-faqīh* (Persian *velāyat-e faqih*). It then describes some recent understandings of those ideas. Necessarily, in a discussion of this length, the treatment of these themes has been selective and much has been omitted.

Considerable scholarly literature now exists on both *marja'īya* and the guardianship of the jurist.[1] Quite properly, discussions of the origin of hierarchy among Twelver Shi'ite ulema go back to the birth of the Uṣūlī school in the time of Waḥīd Bihbahānī, who died in the 1790s, or the early years of the 13th/19th century. The Uṣūlī school is usually held to have reached full development with Murtaḍā Anṣārī (d. 1281/1864), who was

Author's note: This article was first published as: "Shi'ite Political Thought and the Destiny of the Iranian Revolution," in Jamal S. al-Suwaidi (ed.), *Iran and the Gulf: A Search for Stability* (The Emirates Center for Strategic Studies and Research, Abu Dhabi: 1996) 70–80. This article was slightly modified by changing from the present to the past tense when discussing certain events now long past.

1 See my entry, "Wilāyat al-Faqīh," in the *Oxford Encyclopedia of the Modern Islamic World*, ed. John L. Esposito, 4 (Oxford and New York, Oxford University Press: 1995) 320–322, which offers a survey of some of this literature; reprinted in *The Oxford Encyclopedia of the Islamic World*, ed. John L. Esposito, 5 (Oxford and New York, Oxford University Press: 2009) 529–532.

most likely the first *mujtahid* to receive international recognition by the majority of Twelver Shi'ites as the religious "leader" of the community. This leadership, it is claimed, showed its real power when, in December 1891, the great majority of the Iranian Shi'ite community obeyed a fatwa of a subsequent leader of the Shi'ite community, Hajj Mirza Hasan Shirazi, to abstain from the sale and use of tobacco. In this case the Shah had granted a humiliating concession on the production, sale, and export of all Iranian tobacco to a British subject, and the fatwa was so effective that it caused the Shah to revoke the concession. According to this standard account, the prestige gained by Shirazi's success was consolidated in the period between 1947 and 1961 when Ayatollah Borujerdi led the Shi'ite community. In fact, some historians claim that he was the first supreme leader of the Twelver Shi'ites to use his power to organize the clergy properly.

The intellectual underpinning of this evolution was the assertion by the Uṣūlī school that law could be interpreted only by *mujtahid*s (*mojtahed*s in Persian), whose warrants to do so were believed to be handed down in a chain of discipleship that had its origins among the inner circle of the infallible Imams of Twelver Shi'ism. According to the precepts of the Uṣūlī school, the believers who were not *mujtahid*s were to choose from among these *mujtahid*s (who, in this century, have seldom if ever exceeded two hundred individuals) a single jurist whom they believe to be "most learned," *a'lam*. This *mujtahid* is their "source" or *marja'*, to follow on issues affected by Islamic law. Among the *mujtahid*s, only a few of the most prominent issued manuals for the believers who seek to imitate them; most *mujtahid*s would be embarrassed to claim *'alamīya*.

One reading of the logical consequences of this view would point to a political conclusion: if this office of *marja'īya* in some sense represented the authority of the absent Twelfth Imam, then did this not mean that the most learned *marja'* also had the worldly authority of the Twelfth Imam? In 1970 Khomeini drew this conclusion in his celebrated book, *The Guardianship of the Jurist*. The theory was enshrined in the Iranian Constitution of 1979, which treats the leadership of a single supreme *marja'* as the norm. Subsequently, the "logic" of political events led to the 1989 revision of the Constitution that requires the "guide" or "leader" (*rahbar*) of the nation be a *mujtahid* but not necessarily a *marja'*.

Thus far the accepted interpretation among scholars of modern Iran has been given. This interpretation is wrong, not in what it includes, but in what it leaves out. The concept of Islamic government has been present in Islamic thought in many forms for a long time; and "the guardianship of the jurist" is by no means the only context in which it exists in Shi'ite sources.[2] The idea of a leadership among the ulema is strongly advocated by many great Sunni thinkers. Al-Ghazālī (d. 505/1111), for instance, says that a layman should follow the opinion of the jurist who is most learned in the law (*afqah*) over the most pious (*awra'*). Al-Khaṭīb al-Baghdādī (d. 463/1071), in *al-Faqīh wa-l-Mutafaqqih*, assumes that it is popular knowledge in any community as to who is the most learned jurist (*a'lamuhum bi-aḥkām al-dīn*), hence the one to whom the believers should turn. 'Abd al-Wahhāb al-Sha'rānī in his *al-Ṭabaqāt al-Ṣughrā*, says of one of his contemporaries in 10th/16th-century Egypt: "He is now the *marja'* for the people of Egypt in the writing of legal opinions (*fa'innahu al-ān marja' ahl Miṣr fī taḥrīr al-fatāwā*)."[3] It is interesting to note that Sha'rānī lived at the dawn of the period in which the Ottoman Empire would force the ulema under its sway into a hierarchy unmatched in the rigor of its organization by any Twelver Shi'ite government past or present.

Another omission in the traditional scholarly account of the *wilāyat al-faqīh* is the pre-Khomeini history of the "guardianship of the jurist." The idea had existed not only in the very early nineteenth century in the thought of Hajj Mullah Aḥmad Narāqī, who is cited by Khomeini, but had been accepted in limited ways by other jurists. Khomeini's book is, in fact, an extract from his commentary on *al-Makāsib*, the masterwork of Murtaḍā Anṣārī. In its first formulation, when Khomeini in his lectures in Najaf discussed Anṣārī's rejection of "the guardianship of the jurist," he restated the traditional view of the Uṣūlīs that every *mujtahid* must follow his own judgment, which implies that no *mujtahid* need defer to another in matters of government. These lectures were published

2 See the highly important book review by Professor Hossein Modarressi of A.A. Sachedina, *The Just Ruler or the Guardian Jurist: An Attempt to Link Two Different Shi'ite Concepts*, 1988, in the *Journal of the American Oriental Society* 111:3 (July–September 1991) 549–562.

3 Al-Ghazālī, *al-Mankhūl* (Beirut, Dār al-Fikr: 1980) 483; al-Khatīb al-Baghdādī, *Kitāb al-Faqīh wa-l-Mutaffaqih*, II (Beirut: Dār al-Kutub al-'Ilmīya, 1980) 179; al-Sha'rānī, *al-Ṭabaqāt al-Ṣughrā* (Cairo, Maktabat al-Qahīra: 1970) 122. All these citations are taken from the brilliant essay by Devin J. Stewart, "Islamic Juridical Hierarchies and the Office of Marji' al-Taqlid." in L. Clarke (ed. and trans.), *Shi'ite Heritage: Essays on Classical and Modern Traditions* (Binghamton, N.Y., Global Publications: 2001) 137–157. This study by Stewart has influenced much of the thinking in the present article. It should be noted that Stewart's spelling *marji'* reflects the classical pronunciation of this word which has changed to *marja'* in modern times.

in installments the morning after they were delivered. But when the fasciculi were gathered into a book, Khomeini stated that if one *faqīh* (i.e., a *mujtahid* who is a *marja'*) possessing knowledge and justice undertakes the task of government, "he will possess the same authority as the Most Noble Messenger in the administration of society and it will be the duty of all people to obey him."[4] Presumably "all people" includes other *mujtahids*; and it is here that Khomeini may break with tradition, a point to which we will return.

As for the period since the Iranian Revolution, the standard interpretation omits key events leading up to the amendment of the constitution. It was, most importantly, the political success of the ulema who were not *marja's*, principally Rafsanjani, that led to the amendment. But ideologically the concept of *marja'īya* had been undergoing change through the course of events. On April 20, 1982, after Ayatollah Shari'atmadari was associated with Sadiq Qobtzadeh's plot against the government, the Association of Combatant Clerics of Tehran, and then, in rapid succession, the Association of Teachers of Qom and the Council of Guardians announced him stripped of his *marja'īya*. It was not clear how, in traditional Uṣūlī terms, a Shi'ite could be considered "the most learned" jurist by a large segment of the Shi'ite world one day, and on political grounds lose his authority on the next when, to all appearances, only his loyalty to the government and not his learning had decreased.

Political considerations again appeared to have forced a reinterpretation of the guardianship of the jurist when, on March 28, 1989, Ayatollah Hossein Ali Montazeri resigned under pressure. At the end of 1985, Montazeri had been declared "the deputy of the Leader" by the Council of Experts, the group empowered to choose the *marja'* who should be the "leader." From that time on Montazeri was seen as the heir apparent to Khomeini, which implied that when Khomeini remained silent on any issue, Montazeri could speak with high authority. Montazeri exercised the right to intervene in the judiciary and to assume control of the traditional educational system of madrasas and of the universities and other aspects of public life. Although he was an advocate of an aggressive foreign policy, he proved to be a force for moderation in domestic politics. For example, he argued for the transfer of ownership of uncultivated land (*mawāt*) to

4 *Islam and Revolution: Writings and Declarations of Imam Khomeini*, trans. Hamid Algar (Berkeley, C.A., Mizan Press: 1981) 62.

a new cultivator even if the land had known a previous owner, thus placing himself between the conservative views of Ayatollah Golpayegani, who held that land must be certifiably abandoned before its ownership can be transferred, and the radical view of Ayatollah Meshkini-Ardabili, who holds that even a hired laborer cultivating land is performing *iḥyā' al-mawāt*, and thereby becomes—at least for the period of the crop—a partner of the owner.[5]

Montazeri's views proved unpalatable. In a sermon delivered on February 11, 1989, the tenth anniversary of the Revolution, he indulged in self-criticism, as well as in criticism of the government's record over the preceding decade. The slogans of the past ten years, he claimed, had made Iran "isolated in the world and caused the people to view us with pessimism ... The people of the world thought our only task here in Iran was to kill ... Prisons must be emptied and forces mobilized for reconstruction." Iranians should repent their "social and political mistakes." In addition, he criticized restrictions on free expression and said that he himself was sometimes censored.[6]

Those who disliked Montazeri, or regarded criticism of the regime as betrayal, jumped to the defense of the government's record. Khamenei told a large crowd in Azadi Square that Iran had diplomatic relations with all but a few nations that were illegitimate and had a history of plotting against Iran. On February 13, Prime Minister Mir-Hossein Mousavi said that the principal intention of those who cast aspersions on the Revolution was "to make use of weak-spirited people" and "to sow seeds of doubt about the Revolution."[7]

On March 28, following a meeting of the Council of Experts, Khomeini, accepting Montazeri's forced resignation, wrote:

> As you have written, the position of leadership of the Islamic Republic is a difficult task and a heavy responsibility that requires endurance greater than you possess ... I see your interest and that of the Islamic Republic in your being a jurist so that the people and the regime may benefit from your views.

5 Hossein Ali Montazeri, *Kitāb al-Khums* (Qom, n.d.) 369–391.
6 FBIS (Foreign Broadcast Information Service, February 11, 1989.
7 *Ibid.*, February 2, 1989.

Again, one might ask: If Montazeri was chosen heir-presumptive primarily for his learning, why had he lost his position so abruptly?[8]

A complicating factor in understanding the significance of this event was Khomeini's celebrated declaration issued in January of 1988, in which he spelled out the meaning of the statement, already found in his book, that the jurist-leader inherited the authority of the Prophet. It is not clear, given the strong abstract claims already advanced in his book, that this declaration represented an innovation in Khomeini's thinking. But for him to say openly that an Islamic government could suspend fasting, prayer, and pilgrimage to Mecca was electrifying. It provoked some soul-searching and a debate which is outside the scope of this chapter, except to say that the book-length rebuttal of Khomeini's declaration by the former prime minister Mehdi Bazargan offered yet another fully articulated and very different position on the guardianship of the jurist. It is important for this article, however, to note that Khomeini based these powers of the state in part on "the wider interests of the community," here clearly invoking a well-known principle in Shi'ite law, *hifẓ al-niẓām* or "the preservation of order," a commonweal principle for the suspension of law similar to *istiṣlāḥ*, *maṣlaḥa*, and other commonweal principles used in the Sunni schools of law. Those out of sympathy with the government felt that the increasingly frequent use of the principle of "the preservation of order" was turning it into a principle of "reason of state."[9]

With Khomeini's death and the subsequent completion and ratification of the 1989 amendment of the constitution, the government was free to choose as "leader" a *mujtahid* who was not a *marja'*. The former Speaker of the Parliament, Rafsanjani, who had emerged as the most popular elected official after the Revolution, became president—an office that had been largely ceremonial but under the revised constitution received increased power, including control of the budget. Khamenei, holder of the formerly ceremonial presidency, received Khomeini's position as spiritual "leader," although he could not inherit Khomeini's charismatic authority. Khamenei had studied for five years in Qom at the "graduate" level, called *khārij*, "beyond the texts," in which students learn to debate and discuss without a text in front of them, a process which—after a considerable

8 Text of the letter in *Iran Times*, March 31, 1989.

9 The rebuttal is entitled: *Tafṣil va-Taḥlil-e Velāyat-e Moṭlaqeh-ye Faqih*, signed by Nehżat-e Āzādi-ye Irān (specifically the head of that organization Mehdi Bazargan), Farvardin 1347, available online.

period of study—prepares the most talented students to receive the title *mujtahid*. Khamenei, who was in his fifties, received this title only when Khomeini, on his death bed in the presence of two witnesses, reportedly recognized Khamenei as a *mujtahid*. Khamenei, who by and large had been a cooperative player with Rafsanjani, was quickly approved by the significant bodies of the clergy, including the Association of Teachers in Qom, which represents the collective opinion of the most learned ulema. At this point Iranians followed Ayatollah Khoei, Ayatollah Mar'ashi-Najafi, or Ayatollah Golpayegani as their *marja*'s; there was now a more purely religious leadership outside the government and a more politically religious leadership inside the government.

Khamenei turned out to have a mind and aspirations of his own. He adopted with gusto the role of guardian of pristine revolutionary values, which he had foreshadowed in his speech on the tenth anniversary of the Revolution. He worried about slipshod standards of dress and public morality. He kept the issue of Salman Rushdie in the foreground, when Rafsanjani, who had seemed to be Khamenei's patron, wanted it to slip into the background; Khamenei has sided with those who have economic entitlements acquired through the Revolution, while Rafsanjani tried to restore a free-market system.[10]

The cunning of reason was at work in yet another area. It was "reasonable" to expect the spiritual "leader" to find his own voice (and, not coincidentally, his own constituency, since he seemed to strike the populist note that many had felt to be absent since Khomeini had died). It was also both "reasonable" that Khamenei should aspire to reunite true spiritual authority, the *marja'īya*, with the uncertain authority he had gained as "leader," and reasonable that the leading men of the ulema establishment, older and—by most conventional measures—more learned than Khamenei, should reject such aspirations.

The drama unfolded accordingly. On Thursday, December 9, 1993, Ayatollah Golpayegani died; he had been predeceased by Ayatollah Khoei and was at the time of his death recognized by the overwhelming majority of Iranian Shi'ites as their *marja'*. Already at Golpayegani's funeral a split was evident; some of the ulema prevented Khamenei from saying the "prayer for the dead," a task reserved for the most respected associate of

10 See also my discussion of the career of Khamenei and his opponents in "Islamic Movements: The Case for Democratic Inclusion" (Article 27 here).

the deceased and performed by Golpayegani at Khomeini's funeral. The Association of Teachers abandoned its usual meeting place, the library of the prestigious Faiziye Madrasa, and did not invite observers from the Shi'ite communities abroad, such as Shams al-Din and Fadlallah from Lebanon. Instead, they met clandestinely so that the followers of Khamenei could not interrupt their deliberations.[11]

The actual vote within the Association of Teachers was an interesting reflection of the different strategies the leading ulema thought appropriate at that juncture. Many favored the election of Ayatollah Sistani, who lived in Najaf in Iraq. Then, in his early seventies, Sistani was comparatively young by ayatollah standards, but he had great learning, was the *marja'* for the Shi'ites of Iraq, and—most importantly—he believed that the clergy should shun political office completely. A fair number secretly supported Montazeri, believing him to be the most learned; but Khomeini's rejection of him made it impossible to refer to him except obliquely. In the end, the majority of the fifty or so *mujtahids* present persuaded all members to endorse the declaration that "the office of *marja'* is exclusively established in the Grand Ayatollah Hajj Shaykh Muhammad 'Ali Araki."[12]

The choice was not unexpected. Araki had unquestionably acquired the rank of *mujtahid* and had long been famous for his piety, although not for his learning. At the age of ninety-nine, he no longer closely followed what was going on around him and was a candidate whose mere presence as *marja'* would block the ambitions of Khamenei and who could be counted on to take a fairly passive role. Moreover, the choice of Araki coincided with the views of the circle around Rafsanjani, the president, which were that Khamenei had interfered too often in matters of policy. Nevertheless, there were members of the ulema who supported Khamenei's ambitions. On December 12, in a memorial service in Tehran, the head of the Majlis, Nateq Nuri, said, referring to the many mourners present there and at the funeral: "This is a sign of the deep religious faith in and following for his excellency Ayatollah Khamenei, the Leader of the Islamic Revolution." Another issue that remained unresolved was in the interpretation of the Association's statement appointing Araki: if the office was "exclusively established" (*muta'ayyan*) in one person as *marja'* this surely meant that there was exclusive establishment only in the collective public view of

11 On the funeral of Golpayegani, see *Iran Times*, December 17, 1993.

12 *Ibid.* The wording in the report in *Iran Times* has "*muhraz*," but an actual copy of the statement has "*muta'ayyan*."

the ulema, who continued to believe individually that there were other legitimate *marja*ʿs such as Sistani. Had a second semi-official office been created to give the Association of Teachers a united face vis-a-vis the state?[13]

Ayatollah Araki died at the age of one hundred on November 29, 1994, having given only one year's respite from struggles over clerical leadership. This time Khamenei was better prepared, in part because Araki had been at death's door for three weeks. Already in the second week of November, Ayatollah Ahmad Jannati, well known for quixotic statements such as his appeal to the Muslims of Europe to take over the governments of that continent, announced that it was precisely the "enemies" of the Islamic Republic who favored the appointment of a non-political *marja*ʿ. But at first his strategy seemed unclear. Only days before Araki's death the ever-busy Jannati announced that Khamenei, "the Leader of the Islamic Republic, did not accept the position of *marja*ʿ*īya* which had been offered to him repeatedly."[14]

Khamenei's modesty, genuine or strategic, had not left his supporters idle. At Araki's funeral a portion of the crowd shouted: "Khamenei is the Imam; he is the *marja*ʿ of the Shiʿites." Then, the Association of Teachers in Qom endorsed a list of seven candidates, including Khamenei, only a few days after warning the government not to interfere in the choice of the *marja*ʿ. One hundred fifty of the 270 members of the parliament endorsed the list and, in their statement, declared Khamenei to be "the most informed person concerning Islam and the Islamic world and the most qualified authority for the leadership of the Muslim society." On December 9 the head of the judiciary, Ayatollah Yazdi, declared Khamenei as Iran's sole *marja*ʿ and warned the senior clergy not to disobey him. Khamenei was increasingly called "the highest *marja*ʿ."[15]

No one who paused to think could believe that this man, then of fifty-five years, who in Qom had never been permitted to teach a really advanced text, was in the same league of learning as the other six candidates on the list. But some obviously did not consider this, and those who did, and

13 The politics of the clerics in this period are discussed with characteristic thoroughness and depth of insight by Shaul Bakhash in his essay: "Iran: The Crisis of Legitimacy," in Martin Kramer (ed.), *Middle East Lectures*, I (Syracuse, N.Y., Syracuse University Press: 1995) Professor Bakhash makes clear the social and, above all, economic agenda that Iranians have sought to support by their various stands on the *marja*ʿ*īya* and "the guardianship of the jurist."

14 *Iran Times*, December 2, 1994.

15 *Iran Times*, December 9, 1994; December 16, 1994.

yet endorsed Khamenei, clearly believed that political experience and ideological orientation counted for as much as—or more than—learning. Almost as striking was the comment that the Association of Teachers added to their list: they declared it a positive aspect of Shiʿism that the believer could choose his/her *marjaʿ*. The majority of the top clergy were trying to diffuse authority, however much the theory of the guardianship of the jurist might favor uniting political authority with *marjaʿīya*, while at the same time the government was trying to keep clerical leadership ensconced in its midst. Yet, as the Qur'ān (III:54) so eloquently says:

وَمَكَرُوا وَمَكَرَ ٱللَّهُ وَٱللَّهُ خَيرُ ٱلماكِرِين

"They plotted and God plotted, and God is the best of plotters."
(Or, as the English proverb states: Man proposes, God disposes.)

Five days after Yazdi's declaration, Khamenei declined the *marjaʿīya* inside Iran but said he was willing to be the *marjaʿ* for Shiʿites outside of Iran, most of whom in any case are followers of Ayatollah Sistani in Iraq. Iranians now jokingly asked each other whether they should obtain copies of Khamenei's manual on proper behavior to keep in their suitcases for their trips abroad. The cunning of reason—which included both reasons of state and the logical entailment of the political theory behind the Iranian constitution—had left *marjaʿīya* everywhere and nowhere at the same time. Ironically, the many seemingly essential compromises appeared to have left no one, at least for the time being, with the religious legitimacy the leading *mujtahid*s had enjoyed on the eve of the Revolution.

No survey of the evolution of ideas on the guardianship of the jurist would be complete without reference to the fate and ideas of Ayatollah Montazeri. Barred from consideration, harassed, and confined to Qom, he had gained support to be the highest *marjaʿ* because of his very refusal to compromise, a position that Shiʿites have always respected in a clergyman. He had the most popular class at Qom, with about one thousand students, and his reinterpretation of the guardianship of the jurist was the boldest step so far taken by clergymen in favor of this theory. Basically, he said that the heart of the theory is elective government, because—among other reasons—God gave man disposal over his personal resources, and therefore a voice (as well as an inner predilection to have a voice) in the government that taxes him. The guardian-jurist is a representative of all society, which needs to entrust its collective interests to a central authority who, however, remains answerable to society. If this strikes an American reader as somewhere between Tom Paine and Thomas Jefferson, it is buttressed with careful argument from the traditional sources of Islamic law.[16]

Even this survey of one aspect of political thought and its transformation shows how multi-centered political life in Iran had once been. Most importantly, there was a three-way stand-off between a pragmatic administration, represented by the presidency, a socially and economically conservative parliament, and the economic radicals, who wanted more state intervention in everything. From Khomeini's time to the present, much of the argument over the legitimacy and scope of authority of the office of *marja'* has been closely tied to the struggle over conflicting economic and social policies, although it should be remembered that "factions" united on any issue will very seldom completely overlap with factions formed over another issue. Struggles over these conflicts are complicated by the degree to which the present Iranian constitution reflects the French Constitution of the Fifth Republic, which assumed that the president (namely, de Gaulle) and the majority in the legislature would agree, a condition often not realized in either system. Moreover, from a religious point of view, there is a tension in Islam as in so many other religions between individual responsibility and leadership. As Khomeini acknowledged in his first draft of *The Guardianship of the Jurist*, a *mujtahid* cannot submit himself before the fact to the forthcoming opinions of another *mujtahid*. Iranian public life has reached something of a stalemate not only because of the stand-off between the parliament, presidency, and radicals, but also because it was impossible to build a true hierarchy of subordination in the sense of the Catholic Church. Twelver Shi'ism is a system in which the leader can lead, but his most important potential "subordinates" (*mujtahids* who do not claim to be *marja'*s) are obliged by a religious precept not to follow. One can seek the political logic of creating a "papacy," as the ever inventive Ayatollah Jannati has suggested, but such an institution would run against the logic of Twelver Shi'ism's millennium-long construction of the behavior of the believer in the absence of infallible advice.[17]

Nevertheless, this millennium-long discussion has dramatically changed in the past two centuries. The change reflects the increase in communication and travel, which has made it physically possible for the highest *marja'*

16 Hossein Ali Montazeri, *Dirāsāt fī Wilāyat al-Faqīh*, I (Qom: 1408 A.H.) 495–496.
17 For Jannati on the need for "papacy," see *Iran Times*, December 9, 1994.

to be in touch with the faithful throughout the world. The "manuals" for the ordinary believer that are issued by the *marja'* seem to have become common only in the nineteenth century. Organization has developed in the granting of the degree of *ijtihād*, increasingly a formal matter. And, in post-revolutionary Iran, a system of informal deference has given way to a system of election through balloting, whether in the Council of Experts set up by the constitution or in the self-generated Association of Teachers in Qom.[18]

Yet, the greatest influence on the transformation of the clergy has been its interface with the emerging modern state. Already during the Safavid dynasty a bureaucratic government had created hierarchy in the clergy. Al-Karaki (d. 1001/1592–93), for example, as the government-installed head of the religious establishment, was called "the *mujtahid*" of his time, a title that seems to imply that any potential *mujtahids* were not encouraged to offer opinions while al-Karaki was in power.[19] The modern state, however, is a much more powerful affair. As the modern state emerged, the ulema saw the need for more centralized clerical leadership to stand up to the that state, although rivalry and the lack of a real hierarchical principle meant Shi'ites, who theoretically favored a central religious authority, have managed to produce such widely recognized leaders for only limited periods in the past two centuries. The idea of deferential leadership based upon consensus among fairly limited communities of ulema, found in Egypt, Iran, and other parts of the Islamic world, is fairly old, as we have seen. But an activist leadership is new and still, for many of the ulema, goes against the grain.

Machiavelli is often seen as the origin of modern Western political thought because he identified a public realm that had its own interests and named this realm the "state." The name has stuck, and many believe that the morality of government cannot be guaranteed by the personal morality of the ruler, as seemed true when we had "governments" but not yet "states." With the birth of the state, a question opened which has never been closed: Can any individual, by his/her virtue, "irradiate" the state with goodness? With the Iranian Revolution a religious clergy, which

18 Stewart, (*supra* n. 3) discusses the changes in the office of *mujtahid* in the nineteenth century.

19 Eskandar Monshi, *The History of Shah 'Abbas the Great*, trans. Roger Savory, I (Boulder, CO: Westview Press: 1978) 205. Sayyid Husayn ibn Hasan al-Karaki is called simply "the *mujtahid*"; Stewart, (*supra* n. 3).

was only loosely hierarchical, attempted to create a "republic of virtue," in part by creating an individual "source" of virtue, a tradition that goes back at least as far as Plato's *Republic*. [Now, forty-four] years after this experiment began, with revolutionary fervor very much diminished and serious economic and social problems on every side, it remains an open question as to whether the Iranian state and Iranians as individuals can agree on the same single source as a highest arbiter of morality for the state and for the individual. Has the "cunning of reason" irreversibly created a de facto independent statist sphere that will last, or is this sphere only a temporary outcome of the reversible cunning of men?

The Quandaries of Emulation: The Theory and Politics of Shi'ite Manuals of Practice

The dramatic rise in Shi'ite–Sunni sectarianism in 2014 caught the attention of the world. Iraq was then split between Shi'ite and Sunni factions while Syria survived as a quasi-Shi'ite state with significant support from the Lebanese Shi'ite community. Bahrain was riven by Sunni–Shi'ite antagonism. In the face of the conquest of much of northern and western Iraq by Sunni insurgents of the self-proclaimed "Islamic State,"[1] Ayatollah Ali Sistani, the highest Shi'ite religious authority in Iraq, issued a statement in his own handwriting and with his seal that addressed recent security "developments in the province of Nineveh and surrounding areas." This statement issued on July 10, 2014, the date that the "Islamic State" captured Mosul, spoke of "the necessity to unite and strengthen efforts to stand in the face of terrorists and increase protection for citizens."[2] Tens of thousands came forward as volunteers. This statement was posted on Sistani's

---

Author's note: This article was originally published separately as: *The Quandaries of Emulation: The Theory and Politics of Shi'i Manuals of Practice*, The Ninth Farhat J. Ziadeh Distinguished Lecture in Arab and Islamic Studies, May 2, 2011, The Department of Near Eastern Languages and Civilization, the University of Washington, (Seattle, WA, University of Washington: 2014). Reproduced with permission. It was a great privilege to honor Professor Farhat Ziadeh, the doyen of Islamic legal studies in North America by delivering the lecture at the University of Washington in 2011. The original lecture was revised and updated after serious illness delayed its publication until 2014.The article has been slightly modified here by changing certain events to the past tense, adding some information in brackets, and removing some information no longer relevant.

1 The "Islamic State" was formerly called ISIS (the Islamic State in Iraq and Syria) and ISIL (the Islamic State in Iraq and the Levant). [The Islamic State was declared "defeated" in 2019, but it is regrouping in Afghanistan and Pakistan and was still carrying out bombing attacks in Iraq and Syria in 2021.]

2 Sistani.org/arabic/statement/24906 (viewed on August 13, 2014)

website along with two sermons delivered by two authorized "representatives of the highest religious source of emulation"—namely, of Ayatollah Sistani. The first of these sermons was given on June 20, 2014. It made clear that the groups (i.e., the Sunni leaders of the "Islamic State") easily calling other Muslims "infidels" and threatening churches and holy places of all kinds were enemies of all citizens of Iraq. The sermon thanked the "hundreds of thousands" who responded to Sistani's call to volunteer and told them to join the army or security forces but not to form militias. The sermon also called on Parliament to form a new government. A sermon delivered on July 11, 2014, reiterated all of these points while emphasizing the urgency of appointing a new government.[3] On August 14, Nuri al-Maliki, the Prime Minister, resigned and without question the largest influence on his unwilling withdrawal was Sistani.

How did so much power come to rest with such a religious leader? A full explanation would require a lengthy intellectual and social history of Twelver Shiʿism (hereafter Shiʿism) from the nineteenth century to the present. In this article I address only one aspect: the rise and continuing importance of "manuals of practice" by the "most learned" of the Shiʿites, written to stake their claim to leadership. I also consider some recent conflicts and compromises within the Shiʿite ulema about such leadership.

Twelver Shiʿites (hereafter Shiʿites) recognize religious authority in their Imams, who, according to their understanding were infallible in their judgments. The eleventh of these Imams, and the last one to be in some personal contact with his community, was Imam Ḥasan al-ʿAskarī (d. 260/874), who lived in Samarra in central Iraq. The attack in 2006 and 2007 on the shrine where this Imam and his father, the tenth Imam, are buried critically deepened the sectarian war between Shiʿite and Sunni Iraqis. The "Islamic State" attacked Samarra on June 4, 2014, and again on June 11, but was driven off by the Iraqi army and Shiʿite militias. On June 30 an attacker fired three mortar rounds at the shrine killing six and slightly damaging the structure.

According to Shiʿite understanding, at Imam Ḥasan al-ʿAskari's death in 874 he left a son Muḥammad, who was concealed from the hostile rulers of the time. He communicated with his followers through intermediaries until they declared that his absence was total. While some Sunnis expect a messiah, all Shiʿites expect the messianic return of the Twelfth Imam as a savior who will fill the world with justice.

---

3 Sistani.org/Arabic/archive/24925 and/24915 (viewed on August 13, 2014).

In the absence of the messiah, opinion in the Shi'ite community supported the view that those who accurately transmitted the sayings of the Prophet and the Imams were a "source" who could give guidance. As procedures were elaborated for shaping such guidance, including the use of reason, the Shi'ites eventually called such specialists "*mujtahids*," which means "those who exert themselves to determine the Divine Law."

In the Sunni world a consensus gradually emerged that the true *mujtahids* were the founders of the four major Sunni schools of law, the Ḥanafīs, the Shāf'īs, the Mālikīs and the Ḥanbalīs, and these founders are often called "*Imām Mujtahids*." Nevertheless, many later Sunni jurists were de facto *mujtahids* in that they used independent reasoning in their decisions, but many preferred to be called *muftīs*, issuers of fatwas or "legal opinions." In the early period of the formation of Sunni law there developed a fairly extensive use of "opinion" (*ra'y*) by the jurists, a term which Shi'ite jurists totally rejected even when later Shi'ite jurists declared reason (*'aql*) to be a source of legal opinions. Shi'ites were cautious about the term *mujtahid* until the 7th/13th century, perhaps because it seemed a challenge to the position of the earlier infallible Imams from whom they had formerly asked legal advice.

Murtaḍā Anṣārī (d. 1864) is, by general consent among Shi'ite scholars, the most important Shi'ite legal thinker of the past two centuries. He greatly advanced the use of certain procedural principles which had a basis in reason and proved extremely useful for the *mujtahid* in making legal decisions. One unintended consequence was that legal thinking became more abstruse and less accessible to the lay person. It took a lot of training and practice to master the works of Anṣārī, which assumed their place as key texts at the end of the curriculum for those studying to become *mujtahids*.[4]

The admiration for Anṣārī was so great that he was widely (some would say universally) recognized as "the most learned" *mujtahid* living and several of his pupils wrote a summary of his legal opinions for the ordinary believers. This widespread recognition of Anṣārī was made possible by the diffusion of printed books, the telegraph, more reliable postal service and increased safety of travel, all of which played important roles in the

4 See my article "An Introduction to Islamic Law and Islamic Jurisprudence" (Article 4 here), which includes an explanation of the procedural principles.

centralization of Shi'ite authority through the distribution of fatwas and manuals of practice during the nineteenth and early twentieth centuries.

One of the written manuals by a pupil of Anṣārī dramatically states on its opening page the slogan that created the institution of the *marja'*, namely: *al-a'lam fa-l-a'lam* or "[authority is given to] the most learned [*mujtahid* then living] and then [after his death] to the most learned."[5] Similarly, another disciple of Anṣārī begins his collection of Anṣārī's opinions, *Ṣirāṭ al-Najāt* (*The Road to Salvation*), with a discussion of the necessity of emulation, a characteristic of these manuals from this time forward.[6] Gradually, the popularity of such manuals became a gauge by which to measure the acceptance of such would-be "most learned" *mujtahid*s.

Similar manuals exist in the Christian, Jewish, Buddhist and other communities. Somewhat similar books also existed in the Islamic tradition long before the nineteenth century. An early example of this genre is the Mālikī law book, *al-Risāla*, written in 327/938 by Ibn Abī Zayd al-Qayrawānī. This book has been memorized from the time of its production to the present in North and sub-Saharan Africa as an introduction to the Mālikī school of Sunni law. Its differences from the later Shi'ite manuals from Anṣārī onward are significant. This early Sunni book begins with a creed whereas the Shi'ite manuals consider the fundamentals of religion as matters that the believer should prove for him or herself and state that he/she "cannot accept the word of another" concerning these fundamentals.[7]

The Shi'ite manuals do not try to establish the "indisputable" matters of Islamic faith such as the need to fast during Ramadan: while they discuss how one should fast, they do not discuss why one should fast.[8] For Shi'ites the fundamental beliefs of their faith are established through theology, not through manuals of practice. Later Shi'ite manuals gained an authority that neither earlier Sunni nor earlier Shi'ite jurists claimed because the

---

5 Fatwas of Murtaḍā al-Anṣārī collected by Muḥammad 'Alī Yazdī and copied in 1274/1857–58 or 1275/July 1859 well before the death of the Anṣārī in 1864: Princeton University Library Voyager Bib ID 6737936. [The original Arabic spelling for *marja'* was *marji'*, but in practice in both Iran and Iraq it is now *marja'* as given here throughout.]

6 This manual was printed in Tehran in 1300/1883, nineteen years after Anṣārī's death. Library of the University of Southern California I.D. 508015.

7 An exception is a manual by Khomeini in which some editions begin with the fundamentals of faith; see J. Borujerdi, "Translator's Note," in Ruhollah Khomeini, *Clarification of Questions* (Boulder: 1984) xxxi.

8 E.g., Abu al-Qasim Khoei [Khū'ī], *Articles of Islamic Acts*, 3rd ed. (Karachi: 1989) 1.

concept of obedience to "the most learned and then [after him] the most learned" centralized authority as it had never been centralized before.

A collection of fatwas from the Sunni world organized by subject and somewhat similar to Shi'ite manuals of practice has been written in the twenty-first century by "Justice Mufti," Muhammad Taqi Usmani, often considered the intellectual leader of the powerful Deoband movement in South Asia.[9] Another such Sunni manual is *Min Fatāwā Faḍīlat al-Imām al-Akbar al-Shaykh Jād al-Ḥaqq* from a decade earlier.[10] The author was Grand Muftī of Egypt, Minister of Religious Affairs, and Shaykh al-Azhar. Both of these manuals are from greatly respected figures, but they could not expect the total obedience that the leading Shi'ite *mujtahid*s expect in contemporary times.

The post-Anṣārī Shi'ite manuals begin with a section on the authority of the *mujtahid* and the obligations of non-*mujtahid*s to follow a *mujtahid* (or to exercise *iḥtiyāṭ*, "precaution," i.e., to adopt the most cautious position imaginable in each action, such as repeating one's prayers if there is the slightest uncertainty as to whether they were correctly performed). Such an obligation to follow the behavior prescribed by a *mujtahid* is called *taqlīd* in Arabic and Persian and is usually translated as "emulation." "Precaution" as the default position when one does not choose to emulate, is considered intellectually prior to emulation, but few choose this burdensome way of living. From the Shi'ite point of view emulation frees the believer from any responsibility for a mistaken judgment by the *mujtahid*, and the possibility of such mistakes is freely admitted.

At this point [2014], the number of Shi'ite *mujtahid*s who are broadly recognized—as determined by the use of their manuals of practice—number about six, the majority of whom are Iranian even though some, like Sistani, may have lived elsewhere for many years. The manuals obligate the emulator to pay a religious tax to his/her chosen "source of emulation" each year. At present Sistani seems to be the source of emulation for the majority of Twelver Shi'ites in the world, although he has strong rivals. Not surprisingly, there is an unspoken competition for emulators because of the financial power that comes with a large following.

---

9 Muhammad Taqi Usmani, *Contemporary Fatwās*, trans. Muhammad Shoaib Omar (Lahore: 2001).

10 Jād al-Ḥaqq, *Min Fatāwā Faḍīlat al-Imām al-Akbar al-Shaykh Jād al-Ḥaqq* (Cairo: 1990).

Two important changes in recent Shiʿite thought concerning these manuals is the permission for ordinary believers to follow a dead *mujtahid* and permission to divide religious affiliation between different sources of emulation. To understand the earlier situation, I refer to the great bibliographer of Twelver Shiʿism, Agha Bozorg al-Tehrani (d. 1389/1970). Here is his description of these manuals, of which I offer an abbreviated English translation from the Arabic:

> *The Manual of Practice* is a general title for treatises consisting of fatwas that bring together questions which common people need in their daily actions regulated by the Divine Law. They were composed in abundance in the eleventh, twelfth, and thirteenth centuries of the Hijra [17th, 18th and 19th centuries C.E.]. In this [the 14th/20th] century the ulema [Shiʿite clergymen] have satisfied the need for them. In the forefront of the ulema to write them is Sayyid Baḥr al-ʿUlūm [d. 1212/1797][11] and Shaykh Anṣārī [d. 1281/1864] ... Given that recent [ulema] do not allow behavior according to the fatwa of someone who is deceased, consequently these manuals of practice and the commentaries upon them are not a matter for concern after the death of the *muftī* [*mujtahid*] issuing them, except in cases in which these manuals are subject to commentary and revision of their questions according to the fatwa of living ulema.[12]

In most respects, this passage, which was published in 1951, remains valid. Shiʿite leaders, living or dead, are called *marjaʿ al-taqlīd* (in the plural, *marājiʿ al-taqlīd*, but hereafter *marja*ʿs), variously translated as the "source of emulation" or "reference point for imitation." All jurists who claim this distinction must issue a manual of practice. The passage from Tehrani does, however, mention an issue still under dispute, namely, the use of manuals of deceased Shiʿite leaders. The issue remains important because some ordinary believers continue to follow parts of the manuals of practice of Ayatollahs Khomeini and Abu al-Qasim al-Khoei.

The "classic" Shiʿite manual of practice is the *al-ʿUrwa al-Wuthqā* by Sayyid Muhammad Kazim al-Yazdi, who died in 1337/1919. It was very

11 Sayyid Muḥammad Mahdī Baḥr al-ʿUlūm (d. 1212/1797). He did not write a "practical manual" in the style of the later manuals although he did write two short surveys of Islamic law, one in prose and one in poetry.

12 Agha Bozorg al-Tehrani, *Al-Dharīʿa ilā Taṣānīf al-Shīʿa* (Qom: 1951).

clear and, despite the author's reputation as a conservative who opposed elected government, became the point of departure for most subsequent *marja*'s. Commentaries on it have been written by most major *marja*'s including Sistani. Yazdi presents the traditional view that, "It is not permissible to turn from one living person [emulated] to another living person, unless the latter is more learned." Once you choose, you must stick with your choice till his death, unless you are persuaded (presumably by the Shi'ite ulema) that someone else is more learned. In his commentary on *al-'Urwa al-Wuthqā* Khomeini added: "... or is equal [in learning]."[13]

Sistani modifies this approach, both in his comments on the *'Urwa*[14] and more specifically in his fatwas in which he answers questions (pl. *istiftā'āt*, sing. *istiftā'*) posed by others.[15] He strongly supports obedience to "the most learned" (*a'lam*) and even states: "The only excuse on the day of resurrection is the fatwa of the most learned."[16] Sistani is in no doubt that one can still follow someone who is dead if he is considered more learned and specifically refers to his teacher, "his excellency Sayyid Khoei,"[17] in this respect, although to do so completely may be impossible on questions that have not been covered by the deceased *marja'*. Sistani squarely faces the problem that many contemporary Shi'ites want to follow one section of the manual of one *marja'* and another section of the manual of a different *marja'*. This practice is called *tab'īḍ* (apportioning or division) in Arabic (and called *tajzi'a* or *tajazzu'* by some Iranian clergymen). The word *tab'īḍ* has a long history in Islamic law, meaning the division of something into parts, whether it be ritual prayer or the repayment of a debt.[18] Sistani says, "Yes, *tab'īḍ* is permissible. It is incumbent in the specific case when one of the two *mujtahids* is more learned in some chapters [of the manual] and the other is more learned in different [ones]. Consequently, one imitates each

13 Muhammad Kazim al-Yazdi, *al-'Urwa al-Wuthqā ma'a-Ta'līqāt* (Qom: 1428) 15.

14 Muhammad Kazim al-Yazdi, *Sharḥ al-'Urwa al-Wuthqā* (Qom: 1425/2004–5), with comments by Sistani.

15 Sistani.org/Arabic/qa/0369 gives Sistani's Arabic fatwas on *taqlīd* numbered from 1 to 98 and his Persian fatwas numbered 1 to 28; hereafter "*istiftā'āt* Arabic" and "'*istiftā'āt* Persian." The fatwas in each language seem to be completely independent from each other.

16 "*Istiftā'āt* Persian," no. 11.

17 "*Istiftā'āt* Arabic," nos. 2, 4, 15. See also n. 23.

18 See *Al-Mawsū'a al-Fiqhīya* X (Kuwait: 1407/1987) 75–93.

in that [i.e., those chapters] in which he is more learned ..."[19] Of course, the emphasis here is on two *mujtahids* rather than on several.

The convenience of *tab'īḍ*, or what I shall henceforth refer to as the "cut-and-paste method," which allows *marja*'s to share authority with other *marja*'s, was first evident in the time of Khomeini, although some earlier manuals mention this practice. Khomeini was late in issuing his manual of practice, and he was more concerned that he be followed in his political jurisprudence than in a field such as *'ibādāt*, acts of worship. He wanted above all to perpetuate his controversial theory of *wilāyat al-faqīh*, or guardianship of the jurist. Khomeini seemed to be implicitly permitting the cut-and-paste method of choosing "sources of emulation" in order to further acceptance of his views on *wilāyat al-faqīh* among believers who had established allegiances to other *marja*'s.

The cut-and-paste method is also convenient for Sistani as the most widely accepted *marja*' of the Shi'ite world today. Because of this method Sistani (who was born in Iran) is able to share authority (and responsibility) with regionally respected *marja*'s. The cut-and-paste method plus the permission to follow a deceased *marja*' has worked well for the followers of Shaykh Muhammad Husayn Fadlallah of Lebanon (d. 2010), who is still revered as a *marja*' by ordinary believers in Lebanon who may turn to other manuals by other *mujtahids* for guidance on different areas such as politics. It is probably a sign of Sistani's willingness to share authority that many of his fatwas were co-signed by the other three *marja*'s of Najaf, Muhammad Sa'id al-Hakim (d. 2021), who was seen as Arab, Bashir al-Najafi from South Asia, and Muhammad Ishaq al-Fayyad from Afghanistan, all of whom are considerably less widely emulated than is Sistani.

Yet there are a fair number of issues in which Sistani agrees with the more conservative Yazdi across two hundred years of history. How does the ordinary believer recognize his/her *marja*'? For both Sistani and Yazdi the primary way is through recognition by the *ahl al-khibra*, the "people of experience." Functionally, the so-called "people of experience" are the upper-level clergy of the Shi'ite madrasa towns, such as Qom and Najaf. The "people of experience" choose their *marja*' by consensus. Without an election the identification of a *marja*' remains imprecise. Such a system of choice by acclamation among the upper-level clergy does not allow for

19 "*Istiftā'āt* Arabic," no. 1. Cf. my article, "Wilāyat al-Faqīh," In John L. Esposito (ed.), *The Oxford Encyclopedia of the Modern Islamic World*, 4 (Oxford, U.K., Oxford University Press: 1995) 320–322.

the creation of a hierarchical structure among the *marja'*s, especially if opinions on different sections of the law can be chosen by ordinary believers. We have here, in Christian terms, many bishops, but no single clearly elected Pope. Incidentally, election by acclamation instead of election by votes has occurred several times in the history of the papacy. Even after election by votes was established by a papal decree of 1059, Pope Gregory VII, the great reforming Pope, became Pope when he was acclaimed by the populace at the funeral of his predecessor in 1073.[20]

Sistani directly addresses the problem of possible conflict among the people of experience. The question is asked: "What do we do if the people of experience differ in specifying the most learned jurist?" Sistani answers in a fatwa: "One accepts the opinion of the strongest in respect to experience."[21] To the question "Who are the people of experience?" He answers, "They are the *mujtahid*s and those who are near to them in knowledge and excellence (*faḍīla*)." [22]

This Shi'ite system of consensual recognition is important to the financial structure of the madrasa towns, where the *marja'* not only receives contributions, but also the religious tax paid by Shi'ite believers and then redistributes the monies to students and the lower clergy. In practice, believers pay their obligatory, but self-imposed religious tax to the *marja'* whom they follow in "acts of worship" even if they follow another *marja'* in political or other matters. The *marja'* is supposed to receive one-fifth of the profit earned by a follower after his expenses (including personal and family maintenance expenses) have been deducted. This tax is self-imposed. In Sistani's case the income from the tax may well amount to hundreds of millions a year. The extent of the leadership of an individual *marja'* is shown by—among other things—the payout that different *marja'*s in Najaf provide for their students. Sistani gives a good stipend; Fayyad gives only approximately one-third of that amount while Hakim gave a meager one-fifth of that amount, and Bashir pays sporadically, if at all. Payouts are not strictly related to the choice of a *marja'* but do reflect the funds at the disposal of a *marja'*.

A widely influential manual of practice entitled *Tawḍīḥ al-Masā'il* (*The Clarification of Questions*) appeared in Persian in Iran. It was compiled

20 Robert Somerville, "Gregory VII," *The Encyclopedia of Religion*, 6 (New York: 1993) 121–124.
21 "*Istiftā'āt* Arabic," no. 6.
22 "*Istiftā'āt* Arabic," no. 59.

by a relatively unnoticed figure of the Shiʿite revival in Iran, Shaykh Ali Asghar Karbaschiyan, known as ʿAllāma, "the very learned." ʿAllāma Karbaschiyan founded the Alavi School in 1955, whose graduates include the well-known reformer Abd al-Karim Soroush as well as the Foreign Minister of Iran, Javad Zarif. In ʿAllāma Karbaschiyan's *Tawḍīḥ* the fatwas of Ayatollah Borujerdi, the supreme (and perhaps the sole) *marjaʿ* from the mid-1940s to 1961 are organized more or less in the categories set out by Yazdi. The first printing of this *Tawḍīḥ* was in 1333/1954 and it was frequently printed and widely used in Borujerdi's lifetime.[23] The Arabic translation remains a *locus classicus* for later commentary.

Sayyid Abu al-Qasim al-Musawi al-Khoei (d. 1992), the teacher of Sistani, wrote a manual, *Minhāj al-Ṣāliḥīn*, that also achieved high status.[24] His manual explains, as most of these treatises do, that a person who is emulated must be *ʿādil*, upright.[25] Again, local knowledge is invoked: "The sign that a man is upright is that he is apparently a good man so that if enquiries are made about him from the people of his locality or from his neighbors with whom he associates, they should confirm his goodness."[26] Functionally, the upper-level clergy of Shiʿite centers of learning determine who is upright because religious scholars have lived most of their adult life in these centers. Yet in theory, this definition, as well as the definition of the "people of experience," would theoretically allow a wider circle of people to determine who has the character and learning to become a *marjaʿ*.

Khoei solidly supports the possibility of following a deceased *marjaʿ*, as do most recent manuals of practice: "If the jurist who is emulated dies, and the follower has committed his rulings to memory, he can act on them as he acted during his lifetime." This opinion has preserved the popularity of Khoei's manual well after his death in 1992 as a fair number of Shiʿites still follow his manual, which is conservative. Part of the continuing appeal of Khoei's manual is that it has nothing to say about "the guardianship of

23 Maḥdī Hā'irī, "Tawḍīḥ al-Masā'il," in A. Sadr, *et al.*, eds., *Encyclopedia of Shia*, V (Tehran: 1996) 147–148.

24 "Khū'ī " reflects the spelling of this name in Arabic, but he and his family used "Khoei," which more correctly reflects the actual pronunciation in Persian and which is the form used in English-language news sources.

25 See the outstanding article on this subject by Farhat Ziadeh, "Integrity (*ʿadālah*) in Classical Islamic Law," in W. Heer (ed.), *Islamic Law and Jurisprudence* (Seattle: 1990) 73–93.

26 Abu al-Qasim Khoei [Khū'ī], *Articles of Islamic Acts* (Karachi: 1991) 2. This edition mistakenly identifies the Arabic original as *Tawḍīḥ al-Masā'il*, which demonstrates how closely this title became identified with a "manual of practice."

the jurist"—unlike recent manuals written in Iran. Probably his silence is due to his rejection of Khomeini's political jurisprudence. While no new followers are allowed to choose the manual of a deceased *marja'*, the commentaries by living *marja'*s, such as Sistani's on Khoei's manual would permit adherence to this older text in a mediated fashion.

The late Lebanese *marja'* Fadlallah accepted the Iranian political jurisprudence of Khomeini insofar as he says: "All the conditions mentioned for the *muftī-marja'* are sound qualifications for the holder of the guardianship of the jurist, except being most learned, which is certainly not considered." This view was a fairly obvious commendation of the revised Iranian constitution that allowed the somewhat less-learned Khamenei to assume the "guardianship of the jurist" after the death of Khomeini. Many Lebanese Shi'ites admire Khamenei, who has sent extensive monies to his favorite Shi'ite causes in Lebanon. But Fadlallah also took a position as to the "general matters" over which the guardian-jurist has control, namely: "That which refers to the general preservation of order on the basis of which the balance of life among Muslims *and* others exists ... through which their life as a society is preserved." Fadlallah further modified the power of the guardian-jurist by saying, "There is no harm in having a number of *faqīhs* (jurists) taking care of 'general matters' in more than one Islamic region (*quṭr Islāmī*), unless this plurality does harm to all or part [of the Muslim community]." Again, as with Sistani, but more explicitly allowing several *marja'*s as sources for cut-and-paste, we see an accommodation to national communities.[27]

Fadlallah's opinion about the limitations of the guardian-jurist coincides with the opinion of Muhammad Sadiq al-Sadr, the father of Muqtada Sadr, the widely known anti-American cleric. Muhammad Sadiq al-Sadr did not want to openly reject Khomeini's theory of a single guardian-jurist, but at the same time he wanted to claim his own authority in Iraq. To this end, he said that there was nothing wrong with recognizing an overarching Shi'ite religious leader, but there was at the same time often the need for a "national guardian" who would interpret Islam within the context of a national state. As this leader said of himself in an interview, "Everybody in the Shi'ite world knows that Muhammad Sadiq al-Sadr is the *marja'* of Baghdad!" (Since Sadr lived in Najaf, Baghdad signified all of Iraq.)[28]

---

27 Arabic.bayynat.org (viewed on August 13, 2014).
28 Fā'iq al-Shaykh 'Alī, *Ightiyāl Sha'b* (London, 2000) 46.

Returning to Fadlallah, his manual of practice also chips away at the authority of the leading jurist while not sanctioning rebellion. He writes, "When one knows for certain that the guardian-jurist is mistaken, it is *not* incumbent on that person to obey him in matters that are not connected with public order."[29] "Public order" and "preservation of order" are code words for political authority. It is significant that Ali Khamenei is the "Leader" and the only Shiʿite clergyman who is head of state. Khamenei did not issue a manual of practice for a long time because his rank as a *mujtahid* and even his appointment as a *mujtahid* were not accepted in all quarters.[30] Earlier in his career he did publish his fatwas organized in the same order as other manuals of practice and indeed this book is reproduced on his website as "Practical Laws of Islam."[31] To the question, "Is it permissible to follow a *mujtahid* who is not a *marjiʿ* and does not have a book of practical laws?" Khamenei answers, "If it is proven for a *mukallaf* (a sane mature Muslim) who wants to follow this *mujtahid* that he is a qualified *mujtahid*, there will be no problem in following him." In other words, being a *marjiʿ* and having a book on practical laws of Islam are not conditions for the emulation of a qualified *mujtahid* to be correct.[32] This answer is obliquely self-referential and breaks with the principle of "the most learned" that is affirmed in other answers. The authority of the "jurist-leader" [or guardian-jurist] (i.e., Khamenei) is affirmed in other fatwas such as the answer to Question 52: "The edicts of the jurist-leader [guardian-jurist] must be followed with respect to the issues relating to the administration of the Islamic country and general affairs of Muslims; while every *mukallaf* is obliged to follow his own *marja*ʿs in absolutely personal issues."[33]

Another great change in the outlook of the leading Shiʿite authorities consists of the differences among the *marājiʿ*, or sources of emulation, in

---

29 See arabic.bayynat.org (viewed on August 13, 2014).

30 See my article "Shiʿite Political Thought and the Destiny of the Iranian Revolution" (Article 24 here).

31 https://www.leader.ir/tree/index-php?catid+23 (viewed online August 26, 2014) showed Questions 1–68. As of February 3, 2022, the site has been reorganized: https://www.leader.ir/en/book/32/Practical-Laws-of-Islam. Only in Khamenei's case have I used the English (rather than the Arabic or Persian) version of his website.

32 *Ibid.* Formerly Question 9. Here the morphologically correct, but seldom spoken "*marjiʿ*" is given.

33 To drive home the point in his answer to former Question 55, Khamenei writes: "It is obligatory for all to obey the edict of the jurist leader, and the fatwa of a *marjiʿ* cannot make it ineffective."

their attitudes toward mystical Islamic philosophy, also called *'irfān*. The differences in attitude rose to prominence in 2011 when a fairly junior cleric named Hasan Ramazani, who teaches the medieval mystical philosopher Ibn 'Arabī's *Fuṣūṣ al-Ḥikam* (Bezels of Wisdom) in Qom, visited Sistani in Najaf. Ramazani subsequently published an online summary of his interviews. This summary included the following statements about *'irfān* attributed to Sistani:

> Some pursue the goal of making Najaf ugly and its *ḥawza* [the area of the seminaries] arid and completely opposed to these disciplines ... which is not a proper thing to do. [Nevertheless,] *'irfān* (the mystical pursuit of knowledge) is a double-edged sword ... Pursue *'irfān* with proper attention to the Divine Law and possess these two [paths] together.

Immediately, great pressure was put on Sistani to take back this statement. His Najafī colleague, the *marja'* Ayatollah Muhammad Ishaq Fayyad, at the opening of his advanced class in 2012, launched a severe attack and called the medieval Ibn 'Arabī a "heretic" (*zindīq*) lacking in belief in God.[34] All of this opprobrium was heaped upon Ibn 'Arabī whose philosophy Khomeini himself enjoyed teaching.

About two weeks after Ramazani's publication of the statement quoting Sistani, Ayatollah Ja'far Sayyidan from Mashhad sent Sistani a request for a fatwa regarding his opinion of "the author of the *Fuṣūṣ*"—namely Ibn 'Arabī, the font of Islamic mystical philosophy. Sistani replied in early December 2011:

> For my part, in accord with the teaching on belief of the great ulema of the Imāmīya [the Twelver Shi'ites] ... I do not support the above-mentioned method.[35]

This exchange is interesting from every point of view. First, we see the continuing importance of a group called *maktab-e tafkik* in Mashhad. *Tafkik* means "disassociation" and, in this context, means "disassociation

34 See note 33.

35 The episode is told with excellent detail in an article: "Feshār-e Ḥawzah-ye Najaf bar Āyatollāh Sistāni," dated (according to the Persian calendar) 8 Day 1390, on the website www.rahesabz.net/46940. All the quotations given above are given in this article.

of revealed knowledge attained from the Prophet and the Imams, from suppositional knowledge, especially philosophy and mysticism." Ayatollah Sayyidan who requested the fatwa from Sistani is a well-known member of this group, the roots of which go back to the 1950s or earlier. This group believes that too much philosophy was mixed with *uṣūl al-fiqh*, the jurisprudence dealing with discovering the Divine Law or *sharīʿa*, as, for example, shown in the works of such jurisprudential greats as Akhund-e Khorasani and his celebrated student, Shaykh Muhammad Husayn, known as Kumpani. The above-mentioned *marjaʿ* of Najaf, Shaykh Ishaq Fayyad, has also expressed his opposition to philosophical jurisprudence.[36] During a trip to Najaf in February 2014 I asked Ayatollah Fayyad to elaborate on his opposition to philosophy (*falsafa*). He said that he enthusiastically approved of natural philosophy (i.e., science), but that Islamic mystical philosophy includes many "imaginary" (*khayālī*) things. The most significant opponent to philosophy in Qom, where mystical philosophy is in fact popular, may be Ayatollah Vahid Khorasani, who does not speak openly against philosophy, but is thought to have preserved his loyalty to his early *tafkiki* training.

The connection of the movement of *tafkik* with Mashhad, the great shrine city of northeastern Iran, illustrates an ongoing feature in Shiʿism in the last two centuries. The rivalry between Qom, Najaf and Mashhad, cities in which the most important institutions of Shiʿite learning have developed, has played a subtle but discernible role in recent history. While Qom may dominate the discussion on Shiʿite jurisprudence and Najaf the discussion on the substance of Shiʿite law, Mashhad has tried to assert its primacy as the source of "pure" Shiʿite Islam. Ayatollah Mirza Mahdi Isfahani (1885–1945), who taught in Mashhad, felt that Hellenistic influences had corrupted the purity of Islamic thought. His disciple, Shaykh Mahmud Halabi (1900–1998), was a charismatic preacher who taught at the seminary in Mashhad and perpetuated Halabi's anti-philosophical approach. He also founded the formerly powerful association known as the Ḥujjatīya that made opposition to Iranian Baha'is their primary goal.

36 See Robert Gleave, "Continuity and Originality in Shiʿi Thought: The Relationship between the Akhbariyya and the Maktab-i Tafkik," in S. Mervin and D. Hermann (eds.), *Shiite Streams and Dynamics (1800–1925)*, (Beirut: 2010); Sajjad Rizvi, "'Only the Imam Knows Best': The Maktab-e Tafkik's Attack on the Legitimacy of Philosophy in Iran," *Journal of the Royal Asiatic Society*, 3rd series, 22 (2012) 487–503. Both of these articles are impressively deep and thorough.

Khomeini seems to have disliked Halabi, but the essence of Isfahani's and Halabi's thought reemerged a decade after the Iranian Revolution of 1978–79 and remains strong. A clergyman of Mashhad, Shaykh Muhammad Rida Hakimi coined the term *tafkik* and his frequently reprinted book on the subject remains the manifesto of this school.

Sistani does not want to take sides in the quarrels of the Iranian clergy. Through his son-in-law Jawad Shahristani, who resides in Iran, Sistani has some sort of understanding with the present leadership in Iran. It is even said that a fixed portion of the *khums* or religious tax paid by the followers of Sistani is given directly to Khamenei.

It has often been important for Iranians to maintain a certain independence from their own leaders by recognizing a spiritual leader in Iraq. At the same time, it has also been important that this leader in Iraq be an Iranian, as is Sistani, but one not directly under the thumb of the authorities in Iran. Sistani was probably chosen by his predecessor, Ayatollah Khoei, also of Iranian origin, in part for this reason. The Iranian clergy may have reason to be apprehensive about their future as Sistani's position as *marja'* continues to grow throughout the Shi'ite world, including in Iran.

In many ways the *maktab-e tafkik* that originated in Mashhad is reminiscent of the Akhbārī movement that dominated the Shi'ite world in the eighteenth century. The Akhbārīs believed that any clergyman of sound mind who had mastered Arabic and could read the Qur'ān and the authenticated sayings of the Prophet and the Twelve Imams could have an opinion about the Divine Law. A revival of this school of thought would be a threat even to the limited hierarchy that exists in Shi'ism and might well be incompatible with the theory of the guardianship of the jurist.

Although there are only a handful of widely recognized *marja'*s, so many clerics have claimed that status that there are quite a number of Shi'ite manuals of practice online. This large number of manuals demonstrates the huge effect of the internet on even this fairly traditional category of Shi'ite learning. As was said previously, the authority of the *marja'*s grew in the nineteenth century with the appearance of the telegraph, which provided an elegant and expeditious way for Muslims, both Sunni and Shi'ite, to put questions to their *muftīs* and *marja'*s. The internet provides an even more convenient portal. In the Sunni world there are an astonishing number of internet shaykhs who offer a clickable connection for *istiftā'* (a request for a fatwa). Sunni Muslims can and are shopping for opinions on a scale never before imagined in Islamic history. As was demonstrated in the 2011 revolution in Egypt, the youth demographic is so large in the Muslim world and often so tech-savvy that it is empowering a generation looking to the internet for opinions and answers to all sorts of questions, religious or political.

While Shi'ite claimants to *marja'* status, each with his own online manual of practice, are growing in number, they are not proliferating as much as the online Sunni *muftī*s, who range from the recently deceased self-educated jihadist Anwar al-Awlaki in Yemen to the very learned former *muftī* of Egypt, Shaykh Ali Gomaa (al-Jum'a), who was my teacher in Cairo many years ago. An example of an online Shi'ite *marja'* is Ayatollah Muhammad al-Yaqubi (Mohammad al-Yaqoobi), who lives in Basra and has some following there although by education he is an engineer. He was born in 1960 and is a mere teenager in the eyes of most *marja'*s. Yaqubi's following seems to be motivated primarily by local Basran particularism. It remains to be seen if the centrifugal force of the internet will bring further decentralization and diffusion of authority. It can also be argued that, in contrast, for the six or seven widely recognized international *marja'*s, their websites have had a centripetal effect that has made their leadership stronger. Shi'ite manuals of practice, due to the concentration of Shi'ite authority into relatively few hands, offer religious shopping on a "wholesale" level whereas Sunni manuals of practice, due to the diffusion of authority in the Sunni world, offer "retail" shopping.

The question as to which *mujtahid* one should choose is also elaborated in Sunni learning, in which this choice is sometimes called *tarjīḥ*, "preponderance" or "preference." The Shi'ite preference for *ahl al-khibra*, the "people of experience," the upper-level ulema, may allow for a similar eventual expansion of the people involved in the choice of a Shi'ite *marja'*, although we are still far from the practice of some Protestants in which the laity elects the clergy.

Justice Mufti Usmani, who is a Hanafī, faces this problem in the Sunni world, and it is discussed at the beginning of his manual: "Unfortunately there are many persons who claim the mantle of issuing *fatwā* [*sic*] without proper training and without having acquired the necessary experience, thereby causing confusion and misunderstanding amongst the lay public."[37] Usmani explains the need to stay strictly in the tradition of one's law school: "If there is only one juristic view on a question amongst all the Hanafī

37 See Usmani, (*supra* n. 9) 23.

jurists, then that view is binding unless there is cogent textual evidence to the effect that such a view is based on an underlying cause which is absent from the particular case."[38] Relatively little leeway is granted the jurist in following the standard authority: "[The *Muftī*] cannot base his reference [for his decision] upon a classical jurist who is not recorded to be amongst the preferred classical jurists (*aṣḥāb al-tarjīḥ*) [those deserving preference]."[39] It is clear that if Sunni *muftīs* had the same following as the Shi'ite *marja*'s, some of them might demand the same degree of obedience.

To return to Shi'ites, permission to continue to emulate a deceased *marja*' has proved not only politically useful but also a means to broaden the choice available to believers. More important is the permission to "cut-and-paste," to choose different practices from different manuals of practice. Latitude in choosing *marja*'s has expanded the role of the individual believer considerably. One may see a move toward individualization of conscientious belief, although we are still far from the Quaker confidence in a personal "inner light." The individual is given some choice between *marja*'s and between their fatwas. This permission to choose between fatwas seems to be a development in twenty-first-century Shi'ite law without precedent. Permission to cut-and-paste has allowed both partial adaptation to regionally important *marja*'s and competing ideas of political philosophy.

Most significant among these changes is the adaptation of Shi'ite theories of religious leadership to national contexts mentioned above. This adaptation began at least a century ago but gained momentum after Khomeini's successful role in fostering the Iranian Revolution of 1978–79. The desire of local Shi'ite leadership in many places such as Iraq and Lebanon to maintain their national position has led them to justify both a division of areas of emulation and an emphasis on national contexts in which national religious leaders within their own countries presume to know the application of Islamic law better than outsiders. Most striking in this respect is Fadlallah who understood that the Shi'ites in Lebanon were a minority and had to live at peace with their non-Shi'ite and non-Muslim neighbors. He therefore emphasized the responsibility of the *marja*'s to keep the needs of the national community, Muslim and non-Muslim, in

38 See Usmani, (*supra* n. 9) 24.
39 See Usmani, (*supra* n. 9) 25. Muhammad Taqi Usmani elaborates his views in *The Legal Status of Following a Madhab*, trans. Muhammed Amin Kholwadia (Karachi: 1999).

view at all times. This position is a striking instance of open recognition of national religious leadership.

It is important to remember that there was a long period in which Shi'ite jurists rejected *ijtihād*, the derivation of rulings, because of their insistence on literal interpretations of the sources of the law. This literalism reminds us of American constitutional lawyers who lay exclusive emphasis on the original intention of the founders. Manuals of practice did exist among Shi'ites and Sunnis prior to the eighteenth century, but only became common among the Shi'ites in the second half of the nineteenth century. The popularity of *ijtihād* in the last century and a half may lead to a period of wider participation in determining religious law, one in which it might even be possible for every believer to be, in respect to some aspects of the law, his own *mujtahid*. Ayatollah Murtada Mutahhari (d. 1979) and Ayatollah Muhammad Baqir al-Sadr (d. 1980) both advocated collective leadership instead of investing leadership in a single *marja'*. Nevertheless, the speed with which Iraqi Shi'ites in 2014 responded to Sistani's message and his sermons shows that it is important to have unified leadership and that single person leadership may be the only way to achieve widespread unity in the Shi'ite community.

[Ayatollah Sistani is now in 2022 ninety-one years old and recently had a walk in his garden in Najaf with Pope Francis. The question as to who will succeed him as the leading Shi'ite religious authority in Iraq remains very open. Similarly,] in Iran the succession to Ayatollah Khamenei is an open question. [40]

Technically, the "guardian-jurist" is elected by the Council of Experts. In practice, the choice may depend on the degree to which the Pasdaran or Revolutionary Guards continue to be nearly all-powerful. Ayatollah Muhammad Taqi Misbah Yazdi (d. 2021), who made a career of exalting the "guardianship of the jurist" to a cosmically important position, might have been acceptable to the Pasdaran as a successor to Khamenei. So may be the equally conservative cleric Sadiq Larijani, although [at sixty-one in 2022] he is still "young." Whether the high clergy in Iran will remain passive in the face of the problems posed by the succession to Khamenei is very uncertain. Khamenei's relegation of other leading clergy to authority only in "personal" matters cannot be well received in all quarters. The upper

40 See Houchang Chehabi, "Iran and Iraq: Intersocietal Linkages and Secular Nationalisms," in Abbas Amanat and Farzin Vejdani (eds.), *Iran Facing Others: Identity Boundaries in a Historical Perspective* (New York: 2012) 191–216, esp. 198.

ranks of the Iranian clergy may find difficulty in accepting any "guardian-jurist" with claims similar to Khamenei.

At this point the young mullah politicians of Iraq—Ammar al-Hakim and Muqtada al-Sadr—have to satisfy their followers by referring to older more learned scholars. But both movements seem to be self-sustaining and may show that for many people political leadership among the Shi'ites of Iraq is not always associated with clerical leadership. One of the websites of the Da'wa Party,[41] which has provided three prime ministers in contemporary Iraq, most recently including Haider al-Abadi (2014–2018), starts with a picture of Muhammad Baqir al-Sadr, who died over forty years ago. It is unclear which living *marja'* the Da'wa Party presently recognizes. [However, in 2022 it is clear that this party is still active and important in Iraq.]

The tensions among the clergy are numerous and substantial as illustrated by their strongly differing attitudes toward mystical philosophy, often considered an important, but contentious aspect of Shi'ism. These tensions also illustrate the great difficulty in translating leadership based on consensus into politics. Some accommodation to their differences—insofar as they are based on differences of nationality or region—is allowed by the "cut-and-paste" adherence to manuals of practice. In Iran the surface toleration among some clergymen is at places very thin. The expulsion and even imprisonment of some clergy have shown that this surface toleration has friable edges. In Iran the cooperation among the clergy is based as much on a shared fear of a liberal change as on any real solidarity among the clergymen themselves.

41 Islamicdawaparty.org (viewed on August 30, 2014).

RECENT HISTORY IN THE MIDDLE EAST

For a few decades I was deeply absorbed in contemporary events and issues in the Middle East. As a loyal American, I felt that I should enter the discussion with an historian's perspective. During this period, research on my primary interest, the Middle East in the medieval period, was limited. I felt a duty to speak out and try to shed light on the underlying reasons for the continual hostilities in the region in the hope that some progress could be made in resolving these conflicts.

Writing op-eds, appearing on TV news, speaking at conferences, and attending seminars at the State Department of the United States and the Ditchley Foundation in the U.K. while teaching full-time at Harvard filled my life. Eventually, I found that daily reading of Arabic and Persian newspapers laid too heavy a burden on me, and I returned to my research interests in the medieval Middle East. I still feel, however, as my principal teacher H.A.R. Gibb did, that scholars of earlier periods competent in Middle Eastern languages may have something useful to say about the modern Middle East.

Medieval history of the Middle East helps to explain both the ideologies and social forms that exist today. Certain people long dead and events long past have been instrumental in resolving or preventing escalating hostilities in specific places and periods. We urgently need people like this today, particularly in our government. Where are the American or Middle Eastern equivalents of Desmond Tutu and Nelson Mandela?

My study of traditional Islamic learning, although far from complete, allowed me to speak with prominent religious figures in Iraq and in Egypt. I tried to communicate some of my experiences in my book *The Mantle of the Prophet*, and later articles. I had hoped to write a book about some of the more interesting figures, especially Muslim reformers, who were and are largely unknown to the West. I hope younger scholars will pursue this interest. Muslim thinkers, progressive or conservative, are the key to understanding the future of many Middle Eastern societies.

Academic freedom is very fragile. Rulers and governments who give money to academic institutions often hope to bend opinion in their way. In Hungary we have seen a university founded by George Soros forced to close by an ultra-conservative government. Even in the United States foreign donors seek to influence the hiring of professors who would shape opinion in their favor. Universities that do not severely limit donor control are betraying their academic mission. Donations creating opinions favorable to their countries and regimes badly affects American opinion, which in turn affects our foreign policy and national security.

There are only two articles in this section about recent history in the Middle East, but I also wrote a number of op-ed pieces that are not included here but which can be found in my bibliography. Most of my scholarly work and teaching were focused on the medieval period in the Middle East. However, I continued to be gripped by events unfolding in the Middle East and consequently wrote the articles in this section.

The first, on "Iran's Foreign Devils", was written at the height of the "hostage crisis," when American diplomats in Tehran were taken prisoner. It was published in 1980 in the magazine *Foreign Policy*, published quarterly by the Carnegie Endowment for International Peace. This hostile act of hostage taking by Iran was a shocking event, and it influences American thinking up to this day. The hostage crisis brought to light the deep ignorance of many well-educated Americans about the Middle East: I had to explain over and over again where Iran was in the world and that Iranians were not Arabs. After years of cooperation and friendship between Iran and the United States, I, like almost every other American, felt that the taking of American diplomats and their mistreatment was a terrible turn of events, made worse for me by my friendship with one the hostages, John Limbert.

America's role in the overthrow of Mossadegh, the democratic leader of the majority of Iranians in 1953, a fact unknown to most Americans, contributed to the violence of the Revolution of 1978–79. Even today many Americans mistake Iran for our worst enemy, not acknowledging the interference of the United States in Iranian affairs. Our support of Saddam Hussein during much of the Iran–Iraq war of 1980–88 is another reason for the alienation of some Iranians toward the United States. It is important to remember that Iran helped us defeat ISIS in parts of the Middle East. Not surprisingly, given American hostility, Iranians are now turning toward China, our greatest rival.

I wrote the article on "Iran's Foreign Devils" in the hope that people on both sides would feel that their grievances were heard and that the Americans would be sent home soon. I tried to explain that there was little or no precedent in Islamic law for holding diplomats as hostages. Although the article was reprinted in the U.S., I have no idea how many in Iran learned of it.

The second article in this section, "Islamic Movements: The Case for Democratic Inclusion," was published in 1995 in *Contention: Debates in Society, Culture and Science,* edited by my friend Nikki Keddie. It bears all the shortcomings of my understanding of the Islamic Middle East at the beginning of 1995. While I did not try to predict the future, I still stand by most of the views I had at that time. However, I did not understand the degree to which Turkey would change its position on religion and other major matters. I did not foresee that Egypt would experiment with rule by the Muslim Brotherhood or that the Arab Spring would spread across the Middle East or that the Taliban would overcome all others in Afghanistan. (I hope that I am better as an historian than as a prophet.)

Our difficulty understanding the Muslim world (as well as the Muslim world's difficulty in understanding the West) is a very long-term problem in our world, dating back to the Crusades and even further in our past. Episodes of terror by extremists on both sides increased this tension in our recent past; the Muslim world follows Kosovo and Kashmir as closely as the West follows the travails of Christians in Egypt and India. These difficulties in understanding are heightened by dramatic world events such as the two Gulf Wars, the bombing of New York's twin towers on 9/11, and the complete conquest of Afghanistan by the Taliban.

My article about Islamic movements was written almost thirty years ago. It was written without footnotes for a journal subtitled "Debates," and it is essentially an opinion piece by an academic specializing in the Islamic history of the Middle East. Though the leaders of the nations in the Middle East as well as the leaders of the various Islamic movements within them have changed, the struggle for democratic inclusion is still a strong undercurrent in the Middle East. While I began the article poking fun at the *Naked Gun* movie of 1988 (itself a farce), I did so then and now in the hope that the original readers and the present readers would remember the numerous movies and television shows that portrayed almost every

Muslim as a terrorist or criminal for decades. Fortunately, more nuanced portrayals of Muslims are now widely available although one should not forget that the handful of Muslims in our Congress have been repeatedly vilified and threatened for their religion.

In writing this article I had hoped to contribute to a better-informed American understanding of the Islamic world, particularly of the Middle East. Many intellectuals in the Islamic world, some of them my friends, the so-called "Muslim reformers," were working toward a similar end before being silenced or exiled. These Muslim reformers have not gone away and, in some cases, have a large audience. I still believe they will be influential in shaping the modern Middle East. Islamic thought on government is still being reformulated to meet contemporary concerns about democratic representation and similar issues.

In some countries of the Middle East there is no free press. Nevertheless, newspapers and journals published in Paris, London, and Washington, partly by exiles, reach the Middle East through the internet or other means. The press in Lebanon remains relatively free but the political and humanitarian situation in that country is tragic. Without a free press it becomes more difficult to understand social and political ideas that are circulating and forming public opinion. The appearance of the Arab Spring brought great hope to many, including myself, but for the time being it has almost disappeared, even in beautiful Tunisia where it began.

Iran's Foreign Devils

The Ayatollah Ruhollah Khomeini's support for the seizure of the American embassy in Tehran in 1979 and the detention of its diplomatic personnel [for over a year] is a culmination—and a crisis—of two prominent motifs in his life: his desire to free Iran from "the hands of foreigners" and his desire to re-establish the pre-eminence of Shi'ite Islamic law in his homeland.

It has not been generally understood that as early as 1964 both of these motifs played a large role in Khomeini's opposition to the granting of diplomatic immunity to American advisers in Iran. At that time a significant number of Iranians agreed with Khomeini that the granting of such rights was tantamount to a continuation of the humiliating regime of "capitulations," which, until their abolition in 1928, gave extensive rights of extraterritoriality to citizens of powerful Western countries traveling or resident in Iran. Khomeini's strong stand on this issue helped make him a national leader of extraordinary influence.

Many Iranians see Khomeini's support for the embassy takeover as a natural extension of his struggle against Western powers who claimed special authority that put them beyond the laws to which every Iranian is subject. While the detention of diplomats may please some Iranian nationalists, both religious and secular, it poses a dilemma for Khomeini as a champion of Islamic law, since, in his present struggle against extraterritoriality, he has so far disregarded the many passages in Islamic law that emphasize the respect owed to non-Muslim emissaries.

Shi'ite Islamic law is particularly generous in its treatment of diplomatic emissaries and goes so far as to say that non-Muslim diplomats who have entered Islamic territory under the reasonable misapprehension that safe

---

Author's note: This article was first published as: "Iran's Foreign Devils," *Foreign Policy* 38 (Washington, D.C., Carnegie Endowment for International Peace: 1980) 19–34. Reproduced with permission. This article has been slightly modified by changing some verbs from the present to the past tense and adding a Postscript.

conduct has been granted them should be given such safe conduct back to their own people.

Before the eighteenth century, Islamic governments regarded capitulations, or grants of special privileges to non-Muslim foreigners, as normal concessions by powerful governments to favored outsiders, especially trading partners. Such concessions had many origins in the Middle East: the ancient *jus sanguinis*, which held that a man carried the law of his people with him; the commercial practices of the Byzantine Empire; and the so-called millet systems, which, in conformity with Islamic law of all schools, gave Christians and Jews the right to apply their own personal and family law to the members of their communities. However, as the European powers became more than a match for the Islamic governments of the Middle East, these regimes of capitulations turned into devices for economic exploitation and foreign privilege that had to be extorted from the unwilling governments of the region.

RIOTS IN THE BAZAARS

For Iran, the abuse of capitulations began after a crushing defeat by the Russians. In the treaty concluded in the village of Turkmanchai in 1828, the Iranians not only conceded disputed border regions but also virtually conceded territory within Iran itself. In modern Persian the loan-word *kapitulasiyun*, when unqualified, refers to the privileges and immunities of Turkmanchai.

Iranian officials were forbidden to enter the homes and warehouses of Russian subjects in Iran without having recourse to Russian diplomats. Moreover, Russian representatives were given exclusive jurisdiction over disputes among Russians in Iran and disputes between Russians and other non-Iranians, and a representative of the Russian mission was to be present at the trial of any dispute between a Russian and an Iranian. Similarly, if a Russian was implicated in a criminal case in which non-Russians were also involved, the case had to be tried in the presence of a Russian diplomatic official; and if a Russian subject were found guilty, he was to be sent home for any punishment ordered by the court.

In 1829 the Russian minister, A.S. Griboyedov, arrived in Tehran, and his harsh interpretation of the treaty immediately brought home its significance to Iranians. He demanded the return of Georgians and Armenians captured by Iranians in earlier wars. Many of these captives had become Muslim and married Iranians and were unwilling to leave Iran. Nevertheless, Griboyedov's men forcibly entered their homes and removed them. Finally, at the Russian's request, a Muslim commander handed over two Georgian women known to have accepted Islam; a leading Shi'ite jurist, with the support of many clerics, ruled that it would be lawful to rescue them.

The bazaars of Tehran were shut. In the ensuing riots, Iranians stormed the Russian legation and killed Griboyedov and his diplomatic staff. If Russia had not been engaged in a war with the Ottoman Empire, another war with Russia might well have followed. The terrified Iranian monarch, Fath-Ali Shah, was glad to accept the Russian terms that the leading jurist should be exiled and the guilty individuals punished. The parallels between the predicament that the Russians faced 150 years ago and the predicament America faced in Iran [in 1980] are, to say the least, striking.

The Treaty of Turkmanchai was to be the basis for Russo-Iranian relations for the next hundred years. Eventually, other Western countries acquired treaties giving them commercial privileges similar to Russia's, but no other treaty extorted such extravagant rights of extraterritoriality. The matter was complicated by the presence of hundreds of thousands of Muslims in the Caucasus and Central Asia who spoke Persian and considered themselves to be of Iranian culture; some established businesses in Iran and, by virtue of their Russian passports, enjoyed the privileges of Turkmanchai.

Iranians over 70 [in 1980] remember the patchwork of homes and warehouses in Rasht, the Iranian center for trade with Russia, which flew Russian flags to proclaim that they were off-bounds to any official of the Iranian government. Westerners as well as Russians acquired the privilege of having the consuls of their countries at their trials; and since the decision of the court was not effective unless countersigned by the consul, these officials acquired a virtual veto power over Iranian courts.

Discriminatory practices in everyday commercial life were an obvious focus for the anger felt by Iranians at their humiliation by the Western powers. An eloquent but half-forgotten book, representative of the intellectual opposition to these concessions to foreigners, was published in 1914 under the title *Iran and the Regime of Capitulations* [*Kapitulasiun va Iran*, Tehran, 1332]. The author was no less a figure in modern Iranian history than Mohammed Mossadegh who later, as prime minister, would cancel a somewhat different kind of concession to foreigners when he nationalized the Iranian oil industry. Mossadegh wrote:

> For a government to be independent it must govern all those residing in its territory ... In the final analysis, a government which does not govern either its own citizens or foreigners is no government and will become the dependency of another government which possesses this position (of full sovereignty).

In 1921 a treaty was signed by the Soviet government and the Iranian government dominated by Reza Khan, who would soon be Shah, canceling the treaty of Turkmanchai, and in 1928 the Iranian government abolished all capitulations enjoyed by foreign powers. The relative quiescence with which Iranians greeted the many changes initiated by the Shah, including the replacement of much Islamic law by a code based on European models, was in part due to the feeling that Iran finally had a leader who could deal with European governments as an equal. But the hollowness of the Shah's successes in foreign relations, including the abolition of capitulations, became stunningly apparent in 1941. In that year England and the Soviet Union, alarmed at the Shah's sympathy with the Germans and eager to guarantee the supply route from the Indian Ocean to the Soviet Union, forced him to abdicate.

Until then, the United States had played a comparatively minor role in Iran. Washington had secured the usual articles of immunity in the treaty it signed with Iran at Constantinople on December 13, 1856, including the right to have all disputes involving an Iranian subject and an American citizen tried in the presence of an agent of the United States. This treaty was terminated in 1928 and replaced by three agreements, one of which declared what codes governing personal status and family matters would apply to American citizens in Iran. Significantly, non-Muslim Americans were to be subject to American law in all such matters. The principles of Islamic law, allowing Christians and Jews internal regulation in such matters, was clearly being applied, for the law did not exempt Muslim Americans from the jurisdiction of any aspect of Iranian law.

DISTURBING THE ELITE

With the victory of the Allies in World War II the United States inevitably acquired some of the interests that England had previously maintained in Iran. England had long sought to keep Iran out of Russian hands, partly to protect the route to India and partly to prevent Russia from becoming a direct neighbor to India.

Iran and Afghanistan managed to preserve their independence thanks to this Anglo-Russian rivalry, which the Iranians (and the Afghans) had, on occasion, brilliantly manipulated to their own advantage. In accord with this new role, the United States strongly backed those elements in the Iranian government that demanded the withdrawal of Soviet troops from Azerbaijan and was partially responsible for Soviet withdrawal in 1946.

In October 1947, the United States and Iran signed an agreement creating a military mission attached to the Iranian ministry of war. No rights of extraterritoriality were given to American soldiers, but Article XI of the agreement did specify that "members of the Mission in case of violation of the laws and regulations of the Iranian Government, may be separated from the service of the Iranian Army and in such case will have only the right to draw travel expenses back to America." In practice, from this time on, some American military advisers who got into trouble were airlifted out of Iran before they could be prosecuted. This agreement remained in force until the Iranian Revolution.

Subsequent agreements and treaties between Iran and the United States showed some awareness of Iranian resentment of the privileges and de facto immunities that had been given to Americans in Iran. For example, the treaty on "amity, economic relations, and consular rights" between the United States and Iran, which was signed on August 15, 1955, explicitly canceled the 1928 treaty regarding personal status and family law and made no special provision on these questions for Americans in Iran.

The new treaty attempted to apply a strict reciprocity in all rights of nationals and companies of either country when in the territory of the other. Since a sizable community of Iranians existed in the United States, this reciprocity not only implied that the two countries dealt with each other as equals, but it also was potentially useful for Iranian consular officials.

Everyone knew, of course, that the Iranian government was having many internal difficulties, needed American economic and military help, and could hardly treat the U.S. government as an equal. (The Central Intelligence Agency had orchestrated the coup against Mossadegh's National Front in 1953, which restored the Shah.) Internal opposition to the Shah became particularly strong in the early 1960s. Land reform disturbed some members of the elite, regardless of their political and religious loyalties, and Iranians of all economic levels were hurt by a three-year economic depression that began to moderate only in 1963. Egyptian President Gamal Abdel Nasser was at the height of his influence and seemed to offer the example of a Third World leader who could both use and defy the superpowers.

In March 1962, in the midst of this sensitive period, Washington sent a note to the Iranian government asking that all members of the U.S. military advisory missions in Iran who were in the employ of the Iranian government be given full diplomatic immunity. Iran was asked to enact a law extending to such advisers the immunities and exemptions described in Article 1 of the 1961 Vienna Convention on diplomatic personnel, which included immunity from criminal jurisdiction by the host country.

The Iranian opposition had already attacked the bilateral defense agreements between Iran and the United States, signed at Ankara on March 5, 1959, and meant to replace the multilateral Baghdad Pact. Yet another focus for such attacks was the agreement on economic assistance, signed by both governments on December 21, 1961, which stated that the Iranian government would consider the personnel of technical assistance missions "as part of the diplomatic mission of the United States of America in Iran for the purpose of enjoying the privileges and immunities accorded to that diplomatic mission."

IRAN'S SHAME

News that the United States had requested diplomatic immunity for its advisers soon spread and was an important theme in political agitation against the Shah's government in 1963, in which the religious figures played the leading role. Khomeini had already achieved such importance as an activist religious leader that the government sent security forces into his theological college in Qom on March 22, 1963, killing at least one cleric. After this event, Khomeini placed increasing emphasis in his preaching on the shame to Iran and to Islam inherent in the capitulatory rights that had been or would be given to American advisers.

At the beginning of June, pictures of Khomeini and posters of his proclamations appeared throughout Iran, and there were demonstrations in the streets of Tehran and several provincial capitals. The government then arrested Khomeini and sent him to Tehran. Following his arrest, there was a massive and violent demonstration, which was not matched until 1978.

In early August of 1963, Khomeini was released from prison with the government's announcement that he agreed "not to interfere in political matters." By October Khomeini was again arrested for his views, but the political matter with which he was most closely identified was approaching a climax. The interpretation of the Vienna Convention requested by the United States was approved by the Iranian Council of Ministers in accordance with a decree on October 5, 1963, and was soon approved by the Iranian senate. The matter was then submitted to the Majlis, the elected house of parliament, where it was passed a year later.

Even in the most cynical interpretation—that some opposition to the amendment was allowed in a carefully chosen and closely controlled parliament, in order to give the impression that the issue had been openly debated—the severity of the uproar was tremendous. The representatives were asked first to ratify the Vienna Convention, which had been left unratified because a parliament had not been in session for some time.

Surprisingly, the Vienna Convention itself was strongly attacked. One representative asked how he should reply to someone who said that even a foreign refrigerator repairman or apprentice mechanic in Iran enjoyed the immunity that Iran's ambassador enjoyed abroad. "Eighteen times," he continued, "I have underlined the word reciprocal, reciprocal, reciprocal. But if I go to someone's house as a guest, does it mean that I have to receive 200 guests on the return visit?" The Vienna Convention finally was ratified by the great majority and therefore without a count of votes.

The second bill, dealing with the inclusion of American military advisers under the provisions of the Vienna Convention, caused a far more violent debate. The attacks centered on the incompatibility of the bill with Article 71 of the Iranian Constitution, which stated that all Iranian courts must be subject to Iranian law. This article had been devised as a rejection of the regime of capitulations, and even though the word *kapitulasiyun* was not used in the debate, it was well known that the opposition to the government and even some of its friends used this word to describe the immunities proposed for American advisers.

One representative said that for 40 years official American advisory missions had been coming to Iran, "and nothing improper has befallen them which would necessitate giving them the immunities." When the vote was taken, the bill passed by 74 to 61, not even an absolute majority of the traditionally obedient 200-member Majlis. Very shortly thereafter, the Majlis voted to accept a large American loan, which was widely thought to be contingent on the grant of diplomatic immunity.

Khomeini had been released in May 1964, again with the government's announcement that he had agreed not to interfere in political matters. Whatever agreement they may have come to, after the vote in the Majlis he issued a proclamation that was a full expression of the political beliefs he would press for the next 18 years. After an apposite Qur'ānic quote ("Never will God give the unbelievers a way [to triumph] over the Believers," IV:141), he continued:

> Does the Iranian nation know what has happened in recent days in the Majlis? Does it know what crime has occurred surreptitiously and without the knowledge of the nation? Does it know that the Majlis, at the initiative of the government, has signed the document of the enslavement of Iran? It has acknowledged that Iran is a colony; it has given America a document attesting that the nation of Muslims is barbarous, it has struck out all our Islamic and national glories with a black line.
>
> By this shameful vote, if an American adviser or the servant of an American adviser should take any liberty with one of the greatest specialists in Shi'ite law, with one of those respected by the Iranian nation, with one of Iran's men of high station, or treat them dishonestly, the police have no right to arrest the perpetrator and the courts of Iran have no right to investigate. But if one of their dogs is attacked, the police must intervene, and the court must investigate ... I proclaim that this shameful vote of the Majlis is in contradiction to Islam and has no legality; it is in contradiction to the opinions of Muslims ... If the foreigners wish to misuse this filthy vote, the nation's duty will be clearly specified ... The misfortunes of Islamic governments have come from the interference by foreigners in their destinies ... It is America that considers the Qur'ān and Islam to be harmful to itself and wishes to remove them from its way; it is America that considers Muslim men of religion a thorn in its path.

In October 1964 Khomeini preached a sermon to the same effect. "If the Shah should run over an American dog, he would be called to account," he said, "but if an American cook should run over the Shah ... no one has any claim against him." Again, he emphasized the political importance of men of religion: "If the men of religion had influence, it would not be possible for the nation to be at one moment the prisoner of England, at the next, the prisoner of America." This proclamation and speech was the cause of Khomeini's exile from Iran in November of that year.

THE CHAPTER CLOSES

Until the death in 1962 of Ayatollah Borujerdi, the leading authority on Shi'ite Islamic law in Iran, Khomeini had been comparatively unknown among Iranians who did not have a higher education in the religious system, even though he was a respected teacher of philosophy, Islamic law, and the principles of Islamic jurisprudence. By 1963 he was becoming a national figure, and his exile the following year made him one of the two or three likely candidates to succeed Borujerdi. Shi'ism has a strong tradition of religious leaders who win their positions through resistance to governments they find unacceptable and suffer persecution and sometimes martyrdom. Khomeini, in large part through his attack on the capitulations, had won his place in this tradition.

In his 1964 sermon, Khomeini had warned that the United States would vastly expand the number of Americans who would be given diplomatic immunity. His prediction was accurate. Shortly after his exile, the Department of Defense informed U.S. military advisers that, in accord with the Vienna Convention, their dependents too would henceforth have immunity. This contradicted explicit assurances given by the prime minister in the Majlis. The blow was softened only slightly by a previous American assurance that the United States would "consider" requests to allow Iranian jurisdiction over cases involving "heinous and other criminally reprehensible acts."

Not including these dependents, the number of Americans holding "special" passports, which entitled them to immunity, probably never reached 2,000, excluding transient technical experts who came for short periods to install or service expensive hardware. Yet Iranian life seemed clogged with foreigners, most conspicuously the 85,000 Americans resident in Iran before the Revolution.

Although these Americans did not have special passports, many Iranians perceived them as having some standing that made them a community not fully subject to Iranian law. When the Iranian economy slowed down in

1975 and the poor had reason to remember Khomeini's fervent advocacy of their cause against a government that seemed to have devoted incalculable wealth to buying foreign weapons and gadgets, they also remembered that Khomeini had tried to protect them from the seemingly privileged foreign "plunderers" who were now so conspicuous throughout Iran.

On May 13, 1979, the chapter opened by Turkmanchai was closed. Tehran radio broadcast that "the Foreign ministry of the Islamic republic of Iran today announced that the capitulations law has been rescinded." Everyone in Iran, whether Iranian or American, was now subject to Iranian law.

One obvious exception remained—diplomatic personnel. There was no question that Khomeini felt a greater grievance against the American government than against any other foreign power. In a speech broadcast on Tehran radio on October 28, 1979, he declared: "All the problems of the East stem from these foreigners, from the West, and from America at the moment. All our problems come from America. All the problems of the Muslims stem from America." Seven days later the militant Muslim followers of the Khomeini occupied the American embassy and, in their statement broadcast on the same program that day, they announced: "How can we really tolerate seeing these instigating mercenaries safe in our homeland, while their country has become a haven for our enemy, the murderer of hundreds of thousands of our brothers and sisters, martyred by the criminal Shah?"

Khomeini may not have been aware in advance that the embassy would be occupied: however, when he gave his approval, he could not have failed to perceive some of the moral ambiguities of the situation. His campaign against diplomatic immunities for American advisers had been a logical corollary to his belief in the pre-eminence of Islamic law for all inhabitants of predominantly Islamic areas; and his campaign against foreign influence had been the negative expression of the same belief. Both the positive and negative aspects of this belief had coincided with a long-term hatred by Iranian nationalists for capitulations, and Khomeini's campaign against the capitulations had been the most significant factor in making him a national figure. But now he had to condone an act that went beyond any unambiguous warrant of Islamic law.

All Islamic legal schools believe in *amān*, the guarantee of safe conduct, which, given verbally or in writing, has been the basis of diplomatic relations between the Islamic and non-Islamic worlds since the time of the

Prophet. Shi'ite jurists, or *faghīs*, are particularly generous in their treatment of the diplomatic immunity owed to non-Muslim emissaries even in time of war between Muslims and non-Muslims. For example, al-Ṭūsī, a Shi'ite jurist of the 5th/11th century, wrote:

> It is the tradition of followers of our [Shi'ite] school of law that if unbelievers seek the protection of Muslims and the Muslims say, "We do not grant you protection," and the unbelievers (mistakenly) presume that they have safe conduct, a Muslim will not place any obstacle in their way; on the contrary, they should be returned to places where they are secure ... If unbelievers should have confidence that such statements have been made to them and enter the territory of the Muslims, no obstacle will be placed in their way because it was an error based on a reasonable presumption. They will be returned to places where they are secure, becoming (again part of the) non-Muslim foe.[1]

This is not an isolated passage by an obscure *faghī* but is typical of the Shi'ite tradition and was written by a great *faghī* of that tradition. Law texts provided a basis for releasing the Americans without prejudging their innocence or guilt, without even acknowledging that they had regular diplomatic immunity. Their release on this basis would only acknowledge that the Americans in the embassy had come under the reasonable presumption that they had safe conduct and that, even if their presumption were totally mistaken, they should be sent back to places where they would be secure.

Khomeini was a profoundly learned scholar of Shi'ite law, and doubtless could have constructed a case to release or detain the Americans according to the dictates of his conscience and his reading of the law. (There is a precedent in the practice of earlier Islamic states of the Middle East for holding ambassadors—particularly in time of war—as pledges for the good conduct of the nations that had sent them.) It is significant that he did not choose to propose a legal interpretation spelling out why the Americans could or could not have a reasonable presumption that they were in Iran under a guarantee of safe conduct. Perhaps his dilemma was partly political. His consistent stand against foreign interference had created a constituency

1 Shaykh al-Ṭā'ifa al-Ṭūṣī, *al-Mabsūṭ*, II (Tehran: 1967) 14–15.

that was not as concerned as he was with the re-establishment of Shi'ite Islamic law. Perhaps his dilemma was also legal.

Americans and Iranians must talk law to each other. As long as Americans believe Iranians to be inspired by some atavistic longing for a crude, primitive, and simplistic legal system, Iranians will have no reason to discuss the rich and complex tradition of Shi'ite law with Americans. As long as the United States threatens to send military forces to Iran without the invitation of the Iranian government, it aborts the political process in Iran that would allow Iranians to discuss and sort out for themselves the implications of various interpretations of Shi'ite law.

DEFYING THE WEST

Khomeini was a new kind of leader in the modern Islamic Middle East. Like Nasser, he drew part of his popular strength from his ability to defy Western governments that had previously been believed to have coercive powers over Middle Eastern countries. And, like Nasser, he was widely admired for the simplicity of his life. But Nasser, however real his piety as a Muslim may have been, intended to carry on his struggle for national dignity by giving his country an internal structure similar to that of Western countries.

Although Khomeini repeatedly expressed his desire to see Iran strong and prosperous, he saw the validation of his mission more in terms of moral than in terms of material advancement. Even his rhetorical style differed widely from the spirited style of Nasser or the elaborate eloquence of Mossadegh; he spoke with the gravity of a man whose aim, in agreement with the jurists of many centuries, was to establish a nomocracy, a state ruled by divine law in which leaders are only the administrative instruments. Such a nomocracy is international by nature, since its basis is that the same divine law is applicable everywhere.

Nationalism, however, is still very much alive in Iran. While Khomeini was an opposition leader, symbolic of resistance and having suffered persecution, the differences between the nomocracy he believed in and the desires of some less legally and/or religiously minded Iranian nationalists were not as apparent before the Revolution. [Following the Revolution] these differences appeared, and the issue of the detained American diplomats in Tehran and the attitudes that Iranians have expressed toward it are part of the dialectic through which these differences are being worked out.

In his 1914 book, Mossadegh observed that foreigners were able to insist on capitulations because Iran lacked a unified legal code. Instead, several Shi'ite codes existed that judges could have applied at their discretion. During the following decade and a half, in their efforts to "modernize," many Islamic countries—Iran among them—copied European codes. [Following the Revolution] this process has been reversing. As governments move to restore some aspects of Islamic law, they reopen the whole question of adherence to predominantly Western international law. In the years ahead, there may well be conflicts, not only among Islamic jurists, but also between these two legal systems—over the repayment of debts, for instance. And in these cases, unlike the case of the hostages in Tehran, the two systems may not agree. The scope for conflict, philosophic and actual, is apparent.

POSTSCRIPT

After the hostage crisis an important Iranian diplomat told me that he personally brought a Persian translation of this article to Khomeini during the crisis to explain to him that his grievances were understood and it was time to release the American hostages. Khomeini was not persuaded.

Islamic Movements: The Case for Democratic Inclusion

Naked Gun, a popular and often very funny American movie [of 1988], opens to the sound of the Islamic call to prayer—alas, in movieland [back then] an almost certain sign that caricatures of Muslims would follow. The camera sweeps past mosques to a palace in the "Moorish" style, outside of which passing camels are treated to the sight of armored vehicles screeching to a halt and disgorging armed men with half-concealed faces. Someone is late for a meeting of "Islamintern"; the world's leading bad boys are gathering with only a token representation from Comintern, the old bad-boy network [of Communists]. Idi Amin, Yasser Arafat, Muammar Qaddafi, and Ayatollah Khomeini (apparently in the chairman's seat) are meeting to plan the humiliation of the United States. Gorbachev has other concerns; he worries about spoiling his good image among Americans. The only other Communist leader is a shadowy and silent Castro, who disappears after one shot; no Kim Il Sung, no Ho Chi Minh, no Pol Pot. When the top four "Islamintern" members have outdone themselves in outrageous proposals for anti-American terrorist acts, the intrepid Lieutenant Drebin reveals himself and single-handedly punches everyone out. As he escapes to heroic music, he shouts, "And don't ever let me catch you guys in America!"

Perhaps Lieutenant Drebin should also have shouted, "And you guys will never see anything but a caricature of the Islamic world in America!"

Author's note: This article was first published as: "The Islamic Movement: The Case for Democratic Inclusion," in Nikki R. Keddie (ed.), *Contention: Debates in Society, Culture, and Science* 4:3 (1995) 107–127. Reproduced with permission. It has been modified principally by changing the present tense to the past tense when discussing actual events close to the time that the article was written. Some additional clarifying information has been added in brackets and a few sentences that are no longer relevant have been removed. I have also added a postscript.

because *Naked Gun*—admittedly a farce—represented, alas, the level at which American understanding of the political meaning of the Islamic revival remained frozen [at that time]. Beginning in the 1970s a revival of identity among the world's billion Muslims has brought to the fore the extremely varied and changing faces of the encounter between Islam and politics. Most people in the United States (and the West in general) still see this ongoing revival as a springboard for a coordinated conspiracy of single-minded fanatics addicted to violence and sworn to the hatred of America and the oppression of women; in short, the present-day analogue to what our Communist-hunting Senator McCarthy called, "A conspiracy so immense and an infamy so black." And, within the Islamic world [of the twenty-first century], many autocratic regimes hostile to various aspects of the Islamic revival know that this is the button to press in order to get American support no matter how distasteful their policies might be: hence our covert support in the 1980s for Saddam's Iraq, which took on the archetypal Islamic regime, Iran.

Yet the very example of Iran—so important as a test case for many Muslims as well as Americans—shows how the Islamic revival, when it enters the centrifuge of real politics, becomes, like every ideal, exalted or otherwise, hostage to the world and its conflicting forces. Moreover, in Iran, as in Egypt, Turkey, and elsewhere, Muslims have understood the relation of religion and politics in significantly different terms based on long-standing and strongly held local, political and civic traditions. As a result, the Islamic revivalist movements of different countries are strikingly different.

The example of Iran, where such a movement has long been in power, offers a very useful point of comparison with the Islamic revival movements in other parts of the Middle East, which have not achieved power. To the degree that they hope to find or succeed in finding a place in the political process, such aspiring movements are often obliged to run after national political traditions and interests. In Iran, with an Islamic revivalist regime in charge, national political traditions and interests often seem to have completely overtaken "Islamic" ideology. The example of Iran makes it clear that the primary political arena, even for avowed Islamic "internationalists" who take over governments, soon becomes the existing nation-state.

Iran is not only an example of what other Islamic revivalist movements might turn into; it is also—and more importantly—an example of the many conflicting pulls on such a regime if and when it *does* come to power. For, after many years of fairly open debate, continuing disagreement within and between the ruling and religious elites in Iran makes it increasingly uncertain as to whose vision of revived Islam will prevail. In Iran, as seems likely to happen in other Islamic societies if the revivalists take power, religion turns out to be a very important source of public opinion rather than a structuring principle of government. Many Iranians must be reminded of the Persian proverb, "When there is more than one midwife, the baby's head is sure to come out the wrong way." Not only for Iran but for all these movements, the adjective "Islamic" by itself explains very little indeed.

How strangely different from the fantasies of *Naked Gun* were the meetings of real Islamic conclaves summoned after the death of Khomeini to Qom, the Iranian city of shrines and religious colleges, to choose a new spiritual Shi'ite leader, a sort of pope. Such meetings were steeped in traditions of the Shi'ite clergy that were far, far older than the Islamic revival. They resembled congressional caucuses; their purpose, to declare who was "most learned" while avoiding a political incompetent, would greatly disappoint the myth-makers of Hollywood. No camels—so necessary for Westerners to situate anything in the Middle East—circulated outside, because camels are almost as rare in urban areas of Iran as long-horn cattle are in Houston or Dallas. And, alas, for the image of "Islamintern," they did not meet in a palace. For decades the leading religious scholars of Qom (now called the Association of Teachers) have gathered to choose the spiritual leader of the Shi'ites in what is now the handsome library of the most prestigious religious college in Iran. Built by a nineteenth-century Shah as a sitting room for his visits to Qom, this library in its origins represents the tradition of arms-length respect that government and the religiously learned (in Iran called mullahs) have maintained toward each other in most periods and most places throughout the history of Islamic societies. The king would visit the shrine city to pay his respects to religion; but the mullahs had to come to the king's own building to pay their respects to the king.

To understand what happened at these meetings, and the dramatic shift they signaled in the relations between the religious establishment and the state in "the Islamic Republic," one must go back to a meeting [thirty-three] years ago. After Ayatollah Khomeini's death in 1989, when the Association of Teachers met in the former royal sitting room to choose a new supreme leader of the Shi'ites, there were no more Shahs in Iran, and the postrevolutionary Constitution of Iran had given recognition of spiritual leadership new importance. According to this Constitution, "the governance and leadership of the nation" should preferably be given to an individual amongst those very, very few mullahs who were *marja*'s, or Grand Ayatollahs—having the qualifications of "political and social perspicacity, courage, strength and the necessary administrative abilities."

A small number of mullahs—probably never more than two hundred—have the authority to give a recognized opinion on disputed points of Islamic law; these men are qualified "doctors of the law" and usually enjoy the title "ayatollah." Their authority has been received from similarly qualified teachers whose own authority can, according to Shi'ite belief, be traced back in a continuous chain to the founder of Islam, the Prophet Muḥammad, somewhat as apostolic succession is traced back to Jesus. But only a few of these "doctors of the law," seldom as many as eight at one time, get any acceptance as *marja*'s; and normally only one, the "most learned," is "the supreme *marja*'." (Since the mid-nineteenth century the ideal has been to have a "supreme *marja*'" recognized by the great majority of Shi'ites; but in practice, there have been many periods without a leader accepted by the majority.) All *marja*'s are the authors of the most popular manuals about the basic practice of Islam expected of an ordinary believer (who bears no guilt before God for error in disputed matters as long as he/she follows one of the *marja*'s as a "source for imitation").

During the last years of Khomeini's life, the majority of Iranian Shi'ites believed that he embodied all these qualifications: he was a *marja*' and the charismatic leader of the Revolution. Few government officials or mullahs dared to oppose him openly from the time the Constitution was ratified in December 1979, until he died on June 3, 1989. Insofar as one can speak in Iran of religion and state (Western terms, not always useful in non-Western contexts), Khomeini was the embodiment of both.

On Khomeini's death the basic constitutional problem lay bare for everyone to see. In its opening statement the Constitution says that its sixth general principle is that, "The affairs of the country must be governed by reliance on public opinion, as determined by elections"; elsewhere, the Constitution seems to disregard the elective process and gives great direct power to the spiritual "Guide" of the nation, including the power to appoint the highest officials in the armed forces, the head of the judiciary, and so forth.

Constitutions are like caterpillars: they feed frenziedly on events and the hurried decisions of influential people until they emerge as utterly metamorphized creatures unpredictable from their earlier shapes. Macaulay, in prophesying the shipwreck of the American Constitution, said it was "all sails and no anchor"; now it is the oldest written constitution still in use in the world. In the Iranian case, the framers of the Constitution had a clear mandate to create a truly "Islamic government"; what is surprising is not that they created a constitution with ambiguities, but that—given the immense uncertainty and disagreement as to what "Islamic government" might mean—they came up with anything at all.

Islamic government is for many Muslims what the old but recently revived phrase "civil society" is for many liberals: a repository of collective hope and an aspiration that the fundamentally good values at the roots of their traditions be recovered and strengthened. But the actual agreed-upon content of Islamic government remains very limited and, more often than not, severely disputed. According to most Sunni Muslims, approximately 85 to 90 percent of the world's Muslims, true Islamic government existed only from 622 to 661 C.E.—that is, in the latter part of the life of the Prophet Muḥammad and under his four immediate successors. According to most Shi'ite Muslims, about 10 to 15 percent of the Islamic community, such government existed only in the latter part of the life of the Prophet (622–632) and under the rule of 'Alī, his cousin and son-in-law, from 656 to 661. In either case the life of the Prophet was the overwhelming source from which to derive examples of Islamic government.

Yet the Prophet's full "legislative" authority could not be inherited by anyone. Who, for example, should say how the many (and necessarily quite different) arrangements made by the Prophet for the collection of taxes (to be paid in some cases in textiles, in others in coin; in some cases, per head, in others, according to agricultural yield) should be generalized into a uniform and truly "Islamic" system of taxation? In this instance a general consensus was worked out, the details of which, however, have remained disputed among Muslims up to the present. Khomeini, in his manifesto calling for Islamic government, says that the medieval Islamic consensus view of taxation would satisfy all the needs of modern government. Iran has yet to adopt tax laws, such as the pre-modern Islamic flat 20 percent tax on agricultural production, that reflect Khomeini's prescription. Such taxes would seem to most Iranians profoundly irrelevant to their situation.

In fact, it is far from clear that Islamic government requires a constitution; and some ayatollahs openly said as much. Saudi Arabia, which considers itself a truly Islamic government, had no constitution in the Western sense until 1992. Then why did Iran adopt a constitution? Because no government, Islamic or otherwise, without a constitution would be legitimate in the eyes of Iranians, who in 1906 had the first successful constitutional revolution in Asia. Iranians, in their own way, obsess about constitutions nearly as much as Americans do. Islamic government in Iran as elsewhere had to be articulated in the political language known by the articulators, which in Iran is [still in 2022] dramatically different from, for example, the political language of Saudi Arabia, with its tradition of monarchy and tribal consensus, or Libya, with its anticlerical and egalitarian traditions [under Muammar Qaddafi (d. 2011) and unresolved struggle to form a national government through elections].

When, however, the "doctors of the law" met in Qom in December 1993 and December 1994 to choose the spiritual leader for Iran's Shiʿites, they did not go to their customary meeting place in the Shah's sitting room turned library; to avoid pressure from outsiders they met in the house of one of the members. In 1979 the religious establishment had taken over the government; fourteen years later the religious establishment was energetically trying to elude control by elements of the very government that supposedly embodied its interests.

Why had events defeated so many early expectations that Iranians had achieved a consensus about the nature of Islamic government? Before his death Khomeini had foreseen that no one could dominate the government as he had; and shortly after his death a revision of the Constitution was ratified that said that the spiritual "Guide" of the nation need only be a "doctor of the law" and not necessarily a *marjaʿ*. This revision allowed a fast round of musical chairs after Khomeini's death. Rafsanjani, an engaging and politically astute mullah of moderate learning, became the president, an office that was then given real power. Khamenei, holder of the formerly ceremonial presidency, received Khomeini's position as spiritual "Guide," although everyone knew that he would have to struggle to reclaim even a portion of those powers exercised by Khomeini.

If, for Iranians, Islamic government had its origins in the spiritual leadership of an overwhelmingly popular *marjaʿ*, then, with the appointment of Khamenei, not only individuals but also ideas had played musical chairs. Until Khomeini's death, Khamenei, a well-spoken and presentably grey-and-white bearded gentleman in his fifties, had never been considered one of the "doctors of the law" (or ayatollahs) qualified to give an independent opinion. Khomeini's son (not a "doctor of the law") and another "doctor of the law" fortuitously present reported that Khomeini, on his death bed, had recognized Khamenei as a "doctor of the law." Khamenei, who had been a cooperative player with Rafsanjani, was quickly approved for the office of "Guide" by the significant bodies, including the influential Association of Teachers. The brute fact was that politics, and the political needs of elected leaders like Rafsanjani, had made it impossible to keep the most learned religious leaders—who were almost invariably too independent in their political views—in government.

It can be said of Khamenei, as it was said of Truman, that he was put forward by men who, speculating beyond the death of their leader, knew what they wanted but had absolutely no idea what they would get. Chosen as a reliable member of the circle of Rafsanjani, Khamenei felt inspired by his new office to be a genuine holy man. He undertook fasts and prayer vigils; he sometimes returned from these spiritual exercises inspired with opinions that were, in the view of President Rafsanjani's circle, positive embarrassments. He thundered against Salman Rushdie, a question that the Rafsanjani circle hoped would slither into the background; he worried about slipshod standards for modesty in dress; and he urged greater government involvement in the economy when the government was trying quietly to restore a free market. To his critics, Khamenei seemed in eager pursuit of the larger role of "Guide" as it had been understood in the lifetime of Khomeini. To his supporters, he seemed to strike the populist note that was otherwise absent in the government after Khomeini's death.

On Thursday, December 9, 1993, Ayatollah Golpayegani, whom the majority of Iranians recognized as their *marja'*, died at the estimated age of ninety-six. When the Association of Teachers in Qom convened to choose his successor, Khamenei wanted to represent himself as the heir of Golpayegani. Not only the family of Golpayegani (who denied Khamenei an important role in the funeral) but also the leading members of the clergy were determined to prevent him from seizing that chance. In the clergy's view they were putting one aspect of religious tradition out of the reach of the nation's "official" religious "Guide."

In the end the Association of Teachers, by the vote of a not-very-sizable majority, decided that "the office of *marja'* is exclusively established in the Grand Ayatollah Hajj Shaykh Mohammad Ali Araki." This terse statement was not unexpected. Araki, once fairly learned, once a moral example to the young clergymen of Qom, had by now largely turned himself over to the state of contemplation his ninety-nine years had earned him. He seemed to fit the wisdom of the Arabic proverb which says, "Better a mute sage than a fool who speaks." One of the very few clergymen opposed to photographs of people, he now was too old and too diffusely focused to notice that he was being photographed. And the choice of Araki coincided with the wishes of the circle around Rafsanjani, the president.

A year later with the death of Araki on November 24, 1994, the senior Shi'ite clergy stepped back to yet an earlier period in their history. Araki had conveniently been unconscious for about two weeks before his death, which allowed the twentieth century's most bizarre and bellicose ayatollah, Ahmad Jannati, to declare that political shrewdness was the most important quality for the *marja'*, an obvious reference to Khamenei and a complete reversal of one hundred and fifty years of Shi'ite tradition. When Araki died, the Association of Teachers met and, on December 2, issued a list of the seven *marja'*s acceptable for people to imitate, adding the name of Khamenei to the six proposed by a group of clergymen in Tehran, without indicating that any one of the seven was superior to any other. The text accompanying the list was almost as significant: it said that freedom of choice of religious leaders had always been a positive aspect of Shi'ite belief, and in past times lists of several names had been put forward—an obvious reference to what had happened after the death of Ayatollah Borujerdi in 1961. Plurality of leadership in 1961 had been regarded as abnormal; now it was being promoted as a positive step. Elements in the government including Ayatollah Yazdi declared a victory for Khamenei. But Khamenei realized that it was as yet too far-fetched for him to put himself forward. Five days later he said he was willing to be the *marja'* for Shi'ites outside of Iran, most of whom are followers of Ayatollah Sistani in Iraq. Iranians jokingly asked each other whether they should get copies of Khamenei's manual on Islamic practices for guidance on their trips abroad. Khamenei had been included in the list so that there was no open confrontation with the government; but to avoid the government's embrace, the clergy had dissolved (at least temporarily) the hope for any clearly defined "supreme leadership." The Shi'ite clergy might have been weaker as a result, but as a group they were certainly harder to grasp and manipulate.

In 1979 in the person of Khomeini the clergy had gained control of the government. In the 1989 revision of the Constitution the government had sought to install Khamenei, a cleric of modest religious learning, but presumed to be cooperative, as the Islamic "Guide" of the nation. In December 1993 and again in December 1994 in the face of Khamenei's activism, the higher clergy attempted to hold the government at arm's length, first by selecting an ancient candidate who would reign but not rule and then by selecting so many candidates that none could rule.

Now [in 2022] a nation of approximately [85 million] (the overwhelming majority of whom are Shiʿite Muslims), Iran, [forty-six] years after its Revolution, has the longest-running experiment in non-monarchial Islamic government. But the example of Iran shows how unpredictable and how influenced by cultural setting Islamic government can be, particularly when, some element of popular sovereignty remains in the government. Iranian culture, with over two thousand years' memory of itself, is an ancient, artful, and powerful creature. The Islamic tradition, with over fourteen centuries of extremely varied history and [in 2022 approximately 1.9 billion] adherents in the modern world, has all the rich diversity that such length and breadth would imply. It should come as no surprise that the Iranian tradition and the Islamic tradition should find in each other's baggage clothes that would comfortably suit.

Turkey and Egypt are the other two giants in the Middle East, with populations [in 2022 of 84 million and 104 million] respectively. In both countries, "Islamists," or advocates of government by Islamic law, have shown the same openness of agendas and the same adaptability to the political cultures of their countries. Anyone who, like myself, watched the crowds accompany the new Islamist mayor of Istanbul to the town hall after his victory in the elections of March 27, 1994, knew that this was a victory for the "oppressed," the very people whom the founder of Republican Turkey, Ataturk, a century ago had obliged to set aside their Ottoman-style Middle Eastern clothing for Western-style dress. The point was that they were, in fact, wearing Western-style clothing, which is the way most city Turks now dress without a second thought. [However, in the countryside a mix of modern and traditional styles continues.]

Necmettin Erbakan [d. 2011], the leader of the Welfare Party that was [in 1994 when this article was written] the embodiment of the Islamist movement in Turkey, was a quite tall and imposing man, notable for his elegant ties, always carefully color-coordinated with his fine European suits. (In Iran ties are considered symbols of anti-Islamic, pro-monarchist sentiment, and no official would be caught dead wearing one, even abroad.) Erbakan has fully understood that paying homage to the memory of Ataturk, best known in the West as a Westernizing secularist, was essential for any nationally important movement. He performed this symbolic act by paying a public visit to the vast and somber Mausoleum of Ataturk in Ankara, a pilgrimage formerly required of all visiting statesmen and performed by most Turkish politicians. He explained that Ataturk, were he alive today, would be a member of the Welfare Party because he had fought the West for the independence of Turkey at the end of the First World War. After some earlier political failure following idiosyncratic politics that ignored Ataturk, Erbakan learned, as the Turks say, that you must cross the same bridge others cross if you want to meet them on the other side. [Nevertheless, a romantic attachment to the Ottoman past has grown stronger in contemporary Turkey.]

Egypt, the third giant, is heir to yet a different political culture. Anyone who visited [in 1995] the leadership of the Muslim Brothers [as I did, once] Egypt's most powerful association of Islamists, would have been struck by their middle-class respectability and their considerable age. The Muslim Brothers came by their gerontocracy legitimately; founded in 1928, they were probably the oldest successful organization of Islamic revival in the world. They attacked the government and were ruthlessly suppressed in the late forties and early fifties; after this baptism by fire, they emerged as a nonviolent movement for the reintroduction of Islamic law. Officially banned but unofficially tolerated at that time, the Muslim Brothers had representatives in Parliament who ran for office under the cover of an accepted party.

To visit the law offices of Ismail Hudaybi, one of the leading Muslim Brothers in Egypt [during the Mubarak period]—where so many important Brothers were lawyers—was to visit the office of a modestly successful middle-class lawyer unidentifiable by appearance and manner as Islamist or secularist. The offices were located in one of the humbler parts of Cairo's posh Mohandessin section with its Baskin Robbins and TCBY. (Greater Cairo, with over twenty-one million inhabitants [in 2022], is aptly called "the Mother of the World" by Egyptians since a little bit of everything from the Pharaonic period to Art Deco seems to be lodged somewhere in its perpetually growing and perpetually decaying fabric.) Somewhat surprisingly for a lawyer, the front door of his law office was open; and behind a room with two clerks, he sat in an office that looked too small to accommodate his desk, a modest couch, and a few chairs. Typical of people in government and business in the Middle East, he carried on several conversations at once, talking to his visitor, one of his lawyers, and one of his clients while passing on requests for coffee and tea to his office boy. A visitor in the mid-1990s found him complaining about the radical Islamists, "ignorant kids" as he called them, who reject democracy and do not understand the Islamic principle of "the dignity of man."

In their acculturation to national politics, the Egyptian Muslim Brothers found that they had an unexpected protector and an unexpected opportunity. The unexpected protector was the Egyptian judiciary, which had a tradition of independence from the administrative branches of the government, born partly out of the considerable size and self-esteem of Egypt's legal profession. Fear might silence the civilian courts in the days of Nasser's greatest power, but given a chance, the courts have upheld certain civil liberties, and routinely overrule administrative detention of suspects by the government that routinely reverses these challenges in special courts set up to deal with "the emergency." The independence of the civilian judiciary [in the Mubarak period] was embodied above all by the Supreme Constitutional Court, which had overruled the government on its right to suppress political parties. Although many of Egypt's legal institutions were formed under French and British influence, the model for the highest court had clearly become American, since it had increasingly expanded its power of judicial review, in part because its chief justice admired the American Supreme Court. The Egyptian government had used military courts to sidestep the civilian courts it perceived to be "slow" and "unreliable."

The unexpected opportunity presented to the Muslim Brothers was precisely the existence of professional associations, often called syndicates in Egypt. Student unions, faculty clubs and, above all, the syndicates had long maintained the trappings of democratic process for the election of officials; and the Islamists, well represented in the professions, decided that this was an arena in which they could compete. They were right. In campus after campus, in syndicate after syndicate, the members of these organizations woke up to find that determined Islamists knew how to campaign, knew how to find out the concerns left unaddressed by the organizations, and—above all—knew how to get out their voters.

When, in the fall of 1992, the Islamists even took over the Bar Association, long considered a bastion of liberalism, the Egyptian government was stunned (as were secularists, whether leftist or liberal). To some extent the administrations since Nasser had every reason to expect to hear from the Islamists—whom some politicians promoted as a counterweight to the leftist secularists—because these administrations had allowed greater freedom of public expression. But they had not anticipated losing so much ground so quickly. The government was also alarmed by the armed attacks of radical Islamists on politicians and tourists and even the revered Nobel Prize-winning Egyptian novelist, Naguib Mahfouz.

The power of the legal profession and the importance of the syndicate united in 1994 in a drama watched all over the Arab world. On May 12, after a supposedly radical Islamist lawyer died while in police custody, reportedly under torture, the Bar Council, the leadership of the Egyptian Bar Association (which included leftists, Nasserists, and supporters of the governing party as well as a majority faction of Muslim Brothers) unanimously voted to strike. Courts all over Egypt ceased to function. On May 17 some hundreds of lawyers gathered outside the Bar Association to march on the Presidential Palace, and their fury, as they stood clutching their briefcases in one hand and brandishing their fists with the other, became, as one says in Arabic, "more famous than a fire on a high place." Security forces not only drove them back with tear gas and batons but also "violated" what lawyers regarded as the "sanctuary" of their syndicate headquarters. Twenty-seven lawyers were arrested on the spot and ten more were arrested later as ringleaders. The lawyers immediately moved to enlarge the circle of confrontation and took their case to human rights organizations. To most Egyptian lawyers, it seemed nothing but vindictive retaliation when on June 15 the Egyptian government arrested five lawyers including two members of the Egyptian Organization for Human Rights. On June 18 the Secretary General of the Bar Association, a member of the old secularist liberal party of Egypt, the Wafd, began an extremely well-publicized hunger strike (which annoyed the Islamists from whom he stole the show). By July 2 the lawyers arrested were released and the Secretary General ended his hunger strike. The slogan of an activist group of lawyers, "Our cause continues, and no bargaining," showed how defiant the legal profession remained.

In the past two years [1993–94] the Egyptian government tried, with considerable success, to destroy the armed Islamists, the "radicals," root and branch. In Egypt everyone asked: will the government turn against the Muslim Brothers who now had representatives in parliament as well as control of many syndicates? Already, the government decided to exclude the Muslim Brothers from the National Dialogue, which it had sponsored with the hope of creating a broad consensus on reforms in the Egyptian political system. The Muslim Brothers were irritated by the growing distrust shown to them; they claimed a long experience of working inside democratic institutions. They also claimed they had no connections with the armed radicals. [However, there was evident disagreement in the Muslim Brotherhood between a non-violent and a radical faction, both devoted to political change.] Some voices in the government argued that the Muslim Brothers regarded the armed radicals as the vanguard essential to destabilize the state and that their present respect for democratic elections was only temporary and strategic. Their critics said that when the Muslim Brothers gained power through elections, their new-found faith in democracy would melt in the Egyptian heat.

Behind much of the fear of the Islamists in the West lay the largely mistaken idea that they were a coordinated movement, that somewhere a black turbaned ayatollah (presumably in the chairman's seat, as in *Naked Gun*) would meet with the elegantly suited Erbakan and an Egyptian lawyer in his lumpy Cairo-made suit to synchronize watches for the next terrorist act their Western-hating minds would have spawned. And how deeply satisfying this specter was to Western imaginations, for some curious reason more so than imagining a conspiracy of the remaining Communist leaders—some of whom had the worst human rights records in the world.

Alas, for the writers of colorful copy, the nonradical Islamists, in spite of occasional gestures of friendship to each other, are [still in 2022] really no more a coordinated movement than are the animal protection movements and conservation societies of the world. [Witness the 2021 disagreements and insults exchanged between Muslim Brotherhood leaders in Istanbul and London.] Their attitudes toward inter-Muslim conflicts tell the story of their primary connection to local circumstances and their primary concern in protecting their local organizations. Attitudes toward the Islamic government of Iran [still] range from admiration to contempt; the degree of non-Iranian Islamists' involvement in their own political communities is reflected in their astonishing ignorance of Iran's postrevolutionary history. Erbakan, the Turkish Islamist leader, who had personal access to King Fahd of Saudi Arabia, had the same guarded view of Iran as did the Saudi government. Erbakan sometimes spoke of an Islamic United Nations and an Islamic NATO, none of which, however, seemed to decrease his commitment to Turkey's sovereignty as a nation-state. He said that once the West accepted the new Islamic terms that would be created by a Welfare Party victory, Turkey's trade with the West would increase. He laid particular stress on coming to an understanding with Germany whence so many billions in remittances by Turkish workers came.

Interestingly, most Alavis, the Shi'ite minority that made up at least 15 percent of the largely Sunni Turkish population, were frightened by the prospect of a Welfare Party victory [of Erdoğan in 1994]. They strongly favored the maintenance of a secular state—as, for obvious reasons, did many Muslim minorities elsewhere, such as the Kurds of Iraq, the Berbers of Algeria, and the one-hundred-ten-million [209 million in 2022] strong Muslim minority of India.

The Muslim Brothers' attitude toward Iran has varied across time and place. At the time of the Iranian Revolution in 1978–79 the Brothers were overwhelmingly enthusiastic about Khomeini's success. But in 1982 the Syrian regime, then a close ally of Iran, mercilessly suppressed the Muslim Brothers in Syria, claiming that they intended armed rebellion. The Syrian Muslim Brothers felt the Iranian government had, by its official silence about their travail, let them down completely. In contrast, the Muslim Brothers of Sudan were ready to work with Iran because they admired Iran's independent and avowedly Islamic stance. The Egyptian Muslim Brothers fell somewhere in between. (Even though they are the oldest branch of the organization they have only "fraternal" relations with branches in other nations.)

Most curious was the position of the Muslim Brothers of Jordan, who—long protected and in 1984 partly enfranchised by King Hussein—developed a distance from their early support of Iran since they wanted to be seen as a loyal opposition to the King's government. Their loyalty was such that when King Hussein agreed to meet Rabin on the White House lawn, the Muslim Brothers made a totally nonconfrontational move by declaring a Day of Mourning. The late King Hussein—whose political gifts never ceased to amaze—had prepared the country for months for his entry into the peace process by telling Jordanians that the country had to move in unison or it would again fly apart. (Jordanians remained traumatized by the tensions between their citizens of Palestinian origin and those of more anciently Jordanian origin that erupted in a short but bloody civil war in 1970.) On the Day of Mourning, out of loyalty to the King, few Islamists or Jordanians of any stripe chose to mourn in public, however much they may have mourned in private.

At the end of July 1994, the Jordanian Muslim Brothers chose a new leader, predictably enough a lawyer, to replace an extremely aged leader. By his public pledge to continue opposition to the agreement only by—in his words—"legal and constitutional means," this new leader assured

Jordanians that the chosen arena for most Islamists in that country was the unusual building—a kind of marriage between a basketball arena and an oriental palace—in which the Parliament sat in Amman. On a visit to Gaza [in the early 1990s] a friend asked a member of Hamas who directed an Islamic foundation what his model for the future political struggle of Hamas would be: Algeria, Iran, or the Sudan? Without hesitation, he said, "Jordan"—by which he meant that Hamas, anxious that they might be excluded by the PLO, sought fair democratic inclusion in Palestinian politics. [Hamas was expelled from Jordan in 1999 less than a year after King Abdullah took power following King Hussein's death.]

The Gulf War of 1990–91 offered yet further scenes of Islamists reflagging themselves according to changing sentiment and local political interest. The Turkish Welfare Party was at first pro-Saddam, but after a September meeting with King Fahd, it assumed a position that was either neutral or somewhat critical of Saddam. The Muslim Brothers in Egypt were in some disarray; while most were contemptuous of Saddam's new claim to be a pan-Islamic leader, they were alarmed to see Western armies sorting out problems between Islamic countries. The old guard amongst them knew how important in the past financial support from sympathizers in the Gulf had been and did not want to support Saddam openly. The rank-and-file were outraged that the Americans were swaggering about yet another area—part of it a sacred area—of the Middle East and wanted Saddam to survive (which, to everyone's surprise, he did). Ultimately, the Muslim Brothers were less vocal about Egypt's involvement with the coalition against Iraq than had been expected, and the secular left, which was vocal, enjoyed a new popularity on Egyptian campuses.

The Iranians, as the Persian idiom has it, felt their hearts "chill" with relief to see Iraq, their opponent in an eight-year war [1980–88], and the West whom—they knew, well before the Western public, had materially supported Iraq—go to war with each other. But it was the Iranian government's behavior in the aftermath of the First Gulf War that spoke volumes on the limitations of Islamic internationalism: the Iranians may have allowed armed Iraqi refugees in Iran to cross into Iraq when there was a massive uprising of their fellow Shi'ites in southern Iraq, but the government understood the risks and kept well clear of significant direct involvement. Some Iraqi Shi'ites felt betrayed.

Why did large-scale movements of Islamists lack (and sometimes even fail to seek) international Islamic coordination? For all that the winds of religious revival blow strongly among the [almost two] billion Muslims of the world, the majority of Muslims do not regard Islamic government as a priority. For the politically committed, there are other options besides the Islamist movements: liberal Islam is still very much alive and anyone who has lived through an Egyptian Ramadan and seen the devotion with which secularist members of the liberal Wafdist Party or leftists of the Nasserist Party fast, cannot doubt the sincerity of their faith. Yet an enormous number, probably the majority, of Muslims remain politically uncommitted. The pietists, those who emphasize inner religious development, are well represented by the largest Islamic movement in the world, the Tablighi Jamaat, which originated in South Asia and even has a following among the few million Muslims in North America. The assembly of its adherents at yearly meetings, whether in Britain, Canada or South Asia, is second in size only to that of Muslims on the Pilgrimage. Yet the Tablighi Jamaat maintains that it is far more important to get Muslims to pray five times a day than, say, to oppose Hindus in the aftermath of their destruction of the Babri mosque at Ayodhya.

The Islamists know that if they wish to capture the hearts and minds of the Muslim majority, they must offer that majority some of the practical things it wants and expects. And the deeper the Islamists become involved in mass politics, and in particular, in democratic politics, the more they articulate the wants and expectations of their fellow countrymen. The Hezbollah, the Shiʿite organization in Lebanon, has the largest bloc in the Lebanese Parliament [in 2021] and its own radio and television shows. (The religious leaders of the Lebanese Shiʿites became somewhat alienated from the leading Iranian clergymen because they were not invited [by the Iranian clergy] to the election of Araki.) Erbakan told his Turkish followers that his party, which had a fair amount of small merchant support, was the party of free enterprise and the private sector. The Muslim Brothers in Egypt are also free marketeers, although they continually point to their quite considerable social welfare projects as proof that Islam has strengthened their sense of social conscience. In Iran, where virtually all public discourse is Islamic, national politics became stalled between the elected officials in parliament who favored a free market and the statist programs of the economic radicals, who found support in social groups such as militias that owed their existence to the Revolution. In any case, the economic radicalism that was an assumed part of the platform of Islamist groups right after the Revolution now seems to be the platform of fringe groups.

Mass movements also have to deal with long-term expectations about what is right and proper: like Iran, Egypt and Turkey also have ancient and artful cultures. In the eighteenth century the majority of Muslims around the world belonged to mystical brotherhoods, the Sufi orders, whose vivid ceremonials were designed to create mindfulness of God in the believers and were widely popular among the literate and illiterate alike. In no place were these orders more powerful than in Turkey, where the Ottoman sultan was proud to belong to a Sufi brotherhood. Small wonder that the original core of Erbakan's party was a group of adherents to Sufi brotherhoods. But the Iranian Shi'ite clergy has always frowned on Sufis, although they have been unable to suppress them. In Turkey a mass movement of Islamists cannot do without the Sufis; in Iran, Sufi support might be a liability. In Egypt, the power of the Sufis has decreased since the nineteenth century, in part because nineteenth-century Egyptian Muslim leaders saw Sufis as forces of backwardness. The Egyptian Muslim Brothers disapprove of Sufis, but at some political cost.

Yet it would be a mistake to think that the cultural world of Islamic countries is somehow rigid and that we are—in that indirect self-compliment used by Westerners in the past—faced with "the unchanging East." This ignorant fantasy has resurfaced in recent discussions of Islam's supposed incompatibility with democracy. The Prophet Samuel's anointing of Saul as king has not prevented Jews from becoming ardent democrats any more than the declaration of Jesus that his kingdom was not of this world has prevented Christians from supporting kings. The Qur'ān is no more specific than the Bible—and, like it, is more explicit about the ethics than about the form of government.

The enfranchisement of women offers a compelling proof of the ability of Islamic political cultures to evolve. Except in Turkey, women got the vote later in the Islamic Middle East than in much of the West, and Muslim religious conservatives generally opposed the enfranchisement of women. But the Islamist movements of Egypt, Turkey, and Iran now regard women as an absolutely fundamental element in their support and would never dream of disenfranchising women. In Turkey, incidentally, women are more effective as house-to-house canvassers for the Islamists than are men (to whom doors are opened only when adult male members of the family are at home). The enfranchisement of women, however, has no built-in bias that favors Islamists; it is just an irreversible fact of politics. It is no accident that the three female heads of state (none of them Islamists) in the Islamic world at the beginning of 1995 were in parliamentary democracies. Benazir Bhutto of Pakistan, Khaleda Zia of Bangladesh, and Tansu Çiller of Turkey led states with a combined population of more than two hundred eighty million, far larger than the Arab world (which in the West is so often mistakenly assumed to be synonymous with the Islamic world). Incidentally, advocates of Islamic government inside Pakistan have had very limited success in national elections and only flourished under the patronage of dictatorship; and Hassan Turabi, the Islamist ideologue of the former regime in the Sudan, was never able to win a seat in parliament in the days when that country had real elections.

One aspect of the Islamic revival seems to have escaped most observers: it has introduced millions to organized politics. Formerly, relations between central governments and local communities took place through elites: landlords, great merchants, clergy, and the like. Most of these elites have been swept away by reform and the redistribution of wealth or pushed to the side by modern communications that allow ordinary people to see and hear the state directly and to experience its interference in local affairs. Wherever religion has been the most basic element of self-identification, local organization has tended to take on a religious identity, whether in Christian Latin America or in the Islamic Middle East. Before the Islamic revival political parties in the Islamic Middle East were more often than not merely the followings of charismatic public men. The new Islamist organizations have, in some cases, created genuine political parties, some of which may survive their leaders. They are, in this respect, in the vanguard of what the West calls "modernization" (although their views on human rights are often far from "modern").

Does this all mean that it would be in the world's interest, and in particular, in the interest of the world's Muslims to favor inclusion of the Islamists in the political process? Two strong arguments have been raised against such inclusion. One says that the Islamists believe in democracy until their victory, that they believe in one man one vote one time only. Some of them probably do believe in this. This fear caused the Algerian government to stop the democratic process in Algeria in January 1992. But the results seemed to indicate that one cost of stopping the Islamists at the ballot box may be to face them again as a mass movement, which is wholly militant, without any stake in democracy, and without perceptible head or tail. It [was then in 1995] unclear with whom Algerian authorities should talk if they wished to reach a compromise [with their opposition.

In 2022 Algeria has opened both its political system and its economy to some extent, but it is still distant from a fully democratic state.] In Egypt some secularist intellectuals [still] argue for the inclusion of the Islamists [despite the failed Morsi government of 2012] because the Islamists have gained power in various groups through democratic means (and even relinquished power, in the Pharmacists' Syndicate, when voted out). They point to Jordan where the Muslim Brothers, after doing very well in the election of 1989, held positions such as Speaker of the House in Parliament. When a change in election laws and in public sentiment (the Islamist Ministers of Agriculture and Education were judged to have handled their portfolios poorly and to be righteous sloganeers who could not deliver) gave the Islamists fewer seats in the 1993 elections, the loyalty of the Muslim Brothers to the King, who supported their inclusion in politics, seemed, if anything, stronger.

Informed estimates [in the 1990s] used to give Egyptian Islamists about 30 percent of the electorate in free elections. [When they actually came to power in 2012, their record was severely criticized, and they were overthrown by a military coup a year later.] Those who distrust the Islamists say they cannot allow Egypt to play Russian roulette again. Cynics have suggested that even if the estimates are incorrect, one man one vote for one time may be better than one man one vote at no time.

The second strong objection to the inclusion of the Islamists is that there are several human rights issues on which the Islamists refuse to compromise because they believe these to be matters of Islamic law; and the one common element in these Islamist movements is their demand that Islamic law be reintroduced. On this point both sides feel misunderstood and both sides are, in fact, genuinely misunderstood.

For example, Americans are deeply shocked and horrified at the mistreatment of any person on the basis of religion; Iranian authorities seem to be deaf and blind to the reasons for this shock and horror. Consequently, some people in authority in Iran can only understand the several votes of the U.S. Congress condemning their persecution of the Iranian Baha'is as a cynical anti-Iranian plot without real support among Americans or any real basis in American political traditions. Iranians, on the other hand, think that Americans see them only through the lens of the hostage crisis and their human rights record (some aspects of which are indeed deplorable) and refuse to recognize that there is some degree of freedom of expression and popular sovereignty in Iran. Thoughtful Iranians admit that in Iran the subjects of debate are, in fact, restricted, but maintain that very real debate goes on. Likewise, candidacy for parliament is, unquestionably, restricted, but elections are, nevertheless, largely honest [with sharply shrinking participation by the electorate] and, consequently, vigorously contested.

The failure of some democratically minded Islamists to understand that individual rights are a necessary complement to popular sovereignty may prove a fatal weakness in their programs. In terms of religion and/or ethnicity most Islamic nations of the Middle East have enormous "minorities." To the degree that Islamist movements do not conceive of citizenship as full and equal for all, whether the citizens be Muslim, Christian, Baha'i, or atheist, and Palestinian, Berber, Armenian, Turkic, or Kurd, such movements will not create successfully integrated societies and will eventually fail. There is some sign that in Iran, through the practical schooling of politics, an increasing number of young Iranians are coming to realize this.

The Islamic Revolution in Iran has catapulted the shrine city of Qom into a different world in more ways than one. Laws to move factories out of Tehran and a superhighway connecting Qom to Tehran have increased industry in the Qom area and, alongside it, the population has grown several fold to over a million. But the heart of the city belongs to the religious colleges, the number of whose students has also increased many fold. The students follow the classic religious curriculum but are fascinated by new books that discuss the possibility of a radical reconstruction of Islamic thought. They too have been affected by political experience.

The victory of the genuine "doctors of the law" in getting their candidates recognized by the Shi'ite masses as the *marja*'s, the highest points of religious reference, often seems to have little meaning. It is significant that the battle over satellite dishes, extremely popular in Iran where MTV is keenly watched, has passed out of the hands of the ayatollahs with their conflicting rulings and into the hands of Parliament. But in fact the "doctors of the law" knew that they could not create an effective hierarchy because in Shi'ite Islam intellectual subordination of one of them to another is possible only to a limited extent. While tradition favors an appointment of a "most learned" ayatollah as a leader, no "doctor of the law" is supposed to follow anyone except himself. [Although Khamenei is not the most learned, his control of Iran is seen by leftists and liberals as religious dictatorship.]

There was [in the 1990s] a three-way standoff in Iranian politics between a pragmatic administration, represented by the presidency, a socially and economically conservative parliament, and the radicals, who wanted more government intervention in everything. Khamenei, perhaps seeking his own constituency, has come to speak more and more for the radicals, while the other ayatollahs are by and large economic conservatives. For some decades a large segment of the Iranian population, has been terrified that their economy might shortly enter a total meltdown and do not know where to look. For all that there are some loose elements of structure in the Shi'ite clergy, the supreme *marja'* never was a "pope" after all. [However, in 2022 Khamenei seems to control most of the game.] Real combinations of spiritual with political leadership have been rare and usually fraught with compromise. Politics, it seems, always has been, and always will be, politics—whether in the former Papal States, the Holy Roman Empire, Buddhist Tibet, or contemporary Iran. Consciously choosing not to follow in Khomeini's path, many of the "doctors of the law" in Iran after several decades of direct experience have become just as cautious about becoming too involved in politics as their nineteenth-century predecessors had been. The pious Shah who built the sitting room in Qom would probably understand.

POSTSCRIPT

It is disheartening to see the diminishing of democracy and the rise of autocracy in so many parts of the Middle East and the world as a whole.

Iran

I no longer expect to see Iran move in a democratic direction in the near future. An ever more conservative parliament voted in by an ever-shrinking electorate in addition to more extensive control by the Supreme Leader, Khamenei, make the prospect for a genuine democracy ever more slim. Growing restrictions on candidacy for the parliament, the presidency, and other elected offices have resulted in a diminished electorate, in which non-participation may show the public's dissatisfaction. Meanwhile the power of the highest religious figure has steadily grown. Following Donald Trump's cancellation of the nuclear agreement with Iran in 2018, Iran has turned more to Russia and China for support.

Turkey

The Republic of Turkey is defined as a parliamentary democracy; however, it is consciously moving away from alliances with the West and towards alliances with the Islamic Middle East, Russia and China. Recep Tayyip Erdoğan had been head of state since 2018 following many years as an active Islamist politician. He has had to moderate his Islamist policies somewhat due to the strongly secular tradition established by Ataturk. Erdoğan was Prime Minister from 2003 to 2014, drawing much of his popular support from the strong Islamist tradition in Anatolia. A revision of the constitution in 2017 removed the office of Prime Minister, after which Erdogan chose to become president with increased powers. Opposition to his presidency continues even though he put down a coup attempt by a faction in the army.

Egypt

The Muslim Brotherhood survives in exile. It is impossible to gauge the underground strength of the Muslim Brotherhood because the government is actively persecuting members of the organization, forcing some leaders to flee the country. The Arab Spring of 2011 caused Hosni Mubarak, President of Egypt for three decades, to resign. The Muslim Brothers then briefly came to power with the election in 2012 of Mohamed Morsi, who was ousted a year later in a military coup by his Minister of Defense, General Abdel Fattah el-Sisi, who retired in order to appear as a civilian president. Sisi continues to rule Egypt to this day although aspirations for genuine democracy have not died out and tensions remain. Sisi has outlawed the Muslim Brotherhood in Egypt and designated it a terrorist organization. It has been banned in some other Islamic countries as well. If the Muslim Brotherhood rises again in the Muslim world, it is likely to have different policies in different countries.

TOLERATION PAST AND PRESENT

Much of my life as a teacher and a citizen has gone toward fostering an ethic of toleration. I believe the materials for such an ethic are present in most of the great religions. As a child born before America's entry into the Second World War, I was aware of war throughout my life. As a child in school in lower Manhattan, I was taught to sit under my desk in the event of an atomic bomb landing on me. As a child growing up in Manhattan, I got interested in toleration because of the many refugees from Nazism and Fascism living in our midst. My parents were keen supporters of the United Nations, and my mother became a non-voting representative of the Baha'is. I first visited the early campus of the United Nations in Lake Success on Long Island around 1947–48, where, as a child, I shook hands with Eleanor Roosevelt. One of the first adult documents I read was the United Nations Declaration of Human Rights, and I remember my older sister shouting at me that I could not possibly understand what I was reading. I also remember the many antagonisms that existed in New York in the late forties and fifties between the various ethnic and religious groups. At my Quaker high school, the George School in Pennsylvania, I went on occasional weekends to Philadelphia to help rebuild housing for needy people. Quaker ethics affected me greatly.

My Iranian father taught me respect for Muslims and for the Qur'ān. Therefore, in my first year at Harvard, I took Arabic and was taught by my outstanding teacher H.A.R. Gibb to recite the opening chapter of the Qur'ān. There were fanatic Muslims then as there are now, but in my research and writing I wanted to show that there was a tolerant side of Islam.

In 1960 I was given a Shaw Traveling Fellowship by Harvard University and spent a year traveling as far east as Afghanistan. There I saw a country still in the eighteenth or nineteenth century where the Shi'ite minority was often persecuted (as they still are today). While a student at Cambridge in England in 1961–62 I was often reproached by English students for the existence of race prejudice in the United States, which subsequently made its blatant appearance in England with the migration from Britain's former colonies. As a graduate student at Harvard, I went on the 1963 March on Washington for civil rights and heard Martin Luther King give his famous "I Have a Dream" speech.

Working on my Ph.D. dissertation on a Shi'ite dynasty in Iraq and western Iran, I became aware of the long-term dissonance produced by sectarian difference in Islam. Such sectarian difference had a lengthy and troubled history in the Middle East. Necessarily, in some of my early articles I discussed social and religious prejudices that existed in early Islamic history and still exist today.

The first article in this section, "Toward an Islamic Theology of Toleration," was my first article specifically on toleration. It was written for a conference in Norway in 1992 on human rights and the modern application of Islamic law and published in 1993 in *Islamic Law Reform and Human Rights: Challenges and Rejoinders*, edited by Tore Lindholm and Kari Vogt. The topic appealed to me because of my lifelong commitment to human rights. Norway, like many other countries which have experienced immigration from the Islamic world, was interested in fostering a tolerant spirit among its population, non-Muslim and Muslim. Coming from an Iranian background I was very conscious of the persecution of my Baha'i relatives. I also deeply admired Islamic and Iranian culture and sought to underscore the tolerant aspects of both throughout their history. There are many instances of Islamic toleration throughout history and passages in Islamic religious texts, poetry, and prose that promote toleration. Some may think that I have overstated the importance of these instances of Islamic toleration, but their very existence remains significant.

The second article in this section, "Pluralism and Islamic Traditions of Sectarian Divisions," was written for the lecture that I was asked to give after receiving an honorary doctorate in theology from the University of Lund in Sweden. In this article, published in 2006 in *Svensk Teologisk Kvartalskrift*, I focused on sectarian differences among Muslims and tried to show the spirit within Islam that would foster coexistence of these sects without conflict. As in other articles I lean heavily on the Sufi tradition, in particular the works of Jalāl al-Din Rumi, the 7th/13th-century author of the *Masṉavi*, the greatest spiritual epic known to me in the Islamic tradition, or perhaps in any tradition.

The third article in this section, "The Clash of Civilizations: An Islamicist's Critique," was published in the *Harvard Middle Eastern and Islamic Review* in 1995. It was written in response to Samuel Huntington's *Clash of Civilizations*, which I first encountered as an article, to which I was asked to respond in a roundtable discussion at the Harvard Divinity School. Sam was extremely unhappy about my presentation which strongly disagreed with his article. Since Sam was a respected colleague, I showed him a typescript of a tamed-down version of this critique when I first wrote it. To my surprise, his reaction was more of an explosion than a discussion. Sam Huntington, who was in some ways a friend, became furious and shouted, "Who would publish such a thing?" (He may have used ruder language.) After this challenge I wrote an extended version of my critique, which was published and later republished in many versions, including in Arabic and Persian as well as in an anthology about Huntington's book. In the years that have passed since the publication of Huntington's *Clash of Civilizations*, Indonesia, the country with the largest Muslim population, has remained democratic, and the identity of the United States has not been transformed by the presence of immigrants. Nevertheless, the general assumptions of Huntington's thesis remain a festering presence among some Americans, as the ascendency of Donald Trump and the insurrection of January 6, 2021, demonstrate. If I meet Samuel Huntington in heaven, I hope he is no longer angry at me. (If I have to present an article to the Examining Angel to gain entrance, I might offer this one.)

The fourth article in this section, "The Islamic Foundation for Citizenship and Pluralism," was written for a conference at the University of Kufa in Iraq and published in the *Kufa Review* in 2014. My visit to Iraq for the Kufa conference was one of the most memorable events of my old age. Kufa was an important center of culture in the early Islamic period and also an important shrine city, especially for Shiʿites. It is only ten kilometers from Najaf so I was able to visit the Tomb of ʿAlī and other sacred sites. (It is also temptingly close to several Babylonian archaeological sites, but my hosts warned me that the countryside was unsafe.)

Many modern Muslim reformers advocate toleration, both between Muslims and between Muslims and non-Muslims, and they point to the writings ascribed to ʿAlī that support such ideas. The enfranchisement of the entire sane adult population is an ideal in most Muslim countries, but often imperfectly realized. Traditionally, minorities have been underrepresented in terms of enfranchisement. (This is true even in the United States.) However, after a terrible period of suppression under Saddam Hussein, Iraq seems to be well on its way to achieving the ideal of full political participation and universal enfranchisement.

The ethic of toleration touches almost all areas of life, religious, social, and political behavior. Some Muslims will object to anything a non-Muslim has to say about Islam. Conversely, some non-Muslims will object to anything a Muslim says, as Mayor Rudy Giuliani did when he refused the gift of Prince al-Waleed to New York City after 9/11. My four articles on toleration here refer to religious toleration. In many modern societies people leave the judgment of wrong belief to God, but this attitude has not persuaded all people (including some Europeans and Americans) to do so. Carrying ideals of toleration beyond religion to social and political areas of modern life requires a very broad spirit of toleration including citizenship and voting rights for minorities. (I never thought to see the voting rights of citizens under attack in America.) I can think of no attitude of mind more urgently needed in the present world than toleration.

Toward an Islamic Theology of Toleration

Professor Abdullahi An-Na'im in his courageous and innovative book, *Toward an Islamic Reformation* (1990), has put forward a bold methodology with which a jurist may be able to reconstruct major areas of Islamic law. On the question of the relations between Muslims and non-Muslims, discussed in Chapters Six and Eight, he implies that the intellectual tradition of pre-modern Muslim thinkers has fairly uniformly supported a policy of limited toleration toward non-Muslims. This essay suggests that, on the contrary, full toleration (and, consequently, full equality before the law) are principles that can find strong theological roots in the pre-modern Islamic tradition.[1]

I should also make it clear that I am not discussing the degree of toleration actually historically demonstrated by Muslim communities, a subject which has been discussed elsewhere. Nevertheless, we should bear in mind that Muslims were generally more tolerant than Christians in the pre-modern world, and I think that this record of toleration does in part

Author's note: This article was first published as: "Toward an Islamic Theology of Toleration," in Tore Lindholm and Kari Vogt (eds.), *Islamic Law Reform and Human Rights: Challenges and Rejoinders* (Oslo, Nordic Human Rights Publications: 1993) 25–36. Reproduced with permission. It was originally presented at a conference in Oslo in 1992 honoring Professor Abdullahi An-Na'im for his contributions to the understanding of Islam and human rights.

1 This essay owes a great debt to the immense learning of Dr. Ahmad Mahdavi-Damghani who led me to many of the references I cite below. Dr. Abbas Amanat, Dr. Muhammad Y. Siddiq, and Dr. Hossein Modarressi have also suggested sources valuable to this subject, for which I am deeply grateful. The extremely interesting book, *Ghayr al-Muslimīn fī al-Mujtama' al-Islāmī*, by Yusuf al-Qaradawi (Cairo: 1977), has suggested to me some of the categories used in this essay. I realize that some of the Qur'ānic quotations supporting toleration that I cite are considered abrogated, but I feel the whole theory of abrogation needs reconsideration.

reflect the spirit of the passages I will quote below from Muslim thinkers. In practice, Muslims—in spite of the sometimes intolerant attitude of Islamic law toward non-monotheists without a revealed book—were often willing to give the benefit of the doubt to most systems of belief they encountered. When, in the early conquests, Muslims first encountered Hindus in the Sind, the Muslim commander declared that Hindus were "People of the Book," and therefore a tolerated religion, a decision which was by and large respected over the ages.[2]

Similarly, as the Qur'ān mentioned the belief of the Sabeans as one of the most ancient revealed religions, Muslims tended to use the term "Sabean" freely for otherwise unclassifiable religions, as they did for Graeco-Roman religion (which they only knew through texts), and as they did for the planet-worshippers of Harran, a town in Mesopotamia in the heart of the Islamic world. Muslims also showed a fair degree of toleration toward heretics who did not *publicly* voice heretical views. A century after the ferocious rebellion against the Islamic central government by the followers of Bābak in northwest Iran had been put down, the historian and polymath al-Mas'ūdī, while travelling in this area, was interested in interviewing some of them about their beliefs; he had no trouble contacting them in spite of their former rebelliousness, their dualistic beliefs and their supposed advocacy of the forcible redistribution of property.[3]

Sometimes even those who rejected religion found toleration. According to a well-known account, when a Shi'ite upbraided Ibn Abī al-'Awjā' for his disbelief, the disbeliever protested that he did not deserve such treatment since his upbraider's leader, Imam Ja'far, who was an infallible source of guidance for this Shi'ite, allowed Ibn Abī al-'Awjā' to come and debate questions of belief with himself, the Imam, in the very sanctuary of Mecca.[4]

Toleration in the above preceding examples is of the sort found in the more enlightened parts of the pre-modern world, in which minorities were allowed to live peacefully but with some degree of deference, and—often—some degree of obligation to the majority. When, however, we turn to find theology of total unconditional toleration we find that there

2 See Y. Friedmann, "Muḥammad b. al-Ḳāsim," *The Encyclopaedia of Islam*, 2nd ed. (hereafter *EI*²), VII (Leiden, Brill: 1991) 405–406.

3 Maçoudi, *Le livre de l'avertissement et de la revision* (Paris: 1896) 453.

4 G. Vajda, in his article "Ibn Abi 'l-'Awdja'" in *EI*², III (Leiden, Brill: 1971) 682, doubts the historicity of his friendship with Ja'far; but for us the important point is that the anecdote was widely believed.

also exists abundant material for such a theory in the pre-modern Islamic tradition. But—to my knowledge—there was no systematic attempt to build a theology of the subject (any more than there was a pre-modern Jewish or Christian attempt to do so). And we should bear in mind that—as Dr. An-Na'im so rightly emphasizes—many Muslims believed that the Qur'ānic verse on jihad abrogated most of the other Qur'ānic verses which point toward a theology of toleration.

The first principle in the Islamic materials that would support a more general theology of toleration is the principle that difference of belief is divinely willed. One of several verses of the Qur'ān that explicitly says this is verse (X:99):

> If it had been your Lord's will, all on earth, without exception, would have believed; will you then compel mankind to become believers?

The celebrated Qur'ān commentary, *Tafsīr al-Jalālayn*, makes the central emphasis for the verse yet clearer by saying, "Will you then compel mankind to do that which God does not want of them?"[5] By extension of this principle some Muslim thinkers see in the variety of belief an opportunity for every community of belief; *including* Muslims, to learn from other communities. The very important Sufi thinker, 'Ayn al-Quḍāt al-Hamadhānī, who died in 1125 C.E., writes in his *Tamhīdāt*:

> O friend: If you too see in Jesus that which Christians have seen, become a Christian. And if you see in Moses that which Jews have seen, become a Jew. But beyond that, if you see in idolatry that which idol-worshippers have seen, become an idol-worshipper. The seventy-two sects are all way-stations on the road to God. Have you, by any chance, not heard the words of [the famous mystic] Abū Sa'īd Bū al-Khayr when he had come into the presence of a Zoroastrian priest: "Is there anything at present in your religion that we are not presently aware of in our religion?"[6]

5 Jalāl al-Dīn Maḥallī and Jalāl al-Dīn al-Suyūṭī's *Tafsīr al-Jalālayn* (hereafter *Tafsīr al-Jalālayn*) appears in very many editions and this commentary follows verse X:99.
6 See *Moṣannafāt-e 'Ayn al-Qożāt al-Hamadhāni* (Tehran: 1962) 258. The last clause could also be read: "since at present in our religion there is nothing new [being said]."

Another principle, very clearly articulated in the Qur'ān, is that judgment and punishment for wrong belief should be left to God alone, an analogue to the Biblical verse which says: "Vengeance is mine, saith the Lord." The end of the Qur'ānic verse XVI:125 reads: "Truly your Lord knows better than you as to who has gone astray from his path and who receives guidance." The highly respected Qur'ān commentator Bayḍāwī explains that this sentence means "proclamation (*balāgh*) and the call (to Islam) (*da'wa*) are those things which are incumbent on you."[7]

This principle, that judgment and punishment belong to God, is explicitly related to the preceding principle, the divinely willed variety of human belief, in another verse of the Qur'ān (II:272): "It is not incumbent on you that you make people rightly guided. But God guides whom he wills." "It is clear that guidance is from God and by his will and it gives preference to certain people rather than others," Bayḍāwī explains.[8] The *Tafsīr al-Jalālayn* explains: "[It is not incumbent to guide] people to enter Islam; only the proclamation of its message (*balāgh*) [is incumbent on you]." The verse goes on to sanction unconditional generosity to non-Muslims: "And whatever you give [to non-Muslims] in the way of good things, is then for your own souls." The *Tafsīr al-Jalālayn* explains: "Give, seeking only the Face of God."[9]

Another reason for leaving judgment to God alone is the strong belief that hidden under many forms of behavior, which might seem contrary to correct religious practice, is an attitude of true worshipfulness which is completely acceptable to God. In that great epic poem of Islamic piety, the *Masnavī* by Jalāl al-Din al-Rumi, its author tells us the story of the reaction of the prophet Moses to a shepherd who seemed to have conceived of God as some form of a shepherd:[10]

> Moses saw a shepherd on the way, who was saying, O God who chooses (whom, He wills),
> Where are You, that I may become Your servant and sew Your shoes and comb Your head?

7 Bayḍāwī, *Anwār al-Tanzīl*, ed. H.O. Fleischer, I (Leipzig: 1846–9) 531.
8 Bayḍāwī, (*supra* n. 7), I:138.
9 Bayḍāwī, (*supra* n. 7), II:272ff.
10 My translation of the *Masnavī* is slightly adapted from that of R.A. Nicholson, editor and translator of *The Mathnawí of Jalálu'ddín Rúmí*, E.J.W. Gibb Memorial Series, New Series IV.1, *Text* I (London: 1925) and IV.2, *Translation* II (London: 1926, reprint 1960) 310, 311–312.

> That I may wash Your clothes and kill Your lice and bring milk to You, O worshipful One. (Bk. II, vss. 1720–1723)

Moses was horrified:

> The shepherd was speaking foolish words in this manner. Moses said, "Man, to whom is this (addressed)?" He answered, "To that One who created us; by whom this earth and sky were brought to sight."
>
> "Pay attention!" Moses said, "You have become very back-sliding; indeed, you have not become a Muslim, you have become a disbeliever (*kāfer*).
>
> What babble is this? What blasphemy and raving? Stuff some cotton into your mouth!
>
> The stench of your blasphemy has made the (whole) world stink: your blasphemy has turned the silk robe of religion into rags."
>
> (Bk. II, vss. 1725–1729)

After his long speech denouncing the shepherd, God rebuked Moses:

> A revelation came to Moses from God: "You have parted My servant from Me.
>
> Did you come (as a prophet) to unite, or did you come to sever?
>
> So far as you can, do not set foot on (the path that leads to) separation: of (all) things the most hateful to Me is divorce.
>
> I have bestowed on everyone a (special) way of acting: I have given to everyone a (peculiar) form of expression.
>
> In regard to him it is (worthy of) praise, and in regard to you it is (worthy of) blame: in regard to him honey, and in regard to you poison.
>
> I am independent of all purity and impurity, of all slothfulness and alacrity (in worshipping Me).
>
> I did not ordain (Divine worship) that I might profit; nay, but that I might do a kindness to (My) servants.
>
> In the Hindus the idiom (*estelāḥ*) of Hind (India) is praiseworthy; in the people of Sind the idiom of Sind is praiseworthy.
>
> I am not sanctified by their glorification (of Me); it is they that become sanctified and pearl-scattering (i.e., pure and radiant).

I look not at the tongue and the speech; I look at the inward (spirit) and the state (of feeling).
I gaze into the heart (to see) whether it be lowly, though the words uttered be not lowly,
Because the heart is the substance, speech (only) the accident; so, the accident is subservient, the substance is the (real) object.
How much (more) of these phrases and conceptions and metaphors? I want [souls] burning, burning (with passion): become friendly with that burning!
Light up a fire of love in thy soul, burn thought and expression away entirely.
O Moses, they that know the contentions are of one sort; they, whose souls and spirits burn, are of another sort."

(Bk. II, vss. 1750–1764)

We also see in this passage a corollary of the principle that apparent wrong belief is to be punished by God alone, and not corrected by compulsion: worship of God, if not freely given, is a form of barter which—unworthily of God—assumes that God is glorified by human subservience.

A further corollary for a mystic like Rumi is the contention that deep belief so changes the focus of a human being that such a being would regard fanaticism as a spiritually unthinkable attachment to things of this world. He writes:[11]

Only unripe fruit clings fast to the bough, because such fruit during its immaturity is not ready for the palace. On ripeness, fruit becomes sweet and lets go ... (Bk. III, vss. 1294–1295)
To hold tightly, [i.e. to take a severe interpretation of things], and to be fanatical (*ta'aṣṣob*) is unripeness; only so long as you are an embryo is your occupation to drink blood. (Bk. III, vs. 1297)

The next (and partly related) principle for constructing a theology of toleration is the mutuality of respect by human communities of belief. A verse in the Qur'ān enjoins Muslims (VI:108): "Do not revile those who call mankind (to worship) others than God, lest they [in turn] revile God

11 Nicholson, *Text* IV.3, Bk. III (London: 1929), *Translation* IV.4, Bk. III (London: 1930) 73 (my translation).

out of ignorance and spite; thus, have we made each people's behavior alluring to them. In the end their point of return is their Lord, and He will inform them of what they were wont to do." The *Tafsīr al-Jalālayn* explains that "others than God" means "idols," idolatry comprehending, according to many Muslims, worship not only of graven images, but also worship of false ideas that have become objects of extravagant affection. The same commentary explains that: "We have made each people's doings alluring to them" means "both their good and bad [religious behavior has been made alluring to them by God] and so they carry out [such behavior]."[12] Here we see mutuality of respect related not only to the Muslims' desire not to have their religion slandered but also to the principle that judgment and punishment are God's alone since God alone understands the cause and motivation of behavior that is un-Islamic.

Texts that support the importance of mutuality among individuals as well as groups, in overlooking mistaken belief or behavior, are also many. Sometimes mutuality is understood to be a three-way matter involving God; as, for example, in the saying of the Prophet reported in *Shuʿab al-Īmān* by the widely respected 5th/11th-century thinker al-Bayhaqī (d. 458/1066): "No human will draw a veil over something concerning another human in this world without having God [in turn] veil him on the day of judgment."[13]

Many of these themes of mutuality are summed up in a striking and very well-known passage in Saʿdi, the 7th/13th-century Persian poet, in which a dervish upbraids an oppressive king:

> The children of Adam are limbs of one another
> And in their creation come from one substance.
> When the world gives pain to one member,
> The other members find no rest.
> Thou who are indifferent to the sufferings of others
> Do not deserve to be called a man.[14]

---

12 *Tafsīr al-Jalālayn,* (*supra* n. 5), following verse VI:108.

13 Aḥmad ibn al-Ḥusayn al-Bayhaqī, *Shuʿab al-Īmān,* ed. Abu Hajir Muhammad ibn Basyuni Zaghlul, VI (Beirut, Dār al-Kutub al-ʿIlmīya: 1990) 105. The whole section of this work, which begins on this page, is replete with closely similar sayings. This Bayhaqī, writing in Arabic, is not to be confused with the famous Persian historian Moḥammad ibn Ḥusayn Bayhaqi, writing in Persian, who died in 470/1077.

14 Saʿdi, *The Gulistan,* ed. John Platts (London: 1874) 23.

Here, the mutuality of mankind springs from the understanding that mankind is a single body and loses its human nature only when its members hurt each other.

Yet the most deeply rooted principle in Islamic thought that supports a theology of toleration is the belief in a natural religion, inborn in all human beings, and the consequent natural goodness of mankind. Here the central Qur'ānic proof text is (XXX:30):

> So set your face toward religion in a way that is naturally pure according to the God-Given pattern on the basis of which He created mankind ...

The commentator Bayḍāwī, explains various interpretations of "The God-Given patterns on the basis of which he has created mankind," including the interpretation that "it is said to refer to the pact taken from Adam and his progeny." This pact was made in a scene which is virtually universally regarded by Muslims to be central to the moral history of mankind, for the seed of all future human beings was brought forth from the loins of the sons of Adam and asked by God: "Am I not your Lord?" To this question all future human beings answered: "Yes, most certainly." A moral pact recognizing the Lordship of God was established by this acknowledgment, and, as we have seen, some commentators associate an inborn naturally pure religious instinct in humankind with this scene.[15] A second and very beautiful Qur'ānic proof text for belief in the natural goodness of all things is (XIII:15):

> Whatever beings there are in the heavens and the earth bow down to worship God, willingly or unwillingly: so do their shadows in the mornings and the evenings [i.e. even the ephemeral things of the world worship God].

The last phrase connects the subject of this paper with the even more neglected theme, not considered here, of an Islamic theology of reverence for the whole of the natural world. In his *al-Adab al-Mufrad* Bukhārī, the 3rd/9th-century author who is the pre-eminent authority among most Sunnis on the traditions of the Prophet says:

---

15 Bayḍāwī, (*supra* n. 7), II:108.

> The Prophet was asked: "Which of the religions is most beloved by God Almighty?" He said: "The primeval tolerant religion (*al-ḥanifīya al-samḥā'*)."[16]

To me, this passage is yet another piece of evidence that a significant body of opinion in classical Islamic thought held that all humans had "natural" religion, that is, were born with a spiritual and moral "pattern" cast by God into their souls, on the basis of which we should assume the innate goodness of our fellow humans.

Interestingly, Bukhārī quotes in his *Ṣaḥīḥ*, a canonical book of prophet traditions among Sunnis, the saying of the Prophet: "Every human given birth is born according to the innate pattern and it is his parents that make a Jew, or a Christian, or a Zoroastrian."[17] While a majority of Muslim opinion holds that "innate pattern," the same word used in the Qur'ānic passage, XXX:30, quoted above, means Islam, a significant minority holds that it means humankind's primeval, inherent religion, which is indelibly printed on the souls of all humans, an extended meaning of Islam sometimes used by Muslims and authors of the classical period. Acceptance of such natural religion and the consequent natural goodness of mankind make all the above-mentioned principles, the divinely-willed differences of belief, suspension of judgment, and so forth more intellectually coherent and more deeply rooted in the overall theological views of Islam, since the presumption of inborn goodness makes it natural to give others the benefit of any doubt and to extend to them unqualified toleration.

As an historian it has always seemed to me that toleration arose in the West after the wars of religion in the seventeenth century not because Christian theology convinced the combatants of the evils of intolerance but because intolerance seemed on the verge of tearing society apart and was too costly. It took many more generations before we saw developed theories of toleration such as we find in Locke, not to mention institutionalized forms of toleration such as we find in the nineteenth century with the extension of the franchise without test of religious belief. And it also seems to me that there are at least two roots to toleration in the

16 Muḥammad ibn Ismā'īl al-Bukhārī, *al-Adab al-Mufrad*, ed. Kamal Yusuf al-Hut, (Beirut, 'Ālam al-Kutub: 1984) 138.

17 *Ṣaḥīḥ al-Bukhārī* (Lahore: 1979) 262. This saying of the Prophet occurs here and in another paragraph of the same chapter of Bukhārī, "al-Janā'iz," It is repeated in very many Sunni and Shi'ite books of such prophetic sayings.

social traditions of the West. One is feudalism, for I very much believe that the feudal view of a human as a nexus of rights and institutions was a model on which some European societies gradually or by fits and starts extended those rights and obligations to all members of a political community while never losing sight of the rights of minorities. Another source was the view of citizenship born in the Enlightenment and brought to the fore by the French Revolution, in which the general will was understood to be determined by general participation in society and contemporary ideas of citizenship were created.

The social traditions of Islamic societies have not always been and need not necessarily be similar to those of the West. We should also bear in mind that Muslims feel justifiably offended that Islam has become the pre-eminent example of an intolerant religion in the minds of so many Westerners. Some Muslims may therefore read this essay as yet another attempt to say: "Muslims should be more tolerant." The author, on the contrary, hopes that the essay provides Muslims, and admirers of Islam, whether they espouse full toleration or not, to say: "The option of full toleration has long existed in the Islamic tradition."

There are, in fact, historical precedents for full citizenship by non-Muslims. A strong expression of government's responsibility to the governed, regardless of their beliefs, is offered by the well-known and often quoted letter said to have been written by ʿAlī ibn Abī Ṭālib, one of the first Muslims and—as the son-in-law of the Prophet and his confidant—nearly universally held up as an ideal among Muslims. ʿAlī wrote this letter of instructions to Mālik al-Ashtar al-Nakhaʿī on the latter's appointment by ʿAlī as governor of Egypt:

> Know, O Mālik, that I am sending you to a land where governments, just and unjust, have existed before you. People will look upon your affairs in the same way that you were wont to look upon the affairs of the rulers before you. They will speak about you as you were wont to speak about those rulers. And the righteous are only known by that which God causes to pass concerning them on the tongues of His servants. So, let the dearest of your treasuries be the treasury of righteous action. Control your desire and restrain your soul from what is not lawful to you, for restraint of the soul is for it to be equitable in what it likes and dislikes. Infuse your heart with mercy, love and kindness for your subjects. Be not in face of

> them a voracious animal, counting them as easy prey, for they are of two kinds; either they are your brothers in religion or your equals in creation. Error catches them unaware, deficiencies overcome them, (evil deeds) are committed by them intentionally and by mistake. So, grant them your pardon and your forgiveness to the same extent that you hope God will grant you His pardon and His forgiveness. For you are above them, and he who appointed you is above you, and God is above him who appointed you. God has sought from you the fulfillment of their requirements and He is trying you with them.[18]

This universal respect for the governed, who, even if they are not the same as you in belief, are "your equals in creation," is explained by ʿAlī to extend even to matters of the pre-Islamic customary law of the Egyptians.

> Abolish no proper custom (*sunna*) which has been acted upon by their leaders, through which harmony has been strengthened and because of which the subjects have prospered. Create no new custom which might in any way prejudice the customs of the past, lest their reward belong to him who originated them, and the burden be upon you to the extent that you have abolished them.[19]

At present, with the rebirth of civil society in a number of Islamic societies and the accompanying demand for equal citizenship and equal rights, it seems likely that some theological basis for toleration will develop. I hope this essay has shown that the developers of this theology will have a great deal of material to hand.

---

18 The passages quoted here are in M.H. Tabataba'i, trans. W.C. Chittick, *The Spiritual Life* (Tehran: 1982) 6–7 and 9. They correspond to ʿAlī ibn Abī Ṭālib, *Nahj al-Balāgha*, ed. Subhi Salih (Beirut: 1967) 427–428 and 431.

19 Tabataba'i, (*supra* n. 18).

Pluralism and Islamic Traditions of Sectarian Divisions

The first part of this essay analyzes the most common system of categorization used by Muslim writers for sectarian difference. In this period of tragic confrontations between Shiʿites and Sunnis in Iraq, Afghanistan, Pakistan and other places, this subject is more relevant than ever. The second half of this essay studies the use of this tradition by the great poet and mystic, Jalāl al-Din Rumi, and turns to the larger question of pluralism between systems of belief.[1]

The central organizing system for sectarian division among Muslims is a scheme that divides Muslims into seventy-two or seventy-three sects. This scheme is not totally unfamiliar to readers of English literature. In the 1888 edition of Edward Fitzgerald's creative reimagining of Omar Khayyam the forty-third quatrain reads:

> The Grape that can with Logic absolute
> The two-and-Seventy Sects confute:
> The subtle Alchemist that in a Trice
> Life's leaden Metal into Gold transmute.

Now this essay is not written to celebrate the power of wine to dissolve sectarian differences; although such an essay might be much more fun. But I think we should pause for a moment at the name of Omar Khayyam,

Author's note: This article was first published as: "Pluralism and Islamic Traditions of Sectarian Divisions," in *Svensk Teologisk Kvartalskrift* 82 (Lund, Wallin & Dalholm Boktryckeri AB: 2006) 155–161. Reproduced with permission.

1 A revised and expanded version of this article is: "Pluralism and Islamic Traditions of Sectarian Divisions," in Zulfikar Hirji (ed.), *Diversity and Pluralism in Islam: Historical and Contemporary Discourses amongst Muslims* (London and New York, I.B. Tauris: 2010) 3–42.

the Iranian Muslim mathematician and astronomer who died in the early 6th/12th century and whose Swedish translator spent much of his life here in Lund, albeit at St. Lars Mental Hospital and not at the University. Khayyam's skepticism was as thrilling to his medieval contemporaries as it was to our Victorian forefathers who first made Omar Khayyam a figure of interest in the West. Matthew Arnold was scandalized to find out how much he resonated with Omar Khayyam's skepticism.

In fact, it is both one of the virtues and great shortcomings of moderns to believe in a thoroughgoing and homogenized system of thought. A totally apocryphal story is told of the Moghul emperor Akbar who in 1581 founded his own religion, the celebrated Din-e Elāhi or "Divine Religion," which he and his vizier Abu al-Fażl formulated to accommodate the multiple truths of existing religions. When emperor Akbar, who had already purchased four hooves of the donkey that bore Jesus into Jerusalem, agreed to buy a fifth hoof, the vizier Abu al-Fażl said: "But, Your Majesty, no donkey has five hooves." To this the emperor replied: "Who knows? One of them might be genuine." This hopeful but not absolutely committed form of belief helps us to understand the culture in which a text of hedonism, like that of Omar Khayyam, can exist alongside the most rigorous texts on the ascetic and self-denying life written by contemporaries of Omar Khayyam. Incidentally, Akbar's interesting religious experiment did not survive the emperor's death.

At this point let us turn to a discussion of the meaning of the traditional division into seventy-odd sects, a division which to many Muslim authors seemed firmly anchored in sayings ascribed to the Prophet, the ḥadīth or "traditions" which, if seen to be scrupulously transmitted, have a nearly scriptural authority for most Muslims. In one form or another this ḥadīth or saying attributed to the Prophet Muḥammad is quoted by almost every author on religious differences among Muslims and often gives structure to the books written on the subject.

This ḥadīth, often called the ḥadīth al-tafriqa or "tradition concerning division", occurs in one of its most frequent forms as: "The Jews divided into seventy-one sects (*firqa*), the Christians into seventy-two sects, and my community will divide into seventy-three sects." This form of the ḥadīth, is found in Abū Da'ūd al-Sijistānī (d. 275/889), Ibn Māja (d. 273/887), al-Tirmidhī (d. 279/892) and al-Nisā'ī (d. 303/915), four of the six so-called "canonical" Sunni collections of ḥadīth. The ḥadīth also occurs frequently in a different version: "There will befall my nation what befell the children of Israel. The children of Israel divided into seventy-two religious groups (*milla*) and my community will divide into seventy-three religious groups (*milla*), one more than they. All of them are in hell-fire except one religious group."[2]

The addition about hell-fire is sometimes followed by the account of a question addressed to the Prophet as to who are the saved/sacred sect (*firqa*) or religious group (*milla*) not in hell-fire, to which the Prophet answers: "That group/sect which I and my Companions believe in."[3] A variant of this ḥadīth explicitly identifies the saved/sacred sect as the *ahl al-sunna wa-l-jamā'a*, i.e., the Sunnis. The ḥadīth also exists in Twelver Shi'ite texts, however without the coda identifying the saved sect and with the understanding that the saved sect is the Imāmī (Twelver) Shi'ites.[4] The Zaydī Shi'ites likewise use a variant of this ḥadīth.[5]

An important variant of the tradition says that "The children of Israel divided into seventy-one sects (*firqa*) and my community will divide into seventy-two, all of them in hell-fire except one. It is the [majority Muslim] community (*jamā'a*)," presumably the Sunnis.[6] The principle of progression in numbers is preserved here. Not the least curious thing about this family of traditions is the claim that Islam should be superior in number of sectarian divisions (whereas to be superior in number of people of piety, or antecedent prophets, would seem a more reassuring feature of a religious tradition). Perhaps the corruption wrought by time, a frequent theme in traditions, a corruption made more severe by the ever-lengthening time

2 For references to these sources, see Muhammad Javad Mashkur, "Introduction," in Anon., *Haftād va-Seh Mellat* ed. Muhammad Javad Mashkur (Tehran: 1962) 6–7; Mashkur believes (p. 5) the author is of the seventh or eighth century C.E. See also Aḥmad Mahdāvī-Damghānī, *Ḥāṣil-e 'Awqāt* (Tehran: 2002) 615. Dr. Mahdavi-Damghani's outstanding treatment of this subject has greatly aided me in writing the present study.

3 Mashkur, (*supra* n. 2) 6.

4 Keith Lewinstein, "Studies in Islamic Heresiography: The *Khawārij* in Two *Firaq* Traditions," Ph.D. Dissertation, (Princeton University: 1989) 3, n. 3, including the quotation from Ibn Bābawayh. Lewinstein has published a valuable article from the dissertation entitled, "Notes on Eastern Ḥanafite Heresiography," *Journal of the American Oriental Society* 114:4 (1994) 583–598. See also Josef van Ess, *Der Eine und das Andere: Beobachtungen an islamischen häresiographischen Texten* (Berlin and New York, N.Y., De Gruyter: 2011) 47–53; I thank Professor Lewinstein for this reference.

5 Lewinstein, "Studies," (*supra* n. 4), quoting from the unpublished 5th/11th-century *Asās al-Maqālāt* of Abū al-Mā'ah.

6 Mashkur, (*supra* n. 2) 6.

between the revelation of Islam and the end of time, might argue for the greater number of sectarian divisions among Muslims.

The 4th/10th-century geographer al-Muqaddasī says that seventy-two sects are in heaven and one in hell according to what he considers a more sound line of transmission (*isnād*).[7] Similarly, the great theologian al-Ghazālī, who died in 505/1111, supports a reading that "all are in heaven except the *zindīq*s" (Manichaeans, outrageous heretics).[8] The opinion that all but one of the sects was saved was not widely held and was not followed by pre-modern Muslim writers of heresiographies.

Such scholars of Muslim heresies almost invariably quote the tradition of seventy-odd sects in their books on heresies. A large number of them work to fit the heresies into a scheme of seventy-odd. This effort forced them to multiply heresies and to combine heresies as each category might be a single heresy or a category of heretics.

Over a century ago Ignaz Goldziher noticed that a few later writers found the seventy-two- or seventy-three-fold division of sects to be an ill-fitting suit of clothes. He quotes the great scholar Fakhr al-Dīn al-Rāzī (d. 606/1209) who, in his commentary on the Qur'ān, writes: "Some have attacked the authenticity of this tradition. They say that if by seventy-two they mean the fundamentals of religious beliefs (*uṣūl al-adyān*) then they do not reach this number; and if they mean the practices (*furū'*), then the number passes this number by several multiples."[9] Goldziher also suggested that the family of division traditions owed their inspiration to another, possibly older, very well-attested tradition that: "Faith has seventy-odd branches and modesty (*al-ḥayā'*) is one of them."[10] The learned contemporary scholar Mahdavi-Damghani has pointed out that this is an independent sentiment with its own line of transmitters.[11] Indeed, as Goldziher observed, here the "seventy-odd" are all praiseworthy "branches," and this tradition gave rise to an independent genre of literature called *shu'ab al-īmān*, or "branches of faith."[12] It is interesting to notice that, unlike the traditions based on "sect/religious group" distinctions,

7 *Aḥsan al-Taqāsīm* (Leiden: 1906) 38, cited by Lewinstein, (*supra* n. 4) 3, n. 4.
8 Cited by Mashkūr, (*supra* n. 2), 7.
9 *Tafsīr Fakhr al-Dīn al-Rāzī*, XI (Cairo: 1985) 219. My translation is slightly different from Goldziher's. See Ignaz Goldziher, "Le denombrement des sectes mahometanes," in *Gesammelte Schriften*, II (Hildesheim: 1968) 409–410.
10 Goldziher, (*supra* n. 9), 410, where it is also noticed that some say "sixty-odd."
11 Mahdavi-Damghani, (*supra* n. 2), 618.
12 Goldziher, (*supra* n. 9), 411.

this "branches of faith" tradition is found in both Bukhārī and Muslim, who are considered by many Sunnis to be more authoritative sources.[13]

The interest in the number "seventy-odd," however, is a consistent theme and deserves independent attention. As Annemarie Schimmel has noted in her book on number significance, the Islamic tradition follows the Bible in its fascination with heptads, from which the interest in ten times seven springs. The seventy nations, the seventy judges of the Sanhedrin, and the seventy years of Babylonian exile are only a small number of the many Biblical seventies. According to Islamic tradition the Prophet recited the Qur'ān seventy times during his journey to the Divine Presence and also asked forgiveness seventy times a day.[14]

Just as important as seventy was seventy-two because it has links with three, six, eight, nine and twelve. Already in late antiquity, its numerological significance—as, for example, the number of degrees in an arc divided by the sacred pentagram equals seventy-two—was added to the significance of seventy-two in the Bible. According to the New Testament seventy-two disciples were sent to preach the gospel in seventy-two languages of the world. The Bible was translated into Greek by seventy, or seventy-two, scholars, each isolated from all others, and miraculously the seventy or seventy-two translations matched;[15] hence, of course, the Septuagint.

In the Islamic tradition seventy-odds are very frequent. Seventy-two were killed at the martyrdom of the Prophet's grandson, Ḥusayn, at Kerbala. In a tradition (of modest authority but in a respected collection) the Prophet asks: "'Do you know the distance between heaven and earth?' They said: 'We do not know.' He said: 'The distance between the two is seventy-one or seventy-two or seventy-three years and the sky extends for the same distance ...'" The distance to hell was not dissimilar; a tradition relates: "We were with the Messenger of God and heard the sound of something falling ... The Messenger of God said, 'That was a stone that was thrown into Hell seventy years ago and it was still falling into Hell until it reached its bottom.'"[16]

13 Goldziher, (*supra* n. 9), 410.

14 A. Schimmel, *The Mystery of Numbers* (New York: 1993) 132, 263–264.

15 Schimmel, (*supra* n. 14), 264–266.

16 On heaven, see Mahdavi-Damghani, (*supra* n. 2), 617, quoting from *Mishkāt al-Maṣābīḥ* no. 2821 from Tirmidhī. On hell, see Muslim, *Ṣaḥīḥ*, ed. M.F. Abd al-Baqi, IV (Cairo: n.d.) 2184–2185, the 21st ḥadīth in "Kitāb al-Janna."

Interestingly, a Shi'ite source says that God's "Greatest Name" has seventy-three letters, of which Imām Muḥammad al-Bāqir knew seventy-two letters. The medieval Jewish Cabbalists held that YHWH's name consisted of seventy-two letters or that YHWH had seventy-two names.[17] Both the Muslim and the Jewish esoteric traditions believed that God saves those who call on Him using his "Greatest Name."

That seventy meant "a sizeable number" and seventy-odd meant "a sizeable number and then some" is fairly clear. In many (and perhaps most) cases the expressions are meant to be pictorial numbers and not exact "head counts." In Surāt al-Tawba the Qur'ān addresses Muḥammad and says (IX:80): "Whether [O Muḥammad] you ask forgiveness—or do not ask forgiveness—for them [the Hypocrites] seventy times, God will not forgive them because they did not believe ..." Here, clearly, "seventy" is a pictorial number, and current English usage would be as well served if one were to say "whether you asked forgiveness a hundred times ..." since there is no exact number of times, and the number is only rhetorically significant. The commentators I have consulted are in no doubt about the pictorial meaning of the number here. The specialist in rhetoric, al-Zamakhsharī (d. 538/1144), for example, writes on this verse in his Qur'ān commentary that: "Seventy assumed the role of a metaphor for numerousness in their speech."[18]

One of the many traditions that uses seventy-odd to signify numerousness is the following: "The Messenger of God said: 'He who helps a [Muslim] believer [in his difficulty], God—Almighty and Glorious—will remove him from seventy-three afflictions, one of which is this world; and seventy-two afflictions at the time of the Great Affliction, when people will be occupied with their souls in the hereafter.'"[19]

A deeper theological insight into the question of sectarian division, however, comes from the Sufi mystical tradition. Ḥāfeẓ (d. 791 or 792/1389 or 1390) epitomizes this tradition when he says:

> Heaven was too weak to bear the burden of responsibility—they gave it to my poor crazy self.

17 Schimmel, (*supra* n. 14), 265. Mahdāvī-Damghānī, (*supra* n. 2), 618.

18 Al-Zamakhsharī, *Al-Kashshāf*, eds. 'Abd al-Mawjud and 'Adil Ahmad, III (Riyadh: 1998) 74.

19 Al-Kulini, *Tarjoma-e Gozida-e Kāfi*, ed. Mohammad Baqer Behbudi, II (Tehran: 1982) 199.

Forgive the war of the seventy-two warring religions; since they did not see the truth, they have struck out on the road of fancy.

Or, to give this last line in the more poetic translation of Gertrude Bell:

Though the soft breath of Truth readies my ears,
For two-and-seventy jangling creeds he hears,
And loud-voiced Fable calls him ceaselessly.

In the two Ḥāfeẓ translations, "religions" in the former and "creeds" in the latter are *mellat*s (Persian plural for Arabic singular *milla*). "Fancy" in the former and "Fable" in the latter are *afsāna*.[20] For Ḥāfeẓ sectarian divisions are the fancy or fable that preoccupy those who have not struck out on the mystical path.

The highest and the most developed reflection of the Sufi tradition is in the *Maṣnavi* of Jalāl al-Din al-Rumi, known in the West as Rumi (d. 672/1273). Rumi depicts the confrontation between a partisan of predestination or divine "compulsion" (*jabr*) and a partisan of free will:

In just this way there is a dispute (*baḥth*) between the partisans of compulsion and those [partisans of] free will till the resurrection of mankind.
If the disputant had been able to refute his adversary, their schools of thought [*madhhab*] would have fallen out of sight.
Since [presented with unquestionable truth] these [disputants] would not be able to escape [admitting the truth] in reply, they would recoil from that road to perdition.
Yet, in so much as their continuation on that course was divinely ordained, [God] feeds them with arguments,
So that [one disputant] not be compelled by the difficulties posed by [another] disputant, and [each] may be prevented from seeing his opponent's success.
[All happens] so that these seventy-two sects should remain in the world till the day of resurrection.
Since this is the world of darkness and that which is hidden, the earth [and its uncertainties] is necessary for [this] shadow [to exist].

20 *Divān*, ed. Salim Naysari (Tehran: 1993) 161.

> Until the resurrection the seventy-two sects will remain, and the talk of those who introduced ideas without religious foundation will not fail.
> The high value of a treasure is [shown by the circumstance] that there are so many locks upon it ...[21]

As Nicholson, the great commentator on the *Maṣnavi* rightly remarks, the argument of the passage is "that religious heresies are necessary and [even] providential."[22] The whole passage can be seen as a commentary on the first part of the well-known Qur'ānic verse: "And if God wished, He would have made them into a single religious community (*umma*) ... (XLII:8)." God has not given certainty to mankind. On this earth man must puzzle out the correct meaning in the shadow—and not in plain sight—of certain truth. God even nourishes the opposing sides of disputes. As earthly creatures we see only the high value and not the real nature of truth because it is locked away and thus difficult to access.

Rumi has a somewhat different approach to the seventy-two varieties of Muslims in a passage on doubt and faith:

> Take care, O believers, for that [vein of philosophical] doubt is within you; within you is many an infinite world.
> In you are all the seventy-two sects; woe [to you] should [that philosophical] doubt extend its hand from within.[23]

Without question this passage urges the believer to master his/her doubts in the name of belief. And yet it regards the internal world or internal forum as a place where inevitably there are encounters of all sorts of belief, here symbolized by the seventy-two sects. That such an internal forum exists is a consequence of the many infinite worlds inside each human being.

In yet another passage Rumi addresses sectarian difference within a mystical vision of the universal—[if not fully conscious]—worshipfulness of all creation:

---

21 My translation of the *Maṣnavi*, influenced by that of R.A. Nicholson, editor and translator of *The Mathnawí of Jalálu'ddín Rúmí*, E.J.W. Gibb Memorial Series, New Series IV, *Text* V, Bk. V, vss. 3214–3232 (London: 1933) 205; *Translation* VI, Bk. V, vss. 3214–3232 (London: 1934) 194.

22 Nicholson, (*supra* n. 21), *Commentary* VIII, Bk. V (London: 1940) 289.

23 Nicholson, (*supra* n. 21), *Text* I, Bk. I, vss. 3288–3289 (London: 1925) 302; *Translation* II (London: 1926, reprinted 1960) 179.

Each glorifies [Thee] in a different fashion, and that one is unaware of the state of this one. Man disbelieves in the glorification uttered by inanimate objects, but these inanimate objects are masters [in performing] worship.

Nay, the two-and-seventy sects, every one, are unaware of [the real states of] each other and in a [great] doubt. Since two speakers have no knowledge of each other's state how will [it] be [with] wall and door?

Since I am heedless of the glorification uttered by one who speaks, how should my heart know the glorification performed by that which is mute?

The Sunni is unaware of the [predestinarian's] [mode of] glorification. The Sunni has a particular [mode of] glorification; the predestinarian has the opposite thereof in [taking] refuge [with God].[24]

Nicholson well summarizes the passage as saying that everything glorifies God by displaying some of His attributes in a special way known to God alone, Who has the infinite knowledge necessary to understand all the particulars of the world. This glorification is an act of worship, and, willing or not, every object, animate or inanimate, glorifies God. Both the Sunni (and Rumi was a Sunni) and his opponent, the Predestinarian (presumably a Shi'ite), glorify God—even though one may be right and one may be wrong about a specific article of belief—insofar as the beliefs of both express diverse aspects of Divine self-manifestation.[25]

Finally, Rumi explodes the two and seventy "sects" as mere epiphenomena of lesser religious consciousness. In an ecstatic passage on Love of the Divine and the Divine as Love, Rumi writes:

Love is a stranger to the two worlds; in it are two- and-seventy madnesses. It is exceedingly hidden, and [only] its bewilderment is manifest: the soul of the spiritual sultans is pining for it.

Its religion is other than [that of] the two-and-seventy sects: beside it the throne of kings is [but] a split-bandage ...

24 Nicholson, (*supra* n. 21), *Text* III, Bk. III, vss. 1496–1504 (London: 1929) 85, *Translation* IV, Bk. III, vss. 1496–1504 (London: 1930) 84. Nicholson's translation is given, except for substituting "predestinarian" for "Jabri." Incidentally, modern Shi'ites believe in free will and reject predestination.

25 Nicholson, (*supra* n. 21), *Commentary* VIII, Bk. III (London: 1940) 43.

> Then what is Love? The Sea of Not-Being: here the foot of the intellect is shattered [when it tries to swim] ...
> Would that Being had a Tongue, that it might remove the veils from existent Beings!
> O breath of [phenomenal] existence, whatsoever thou mayest utter, know that thereby thou hast bound another veil upon it [the mystery].[26]

While the intellect may be destined to speculate, the religion of love passes beyond sectarian difference. Love manifests itself in great variety, called here seventy-two madnesses, and ultimately takes the lover beyond the phenomenal world. Ultimately, beyond the babble of sectarian differences, the soul seeks a mystery which language cannot express.

Rumi has brought us to the end of our quest. The scheme of seventy-odd sects may be inspired by an earlier tradition about sixty-odd or seventy-odd branches of faith. Seventy-odd is very likely meant to convey the idea of considerable number. Whether one agrees with the usual interpretation, that only one sect is saved, or the minority interpretation, that only one is lost, the only punishment for right or wrong belief mentioned in these traditions is otherworldly, i.e., heaven or hell.

The Sufi tradition goes beyond these commonsensical understandings of religious pluralism among Muslims. Arguments for pluralism often depart from the suppositions that there are good impulses in all humans, or that most forms of belief are refractions of the vision of God. Rumi would accept both suppositions and transcend them. For him it is a logical necessity that people dispute about religion, even among Muslims. God put the arguments inside us, each of whom continues a wide variety of opinions, symbolized by the seventy-two sects, in our internal forum. This plurality arises from flaws, created by the intellect, yet each opinion is in its way an attempt to worship God. The deeper religion is the trans-religious mystery of love of God which the intellect can never really understand. This love manifests itself in many (that is, seventy-two) madnesses and takes the soul beyond the world of being. Ultimately, we not only accept pluralism among Muslims but among all the mysterious paths of the love of God.

---

26 Nicholson, (*supra* n. 21), *Text* III, Bk. III, vss. 4719–4726, omitting 4722 and 4724 (London: 1929) 270 and *Translation* IV, Bk. III (London: 1930) 263.

Rumi, whose *Maṣnavi* may be the greatest spiritual epic of the Islamic tradition, proves to be above categorization as a "pre-modern" or "modern" sensibility. He believes that there are right and wrong opinions about Islam (and, indeed, about religion in general). But he leaves such judgment to God since we live in the world of "shadow" where conflict is inevitable. He urges upon us the ultimate pluralism: to respect the other's quest as springing from the same impulse as our own, without giving up faith in our own spiritual belief.

The Islamic tradition offers more than one path to pluralism. I think a strong argument for pluralism can be made on the basis of some thinkers' view of innate human nature, *fiṭra*. In any case, Rumi's path seems to me spiritually and intellectually powerful. But it also tells us something about the uses of tradition. Hundreds of millions of Muslims have lived over the past fourteen centuries since the life of the Prophet and there are many voices and approaches in this vast and varied tradition.

Given the sociological realities of the religious world in which we live, Muslims must and can find in their tradition authentic voices that speak for an acceptance of pluralism. The wanton killing of Iraqis in the aftermath of the Second Gulf War in an attempt to ignite a civil war between Sunnis and Shi'ites warns us of the need to establish a strong ethical basis for pluralism among Muslims. And the fates of Muslim minorities—in the case of India, the second largest Muslim community in the world—show that if one urges Muslims to embrace pluralism, one should also urge their non-Muslim neighbors to embrace difference. Here I address a criticism to the stubborn secular religion of France. Surely a Muslim woman should be free to wear a head scarf to school, as a Jewish man should be free to wear a yarmulke and a Catholic nun to wear a habit.

The message of Rumi is not some mealy-mouthed multiculturalism. Rumi is a devout believer. Yet he recognizes that others are not only free to disagree with him but that God Him or Herself supplies the arguments of disagreements. Certainty is structurally impossible in the mundane realm and, as the Sufi theologian al-Ghazālī had said, instead of "true religion" we have human knowledge of religion. Yet we all see the high value of truth and right belief and would surrender to it if it were self-evident. Correct belief may be one path, but all imaginable forms of belief live inside us, and their presence is not to be denied. The seventy-two sects are not even fully aware of each other's existence, although the members of these sects—like every inanimate object—knowingly or unknowingly, worship God.

And let no one say Rumi is impossibly far from the Qur'ān, the pivotal text which for so many Muslims remains central to their belief. In the Sūra V of the Quran, Sūrat al-Mā'ida, the long verse 48 reads:

> To you We sent the scripture with truth, confirming the scripture that came before it, and guarding it in safety; so, judge between them by what God has revealed, and follow not their vain desires, diverging from the truth that has come to you. To each among you have We prescribed a law and a clear way. If God had so willed, He would have made you a single people, but [God's plan] is to test you in what He has given you; so vie with each other in good works. The goal of all is [to hasten] toward God; for it is [God] who will show you the truth of the matters in which you differ.

For the Qur'ān, too, diversity of belief is divinely initiated, and the common goal, known or unknown, is God. God urges all communities of belief to strive with each other as in a race in all virtues. We can see this passage as a direct inspiration to Rumi.

The Clash of Civilizations: An Islamicist's Critique

The twentieth century has had two great prophet-philosophers of history, Spengler and Toynbee. Each of them spoke to the West about its future after a major change in circumstance, prophesied for the West on the basis of a long historical view of the destiny of civilizations, and led careers that spanned the world of scholarship and public policy. Both of them, Spengler and Toynbee, started out as historians but came to despise their fellow professional colleagues as narrow-minded slaves of detail who made niggling objections to their larger schemes. Now [1995], Samuel Huntington, a political scientist who has plunged into history, seems ready to join this pantheon. In his celebrated article, "The Clash of Civilizations," soon to be published in expanded form as a book [in 1996], Huntington also reflects on the course of civilizations, past and, more especially, future. As a by-product he has given the United States of the 1990s what it most desires: a principle with which to make order of the post-Cold War era, and a sense of purpose. It is, moreover, a testimony to the protean creativity of its highly intelligent author that he has not fallen captive to the "scientism" that has fostered so many arid debates in the discussion of foreign policy. The "clash of civilizations" thesis has also strengthened the reintroduction

Author's note: This article was first published as: "The Clash of Civilizations: An Islamicist's Critique," in *Harvard Middle Eastern and Islamic Review* 2:2 (1995) 1–26. Reproduced with permission. This journal, dated 1995, only went to press in 1996 and some information from early 1996 is included. The examples cited in this article to challenge Huntington's thesis reflect the time in which the article was written. I have not changed these examples although I have included in brackets some clarifications and additional information. I have also added a postscript at the end.

of culture into the discussion of politics; the development theories of the 1960s, which heavily discounted culture, now seem sadly naive.[1]

As an historian, I had very much hoped that Samuel Huntington [d. 2016] would remain an empiricist and care about detail. Ultimately, Spengler's contempt for empiricism made him an honorable but largely irrelevant episode in twentieth-century thought. Toynbee, who maintained throughout that he was an empiricist and tried mightily to be civil to his professional detractors, could not accommodate, or even take in, the many (largely empirical) criticisms of his work; and the judgment of most professional historians was summed up by the English historian John Kenyon, who wrote that "the great Toynbee Cult, which some had seen as an indirect threat to Western civilization, proved less enduring and no more significant in the long run than the similar Tolkien Cult."[2]

The heart of the Huntington thesis lies precisely in the claim, based on a trend which Professor Huntington attempts to establish empirically, that, in a new phase of world politics, culture will be the mainspring of the great divisions among peoples and the "dominating" source of international conflict. According to Huntington (who is strongly influenced by Toynbee's categorization of civilizations), at present the major civilizations are the Western, Confucian, Japanese, Islamic, Hindu, Slavic-Orthodox, Latin-American, and—possibly—African. "Western ideas of individualism, liberalism, constitutionalism, human rights, equality, liberty, the rule of law, democracy, free markets, and the separation of church and state often have little resonance in Islamic, Confucian, Japanese, Hindu, Buddhist or Orthodox cultures." (It is interesting that Buddhism appears as a fugitive category throughout the article.) The policy implications are clear: "The

1 Samuel P. Huntington, "The Clash of Civilizations?" *Foreign Affairs* 72:3 (1993) 22–49. The Huntington quotations here are all taken from this article unless otherwise noted. Huntington has a later article published in the same year: "If Not Civilizations, What? Paradigms of the Post-Cold War World," *Foreign Affairs* 72:5 (1993) 186–194. Huntington's book, *The Clash of Civilizations and the Remaking of World Order* (New York, Simon & Shuster: 1996), was published after my critique was published. I would like to thank several Harvard colleagues, Professors Edward Keenan, Roger Owen, Roderick MacFarquhar, and Thomas Scanlon, for their extremely useful comments on this paper. I would also like to thank Professor Thomas S. Kuhn of MIT. All opinions expressed here are, of course, entirely my own. Although I am an historian of the medieval Middle East, my interest in the comparative study of Islamic societies dates back to a conversation with Vartan Gregorian in Afghanistan in 1961, to whom I dedicate this paper.

2 John Kenyon, *The History Men* (London: 1983) 282.

fault lines of civilizations are the battle lines of the future." The West must be accommodating to "alien" civilizations, if possible, but confrontational if necessary. For this purpose, the United States must forge alliances with similar cultures. Whereas Huntington hopes to "incorporate" into the West societies in Eastern Europe and Latin America, there is—apparently—no such hope in the near future for the rest of the non-West. In the case of the Confucian and Islamic world, the West must "limit" the expansion of their military strength by, among other measures, maintaining "military superiority in East and Southwest Asia," and by seeking "to exploit differences and conflicts among Confucian and Islamic states." But, in the final analysis, "all civilizations should learn to tolerate each other."

Huntington's thesis is arresting because it offers a broad picture of world events that seems to be supported by a wealth of examples. Yet for an Islamicist—a scholar whose primary interest touches in some way on the Islamic world—some of the examples taken from the Islamic world are far more ambiguous than they first appear, and counterexamples seem to be abundantly to hand. Not only is the "empirical" basis of the thesis a matter for dispute, but the theoretical structure proposed to explain the relation between "culture" and political behavior seems to the present author very much open to question. And, unfortunately, some of these examples are presented in a way that unwittingly panders to the less constructive stereotypes of the history of the non-Western world.

For example, in his capsule history of the Islamic world Huntington tells us that after "the Arab and Moorish surge west and north, the Crusaders attempted with temporary success to bring Christianity and Christian rule to the Holy Land." As Professor Huntington knows but the less informed reader of this sentence may forget, the Crusaders could not bring Christianity to the Holy land because Christianity continued to exist (and profit from Christian pilgrimage) both in the Holy Land and in the rest of the Middle East because of the principle of tolerance toward Christians (as well as Jews) in Islamic law. As often as not, the indigenous Christians of the Holy Land found Crusader Christian presence a burden since the Crusaders could be extremely intolerant of the indigenous Christian groups present there.

Huntington continues his history of the relations of the Islamic world and the West by giving an accurate summary of the relations between the Arab world (with one reference to Iran) and the West. He then concludes: "This warfare between Arabs and the West culminated in 1990, when the United States sent a massive army to the Persian Gulf." (Of course, the Egyptians, the Syrians, the Saudis and other members of the Gulf Cooperation Council, Arab nations with a collective population many times Iraq's population, also sent troops.) "This centuries-old military interaction between the West and Islam is unlikely to decline. It could become virulent." While there have been efforts to introduce democracy, "the principal beneficiaries of these openings have been Islamist movements. In the Arab world, in short, Western democracy strengthens anti-Western political forces. This may be a passing phenomenon, but it surely complicates relations between Islamic countries and the West."

Of course, Professor Huntington, in spite of the alternation between "Arab" and "Islamic" in these paragraphs, knows that the categories "Arab" and "Muslim" do not even approximately overlap. At the very most one in five Muslims is an Arab. The Arab nations [in 1995] claim a population of about two hundred million [436 million in 2022] out of the world's approximately one billion [1.9 billion in 2022] Muslims, but this number includes several millions of Berbers and Kurds. The Arab world also, incidentally, includes at least fifteen million Christian Arabs [unchanged in 2022 due to emigration from the Arab world], some of whom, such as [the late] George Habash, the leader of the Palestinian Front for the Liberation of Palestine (PFLP), were considerably less sympathetic to the West than a Muslim such as [the late] Yasir Arafat. [In 2022 Muslims worldwide number approximately 1.9 billion and Muslim Arabs represent at most 421 million of that number.] Therefore, a summary history of the hostilities between the Arab world and the West by itself can hardly support the conclusion that "this centuries-old military interaction between the West and Islam is unlikely to decline." In fact, even if we were to concentrate only on the Mediterranean world and disregard such peripheral matters as the British conquest of Moghul India and the Dutch conquest of Indonesia, the most important conflict between Christians and Muslims of the past five centuries of Mediterranean history would seem to be the West's struggle with the Ottoman Turks, hardly an "Arab" opponent.

Yet an important intellectual problem is raised by the conflation of Arabs and Muslims at the conclusion of this summary history: "In the Arab world, in short, Western democracy strengthens anti-Western forces. This may be a passing phenomenon, but it surely complicates relations between Islamic countries and the West." Professor Huntington's idea of civilization is such that other Muslims should behave the way Muslim Arabs behave—but they do not. In early 1996, the two non-Arab parliamentary democracies in Muslim lands led by women prime ministers—Pakistan and Bangladesh—alone had a combined population of approximately two hundred and twenty million [approximately 491 million in 2022], significantly larger than that of the Arab world. Turkey, a parliamentary democracy until recently also led by a woman prime minister [1993–96], has a population of sixty million [84 million in 2022]. Is it possible that, in spite of being fellow Muslims, the Muslims of South Asia and the Muslims of Turkey have a different political culture than Arab Muslims? I believe the case that they do have such individual political cultures to be overwhelming.

Even within the Arab world the principal beneficiaries of democratic openings have not always been the Islamists: Hasan Turabi [died 2016], the Islamist ideologue of the present [1996] government of the Sudan, was unable to win a parliamentary seat when that country had a democratic system. Other Islamic countries offer many parallels: in Pakistan, for example, Islamists rode high under the authoritarian rule of Zia ul-Haq [1978–88] but have done poorly in popular elections both before and after his time [up to 1996].

Huntington, in fleshing out his theory of "the bloody borders" of Islam, tells us that in Africa the conflict between "Arab Islamic" civilization and the non-Islamic peoples to the south, in the past "epitomized in the image of the Arab slave dealers and black slaves," is now "reflected in the on-going civil war in the Sudan between Arabs and blacks, the fighting in Chad between Libyan-supported insurgents and the government, the tension between Orthodox Christians and Muslims in the Horn of Africa, and ... [the] conflicts ... between Muslims and Christians in Nigeria." But the Ethiopians, the only substantial Christian community near the Horn of Africa, are Miaphysite, a variety of Christians once vigorously persecuted and still regarded as scandalously heretical by the Eastern Orthodox. In Chad [in the 1980s], Goukouni Weddeye, a Muslim, received Libyan support, while his Muslim opponent Hissein Habré was supported by Sudan, Egypt, and Saudi Arabia as well as the United States. At certain stages, Libyan-backed Goukouni Weddeye had more sympathy in the non-Muslim south than his opponent, the anti-Libyan Habré, who had to reconquer the south before he drove the Libyans from the north. As one scholar of Libyan and Chadian affairs has remarked, while feelings among Muslims were a factor in the outbreak of civil war in Chad, "Islam proved a remarkably feeble counterweight to the divisive forces of ethnicity and regionalism."[3] [In 2022 Chad may emerge as a democracy after the present transitional military council although many feel its chances are slim.] As for the Arabs of the Sudan (which in Arabic means "land of the blacks"), they are in majority black by the understanding of the (admittedly artificial) racial categories used in the United States and Egypt, something that only victims of stereotypes about "white" Arab slave traders would forget. The "communal violence" between Muslims and Christians in Nigeria to which Huntington refers is very real but at present [in 1995] it is far overshadowed by the conflict between Mashood Abiola, the Yoruba Muslim from the south who won at the polls in 1992, and the military government, dominated in part by Muslims of the north, which cancelled the result of those elections. [Nevertheless, in 2022, Nigeria, as a federal republic, has a functioning democracy.]

"On the northern border of Islam," Professor Huntington tells us, "Conflict has increasingly erupted between Orthodox and Muslim peoples." Included in this formula is the "simmering violence between Serb and Albanian," Albanians being an overwhelmingly Muslim people. This "simmer" seems at the moment partly to consist of fuel sales, including jet fuel, to the officially embargoed Serbs by Albania, which is selling more oil to the Serbs than all other sources combined.[4] And, real as the historical antipathy between the Serbs and Albanians may be, it is no less real than the antipathy that simmers between the Orthodox Slavs and Orthodox Greeks in neighboring Macedonia. [In 2022 democracy is more secure in Albania than in Serbia].

For the Caucasus Professor Huntington offers us two examples of the Orthodox-Muslim conflict: one is "the violence between Ossetians and Ingush, and the other the unremitting slaughter of each other by Armenians and Azeris." While including the not very important example of the Muslim Ingush and the Ossetes, who are in majority Orthodox (although with a twenty to thirty percent Muslim minority), Professor Huntington neglects many far more important counterexamples. Under Gamsakhurdia's presidency [1991–1992], (Orthodox) Georgia waged a bloody war against its (largely Orthodox) Ossetian minority. Since Shevardnadze assumed leadership of Georgia in 1992 there have been

3 Rene Lemarchand, "Chad," in *the Oxford Encyclopedia of the Modern Islamic World,* 1 (New York: 1995) 276.

4 See the reports of Raymond Bonner in *the New York Times,* April 30, 1995, p. 4, and April 2, 1995, p. 10.

efforts (not altogether successful) to heal this rift; but meanwhile [in 1995] (Orthodox) Russia has helped the (largely Muslim) Abkhazians to declare themselves independent of (Orthodox) Georgia. No surprise that Georgia has felt more sympathy to (Muslim) Azerbaijan, which has been resistant to Russian influence. No surprise, either, that Iran—the archetypal Muslim state in Western thinking—has been so careful to be neutral in the struggle between Christian Armenians and Muslim Azerbaijanis, since Iran wishes to discourage Azerbaijani separatists within its own borders and sees friendship with Russia as a key to its foreign policy. Orthodox Russia, Christian Armenia—the majority of whose population has, for over a millennium, totally rejected the authority of the Orthodox churches as normally understood—and Islamic Iran are emerging as covert allies in Caucasian affairs [in 1995]."[5] [In 2022 Georgia continues to be a functioning democracy and Azerbaijan, while still authoritarian, seems to be moving toward democracy.]

Central Asia is another arena in which Muslim-Orthodox differences have a weak explanatory power. Iran has joined Russia and India in strongly backing the Rabbani government in Kabul [1992–96] against the more "Islamist" forces of the Taliban in Afghanistan. [In 2022 almost three decades later Islamists control almost all of Afghanistan, and large segments of its population are seeking refuge in Iran and Pakistan.] By and large Iran has not helped Muslim religious rebels in Tajikistan, where it could have great influence because of shared language, but has restricted its dealings to the pro-Russian official government. To view the relations of (Orthodox) Russia with its Caucasian and Central Asian neighbors, or even to view the relations between these neighbors as primarily a Muslim-Orthodox question is a bit like viewing American relations with the Caribbean and Central America as dominated by religious questions. Russia and the United States have strong geopolitical interests in what they consider their backyards; and in sorting out conflicts in these regions, religion, more often than not, has nothing to do with the case.

So far we have been discussing civilization largely as an explanation for lines of conflict. Now we should turn to civilization as an explanation for the motives of its "members." There is a very great danger that using the term "civilization" will lead us to underestimate the variety within that

5 See the excellent article by Mohiaddin Mesbahi, "Russian Foreign Policy Security in Central Asia and the Caucasus," in *Central Asian Survey* 12:2 (1993) 181–215.

designation and the rapidity with which it can change over time. There is the even greater danger that units proposed as "civilizations" but still far from being proved to be such will be treated as realities before they are shown to be such. Professor Huntington allows that civilizations have "variants," and that they are "dynamic; they rise and fall; they divide and merge." But his overall message is that civilizations are highly stable units, each internally united by a large number of characteristics: "Differences among civilizations are not only real; they are basic. Civilizations are differentiated from each other by history, language, culture, tradition and, most important, religion. The people of different civilizations have different views on relations between God and man, the individual and the group, the citizen and the state, parents and children, husband and wife, as well as differing views of the relative importance of rights and responsibilities, liberty and authority, equality and hierarchy. These differences are products of centuries. They will not soon disappear."[6]

The degree to which each civilization is closely tied to its assumed primary carriers is brought home by a paragraph in Professor Huntington's reply to his critics in a subsequent issue of *Foreign Affairs*. He notes that "the Census Bureau estimates that by 2050 the American population will be 23 percent Hispanic, 16 percent Black and 10 percent Asian-American." In the past the United States has successfully absorbed immigrants because they have "adapted to the prevailing European culture and enthusiastically embraced the American Creed of liberty, equality, individualism, democracy. Will this pattern continue to prevail as 50 percent of the population becomes Hispanic or nonwhite?" There is, he feels, a real possibility that this Hispanic and nonwhite population may not adapt to European culture and the American Creed, which would lead to "the de-Westernization of the United States" because it will have become "truly multicultural and pervaded with an internal clash of civilizations," and therefore unable to survive as a liberal democracy. In this case, "the United States as we have known it will cease to exist and will follow the other ideologically defined superpower onto the ash heap of history."[7] Why the 16 percent black Americans of 2050, overwhelmingly descended from black Americans who arrived here long before the Slavic, Italian and other post-Civil War white immigrant groups, are considered not only not successfully absorbed but

6 Huntington, "Clash of Civilizations," (*supra* n. 1), 24–25.
7 Huntington, "If Not Civilizations, What?" (*supra* n. 1), 190.

a potential source of "de-Westernization" of the United States remains to be explained in Huntington's forthcoming book.

Let us, however, examine one of the global traits that Professor Huntington ascribes to Islamic civilization. When Professor Huntington tells us that, "western ideas of ... free markets ... often have little resonance in Islamic (culture)," the "often" preserves him from a totalizing description; but what are we left with? Anyone who has read pre-modern Islamic law knows how frequently the saying of the Prophet Muḥammad, "God sets prices," is quoted, and how deeply suspicious this legal tradition is of price-setting. The overwhelming majority of the pre-Ottoman Islamic societies of the Middle East were free market economies. Is Professor Huntington thinking of the use of price fixing in certain periods of Ottoman history? As a student of the Islamic world, I would guess (although without great conviction) that most Muslims in most places and in most periods were free marketeers. But I do know that in the 1950s and 1960s in many Muslim countries socialist leaders such as Sukarno and Nasser insisted that Islam was inherently socialist (another totalizing assumption) and created laws accordingly. In fact, Nasser had Shaykh Makhlouf, the highest religious authority in Egypt, dismissed when Makhlouf rejected Nasser's contention that Islam was essentially socialistic. Therefore, I know that Muslims can oppose a free market and know that they often have enthusiastically endorsed free markets. Although perfect market economies probably only exist in the minds of Chicago economists, at present among Islamic Middle Eastern countries alone relatively free markets exist in Morocco, Tunisia, Turkey, Kuwait, and most of the other Arab Gulf states. Can anyone say empirically that the idea of the free (or, for that matter, the controlled) market has "little resonance" in "Islamic civilization"? And, given the vast geographical spread and long historical varieties of the experience of Muslim peoples, is the question in any way useful, or even meaningful?

Behind this assumption of the very close ties between ideas and their assumed primary carriers are several other assumptions hard to accept. One is that people are not merely influenced, sometimes shallowly, sometimes very deeply, by their cultures, but are intellectually subjugated to them. Another is that ideas live most authentically in their place of origin. Thus Professor Huntington tells us that "the very notion that there could be a 'universal civilization' is a Western idea," and, we are to understand therefore, difficult to export; it is "at odds with the particularism of most

Asian societies and their emphasis on what distinguishes one people from another."[8] Even historically this claim may be questionable, as Christianity and Islam—both, incidentally, Near Eastern in origin-are proselytizing monotheisms with ambitions to convert the entire world. But even granting that (on some definition of civilization) "universal civilization" may well be a "'Western idea," what does this tell us? Does it tell us that "particularisms of most Asian societies and their emphasis on what distinguishes one people from another" have an iron grip on the minds of Asians, and that such Asians cannot, except in some remote future, make such alien concepts as "universal civilization" their own?

To many historians, claims that cultures are largely impervious and that "imported" ideas flourish less fully and authentically outside their places of origin seem strange indeed. Does the idea of casting ballots in elections flourish more authentically in its country of origin, Greece, than in Great Britain? The idea of courtly love certainly existed in early Arabic literature, and probably passed from there to the West; is Chaucer's *Troilus and Criseyde* therefore less authentically English and European? Pseudo-scientific theories of race and a rigorous idea of "the color bar" are also a European invention; have they proved impossible to export?

Professor Huntington tells us that "modern democratic government originated in the West. When it has developed in non-Western societies it has usually been the product of Western colonialism or imposition." For anyone who sees a culture or "civilization" as a set of handmade Russian nesting dolls, each of which is almost certain never to fit into any other set, this view of culture, which regards "cultural grafts" as suspect *a priori*, will be convincing. But, of course, culture is not made of nesting dolls or precisely shaped puzzle pieces; and large elements of Western culture introduced by colonialism, imposition, or mere imitation have developed deep and authentic roots in non-Western societies, to a degree that these societies often no longer sense these elements to be alien. Nothing in the pre-modern Islamic tradition drives modern Muslims to give the vote to women, and many Muslim conservatives opposed the enfranchisement of women. But in countries such as Turkey, Egypt, and Iran the overwhelming majority of Islamists—advocates of the reintroduction of some measure of Islamic law—would now never raise a whisper against votes for women, who form an important part of their constituents. Even Ayatollah

8 Huntington, "Clash of Civilizations," (*supra* n. 1), 41.

Khomeini, though he had been opposed to the Iranian law of 1962 that enfranchised women, never suggested that Iran's new constitution, over which he could have exercised great power, should deny women the vote. The direct electoral participation of women is an irreversible fact in the life of many Islamic countries, regardless of whether or not it is an "imposition" and/or a "product of Western colonialism." The same can be said for written constitutions and national law codes.

The history of the West itself offers many striking illustrations of the sometimes gradual, sometimes rapid circulation of ideas from one area of the West to another, the virtual "colonization" of one part of the West by another, in a way that the nesting doll or rigid puzzle piece theory of culture would consider highly unlikely. And it also offers many examples of earlier Huntingtonians. It was once commonly said, for example, that democracy could only live fully and authentically in Protestant countries. The supposedly anti-liberal nature of Catholicism was a significant element in the struggle between Protestants and Catholics in nineteenth-century Germany called the *Kulturkampf*. The struggle took its name from the words of Rudolf Virchow, who in 1873 declared in the Prussian diet: "The contest has taken on the character of a great cultural struggle," all of which should sound enchantingly familiar to the new theorists of "the West against the rest." It was "self-evident" to many Protestants that Catholics were obedient to the Pope and could not be true democratic participants in a German state; anti-Catholic sentiment was so strong that Prussia enacted a law to expel all Jesuits [1872]. Many Americans will remember the joke that the Catholic politician Alfred E. Smith, on losing his bid for the presidency in 1928, telegraphed the Pope to "unpack immediately." In America this distrust of Catholicism seems only to have died with the election of John F. Kennedy as President in 1960. In 1944, the most distinguished American Protestant theologian of his time, Reinhold Niebuhr, lamented the chasm "between the presuppositions of a free society and the inflexible authoritarianism of the Catholic religion."[9] To distrust the ability of sincere Catholics to be true democrats seems as quaint and fanciful to

9 Reinhold Niebuhr, *The Children of Light and the Children of Darkness: A Vindication of Democracy and a Critique of Its Traditional Defense* (New York: 1944) 319. I owe this quote to John T. McGreevy's article, "Thinking on One's Own: Catholicism in the American Intellectual Imagination, 1928–1960," in *The Journal of American History* 84:1 (Bloomington, IN: June 1997) 97–131.

us at the end of the twentieth century as will seem, in a generation, our present distrust of the ability of sincere Muslims to be true democrats.

This tendency to assume that a group has uniformities of attitude that originate in its religious identity, and that are changed only with the greatest difficulty, has an earlier and dark chapter in Western Christian assessments of the Jews. In 1782 David Michaelis, a German professor of Oriental languages at the University of Göttingen and reputed to be a Christian expert on the Jews, wrote: "Does the Law of Moses make citizenship, and the full integration of the Jew into other peoples, difficult or impossible? I think it does!" Soon, this line of thought reached its full development as a theory of culture and citizenship, as when Bruno Bauer, a German Protestant theologian, wrote in 1843: "Human rights are the result of education, and they can be possessed only by those who acquire and deserve them. Can the Jew really possess them as long as he lives as a Jew in perpetual segregation from others, as long as he therefore must declare that the others are not really his fellowmen? As long as he is a Jew, his Jewishness must be stronger in him than his humanity and keep him apart from non-Jews. He declares by his segregation that this, his Jewishness, is his true, highest nature, which has to have precedence over his humanity."[10] It should be noted that Bauer's sense of alienation from Jews was purely cultural and not racial; hence Bauer's important influence on Karl Marx, who, although of Jewish origin, agreed that Jews should strip themselves of all "Jewishness" in order to join the body politic.

One last general observation would seem to weaken the strength of the Huntington thesis: its neglect of the distinction between peoples and governments. At the 1993 World Conference on Human Rights in Vienna the majority of Chinese organizations not controlled by the Chinese government supported the Dalai Lama's right to speak, which the Chinese government unyieldingly opposed. The Dalai Lama rejected the position of China and some other Asian and African countries that human rights in less-developed countries need not be as liberal as elsewhere. "I do not share this view," he said, "and I am convinced that the majority of Asian people do not support this view either."[11] Are we really supposed to believe

10 *The Jew in the Modern World: A Documentary History*, eds. Paul R. Mendes-Flohr and Jehuda Reinharz (New York: 1980) 37 (Michaelis) and 263 (Bauer). These remarks are not meant to suggest that Professor Huntington's name can by any stretch of the imagination be associated with anti-Semitism or racism of any kind.

11 Associated Press Report by Alexander G. Higgins, Vienna, Austria, June 15, 1993.

that the Chinese Communist government is more truly Buddhist and/or Confucian than the Chinese people and/or the Dalai Lama? The United States Congress has agreed to join the over one hundred nations that have ratified the 1948 convention on genocide only with reservations that nullify its commitments. Is this a sign that the American people are less truly attuned to the values of Western civilization than most other nations in the world, or that our legislative process often ties us in knots?

The sad but shocking truth is that readers less sophisticated than Professor Huntington will use his thesis to feed fantasies already too prevalent about a massive coordinated Islamic movement that sees as its primary objective the humiliation of the West. Of course, in a community of a billion [now in 2022 1.9 billion] souls, the Muslim world contains its analogues to our home-grown organizations of bigots such as the anti-Semitic Christian Patriot's Defense League in the United States or the die-hard fanatics in Northern Ireland. But Muslims—marvelous to say—are human beings, subject to all the pulls of economic need, local community, and all the other interests that influence humans everywhere; and only lavish, ignorant and sensationalizing uses of words like "fundamentalism" have blinded us to their humanity and diversity.

There is a group of Muslims, in my opinion very distinctly a minority, who are properly called Islamists, who call for some degree of reimposition of Islamic law, and who tend to view the West as a more or less unified and universal "alien civilization" to be treated in the spirit of the "clash of civilizations" thesis—with accommodation, if possible, but with "confrontation" if necessary. I do not speak here of the very small if noisy minority of militant extremist Muslims, who should not be allowed to set anyone's agenda for anything. I strongly believe this group will remain a distinct minority, because it disregards the large historical variation in the Islamic tradition (even in the area of law), because its followers have large areas of internal disagreement, and because it has no real answers to the problems of economic and social justice that beleaguer the majority of Muslims.

In addition to the examples from the Caucasus, Balkans and Central Asia cited above, certain recent events have shown us the very considerable diversity of opinion on foreign policy even among this minority of Muslims who are "Islamists." This diversity was dramatically illustrated by the variety of Islamist reactions to the Gulf Crisis of 1990–91[caused by the invasion of Kuwait by Saddam Hussein]. In Egypt the Muslim Brothers were for some time unable to agree on the crisis, since Saudi Arabians had long supported them, but many members found the sight of non-Muslims sorting out a quarrel between Muslim nations unacceptable. Tunisian Islamists were similarly divided. Jordanian Islamists followed King Hussein in taking a pro-Iraqi stance [although the King may well have preferred to be neutral]. The principal Turkish Islamist party was at first favorable to Saddam, but then its leaders, after a September meeting with King Fahd of Saudi Arabia, became either neutral or somewhat critical of Saddam.[12] Professor Huntington writes, however, that "ignoring the rivalry between Iran and Iraq, the chief Iranian religious leader, Ayatollah Ali Khamenei, called for a holy war against the West."[13] In fact, Iranian actions, such as the seizure of the Iraqi aircraft that fled the fighting to land in Iranian airports, are a far better gauge of how mindful the Iranian leadership was of its eight-year war with Iraq [1980–88]. It is mistaken information indeed that has persuaded Samuel Huntington to write, "Islamic fundamentalist movements universally supported Iraq rather than the Western-backed governments of Kuwait and Saudi Arabia."

Many parallel cases, in which actual policy was determined by particularistic interests over pan-Islamic interests, will suggest themselves to anyone who follows the politics of nations in which Muslims are significantly represented. For example, Khomeini, for all his fierce rhetoric about Palestine, was far more concerned with Iraq. 'Ali-Akbar Mohtashemi, the Iranian ambassador to Syria in the early eighties and later the hard-line Minister of the Interior, in a recent interview in *Jahan-e Islam* claimed that in 1982 Khomeini personally stopped the Revolutionary Guard of Iran from going to Lebanon to fight Israel; "the Imam explained that it was not appropriate for Iran to confront Israel from a long distance without any common border, and to do a job that the Arabs themselves should do."[14]

A major problem in discussing the validity and/or importance of a thesis such as that proposed by Samuel Huntington is the weighing of evidence. Presumably, insofar as his examples of intercivilizational conflict prove to be incorrect—as for instance in the case of Chad—the evidence for his theory becomes thinner and the theory less sustainable. And, if ideas

12 See François Burgat, "Islamists and the Gulf Crisis," in *The Arab World Today*, ed. Dan Tschirgi (Boulder: 1994) 205–211, and my article "Islamic Movements: The Case for Democratic Inclusion" (Article 27 here).
13 Huntington, "Clash of Civilizations," (*supra* n. 1), 35.
14 Quoted by William Scott Harrop, "Iran's Revolutionary Paradox," in *Mind and Human Interaction* 6:1 (Feb. 1995) 26.

about civilization-wide traits, such as the presumed lack of "resonance" in Islamic civilization to Western ideas, turn out to be neither historically true nor true at present, the evidence for the Huntington thesis would seem to have less weight. At this point, however, a problem arises for everyone who seeks to evaluate the Huntington thesis. Non-Western civilizations are not likely to change soon, we are told, because they have been the way they are for a long time. At the same time, much of the evidence for the nature of their long-held traits is shown in their recent behavior. Moreover, the Huntington essay is in significant part a prophecy about the future.

About the evidence that the future will provide we can (or, at least, should) agree to be silent. But if "civilizations" have proved fairly rapidly adaptive to *some* imported institutions, as this essay argues many Islamic societies (including their minorities of Islamists) have proven to be—for example, in accepting the enfranchisement of women—then which long-term traits are predictive of future behavior? There is a good argument to be made that such traits can be identified in local cultures (much smaller units than the proposed "civilizations"). We must hope that in his book Samuel Huntington will provide us with a theory that will explain why there is this significant variation in local adaptability to change within each civilization. Such an explanation would advance social theory immeasurably.

If, however, only very recent events count as evidence for such a theory, then how are we to weigh examples against counterexamples? Is the supposedly intercivilizational conflict between the Ossetes and the Ingush more or less important than the intracivilizational conflict between the Ossetes and the Georgians (and so on and so forth)? Of course, the world system was partly frozen in place by the Cold War, and now is in motion again with an attendant number of small wars. But is this motion a new trend, or is it back to history all over again? The nineteenth century saw the expansion of some empires on the basis of (conflictingly described) civilizational missions, as well as the contraction of others, such as the Ottomans, who energetically (but, in the end, futilely) evoked first a pan-Islamic, then a pan-Turkic civilizational claim. First, the case has to be made that long-existing non-civilizational causes, such as the mutual distrust of Caucasian peoples, do not satisfactorily account for the conflicts brought forward as civilizational conflicts. Second, the truly abysmal record of civilization-wide movements, from pan-Slavism and pan-Islam in the nineteenth century to the international Islamic organizations of today, to deliver effective backing for political action will have to be accounted for.

Pan-Islamic movements have often loomed unaccountably large in the mind of the West. In 1916 a missionary and supposed expert on the Middle East, the American Samuel M. Zwemer, wrote in *Mohammed or Christ*: "The coming struggle will not be solely religious, but an educational, industrial, social, and political upheaval in which religion plays a chief part ... It is a struggle between two civilizations; between the ideals of the Moslem world and those of Christendom."[15] In the First World War the opposing sides in Europe nurtured hopes that they could arouse Islamic holy wars led by the (pro-German) Ottomans or the (pro-British) Hashemites (Hāshimīs). In the event these hopes aroused the Western European imagination far more than they aroused the Middle Eastern Islamic imagination. Huntington, who has been a pioneer in developing mathematical expression of political trends, will have to give us some basis on which to weigh the comparative importance of examples and to demonstrate that the examples he cites do, in fact, show a strong new trend, and are not a miscellany that could be matched in the 1890s or 1910s.

One argument implicit in Huntington's proposal—namely, that his "civilizational approach" should be accepted because it has no plausible competitors that explain contemporary international politics—seems to me to be a complete non-starter. In his reply to his critics Huntington tells us: "When people think seriously, they think abstractly; they conjure up simplified pictures of reality called concepts, theories, models and paradigms." Without such intellectual constructs, there is, William James said, only "bloomin' buzzin' confusion."[16] William James uses this phrase in only two places I know of, and in neither does he use it in the same sense as Huntington.[17] James seems to be arguing for the need for such basic concepts as "sea" or "grass" in order for us, in his terminology, to "disassociate" discrete elements from the continuum of perception—the blooming, buzzing reality he assumes that babies feel. He goes on to say that our desire to harmonize these concepts leads to "explanatory systems." If people fail to find an explanatory system, however, it does not mean that they have regressed to seeing the world as a "blooming,

15 Samuel M. Zwemer, *Mohammed or Christ* (London, Fleming H. Revell: 1916) 121 and 124. I am grateful to the ever-learned Yvonne Haddad for calling these quotations to my attention.

16 Huntington, "If Not Civilizations, What?" (*supra* n. 1), 186.

17 William James, *Principles of Psychology*, I (Cambridge, MA: 1981) 461 and *Some Problems in Philosophy* (Cambridge, MA: 1979) 32.

buzzing confusion." When Locke saw states living in a world of unregulated competition and wrote that, "[T]he whole community is one body in the state of nature in respect to all other states," he had not with that remark entered his second infancy.[18]

Even if we were to assume that our perception of international relations would be a "blooming, buzzing confusion" without an "explanatory system," however, we need not follow Huntington's claim that his theory is better than others because "intellectual and scientific advance, as Thomas Kuhn showed ..., consists of the displacement of one paradigm, which has become increasingly incapable of explaining new or newly discovered facts, by a new paradigm that accounts for those facts in a more satisfactory fashion." Margaret Masterman, in an essay which Kuhn has largely endorsed, has shown that Kuhn uses "paradigm" in a number of different ways, but only rarely as a hypothesis, pure and simple, although this understanding of paradigm seems to be the only one that has entered popular usage (which is one of several reasons that Professor Kuhn no longer uses the term himself). What Kuhn is talking about, as he repeatedly says, is "normal science," so well accepted that experimenters who find results that contradict the paradigms of normal science blame themselves rather than "normal science."[19] For Kuhn, a paradigm is never an individual possession, but is constitutive of a group. No one doubts Huntington's enormous, perhaps unmatched, distinction among political scientists. But would even he, in the unlikely event that his modesty should fail him, claim that he has created a "normal" political science of international relations, in the face of which other political scientists discredit contrary examples?

A large number of international-relations specialists continue to argue vigorously that "Realism," the school of international relations that claims that states act largely to protect their interests and are the predominant players in world politics, explains more events than any other. Against this theory Huntington has fielded some interesting possible counterexamples. Kuhn believes most of the social sciences to be in the pre-paradigm stage, in which examples and counterexamples are adduced and competing

18 John Locke, *The Second Treatise of Government*, chapter 12, paragraph 145.

19 Margaret Masterman, "The Nature of a Paradigm," 59–89, and Thomas S. Kuhn, "Reflections on My Critics," 231–278, in Imre Lakatos and Alan Musgrave (eds.), *Criticism and the Growth of Knowledge*, Proceedings of the International Colloquium in the Philosophy of Science, London, 1965 (Cambridge, U.K., Cambridge University Press: 1970).

theories easily coexist. He writes: "In the physical sciences disagreement about fundamentals is, like the search for basic innovations, reserved for periods of chaos. It is, however, by no means equally clear that a consensus of anything like similar strength and scope ordinarily characterizes the social sciences." It is not clear that by Kuhn's standards either history or international relations will ever emerge from the pre-paradigm phase, but he offers historians like myself and other social scientists the wise advice: "As in individual development, so in the scientific group, maturity comes most surely to those who know how to wait."[20]

Yet does the "clash of civilizations" hypothesis actually offer us a "theory," in William James's sense of an "explanatory system?" It seems to me far more a description (and prescription) than an explanatory system. It offers a long list of things that the West is—the bearer of individualism, liberalism, democracy, free markets and the like—but, by and large, just tells us that the non-Western, in the great American language of the multiple-choice test, is "none of the above." There are a few tantalizing hints, as when Huntington says that the Western notion of universal civilization is "at odds with the particularism of most Asian societies and their emphasis on what distinguishes one people from another." But even if we were to grant that particularism is non-existent in the West or far weaker than in some unit transcivilizationally or geographically defined as "Asian," we are left with very little in the way of explanation as to why others act differently from the West, insofar as they do act differently. Huntington tells us that "civilizations are differentiated from each other by history, language, culture, tradition and, most important, religion." Is it, then, religion as a set of beliefs that determines social, economic, and political attitudes, and if so, are these beliefs really stable, determining the behavior of those who hold them, and clearly different from the list of beliefs Huntington ascribes to the West?

As an Islamicist, I believe that the result of our examination of the assumption about free markets given above could be multiplied many fold. Islam exists as a normative set of beliefs chiefly at the level of Islamic law, which, as I have said, is very largely in favor of free markets. But I would not *a priori* expect this normative legal system actually to influence social and governmental behavior. If I did, I would be led into a set of totally mistaken assumptions about the behavior of Muslim societies in various

20 Thomas S. Kuhn, *The Essential Tension* (Chicago: 1977) 221–222.

times and places, past and present. As an Islamicist, it seems to me that to assume a set of normative beliefs over a vast area, such as a Huntingtonian civilization, is an extraordinarily difficult task even for the Islamic world which supposedly had a normative system of law. This distinct variety among the cultures of Muslims was even true before the mid-nineteenth century, up to which time there was some limited uniformity in the training of legal experts in much of the Islamic world, a small but important "class" of bearers of this normative law. And, as a social historian, it seems to me an extraordinary assumption that, even if we were to identify a large and clear set of normative beliefs for one of these civilizations, that these beliefs should easily determine the behavior of those who formally ascribe to them.[21] As someone born into an American Christian milieu and a product of twelve happy years of Quaker education, in order for me to believe that Christians when abused are supposed to turn the other cheek, I must forget the example of almost all the Christians I have ever met.

If we set aside the problem of what beliefs shape a civilization and how they do so, we are still left with Huntington's definition of a civilization as the largest "identity"; the civilization is "the broadest level of identification with which he [i.e., one of its members] intensely identifies." If we disregard the question of intensity, this statement gives us a functional definition of civilization, and one that probably has more significance for Muslims than for most other groups identified by Huntington. But let us examine what this means for a specific people who are overwhelmingly Muslim: the Iranians. Why is one of the best known and most frequently quoted lines of Persian verse, "The sons of Adam are limbs of each other?" Is it possible that Iranians identify not only with Muslims but also, like the rest of us, with the human race? Over sixteen years [forty-six years in 2022] have passed since the "Islamic Revolution" [of 1978–79] in Iran; if you asked Iranians individually, "Who are you?" I would guess that the first answer would be, "an Iranian," their identity, therefore, of greatest intensity. I would also guess that the great majority of Iranians would agree that, after sixteen [forty-six] years of searching for an Islamic identity, the contents of such an identity (including the content of an Islamic foreign policy) is far less clear to them now than it has ever been.

---

21 One of the greatest anthropologists of our time, in comparing Morocco and Indonesia, discussed the extraordinary difficulty in identifying features of a society as Islamic; see Clifford Geertz, *Islam Observed* (New Haven: 1968).

Columbus died thinking that he had discovered the easternmost parts of Asia; his discovery is no less considerable for his mistake. Huntington has discussed the revival of identity politics, even if this identity is usually (though not always) felt "intensely" in units far smaller than his "civilizations." The social and economic revolutions of recent history have swept aside traditional elites in many parts of the world, and the revolution in communications and education has persuaded peoples all over the globe to assert themselves directly in a wider political world, and not through the intermediacy of elites. At first, many of these new political actors will form groups based on a variety of identities. In some cases such an identity will take its name from a religious group, as in Bosnia, where membership in the category "Muslim" has nothing to do with actual religious belief. (In Bosnia, many so-called Muslims are agnostics or atheists.) In other places, as in the Caucasus, identity seems overwhelmingly to correspond to language, so that a group such as the Ossetes, in majority Christian and in minority Muslim, nevertheless feel a strong ethnic identity and have, by and large, worked in concert. Overlapping identities are a feature of all societies and asking questions appropriate to these identities will yield different answers. Mexico, considered as a state that belongs to NAFTA [the North American Free Trade Agreement that was replaced in 2020 by the USMCA, the United States-Mexico-Canada Agreement], to Latin America, to the successor states of the Aztecs, to the Catholic world, and so on and so forth, will yield different explanations for its conduct in its international relations as each of those identities is considered; is it really evident that any of these identities has clear primacy for all major questions? Might not NAFTA, in some respects a weak identity, still be the central identity for a discussion of economic foreign policy?

Some identities are, indeed, transnational, and hence, to use Huntington's felicitous phrase, transnational "resonances" exist. They have some (though, more often than not, secondary) importance in explaining political behavior. Orthodox Russia feels a certain sympathy for Orthodox Serbia, Catholic Europe for Catholic Croatia, and the Muslim world for Muslim Bosnia, although invoking these three civilizational ties would lead us only a very limited way toward understanding outside reaction to the tragedy that unfolded in the former Yugoslavia [which, after years of civil war, dissolved into five successor states in 2001 and are now seven sovereign states]. Yet in Bosnia, where the United States proved the decisive outside actor, as in Northern Ireland and so many other places, these animosities based on identity seem only to flourish when they are cultivated by desperate leaders. Many observers believe that, without Milosevic's use of "Serbian" identity, Yugoslavia might well not have unraveled. Not the least contribution of Professor Huntington is that he has increased our ability to see that appeals by leaders to the defense of "cultural" values may be increasingly used by politicians (as seems to be the case in the United States). Politicians, like writers of panegyrics, tend to be maximizers, who use every claim possible to achieve some minimal credibility. Perhaps we are reentering a period in which claims that are in some loose sense "cultural" have become more frequent. Necessarily, such a contention is hard to quantify, but if demonstrated, it offers an important insight into contemporary politics.

It would, however, be a very great mistake to buy into the cultural claims of these desperate leaders and to construct policy on their claims. As for the policy recommendation that we should seek "to exploit differences and conflicts among Confucian and Islamic states," we hope that Professor Huntington is only thinking of the pan-Asiatic games. Some of us, perhaps including Professor Huntington, actually believe that the United States has higher interests than seeking the exploitation of harmful conflicts. If we were to discover a secret memorandum circulated among the Chinese leadership that claimed a policy interest in exploiting "differences and conflicts" between Catholics and Protestants in Northern Ireland, or between the races in the United States, we would want further explanation as to what was intended. Professor Huntington, whose intentions are surely benign, should not be surprised that this aspect of his recommendations for policy has aroused great suspicion in the parts of the world he characterizes as "Confucian" and "Islamic."

By early August 1990 Saddam Hussein's initial rationale for the invasion of Kuwait—that he had come at the invitation of a "Free Kuwaiti Interim Government"—had collapsed because no Kuwaiti collaborators could be found. On 10 August Saddam decided to play the "civilizational card," as Huntingtonian theory would have predicted, and [playing the pious Muslim] called for an Islamic "holy war" against "aggressive invaders" and their "collaborators." He based his call in part on the linkage he claimed to have established between his withdrawal from Kuwait and [the long-sought] Israeli withdrawal from the Occupied Territories. Saddam had a long record as a secularist who advocated the complete divorce of religion from politics, and he was nobody's model of a pious Muslim. Yet he found a certain, though decidedly limited (and ultimately ineffectual), response among Muslims to his call for a "holy war." It has taken one of our most perceptive political scientists to show us that, for some political leaders at the end of the twentieth century, civilizationism, and not nationalism, has become the last refuge of scoundrels.

It is, perhaps, appropriate in our conclusion to return to our two prophet-philosophers of history. Spengler believed that each culture has its unique "soul" and, hence, sought to define that soul; he also believed decline to be the result of the betrayal of that soul. (Strangely, in the German context he saw parliamentary democracy as the great betrayal.) Toynbee, like Spengler, was driven to his civilizational analysis by the shock of the First World War. But, unlike Spengler, who was a deep pessimist, Toynbee was optimistic about the coming of a successor civilization to the West. Toynbee, who struggled mightily—but not always successfully—to avoid ethnocentrism, believed that alien elements in the West such as "Negro rhythms" were evidence of its decline. (The spirit of jazz might have done a lot for Toynbee's impressive—but ultimately exhausting—stately prose style.) Since Toynbee saw many civilizations as emanating from religious and/or cultural bases, he had to classify the more ancient minority religions still living as "fossilized relics." These fossils of earlier civilizations included "the Monophysite Christians of Armenia, Mesopotamia, Egypt, and Abyssinia and the Nestorian Christians of Kurdistan and Malabar, as well as the Jews and Parsees," to which he subsequently added "the Lamaistic Mahayana Buddhists of Ceylon, Burma, and Siam, as well as the Jains in India."[22] This somewhat strange list (Are Armenians and Jews really so unlike the peoples surrounding them as to be described as "fossilized relics"?) shows that even an extremely learned would-be empiricist such as Toynbee could be led astray by a mania for order. Such manias, alas, have all too often led theorists like Toynbee to strain the evidence in order to discover lists of traits that "essentially" characterize the units they call "civilizations." (In this respect Toynbee came in the end to resemble Spengler, as a discoverer of the "souls" of civilizations, an approach which he claimed to dislike.)

Samuel Huntington has raised the challenge for us to define in a really empirical fashion large transnational cultural entities, to explain to what

22 A.J. Toynbee, *A Study of History*, I (Oxford, U.K.: 1934) 35.

degree their systems of belief affect their behavior, and to explain why various traits of these civilizations migrate, sometimes quickly, sometimes slowly, and sometimes not at all, between these entities. Only when this challenge has been met can there be any meaningful discussion on an academic level about the nature of the "West" and its relation with "the rest." But even if (as I very much doubt) it is empirically established that the "West" is a well-defined area that is the sole bearer of many beliefs, beliefs which will not for some time be adopted by other "civilizations," do we want to construct a policy of pessimism on this finding? If we were to discover growing racism in America, we would feel a sense of urgency to strive against it. Similarly, if there really is growing alienation between civilizations, we should not limit ourselves to an austere policy that only in passing mentions accommodation, when possible, to "alien" civilizations. My reading of the American tradition is that we should seek to create such possibilities even if, at first, they seem impossible. We are too great a people to do anything less.

POSTSCRIPT

Over twenty-five years have passed since I wrote this critique of Huntington's theory of the "Clash of Civilizations." Subsequent history has not been kind to Huntington's theory. His civilizational division of the world has produced few of the predicted alliances and hostilities. Morocco and some smaller Arab states have recognized Israel. The "bloody" borders of Islam in the former Yugoslavia have stopped bleeding. Most Islamic countries have even freer markets than they had twenty-five years ago. Pan-Islamic conferences have not been able to agree on much beside the value of Islamic belief. The examples I used to challenge Huntington's theory were valid twenty-five years ago and most are still valid today. More examples to challenge Huntington's theory are easily found.

The Islamic Foundation for Citizenship and Pluralism

Human diversity is an assumption of most people in most places. The reality of such diversity is handsomely and clearly stated in a famous and often quoted verse of the Qur'ān.

Verse 13 of Sūra XLIX reads:

> Oh men, We have created you from a male and a female, and We have made you into groups (*shuʿūb*) and tribes (*qabāʾil*) that you may come to know one another; truly, the noblest (*akram*) among you before God is the most righteous (*atqā*) among you; truly God is the All-knowing, the All-seeing.

I have deliberately chosen the colorless translation "groups" for *shuʿūb*, singular *shaʿb*, to avoid prejudicing the interpretations of commentators. This verse was a point of reference for a celebrated controversy among Muslims from the 3rd/9th century to the 5th/11th century. A group of Muslims calling themselves (after the word in the verse) *shuʿūbī*s claimed that the verse advocated equality among Muslims. As Ibn ʿAbd al-Rabbih (d. 328/940), a highly talented Andalusī scholar, tells us, the *shuʿūbī*s asserted:

> The believers are brothers, whose lives are equal in value before the law (*tatakāfaʾu dimāʾuhum*) ... As [Muḥammad] said in the farewell pilgrimage in the speech in which he bade farewell to his

---

Author's note: This article was first published as: "The Islamic Foundation for Citizenship and Pluralism," in *Kufa Review* 7 (2014) 9–15, International Academic Journal Sponsored by the University of Kufa, Iraq (Dar attanweer: 2014). Reproduced with permission. Some important examples of Islamic toleration cited in this article are also cited elsewhere in my discussions of toleration.

> community and with which he set a seal on his prophecy: "O man, God has removed from you the baseless pride of the period of ignorance (*nakhwat al-jāhilīya*) and its glorying in ancestors. You are all from Adam, and Adam was from the dust. The Arab has no superiority to the non-Arab (*'ajamī*) except by virtue of righteousness (*taqwā*)." These words of the Prophet [add the *shu'ūbīs*] are in agreement with the words of God: "Truly the noblest among you before God is the most righteous."[1]

The *shu'ūbīs* tended to be of Persian or Iberian (i.e., Andalusī) descent, although anti-*shu'ūbīs* also include many scholars of Persian descent such as Ibn Qutaybạ (d. 276/889), one of the greatest figures in classical Arabic literature. While the *shu'ūbīya* controversy died out in the 6th/12th century, it was tragically resurrected in a most unbecoming way by the otherwise excellent Iraqi historian 'Abd al-'Aziz al-Duri in the twentieth century. Duri stated that the *shu'ubīya* represented "a literary, cultural, historical, linguistic and religious attack" on Sunni Arab society that has reappeared throughout history.[2]

The reactions to this verse show that ethnicity and religious difference are issues that often become confused. Two cases of the confusion of religion and ethnic identity are offered by [the civil wars in] Bosnia [in 1992–1995] and in Sri Lanka [1983–2009, where hostilities have continued to this day.] This confusion is well illustrated by the remarks of a Serbian mayor who, forgetting that Bosnians are southern Slavs like himself, said that Bosnian Muslims should go back to Turkey from where they came.[3]

In some understandings of ethnicity, the shadow of racism can also be clearly seen. Community is created by the sense of social solidarity, the *'aṣabīya* that Ibn Khaldūn so well described as the basis of social organization. "Race" is also a social construct. The Qur'ān regards social solidarity

1 I discuss the commentaries on this verse extensively in my article "The *Shu'ūbīyah* Controversy and the Social History of Early Islamic Iran" (Article 9 here). The passage from Ibn 'Abd Rabbih is from *al-'Iqd al-Farīd* ed. 'Abd al-Majid al-Rahini, III (Beirut, Dār al-Kutub al-'Ilmīya: 1983, 3rd printing, 1987) 356. This speech of the Prophet is quoted in commentaries and in ḥadīth books in slightly variant forms, some of which include quotation of Qur'ān XLIX:13.

2 See Eric Davis, *Memories of State* (Berkeley: 2005) 131, who quotes 'Abd al-'Aziz al-Duri, *al-Judhūr al-Ta'rīkhīya li-l-Shu'ūbīya* (Beirut: 1980).

3 See my "Foreword," in Mark Pinson (ed.), *The Muslims of Bosnia-Herzegovina: Their Historic Development from the Middle Ages to the Dissolution of Yugoslavia* (Cambridge, MA, Harvard University Press: 1994) vii–viii.

to be a natural aspect of society yet ranks individual piety ahead of any affiliation of group or tribe.

I see the verse about groups and tribes as promoting a concept of citizenship in which people, while dividing themselves into religious or language or lineage groups, believe that everyone (that is, every citizen) has an equal right to strive for virtue and that righteous acts may come from individuals of any group.

Such equality in citizenship can also draw strong support from the Qur'ānic concept of *fiṭra*, which can be translated as "innate pattern" meaning the inborn pattern of religiosity that God has created in every person. In Sūrat al-Rūm, verse 30 reads:

> So set your face towards religion as (or "supporting") a true monotheist (*ḥanīfan*), according to the innate pattern on the basis of which He created people. There is no exchange for what God's creation has ordained, which is the upright religion. Yet most of mankind do not know it.

This verse makes clear that we are talking about the inborn pattern of goodness and right belief. Many of the commentators explain *fiṭra* as "Islam" and certainly in the large sense of Islam, the virtuous and Godly religion that existed for Adam and his descendants, this explanation is correct.[4]

According to the classical Arabic dictionaries *fiṭra* is "the natural constitution with which a child is created in his mother's womb."[5] A famous ḥadīth is often associated with this verse. It reads: "Every child is born according to his natural constitution (*fiṭra*), and it is his parents who make him a Jew or a Christian or a Zoroastrian."[6] In my view these scriptural sources are very close to the concept of "natural religion." It is implied that this kind of "natural religion" is Islam in its widest sense, meant to include all those who, like Adam, understand the oneness of creation.

---

4 The importance of this verse (XXX:30) for an ethic is argued for persuasively in the last chapter of Murtada Mutahhari's *al-'Adl al-Ilahī* in Arabic (Qom: 1405 A.H.); Mutahhari's book is also available in Persian, *'Adl-e Ilāhi*, and in English, *Divine Justice* (Qom: 2004).

5 Ibn Manẓūr, *Lisān al-'Arab*, V (Beirut: 1990) 56–58.

6 This famous ḥadith is quoted in slightly variant forms in many books of ḥadīth as well as in numerous other sources. The version quoted here is from Shaykh Muḥammad ibn al-Ḥasan al-Ṭūsī, *al-Tibyān* under the commentary on verse XXX:30.

The very perceptive Shi'ite Fayḍ al-Kāshānī (d. 1090/1679) says in agreement with many others that the innate pattern of each human is the recognition of the unity of God (*tawḥīd*) and quotes Imām Muḥammad Bāqir, the fifth Shi'ite Imām, as saying that: "Their innate pattern is based on recognition of Him (*al-ma'rifa bihi*)." He also quotes Imām Bāqir as saying that this recognition is based on the primal covenant between God and mankind when God asked all potential humans, "Am I not your Lord?" and was answered, "But yes!"[7]

'Allama Tabataba'i the great twentieth-century commentator on the Qur'ān interprets the verse even closer to a universal vision of the innate goodness of men. He understands *ḥanīf* to refer to "the inclination of the ancients to the golden mean, that is to say, to balance (*al-i'tidāl*)." As for *fiṭra*, he explains that this innate religion is "nothing less than the customary behavior (*sunna*) of life and the path that a person must follow so that he attains felicity in life."[8]

The highly respected and deeply thoughtful Ayatollah Murtada Mutahhari (d. 1979) discussed this verse:

> Inherent in every being who has deviated from its original path there is a propensity toward returning to its primordial state. In philosophical terms, in every nature that suffers from an impediment there exists an inclination to revert to its original state, i.e., there always exists in the universe a force to escape from disequilibrium and move toward health and equilibrium.[9]

Mutahhari rightly sees in this religious principle an argument to give mercy precedence over anger and to forgive rather than to pursue people for their shortcomings.

To my mind the concept of *fiṭra* is a strong argument for toleration and pluralism. Do we encourage people's better natures to emerge by beating them or, rather, by encouraging them? I believe that society will only get sincere expressions of our inborn better natures by encouragement. This sentiment fits in with the idea that regardless of tribe or group we should

7 Fayḍ Kāshānī, *al-Ṣāfī*, accessed under altafsir.com on 6/23/2014.
8 Muhammad Husayn Tabataba'i, *Tafsīr al-Mīzān*, accessed under altafsir.com on 6/23/2014.
9 Mutahhari, *al-'Adl al-Ilāhī*, p. 249.

recognize that God respects piety and virtue over other characteristics, such as belonging to a specific group.

Another clear call to toleration comes from the many verses of the Qur'ān which say that no one foretells the judgment of God. Verse 9 of Sūra XLVI reads: "Say, I am not a novelty among the Messengers [of God] and I do not know what will be done with me or with them." As the Prophet is assured of his salvation in other verses, why was this verse revealed? As Mutahhari suggests, it is to warn us that no person no matter how sanctified can assume to know what God will do with us after Judgment. No believer questions the salvation of the Prophet, but the rhetoric of this verse strongly reinforces the view that humans cannot know the mind of God and be certain of anyone else's salvation or damnation.[10]

Then how are we in a position to punish people in this world as a prelude to God's as yet unknown decision as to how they should be punished in the next world? Moreover, the Qur'ān (XVII:20) says God's bounty will extend to all groups: "Each we assist out of the bounty of our Lord, both this group and that one, and the bounty of your Lord is not restricted."

To some extent the actual historical experience of Muslim communities through many centuries reflects the admirable ethic of pluralism. As is well known, the moon-worshippers of Ḥarrān in northern Mesopotamia preserved their religion in the early 2nd/8th century by claiming to be Sabeans, the monotheists of southern Arabia mentioned in the Qur'ān.[11] When Muslim armies conquered Sind, then a largely Hindu province of India in 92/711, the general in charge declared the Hindus to be a "People of the Book," a decision that has by and large been respected ever since.[12] The toleration of Jews and Christians in Muslim lands in the pre-modern period stands in considerable contrast to the predominant attitude toward non-Christians in Christian Europe of that period. At the same time no serious historian would deny that there have been and continue to be unfortunate episodes of intolerance in the historical record on all sides.

An outstanding example of tolerance, however, is offered by the Shi'ite Imām Ja'far al-Ṣādiq (d. 148/765). According to a well-known account, a Shi'ite began to upbraid a famous *zindīq* or heretic, Ibn Abī al-'Awjā',

10 Mutahhari, *al-'Adl al-Ilāhī*, p. 265.

11 Ibn al-Nadīm, *The Fihrist of al-Nadīm: A Tenth-Century Survey of Islamic Culture* II, trans. Bayard Dodge (New York: 1970) 751–753.

12 Y. Friedmann, "Muḥammad b. al-Ḳāsim," *The Encyclopaedia of Islam*, 2nd ed., VII (Leiden: 1991) 405–406.

for his disbelief. Ibn Abī al-ʿAwjā' protested that he did not deserve such treatment because Imām Jaʿfar allowed him to come to the Kaʿba of Mecca and dispute religious questions with the Imām himself.[13] Perhaps Imām Jaʿfar believed that one's faith could be strengthened through peaceful disputation.

Even in the worst period of Sunni–Shiʿite sectarianism there were signs of the desires of leaders to rise above such intolerance. In 403/1012–13 the Sunni Abbasid caliph granted the traditional black cloak of honor to the very great Shiʿite poet, al-Sharīf al-Raḍī, when the latter was appointed *naqīb al-ṭālibīyīn.* He was the first Ṭālibī, or descendant of ʿAlī ibn Abī Ṭālib, to wear the Abbasid black cloak. Although he and his brother, Sharīf al-Murtaḍā, were among the most prominent Shiʿite scholars of their day, they were both accepted (and were pleased to go) quite frequently to the palace of the Sunni, and indeed rather Ḥanbalī caliph, al-Qādir bi-llāh.[14] In the same setting, with the same caliph and his successors, the very distinguished Sunni jurist al-Māwardī often acted willingly as an intermediary to resolve differences between the Shiʿite Buyids and the Sunni Abbasid caliphs.

A striking case of cooperation between Sunnis and Shiʿites occurred in 442/1050–51. An extremely harsh police chief, Abū Muḥammad al-Nasawī caused the Sunni and Shiʿite toughs to unite against this man. So great was the fellow feeling of the two groups that Shiʿite muezzins in the Karkh neighborhood of Baghdad gave the Sunni call to prayer while the Sunnis of Bāb al-Baṣra gave the Shiʿite version with its characteristic: "Come to the best of deeds."[15]

A new imperative for pluralism and toleration exists for Muslims in the modern world. There are now Muslim minorities in many countries throughout the world. Indeed, the second (or perhaps third) largest Muslim community is in India, a predominantly Hindu country. The 175 million [209 million in 2021] Muslims of India are approximately ten percent of the Muslims in the world. If Muslim minorities very rightly ask for toleration in predominantly non-Muslim countries (and in some places receive toleration or at least protection in the law), do not predominantly Muslim communities owe similar toleration and protection to non-Muslims in

13 See "Ibn Abī al-ʿAwjā'," *Dā'erat al-Maʿāref-e Bozorg-e Eslāmi*, II (Tehran: 1368) 688–690.

14 Ibn al-Jawzī, *Muntaẓam*, VII (Haydarābād: 1358) 260.

15 Ibn al-Jawzī, *Muntaẓam*, VIII (Haydarābād: 1359) 145.

nations that are largely Muslim? Religious conflict is not only contrary to the spirit of the Qur'ān's verses quoted above, but it is also contrary to the interest of Muslim majorities because they can only build powerful and prosperous nations through concepts of cooperation and equality based on the friendship between members of the seventy odd versions of Islam as well as the other varieties of religion.

In the sixteenth and seventeenth centuries Europe was dominated by wars of religion, mainly between Catholics and Protestants. Estimates of the loss of population from this intra-Christian war in the German-speaking regions alone go from 25 to 40 percent of the population. After this horrible experience most Europeans realized that the cost of such opposition to pluralism was the destruction of their communities and their economies. In the late seventeenth century philosophers of tolerance such as John Locke began to put forth powerful arguments for pluralism.

God forbid that the Islamic Middle East or any part of the modern world goes through an experience as bad as the European Wars of Religion. As concerned advocates for religious pluralism seek everywhere, in the face of the horrors of intolerance and the problems of exclusivity, to strengthen the ethic of pluralism, they are able to find important support in the Islamic tradition as well as in Islamic history. We will always be tribes and peoples but let us compete in honoring the virtuous whose deeds will not be lost.

REMEMBERING THE PRE-ISLAMIC PAST

The past has importance for the present, not least of which is to remind us of the evanescence of all worldly things. Surrounded by the ruins of impressive monuments from the past like Persepolis as well as ancient Greek and Roman sites, medieval Muslims were naturally interested in their past, particularly the pre-Islamic past of the Middle East.

Continuity in the history of Western Asia is an important concern for historians of the Islamic Middle East. For example, so much of the land tax system used by Muslims was inherited from earlier empires in this region, such as the Byzantine and the Sasanian empires. The rivalry between Egypt and states centered in the Fertile Crescent or Iran reappears again and again in the history of the Middle East. The translation of ancient Greek science and philosophy into Arabic had a great intellectual impact on the Muslim world. Zoroastrian, Christian, and Jewish ideas of heaven and hell have echoes in the Islamic tradition. The Qur'ān accepts some of the Old Testament and New Testament figures as prophets, and a considerable literature on the lives of prophets was written by Muslim authors which includes Abraham, Noah, Moses, David, Solomon, Jesus, etc. Some festivals and practices in pre-Islamic societies also survived into the Islamic world, often re-explained, such as the Persian New Year called Nowruz. Often new legends associating ancient practices with Islam were created by Muslims in an effort to sanitize the pre-Islamic practices. Interpretation of ruins from the past with great figures was also common. Islamic rulers wanted to associate themselves with ancient traditions of kingship, particularly in the eastern Islamic world, in order to make their rule legitimate.

Much more scholarship remains to be done on the subject of continuity in the history of the Middle East. Muslim historians have received a fair amount of attention in modern times. The extremely learned and kindly professor of Islamic studies at Yale, Franz Rosenthal, wrote on historiography as did the very insightful Iraqi professor Abd al-Aziz al-Duri. As more and more primary sources by Muslim authors are published, a more rounded picture of their understanding of their pre-Islamic history will be revealed. Qur'ān commentaries are another possible source for such study.

The first article in this section, "Some Islamic Views of the Pre-Islamic Past," was published in 1994 in the *Harvard Middle Eastern and Islamic Review*. The subject of the pre-Islamic past, the period before Muḥammad, is vast. Medieval Muslims had a little knowledge of Greek and Byzantine history, some knowledge of Biblical history, and a somewhat fantastic knowledge of the pre-Sasanian history of Persia. This article only considers a few prominent pre-modern Muslim historians such as the great Ṭabarī and the less well-known Ṣā'id al-Andalusī, who discuss the pre-Islamic past. The Muslim historians of the Middle East inherited different and often contradictory accounts of the ancient world from the Greek, Syriac, and Persian traditions. They tried to connect these accounts with their own history using comparative chronology. Therefore, some Muslim historians identified the Greek poet and pre-Socratic philosopher Empedocles as living in the time of King David although modern scholars date them half a millennium apart. The emphasis among pre-modern Muslim historians on writing universal histories from Adam to their time resulted in many interesting speculations, such as: was Socrates a prophet? Similarly, the correlation of Biblical history with ancient Mediterranean history was a preoccupation of Europeans from the Renaissance through the seventeenth century. Some of this correlation was done by identifying figures from different traditions just as the Iranian Islamic tradition identified Jamshid with Solomon. Both were culture heroes.

The second article in this section, "The Eastern Travels of Solomon: Reimagining Persepolis and the Iranian Past," was published in 2012 in *Law and Tradition in Classical Islamic Thought: Studies in Honour of Professor Hossein Modarressi*, edited by Michael Cook, Najem Haider, Intisar Rabb, and Asma Sayeed. This article was written for my close friend Hossein Modarressi of Princeton University, who has taught me so very much over our more than four-decade-long friendship and shared interest in the history of the Islamic Middle East. It examines the role of Solomon in the Islamic tradition, using literature and history to trace his works and track his travels throughout the Muslim world. Solomon, already such an important prophet-king in the Bible, became even more important in the Islamic tradition. He owes this prominence to being one of the four universal kings according to medieval Muslim historians. Two of these kings were bad, and the other two were righteous rulers, one of whom was Solomon. Thanks to Solomon's control of the amazing creatures called *jinn*, he could construct colossal palaces and buildings and travel a month's journey in a morning or an afternoon. Therefore, Muslim historians attributed imposing ruins like Persepolis to Solomon. Echoes of his greatness make their way into folk literature of the Muslim world, such as *The Thousand and One Nights*.

The third article in this section, "The Idea of Iran in the Buyid Dominions," was delivered in 2010 at a symposium on "The Idea of Iran" held in London, and subsequently published in 2012 in *Early Islamic Iran: The Idea of Iran*, 5, edited by Edmund Herzig and Sarah Steward. The ancient Persian designation of Iran (which also included southern Iraq) lived on into the Islamic period. One of the world's best Iranologists, the distinguished Austrian scholar Bert Fragner (d. 2021), has written that the concept of Iran only fully revived in the Ilkhanid period of the 7th/13th and 8th/14th centuries. The question remains how much revival constitutes a new consciousness of Iran. Certainly, under the Ilkhanids a territorial government more or less congruent with pre-Islamic ideas of Iran came into being. Nevertheless, the consciousness of Iran as a coherent region existed to some degree in earlier Islamic periods. The kings of the Buyid dynasty of the 4th/10th and 5th/11th centuries certainly subscribed to their own descent from ancient Iranian kings and fostered an Arabic literature that recognized the idea of Iran. The preservation of Arabic as the language of administration and panegyric in western Iran (as contrasted with eastern Iran) is due to several factors. The language of New Persian first appeared in eastern Iran in part due to the more rapid disappearance of Zoroastrianism and other pre-Islamic religions such as Buddhism in the East, whereas Zoroastrians remained more present in the West, especially in Fars province around Persepolis. Therefore, some form of Iranian identity survived in western Iran (and, in part, in southern Iraq), which expressed itself in royal titles, royal regalia, and royal genealogy. For this reason, the great Russian Iranologist V.V. Minorsky (d. 1966) characterized this area in the tenth and early eleventh centuries as the "Iranian intermezzo," which very much includes the Buyids.

Some Islamic Views of the Pre-Islamic Past

This paper examines the view of the pre-Islamic past held by some writers in the Islamic world in the tenth and eleventh centuries C.E.; it should be emphasized that I do not believe that there is such a thing as a reified Islam or an archetypal Islamic view of the past. Moreover, it is not my object to determine how much the inhabitants of the Islamic world in this period knew about the past, or how accurate or inaccurate that information was. Many scholarly studies have already been devoted to this topic. Instead, I will discuss certain attitudes or points of view that influenced these authors in their approach to the pre-Islamic past.[1]

Although it would be incorrect to speak of an archetypal Islamic view of the past, nevertheless there are passages in the Qur'ān which point towards a theory of history. Since Muslim historians elaborated on this theory of history, and since virtually all Muslim historians used Qur'ānic proof texts, it is to the Qur'ān that we should turn first if we are going to understand the discussions of later Muslim historians.

The theory of history partially elaborated in the Qur'ān during the period 610 to 632—the dates traditionally held by Muslims to encompass its revelation to the Prophet Muḥammad—holds that there never has been a community that did not ultimately owe its origin to a prophet. One classic proof text for this assertion is a verse of the Qur'ān (XXXV:24)

Author's Note: This article was first published as: "Some Islamic Views of the Pre-Islamic Past," in *Harvard Middle Eastern and Islamic Review* 1:1 (1994) 17–26. Reproduced with permission.

1 This paper was first delivered at a conference on "Heritage and Memory" held July 8–11, 1991, at the Humanities Research Centre of the Australian National University. I am happy to have an opportunity to express my deep appreciation for the generosity and hospitality shown me by the Centre and its members, in particular Professor Ann Curthoys, the Convenor, and Professor Graeme Clarke, the Director.

that states: "In truth we have sent you [Muḥammad] as a bearer of glad tidings and as a warner; and there never has been a community (*umma*) that did not have a warner." Another is the verse (X:47) which states: "To every people (*umma*) [was sent] a Messenger (*rasūl*)." The Qur'ān makes this scheme especially clear in its treatment of Abrahamic religion with its many branches, the most significant, other than Judaism, being Christianity and Islam, each founded by a prophet whose revelation and example were held to have created a community.

As Muslims came into contact with increasing numbers of communities, this theory was elaborated to explain the large number of religions and communities in the world. For example, in *The Book of Creation and History*, generally attributed to Muṭahhar ibn Ṭāhir al-Maqdisī, which was written in Sistan in eastern Iran in 355/966, the author tells us that, according to the tradition of the Muslims, there have been one hundred and eighty thousand prophets (*nabī*), among whom three hundred and thirteen were Messengers (*mursal*), that is, bearers of revelation, although it has been said that the Messengers numbered only fifteen.[2] By necessity, within this scheme, Adam, founder of the first human community, must be a prophet; and al-Maqdisī even reports a tradition that God gave him a scripture of twenty-one folios which included interdictions against eating blood and pork.[3]

Yet some prophets have been ignored, and all revelation and scripture before the Qur'ān have been subject to the corruption wrought by time. Therefore, the basis of community has been weakened, and some communities, given a chance to renew themselves morally by a warner-prophet, have rejected the opportunity. Here a Qur'ānic proof text that would come to the minds of many Muslims is III:137: "Many were the ways of life (*sunan*) that passed away before you: travel through the earth and see what was the end of those who reject truth." Commentators see this verse as a positive injunction to study the history of communities that precede Islam, at least insofar as moral lessons were to be derived from their example. Thus, the commentator al-Ṭūsī, who died in 460/1067,

2 *Le livre de la création et de l'histoire de Moṭahhar ben Ṭāhir el-Maqdisī: attribué à Abou-Zéïd Aḥmed ben Sahl el-Balkhī publié et traduît d'après le manuscrit de Constantinople*, trans. Clément Huart, III (Paris: 1903) 1. Cf. *Kitāb al-Bad' wa-l-Ta'rīkh*, ed. Clément Huart (Paris, Leroux: 1918); the editor identifies the author as Aḥmad ibn Sahl al-Balkhī, who wrote under the authority of the Sāmānid official Ibn Muṭahhar al-Maqdisī.
3 *Le livre de la création*, III:2.

glosses the end of this verse as follows: "So God orders that they travel the earth and become acquainted with accounts of them and what befell them in order that they may take warning from that, and avoid doing what they have done."[4]

The explanation of the decay of earlier communities is built into an anthropology of empires, which finds further support in the Qur'ān. Just three verses after the order to travel through the earth, a clause in a verse (III:140) tells us: "Such days [of varying fortunes] we cause to pass by turns (*nudāwilu*) among men." Here the thrust of the verse is that misfortune strikes even the righteous and tests them. But a belief that religions, communities, and ruling families had divinely allotted turns of pre-eminence became strongly rooted in the historical thinking of the classical Islamic tradition and *dawla*, the divinely allotted term in power, came to mean "dynasty" in pre-modern Arabic and to mean "state" in modern Arabic.[5]

Notice the extreme linearity of a scheme which begins with the prophet Adam and in which all communities are built on a prophetic tradition that is ultimately derived from Adam. This linearity made many classical Islamic historians what we would call diffusionist: they believed that things are only discovered or invented one time and diffused from that early source. Hence, we find in classical Arabic literature a fair number of lists of "firsts," and even books of "firsts," the first person to have held a view or invented a technique and the like.[6]

Another result of this quasi-genealogical linearity with its pattern of prophetic archetypes was to regard as prophets those founders and principal figures of important traditions of the pre-Islamic past accepted by the Islamic world. Greek philosophy, as received from late antique sources, seemed to some Muslims an intellectually coherent and highly valuable tradition, hence these Muslims held that Socrates and Aristotle were prophets, or at least were considered to be prophets by the "ancients."

Correspondingly, Islamic features were retrojected to earlier, supposedly prophetic traditions. Socrates was not only a prophet, but he was also—according to one source—a bringer of "religious laws" (*sharā'i'*).[7] Similarly, the Spanish Arabic "anthropologist" of cultures, Ṣā'id al-Andalusī,

4 Abū Ja'far Muḥammad ibn al-Ḥasan al-Ṭūsī, *Tafsīr al-Tibyān*, III (Najaf: 1957) 597.
5 Franz Rosenthal, "Dawla," *The Encyclopaedia of Islam*, 2nd ed. (hereafter *EI²*), II (Leiden, Brill: 1965) 177–178.
6 Franz Rosenthal, "Awā'il," *EI²*, I (Leiden, Brill: 1960) 758–759.
7 See Ilai Alon, *Socrates in Medieval Arabic Literature* (Leiden: 1991) 88.

who died in 462/1070 in his fascinating book entitled *The Succeeding Generations of Peoples* (*Ṭabaqāt al-Umam*), discusses the attitude of the major Greek thinkers toward the relation between the Divine Being and its attributes, a problem as central to Islamic theology as is the relation of the persons of the Trinity to Christian theology.[8]

One consequence of this linear and quasi-genealogical approach to the pre-Islamic past was a great interest in comparative chronology. The Islamic world had inherited separate chronologies for the sages of the Greeks, the prophets of the Jews, and the kings of the pre-Islamic empires, especially of the Iranian empires; which of these sages, prophets and kings were contemporaneous with each other?

The problems posed by comparative chronology and the assumed filiation of all traditions were "solved" in a variety of ways. Sometimes an actual genealogical connection was forged, as when al-Mas'ūdī, an historian of the central Islamic world who died in 345/956, tells us that the Greeks were descendants of Shem, the son of Noah and ancestor of the Semites.[9] Another technique was to create a quasi-genealogical filiation that connected all known thinkers of the past in chains of teachers and students. Thus, Ṣā'id al-Andalusī says that Empedocles lived at the time of King David and, before going to Greece, studied philosophy in Syria with Luqmān.[10] Luqmān, mentioned in the Qur'ān as a sage who uttered many aphorisms, became in the first few Islamic centuries a many-sided figure around whom material of a wide variety gathered, including an Arabic translation of a selection of Aesop.[11] Ṣā'id al-Andalusī also tells us that Pythagoras studied philosophy with Solomon and that Socrates was one of the pupils of Pythagoras. Thus, this Muslim writer believed he had satisfactorily worked out the comparative chronology and interaction of the Greek and Jewish traditions.[12]

Yet another technique for working out problems of comparative chronology was identification, not the unconscious identification which ascribed the writings of Aesop to Luqmān, but conscious identification of figures with different names. For example, the Qur'ān mentions Idrīs as a

8 Al-Andalusī, *Kitâb ṭabaḳât al-umam; où, livre des catégories des nations*, trans. Régis Blachère (Paris: 1935) 59 and 61.

9 Maçoudi, *Le livre de l'avertissement*, trans. B. Carra de Vaux (Paris: 1896) 162.

10 Al-Andalusī, (*supra* n. 8), 58–59.

11 B. Heller and N.A. Stillman, "Luḳmān," *EI²*, V (Leiden, Brill: 1983) 811–813.

12 Al-Andalusī, (*supra* n. 8), 60.

prophet but gives no information about him except that he was upright, patient, and "was raised to a high place" (XIX:57). Since the Biblical prophet Enoch was a pious man who was taken by God (Gen. V:24) the Islamic tradition is virtually unanimous in attributing to him certain aspects of the story of Enoch, such as a terrestrial life of three hundred and sixty-five years. It also identifies him with the cook of Alexander, a figure mentioned (though not named) in the Qur'ān, who—according to late antique sources—achieved some sort of immortality as did Enoch in the Jewish tradition. A further identification of Idrīs with Hermes Trismegistes allowed Idrīs not only to be a culture hero in practical matters—among other things he was the first person to sew and wear clothes instead of wearing skins—but also in semi-scientific and occult matters related to the Hermetic tradition.[13] Al-Maqdisī, in an attempt to complete the comparative chronology of Idrīs, says that the claim of the Persians that Hūshang, one of their earliest kings and culture heroes, was the first person to invent clothes, proves that Hūshang lived before or in the time of Idrīs.[14] Why al-Maqdisī should give precedence to a Persian over a Biblical and Qur'ānic cultural hero I do not fully understand.

Incidentally, extraordinarily careful attempts to work out the chronology of these peoples were occasionally made, although the general level of educated speculation seems to have been at the level of al-Maqdisī's assertion that Idrīs lived in the time of Hūshang. Outstanding among such serious specialists on ancient chronology was al-Bīrūnī, one of the truly luminous minds of the pre-modern Islamic tradition of the Middle East. For example, in his book, *The Vestiges of the Past*, written in 390/1000, he takes on the vexed problem of the chronology of the Parthian or Arsacid kings who ruled Iran and surrounding areas for most of the period between Alexander and the rise of the Sasanian dynasty in the early third century C.E. After giving several dramatically different king lists (with lengths of individual reigns), al-Bīrūnī is able to limit the maximum length of the reign of the Parthian dynasty as a whole because he knows approximately when the Sasanian dynasty began in the era which starts with Alexander. Moreover, he realizes that other successor states ruled Mesopotamia before it fell under the sway of the Parthians. He finally comes up with an amazingly accurate figure for the length of Parthian rule.

13 G. Vajda, "Idrīs," *EI*², III (Leiden, Brill: 1971) 1030–1031.
14 *Le livre de la création*, (*supra* n. 2), 15.

Surprisingly, as confirmation for this estimate Bīrūnī cites a book ascribed to the dualist Mani, who was as overwhelmingly disapproved of in the Islamic tradition as he was in the Christian tradition. His reasons for doing so are very interesting. Bīrūnī writes: "[Of] all Persian books, [Mani's *Shaburkan*] is one that may be relied upon [as a witness] for the time immediately following the rise of Ardashīr. Besides, Mani in his law has forbidden telling lies, and he has no need whatsoever to falsify history." The first and third reason—that Mani lived relatively soon after the end of Parthian rule, and that he had no motive for changing their chronology—would appeal to a modern historian.[15] The second, that Mani was (at least in al-Bīrūnī's view) a scrupulous transmitter of information, is an argument that would have some weight with a modern historian but had far greater weight with a pre-modern Muslim historian for whom the veracity of transmitters is often the central issue in determining the historicity of any account. This view of the past as something most authentically recovered through a chain of reliable transmitters—called in Arabic an *isnād*, literally, "a propping up"—is fundamental to the science by which Muslims derive much of their law and theology. Incidentally, al-Bīrūnī's careful reconstruction of the length of Parthian rule is forgotten by the overwhelming majority of later pre-modern Islamic historians. Just a generation after al-Bīrūnī the author of the Persian national epic cavalierly reduces their reign to two hundred years."[16]

The "chain" extending into the past is in fact fundamental to many of the approaches described above. The genealogy, the chain of prophets, the consequent quasi-genealogical anthropology of communities and, especially, of empires, the chains of teachers, the chain of transmitters of inventions and discoveries from culture heroes, and the chain of transmitters of historical accounts were all ways of viewing history that supported each other.

They also strongly supported the social map of the Islamic world as it appears in many writers of the 4th/10th and 5th/11th centuries. In this society, many institutions were understood vertically; that is, people often saw themselves not so much linked with their contemporaries as common members of a religious school of thought or profession as they saw themselves linked vertically as common descendants of teachers and

15 Al-Bīrūnī, *The Chronology of Ancient Nations*, trans. C.E. Sachau (London: 1879) 121.

16 Firdausi, *Shāhnāma*, ed. A. Bertels *et al.*, VII (Moscow: 1968) 116.

transmitters. This vertical view of institutionalization could extend to even quite humble occupations; thus, tailors regarded the prophet Idrīs as the founder of their profession, with whom they were ultimately linked through traditions of apprenticeship.[17]

Not only was the pre-Islamic past the key to the social map of the present, it was also the essential prolegomenon to the last overall chapter in the moral history of mankind. In a famous clause in the third verse of the fifth chapter of the Qur'ān, God tells mankind, "This day have I perfected your religion for you, completed my favor to you and have chosen Islam as your religion." Not surprisingly, Muslims believe this verse to be the last revealed to Muḥammad. Yet this scheme of salvation or *Heilsgeschichte* did not exclude the falling of people away from religion after the coming of Islam; and the pre-Islamic past is the most important repository of moral warnings for people of the Islamic era. Verse 111, the concluding verse of the twelfth chapter of the Qur'ān, which is largely devoted to the story of the Prophet Joseph, says: "There is in the story [of the Messengers of God] an admonitory lesson (*'ibra*) for men endowed with understanding. It is not a tale invented, but a confirmation of what went before it and a detailed exposition of all things, and a guide and a mercy to any such as believe." It is altogether appropriate that the fourteenth-century Muslim philosopher of history, Ibn Khaldūn, whose work falls outside the scope of this paper, called his history *The Book of Admonitory Lessons*.[18]

As an extension of this view of history as a repository of moral lessons, the past became particularly important to literary works which emphasize the poignancy of the past. This view drew some strength from a retrojection of the very idea that Muḥammad had by the end of his life brought the most perfect revelation that mankind would ever know, as we have seen in the verse quoted above. Similarly, Muḥammad was held to have created the perfect Islamic community in his lifetime, and in the view of many Muslim thinkers later Islamic communities had almost necessarily to be morally deficient in comparison. Correspondingly, many Muslim thinkers—though not all—tried to point to an apogee for other human activities in the past, and very often, in the pre-Islamic past. Thus Ṣā'id al-Andalusī says that Ptolemy carried knowledge of the stars and celestial

17 Vajda, (*supra* n. 13), 1030.
18 See the brilliant discussion of *'ibra* in Muhsin Mahdi, *Ibn Khaldun's Philosophy of History* (London: 1957) 64–73.

secrets to perfection, as did Aristotle with the science of logic and Sībawayh (a figure of the Islamic period) with the science of grammar.[19]

The poignant past, with its lost moments of grandeur and its ruined physical monuments, often became a source of consolation to those who saw the present as itself corrupt, or at least filled with vicissitudes. Thus, the 3rd/9th-century Arab poet al-Buḥturī says that he went to Ctesiphon, the palace of the ancient kings of Iran:

> Consoling myself for what chances have come upon me, and grieving for a decayed abode of the House of Sasan.
> Successive vicissitudes reminded me of them—and vicissitudes are apt to make a man remember and forget—
> When they dwelt at ease in the shadow of a tall palace overlooking the surrounding land, wearying and weakening the eyes that gazed upon it.[20]

The very same monument, the palace of the Sasanian kings at Ctesiphon, is also used by the 5th/11th-century Persian poet Khāqānī to evoke the poignancy of the past. Khāqānī not only tells the mighty to look on and despair, not only does he find consolation in the thought that past grandeur has suffered vicissitudes as he must personally suffer vicissitudes, but he also finds in the ruined monument of the past a source of wonder at the infinite mutability of the physical and psychic world, a theme that will be familiar to many from the poetry of Omar Khayyam. Khāqānī writes:

> The earth's belly is eternally pregnant with them ...
> That wine which the vine gives is the blood of Shīrīn;
> The pitcher which the vintner sets out is made of the clay of [King] Parvīz.
> Although this earth has swallowed up many tyrants,
> This hungry one still has not been filled up by them.
> It makes rouge from the blood of children's hearts,
> This white-browed ancient, this black-dugged mother.
> O Khāqānī beg admonitory lessons (*'ibrāt*) from this court,
> So that afterward the emperor of China will beg at your door ...

19 Al-Andalusī, (*supra* n. 8), 73.
20 In A.J. Arberry, *Arabic Poetry: A Primer for Students* (Cambridge, U.K.: 1965) 74–75.

> Note well the secret he repeats throughout this poem:
> The dead man with a Christ-like heart, the madman with a wise soul.[21]

Of all its meanings for writers of this age, perhaps the pre-Islamic past was most significant as a locus of poignancy, for the consolation, the moral warning, and the amazement at the world's mutability which contemplation of that poignant past evoked.

21 Jerome W. Clinton, "The Madaen Qasida of Xaqani Sharvani, I," *Edebiyât* 1:2 (1976) 166–167.

The Eastern Travels of Solomon: Reimagining Persepolis and the Iranian Past

In the Muslim tradition few prophets traveled with the speed—and none in the grand style with his entire court—of King Solomon, who was not only a revered prophet but also a universal ruler. The very sober and conservative scholar Baghawī (d. 510/1117 or 516/1122) quotes one of the earliest Qur'ān commentators, Muqātil ibn Sulaymān (d. 153/770), who describes Solomon's mode of transportation as follows:

> The satans wove a carpet one *parasang* square for Solomon out of gold and silk, and they placed for him there in the middle of the carpet a pulpit of gold. Around it were three thousand seats of gold and silver, the prophets sitting on the seats of gold and the men of religious learning on the seats of silver, and around them were the *jinn* and satans. The birds with their wings gave Solomon shade so no sun fell upon him. The morning wind that blows from the East would raise the carpet so that it would travel a month's journey

Author's note: This article was first published as: "The Eastern Travels of Solomon: Reimagining Persepolis and the Iranian Past," in Michael Cook, Najam Haider, Intisar Rabb, and Asma Sayeed (eds.), *Law and Tradition in Classical Islamic Thought: Studies in Honour of Professor Hossein Modarressi* (New York, Palgrave Macmillan: 2013) 247–267. Reproduced with permission of Palgrave Macmillan.

I am sincerely grateful for bibliographic help from Professor Hossein Kamaly, for some wise emails from Professor David Stronach, for thoughtful advice from Professor Abbas Amanat on an early version, for advice on Middle Persian languages from Professor Daniel Sheffield, for invaluable advice in the archaeological literature from Professor Donald Whitcomb, and for deeply informed advice from Professor Sarah Savant, who completed a book on a similar theme after this article was published: Sarah Savant, *The New Muslims of Post-Conquest Iran* (Cambridge, U.K., and New York, Cambridge University Press: 2013).

> from the morning to the afternoon, and [an equal trip] from the afternoon to the morning.[1]

Other commentators insist that the flying carpet is actually a wooden platform and add details about Solomon's elaborate kitchens and stables. Such descriptions are to be found from the earliest to the early modern commentaries and are not the product of late traditions among Muslims.

In analyzing Solomonic stories in the Qur'ān it is important to remember what a remarkable figure Solomon cuts in that holy book. Verse twelve of Sūrat Saba' is most significant for Solomon the great traveler:

> And we made the wind [subservient] to Solomon, its morning stride was [the journey of] a month, and its afternoon stride was [the journey of] a month. (XXXIV:12)

Solomon's varied entourage as he traveled is determined in part by his command over creatures of all sorts. Verses 16 and 17 of Sūrat al-Naml read:

> Solomon was the heir of David. He said: "O mankind we have been taught the language of birds, and we have been given all things. This most surely is a manifest grace." His host of the *jinn*, humankind, and the birds were all drawn up in order. (XXVII:16–17)

The *jinn* are valuable skilled laborers whose capacity seems at times to exceed that of humans:

> They made for him what he pleased in the way of fortresses and images (*tamāthīl*) and basins as large as reservoirs and immoveable cauldrons. (XXXIV:13)

These qualities are manifested in Solomon's staunch support of Islamic monotheism. His letter to the Queen of Sheba, as quoted in the Qur'ān, begins:

> In the name of God, the Merciful, the Benevolent: Do not exalt yourself against me, but come to me as Muslims [or, "as ones submitting"]. (XIX:30–31)

1 Baghawī, *Ma'ālim al-Tanzīl* (Riyadh, Dār al-Ṭiba: 1993) commentary on XXI:81. A *parasang* is about three miles. Satans are a subcategory of *jinn*, the alternate creation to mankind and, like humans, subject to judgment of heaven or hell.

In light of Solomon's ability to command great building works, to make images, and to travel in half a day the distance of a month's journey by ordinary means, it is no surprise that many impressive pre-Islamic sites are ascribed to him by Muslims in pre-modern times.

Equally early and persistent in Qur'ān commentaries are the descriptions of the universality of Solomon's rule. Būshanjī, an important 4th/10th-century author of biographies of prophets mentioned in the Qur'ān, writes:

> Some transmitters tell us that the whole earth was [Solomon's] kingdom, a thing true for only one other believer, Alexander the Great, and for two unbelievers, Nimrod and Nebuchadnezzar.[2]

In this and many similar quotations, universal rule is limited to four persons, two of whom are arch villains mentioned in the Bible. The inclusion of Alexander alongside Solomon as a pious universal ruler in the Muslim tradition will be discussed later.

Some commentaries describe Solomon's unconquerable army of *jinn*, men, and birds. A comparatively early historian of the prophets, Tha'labī (d. 427/1035), transmits stories supposedly attested by Muḥammad ibn Ka'b al-Quraẓī, a Companion of the Prophet and early Jewish convert to Islam, that Solomon had an army of a hundred *parasang*s in extent: "one quarter men, one quarter *jinn*, one quarter beasts, and one quarter birds."[3]

Solomonic flights on the winds led to the identification of the palaces, quasi "airports," from which he took off and where he landed on his extensive travels. All of these are—not surprisingly—in Greater Syria. When the geographer Ibn al-Faqīh al-Hamadhānī (fl. 290/903) visited the Palestinian town of Ludd (Lydda) and asked if its ruins had been built by Solomon, an inhabitant shrewdly responded:

> All you city people attribute impressive old buildings to *jinn* and demons but Ludd is far older than Solomon.[4]

2 Al-Haytham ibn Muḥammad Būshanjī, *Qiṣaṣ al-Qur'ān al-Karīm* (Amman: 2006) 470. Some scholars date Būshanjī to the early 5th/11th century.

3 Tha'labī, *'Arā'is al-Majālis fī Qiṣaṣ al-Anbiyā'*, trans. William M. Brinner (Leiden, Brill: 2002) 492.

4 Antoine Borrut, "La Syrie de Salomon," *Pallas* 43 (2003) 112.

An even more impressive ancient site in Greater Syria was Baalbek (Baʿlabakk). The traveler Harawī of the 6th/12th century writes in his guide to places of pilgrimage:

> The citadel of Baalbek is one of the wonders of the world. There is nothing like it in Syria or the Islamic lands, save the ruins of Istakhr in Fars. These ruins were built by the *jinn* or by Ḍaḥḥāk, which is to say Solomon, son of David.[5]

The great encyclopedist Yāqūt (d. 626/1229), who is a near contemporary of Harawī, explains that Baalbek is supposed to have been the dowry of the Queen of Sheba and contains a castle that belonged to Solomon.[6]

Palmyra (or, in Arabic, Tadmur) figures in these lists of Syrian Solomonic sites. The literary critic Thaʿālibī (d. 429/1038) even quotes from the work of Jāḥiẓ, the celebrated 3rd/9th-century essayist from Basra, who ascribes to a pre-Islamic poet a verse that reports that the *jinn* built Palmyra for Solomon. Thaʿālibī is so scrupulous with his sources that this verse, whether genuinely pre-Islamic or not, seems to go back at least to 255/868, the date of Jāḥiẓ's death.[7]

There is one other place in Palestine mentioned as a point of departure for Solomon's travel, a large stone platform in the middle of Lake Tiberias. Yāqūt rather mysteriously reports that this rock may have been built by the ancient Iranian king Ṭahmūrath.[8] This king was the third ruler of the world and appropriate as a precursor of Solomon in that he subdued the demons (*div* in Persian) and was active in Fars province, an area important to Solomonic legend. The town of Tiberias already had Solomonic associations, as the prophet-king was said to have built the famous baths next to Lake Tiberias.[9]

Historians and geographers were in no doubt that Solomon was the ruler of Greater Syria, namely, Lebanon, Israel, Palestine, Jordan, present-day Syria, and small parts of Turkey. Therefore, any of these "Syrian"

5 Borrut, "La Syrie," 112. According to the Iranian tradition, Ḍaḥḥāk was a universal ruler, but as he was generally considered a "wicked" king, he is seldom equated with Solomon.

6 Yāqūt, *Muʿjam al-Buldān*, ed. F. Wuestenfeld, I (Leipzig, Brockhaus: 1886) 684.

7 Thaʿālibī, *Thimār al-Qulūb* (Cairo, Dār Nahḍat Miṣr: 1965) 17.

8 Yāqūt, *Muʿjam*, (*supra* n. 6), I:515.

9 See the excellent article by Priscilla Souchek, "Solomon's Throne/Solomon's Bath," *Ars Orientalis* 23 (1993) 109–136.

points of departure seemed plausible to pre-modern interpreters of the Qur'ān. Jerusalem is mentioned as a place from which Solomon departed and may predominate over these other sites by a slim margin. Yet, famous as Jerusalem was as the site of the Temple of Solomon, there was no enormous palatial architecture in that city that could be associated with him.

Once Solomon took off, he traveled almost exclusively to destinations farther east. (The one exception is the fabulous city of brass, supposedly built by the *jinn* at Solomon's command somewhere in the Sahara.) One of the most dramatic of Solomon's eastern destinations is Takht-e Solaymān in the northwestern Iranian province of Azerbaijan. At this site a collection of impressive ruins surrounds a crater lake that is of a vivid blue color. One of the buildings has been identified as a Zoroastrian fire temple, one of the three "Great Fires" that were associated with kingship in the Sasanian period before the advent of Islam. Calling these ruins the "Throne of Solomon" suggests that the buildings were thought to be a royal palace built and used by the great traveling prophet.

Another eastern site quite grandiosely assumed to be associated with Solomon is the group of mountains in Baluchistan now called the Solomon Mountains. This is a fairly ancient association as the great 8th/14th-century traveler Ibn Baṭṭūṭa mentions them in an important passage:

> We traveled on to Kabul, formerly a vast town, the site of which is now occupied by a village inhabited by a tribe of Persians called Afghans. They hold mountains and defiles and possess considerable strength and are mostly highwaymen. It is told that the Prophet Solomon ascended this mountain and, having looked over India, which was covered with darkness, returned without entering it.[10]

And indeed to this day the high peak in these mountains is called Takht-e Solaymān, the Throne of Solomon.

A mountain with prominent rock outcroppings next to the city of Osh in Kyrgyzstan is also called the "Throne of Solomon." The mountain, which has been held sacred by Muslims and non-Muslims, contains a shrine that claims to hold Solomon's grave. At the peak is a mosque built by the emperor Babur, the founder of the Moghul dynasty of India, in 1510.

10 Ibn Baṭṭūṭa, *Travels in Asia and Africa*, trans. H.A.R. Gibb (London, Routledge: 1939) 180.

The most dense and elaborately wrought associations of places with Solomon are, however, sites in the provinces of Fars and Khuzestan in southwestern Iran. Overlooking the present-day town of Masjed-e Solaymān (or the "Mosque of Solomon") in Khuzestan stands a hill with ruins called Sar Masjed, perhaps to be translated as the "Front of the Mosque." This is a vast platform made of large stones with the remains of columns, which is understood to have been constructed by the *divs*, or Persian creatures similar to the Arabic *jinn*, who worked for Solomon. This town is recognized as yet another destination built by Solomon with a mosque to pray in.[11]

In the heart of Fars, the association with Solomon became even more frequent. The monument at Pasargadae that is now considered the tomb of Cyrus the Great was until recently called the "Tomb of the mother of Solomon" by the people of Fars. Ibn al-Balkhī, the great historian and geographer of Fars, who wrote in the 6th/12th century, says:

> Anybody who looks into the interior of the tomb of the mother of Solomon becomes blind, but I have never met a victim.[12]

Also in Pasargadae is a very tall fragment of a wall, called the "Prison of Solomon," most probably because Solomon was assumed to have imprisoned there some of the strange creatures who worked for him.

Pride of place among Solomonic destinations goes to Istakhr (Persian Estakhr), not very far from Pasargadae. The Qur'ān commentators and relaters of Stories of the Prophets (*Qiṣaṣ al-Anbiyā'*) are almost united in their opinion that Istakhr was the preferred destination for Solomon's month-in-a-day trips. The great historian and commentator Ṭabarī (d. 310/923) relates on two different chains of authority that Solomon "used to go out in the morning and nap at Istakhr, then leave there in the evening for Kabul."[13] An inscription is cited as proof of these trips by Qur'ān commentaries from that of Ṭabarī right up to that of Abū Su'ūd, who was made Grand Mufti or Shaykh al-Islam of the Ottoman Empire by Süleyman the Magnificent in 939/1537. The inscription, which was supposedly found near the Tigris, reads:

---

11 Ahmad Iqtidari, *Khūzestān* (Tehran, Anjoman-e Āṣār-e Melli: 1359/1980) 7.

12 Assadullah Souren Melikian-Chirvani, "Le royaume de Salomon," *Le monde iranien et l'Islam*, 1 (1971) 18.

13 Ṭabarī, *Jāmi' al-Bayān*, XVII (Cairo, Muṣṭafā al-Bābī al-Ḥalabī: 1954) 55.

> We have alighted at it [to be understood, "this ruin"] and did not build it but found it built already. We came in the morning from Istakhr and napped here. We will now depart in the evening, spend[ing] the night in Syria.[14]

Why was Istakhr chosen out of the many possible sites where Solomon might have landed? Surely much of the answer lies in sacred geography. According to the normative legend established by the Sasanians, who ruled for four centuries before the Islamic conquest, Istakhr was the site of the temple to Anahita at which Pāpak, father of the founder of the Sasanian dynasty, Ardashir I, was supposed to have been a priest. It may have been a place for rallying local Iranian champions of a warrior cult dedicated to Anahita. Part of the official story about Pāpak includes the intriguing genealogical assertion that he was a descendant of Darius III, the last ruling Achaemenid, who was defeated by Alexander the Great. Therefore, Pāpak unites the lineage of the Sasanians with their glorious predecessors. Istakhr remained the cultic center of the Sasanian dynasty from the third century C.E. right down to the last Sasanian, Yazdagird III, who was crowned there in 632. The site was also the repository of the Sasanian treasury and the sacred books of the Zoroastrians.[15]

Sacred geography alone cannot, however, account for the continuing importance of Istakhr in Muslim sources from the 2nd/8th to the 13th/19th centuries. Only the persistent conflation of the city of Istakhr, continuously inhabited since ancient times, with the impressive Achaemenid ruins of Persepolis, located outside the city, can account for Istakhr's long association with Solomon. Persepolis was a mere one *parasang* from the city of Istakhr. According to the important testimony of the polymath Masʿūdī, writing in the 4th/10th century:

> The Persians have a fire temple in Istakhr which the Zoroastrians venerate ... The people in our times, which is the year 336[/947–48] relate that it [the site of Persepolis] is the mosque of Solomon and that is the way it is known. I have entered it, being about one *parasang* from the city of Istakhr. I saw an amazing building and an enormous temple as well as amazing stone columns on the top of which were depictions in stone of a cavalcade of horses and other

14 *Ibid.*

15 A.D.H. Bivar and Mary Boyce, "Estakhr," *Encyclopaedia Iranica*, viewed online May 30, 2011.

> animals, all amazingly large in bulk and shape. All this is surrounded by a great wall and a formidable barrier of stone in which images of people have been shaped. These images have been skillfully executed. Those who live adjacent to this place claim that they are images of the prophets.
>
> It is at the foot of the mountain. A wind, which comes out of that temple and blows at night—but never in the daytime—is both strong and booming. The Muslims from there say that Solomon imprisoned the wind in that place. They say he used to have lunch in Baalbek in the land of Syria and take dinner in this mosque [in Istakhr] and alight between the two at Palmyra. This location was the place where he took recreation.[16]

To this remarkable testimony, Mas'ūdī adds in another book a description of the kind of illustrated books of history that are assumed to have survived from the Sasanian period among the noble families still living in the actual city of Istakhr:

> In the year 303[/915–16], at the house of a very noble Persian family in Istakhr in the province of Fars, I saw a large book which contained, along with a discussion of several scenes, the history of the kings of Persia, their reigns and the monuments they built ... The book I saw was edited according to the documents found in the treasure of the kings of Persia.[17]

In these two passages we have many hints as to the importance of the ruins of Persepolis near Istakhr. The vastness of the site suggested that only humans of very superior power or *jinn* and satans could have constructed it. The amazing capitals on the columns with sculpture of animals clearly point to some significant pre-Islamic building. The city of Istakhr was known in the Sasanian period to have had a great repository of royal books. Perhaps some of these books were rescued or survived the Muslim conquest. Hence Mas'ūdī could find such a book there in the 4th/10th century, about three centuries after the fall of the Sasanians.

The great wall surrounding the ruins of Persepolis outside Istakhr suggested to the Muslims of the area the presence of another Solomonic

16 Mas'ūdī, *Murūj al-Dhahab*, II (Beirut, al-Jāmi'a al-Lubnānīya: 1966) 399–400.
17 Maçoudi (Mas'ūdī), *Livre de l'avertissement et de la revision* (Paris, Imprimerie nationale: 1896) 150–151.

destination. A dramatic remnant of Solomon's attested command of the winds is the booming wind that blows inside the enclosure at night. Although Mas'ūdī thinks that he is looking at an ancient Persian site, he acknowledges its reinterpretation as a proto-Islamic site by noting that the inhabitants who live nearby identify the depictions on its walls as "prophets," and that Muslims regard Istakhr (here meaning the ruins of Persepolis) as the place where Solomon took his dinner.

The presence of a famous library at Istakhr is a subject for comment by many early Muslim authors. Istakhr and Persepolis were held to be one city and the story of Alexander's burning of Persepolis may also be part of a narrative of an earlier destruction or dispersal of the library at Istakhr that took place during the repeated attempts at Muslim conquest. Ibn al-Nadīm, a bibliophile who died in the late 4th/10th century, gives us one version of the story:

> He [Alexander] destroyed the cities and the castles that satans and proud men had built. His destruction [ruined] whatever there was in the different buildings in the way of scientific material, whether inscribed on stone or wood. Along with this demolition there were conflagrations, with the scattering of the books. Such of these things, however, as were gathered in collections and libraries in the city of Istakhr, he had transcribed and translated into the Greek and Coptic tongues. Then, after he had finished copying what he had need of, he burned the material written in Persian.[18]

An even more unfavorable report of Alexander is to be found in later books, where Zoroastrians recounted the supposedly brutal oppression of their culture and their aristocrats by Alexander and his successors. In the *Arda Wiraf Namag*, perhaps a Sasanian book that was redacted as late as the 3rd/9th or 4th/10th century, we read:

> [Alexander] killed the ruler (*dahibad*) of Iran. He destroyed and ruined the court and the nobility. This religion, the entire Avesta and Zand, was written with gold ink on prepared cowhides and deposited at Istakhr of the dynasty of Papag in the fortress of the

18 Ibn al-Nadīm, *The Fihrist of al-Nadīm: A Tenth-Century Survey of Muslim Culture*, ed. and trans. Bayard Dodge (New York, Columbia University Press: 1970) 574.

> Scriptures. This miserable (*bad-bakht*) enemy, heretical and evil and maleficent, brought [the Scriptures] out and burned them. He killed many priests and judges and *herbed*s and Magi, the faithful, the specialists, the wise men of Iran. He cast mutual hatred and discord among the great and the masters of households. He himself, however, was broken and thrown into hell.[19]

The dramatic qualities of this account do not match its historical accuracy. It represents one version of history current among the Sasanians, who claimed, from the time of Ardashir in the third century C.E. until the Muslim conquest in the seventh, that they were the upholders of the Zoroastrian faith. The point of great interest here for us is that Alexander is represented as burning Istakhr of the dynasty of Pāpak, ancestor to the Sasanian dynasty, which must mean the city itself rather than Persepolis. All historians nearer to the time of Alexander agree that he burned Persepolis as opposed to Istakhr.

The reason for the exchange of city names is partly found in the Arabic geographers of the 4th/10th and 5th/11th centuries. As the very observant 10th-century geographer Muqaddasī tells us, Istakhr was the largest subdistrict of the province of Fars in southwestern Iran. Istakhr remained the capital of the province for about a century after Shiraz, the later capital, became more populous:

> A *parasang* from Istakhr is Solomon's pleasure palace (*mal'ab*), to which one ascends by handsome stairs cut in the rock. Here are black pillars, and statues in niches and remarkable constructions like the theatres of Syria. Between the pillars are the baths and the Mosque of Solomon.[20]

In this passage we can see that Persepolis, which is indeed about a *parasang* from Istakhr, is regarded as a "pleasure palace" associated with it, much as Versailles is associated with Paris.

---

19 Philippe Gignoux, *Le livre d'Ardā Vīrāz* (Paris, Editions recherche sur les civilisations: 1984) 145–146. Middle Persianists now would transliterate the name Papag as Pābag. The customary form of this name in the *Shāhnāma* is Pāpak. Middle Persianists would also render *bad-bakht* as *wad-baxt*.

20 Muqaddasī, *Best Divisions far Knowledge of the Regions*, trans. Basil Collins (Reading, U.K., Garnet: 2001) 36.

This description of Persepolis is confirmed by the great Bīrūnī, who died about 442/1050. First, Bīrūnī explains the widespread but mistaken chronology that abbreviates the period of Alexander's successors in the East, the Parthians, to two hundred-odd years when they actually ruled parts of Iran for over five hundred years only to be replaced by the Sasanians:

> Such were the calamities which Alexander and his Greek lieutenants brought upon them—and yet further conflagration of all the literature in which the people delighted, the ruin of all fine arts which were the recreation and desire of the people. And more than that, Alexander burned the greatest part of their religious code, he destroyed the wonderful architectural monuments, e.g., those in the mountains of Istakhr, nowadays [in the time of Bīrūnī] known as the Mosque of Solomon, son of David, and delivered them up to the flames.[21]

Although Bīrūnī was a Muslim, this passage reflects the Zoroastrian view of Alexander as the "Destroyer of ancient Iran," which survived among some Persianate Muslims well into the twentieth century. There can be no question that the reference in Bīrūnī to the Mosque of Solomon is to Persepolis, along with some aspects of its very near neighbor Istakhr, where the royal books of the Sasanians were kept.

At this point some of the features of Persepolis should be mentioned. Unlike Istakhr, which had its own river and lake, Persepolis is built in an area that required great feats of irrigation to make it habitable, not all of which are as yet fully understood by archaeologists.[22] The destruction and neglect of the water supply may well explain why the site remained largely uninhabited after Alexander.

The enormous hypostyle columned hall on the great platform of Persepolis so impressed the ancient East that *apadana*, the word for such a hall in Old Persian, traveled directly—or through other languages—into Hebrew, Aramaic, Syriac, Palmyrene, and eventually into Arabic, where the word is already in use among the pre-Islamic poets. The classical

---

21 Bīrūnī, *Chronology of the Ancient Nations*, trans. C.E. Sachau (London, Oriental Translation Fund: 1879) 127, with some modifications by this author; *Kitāb al-Āthār al-Bāqīya* [Chronologie orientalischer Völker] (Leipzig, Brockhaus: 1878) 129.

22 Mahdi Moradi-Jalal, Siamak Arianfar, Bryan Karney, and Andrew Colombo, "Water Resource Management for Iran's Persepolis Complex," in *Ancient Water Technologies*, ed. Larry W. Mays (Dordrecht, Springer: 2010) 87–102.

dictionaries of Arabic say that this loan word, *fadan*, signifies a pavilion or building of the kind called castle (*qaṣr*), raised high or made lofty.[23]

The great audience hall of Darius and Xerxes with its 72 columns, each 20 meters or 66 feet high, was one of the awe-inspiring spaces of the ancient world. It is no wonder that its architectural reputation continued to ring in later languages as a word for lofty palaces. And it is no wonder that Solomon, conceived to be a universal and universally traveled ruler in Islamic lore, was understood to be the builder of Persepolis. Had not Solomon erected two famous pillars in front of his temple in Jerusalem, which he had personally named (1 Kings 7:21 and 2 Chronicles 3:17)? And was not Solomon the only builder to command the satans and the *jinn* and therefore the only one able to create such colossal architecture?

The modern name for Persepolis has become fixed as Takht-e Jamshid or the "Throne of Jamshid," Jamshid being an ancient king and great culture hero of the Persian tradition. The widespread identification of Jamshid with Solomon will be discussed below. But earlier sources as frequently—or perhaps more frequently—described the site only with references to Solomon (or to the many columns) without reference to Jamshid. The first modern European known to have correctly identified the ruins of Persepolis, García de Silva y Figueroa, the Spanish diplomat who visited Persia from 1617 to 1619, said the site was called "Chil'minara." This word is unmistakably *chehel menār* or *chehel menāra*), the "Forty Columns'' or "Forty Minarets,"[24] a local name that has long coexisted with other names. The tradition of architecture inspired by these 40 columns is attested not only by the palace of Shah Abbas at Isfahan but by other palaces as far-flung as Akbar's palace in Allahabad. In fact, the Pahlavi inscription left by the Sasanian king Shapur II in 311 C.E. calls the site of Persepolis *Sad Stun*, "One Hundred Columns," and some later sources call it *Hazār Sotun*, "One Thousand Columns."[25] In the *Shāhnāma*, the Persian epic composed by Firdausi and traditionally dated to 401/1010, the site is sometimes called "Takht-e Jamshid," but also *Sad Sotun*) "One Hundred Columns."[26] In all likelihood, the sources just mean "a great many columns," the number

23 E.W. Lane, *An Arabic-English Lexicon*, VI (London, Williams and Norgate: 1877) 2353, with references to the classical lexicons.

24 Michele Bernardini, "Figueroa," *Encyclopaedia Iranica* online, viewed online January 10, 2011.

25 For Shapur's inscription, see n. 39.

26 Josef Wiesehoefer, *Ancient Persia* (London, I.B. Tauris: 1996) 226.

perhaps diminishing to 40 from 100 due to attrition over time. Nonetheless, the site has indeed been associated with the largely mythic Jamshid from a comparatively early period. The reason is not far to seek.

Ibn al-Muqaffaʿ, a Persian who in the early 2nd/8th century was regarded as one of the masters of Arabic prose, is quoted in a 3rd/9th-century work as saying:

> Ignorant Persians and such as have no systematic learning suppose that King Jam was Solomon, the son of David, but this is an error, for between Solomon and Jam was an interval of more than three thousand years.[27]

The comparative chronology mentioned in this quote will be discussed herein. In spite of Ibn al-Muqaffaʿ's negative assessment, the persistent identification of these two figures, Jam and Solomon, remains a frequent theme in later works. Two Persian histories written in the early 6th/12th century accept the identification without question. Ibn al-Balkhī says that Kayumarṣ, who came after Noah, was the first person to be king. One of his successors was Jamshid, who made Istakhr his capital and turned it into a great city by laying out the palatial complex of Persepolis outside the ancient city:

> He laid out an immense platform of black solid stone. There are two staircases so broad that knights can drink on horseback ... There is a portrait of Burāq with the face of a human with a beard, curls, and a crown, and he has wings and a body and legs and a tail like a cow. Everywhere one sees the image of Jamshid, which has been incised [into the stone]: a powerful man with a full beard and a handsome face and curly hair. In one place he has a case in one hand and a censor in the other. Elsewhere there is a lion on the left hand or the head of an onager, and a dagger in his right hand which he is plunging into the belly of the lion or unicorn.[28]

This last scene is unquestionably a reference to the bas-relief in the palace of Darius at Persepolis, which shows the king killing a winged lion. The

27 Dīnawarī, *al-Akhbār al-Ṭiwāl*, ed. Vladimir Guirgass (Leiden, Brill: 1888) 9. Jam is a common alternate for Jamshid because the latter means "Jam the Shining."
28 Ibn al-Balkhī, *The Fārsnāma*, ed. Guy Le Strange and R.A. Nicholson (London, Luzac: 1921) 26.

description of the king with a cane and "censor" is unquestionably a reference to an audience scene, also in the palace of Darius at Persepolis. The many portraits of "handsome" Jamshid are actually those of Iranian soldiers and nobles represented in the many bas-reliefs found throughout Persepolis (with the characteristic curve of the nostrils frequently seen in Iranians up to the present). As a native of Fars, Ibn al-Balkhī understands the distinction between the palace at Persepolis and the Sasanian city of Istakhr, but apparently believes them to be contemporary with each other.

The nearly contemporary source, *Mojmal al-Tavārikh*, correlates the ancient Persian kings with the prophets:

> Abraham is Siyāvash, because both went into the fire. Solomon was Jamshid, Noah was Nariman, and Lohrasp was Nebuchadnezzar.[29]

These sorts of identifications and sometimes elaborate attempts to wed Biblical and ancient Iranian history were foreshadowed in several Arabic works. Perhaps the most striking of these accounts is contained in the work of the early historian Abū Ḥanīfa al-Dīnawarī, an erudite scholar from western Iran who died in the late 3rd/9th century.

Dīnawarī's work is one of the earliest surviving histories describing both the pre-Islamic and the Islamic past. He tells us that Shem was the heir of Noah and settled in Iraq, which he called *Irānshahr*.[30] His son, Shalih, succeeded him, and Shalih in turn was succeeded by his nephew Jam or Jamshid, who:

> laid the foundation of royal sovereignty, solidly planted its pillars, erected its characteristics, and adopted Nowruz as a festival.[31]

This amazing feathering together of the Persian and Biblical traditions is followed by an even more amazing statement: From Arfadhshadh, the grandfather of Jamshid, who is called "Iran" by the Persians, "are descended all Arabs and all rulers and nobility among the Persians." We know that Dīnawarī was a keen student of Arabic philology, studying with, among others, Ibn al-Sikkīt. He found a way to make Jamshid the ancestor of both the Abbasids, the rulers of his day, whom he respected as legitimate,

---

29 Anon., *Mojmal al-Tavārikh*, ed. M. Bahar (Tehran, Mu'assasa-yi Khāvar: 1318) 38.
30 On the term *Irānshahr*, see my article "The Idea of Iran in the Buyid Dominions" (Article 34 here).
31 Dīnawarī, *al-Akhbār al-Ṭiwāl* (Beirut, Dar al-Kutub al-'Ilmīya,: 2001) 32.

and of himself and other well-born Persians. Dīnawarī even adds that the Pharaoh of the time of Abraham is a descendant of Jamshid.[32] Dīnawarī's great contemporary, Ṭabarī, has a generally similar account.

There are many similarities between the narratives of Jamshid and Solomon. Both sit on greatly admired thrones. Both command the obedience of nonhuman helpers: for Solomon the *jinn* and for Jamshid the *divs*. Both travel rapidly through the air. The Qur'ānic story of Solomon's conversation with an ant seems to have created a parallel story about Jamshid, as has the story of Solomon's signet ring that symbolized his power. In turn, the story of Jamshid's famous cup, in which he could see events unfolding in any place within the seven climes, influenced the stories of Solomon.[33]

The identification of southwestern Iran as the realm of Solomon, already attested in the work of Ibn al-Balkhī, reached its apotheosis in the 7th/13th and following centuries. The great Iranian scholar Mohammad Qazvini wrote in 1317/1938 a classic essay on the recipients of the panegyrics composed by the pre-eminent Persian poet of the 7th/13th century, Sa'di of Shiraz. In praise of his patron, the Atabeg Abu Bakr Moḥammad ibn Sa'd Zangi, who ruled Fars from 628/1231 to 658/1260, Sa'di calls this ruler "Lord Commander of the Kingdom of Solomon, the just *Shāhinshāh*." Already in the reign of his father, Sa'd Zangi, the dynasty had adopted the officially elaborated royal signature "Heir to the Kingdom of Solomon" (*vāreṯ-e molk-e Solaymān*). Sa'di thoroughly mixes Qur'ānic and Iranian history in an ode in which he praises this ruler as "Heir to the throne of Solomon, with the kingly glory of Khosraw [Chosroes] and Jamshid." Many verses of Sa'di and passages quoted by Qazvini show that this local dynasty of Fars province gloried in associations so richly attested by the identification of its ruins with Solomon.[34]

Another of Sa'di's works, the dedication of his *Golestān*, testifies to the Solomonic heritage of the kings of Shiraz. Almost certainly the most copied and memorized Persian book in the Persianate Muslim world that stretched from Sarajevo in Eastern Europe to Urumchi in Western China, Sa'di's *Golestān* was written in 656/1258 and dedicated to the son of the

32 Dīnawarī, *al-Akhbār*, 32 (on Jamshid), 40 (on Pharaoh).
33 Manuchehr Mortazavi, *Maktab-e Ḥāfeẓ*; (Tabriz, Setuda: 1370) 225. In the *Shāhnāma*, it is the legendary king Kay Khosraw (and not Jamshid) who possesses the world-viewing cup. In later Persian poetry the cup is almost universally attributed to Jamshid.
34 Mohammad Qazvini, *Mamduḥin-e Shaykh Sa'di* (Tehran, Vezārat-e Ma'āref,: 1317).

Salghurid king of Shiraz. In the florid style of the period, the author says that his book is not complete until it is found pleasing in the court of:

> the beauty of humankind, the pride of Islam, Saʿd, son of the greatest Atabeg, the glorious king of kings, master of the kings of the Arabs and Persians, Sultan of the land and the ocean, heir to the kingdom of Solomon, Moẓaffar al-Dīn Abū Bakr ibn Saʿd ibn Zangi, may God perpetuate their good fortune and redouble their glory.[35]

One might not guess from this description that the Salghurids, also called the Zengids and Muzaffarids (Mozaffarids), were local rulers who recognized the Mongols as overlords.

There is ample testimony to the continuation of this tradition of Solomonically-styled kingship in the poetry of Saʿdi's successor as the leading poet of Shiraz, Ḥāfeẓ, usually considered the greatest lyric poet of the Persian tradition. Ḥāfeẓ also mixes references to Jamshid and Solomon, who lost his signet ring and hence his kingship for a moment.[36] He writes:

> A heart which has the ability to see the unseen and has the cup of Jamshid,
> Why should it feel sad for the signet ring that it has lost for a moment? (*ghazal* 119)

In like manner Ḥāfeẓ defies conventional religion by mixing Zoroastrian and Islamic terminology when he writes:

> When, like Solomon, I boast of seizing her ruby red signet ring [the lips of the beloved?]
> What fear should I have of Ahriman [the Zoroastrian embodiment of evil who defiles the ring]
> Since it [the boast] will be like the greatest name [that name to which God responds]. (*ghazal* 327)

---

35 Saʿdi, *Kolliyāt*, ed. Baha' al-Din Khurramshahi (Tehran, Enteshārāt-e Nāhid,: 1379) 28.

36 Ḥāfeẓ, *Divān*, ed. M. Qazvini and Q. Ghani (Tehran, Sinā, n.d.) 69–70, *ghazals* 100–101; 89, *ghazal* 119; 223, *ghazal* 327.

In effect, in the works of Ḥāfeẓ, the imagery used passes into a totally metaphoric understanding of the Islamic and Iranian past in which names are virtually interchangeable. In these *ghazals* Ḥāfeẓ refers to the "Throne of Solomon" and the "Throne of Jamshid" along similar lines:

> May your efforts be in vain if you set your heart on nothing
> In a setting where the Throne of Solomon has vanished with the wind ... (*ghazal* 100)

> Do not be amazed at the changes wrought by time, for the wheel of heaven
> Remembers thousands upon thousands of such stories ...
> Who understands how the Throne of Jamshid (*Takht-e Jam*) disappeared on the wind? (*ghazal* 101)

The reference to the Throne of Solomon may be the only one to the great ruins of Ḥāfeẓ's homeland in his work, if indeed the reference is more than symbolic. A survey of all of the imagery in Persian poetry with associations to Solomon would fill a work of many volumes.

Interestingly, there exists one reference to the Solomonic past of Fars in a work of art preserved from the time of Ḥāfeẓ. It is a brass bucket inlaid with gold and silver made in Shiraz in 733/1332–33 by an artisan who identifies himself as the servant of the sultan who is called "the Heir to the kingdom of Solomon" (*vāreṣ-e molk-e Solaymān*) but also "the Alexander (Iskandar) of his time."[37]

The record of inscriptions and graffiti, royal and otherwise, left at Persepolis tells a similar story of strong associations giving way to diffuse ones. There are a series of inscriptions and graffiti at Persepolis attesting to the homage paid to the site by the local kings of Fars in the period after Alexander. One of these inscriptions is ascribed to Pāpak, the priestly father or ancestor of the first Sasanian king, who was the guardian of the nearby shrine of Anahita at Istakhr.[38] Another inscription written in the

37 Adel T. Adamova, "The St. Petersburg Illustrated Shahnama of 733. Hijra (1333 AD) and the Injuid School of Painting," in *The Visual Language of the Persian Book of Kings*, ed. Robert Hillenbrand (Aldershot, U.K., Ashgate: 2004) 58.

38 See Pierofrancesco Callieri, "At the Roots of the Sasanian Royal Imagery: The Persepolis Graffiti," in *Eran ud Aneran: Studies Presented to Boris Ilic Marshak* (Venezia, Cafoscarina: 2006) 129–148, especially p. 138.

name of Shapur II (309–373) at Persepolis shows that, however much the Sasanians built in neighboring Istakhr, they nonetheless greatly revered the site. Part of this inscription reads:

> The Mazda-worshipping Lord, Shapur, the king of kings of Iran and An-Iran [non-Iran] ... traveled on this road from Istakhr to Sakistan [Sistan] and graciously came here to *Sad Sotun* [Pahlavi: *Sad Stun*] (One Hundred Columns); he ate bread in this building [the Palace of Darius] ... And he organized a great feast, and he had the rituals performed and he prayed for his father and his ancestors, and he prayed for his own soul, and he also prayed for the one who had this building constructed.[39]

Scholars have noticed that Shapur refers to Persepolis not by its old name, Parsa, but as the "Hall of Many Columns," the name by which it will often be called throughout the pre-modern period.

The three Buyid inscriptions at Persepolis are well known and respectful if less well informed about the site. The first, by the ruler Abū Shuja' Fannā Khosraw, the future 'Aḍūd al-Dawla, simply says: "He was present at it (*ḥaḍarahu*) [i.e., at this site] ... in the year 344 [/955–56]." In fact, the inscription is placed next to the inscription of Shapur II, which, according to the plausible explanation in 'Aḍūd al-Dawla's inscription, was read to him by "one who read the inscription in these remains (*āthār*)." Henceforth it became a royal custom to leave an inscription at Persepolis. 'Aḍud al-Dawla's son, Bahā' al-Dawla, a wily though far less enlightened ruler, left an inscription nearby in 392/1001–2, saying that "he came to this place with a mighty army."[40]

Of the many later Arabic and Persian inscriptions at Persepolis, this chapter will only discuss two Persian examples, one from the time of the Īnjū'ids and the other from the later period of the Aq-Qoyunlu, who ruled Shiraz in the 9th/15th century. The Īnjū'id patron of Ḥāfeẓ, Abū Isḥāq Jamāl al-Dīn Shāh, ruled Shiraz until his death in 758/1357. Ḥāfeẓ laments his absence in the last lines of one of his beautiful lyric poems:

39 Vesta Sarkhosh Curtis, "The Legacy of Ancient Persia," in *The Forgotten Empire*, ed. John E. Curtis and Nigel Tallis (London, British Museum Press: 2005) 252.
40 John J. Donahue, "Three Buwayhid Inscriptions," *Arabica* 20: 1 (1973) 74–80 on the inscription and the Zoroastrian priest named in 'Aḍud al-Dawla's second inscription.

The turquoise signet ring of Abū Isḥāq shone beautifully indeed;
But it was a good turn of fortune—that leaves in haste.
O Ḥāfeẓ, do you hear that cry like laughter from the strutting partridge
Which had forgotten the claws of the falcon of destiny?[41] (*ghazal* 207)

The first of the two Persian inscriptions, in spite of several lacunae, reflects both the "ubi sunt" and "eheu fugaces" atmosphere of the preceding poem and also the understanding by rulers of the significance of Persepolis itself:

Where are the mighty rulers of early times?
They put away treasures which have not remained just as they did not remain.
Did not the Throne of Solomon, on him be peace, use to go on the wind in the morning and in the evening?
Did you not see that in the end he disappeared with the wind?
Fortunate is the learned and just person who has so departed.

In the first days of Rabīʿ I, seven hundred and forty-eight (*lacuna*) the ruler (*Pādishāh*) of Islam, the King of Kings of the seven climes, the Alexander of his time, and the heir to the kingdom [of Solomon] (*lacuna*) Jamāl al-Dunyā wa-l-Dīn, the Ruler (*farmān-farmā*) of the world (*lacuna*) Shaykh Abū Isḥāq, may God make his reign eternal (*lacuna*) And at an auspicious time he ordered that this exalted place and wondrous construction (*bonyān-e badiʿ*) [be used for] the pitching of his Majesty's tent and the encampment [of the army].[42]

This inscription is important in many ways. Its Solomonic language tells us how the site is perceived historically. Its description of the structure as "wondrous" (*badiʿ*) tells something about aesthetic appreciation of the site.

The second Persian inscription is, to our great good fortune, discussed in a small treatise that admirably explains its context. This treatise describes how Sultan Khalil, a son of the great Uzun Ḥasan, came with a great procession of his subjects to Persepolis and Istakhr in 881/1477. It was written by the polymath (and, according to some scholars, all-around second-rater) Jalāl al-Din Davāni, in the most bombastic style of post-Mongol Persian.

41 Ḥāfeẓ, *Divān*, 141, *ghazal* 207.
42 Mohammad Taqi Mostafavi, *Eqlim-e Fārs* (Tehran, Anjoman-e Āṣār-e Melli: 1343) 346–347.

This inscription at Persepolis is mostly in Persian verse (with some words and phrases in Arabic). Here only the third and fourth lines as well as the last three lines are quoted:

> Do not seek the kingdom of Solomon, for that is [now] dust;
> Of these jewels and treasures which were beyond counting, what has [the hero] Jam carried away,
> What has Solomon borne off? 'Ali son of Sultan Khalil son of Sultan
> [Uzun] Ḥasan—May God favor their rule— in the year eight hundred and eighty-one,
> One of God's graces is that I am nine years old and wrote in this manner.[43]

Indeed, the treatise by Davāni talks about the precocity of Sultan Khalil's son, whom he calls "the pearl of the shell of world rulership, young in years but old in knowledge."[44]

The account by Davāni deserves a full analysis for its Solomonic and non-Solomonic imagery, which I will only briefly describe here. Whereas Uzun Ḥasan is the "caliph of God" and his genealogy is a continuous chain of great sultans stretching back to Jamshid, his son Sultan Khalil is the "one occupying the place (and dignity) of Solomon" (*Solaymān-makāni* or *Solaymān-makān*).[45] Sultan Khalil is specifically said to have moved the site of his parade "from his summer quarters of Tang-e Bolāq to his winter quarters ... in the direction of the kingdom of Solomon."[46] The actual review took place at Band-e Amir, the famous dam built by 'Aḍūd al-Dawla near Persepolis on the Pulvar River.

> When the banners that are the signs of victory arrived at Istakhr in Fars ... he stopped for one day in that place of amazing remains and contemplated the wondrous images (*tamāthil-e badi'*).[47]

Davāni then proceeds to a digression to explain the site:

43 Mostafavi, *Iqlīm*, 339.

44 For Davāni, see Vladimir Minorsky, "A Civil and Military Review in Fars in 881/1476," *Bulletin of the School of Oriental and African Studies* 10: 1 (1939), corrected here on the basis of Iraj Afshar's excellent edition of Davāni, "*'Arẓ-e Sepāh-e Uzun Ḥasan*," *Majalla-ye Dāneshkada-ye Adabiyāt* 3: 3 (Tehran, Farvardin: 1325) 26–55.

45 Davāni, "*'Arẓ*," 36ff. See Minorsky, "Civil," 149.

46 Davāni, "*'Arẓ*," 40.

47 Davāni, "*'Arẓ*," 41.

> In some histories ... it is written that they called this place the "Thousand Columns" in the time of the kings of Persians. In the time of Jamshid who, according to the assertion of some historians, is Solomon, that [place] was founded.[48]

There is mention of Sultan Khalil's son, 'Ali, and his presentation of the verses that are to be found in his inscription. Then follows the detailed description of the parade of the army, bureaucracy, turbaned men, descendants of the Prophet, dervishes, and many others who passed in review in front of the Sultan as he sat in the Castle of Sar-band at the Lake of Istakhr. One of the first officials mentioned is "the supreme commander (*amir-e a'ẓam*), the Lord Keeper of the Seal, who has the seal-ring of eternal felicity at the disposal of his palm and the bezel of Solomon in the hand of authority."[49]

As would be expected in such verbose and overwrought Persian prose there are ample references to other kings of the Persian and Islamic traditions. Moreover, the "kingdom of Solomon" (*molkei Solaymān*) can sometimes be translated as "the kingship of Solomon," a metaphoric use to which many Islamic rulers might lay claim. Yet some of the references in this and other documents and inscriptions show that the kingdom of Solomon located in southwestern Iran is the intended meaning, as when we are told that Sultan Khalil, in moving from his winter quarters to Istakhr and Persepolis, went "in the direction of the kingdom of Solomon."

Following the Solomonic (and, secondarily, Jamshidic) identification of Persepolis and Istakhr, the creation of a royal palace of 40 (or one hundred or one thousand) columns became an important symbol of sovereignty. In Iran itself two of the most famous examples were built by Shah 'Abbas in 11th/17th-century Isfahan. Ebba Koch has written extensively with great learning on the numerous palaces called "Forty Pillars" in South Asia.[50] This connection has been doubted but the weight of the written evidence, including the inscriptions at Persepolis, seems to make it overwhelmingly likely that the Solomonic model of Persepolis was being invoked in these palaces.

One of the first lessons to be drawn from this example of place and memory is the importance of correlative chronology. The Muslim Middle East before 1500 was heir to a little bit of Roman history transmitted

48 Davāni, "'Arẓ," 41.
49 Davāni, "'Arẓ," 47.
50 Ebba Koch, *Mughal Art and Imperial Ideology* (New Delhi, Oxford University Press: 2001).

through Syriac, a little bit of ancient history of the Yemen, and a great deal of Biblical history and post-Biblical embroidery upon that history. It was also heir to a great deal of Iranian history, some as reconceived by the Sasanians or by the Zoroastrian priests under Muslim rule in the 3rd/9th and 4th/10th centuries or by many generations of interested Muslims.

The pre-eminent specialist on Alexander's eastern conquests, Pierre Briant, says that "Alexander's decision to burn Persepolis in May 330 B.C. was practically imposed on him by his own strategy and war propaganda: he arrived as avenger of the Greeks."[51] Others have construed Alexander's motives differently. Whatever his motives, the burning of Persepolis, which was, among its other functions, a ritual center for Achaemenid Iranians, must have been a shock to the Iranian aristocracy and religious functionaries. During the third century B.C.E. this royal and ritual center, in ruins and perhaps having lost its water supply, had moved to the nearby city of Istakhr, which then became the seat of the local rulers of Fars, the Fratarakas. The city reached its zenith under the Sasanians, the first of whom was Ardashir, the son or grandson of Pāpak, a local ruler who is also identified as a keeper of one of the most venerated Zoroastrian fires.[52]

The Sasanian dynasty, which Ardashir founded, posed as the restorers of Zoroastrianism or, as it is more properly called, Mazdayasna. By this period there was a fairly well-established Zoroastrian priesthood. In his inscription at the monument locally called the Kaʿba of Zoroaster, the *herbed* or "high priest" Kartir proudly announces his close relationship with the son and successor of Ardashir, Shapur I (r. 241–272) and Shapur's son Hormizd, as well as Hormizd's successor and brother, Bahram I, and Bahram's son, Bahram II. Of Bahram II, Kartir says:

> He is devout, sincere, faithful [to promises], well-behaved and beneficent ... He made me master of ceremonies and powerful overlord at the fire of Anahid-Ardashir and of Anahid, the Lady of Istakhr.

Istakhr is the only place name in this long trilingual inscription. Kartir makes clear the fire temple's intimate connection with homage to the Sasanian dynasty.[53]

51 Pierre Briant, *Alexandre le Grand* (Paris, Presses universitaires de France: 1977) 96.
52 Richard Frye, "Papak," *Encyclopaedia Iranica*, viewed online May 3, 2011.
53 Marie-Louise Chaumont, "L'inscription de Kartir à la Kaʿbah de Zoroastre," *Journal Asiatique* 248 (1960) 339–380. See also the more recent synoptic edition of

The pre-Islamic Arabs knew about Istakhr and its importance to the Sasanians. In the reign of Khosraw Anushirvan (r. 531–579 C.E.) at the "Battle Day of Mushaqqar" (*yawm al-Mushaqqar*) in Arabia a Sasanian official massacred members of the tribe Banū Tamīm. It was a severe defeat and some of the captured Arabs were sent to Istakhr. Ṭabarī notes that years later, during the Muslim conquest of the Sasanian homeland in Fars, some of the Arab deportees from this earlier battle were still living in Istakhr, where they had been sent as prisoners of war.[54]

With the advent of Islam and the Muslim conquests, the fortunes of Istakhr might seem to have been sealed. And indeed Ṭabarī tells us that at the birth of the Prophet Muḥammad "the [sacred] fire of Fars, which had not previously been extinguished for a thousand years, was extinguished." As the translator of this passage says in his notes, this was "presumably the great fire temple at Istakhr."[55] The people of Istakhr do not seem to have gotten the message. Ṭabarī reports that in 23/643 the Muslims and "the army of Istakhr ... fought a long battle." After the Muslims won a victory, they conquered Iṣtakhr. Then Fars threw off allegiance to the Muslims in 28/649–650 and had to be reconquered the following year (29/649–650).[56]

For Iranians attracted to Islam, the career of the famous Companion of Muḥammad, named Salmān al-Fārisī or "Salmān the man from Fars," was an important precursor. It should be noted in passing that Solaymān (i.e., Solomon) is understood in Arabic to be a correct diminutive of Salmān.[57] Balādhurī, an historian of the second half of the 3rd/9th century, tells us that Salmān was born at Istakhr into a Zoroastrian family. He converted to Christianity and went to Syria to understand his new religion and was told there, by a monk, to seek someone with "the marks of a prophet." Sold into slavery by a Bedouin, Salmān arrived in Medina shortly after Muḥammad. He recognized in Muḥammad the marks he had been told to find in a prophet, and in Muḥammad's message the pure monotheism he had been seeking.[58]

---

this inscription by D.N. MacKenzie, "Kerdir's Inscription," in Georgina Herrmann, *The Sasanian Rock Relief at Naqsh-i Rustam* (Berlin, Dietrich Reimer Verlag: 1989) 35–72.

54 Ṭabarī, *Ta'rīkh*, I (Leiden, Brill: 1965) 986.

55 Ṭabarī, *The Conquest of Iran*, trans. G. Rex Smith (Albany, N.Y., SUNY Press: 1994) 285 and note 667.

56 Ṭabarī, *The Conquest*, 66–68.

57 *Mu'jam Asmā' al-'Arab*, ed. Muhammad ibn al-Zubayr *et al.*, I (Beirut, Maktab Lubnān: 1991) 827.

58 Balādhurī, *Ansāb al-Ashrāf* (Damascus, Dār al-Yaqẓa al-'Arabīya: 1997) 213.

Salmān's Zoroastrian origin made him an accessible and appealing example to Iranians of one of their community who became a prominent Muslim. In Persian he became known as Salmān Pāk, Salmān the Pure, the man who was born into a good family. According to Balādhurī, he was born at the seat of Iranian royalty, Istakhr, although some say he was born at Isfahan, but that is "wrong." He found his way to Islam at the end of a personal quest for a prophet of the purest monotheism. Thus, Salmān became a bridge to Islam for his countrymen. Admiration for his story made Salmān the inspiration for asceticism, mystical traditions, and guild traditions throughout the Islamic world but, in particular, in the Persianate world.

Several accounts of the Prophet's sayings are told on the authority of Salmān, two of which are especially significant for Iranians. In one of the accounts the Prophet has just recited the verse:

> And He has sent him [Muḥammad] to others among them [Muslims] who have not yet joined them. And He is the Mighty and the Wise (Qur'ān LXII:3).

"Abū Hurayra, a Companion of Muḥammad, said, 'Who are they, O Apostle of God?' The Apostle of God put his hand on Salmān saying, 'If Faith (*īmān/dīn*) were [as far away as] in the Pleiades, one from among them [the Persians] would surely attain it.'" According to the second account, the Prophet said: "Salmān is one of us, a member of our lineage (*ahl al-bayt*)." The somewhat unlikely claim is made that Salmān translated part of the Qur'ān.[59]

With the spread of Islam in Iranian lands, opinion regarding Alexander, the conqueror of the Persians, split. A part of the tradition, as represented by the previously cited quotations, regarded Alexander as deeply wicked. But the majority of Muslims, including Iranian Muslims, regarded Alexander as the prophet referred to in the Qur'ān (XVIII:83) as the "The Possessor of Two Horns" (apparently from his widely circulated coin and sculptural images in which he sports rams' horns). The legendary Alexander also built the barrier of metal that kept Gog and Magog walled up. He, along with Solomon, is usually considered "Muslim" by Muslim historians, as

59 Sulayman Bashir, *Arabs and Others in Early Islam* (Princeton, Darwin Press: 1997) 76.

are all monotheists before Muḥammad. Thaʿālibī, the prominent 4th/10th-century Arabic writer mentioned above, explains:

> Some of the specialists in historical accounts (*akhbār*) have said that the prophet-kings were Adam, Joseph, David, Solomon, Alexander, and Muḥammad. They added the support of kingship to prophecy and thus became the most glorious of prophets. They could manifest their call to God and exalt His [God's] authority (*kalima*) and give power to his Divine Law and prepare through His kingship for Him to enact what He legislates.[60]

The alternate tradition of Alexander the destroyer did survive, though it was only espoused by a minority of learned Muslims. A strong trend in Zoroastrian learning arranged history in thousand-year cycles. Alexander the destroyer is placed at the end of one of these cycles, and at the end of the next millennial cycle came the onslaught of the Islamic conquests, with the attendant end of Sasanian Zoroastrian kingship. Some Zoroastrians believed that after another thousand years a cycle would begin in which Zoroastrian belief would be victorious.

From the 1st/7th century on, Zoroastrianism was confronted with the Muslim doctrine that a revealed religion should have a central revealed scripture. The Zoroastrians may well have started the canonization of their scripture long before Islam and may have had other motives for doing so after the advent of Islam. Nevertheless, the context of Islamic scripturalism hastened that canonization and an important part of the codifying and recreating of Zoroastrian scripture was justified by the explanation that it once existed in Istakhr written in gold ink on ox hides, all of which had been burned by Alexander. The account that Alexander had ancient Persian books translated into Greek may be the reason that so much Greek learning was later translated into Pahlavi, a movement that has only been appreciated recently.[61] The memory of the treasury of "scripture" that the Sasanians kept at Istakhr, whatever this treasury may have been, was projected back to the time of Alexander's conquest of the Achaemenids. It is not surprising that in the time of Ibn al-Balkhī, one of the hills next to Istakhr was still called Kuh-e Nafasht, "Mountain of Writing/Scripture,"

60 Thaʿālibī, *Ghurar al-Siyar* (Paris, Imprimerie nationale: 1900) 4.
61 Dimitri Gutas, *Greek Thought, Arabic Culture* (New York, Routledge: 1998).

which is presumably the same as the *dezi nebesht* (i.e., "fortress of the Scriptures") mentioned in the *Arda Wiraf Namag* quoted above.[62]

With the passage of time, and the conversion of the Zoroastrians of Fars to Islam, a more relaxed view of the past became possible. Again, Ibn al-Balkhī represents this trend. He reports history as recounted by the "Pārsiyān," without any concern as to whether he is talking of Zoroastrians or Muslims. Not only the inscriptions at Persepolis but also many important literary sources written by Muslim Persians amply testify to the complete acceptance of the remains of the pre-Islamic past. They have been successfully rebaptized as both Solomonic and Jamshidic remains. The Solomonic heritage of Fars, evident from the earliest Qur'ān commentaries, had now become widely accepted and the rulers of Shiraz began to add to their titles, both in inscriptions and in the poems by their accepted panegyrists, "Heir of the Kingdom of Solomon."

There are many aspects of the stories of Solomon's earlier journeys that illustrate the larger contexts in which these stories existed. One context is provided by what I have called earlier in this essay "correlative chronology," although the phrase "comparative chronology" bears a similar meaning. Interest in correlating chronologies is no stranger to the Western tradition. The "father of history," Herodotus, is troubled that the Egyptians reckon Hercules to be seventeen thousand years before the Pharaoh Ahmose II (r. 570–526 B.C.E.) whereas the Greeks know him to have lived less than a thousand years earlier (Bk. II). Similarly, one of the greatest minds of the Enlightenment, Sir Isaac Newton, in his last work, *The Chronology of Ancient Kingdoms Amended,* dates Hercules to 956 B.C.E., and in "correlating" him with Biblical history, Sir Isaac states that Hercules lived in the time of "Asa King of Judah."[63]

Correlating Biblical history with ancient Iranian history was a major concern for many premodern Muslim historians. The anonymous 5th/11th-century Persian work *Mojmal al-Tavārikh* says that King Khosraw, a great ruler in Iranian history, asked Solomon, who was king of Syria, "to send him some *div*s so that they could erect buildings for him. These [the author says] are the gigantic structures one finds in Pars

62 Ibn al-Balkhī, *Fārsnāmah*, trans. Guy Le Strange, *Journal of the Royal Asiatic Society* (1912) 137.

63 Isaac Newton, *The Chronology of Ancient Kingdoms Amended* (London, J. Tonson *et al.*: 1728) 191–264 (Chapter II, "Of the Empire of Egypt").

and other places that are called the Throne of Solomon."[64] Other authors suggest further correlations. In the Sufi or Sufi-esque poetic sensibility of the time of Sa'di and Ḥāfeẓ, which favored easy interchange of heroes and symbols, the equation of Solomon and Jamshid was made so frequently that poets even called Asaf, the Biblical adviser to Solomon, the minister of Jamshid. A 4th/10th-century eastern Iranian author, once thought to be Ibn Muṭahhar al-Maqdisī, confesses his total confusion as to the identity of Jamshid:

> The Persians describe the king Jamshadh as having the qualities of Solomon. I do not know if they are the same man, or he is the Persian Solomon, or neither. If their accounts are true, the man must be one of the prophets, for no one else could do the miracles [ascribed to him].[65]

The mutual accommodation of the Persian and Muslim traditions is a vast topic that can be only very briefly treated in this chapter. Such accommodation used to be called "syncretism," a term which the veteran scholar of religions (and accomplished Iranist) Carsten Colpe still thought useful in his article on the subject published in 1987.[66] Colpe did complain of the looseness of the term and its negative overtones, as well as its implicit reference to supposedly "pure" and "uncontaminated" traditions. Nevertheless, he felt that it applied to situations in which "a unity of type is preserved." This approach seems to create a new barrier for students of religion, insofar as it demands that such a unity be demonstrated, an easier task for Colpe's work on Manichaeism than in the many diffuse systems of belief actually found in most societies in most periods.

Colpe carefully distinguishes between syncretism and various parallel phenomena, such as symbiosis and acculturation, and these classifications may be useful to some religionists. But an application of Occam's Razor might be appropriate, especially as categories, like essences, draw

---

64 Anon., *Mojmal*, (*supra* n. 29) 47.

65 *Kitāb al-Bad' wa-l-Ta'rīkh*, ed. Clément Huart, III (Paris, Leroux: 1918) 106; the editor identifies the author as Aḥmad ibn Sahl al-Balkhī, who wrote under the authority of the Sāmānid official Ibn Muṭahhar al-Maqdisī.

66 Carsten Colpe, "Syncretism," in *The Encyclopedia of Religion*, ed. Mircea Eliade, vol. 14 (New York, Macmillan: 1987) 218–227.

attention away from the phenomena themselves, in particular, from their context and fluidity.[67]

Sometimes identities from one tradition to another are sincerely adopted. Herodotus believed in the identity of the Egyptian and the Greek Hercules. In other cases, they are hopefully adopted. In an anecdote about the Moghul emperor Akbar (still current in India) it is said that when he was buying relics for his new religion, his vizier remarked, "Your majesty, you have just bought a fifth hoof of the donkey that bore Jesus into Jerusalem." Akbar replied: "Who knows: one of them may be genuine."

Belief that the great pre-Islamic ruins in Fars were built by King Solomon was held in part devoutly, as is seen from the insistence of the entire tradition of Qur'ānic commentary that Istakhr was a palatial construction and remote destination of Solomon. It was also held with various levels of hopefulness, as is seen from the variety of commitments to the identification of Jamshid with Solomon. This identification is part of the cultural language of pre-modern Muslims of the Persianate world. As in language itself, the etymology of the words (or symbolic images and heroes) used means little to speakers of the language. Pre-modern Persianate Muslims did not "paste" their own traditions onto Muslim traditions just as they did not "paste" their own tradition onto Islam. Rather, the elements of what they considered to be history were integrated by them into plausible historical accounts.

The resonances of these accounts in the minds of pre-modern Persianate Muslims and, in particular, the inhabitants of Fars in southwestern Iran were sufficient to keep ancient sacred places still revered in Islamic times. These resonances came to permeate Persian literature. Historical accounts created a tradition and a site, Persepolis-Istakhr, to pay homage in the Islamic period to an ongoing narrative of Persian kingship. What may have seemed to Zoroastrians a poignant past emerged among pre-modern Persianate Muslims as an affirming past lending glory to both Persepolis and Jerusalem.

---

67 For a different but important critique of Colpe, see Fritz Graf, "Syncretism (Further Considerations)," in *Encyclopedia of Religion*, 2nd ed., ed. Lindsay Jones, vol. 13 (New York, Macmillan: 2004) 8934–8938, viewed online May 28, 2011.

The Idea of Iran in the Buyid Dominions

At the beginning of the tenth century C.E. fierce spear-carrying warriors from the Caspian provinces, that great reservoir of Iranian identity, began to establish dynasties on the Iranian plateau.[1] The most successful of these warriors were the Buyids who came from the region of Daylam, a name that, by extension, came to be used for most of the southern Caspian region. It is important to remember that, according to the legends of Ṭabaristān, the sons of Qārin, a great Sasanian family, ruled much of this area from the time of their appointment as governors in the reign of Chosroes I, or Khosraw Anushirvān. Ibn Isfandiyār gives some members of the Qārinid dynasty the title *pādeshāh,* which they may well have assumed after the Muslim conquest of the Iranian plateau.[2]

From the 1st/7th to the 3rd/9th century the Muslim conquest of the Caspian provinces was never complete and, in most cases, temporary. Right through the 3rd/9th century Qazvin was considered a garrison city that faced the dangerous Daylamīs.[3] The conversion of the province to Islam may have happened at the hands of Zaydī Imams who ruled in the 3rd/9th century. In any case, the history of the local dynasties of the Caspian provinces such as the Bāvandids, the Bāduspānids and their respective titles

---

Author's note: This article was first published as: "The Idea of Iran in the Buyid Dominions," in Edmund Herzig and Sarah Steward (eds.), *Early Islamic Iran: The Idea of Iran*, 5 (London and New York, I.B. Tauris: 2012) 153–160. Both Persian and Arabic transliteration are used in this article. Reproduced by permission of Bloomsbury Publishing Plc.

1 The weapon associated with the Daylamīs is the *zūbīn* or *zhūbīn.* Cf. 'Ali-Akbar Dehkhoda, *Loghat-Nāma*, V (Tehran, Tehran University: 1373 A.H.) 11, n. 453.

2 Mohamed Rekaya, "Ḳārinids," in *The Encyclopaedia of Islam*, 2nd ed. (hereafter *EI²*), IV (Leiden, Brill: 1978) 644–647.

3 'Abd al-Karīm ibn Muḥammad Rāfi'ī, *al-Tadwīn fī Akhbār Qazwīn*, 4 vols, (Tehran, Atarid: 1374 A.H.) *passim.*

would be the work of another article. Here I discuss the Daylamī Buyids, who controlled Rayy, Isfahan, Shiraz, Baghdad and Basra.

The Buyids are seen as having revived the Iranian tradition of kingship, an interpretation that is partly true. ʿAḍud al-Dawla (ʿAżod al-Dawla) revived the ancient Persian title of *shāhānshāh*, which was written on his coins and used in many other contexts.[4] In conscious imitation of the Sasanian monarchs he founded a city in Fars named Kard-e Fannā Khosraw, Fannā Khosraw being ʿAḍud al-Dawla's given name.[5] According to Bīrūnī he revived the Persian festivals of Sadah and Mehregān.[6]

ʿAḍud al-Dawla's most moving tributes to the Iranian past are his inscriptions at Persepolis inscribed over the doorway of the Palace of Darius. The longer of his two Arabic inscriptions reads:

> In the name of God: The illustrious *amīr*, ʿAḍud al-Dawla Fannā Khusraw, son of al-Ḥasan, was present here in the year 344 on his victorious return from the conquest of Isfahan, the capture of Ibn Mākān, and the defeat of the army of Khorasan. He ordered that there be brought before him one who read the inscriptions on these ruins.[7]

A second short inscription, engraved at the same time as the first, names the *mobad* who read the writing on the ruins for ʿAḍud al-Dawla; he was Mārasfand of Kāzerun, a known Zoroastrian scholar of the time. These inscriptions are placed next to the inscription written for the infant Shāpūr II who was brought on a visit to Persepolis in 311 C.E. In his inscription Shāpūr wrote that: "He prayed for the one who had this building

4 On the assumption of the title *shāhānshāh*, see the learned articles by Lutz Richter-Bernburg, "'*Amīr-Malik-Shāhānshāh*: 'Adud ad-Daula's Titulature Re-examined," *Iran* 18 (1980) 83–102 and Wilfred Madelung, "The Assumption of the Title Shahanshah by the Buyids and the Reign of the Daylam (Dawlat Al-Daylam)," *Journal of Near Eastern Studies* 28: 2 (1969) 84–108.

5 Richter-Bernburg, (*supra* n. 4), 89 gives this place name with an *ezāfa*, but an equally good case can be made for reading it without the *ezāfa* to mean "Fannā Khosraw did/built it."

6 See Christof Bürgel and Roy Mottahedeh, "ʿAzod al-Dawla," *Encyclopaedia Iranica*, III (London and New York, Routledge & Kegan Paul: 1989) 265–269.

7 Translation adapted from the excellent article by John J. Donohue, "Three Buwayhid Inscriptions" in *Arabica* 20: 1 (1973) 74–80. Of philological interest in this inscription is the spelling of the second element in the ruler's name as "Khusra." Isfahan is written in the standard Arabic form, Iṣfāhān.

constructed."[8] The Buyids claimed royal Iranian lineage.[9] That 'Aḍud al-Dawla and later his son Bahā' al-Dawla placed their inscriptions next to that of one of the great Sasanian kings is totally fitting.

The third Buyid inscription, written for Bahā' al-Dawla, is significant in that it explicitly mentions the Iranian title "king of kings" in its Sasanian form, *shāhānshāh*, but only after it has given the Arabic equivalent, *malik al-mulūk*. Bahā' al-Dawla, moreover, seems to have been equally interested in giving the multiple Arabic titles granted him by the caliph, *ḍiyā' al-milla* and *ghiyāth al-umma*, which are repeated twice in the inscription. The inscription is dated to 392/1001–2.[10]

Yet 'Aḍud al-Dawla also displayed the limitation of the Buyids in their self-Iranization. He commissioned a would-be definitive Arabic grammar, the famous *al-Iḍāḥ al-'Aḍudī* (*'Aḍud's Clarification* [*of Arabic Grammar*]), so named by the author Abū 'Alī al-Fārisī, as a tribute to the ruler. Abū 'Alī al-Fārisī also composed a work on grammatical questions asked of him while at the Buyid court in Shiraz called, amusingly, *al-Masā'il al-Shīrāzīyāt* (*The Shirazi Questions*). One manuscript of this work introduces the book by quoting Abū 'Alī al-Fārisī as saying, "I have written it for our master, the glorious king 'Aḍud al-Dawla, may God prolong his reign and perpetuate his rule and make his royal sovereignty firm."[11] The very distinguished grammarian Ibn al-Jinnī is said by Yāqūt to have written a fifty-page book entitled *al-Bushrā wa-l-Ẓafar* as a commentary on a single (in my view, rather mediocre) verse of Arabic poetry by his patron 'Aḍud al-Dawla.[12] As far as I know, this mighty ruler never showed any interest in New Persian.

Richard Frye has argued persuasively that western Iran under the Buyids was still dominated by the Zoroastrian clergy who specialized in Avestan and Pahlavi texts and therefore had little interest in using New

8 Vesta S. Curtis, "The Legacy of Ancient Persia," in John Curtis and Nigel Tallis (eds.), *The Forgotten Empire: The World of Ancient Persia* (London, The British Museum Press: 2005) 250–257, 252.

9 Clifford E. Bosworth, "The Heritage of Rulership in Early Islamic Iran and the Search for Dynastic Connections with the Past," *Iranian Studies* 11:1/4 (1978) 7–34.

10 Donohue, (*supra* n. 7), 78–80.

11 Al-Fārisī, *al-Masā'il al-Shīrāziyāt*, ed. by Hasan Hindaw, I (Riyadh, Konuz: 2004) p."h."

12 Yāqūt, *Irshād al-Arīb ilā Ma'rifat al-Adīb*, III (Beirut, Dar al-Kutub al-'Ilmīya: 1991) 479.

Persian.[13] This estimate seems generally correct for southwestern Iran. In his late 4th/10th century geography Ibn Ḥawqal writes:

> They speak three languages. [First, there is] Farsi, which they all understand and speak to each other. However, they use expressions that differ, without making their speech incomprehensible to the majority of the people. There is, moreover, the language in which the works of the Persians as well as their annals, including the correspondence of Zoroastrians among each other is composed: this is Pahlavi, which needs to be explained to be accessible to Persians. [Finally,] there is Arabic, which is used in all documents of state and ministries as well as for people in general.[14]

It should be noted that the Buyids of Iraq and their viziers were great patrons of literature and learning in Arabic. Al-Muhallabī, the vizier at the Buyid court in Baghdad for decades before his death in 352/963 was surrounded by a brilliant circle of poets and literary scholars including Ibn al-Hajjāj, Ibrāhīm al-Ṣābi and Abū al-Faraj al-Iṣfahānī, the author of the *Kitāb al-Aghāni*.

The Buyid court at Rayy was dominated for a long time by the celebrated vizier Ṣāhib ibn ʿAbbād, who is said to have preferred Arabic to his native Persian and who, as far as I know, wrote only in Arabic. Ibn ʿAbbād certainly accepted panegyrics directed to him in New Persian. Moḥammad ʿAwfi, an admittedly later source, as he wrote in the early 7th/13th century, mentions Manṣur ʿAli al-Manṭeqi al-Rāzi as a Persian poet who praised Ibn ʿAbbād, but almost all of the surviving poetry about this vizier is in Arabic.[15] Ibn ʿAbbād even supported claims to the superiority of Arabic literary culture as against the *shuʿūbīya* movement, which emphasized the equality of all cultures embraced by Muslims.[16]

Buyid courts in southwestern Iran both cooperated and competed to give similar patronage to Arabic letters. The well-known story of

---

13 Richard N. Frye, "Die Wiedergeburt Persiens um die Jabrtausendwende," *Der Islam* 35 (1960) 42–51.

14 Ibn Ḥawqal, *Kitāb Ṣūrat al-Arḍ*, eds. Johannes H. Kramers and Gaston Wiet (Leiden, Brill: 1939) 289.

15 Moḥammad ʿAwfi, *Lubāb al-Albāb* (Tehran, Etteḥād: 1335 A.H.) 254–256.

16 See Erez Naaman, *Literature and the Islamic Court: Cultural Life under al-Sahib Ibn ʿAbbad* (New York: 2016), based on his outstanding Harvard University dissertation (2009).

the enthusiastic reception of Mutanabbī, the greatest of the medieval Arabic poets, at the court of ʿAḍud al-Dawla in Shiraz is one striking example of Buyid patronage of Arabic literature in western Iran.[17] All the preceding, and much more, is to say that although the Buyids had a sentimental attachment to the Iranian past and, in particular, to an Iranian tradition of kingship, they were not attracted to the New Persian learning of eastern Iran.

Now I will discuss briefly a largely contemporaneous phenomenon, by no means confined to the Buyid kingdoms, namely, the revival of interest in the concept of "Īrānshahr." The idea of Īrānshahr is present in the works of geographers writing in Arabic from the beginning of that discipline. Most of these geographers happened to be Iranian. Iṣṭakhrī (Eṣṭakhri), from the province of Fars as his name implies, was a subject of the Buyids during the late 4th/10th century for at least some of his lifetime. He writes:

> The best cultivated (*ma'mūr*), fairest and most fertile part of the world, and the most established in its political life is the kingdom of *Īrānshahr*.[18]

Īrānshahr at that time was understood to include southern Iraq, called Babylon (Bābil) in these sources, and it is tempting to see the union under the Buyids of western Iran with southern Iraq as an encouragement to this ancient geographical unit.

Somewhat unexpected is the exaggerated version of the claim as to the paradisiacal character of Īrānshahr combined with distasteful racism found in the famous *Kitāb al-Bad' wa-l-Ta'rīkh* ascribed to al-Muṭahhar ibn Ṭāhir al-Maqdisī, a Sāmānid official writing around 355/966:

> They say the most temperate and delicious clime of the world is Īrānshahr, the clime of Bābil, between the river Balkh up to the Euphrates longitudinally and between the Caspian down to the Persian Ocean and Yemen then to Makrān and Kābul and Tukharestān and the confines of Azerbaijan. It is the choicest part

17 On the flourishing Arabic-language culture of the Buyid courts, see the classic study by Joel L. Kraemer, *Humanism in the Renaissance of Islam: The Cultural Revival during the Buyid Age* (Leiden and New York, Brill: 1992).

18 Iṣṭakhrī, *Kitāb Masālik al-Mamālik* (Leiden, Brill: 1927) 4.

> of the earth, the *omphalos*, because of the balanced nature of the colors of its people and the proportions of their bodies and the soundness of their intellect. They are free of the "ruddiness" of the Romans and the "harshness" of the Turks and the "unseemliness" of the Chinese and the "short stature" of the Gog and Magog and the "blackness" of the Ethiopians and the "stupidity" of the Zanj and therefore it is called Īrān, meaning the "heart of lands," since *īrān* meant "heart" in ancient Babylonian. [Iran is the land] of the wise and the learned and the home of generosity, mercy, subtle distinguishing, and apprehension [as well as] every praiseworthy characteristic the absence of which distinguishes [other] people on earth ... acquaintance with these lands is sufficient for you so that anyone who visits from elsewhere must feel in his soul [a wish] to return there, their own lands not being like that at all. But God knows best.[19]

An extremely expansive definition of Irānshahr is offered by the mid-4th/10th-century author Abu Manṣur Maḥmud ibn ʿAbd al-Razzāq al-Ṭusi, who, according to the great Iranian scholar Mohammad Qazvini, wrote one of the oldest passages in New Persian prose that survives. In his introduction to a lost *Shāhnāma* Ṭusi says that Irānshahr "extends from the Oxus River to the Nile."[20] Incidentally, his Islamic warrant for transmitting knowledge of the ancient Iranians is a famous ḥadīth considered to be the warrant for the Isrāʾīlīyāt. Ṭusi writes:

> Those who are the enemies of knowledge consider these stories of the ancient Persians unseemly; but in this world amazement finds abundant cause. As the Apostle of God said: "Transmit accounts from the Israelites without hesitation." [Ṭusi then translates this saying into Persian as]: "Everything you hear from the Israelites, listen to all of it, for all of it actually happened and is not a lie."[21]

---

19 The actual author is identified as Aḥmad ibn Sahl al-Balkhī by the editor and translator; *Kitāb al-Badʾ wa-l-Taʾrīkh*, ed. Clément Huart, IV (Paris, Ernest Leroux: 1899–1919) 97–98.

20 Qazvini, "Moqaddama-ye Qadim-e Shāhnāma," *Bist Maqāla* 2 (Tehran, Adah: 1332 A.H.) 49. I thank Professor Touraj Daryaee for calling my attention to this introduction by Ṭusi. In Persian, Irānshahr does not have a long I.

21 Qazvini, (*supra* n. 20), 38.

We should remember that a large number of writers of this period considered the Persians to be descendants of Isaac or Isḥāq.[22]

It is not surprising that the most perceptive definition of Īrānshahr comes from the nearly incomparable Abū Rayḥān al-Bīrūnī, who is thought to have died in 442/1050. In the *Taḥdīd Nihāyāt al-Amākin* he writes:

> First, I say that for political reasons and for fixing the demarcation lines between kingdoms, the inhabited world was partitioned into seven circular parts, like the six circles which encircle (tangentially) a seventh circle, when all circles are equal. The reason for this division is that the great kings were natives of Īrānshahr which consists of 'Iraq, Fars, Jibāl, and Khorasan ...
>
> This partition has nothing to do with natural climatic conditions, nor with astronomical phenomena. It is made according to kingdoms which differ from one another for various reasons—different features of their peoples and different codes of morality and customs.[23]

It is important at this point to consider the kind of Persian spoken in the Buyid kingdoms of western Iran. There are a number of examples of Persian prose and poetry translated into Arabic. We have an example of the great Arabic prose stylist from Hamadan, Badī' al-Zamān, spontaneously translating Persian verses into Arabic in a Buyid court setting.[24] Furthermore, we know from Māfarrokhi's Arabic *History of Isfahan*, of which we have the medieval Persian translation, that an Iṣfahānī insulted Rokn al-Dawla "in the Iṣfahānī tongue" (*be zabān-e Eṣfahāni*).[25]

This and much other evidence indicates that, when not cultivating Arabic, the Buyid courts of western Iran spoke western dialects of Persian, the famous *fahlavīyāt*, which continued to be used into the Seljuk period. The area called *Fahla* included Isfahan, Rayy, Hamadan, Nihāvand and

22 My former student, the talented Sarah Savant, discusses the genealogical claims of the Iranians exhaustively in her book, *The New Muslims of Post-Conquest Iran: Tradition, Memory and Conversion* (Cambridge, U.K., and New York, Cambridge University Press: 2013).

23 Bīrūnī, *Taḥdīd Nihāyāt al-Amākin* (Ankara, Dogus: 1962) 105–106; *The Determination of the Coordinates of Positions for the Correction of Distances between Cities*, trans. Jamil Ali (Beirut, American University of Beirut Press: 1967) 101–102.

24 'Awfi, (*supra* n. 15), 255.

25 Māfarrokhi, *Mahāsen-e Eṣfahān* (Eṣfahān, Markaz-e Eṣfahān-Shenāsi: 1385 A.H.) 119. I thank my former student Professor Alexander Key for drawing my attention to this passage.

Azerbaijan, almost all of which were ruled by the Buyids. There was a genre of poetry in the western Iranian dialects of this area that may have competed with the New Persian of eastern Iran.[26] It is significant that Asadi Ṭusi, writing at the very end of the Buyid period, introduces his dictionary of Persian, *Loghat-e Fors*, by saying that, "It is the tongue of the people of Balkh and Transoxiana and elsewhere."[27] Specialists have always considered New Persian to be the language of Fars, as spoken by the people of eastern Iran, somewhat analogous to the famous formulation of Italian as "la lingua Toscana in bocca Romana."

Considered together the preceding materials offer important clues to the question of Iranian identity under the Buyids. In the first instance we have rulers who are unashamedly Iranian and who sought by genealogy, title and homage to Persepolis to show their connection with the pre-Islamic Iranian past. At the same time, the inhabitants of the Buyid kingdoms and eastern Iranians showed a sometimes embarrassingly high level of self-esteem as the people of Īrānshahr.

Then why did the Buyids fail to cultivate New Persian, which they undoubtedly understood? First, as I have mentioned, the Buyids were influenced by their presence in Baghdad and were in competition to be great patrons of Arabic letters. Secondly, the influence of the *mobads*, Zoroastrian priests who wrote in Pahlavi in provinces such as Fars, might have deterred the use of New Persian. A third reason could be that the New Persian of eastern Iran was still at variance with the Persian dialects of western Iran, such as the Iṣfahānī dialect mentioned above, and was not yet widely accepted outside of eastern Iran.

Yet another reason for the lack of interest of the Buyids in New Persian might be religion. This suggestion is highly speculative. The true beginning of the dissemination of New Persian as a prose medium is associated with a Sāmānid program to create a popular Islamic literature in New Persian, which is widely associated with the Persian adaptation of the great world history of Ṭabarī.[28] A somewhat neglected part of this program was the translation into New Persian in 370 A.H., at the order of the Sāmānid ruler

26 The classic article on the subject is by Ahmad Tafazzoli, "Fahlavīyāt," *Encyclopaedia Iranica*, IX/2 (Leiden, Brill: 1999) 158–162, (viewed online January 5, 2011). Tafazzoli quotes only one example of *fahlavīhyāt* from Fars province.

27 Asadi Ṭusi, *Loghat-e Fors*, ed. M. Dabir-e Siyaqi (Tehran, Tahuri: 1977) 1.

28 See the learned work of Andrew C.S. Peacock, *Mediaeval Islamic Historiography and Political Legitimacy: Bal'amī's Tārīkhnāma* (London, Routledge: 2007).

Nūḥ, of a strongly Sunni creed by the Ḥanafī scholar from Transoxiana, Abu Esḥāq ibn Moḥammad al-Samarqandi.[29] The Buyids were Shi'ites without belonging to any specific Shi'ite group. They were not interested in converting their Sunni Muslim subjects to Shi'ism and probably realized they would rouse resistance among their subjects by a translation project favoring Shi'ism. They did, however, patronize Shi'ite learning, which was largely centered in Iraq at that time and therefore written in Arabic.

It would await the coming of the Seljuk Turks and their many eastern Iranian officials in the mid-5th/11th century before western Iran would openly delight in the beautiful New Persian language. Paradoxically, New Persian, which was so ably promoted in the Turkish court of Maḥmūd of Ghazna, continued to be cultivated by the Turkish rulers of their successor state, the Great Seljuks. All these Turkish rulers hoped to connect themselves with the kingly tradition represented by the *Shāhnāma* which offered an ideal of rulership that they could easily and happily embrace.

29 Samarqandi, *Tarjoma-ye al-Savād al-A'ẓam* (Tehran, Enteshārāt-e Bonyād-e Farhang-e Īrān: 1969).

ISLAMIC LITERATURE

Half of my Harvard career was devoted to teaching Arabic and Persian texts, and I have been a text-driven historian of the Islamic world. Islamic literature of the pre-modern period addresses every kind of subject. Persian and Arabic poetry and prose is known to the Western world because of people like Omar Khayyam and classics like *The Thousand and One Nights*. However, there are many equally deserving classics in both languages as well as masterpieces on other subjects such as Rumi's *Maṯnavi* in Persian on the mystic love of God and Avicenna's (Ibn Sīnā's) medical and philosophical works in Arabic. There are histories, biographies, geographies, medical studies, botanical studies, philosophy, etc.

It is important to note that the Islamic Middle East greatly admired some works of antiquity before Western Europe paid attention to these works. Aristotle was so well respected that some medieval Muslims thought him to be a prophet sent by God. Many other Greek texts of antiquity were known and used as the basis for further study in the Islamic world, including those by such well-known authors as Hippocrates, Euclid, and Ptolemy. The Islamic world knew less about Latin texts because the Muslims conquered territories that had been Greek centers of learning, such as Alexandria in Egypt, Antioch in Syria, and Konya (Iconium) in Turkey, as well as later Byzantine centers such as Constantinople. The great 7th/13th-century Sufi mystic Jalāl al-Din Rumi even wrote some poems in demotic Greek.

As an historian, my focus in teaching was largely on historical and, to a lesser extent, legal texts, but I would have happily taught Islamic literature if there were not others better qualified. It would be wonderful if more of these texts were published in their original language with facing translations, as was done in the Loeb Library for Latin and Greek classics.

My first article in this section, "*'Ajā'ib* in *The Thousand and One Nights*," was delivered at a conference in 1989 on the *The Thousand and One Nights* honoring André Miquel, held at UCLA and published in the Giorgio Levi della Vida Series in Islamic Studies in 1997. The *Nights* surprisingly gained its status as a literary classic in the Western world before it achieved this standing in the Islamic world, where originally it was admired only as folk literature. It picked up and dropped stories as it went through the centuries because no one thought it a "classical" book with a definitive text. In *The Thousand and One Nights* curiosity is provoked by contradictions. There is an appeal for patience in most tales; then some participants lose patience and demand to know what is happening. They are subsequently punished for their impatience. The hitherto unexplained reasons for their curiosity are "amazing" and "astonishing" things or events. The narrators of the *Nights* present themselves as topping one another in their tales of the amazing and astonishing partly to draw the reader on.

More than a decade earlier I had become interested in the subject of *'ajā'ib* when some of my colleagues in European history began discussing *mirabilia* or "marvelous things" in the Renaissance. Subsequently, I discovered that a similar genre of literature existed in both Arabic and Persian, the most famous exemplar being the *'Ajā'ib al-Makhlūqāt* (*The Marvels of Creation*) by Qazwīnī, written in the 7th/13th century. I gave a series of three invited lectures at the British Library in 1991 on this text and its many illustrations, and then repeated this series of lectures in the United States and elsewhere. I never published this work but allowed recordings to be made so that younger scholars could carry my research further.

My second article in this section, "Finding Iran in the Panegyrics of the Ghaznavid Court," was written for a conference on "Eastern Iran and Transoxiana, 750–1150," at St. Andrews in Scotland in 2013. It was published in 2015 in *Medieval Central Asia and the Persianate World: Iranian Tradition and Islamic Civilisation*, edited by A.C.S. Peacock and D.G. Tor. This article developed from my long interest in early Persian poetry, especially in the Ghaznavid and Seljuk courts. I first read parts of Firdausi's (Ferdawsi's) famous *Book of Kings* (*Shāhnāma*), written in the early 5th/11th century, in second-year Persian. However, I soon realized that the secondary literature on this Iranian national epic would take more than a lifetime to consume. In the end I settled on writing about Firdausi's contemporaries at the court of Maḥmūd of Ghazna. They were, in some ways, a more manageable subject and, in their panegyrics, I focused on their understanding of Iran.

Leading poets in the medieval period made a living in large part by writing panegyrics. We forget that once upon a time well-known English poets like Dryden, who became the first Poet Laureate of England in 1668, supported themselves in the same way. Panegyrics were a very significant part of kingly glory in the medieval world, especially as they could long survive such kings. The relationship between poet and ruler was mutually beneficial. The "immortality" sought by the ruler could be gained through the lasting influence of the poet's panegyric, often officially recorded by the court. The wealth and repute sought by the poet could be gained through the patronage of the ruler and others. This network of mutual expectation not unexpectedly restrained rulers and mighty subjects like viziers on some occasions.

It is noteworthy that so many panegyrists of the 5th/11th and 6th/12th century mention Iran as a country deserving to be ruled by a proper king such as the one being praised by the panegyrist. An extremely learned Iranologist has claimed that awareness of Iran as a geographical polity only reappeared in the Ilkhanid or Mongol period following its disappearance with the Arab conquest. However, the panegyrics (largely untranslated) from the Ghaznavid period reveal Iran as a political unit ruled by kings who celebrate themselves as rulers of Iran specifically well before the Mongol period. In these Ghaznavid panegyrics the frequent reference to Iran as the kingdom of Maḥmūd shows that this milieu, in which Firdausi lived, recognized the designation of the country called Iran in their work.

Poetry does not have the central place in our society that it once had, and panegyrics have largely disappeared to be replaced by eulogies at funerals. However, it is still common practice among aspiring candidates for political office and applicants for other positions to attempt to promote themselves or gain prestige by associating themselves with earlier figures of significance, especially if they happen to have been taught or trained by that important person.

For this reason, the Republican Party in the United States used to call itself the party of Lincoln, and young lawyers clerking at the Supreme Court for Ruth Bader Ginsburg and Antonin Scalia used to emphasize their association and training with these important figures who came from opposite ends of the political spectrum.

'Ajā'ib in *The Thousand and One Nights*

My title, "'Ajā'ib in The Thousand and One Nights", may suggest a fairly straightforward project; namely, to relate that genre of literature called, in Arabic, *'ajā'ib* (loosely: marvels, wonders, and astonishing things) to its obvious cognates and possible derivatives in *The Thousand and One Nights*. This project has been alluded to many times, even by the careless but fascinating Richard Burton, who, over a century ago, in his notes to his celebrated translation, said that Sindbad:

> is a fanciful compilation, like Defoe's "Captain Singleton," borrowed from travelers of an immense variety and extracts from al-Idrisi, al-Kazwini [referring, of course, to the *'Ajā'ib al-Makhlūqāt* by al-Qazwīnī] and Ibn al-Wardi ... [We also find, among other things,] sundry cuttings from Moslem writers dating between our ninth and fourteenth centuries. [And he adds in a separate note:] E.g. *'Ajā'ib al-Hind* [of the] ninth century.[1]

This project, in spite of its obvious importance, has to my knowledge been accomplished only in the most fragmentary way.

My project here, however, is both less ambitious and more treacherous: to describe the place of the emotion of astonishment called *'ajab* or *ta'ajjub*,

---

Author's note: This article was first published as: "*'Ajā'ib in The Thousand and One Nights*," in Richard G. Hovannisian and Georges Sabagh (eds.), *The Thousand and One Nights in Arabic Literature and Society*. Giorgio Levi della Vida Series in Islamic Studies 12 (Cambridge, U.K., and New York, N.Y., Cambridge University Press: 1997) 29–39. Reproduced by permission.

1 *The Book of The Thousand Nights and a Night*, trans. Richard F. Burton (New York: 1962) 3713 and 3841. The *'Ajā'ib al-Makhlūqāt* by Qazwīnī, to which he refers, begins with an important discussion of the meaning of the *astonishing* and *strange*.

and the *'ajā'ib*, those objects or events that inspire this astonishment, in *The Thousand and One Nights*. At the outset we should recall that astonishment is one of a vast range of similar words that we use in English, words between which, at least in the past, we could make important distinctions. Many of you will recall the story of the wife of an early nineteenth-century lexicographer who, chancing upon her husband at dalliance with the housemaid, said: "Sir, I am surprised," to which the lexicographer is supposed to have replied, "No, madam, *I* am surprised, *you* are astonished." And what a rich vocabulary English has: we speak of the surprising, the astonishing, the amazing, the wonderful, the fabulous, the curious, the marvelous, and so on and so forth. The marvelous, incidentally, brings us etymologically closest to *mirabilia*, the true Latin equivalent of *'ajā'ib*, since the late antique and medieval European literature on *'ajā'ib* is called *mirabilia*, hence our "seven marvels of the world," and the like.

Arabic has a rich vocabulary for emotions of astonishment, and this paper does *not* deal with all of them. Here I am concerned with *'ajab* and its derivatives; to a lesser extent with *gharīb* and its derivatives; and—very tangentially—with *ḥayra*. *'Ajab* and its derivatives are used several times in the Qur'ān. Significantly, of the Ahl al-Kahf, the Companions of the Cave, or the seven sleepers of Ephesus, the Qur'ān says: "They were wonders [*'ajaban*] among our signs" (Sūra XVIII:9). The common Qur'ānic theme of the world as replete with signs of God evident so as to make any aware person mindful of God, is in this verse further refined. Some of these signs, in distinction from others, are "wonders." This category of wondrous signs quite naturally forms an important theme in homiletic literature. The celebrated sermons of the bat, the peacock, and the ant ascribed to 'Alī in the *Nahj al-Balāgha* are examples of this theme of wondrous signs of God. In his justly admired discussion of Qur'ānic vocabulary, al-Rāghib al-Iṣfahānī, who lived in the late 4th/10th century, explained that "*'ajab* and *ta'ajjub* are states which come to a person at the time of that person's ignorance of the *sabab* [cause] of something."[2] A definition along these lines becomes standard in the scholastic tradition; hence Jurjānī, whose book of definitions was much used by scholastics, says that *'ajab* is "the change of the *nafs* [spirit or soul] through something the cause of which is unknown and goes out of the ordinary."[3] This last element of *'ajab*,

2 *al-Mufradāt fī Gharīb al-Qur'ān*, ed. Muhammad Kaylani (Cairo: 1961) 322.
3 *Kitāb al-Ta'rīfāt*, ed. G. Flügel (Leipzig: 1845) 152.

the perception that something is out of the ordinary, is, of course, the element, that gives *'ajā'ib* their larger career in Arabic and Islamic thought and accounts for the diversity of things that are sometimes considered wondrous and marvelous according to the varying taste of the medieval authors. *'Ajā'ib* can be everything from the remote and unique (like the land of Waq-Waq, at the end of the world, where according to Jāḥiẓ the inhabitants are a cross between plants and animals) all the way to the familiar best-buy items, such as the dates of Basra, which are scrupulously listed by the class of geographers who use *khaṣā'iṣ* (specialities) and *'ajā'ib* almost interchangeably. All such matters are wonderfully well discussed in Professor André Miquel's magisterial *La géographie humaine du monde musulman*, which also makes clear the role of *'ajab* as a source of *adab* in a broadened sense, that is, *adab* as recreative knowledge.

That *The Thousand and One Nights* represents itself as a work that inspires *'ajab* and *gharāba* cannot be doubted. In Muhsin Mahdi's magnificent new edition of the *Nights* the great majority of nights in the first third of the book begins with a formula such as "among the astonishing [*'ajīb*] and strange [*gharīb*] stories of *The Thousand and One Nights* ..."[4] Our second term here, *gharīb*, often appears paired with *'ajīb* in *The Thousand and One Nights* (as elsewhere in Arabic literature) and, again, al-Rāghib al-Iṣfahānī is one of our shrewdest commentators on its meaning: "One says," he explained, "of anything separated away, that it is *gharīb*, and of anything which is not similar to its species [*jins*] that it is *gharīb*. Hence the Prophet said: Islam appeared *gharīb* and it will again be as it then appeared."[5] An important element often present in the *gharīb*, but not in the *'ajīb*, is precisely this sensation of separation and hence loneliness.

The *'ajīb* and, to a lesser extent, the *gharīb* are not only the self-description of the *Nights* in the rubrics of its subsections but they also lie at the very heart of the self-description of the frame tale in which the *Nights* exists. *'Ajab* plays some role in this strange tale of *Schadenfreude* between the two brother kings, Shāhriyār and Shāhzamān, at the very beginning of the *Nights*. When the kings find themselves betrayed by their women, they seek *sulwān* (consolation) for both the *hamm* (distress or anxiety) and—a most important word to which I shall return—*waswās* that they feel. And, in fact, when the two kings hear the story of the woman captured by the

4 *Kitāb Alf Layla wa-Layla* (Leiden: 1984) 124.
5 *al-Mufradāt*, (*supra* n. 2), 359.

ʿifrīt, who nevertheless deceives the *ʿifrīt* about her encounters with men, "they [that is, the two kings] were struck with the utmost astonishment (*taʿajjabū ʿajaban ʿaẓīman*) and rejoiced and said, 'The deceit of women is great.'"[6] Shāhriyār decides that his *sulwān* is to this degree sufficient that he could bear to return to his kingdom, though only at the cost of killing his consort at the end of each night.

ʿAjab, however, appears with its full force in the frame tale when Scheherazade assumes her role as storyteller to Shāhriyār; for, at the end of the very first night, her sister Dīnārzād says to her: "How good your story is and how astonishing," to which Scheherazade answers: "What is this compared to the story I will tell on the next night, if I live and this king spares me; for it is better and more astonishing."[7] Here the *Nights* enters into collusion with the reader in the construction of a system of what we might call suspense: if something astonishing is produced and something more astonishing promised, there is interest and, consequently, hope; and the very next night Dīnārzād says: "How astonishing your story is and how strange"; and Scheherazade again says that on the next night she will tell a story "more astonishing and yet more strange"; and they repeat variants of this formula for many nights to come.[8] Incidentally, its connection with suspense is shown by the reaction of Scheherazade's father, the vizier, when he finds his daughter still alive after her first night with Shāhriyār: "The vizier, the father of Scheherazade, was astonished at that and rejoiced."[9]

This dynamic of astonishment, consolation, temporary reprise, suspense, and hope is reinforced by the very first story that Scheherazade tells, namely "The Merchant and the Genie." When the three sheikhs (*shaykhs*) see that the genie is about to kill the merchant, one of them approaches the genie and says: "Oh thou Satan and crown of the king of genies, if I relate to you the story of myself and this gazelle and you find it astonishing and strange [*ʿajīb* and *gharīb*] in comparison, more so than what happened to the merchant, will you give up to me a third of your claim on the merchant's life?" The genie agrees and finds the story as promised, just as he finds the story of each of the other two sheikhs more astonishing and strange than the story of the preceding sheikh, as promised, until he reaches an ecstatic state of astonishment (*taʿajjub*): "So the genie was

6 *Kitāb Alf Layla*, (*supra* n. 4), 64.
7 *Kitāb Alf Layla*, (*supra* n. 4), 73–74.
8 *Kitāb Alf Layla*, (*supra* n. 4), 76.
9 *Kitāb Alf Layla*, (*supra* n. 4), 74.

astonished to the utmost limit of astonishment, and shook with ecstasy [*ihtazza min al-ṭarab*]." And, of course, having been adequately paid off in the coin of astonishment, he frees the merchant.[10]

Centrally important as astonishment is to the frame story, it is also extremely important to the internal dynamics of many of the stories enframed; and I hope to demonstrate this importance within the context of the celebrated story of "The Porter and the Three Ladies of Baghdad," and, in particular, the story of "The Third Qalandarī Dervish." Readers of *The Thousand and One Nights* will recall that early in the story of "The Porter and the Three Ladies" when the porter (who has met the ladies only on this day) and the three ladies have settled down to an evening of unrestrained enjoyment, there appears at the door of their house three dervishes, all with heads, eyebrows, and chins shaven and all blind in the right eye. As one of the three ladies appropriately remarks, "This is one of the most amazing of happenings" (or, more accurately in this context, "coincidences": *hādhihi min a'jab al-ittifāqāt*). This turn of phrase points to a variety of "astonishing things" which are important in many stories in *The Thousand and One Nights* and are particularly important in this cycle of stories. These are events that are "astonishing things," not just objects such as magnetic mountains or rocks or self-transforming *'ifrīts*. Such events are "strange and astonishing things" because the cause of their appearance in the sequence of events is, to use Jurjānī's definition, at least at first unknown and out of the ordinary.

To return to the story of "The Porter and the Three Ladies," Hārūn al-Rashīd and Ja'far the Barmecide come along and ask to join the party and the three ladies admit them but only on the condition: "That you be eyes without tongues and that you do not speak of that which does not concern you, lest you have that which will not please you."[11] "And they, like the preceding guests, accept the condition. Not unnaturally when Hārūn sees the three one-eyed dervishes he is astonished (*ta'ajjab*); but when he and the other male guests see one of the ladies flog two dogs violently, then hug and kiss them, all the guests are totally astonished and the caliph loses his patience completely (*'īla ṣabruhu*). But Ja'far the Barmecide, who is consistently wiser than Hārūn al-Rashīd, tells him by a sign: "This is no time for meddling (*fuḍūl*)."[12]

10 *Kitāb Alf Layla*, (*supra* n. 4), 86.
11 *Kitāb Alf Layla*, (*supra* n. 4), 137 (coincidences); 140 (do not speak).
12 *Kitāb Alf Layla*, (*supra* n. 4), 141.

Against Ja'far's advice to Hārūn to be patient throughout the night, as he promised the three ladies, and to question them only in the morning, Hārūn, the porter, and the three dervishes eventually lose control and ask what is going on. At a signal from the ladies armed slaves appear and seize the questioners and prepare to kill them. The porter recites a poem and the ladies relent on the condition that they tell their stories: and the first dervish begins by saying his story is "astonishing" and "strange" (*'ajīb* and *gharīb*) and a "sign to one who can learn from signs" (*'ibra li-man i'tabara*).[13] (Here, incidentally, we again see the relation, noticed in the Qur'ānic verse quoted above, of signs to wonders.) The adventures of the first dervish are full of astonishing and strange things but he is largely a passive participant in them.

The second dervish is somewhat more responsible for his fate (his drunkenness causes him to make an *'ifrīt* aware that he is having an affair with the *'ifrīt*'s wife). The *'ifrīt* transforms the second dervish into a monkey but a monkey with all former human abilities except speech. As this dervish, like all three of the one-eyed men, turns out to be the son of a king, who has received an excellent education, he is soon able to save his life through these abilities. When the monkey jumps onto a ship that comes to the land in which he is stranded, the passengers are about to kill him until the captain and some of the ship's company see the monkey's "astonishingly" human tears and his "astonishingly" human gestures of supplication. Again, astonishment has averted death. Then the monkey indicates he can write, and he proceeds to write seven different poems in seven styles of handwriting beginning with *ruq'a* and ending with *ṭūmār*. Naturally, everyone who encounters the monkey is in a high state of astonishment (as well as *taḥayyur*, or bewilderment),[14] not only because of his literacy but also because of the exquisite courtly manners the monkey now displays when presented to the monarch. Eventually, he regains his human form but loses an eye, is banished, and becomes a dervish.

The third dervish starts by saying, "My story is stranger [*aghrab*] and more astonishing [*a'jab*] because the other two were badly treated by fate [*al-qaḍā' wa-l-qadar*] but I am the one who pulled my fate to me with my hand and pulled distress [*hamm*] to my soul."[15] It is not a coincidence that this third dervish is actually named 'Ajīb, "The Astonishing One." 'Ajīb is

13 *Kitāb Alf Layla*, (*supra* n. 4), 147.
14 *Kitāb Alf Layla*, (*supra* n. 4), 172.
15 *Kitāb Alf Layla*, (*supra* n. 4), 178.

a curious man, and his curiosity leads him to all sorts of *'ajā'ib*, including the accidental manslaughter of a youth he deeply admires. In yet another episode his patience is taxed in a strange parallel to the circumstances that taxed the patience of the men at the house of the three ladies: he meets ten one-eyed men who live in a palace and who welcome 'Ajīb on the condition that he not ask their story, especially the cause of their blindness. Nevertheless, after witnessing for many nights the ten men blacken their faces and strike their cheeks, crying, "We were at ease as long as our meddlesomeness left us alone," 'Ajīb explains: "Wicked inner suggestions [*waswās*] became too much for me and my patience was lost [*'īla ṣabrī*]." And he tells them, in a phrase that is almost an echo of what the ladies told Hārūn al-Rashīd and the other guests when they came, that he will leave the ten men if they do not tell him their story, since "What the eye does not see, the heart does not grieve for."[16] Clearly, in 'Ajīb's view, the need to find the cause (*sabab*) of an astonishing thing overrules all other considerations.

At first the result of his impertinent curiosity seems not at all bad, as he is transported to an incomparably splendid palace, where he is wonderfully entertained for forty days by forty incomparably beautiful princesses, who, however, then leave him for the next forty days on the condition that he not open one specific door among the forty doors in the palace. Behind each of the thirty-nine permitted doors he finds treasures and delights, and with the opening of each door he feels a little less anxiety (*infaraja hammī*).[17] Then, finally, he cannot control his impertinent curiosity: "My inner mind was preoccupied and my soul whispered wicked suggestions to me and Satan passed judgment against me because of my wretchedness, and I did not find the patience (*ṣabr*) to control myself from opening it."[18] And, of course, as a consequence of opening this door he loses sight in one eye and is expelled from this earthly paradise. On encountering the ten blind men who had once taken him in, they tell him that their meddlesomeness (*fuḍūl*) caused each of them in their turn to suffer the same fate. Now they too expel 'Ajīb from their company, and he ends as a dervish at the house of the three ladies of Baghdad.

The story of "The Porter and the Three Ladies of Baghdad," while one of the most entertaining stories in *The Thousand and One Nights*, is by no

16 *Kitāb Alf Layla*, (*supra* n. 4), 190 (patience); 191 (grieve).
17 *Kitāb Alf Layla*, (*supra* n. 4), 197.
18 *Kitāb Alf Layla*, (*supra* n. 4), 198.

means peculiar in the features that interest us, namely: the psychological dimensions of the characters within the stories and the psychological dimensions that the *Nights* suggest should exist between the readers and the text. While medieval Arabic literary criticism gives us an unusually rich analysis of certain formal aspects of language, it has always seemed to me—and, I believe, to other students of that tradition—uninterested in structural analysis of the development of characters and of plot. Do we have really satisfactory discussions of, or even terms for, such elements as suspense and irony, two terms which I think well apply to the stories discussed above? Such analysis is, I argue, not present, at least in part, because two other kinds of analysis took its place: analyses of states of mind and analyses of the moral value of these states of mind and their relation to events.

What in the language of *The Thousand and One Nights* is suspense, that emotion with which this book engrosses us so skillfully and which also engrosses so many of its characters such as Shāhriyār to whom Scheherazade tells the story, or Hārūn al-Rashīd when he wants to know why the lady beats the dogs then kisses them? The encounter with things and events, the *sabab* or reason for which is unknown, creates suspense; and it is the promise that things more astonishing and strange, *a'jab* and *aghrab*, lie ahead that sustains suspense. In his fine essay on *The Thousand and One Nights*, Todorov rightly remarks that in the *Nights* the cry is not "Your money or your life," but "Your story or your life";[19] but we should add to this that, very often, the cry is: "A more amazing story or your life!"

Suspense implies curiosity, and here the moral dimension of the structural analysis of plot and character comes into play. Curiosity is of more than one kind and the third dervish makes it fully clear that what I have translated as "impertinent curiosity" or "meddlesomeness" (*fuḍūl*) is responsible for his misfortune. But *fuḍūl*, meddlesomeness, is one of several bad character traits that spring from *waswās*, "wicked inner suggestions" or "inner disquiet," which, along with *hamm* (anxiety) is supposed to be stilled by the stories of the astonishing things that have been encountered by others. For we are explicitly told on certain occasions that astonishing things gave consolation, *sulwān*, for the inner disquiet and anxieties that exist in figures such as Shāhriyār and the third dervish. Some stories drive

19 Tzvetan Todorov, "Narrative Men," in *The Poetics of Prose*, trans. R. Howard (Ithaca: 1977) 75.

home the moral need to accept suspense by explicit instructions to one or several characters not to ask the reason for the astonishing things they see, or else they will suffer terrible consequences, as Hārūn al-Rashīd is told by the three ladies, and the third dervish, 'Ajīb, is told by the ten blind men.

The self-control that they are asked to exercise is *ṣabr*, "patience" or "patience to control one's self" as I translated it in 'Ajīb's statement about his surrender to the temptation to open the forbidden door. Hārūn al-Rashīd explains his lack of self-control by saying: "My patience was exhausted." And here patience to control oneself emerges as partly cognate in meaning with suspense itself. *Ṣabr* is the quality that should sustain us between the appearance of astonishing things and their explanation, or, at least, stop the murderous king or *'ifrīt* until he hears something more astonishing and yet stranger.

The need for *ṣabr* is driven home by a story in *The Thousand and One Nights* about a sage who, when threatened by the king with death, tells the king that his behavior is like the reward of the crocodile. "What is the story of the crocodile?" demands the king. The sage tells the king that in the face of death he is in no condition to tell the story of the crocodile. Despite much pleading by the sage, the king orders his execution. Just before the sage is decapitated, he offers the king a book to read. The king opens the book while the execution is taking place, finds the pages stuck together, and wets his finger several times to turn the pages until he comes to the seventh leaf, at which point the king says to the sage's severed head, which is still talking though close to death, "I see nothing." "Keep turning the pages," replies the head and the king does so only to find more blank pages. Suddenly, the poison that impregnates the book takes effect and the dying sage has the satisfaction of seeing the king stagger forward and die himself.[20] Not only is the cry of *The Thousand and One Nights* "Your story or your life," it is also "Have the *ṣabr* to listen to *my* story or *you* will lose your life."

Beyond this, astonishment and patience also would seem to be the relation that the *Nights* wishes to establish between the reader and the text; there are astonishing things to explain, and astonishing things to anticipate, and the reader or listener must have *ṣabr* until the narrative explains them. This nexus of astonishment and *ṣabr* is, to my thinking, somehow a cognate of suspense.

20 *Kitāb Alf Layla*, (*supra* n. 4), 103–104.

Irony presents us with a similar problem. Who can doubt the existence of irony in pre-modern Arabic literature in general and in the *Nights* in particular? In *Kalīla wa-Dimna*, there is a wonderful story (not in the *Panchatantra*) of a man who, each time he escapes one pursuer finds himself confronted with a new pursuer, be it a lion or a robber or whatever; and when, finally, totally out of breath, he has escaped them all, he leans against a wall, and the wall falls down and kills him—an example of irony if ever there was one. But what would we call it, in the vocabulary of medieval Arabic criticism, or in the terms mentioned by *The Thousand and One Nights* itself? Certainly, irony is abundantly present in the *Nights*, particularly in the partial and—I would say—ironical duplication of events, as when the third dervish, 'Ajīb, later to be partly blinded, takes us to the society of ten partly blind dervishes, who warn him—as the three dervishes in the frame tale were warned by the ladies of Baghdad—not to be curious. The term for such irony is not *sukhrīya*, which, though present in medieval Arabic literary criticism, corresponds more to mockery. It is interesting to note that one of the better English-Arabic dictionaries offers, among possible translations for "ironic": *fīhī tawrīya ta'jjubīya*, "containing astonishing concealments."[21] Again, I think that a certain kind of astonishment is the emotion that such irony evokes, and one of the important occasions for it is given in the phrase that one of the three ladies of Baghdad used when the three dervishes, all blind in one eye, turn up together on her doorstep: "This is one of the most astonishing happenings" (or "coincidences"); that is, structurally amazing events are a category of astonishing things which, I think, comprehends a great deal of what we consider dramatic irony. Appreciating and accepting such structurally astonishing things is another aspect of patience or *ṣabr*.

It has been argued that irony is a close relative of allegory; because, while allegory tells us one story by telling us another, irony often implies that the reader knows parts of the story of which the participants are not aware. We know that 'Ajīb will end up blind in one eye like his ten one-eyed hosts from the minute he joins their company even though he does not, and we guess that impertinent curiosity, *fuḍūl*, is responsible for the blinding of all involved. Several critics have argued persuasively for allegorical readings of *The Thousand and One Nights*, in particular Andras

---

21 Hasan S. Karmi, *al-Mughnī al-Kabīr* (Beirut: 1987) 650.

Hamori, and I think it is important to emphasize that partial replication, so important to allegory, is also important to irony.

When I argue that a moral vocabulary is used in *The Thousand and One Nights* to explain its own mechanics and that this vocabulary offers us a useful language for literary criticism of the *Nights*, I do not mean a moralistic or moralizing vocabulary. It is important to remember that Arabic literature has several genres which began as overtly homiletic literature and subsequently became profane. One example is the genre called *al-faraj ba'd al-shidda* (Relief after Stress), which is religious in a writer like Ibn Abī Dunyā but profane in Tanūkhī (although both religious and profane examples were written after Tanūkhī). Notice, incidentally, 'Ajīb's phrase quoted above when his curiosity is partly satisfied: "My anxiety was relieved a little" (*infaraja hammī qalīlan*). Similarly, the *Maqāmāt* started as a homiletic genre but are not so in Badī' al-Zamān or Ḥarīrī. In both these genres I think one can argue that a moral though not a moralistic vocabulary is used to describe the dynamics of character and suggest a dynamic between reader and text.

If, as Hamori has so persuasively argued, the story of "The Porter and the Three Ladies" gives us a sense of the "labyrinthine" quality of justice,[22] it and the entire *Thousand and One Nights* convey a sense of a labyrinthine world in which we are carried forward by suspense and curiosity but always with the ironical realization that there will never be any complete squaring of accounts within the world itself. To view things and events as astonishing is to have this realization. It is to accept with patience the gradually revealed but never fully understood causes of astonishing things that present themselves to us, to greet them with wonderment, and transform them, as *The Thousand and One Nights* so successfully does, into entertainment.

22 Andras Hamori, *On the Art of Medieval Arabic Literature* (Princeton: 1974) 178.

Finding Iran in the Panegyrics of the Ghaznavid Court

Persian panegyric poetry is both painful and revealing. It is painful to the modern reader who fears its exaggerated and far-fetched nature and who is embarrassed by its extravagant style. In 1909 Richard Gottheil, a professor at Columbia University, after praising Firdausi (Ferdawsi), explained his unfavorable view of classical Persian literary style as follows:

> We feel grateful that the battle of Salamis [in 480 B.C.E.] stopped the Persian invasion of Europe, which would doubtless have resulted in changing the current of literature from that orderly and stately course which it had taken from its fountain in a Greek Parnassus and diverted it into the thousand brawling rills of Persian fancy and exaggeration.[1]

To its original patrons, however, for whom feasting and fighting were central activities that had to be memorialized, Persian panegyric poetry

---

Author's note: This article was first published as: "Finding Iran in the Panegyrics of the Ghaznavid Court," in A.C.S. Peacock and D.G. Tor (eds.) *Medieval Central Asia and the Persianate World: Iranian Tradition and Islamic Civilisation* (London and New York, I.B. Tauris: 2015) 129–142. Reproduced by permission of Bloomsbury Publishing Plc. In the article here I have rendered Persian terms and names according to a widely agreed transliteration system for Persian so that Farrukhī becomes Farrokhi and ʿUnṣurī becomes ʿOnsori, etc. However, I have preserved Arabic transliteration for prominent people such as Sultan Maḥmūd as well as for Arab authors and books in Arabic. Firdausi, whose name is in English dictionaries, is not transliterated.

1 Richard Gottheil, *Persian Literature* (New York: 1909). I would like to thank several scholars who helped me in my research: Mohsen Ashtiany, Hossain Kamaly, Justine Landau and above all Tajmah Asefi-Shirazi who complemented my search through two readings of Farrokhi by a yet more serious search. Unfortunately, I did not have access to the Persian poetry database *Dorj*.

must have been exhilarating. To its modern readers, this panegyric poetry is revealing in its portrayals of the aspirations of these patrons to a world just beyond their grasp.

The panegyrists who served the Ghaznavid Sultans Maḥmūd (r. 387/997 to 421/1030) and Mas'ūd (r. 421/1030 to 432/1040) give new insights into the ideologies and the courts of both rulers. In this article I discuss how these poets understood the word "Iran" and also how they themselves viewed the role of the panegyrist. I conclude with some general considerations about Persian panegyric poetry.

We should always keep in mind how central Persian poetry was and is to Iranian culture. Most Russians at some time in their life try to play chess. Similarly, most literate Persian speakers at some time in their lives try to compose poetry. A repeated subject of illustration in Persian miniatures and other illustrations of the *Shāhnāma* from the 7th/13th century onward shows Firdausi, soon to be admired as Iran's greatest epic poet for his *Shāhnāma*, being introduced by three court poets, 'Onṣori, 'Asjadi and Farrokhi, to the mighty Sultan Maḥmūd. From this time onward no great Persian court was complete without its poets.[2]

The four poets shown in the miniatures of the *Shāhnāma*,[3] the three court panegyrists and the poet of epic, Firdausi, are the principal subjects of this essay. They are all figures of the first half of the 5th/11th century. The senior figure among them is 'Onṣori, who lived at least until 422/1031. A fifth poet, Manuchehri, of a somewhat younger generation, who entered the court after the reign of Sultan Maḥmūd, acknowledges the primacy of 'Onṣorī, whom he calls "the master of the masters of the present time."[4]

2 Julie Scott Meisami, *Medieval Persian Court Poetry* (Princeton: 1987) is a good general reference. Meisami has written several articles on panegyrics of which "Ghaznavid Panegyrics: Some Political Implications," *Iran* 28 (1990) 31–44 and "The Poet and his Patrons," *Persica* 17 (2001) 91–105 are particularly relevant. G.E. Tetley's *The Ghaznavid and Seljuk Turks: Poetry as a Source for Iranian History* (London: 2009) is an extremely helpful book on the subject. C.E. Bosworth's "Farrukhī's Elegy on Maḥmūd of Ghazna," *Iran* 29 (1992) 43–49 is an exemplary study of a specific panegyric. See also the valuable article of Franklin Lewis, "Sincerely Flattering Panegyrics: The Shrinking Ghaznavid *qasida*," in F. Lewis and S. Sharma (eds.), *The Necklace of the Pleiades: 24 Essays on Persian Literature, Culture and Religion* (Leiden: 2010) 209–250. Among the many excellent books on Arabic panegyric, I have found Andras Hamori, *The Composition of Mutanabbī's Panegyrics to Sayf al-Daula* (Leiden: 1992) particularly helpful.

3 See, for example, *The Houghton Shahnameh*, eds. M.B. Dickson and S.C. Welch, II (Cambridge, MA, Harvard University Press: 1981) pl. 2 (folio 7 recto).

4 François de Blois, *Persian Literature: A Bio-Bibliographic Survey*, V: *Poetry of the Pre-Mongol Period*, (London: 2004) 201.

Farrokhi, perhaps the most talented of the court panegyrists, wrote an elegy on the death in 432/1040 of Mas'ūd, the son and successor of Maḥmūd, which gives a *terminus post quem* for his death date. As for 'Asjadi, very little remains of his poetry, but he seems to have survived into the reign of a later Ghaznavid ruler, Mawdūd (r. 432/1041 to 440/1048).[5] Some of these poets composed panegyrics in praise of Mas'ūd's half-brother, Muḥammad, who ruled briefly in 421/1030 and then again in 432/1040–41.

Firdausi's traditional death date is 411/1020. It is said that Firdausi presented himself to 'Onṣori, 'Asjadi and Farrokhi when just arrived in Ghazna, Maḥmūd's capital. 'Onṣori said: "O brother, we are the king's poets, and none but poets may enter our company." Each poet produced a poem of three lines, and Firdausi capped each of them with a perfectly metrical and rhyming fourth line.[6]

The younger Manuchehri attached himself to Mas'ūd in the early 420s/1030s and stayed with him until Mas'ūd's death, at which time he moved to the new court of the Seljuks. Except for Firdausi,[7] he is the best preserved of the five poets discussed here. He is a skillful poet, much admired in the Persian tradition.

Moḥammad 'Awfi, the celebrated anthologist of the early 7th/13th century, presents a stunning portrait of 'Onṣori's first patron, Sultan Maḥmūd (here given according to A.J. Arberry's robust translation):

> He was such a king, that his name stands as a frontispiece to the scroll of world-empire by reason of his noble qualities and proud exploits; the robe of glory and grandeur was richly embroidered by his virtues and triumphs. From the centre of his kingdom, like a circle's circumference he encompassed all the climes of earth; his bidding and forbidding embraced in absolute authority every land and sea. Omnipotent as heaven straddling the earth, the whole world shone in reflected splendor of his sun ... [D]espite all [his] preoccupations he did not neglect for a moment to care for the learned and the eminent. For their conversation he entertained a

5 'Asjadi, *Divān*, ed. Taheri Shehab (Tehran: 1334); de Blois, (*supra* n. 4), 97–98.

6 Edward G. Browne, *A Literary History of Persia* II: *From Firdawsī to Sa'dī* (London: 1906) 129. Browne summarizes the account of Dawlatshāh from his *Tadhkirat al-Shu'arā'*, ed. Fatima 'Alaqa (Tehran: 1385) 92.

7 I do not discuss the meaning of "Iran" in Firdausi because this subject has been thoroughly covered by Dr. Hasan Anvari in his article, "Irān dar Shāhnāma," *Namiram az in pas* (Tehran: 1374) 719–729.

> sincere passion, and he always sought every occasion to associate with them. He lavished noble gifts and splendid prizes upon poets, so that inevitably everyone according to the limits of his capacity strove to immortalize his fair fame and goodly name, filling many volumes of Arabic and Persian verse and prose with the record of his laudable attributes and mighty achievements.[8]

As this passage suggests it was wise for panegyrists to depict the ruler as a universal ruler. In this vein, Farrokhi writes:

> يمين دولت محمود شهريار جهان ** بشهرياري ورادى وخسروى بزياد
> سپهر با او پيوسته تازه روى ومطيع ** چنانكه مادر دختر پرست با داماد

> Maḥmūd, auspicious in Fortune, [a play on Maḥmūd's title "Right Hand of the Caliph"], the ruler of the world, is one with abundant rulership, generosity, and kingliness (*khosravi*). In his presence Heaven is always smiling and obedient, just as a mother who adores her daughter behaves towards the bridegroom.[9]

Nevertheless, these poems make it absolutely clear that the specific area that Maḥmūd ruled and defended was Iran. Farrokhi calls Maḥmūd's highest official "the vizier of the *Irānshāh*."[10] In a poem of apology to Maḥmūd he calls this sultan "Khosraw of Iran," a more historically specific title for an Iranian king.[11] 'Onṣori calls Maḥmūd "the mighty Lord of Persian speakers" (*khodāyegān-e 'Ajam*).[12] Farrokhi in a poem to a boon companion of the king says:

> پاداش همي يابد از شهنشاه ** بر دوستى وخدمت فراوان
> هستند ز نيم روز تا شب ** در خدمت او مهتران ايران

8 'Awfi, *Lubāb al-Albāb*, ed. Sa'id Nafisi, (Tehran: 1333) 24–25; trans. A.J. Arberry, *Classical Persian Literature* (London: 1958) 53 (slightly abbreviated).

9 Farrokhi, *Divān*, ed. Mohammad Dabir-Siyaqi (Tehran: 1333) 35–36. I use *Shāhanshāh* instead of the Parthian and later Persian usage of *Shāhinshāh* because the coins of the Ghaznavid period often write out this title as *Shāhānshāh*, based on a mistaken etymology of the word as "of the Kings' King." From this mistake the shortened form becomes *Shāhanshāh*.

10 Farrokhi, (*supra* n. 9), 356; see also p. 355 in the panegyric for Yusof, son of Sebüktegin; again, on p. 138.

11 Farrokhi, (*supra* n. 9), 267.

12 'Onṣori, *Divān*, ed. Mohammad Dabir-Siyaqi, (Tehran: 1342) 195.

He continuously finds reward from the Shāhanshāh for his abundant
friendship and service,
The great men of Iran are at his [the Shāhanshāh's] service from
mid-day till night.[13]

Iran is frequently mentioned as the country of the King of Kings in contrast with Turān, the area to the north and east of the Oxus, very approximately the area we associate with Turkish Inner Asia. ʿOnṣori, in a poem of praise for Sultan Maḥmūd, says that when the banner of the non-Iranian ruler, the Qarakhanid Īlak Naṣr, moves toward "the clime (*keshvar*) of Iran and consequently comes to do battle with the Shah, he [the Īlak] flees with his neck lacerated [back] towards Turkestan."[14]

This understanding of Iran and Turān is mentioned as well in the very laudatory Arabic prose description of Maḥmūd's rule by al-ʿUtbi. This historian writes that a certain religious figure "carried a priceless pearl from the Sea of the Turks to the land (*ʿarḍ*) of Iran."[15] Farrokhi makes it clear that the people of the two regions are named after their respective "climes":

بایرانی چگونه شاد خواهد بود تورانی
پس از چندین بلا کامد ز ایرانشهر بر توران

How will the Turāni be happy with the Irāni
After so much calamity has been visited on Turan by Irānshahr?[16]

Manuchehri is even more fulsome on the subject of the conflict of Iran and Tūrān, perhaps reflecting Sultan Masʿūd's struggle with the invasion of the Ghuzz Turks under the Seljuk leadership. In rather wild exaggeration he writes:

ملکت تورانیان همه بستاند ** بر در ماچین خلیفتي بنشاند
مرز خراسان به مرز روم رساند ** لشکر شرق از عراق در گذراند

13 Farrokhi, (*supra* n. 9) 323; Manuchehri calls Masʿūd "the commander of the commanders," which the editor of his poems understands to mean "King of Kings of Iran." Manuchehri, *Divān*, ed. Bar'at Zanjani, (Tehran: 1387) 282.
14 ʿOnṣori, (*supra* n. 12), 197; presumably the reference is to the Īlak/Ilig Naṣr ibn ʿAlī, who invaded Khorasan in 396/1006.
15 Abū Naṣr al-ʿUtbi, *al-Yamīnī*, ed. Ihsan al-Thamiri (Beirut: 2004) 257.
16 Farrokhi, (*supra* n. 9), 256. See a similar verse in Manuchehri, (*supra* n. 13), 74, line 26.

He will seize the kingdom of the Turānians in its entirety;
He will set up a representative in outer China;
He will cause the border land of Khorasan to stretch to the border land of Byzantium;
He will cause the army of the East to pass onward from Iraq.[17]

ʻOnṣori echoes this sentiment in another poem written in praise of Maḥmūd:

زچین وماچین یکرویه تا لب جیحون
ز ترک وتاجیک از ترکمان وغز وخزر

From China and outer China continuously up to the Oxus,
[The invaders] consist of Turks and Persian-speakers (Tājiks) and of Turkomans and Ghuzz and Khazars.[18]

The first passage clarifies the ambition of the Ghaznavids to expand to the borders of the Byzantines, which would create a kingdom that would approximately correspond with the 5th/11th-century understanding of the land of Iran. The second passage, by mentioning Persian-speakers among the Central Asians, makes clear that for ʻOnṣori Iran was primarily a territorial concept that ends at the Oxus.[19]

Farrokhi in his poetry frequently invokes another well-known instance of contrastive pairs, *ʻArab* and *ʻAjam*, the latter of which in this context means Persian-speakers. In a poem in praise of Muḥammad, the younger son of Maḥmūd, Farrokhi offers an interesting reflection on royal legitimacy using this contrast:

خسرو خسرو نسب
پادشه زاده محمّد خسرو پیروز بخت ** سرفراز تاجداران عجم وآن عرب

17 Manuchehri, (*supra* n. 13), 282. In reading these lines it is important to remember that Mas'ūd had conquered Isfahan which was considered part of "'Ajami Iraq." Compare Farrokhi, (*supra* n. 9), 81, where the younger son of Maḥmūd is called "Shah of the East," perhaps because Maḥmūd left him (Muḥammad) the eastern half of his kingdom. In a letter of 421/1030 to the Turkish ruler Qādir Khān, Sultan Mas'ūd announces his intention to assume control of Iraq (and raid Byzantium); see Bayhaqi, *The History of Beyhaqi*, trans. C.E. Bosworth and Mohsen Ashtiyani, I (Boston: 2011) 159–166.
18 ʻOnṣori, (*supra* n. 12), 122.
19 See my article "The Idea of Iran in the Buyid Dominions" (Article 34 here).

A king (*khosraw*) of kingly lineage;
Muḥammad, born of a ruler (*pādshāh-zāda*) and king (*khosraw*) with the good fortune to reach victory;
The one exalted among the Persian bearers of crowns as well among those of the Arabs.[20]

The Ghaznavid desire to forget that they are descended from a Turkish slave soldier comes through very strongly in this verse. In one case Farrokhi lays out this contrast with the somewhat rarer word, *Pārsiyān*, which seems to mean Persian-speakers:

اندر عرب در عربي گويى او گشاد ** واو باز كرد پارسيان را در درى

He opened by speaking in Arabic amongst the Arabs
Then spoke on to the *Pārsiyān* in court Persian (*dari*).[21]

How comfortable these claims to Iranian kingship sat with the religious claims of Maḥmūd and his sons Muḥammad and Mas'ūd is shown in verses by 'Onṣori. In a poem in praise of Maḥmūd, a very zealous Sunni ruler, he writes:

خداى طاعت خويش ورسول وسلطان خواست نكرد فرق بدين هر سه
امر در فرقان
نجات خلق بحمد محّمد و محمود ** سر نبى ونبى خدايگان جهان
از آنكه بد بحجاز آن واين به ايرانشهر ** حجاز دين را قبله است وملک را ايران

God has asked for obedience to Himself, the Prophet and the Sultan,
Having never made any distinction in these three [matters] in the Qur'ān (*Furqān*),
The salvation of humankind lies in praising [the Prophet] Muḥammad and [the Sultan] Maḥmūd,
The chief Prophet and the most exalted of the Lords of [this] world.

20 Farrokhī, (*supra* n. 9), 5; on *'Arab* and *'Ajam*, see also pp. 14, 139 (books of *'Arab*s and *'Ajam*) 242, 245; see also 'Onṣori, (*supra* n. 12), 195: "Those who were in opposition to [Maḥmūd] the Lord of the *'Ajam* became nothing." Compare n. 17.

21 Farrokhi, (*supra* n. 9), 381; see the discussion of *Pārsiyān* in my article "The Eastern Travels of Solomon: Reimagining Persepolis and the Iranian Past" (Article 33 here).

Since the former [i.e., Prophethood] occurred in the Hijaz and the latter in Irānshahr,
Hijaz is the *qibla* for religion and Iran is the *qibla* for kingship.[22]

Farrokhi expresses somewhat similar sentiments. In his poem praising Sultan Muḥammad mentioned above, he writes:

شاه جهاد محّمد محمود کز خدای ** هر فضل یافتست برون از پیمبری

King of the world, Muḥammad son of Maḥmūd, who has received from the Lord
Every excellence in the world except Prophethood.[23]

The *qibla*-like nature of the ruler is attested everywhere in these poets. Farrokhi writes: "Your house has become the *qibla* for humankind."[24] A poem by Bu Ḥanīfa Eskāfi addressed to the Ghaznavids flatly states that their capital, Ghazna, is: "The Ka'ba of the world's kingship."[25]

All of these references point to a strong belief on the part of Iranians that traditions of kingship are most perfectly preserved and still fully flourishing in Iran. As 'Onṣori tells Maḥmūd, "While you have the eloquence of the Arabs (*Muḍar*), you have the governmental skills of the Iranians (*siyāsat-e 'Ajami*)."[26]

Readers may well ask whether this approach is partly or entirely exclusive to Eastern Iran. A good way to consider this question is to study the almost contemporary divan of the poetry of Qaṭrān, who was born near Tabriz in Azerbaijan, the northwest province of Iran. He wrote for local rulers in this area, chiefly for the rulers of Tabriz and Ganja (now in the Republic of Azerbaijan). He was active as a poet before 438/1046, when he met Nāṣer-e Khosraw, and afterwards at least until 462/1070, a date mentioned in his poetry.[27]

22 'Onṣori, (*supra* n. 12), 201. The word *qibla* refers to the direction of prayer.
23 Farrokhi, (*supra* n. 9), 381.
24 Farrokhi, (*supra* n. 9), 41.
25 *The History of Beyhaqi* I (*supra* n. 17), 390.
26 'Onṣori, (*supra* n. 12), 280.
27 De Blois, (*supra* n. 4) 186–189. De Blois conveys a rumor that the single manuscript of this divan, no longer extant, is a fake, an issue on which I am not qualified to judge. If so, the forger has offered false information on Azerbaijani history not available

Qaṭrān repeatedly mentions Iran and Tūrān together although Tabriz is about a thousand miles from the Oxus.[28] He also repeatedly calls the minor rulers he praises the Shāhanshāhs of Iran. As he tells Abu Khalil Ja'far, a Shaddādid ruler, a king so obscure that his dates remain uncertain:

تو سالار دلیرانی تو شاهنشاه ایرانی
هم از دل فضل بی عیبی هم ازتن فخر بیعاری

You are the courageous leader [or, commander of the brave],
You are the Iranian Shāhanshāh
Both in respect to your heart your excellence is without fault,
And in respect to your body your honor is without blemish.[29]

In a panegyric addressed to Abu Nāṣer Jostān (or Jastān), an equally obscure member of a ruling family, Qaṭrān says:

مباد ایران از تو خالی که هستی قبله ایران
که ایران ان بی وجود تو بیکساعت شود ویران

May Iran never be empty of you since you are the *qibla* of Iran,
For if Iran for one second were without your existence it would be ruined.[30]

For another ruler, the slightly more important Abu al-Ḥasan 'Ali Lashkari of Ganja, Qaṭrān writes:

قبله شاهان نباشد جز مقام لشکری

There is no *qibla* for Shahs except for the place Lashkari is.[31]

---

elsewhere. I. Dehgan, "Ḳaṭran," *The Encyclopaedia of Islam*, 2nd ed., IV (Leiden, Brill: 1978) 773, says that one reference in his poems can be dated to 481/1088.

28 Qaṭrān-e Tabrīzī, *Divān*, ed. Mohammad Nakhjavani, (Tehran: 1362) 64, 359, 452.

29 Qaṭrān-e Tabrīzī, (*supra* n. 28), 391; see also pp. 381, 432, 448.

30 Qaṭrān-e Tabrīzī, (*supra* n. 28), 271.

31 Qaṭrān-e Tabrīzī, (*supra* n. 28), 432.

In short, even minor rulers of this period in Iran, who lived in the east or the west of that "clime," wanted to be remembered in the canon of the kingly tradition that was established in the first half of the 5th/11th century.

What did these poets understand themselves to be doing in writing these panegyrics? The ever observant and ever perceptive Bayhaqi, who served as historian to Sultan Mas'ūd devotes a long aside to this question. He holds that the best panegyric tells the truth:

> Such honest and blunt advice must be proffered repeatedly to exalted and blessed monarchs so that it may be written down. Mighty rulers must be impelled to construct an edifice of noble deeds, for although the intention itself is engrained in their natures, it will be awakened and aroused by external prodding and wise counsel. Truly indomitable and resolute monarchs always made a treasury out of wise words.[32]

In this passage we get hints as to some uses of panegyrics. First, it is speech "that may be written down"—that is, the kind of speech, namely poetry, which is most memorable and worth recording in the canons of this culture. Furthermore, panegyric not only memorializes the "good deeds" shown by rulers, but it also holds rulers up to a standard "by external prodding." Memorialization is one of the reasons that great kings "have always made a treasury out of wise words." In another passage Bayhaqi declares that "As long as the world continues to exist, monarchs will do mighty deeds and poets will relate them in verse."[33]

However, Bayhaqi gives us an ambiguous message as to what would be appropriate or inappropriate in panegyric poetry. On the subject of a panegyric poem in Arabic, he says, "Had he not possessed these virtues [described in the poem], how would [the poet] ... ever have had the courage to describe him thus, since great men cannot stomach ridicule (*ṭanz*)?" Yet on the very same page Bayhaqi writes of his later patron, Sultan Ibrāhīm, grandson of Maḥmūd, that "people will see exploits like those of Sultan Maḥmūd from this great Sultan Ibrāhīm, so that cavaliers of poetry and prose will enter the arena of eloquence and display such virtuoso performance that they will put preceding generations in the shade."[34] Clearly,

32 *The History of Beyhaqi* II (*supra* n. 17), 31.
33 *The History of Beyhaqi* II (*supra* n. 17), 33.
34 *The History of Beyhaqi* II (*supra* n. 17), 33; see 'Awfi, *Lubāb* (*supra* n. 8) 25.

for all his pious condemnation of undue praise, Bayhaqi could not restrain himself from offering such praise to a comparatively minor ruler. Of course, Bayhaqi's claim to be a reluctant panegyrist may well have been intended to reinforce the strength of his panegyric.

Farrokhi directly addresses the issue of panegyrics and his role in composing them, as in this poem addressed to a high official:

من ثناگوی بزرگانم ومدّاح ملوک ** خاصه مدحتگر آن راد عطا بخش کریم

I am the praiser (*ṣanā-gu*) of the great and the panegyrist of kings (*maddāḥ-e moluk*),
In particular the panegyric-maker (*medḥat-gar*) for that happy, generous, noble person."[35]

In another poem, this time directed to Muḥammad, son of Sultan Maḥmūd, Farrokhi says:

از زائر و سائل وخدمتگر ومداح ** هر روز بدان درگه چندین نفر آید
مادح بر او پوید زیرا که ز مدحش ** الفاظ نُکت گردد ومعنی غُرر آید
من مدحت او چونکه همی مختصر آرم ** آری چو سخن نیک بود مختصر آید

Every day several people from among the visitors, petitioners, servitors and panegyrists come to that court.
The panegyrist (*mādeḥ*) seeks after him because in praising him mere words become subtle conceits and their ideas become points of brilliancy.
Since I always bring praise for him in brevity,
Let you so bring it since the best speech is that which is brief.[36]

Of course, reward remains a very strong and openly acknowledged motive for panegyric. Farrokhi writes:

زبس بر سختن زرّش بجای مادحان هزمان ** زناره بگسلد کپان زشاهین بگسلد پله

35 Farrokhi, (*supra* n. 9), 244.
36 Farrokhi, (*supra* n. 9), 40. The last line is a reference to a famous Arabic proverb. See parallels: p. 153 (*shā'erān-e ṣanā-gu'i*) and p. 381 (*medḥat-garān*).

From the quantity of gold that he continually weighs out for panegyrists (*mādeḥān*)
The tongue of the balance/steelyard is detached and the pan breaks off from the beam.[37]

Bayhaqi actually records the distribution of gifts by Sultan Mas'ūd at the festival for the end of the Fast in 422/1031: "The Amir [Mas'ūd] ordered that the less well-known poets should receive 20,000 dirhams. Fifty thousand dirhams were conveyed to the house of [the poet] 'Alavi Zaynabi on an elephant. 'Onṣori was given one thousand dinars."[38]

A poem in Arabic by Abū al-Fatḥ al-Bustī (d. *circa* 400/1009), a sometime panegyrist for Sultan Maḥmūd, addresses rulers in general:

نصحتكم يا ملوك الأرض لا تدعوا
كسب المكارم بالإحسان والجود
وانفقوا بيضكم والحمر في شرف
لا ينتهي باختلاف البيض والسود
هذا ذخائر محمود قد انتهيت
والا انتهاب لنا في ذكر محمود

I advise you, kings of the earth, do not let go acquisition of noble characteristics through generosity and good deeds.
Spend your white and red [silver and gold] for the sake of honor (*sharaf*)
That will not cease with the alternation of black and white [night and day].
These are the treasures of Maḥmūd that you have brought to an end.
Was there not plunder for us in the mention of one praiseworthy? (*maḥmūd*)[39]

37 Farrokhi, (*supra* n. 9), 350 and Jan Rypka and Milos Borecky, "Farrukhī," *Archív Orientální* 16 (1947–49) 68.
38 *The History of Beyhaqi* I (*supra* n. 17), 383. Zaynabi is often counted as one of the poets of the early Ghaznavid court. Of the few poems that survive one can be dated to 422/1031. See De Blois, (*supra* n. 4), 207–208. The exchange rate between dirhams and dinars varied. Sometimes it was ten dirhams to one dinar; other times it was fourteen dirhams to one dinar.
39 Dawlatshāh, *Tadhkirat*, (*supra* n. 6), 47; cited in Browne, (*supra* n. 6), II:99, with his different translation.

In this passage the "cash and carry" exchange between patron and panegyrist is combined with the offer of eternal human remembrance through the poetry purchased.

Another aspect of panegyrics in this tradition is that it uses a self-replenishing repertoire of images. Not only are these images shared by 'Asjadi, 'Onṣori, Farrokhi and Manuchehri but many of them come out of the Arabic tradition of panegyric. Farrokhi mentions the relation of the much-admired Arabic poet, Mutanabbī, with one of his patrons, Kāfūr, the ruler of Egypt, and mentions Buḥturī (d. 284/897), the great panegyrist of the Abbasids, with high praise.[40]

One theme, the renewal of the land and its people through the good king, is continuous from the ancient Near Eastern kings to our Iranian kings of the 5th/11th century. Farrokhi addresses Maḥmūd as:

خداوند ما شاه کشور ستان ** که نامی بدو گشت زاولستان
سر شهریاران ایران زمین ** که ایران بدو گشت تازه جوان

Our Lord king who grasps whole regions through whom Zavolestān
[which is the province around Ghazna] became famous,
Chief of the kings of the land of Iran (*Irān-zamin*), Iran through him
has again become young.[41]

Firdausi in a similar vein writes in his panegyric to Maḥmūd at the beginning of the *Shāhnāma*:

زفرش جهان شد چو باغ بهار
هوا پر ز ابر وزمین پر نگار

From his kingly glory the world has become like a spring garden;
The air is full of rain clouds, the earth is full of beauty.[42]

40 Farrokhi, (*supra* n. 9), 196 (Mutanabbī), p. 381 (Buḥturī).

41 Farrokhi, (*supra* n. 9), 248. See the outstanding essay on this subject by Stefan Sperl, "Islamic Kingship and Arabic Panegyric Poetry in the Early 9th Century," *Journal of Arabic Literature* 8 (1977) 20–35.

42 Firdousi (Firdausi), *Le livre des rois*, ed. and trans. Jules Mohl, I (Paris: 1876) 24, line 218.

Panegyric is, therefore, highly valued memorialization since good poetry (and with it the events and settings it describes) survives ordinary speech. Neẓāmi ʿAruẓi, writing almost exactly a century after these poets, says:

> A king cannot dispense with a good poet, who shall provide for the immortality of his name, and shall record his fame in divans and books. For when the king receives that command which none can escape, no traces will remain of his army, his treasure, and his store; but his name will endure forever by reason of the poet's verse.[43]

It was the mark of a great ruler to have great panegyrists. Panegyrics involve exchange between the poet and the recipient. The lavish size of some of the rewards paid to the panegyrists indicates the ruler's appreciation or judgment of their worth to him and his reign.

Neẓāmi ʿAruẓi reports that the panegyrist Rashidi, who wrote Persian lyrics for the Īlak Khān, was generously rewarded by that ruler:

> On this day he ordered Rashidi to receive all four trays [made of gold and silver], so he obtained the highest honor, and became famous. For just as a patron becomes famous by the verse of a good poet, so do poets likewise achieve renown by receiving a great reward from the King, these two things being interdependent.[44]

Dishonoring the poet might also hurt the ruler's chances for "fair fame." Neẓāmi ʿAruẓi tells us of the negative consequences of the decision of a slightly later Ghaznavid ruler to imprison another prominent panegyrist, Masʿud Saʿd Salmān: "The ill repute of this deed remained on this noble house [of the Ghaznavids]."[45]

The performance of the panegyric is an important part of its meaning. It is a ritual that can only have its full impact in a court setting. Since the practice of writing panegyrics was already several centuries old in the Islamic Middle East, a self-renewing repertoire existed for panegyrists that made these poems instantly recognizable to ruler and audience alike as an essential ritual for affirming kingship.

---

43 Neẓāmi ʿAruẓi Samarqandi, *Chahār Maqāla*, ed. Mohammad Moʿin (Tehran: 1336/1952) 29.
44 Neẓāmi ʿAruẓi Samarqandi, (*supra* n. 43), 53.
45 Neẓāmi ʿAruẓi Samarqandi, (*supra* n. 43), 51.

One way to reconstruct the 5th/11th-century Iranian world in which these panegyrists worked is to see it as a network of mutual expectations. The ruler expects his ceremonial occasions and significant deeds to be memorialized in the most highly wrought and indelible speech, poetry. The ruler also expects this speech to resonate with the speech offered to other rulers so that the ruler is seen as, at least, their equal and, preferably, their superior. He expects, moreover, to be portrayed as the ideal king as understood in this tradition, in which justice and protection of the weak were so highly prized. His reign is supposed to make the world young again and to renew the land. Rulers surely wanted such portrayals both for their own self-esteem and for the esteem it would engender among their subjects. Their portrayal as fonts of true generosity would be reinforced by the lavish rewards given to their chosen poets—rewards that, in turn, conveyed the immensity of resources at the rulers' disposal.

The public inside the ruler's kingdom might find in the panegyrics hope that the ruler was an approximation to the ideal king. They might also hope that the ruler would be encouraged toward the ideal because the poet had portrayed him as upholding it. The subjects of the ruler would certainly see him in the spiritual lineage of kings because this ritual was performed for him. The public outside the kingdom would know that this ruler wanted to be considered a proper king and a possible source of both patronage and protection.

The poet would of course understand that his poem and its performance was the basis of his livelihood. He probably wished to inculcate the traits of the ideal king in the real king by recounting them in his poem and ascribing them to the subject of his poem. He would certainly hope that his skill as a panegyrist would make him a desirable commodity in competing courts. (Manuchehri left the Ghaznavids as the Seljuks emerged as richer and more powerful patrons.) He would probably hope to be remembered for his contribution to both the genre of panegyric and to the memory of great events.

These poems also greatly clarify the geographic boundaries of the land designated by the word "Iran" in the eyes of early 5th/11th-century Iranians. More than that, they tell us that in Persian-speaking lands kingly glory in the eyes of the poet, patron and public alike was intimately associated with Iran. To be the Shah of Iran was to be a proper king. However much Maḥmūd and Mas'ūd's ancestor may have begun life as a Turkish slave, his descendants bravely shouldered their duty as Iranian rulers and defended Iran against outsiders, particularly the people of Turān.

Author Bibliography

1967

1. "Sources in the Study of Iran," *Iranian Studies* 1:1 (1967) 4–7.

1973

2. "Administration in Buyid Qazwīn," in D.S. Richards (ed.), *Islamic Civilisation 950–1150* Papers in Islamic History, III (Oxford, U.K., Cassirer: 1973) 33–45.

1975

3. "The 'Abbasid Caliphate in Iran," in R.N. Frye (ed.), *The Cambridge History of Iran*, 4 (Cambridge, U.K., Cambridge University Press: 1975) 57–89.

1976

4. "The *Shu'ūbīyah* Controversy and the Social History of Early Islamic Iran," *International Journal of Middle East Studies* 7:2 (1976) 161–182.

1980

5. *Loyalty and Leadership in an Early Islamic Society* (Princeton, N.J., Princeton University Press: 1980).
6. "Some Attitudes towards Monarchy and Absolutism in the Eastern Islamic World of the Eleventh and Twelfth Centuries A.D." in Joel L. Kraemer, Ilai Alon (eds.), *Religion and Government in the World of Islam*, Proceedings of the Colloquium held at Tel-Aviv University 3–5 June 1979, *Israel Oriental Studies*, X (Tel-Aviv, Tel Aviv University: 1980) 86–91.
7. "Iran's Foreign Devils," in *Foreign Policy* 38 (Washington, D.C., Carnegie Endowment for International Peace: 1980) 19–34.

1981

8. "A Note on the '*Ṭasbīb*,'" in Wadad al-Qadi (ed.), *Studia Arabica et Islamica: Festschrift for Ihsān 'Abbās on his Sixtieth Birthday* (Beirut, American University in Beirut: 1981) 347–352.

1983

9. "Bureaucracy and the Patrimonial State in Early Islamic Iran and Iraq," in Ihsan Abbas (ed.) *al-Abḥāth* 29 (1981) 25–36, Journal of the Center for Arab and Middle East Studies, Faculty of Arts and Sciences, American University of Beirut.

1984

10. "The Foundations of State and Society," in Marjorie Kelly (ed.), *Islam: The Religious and Political Life of a World Community* (New York, Praeger Publishers: 1984) 55–72.

1985

11. *The Mantle of the Prophet: Religion and Politics in Iran* (New York, Simon and Shuster: 1985).

1987

12. *Der Mantel des Propheten oder das Leben eines persischen Mullah zwischen Religion und Politik* (Munich, Verlag C.H. Beck: 1987). German translation of 11 by Klaus Krieger.

1988

13. "Shi'i Education," in Seyyed Hossein Nasr, Hamid Dabashi, Seyyed Vali Reza Nasr (eds.), *Shi'ism* (Albany, N.Y., State University of New York Press: 1988) 282–286.

1989

14. "Consultation and the Political Process in the Islamic Middle East of the 9th, 10th, and 11th Centuries," in Moawiyah M. Ibrahim (ed.), *Arabian Studies in Honour of Mahmoud Ghul: Symposium at Yarmouk University, December 8–11, 1984*, Yarmouk University Publications, Institute of Archaeology and Anthropology Series 2, (Wiesbaden, Otto Harrassowitz: 1989) 83–88.

15. With Christoph Bürgel, "'Azod-al-Dawla," in *Encyclopaedia Iranica*, III (London and New York, Routledge & Kegan Paul: 1989) 265–269.

1990

16. "Foreword," in Philip S. Khoury and Joseph Kostiner (eds.), *Tribes and State Formation in the Middle East* (Berkeley and Los Angeles, University of California Press: 1990) ix–x.

1991

17. With Antonia Chayes, "Security Diplomacy for the Middle East," in *The Aspen Quarterly* 3:4 (1991) 74–97.

1992

18. "Afkār ḥawl Taswīya mā ba'd al-Azmah fī al-Sharq al-Awsaṭ [Stabilization after the Gulf Crisis]," in Sa'd al-Din Ibrahim and Hasan Wajih (eds.), *Azmat al-Khalīj wa-Mustaqbal al-Sharq al-Awsaṭ: Ru'ā 'Arabīya wa-Amrīkīya [The Gulf Crisis and the Future of the Middle East]*, (Kuwait, Dār Su'ād al-Ṣabāḥ and Cairo, Markaz Ibn Khaldūn li-l-Dirāsāt al-Inmā'īya: 1992) 51–65.
19. "Du wirst das Licht sehen," "Aufruhr im Basar," "Jugend eines Mullah," and "Die islamische Welt blickt auf Algerien," in Maria Haarmann (ed.), *Der Islam: Ein Lesebuch* (Munich, Verlag C.H. Beck: 1992) 51–54, 141–145, 181–187. German translation of extracts from **11**.

1993

20. "Toward an Islamic Theory of Toleration," in Tore Lindholm and Kari Vogt (eds.), *Islamic Law Reform and Human Rights: Challenges and Rejoinders* (Oslo, Nordic Human Rights Publication: 1993) 25–36.
21. "Consultation and the Political Process in the Islamic Middle East of the 9th, 10th, and 11th Centuries," in Chibli Mallat (ed.), *Islam and Public Law: Classical and Contemporary Studies*, (London and Boston, Graham and Totman: 1993) 19–28. Reprint of **14**.

1994

22. "Foreword," in Mark Pinson (ed.), *The Muslims of Bosnia-Herzegovina: Their Historic Development from the Middle Ages to the Dissolution of Yugoslavia* (Cambridge, MA, Harvard University Press: 1994) vii–viii.

23. "Some Islamic Views of the Pre-Islamic Past," in *Harvard Middle Eastern and Islamic Review* 1:1 (1994) 17–26.

1995

24. "Traditional Shi'ite Education in Qom," in *Harvard Middle Eastern and Islamic Review* 2:1 (1995) 89–98.
25. "The Islamic World 1400–1700," in Mark Kishlansky et al. (eds.), *Societies and Cultures in World History* (New York, Harper Collins: 1995) 440–471.
26. "The Islamic Movement: The Case for Democratic Inclusion," in Nikki R. Keddie (ed.), *Contention: Debates in Society, Culture, and Science* 4:3 (1995) 107–127.
27. "The Clash of Civilizations: An Islamicist's Critique," in *Harvard Middle Eastern and Islamic Review* 2:2 (1995) 1–26.
28. "Wilāyat al-Faqīh," in John L. Esposito (ed.), *The Oxford Encyclopedia of the Modern Islamic World*, 4 (Oxford, U.K., Oxford University Press: 1995) 320–322.

1996

29. "Shi'ite Political Thought and the Destiny of the Iranian Revolution," in Jamal S. al-Suwaidi (ed.), *Iran and the Gulf: A Search for Stability* (Abu Dhabi, The Emirates Center for Strategic Studies and Research: 1996) 70–80.
30. "al-Fikr al-Siyāsī al-Shī'ī wa Maṣīr al-Thawrah al-Īrānīya," in Jamal Sanad al-Suwaydi (ed.), *Īrān wa-l-Khalīj: al-baḥth 'an al-istiqrār* (Abu Dhabi, Markaz al-Imārāt li-l-Dirāsāt wa-l-Buḥūth al-Istirātījīya: 1996), 103–115. Arabic translation of **29**.
31. "Astonishment in the 1001 Nights," *Ḥadīth al-Dār* 4 (1996) 21–24.
32. "Chand Naẓargāh-e Eslāmi dar bārah-ye dawrān pish az Eslām," in *Mehregān* 2 (Tehran: 1375/1996–97) 118–126. Persian translation of **23**.
33. "Naẓariyah-e Huntington az Didgāh-e yak-Eslām-pazhuh (On Huntington's Theory: Clash of Civilizations)" in *Eṭṭelā'āt-e Siyāsi-Eqteṣādi* (*Political and Economic Ettela'at*) 109–110 (1996) 14–24. Persian translation of **27**.

1997

34. "*'Ajā'ib* in *The Thousand and One Nights*," in Richard G. Hovannisian and Georges Sabagh (eds.), *The Thousand and One Nights in Arabic*

Literature and Society. Giorgio Levi della Vida Series in Islamic Studies 12 (Cambridge, U.K., and New York, N.Y., Cambridge University Press: 1997) 29–39.

35. "The Transmission of Learning: The Role of the Islamic Northeast," in Nicole Grandin and Marc Gaborieau (eds.), *Madrasa: la transmission du savoir dans le monde musulman* (Paris, αρ Éditions Arguments: 1997) 63–72.

36. "The Islamic Movement: The Case for Democratic Inclusion," in Gary G. Sick and Lawrence G. Potter (eds.), *The Persian Gulf at the Millennium: Essays in Politics, Economy, Security, and Religion* (New York, St. Martin's Press: 1997) 297–318. Reprint of **26**.

1998

37. "Traditional Shi'ite Education in Qom," in Amélie Oksenberg Rorty (ed.), *Philosophers on Education: New Historical Perspectives* (London, Routledge: 1998) 449–454. Reprint of **24**.

38. "In memoriam: Jeanette Ann Wakin (1928–1998)," *Middle East Studies Association Bulletin* 32:1 (1998) 141–142.

1999

39. "Fī Naqd ... Ṣidām al-Ḥaḍārāt," in Dr. Samīr Sulaymān (ed.), *Ṣidām al-Ḥaḍārāt* [*The Conflict of Civilizations*], (Beirut, The Consulting Center for Studies and Documentation: 1999) 205–223. Arabic translation of **27**.

2000

40. *The Mantle of the Prophet: Religion and Politics in Iran* (Oxford, U.K., Oneworld: 2000). Reprint with a new Introduction of **11**.

2001

41. *Loyalty and Leadership in an Early Islamic Society* (London and New York, I.B. Tauris: 2001). Reprint with a new Introduction of **5**.

42. With Angeliki E. Laiou, (eds.), *The Crusades from the Perspective of Byzantium and the Muslim World* (Washington, D.C., Dumbarton Oaks Research Library and Collection: 2001).

43. "The Idea of *Jihād* in Islam before the Crusades," with Ridwan al-Sayyid, in Angeliki E. Laiou and Roy Parviz Mottahedeh (eds.), *The Crusades from the Perspective of Byzantium and the Muslim*

World (Washington, D.C., Dumbarton Oaks Research Library and Collection: 2001) 23–29.

44. "A Just War? Judeo-Christian and Islamic Perspectives: A Conversation with J. Bryan Hehir and Roy Mottahedeh," *American Academy of Arts and Sciences*, Cambridge, Massachusetts, Dec. 10, 2001, 1–21. Available at www.amacad.org/sites/default/files/academy/pdfs/justwar.pdf
45. "Brother and Brotherhood," in Jane Dammen McAuliffe (gen. ed.) *Encyclopaedia of the Qur'ān* 1 (Leiden, Brill: 2001) 259–263.

2002

46. "Islam: A Primer," in *Center Conversations* 15 (2002), An Occasional Publication of the Ethics and Public Policy Center, Washington, D.C., transcribed from a taped conversation and published online without the author's corrections.

2003

47. "Introduction," in Muḥammad Bāqir aṣ-Ṣadr, *Lessons in Islamic Jurisprudence*, translated and with Introduction, Glossary and Summary by Roy Parviz Mottahedeh (Oxford, U.K., Oneworld: 2003) 1–33.
48. "Keeping the Shi'ites Straight," in Mark Silk (ed.) *Religion in the News* 6:2 (2003) 4–6, 27, Journal of the Center for the Study of Religion in Public Life, Trinity College, Hartford.
49. "Public and Private as Viewed Through the Work of the 'Muhtasib,'" with Kristen Stilt, *Social Research: An International Quarterly of the Social Sciences* 70:3 (2003) 735–748.
50. "The Clash of Civilizations: An Islamicist's Critique," in Emran Qureshi and Michael A. Sells (eds.), *The New Crusades: Constructing the Muslim Enemy* (New York, Columbia University Press: 2003) 131–151. Reprint of 27.
51. *Peygamberin Hirkasi: İran'Da Din ve Politika Bilgi ve Güç* (Istanbul, Istanbul University Press: 2003). Turkish translation of **11** by Ruşen Sezer.

2004

52. "Foreword," in Birgit Schaebler and Leif Stenberg (eds.), *Globalization and the Muslim World: Culture, Religion, and Modernity* (Syracuse, N.Y., Syracuse University Press: 2004), vii–ix.

53. "An Interdisciplinary Roundtable Discussion held in Vouliagmeni, Greece, October 1999," Organized by the Harvard Law School Human Rights Program, in *Religion and State* (Cambridge, MA, Harvard Law School Human Rights Program: 2004) 40, 58, 63, 74.

2005

54. *Profetens kappe laerdom og magt i Iran* (Copenhagen, Forlaget Vandkunsten: 2005). Danish translation of **11** by Claus Bech.
55. "Foreword," in Hamid Enayat, *Modern Islamic Political Thought: The Response of the Shīʿī and the Sunnī Muslims to the Twentieth Century* (London, I.B. Tauris: 2005) ix–x.
56. "Islam: A Primer," in Michael Cromartie (ed.) *Religion, Culture, and International Conflict: A Conversation* (Lanham, MD, Rowman & Littlefield Publishers: 2005) 53–59. Reprint of **46** without author's corrections.

2006

57. "Pluralism and Islamic Traditions of Sectarian Divisions," *Svensk Teologisk Kvartzalskrift* 82 (Lund, Wallin & Dalholm Boktryckeri AB: 2006) 155–161.

2007

58. "*Afterword*," in A. Amanat, F. Griffel, Shariʿa: Islamic Law in the Contemporary Context (Stanford, CA, Stanford University Press: 2007) 178–182.
59. Burdat al-Nabī: al-Dīn wa-l-Sīyāsa fī Īrān (Beirut, Dār al-Madār al-Islāmī: 2007). Arabic translation of **11** by Ridwan al-Sayyid.

2008

60. "Oaths and Public Vows in the Middle East of the Tenth and Eleventh Centuries," in Marie-France Auzépy and Guillaume Saint-Guillain (eds.), *Oralité et lien social au Moyen Âge (Occident, Byzance, Islam): parole donnée, foi jurée, serment*, College de France-CNRS, Centre de recherche d'histoire et civilisation de Byzance, Monographies 29 (Paris, ACHCByz: 2008) 117–122.

2009

61. Owzāʿ-e ejtemāʿi-ye dowreh-ye Āl-e Buyah (Mashhad: 2009). Persian translation of **5** by Mohammad Reza Reza Mosahebi and Ali Yahyayi.

62. "Wilāyat al-Faqīh," in John L. Esposito (ed.) *The Oxford Encyclopedia of the Islamic World*, 5 (Oxford, U.K., and New York, Oxford University Press: 2009) 529–532. Reprint of **28**.

2010

63. "Faith and Practice: Muslims in Historic Cairo," in Farhad Daftary, Elizbeth W. Fernea and Azim Nanji (eds.), *Living in Historic Cairo: Past and Present in an Islamic City* (Seattle, WA, Azimuth Editions, London, in association with the Institute of Ismaili Studies; University of Washington Press: 2010) 104–116.

64. "Pluralism and Islamic Traditions of Sectarian Divisions," in Zulfikar Hirji (ed.), Diversity and Pluralism in Islam: Historical and Contemporary Discourses amongst Muslims (London and New York, I.B. Tauris: 2010) 3–42.

2012

65. "The Idea of Iran in the Buyid Dominions," in Edmund Herzig and Sarah Steward (eds.) *Early Islamic Iran: The Idea of Iran*, 5 (London and New York, I.B. Tauris: 2012) 153–160.

66. "Qur'ānic Commentary on the Verse of *khums* (al-Anfāl VIII:41)," in Kazuo Morimoto (ed.), *Sayyids and Sharifs in Muslim Societies: The Living Links to the Prophet* (London and New York, Routledge: 2012) 37–48.

2013

67. "The Eastern Travels of Solomon: Reimagining Persepolis and the Iranian Past," in Michael Cook, Najam Haider, Intisar Rabb, and Asma Sayeed (eds.), *Law and Tradition in Classical Islamic Thought: Studies in Honour of Professor Hossein Modarressi* (New York, Palgrave Macmillan: 2013) 247–267.

2014

68. *The Quandaries of Emulation: The Theory and Politics of Shi'i Manuals of Practice*, The Ninth Farhat J. Ziadeh Distinguished Lecture in Arab and Islamic Studies, May 2, 2011, The Department of Near Eastern Languages and Civilization, University of Washington (Seattle, University of Washington: 2014).

69. "The Islamic Foundation for Citizenship and Pluralism," in *Kufa Review* 7 (2014) 9–15, International Academic Journal Sponsored by the University of Kufa, Iraq (Dar attanweer: 2014).

2015

70. "Finding Iran in the Panegyrics of the Ghaznavid Court," in A.C.S. Peacock and D.G. Tor (eds.), *Medieval Central Asia and the Persianate World: Iranian Tradition and Islamic Civilisation* (London and New York, I.B. Tauris: 2015) 129–142.
71. *Tārikh-e ejtemāʿi-ye Irān dar ʿaṣr Āl-e Buyah*, (Tehran, Nāmak: 1394/2015–16). Persian translation of 5 by Mohammad Dehqani.

2016

72. "Friendship in Islamic Ethical Philosophy," in Alireza Korangy, Wheeler M. Thackston, Roy P. Mottahedeh and William Granara (eds.), *Essays in Islamic Philology, History, and Philosophy*, Studies in the History and Culture of the Middle East 31, A Festschrift in Celebration and Honor of Professor Ahmad Mahdavi Damghani's 90th Birthday (Berlin and Boston, De Gruyter: 2016) 229–239.
73. "The Najaf Ḥawzah Curriculum," in *Journal of the Royal Asiastic Society*, 3rd series, 26:1–2 (2016) 341–351. Also posted online by Ali Teymoori, January 29, 2017: www.ijtihadnet.com/article-najaf-ḥawzah-curriculum

2017

74. "Caliphate," in Bryan S. Turner *et al.* (eds.), *The Wiley Blackwell Encyclopedia of Social Theory* (Oxford, U.K., John Wiley & Sons Ltd: 2017; also published online) 203–206.

2018

75. With David Durand-Guédy and Jürgen Paul (eds.), *Cities of Medieval Iran*, *Eurasian Studies* 16 (Leiden, Brill: 2018).
76. "Medieval Kashan: Crossroads of Commerce and Culture," with Mehrdad Amanat, in David Durand-Guédy, Roy P. Mottahedeh and Jürgen Paul (eds.), *Cities of Medieval Iran*, *Eurasian Studies* 16 (Leiden, Brill: 2018) 395–429.
77. "Medieval Lexicography on Arabic and Persian Terms for City and Countryside," in David Durand-Guédy, Roy P. Mottahedeh and Jürgen

Paul (eds.), *Cities of Medieval Iran, Eurasian Studies* 16 (Leiden, Brill: 2018) 465–478.

2020

78. With David Durand-Guédy and Jürgen Paul, *Cities of Medieval Iran* (Leiden, Brill: 2020). Separate Reprint of 74.

2022

79. "Does Pre-Modern Islamic Thought Allow for a Secular Realm?" in Bruce Fudge, Kambiz GhaneaBassiri, Christian Lange, and Sarah Bowen Savant (eds.), *Non sola scriptura: Essays on the Qur'an and Islam in Honour of William A. Graham*, Routledge Studies in the Qur'an (London and New York, Routledge: 2022) 215–224.

Select Book Reviews

80. "Review of Bernard Lewis, *The Assassins: A Radical Sect in Islam* in *Speculum* 44:3 (1969) 477.
81. Review of R.W. Bulliet, *The Patricians of Nishapur: A Study in Medieval Islamic Social History* in *Journal of the American Oriental Society* 95:3 (1975) 491–495.
82. Review of J.J. Saunders and G.W. Rice (eds.), *Muslims and Mongols: Essays on Medieval Asia* in *Speculum* 54:2 (1979) 425–426.
83. Review of Nissim ben Jacob ibn Shāhīn, *An Elegant Composition concerning Relief after Adversity* in *Journal of the American Oriental Society* 103:4 (1983) 771–772.

Select Op-eds

84. "The Mideast Madness," the *New York Times*, September 21, 1982.
85. "Why does Iran Kill Bahais?" the *New York Times*, June 22, 1983.
86. "With Democratization Comes the Revival of Ethnicism," the *Boston Globe*, April 7, 1990.
87. "Danny Thomas: A Beloved Arab-American," the *Christian Science Monitor*, March 8, 1991.
88. "Rebuild Iraq—After Saddam Goes," the *New York Times*, March 23, 1991.
89. "In Iran, Power is Broadly Defined," the *New York Times*, January 9, 1998.

90. "Islam and the Opposition to Terrorism," the *New York Times*, September 30, 2001.

91. "Arabs and America: Education is the Key," the *Washington Post*, February 12, 2002.

92. "Ahammīyat al-ʿInāya bi al-Taʿlīm al-Mutaqqadim fī al-Buldān al-Islāmīya," *al Mustaqbal*, February 17, 2002. Arabic Reprint of **90**.

93. "Reevaluating the Plan to Transfer Power to Iraq," the *Boston Globe*, January 26, 2004.

Index

References to images are in *italics*.